DICTIONARY OF GEOLOGICAL TERMS

DICTIONARY
OF
GEOLOGICAL TERMS

Prepared under the direction of the
AMERICAN GEOLOGICAL INSTITUTE

Anchor Books
Anchor Press/Doubleday
Garden City, New York

ISBN: 0-385-01491-0
Copyright © 1957, 1960, 1962 by the National
Academy of Sciences for the American Geological
Institute
All Rights Reserved
First Edition: June 1957
Second Edition: November 1960
Anchor Books Edition: 1974
Printed in the United States of America

PREFACE

This dictionary contains 7500 of the more commonly used terms in geology and related sciences. It is intended for use by elementary and secondary school science teachers, beginning students of geology, and hobbyists studying rocks, minerals, and fossils. The dictionary is an abridged and revised edition of the *Glossary of Geology and Related Sciences,* 2nd Edition, 1960, published by the American Geological Institute, Washington, D.C. The unabridged glossary contains nearly 17,000 terms.

In the preparation of this abridged edition of the AGI *Glossary of Geology and Related Sciences,* a team of geologists from the Department of Geology, Iowa State University, selected and in some instances revised terms appearing in the second edition, 1960. Members of this editorial team were: Dr. Donald L. Biggs, Dr. Keith M. Hussey, Dr. John Lemish, aided by Mrs. Isabelle Lyons, Mr. Lyle V. Sendlein and Dr. Leo A. Thomas.

The first edition of the AGI glossary was published in 1957 as an outgrowth of a compilation project which was started early in 1953 after several years of planning. The Glossary Proj-

ect was financed by a grant from the National Science Foundation supplemented by a loan from the Geological Society of America.

The success of the Glossary Project was due in large part to the persistent efforts and enthusiasm of Dr. J. V. Howell, consulting petroleum geologist of Tulsa, Oklahoma, who served as Chairman of the Steering Committee which marshalled the efforts of nearly one hundred scientists serving on the contributing subcommittees. The names of those participating in the Glossary Project follow this preface.

The glossary was received with great enthusiasm when it first appeared in 1957 and rapidly became the standard reference of geological scientists for geologic terms. Provisions were made by the American Geological scientists for geologic terms. Provisions were made by the American Geological Institute for a Glossary Review Committee headed by Dr. J. Marvin Weller, Professor of Geology, University of Chicago. This committee received suggestions for revisions and additions to the first edition; their work culminated in the second edition vi

which included supplement and was published in 1960.

A more detailed account of the original Glossary Project and the review procedure may be found in the introductory pages to the second edition, 1960.

The American Geological Institute is a federation of scientific and technical societies serving the geological sciences in the areas of education, public relations, professional relations, and government relations. The Institute operates under the National Academy of Sciences —National Research Council.

The Member Societies include: American Association of Petroleum Geologists; American Geophysical Union; American Institute of Mining, Metallurgical, and Petroleum Engineers; Association of American State Geologists; Geochemical Society; Geological Society of America; Mineralogical Society of America; National Association of Geology Teachers; Paleontological Society; Seismological Society of America; Society of Economic Paleontologists and Mineralogists; and Society of Vertebrate Paleontology.

AGI GLOSSARY PROJECT

STEERING COMMITTEE
J. V. Howell, *Coordinating Chairman*

Chalmer L. Cooper
Paleontological Society
Kenneth Cottingham
A.A.P.G.
Edwin B. Eckel
Geological Society of America
J. D. Forrester
A.I.M.E.
George M. Fowler
Society of Economic Geologists
Michael Fleischer
Mineralogical Society of America
Richard A. Geyer
Society of Exploration Geophysicists

J. E. Gill
Geological Association of Canada
Willard D. Pye
S.E.P.M.
Charles F. Richter
Seismological Society of America
George M. Schwartz
Association of American State Geologists
David J. Varnes
American Geophysical Union
John A. Wilson
Society of Vertebrate Paleontology

STAFF

Editor: Dr. A. C. Trowbridge, State University of Iowa
Technical Editor: L. M. Nichlos, Oil and Gas Journal
Typing: Mrs. Lorraine Littlefield, Tulsa, Oklahoma
Mrs. Gertrude Maebius, Tulsa, Oklahoma

CONTRIBUTING SUBCOMMITTEES

Selection of definitions used was made by the members of the subcommittees listed below. Unaccredited definitions were written by these committees or individuals:

COAL
Kenneth E. Clegg, Illinois Geological Survey
ECONOMIC GEOLOGY
G. M. Schwartz, *Chairman,*

Minnesota Geological Survey

Murl H. Gidel, Anaconda Copper Mining Company

ENGINEERING GEOLOGY

Edwin B. Eckel, U. S. Geological Survey

GEOCHEMISTRY

Konrad B. Krauskopf, Stanford University

GEOMORPHOLOGY

J. Hoover Mackin, *Chairman*, University of Washington

Luna B. Leopold, U. S. Geological Survey

A. D. Howard, Stanford University

W. Armstrong Price, Texas A. & M. College

Harold T. U. Smith, University of Massachusetts (Wind Action)

GEOPHYSICS

Paul L. Lyons, *Chairman*, Sinclair Oil & Gas Company

E. A. Eckhardt, Gulf Research & Development Company

Sigmund I. Hammer, Gulf Research & Development Company

Thomas A. Elkins, Gulf Research & Development Company

L. L. Nettleton, Gravity Meter Exploration Company

Henry Faul, U. S. Geological Survey (Nuclear Geology)

GLACIAL GEOLOGY

Richard Foster Flint, *Chairman*, Yale University

Paul MacClintock, Princeton University

A. L. Washburn, Dartmouth College

GLACIOLOGY

Robert P. Sharp, *Chairman*, California Institute of Technology

G. William Holmes, U. S. Geological Survey

GLOSSARIES

Mark W. Pangborn, Jr., Librarian, U. S. Geological Survey

HYDROLOGY & UNDERGROUND WATER

A. N. Sayre, *Chairman*, U. S. Geological Survey

V. T. Stringfield, U. S. Geological Survey

Robert Carson Vorhis, U. S. Geological Survey

A. G. Fiedler, U. S. Geological Survey

INVERTEBRATE PALEONTOLOGY

Raymond C. Moore, University of Kansas

Caroline H. Kierstead, Smith College

J. Marvin Weller, University of Chicago

MARINE ECOLOGY, OCEANOGRAPHY

Francis P. Shepard, *Chairman*, Scripps Institution of Oceanography

W. Armstrong Price, Texas A. & M. College

METEOROLOGY

Charles C. Bates, U. S. Navy Hydrographic Office

MILITARY GEOLOGY

Frank C. Whitmore, Jr., *Chairman*, U. S. Geological Survey

W. S. Benninghoff, University of Michigan

Cornelia C. Cameron, U. S. Geological Survey

William E. Davies, U. S. Geological Survey

Donald H. Dow, U. S. Geological Survey

Arthur T. Fernald, U. S. Geological Survey

Paula Franchina, U. S. Geological Survey

Allen H. Nicol, U. S. Geological Survey

Arnold C. Orvedal, U. S. Geological Survey

Louis C. Peltier, U. S. Geological Survey

Charles R. Warren, U. S. Geological Survey

MINERALOGY

Michael Fleicher, *Chairman,* U. S. Geological Survey

C. B. Slawson, University of Michigan

Horace Winchell, Yale University

Richards A. Rowland, Shell Development Company (Clay Minerals)

PALEOBOTANY

Robert M. Kosanke, *Chairman,* Illinois Geological Survey

J. Harlan Johnson, Colorado School of Mines

PERMAFROST

Frank C. Whitmore, Jr., *Chairman,* U. S. Geological Survey

Arthur T. Fernald, U. S. Geological Survey

Gerald M. Richmond, U. S. Geological Survey

A. L. Washburn, Dartmouth College

PETROLEUM GEOLOGY

Kenneth Cottingham, *Chairman,* Ohio Fuel Gas Company

E. Russell Lloyd (deceased)

Walter A. Ver Wiebe, Detroit, Michigan

Ronald K. DeFord, University of Texas

Kenneth K. Landes, University of Michigan

PETROLOGY

Earl Ingerson, *Chairman,* U. S. Geological Survey

Igneous & Metamorphic Petrology

Igneous Rock Names:

Robert L. Smith, U. S. Geological Survey

Roy A. Bailey, U. S. Geological Survey

Descriptive Igneous Petrology:

Charles Milton, U. S. Geological Survey

Robert G. Schmidt, U. S. Geological Survey

Marland P. Billings, Harvard University

Experimental and Theoretical Igneous Petrology:

Edwin W. Roedder, U. S. Geological Survey

Descriptive Volcanology:

Robert G. Schmidt, U. S. Geological Survey

Structural Petrology:

Harold W. Fairbairn, Massachusetts Institute of Technology

Marland P. Billings, Harvard University

Metamorphic Rock Names:

Donald B. McIntyre, Pomona College

Metamorphic Petrology: Gordon MacDonald, Massachusetts Institute of Technology

SEDIMENTOLOGY

Jules Braunstein, *Chairman,* Shell Oil Company

William C. Krumbein, Northwestern University

H. Andrew Ireland, University of Kansas (Insoluble Residues)

Roger Lewis Corbeille, Shell Oil Company

Robey H. Clerk, Magnolia Petroleum Company

McLain Jay Forman, Gordon Atwater, Consultant

August Goldstein, Jr., Stanolind Oil & Gas Company

J. Harlan Johnson, Colorado School of Mines (Reefs)

Willard D. Pye, North Dakota Agricultural College

SEISMOLOGY

Don Tocher, University of California

SPELEOLOGY

William E. Davies, U. S. Geological Survey

STRATIGRAPHY

John G. Bartram (deceased)

George V. Cohee, U. S. Geological Survey

John B. Reeside, Jr., U. S. Geological Survey

STRUCTURE

Marland P. Billings, *Chairman,* Harvard University

John Rodgers, Yale University

Clarence R. Allen, California Institute of Technology

Eugene C. Robertson, U. S. Geological Survey

Hugh E. McKinstry, Harvard University

James E. Gill, McGill University

SURVEYING & MAPPING

Julian W. Low, The California Company

GLOSSARY REVIEW COMMITTEE
Second Edition, 1960

J. Marvin Weller, *Chairman*

G. C. Amstutz
Charles C. Bates
Marland P. Billings
Kenneth E. Clegg
William E. Davies
George W. DeVore
Richard Foster Flint
Robert J. Foster
Clifford Frondel
H. R. Gault
Richard A. Geyer
J. V. Howell

Robert Max Kosanke
W. C. Krumbein
J. Hoover Mackin
Mark F. Meier
Robert V. Ruhe
A. Nelson Sayre
George M. Schwartz
Francis P. Shepard
Don Tocher
Charles R. Warren
Frank C. Whitmore, Jr.
Ray E. Wilcox

James H. Zumberge

DICTIONARY OF GEOLOGICAL TERMS

a- (direction) *Struct. petrol:* The direction of tectonic transport, similar to the direction in which cards might slide over one another. Striae in a slickensided surface are parallel to a.

aa A Hawaiian term ‾for basaltic lava flows typified by a rough, jagged, spinose, clinkery surface. *Cf.* PAHOEHOE

Aalenian Lowermost Middle or uppermost Lower Jurassic.

a-axis *Struct. petrol:* The direction of movement or transport in a tectonite. This may be parallel to lineation, as in many shear zones (slickensides), or normal thereto, as in regionally folded metamorphic terranes.

ab Abbreviation for albite. *See* PLAGIOCLASE

abaxial The side of an organ away from the axis or center of the axis; dorsal.

aberration *1.* The failure of light from a point on an object to converge to a point on the image after passing through a lens. *2.* Single organism differing in some conspicuous way from all others. *Cf.* VARIETY

ablation The combined processes by which a glacier wastes.

ablation cone Ice cone; ice pyramid. A debris-covered cone of ice, firn, or snow formed by differential ablation.

ablation factor The rate at which a snow or ice surface wastes away. *See* ABLATION

Abney hand level Hand level with movable bubble tube that can be used to measure vertical angles.

abnormal anticlinorium Anticlinorium in which axial planes of subsidiary folds diverge downward.

abnormal synclinorium Synclinorium in which axial planes of subsidiary folds converge downward.

aboral cavity *Paleontol:* Escutcheon, *q.v.*

ab-plane *Struct. petrol:* The surface along which differential movement takes place. a is the direction of displacement—that is, the direction of tectonic transport; b lies in this surface of movement and is perpendicular to a.

abrade *1.* To rub or wear off; to waste or wear away by friction, as to abrade rocks. *2.* As used in the sharpening-stone industry; abrading means cutting, as the steel composing the tool is cut away rather than worn away.

abrasion pH Characteristic pH developed when a mineral is pulverized under water, resulting from OH or H ions being absorbed by the mineral particles.

absarokite A variety of alkalic basalt consisting of about equal amounts of olivine, augite, labradorite, and sanidine, with accessory biotite, apatite, and opaque oxides. Leucite is sometimes present in small amounts. Absarokite forms a series with shoshonite and banakite and is transitional into shoshonite with decreasing amounts of olivine and increasing amounts of plagioclase and sanidine.

absolute age See GEOCHRONOLOGY

absolute atmosphere An absolute unit of pressure, equal to one million times the pressure produced on a square centimeter by the force of one dyne.

absolute permeability A measure of the possible flow under fixed conditions of a standard liquid through a porous medium when there is no reaction between the solids and the liquid. This measure is arbitrarily taken for isothermal, viscous flow. It can be duplicated with gases if tests are so conducted that extrapolation to infinite pressure can be made. Specific permeability.

absolute pressure Pressure indicated by a pressure gauge plus the atmospheric pressure.

absolute temperature Temperature measured in degrees centigrade from absolute zero, −273. 18° C. Absolute temperatures are given either as "degrees absolute" (e.g., 150° A.) or as "degrees Kelvin" (e.g., 150° K.).

absolute time 1. Time in abstract sense. 2. Geologic time as determined by radioactive decay.

absolute viscosity See VISCOSITY, ABSOLUTE

absolute zero The temperature at which all thermal motion of atoms and molecules ceases: −273. 18° C.

absorption 1. Taking up, assimilation, or incorporation; as the absorption of gases in liquids, as distinguished from adsorption, q.v. Sometimes loosely used in place of adsorption. 2. In optics, the reduction of intensity of light in transmission through an absorbing substance or in reflection from a surface. In crystals, the absorption may vary with the vibration-direction of the transmitted light. See PLEOCHROISM. 3. The process by which energy, such as that of electromagnetic or seismic waves, is converted into other forms of energy, e.g., heat. 4. *Hydrol:* A term applied to the entrance of surface water into the lithosphere by all methods.

abstraction 1. A method of shifting waterways related to the shifting of divides. 2. A stream which for any reason is able to corrade its bottom more rapidly than do its neighbors, expands its valley at their expense, and eventually "abstracts" them. And conversely, a stream which for any reason is able to corrade its bottom less rapidly than its neighbors, has its valley contracted by their encroachments, and is eventually "abstracted" by one or the other.

abstract time 1. Time in abstract sense; absolute time. 2. Uncalibrated time.

abtragung That part of degradation not resulting directly from stream erosion, i.e., preparation and reduction of rock debris by weathering and translocation of waste.

abysmal sea That part of the sea which occupies the ocean basins proper.

abyssal 1. Of, or pertaining to, deep within the earth; plutonic. 2. Of, or pertaining to, the oceanic deeps below 1000 fathoms (6000 feet). 3. Referring to the great depths of seas or lakes where light is absent.

abyssal gap Gap in a sill, ridge,

or rise separating two abyssal plains through which the sea floor slopes from the level of one plain to that of the other.

abyssal hill Relatively small topographic feature of the deep ocean floor ranging to 2000 or 3000 feet high and a few miles wide.

abyssal plains Flat, nearly level areas which occupy the deepest portions of many ocean basins.

Ac Abbreviation for acmite in normative calculations of igneous rocks and for actinolite in similar calculations for metamorphic rocks.

Acadian Middle Cambrian.

Acadian orogeny Late Devonian diastrophism.

acanthite A mineral, Ag_2S, orthorhombic.

acceleration *1.* The rate of change of velocity. *2.* The appearance of modifications earlier and earlier in successive generations in the evolution of species. *3.* In Paleozoic corals, the addition of more secondary septa in one pair of quadrants than in the other pair.

acceleration of gravity The acceleration of a body falling freely in a vacuum due to the gravitational attraction of the earth. The International Committee on Weights and Measures has adopted as a standard or accepted value 980.665 cm./sec.^{2} or 32.174 ft./sec.^{2}, but its true value varies with latitude, altitude, and the nature of the underlying rocks.

accelerometer An instrument used to measure acceleration; specifically, a seismograph designed to measure earth particle accelerations.

accessory *1.* A term applied to minerals occurring in small quantities in a rock, and whose presence or absence does not affect its diagnosis. *2.* Applies to pyroclastic materials derived from previously solidified volcanic rocks of consanguineous origin, i.e., the debris of earlier lavas and pyroclastic rocks from the same cone.

accessory elements Minor elements; trace elements, *q.v.*

accessory minerals Those mineral constituents of a rock that occur in such small amounts that they are disregarded in its classification and definition. Opposed to essential minerals.

accidental inclusions Enclosed crystals or fragments having no genetic connection with the igneous rocks in which they occur. Xenocryst or xenolith, enclave enallogene of Alfred Lacroix, allothogenous ejectum of Ferdinand von Wolff, exogenous inclusion of Albert Johannsen.

acclivity An ascending slope, as opposed to declivity.

accordant fold One of several similarly oriented folds.

accordant summit levels Evencrested ridges, *q.v.*

accretion. *1.* The gradual addition of new land to old by the deposition of sediment carried by the water of a stream. In Canada the terms avulsion and dereliction have been used. *2.* The process by which inorganic bodies grow larger, by the addition of fresh particles to the outside.

accretionary ridge Beach ridge located inland from the modern beach showing that the coast has been built out seaward; ridges of this kind may be accentuated by the development of dunes.

accretion hypotheses Any hypothesis of the origin of the earth which assumes that it has grown from a small nucleus by the gradual addition of solid bodies, such as meteorites, asteroids, or planetesimals, formerly revolving about the sun in independent orbits, but eventually drawn by gravitation to the earth and incorporated with it.

accretion theory A theory of the origin of the solar system involving the development of the planets from vortices in a diskshaped mass of gas.

accretion topography Topographic features built by accumulation of sediment, e.g., meander scrolls.

accretion veins Veins formed by the repeated filling of channelways and their reopening by the development of fractures in the general zone undergoing mineralization.

accumulator plant *Geobot. prospecting:* Plant or tree that acquires an abnormal content of a metal where growing in metalbearing soil.

A C F diagram Triangular diagram showing the chemical character of a metamorphic rock in which the three components plotted are: $A=Al_2O_3+Fe_2O_3-(Na_2O+K_2O)$, $C=CaO$, $F=FeO+MgO+MnO$.

ac-fracture *Struct. petrol:* A tension fracture parallel with the ac fabric plane and normal to b. Where ac-fractures are well developed, b is usually a strong lineation coincident with flexure fold axes.

ac-girdle *See* GIRDLE, AC.

achondrite Rare stony meteorite without chondrules.

acicular Needle-shaped; slender, like a needle or bristle, as some leaves or crystals.

aciculate Needle-shaped (pertaining to shape of gastropod shells).

acid, *n. 1.* A substance whose water solution has a sour taste, changes the color of certain organic dyes, and dissolves active metals with the liberation of hydrogen. *2.* A substance containing hydrogen which dissociates to form hydrogen ions when dissolved in water (or which reacts with water to form hydronium ions). *3.* A substance capable of donating protons to other substances. *4. Adj:* A term applied to igneous rocks having a higher percentage of silica than orthoclase, the limiting figure commonly adopted being 66%.

acid clay A clay which, when in water suspension, gives off H ions. Hydrogen clay.

acidic *1.* A descriptive term applied to those igneous rocks that contain more than 66% SiO_2 as contrasted with intermediate and basic. Sometimes loosely and incorrectly used as equivalent to felsic and to oversaturated, but these terms include rock types (e.g., nepheline, syenite, and quartz basalt, respectively) which are not generally considered acidic. *2.* Less frequently used in reference to composition of feldspars, based on their content of silica. *3.* When referring to hydrothermal, pegmatitic, or other aqueous fluids the term is used in its chemical sense of high hydrogen ion concentration (low pH); very loosely used to refer to solutions containing salts of the strong acids (chlorides, sulfates, etc.) regardless of pH. *4.* In furnace practice, a slag in which silica is present in excess of the amount required to form a "neutral" slag with the earthy bases present.

acidization The process of forcing acid into a limestone, dolomite, or sandstone in order to increase permeability and porosity by removing a part of the rock constituents. It is also used to remove mud injected during drilling. The general objective of acidization is to increase productivity.

acid rock A term rather loosely used in petrology, generally to mean one of the following: *1.* An igneous rock containing 66% or more of silica, free or combined, in this sense being nearly equivalent to acidic. *2.* An igneous rock in which minerals high in silica, such as quartz, alkaline feldspar, and muscovite, are dominant. *3.* Very loosely, an igneous rock composed dominantly of light-colored minerals. In all three senses contrasted with basic.

The term is misleading and undesirable and is going out of use. As used in the first sense it is being replaced by silicic or persilicic, and as used in the second sense it should be replaced by felsic or by a term denoting the dominant mineral. As used in the third sense it should be replaced by leucocratic. *See* ACIDIC

aclinic Having no inclination or dip; situated where the compass needle does not dip, as the aclinic line, or magnetic equator.

acmite Aegirite. *See* PYROXENE

acoustical well logging Any determination of the physical properties or dimensions of a bore hole by acoustical means, including measurement of the depth of fluid level in a well.

acoustic waves The waves which contain sound energy and by the motion of which sound energy is transmitted in air, in water, or in the earth. The wave may be described in terms of change of pressure, of particle displacement, or of density.

ac-plane *Struct. petrol:* A plane at right angles to the surface of movement. The ac-plane contains *a*, the direction of tectonic transport, and *c*, the axis perpendicular to the surface of movement.

acquired character Character not inherited but acquired by an individual organism during its lifetime as a result of use or disuse according to its mode of life or the conditions under which it lived.

acre A measure of surficial land area, containing in the United States and England 43,560 square feet.

acre-foot The volume of liquid or solid required to cover 1 acre to a depth of 1 foot.

acre-inch The quantity of water, soil or other material that will cover 1 acre 1 inch deep.

acre-yield The average amount of oil or gas or water recovered from 1 acre of a reservoir. The amount of any product obtained from 1 acre.

actinolite *See* AMPHIBOLE

activation, energy of The extra amount of energy which any particle or group of particles must have in order to go from one energy state into some other energy state. Applied to changes in phase, as in chemical reactions, and to movement of particles, as in diffusion ("activation energy migration"). The greater the amount of energy involved, the higher the "barrier" preventing the change.

active glacier A glacier in which some of the ice is flowing.

active layer Annually thawed layer; mollisol. Layer of ground above the permafrost which thaws in the summer and freezes again in the winter.

active permafrost Permafrost

which, after having been thawed due to natural or artificial causes, is able to return to permafrost under the present climate.

active volcano *See* VOLCANO

activity, chemical *1.* Tendency to react spontaneously and energetically with other substances. *2.* Effective concentration; concentration as modified by the effects of the solvent and other dissolved substances. When activities are used in place of concentrations, dissociation constants and solubility products are true constants instead of approximate ones.

activity ratio Ratio of plasticity index to percentage of clay-sized minerals in sediment.

acute bisectrix The line which bisects the acute angle of the optic axes of biaxial minerals. *See* BISECTRIX

adamantine Like a diamond in hardness or luster. Some consider hardness is not a part of definition.

adamellite Synonymous with and perhaps a preferable name for QUARTZ MONZONITE.

adaptation Adjustment of organisms to their environments that involves development of new or better functioning structures or other improvements.

adaptive grid Discontinuities that separate closely related adaptive zones.

adaptive norm That part of an organic population which can survive and reproduce in the environment usually occupied by the species; the remainder carries hereditary defects and diseases.

adaptive radiation Term proposed for the spreading or phyletic ramification of a group of animals from a common ancestral type into divergent descendant types, each with a distinct

and characteristic adaptive status and ecological relationship.

additive metamorphism Pneumatolitic metamorphism.

adhesion The attraction of the molecules in the walls of interstices for molecules of water.

adiabatic *Thermodyn:* The relationship of pressure and volume when a gas or other fluid is compressed or expanded without either giving out or receiving heat. *See* ISOTHERMAL

adiabatic gradient A temperature gradient in a column of material such that essentially no heat enters or leaves the system upon such processes as convection.

adit *1.* A nearly horizontal passage from the surface by which a mine is entered and unwatered. In the United States an adit is usually called a tunnel, though the latter, strictly speaking, passes entirely through a hill and is open at both ends. Frequently called drift, or adit level. *2.* As used in the Colorado statutes it may apply to a cut either open or under cover, or open in part and under cover in part, dependent on the nature of the ground.

adjusted stream Stream which flows essentially parallel to the strike of underlying beds.

adobe *1.* Unburnt sun-dried brick. *2.* Clayey and silty deposits found in the desert basins of southwestern North America and in Mexico where the material is extensively used for making sun-dried brick. The composition is a mixture of clay and silt together with other materials. Most adobes are calcareous. Similar deposits are found in other desert basins. The agent of deposition seems to have been mainly water, and the places of deposition are more or less flat areas in the central and lower parts of desert basins.

adolescence The state of early maturity in which the following features of maturity are only partially developed: flood plains and meanders, moderately sloping valley walls, a well-defined drainage system with many tributaries and definite divides, a fairly established grade, and the absence of waterfalls and lakes.

adsorption 1. Adhesion of molecules of gases, or of ions or molecules in solutions, to the surfaces of solid bodies with which they are in contact. 2. The behavior of a multicomponent fluid system which results in a dissolved material becoming more concentrated, or less concentrated, at an interface than in the body of the solution.

adularia A variety of orthoclase.

advance 1. **of a beach** A continuing seaward movement of the shore line; a net seaward movement of the shore line over a specified time. *Syn:* PROGRESSION. 2. **of a glacier** The forward movement of a glacier front.

aegirite Acmite. *See* PYROXENE

Aeolian, *Obs.* Eolian, *q.v.*

aerate To expose to the action of the air. Supply or charge with air.

aeration, zone of *See* ZONE OF AERATION

aerial Relating to the air or atmosphere. "Subaerial" is applied to phenomena occurring under the atmosphere; "subaqueous" to phenomena occurring under water.

aerial magnetometer A device used to measure variations in the earth's magnetic field while being transported by an aircraft. Same as airborne magnetometer.

aerial photograph A photograph of the earth's surface taken from the air. It is usually one of a series taken from an aircraft moving in a systematic pattern at a given altitude in order to obtain a mosaic for mapping land divisions, geology, soil, vegetation, topography, etc.

aerobic 1. Living or active only in the presence of oxygen. 2. Pertaining to or induced by aerobic organisms.

aerolite A type of meteorite consisting largely of silicates; also called stones.

aeromagnetic Refers to magnetometer observations made from a moving airplane.

aff Affinity. *Paleontol:* Indicates a specimen or specimens believed to be closely related to but not exactly the same as the named species.

affine Refers to deformative movements in which, at the scale considered, individual particles move uniformly with respect to each other and originally straight lines and even planes are not distorted but a sphere is transformed into an ellipsoid.

affine deformation Homogeneous deformation. Deformation in which very thin layers slip against each other in such a way that each moves equally with respect to its neighbors; generally does not result in folding.

aftershock An earthquake which follows a larger earthquake and originates at or near the focus of the larger earthquake. Generally, major earthquakes are followed by a large number of aftershocks, decreasing in frequency with increasing time. Such a series of aftershocks may last many days or even months.

Aftonian Post-Nebraskan interglacial.

agate 1. A variegated waxy

quartz in which the colors are in bands, in clouds, or in distinct groups. 2. Kind of silica consisting mainly of chalcedony in variegated bands or other patterns commonly occupying vugs in volcanic and some other rocks.

age 1. Any great period of time in the history of the earth or the material universe marked by special phases of physical conditions or organic development; an eon, as the age of mammals. 2. Formal geologic time unit corresponding to a stage. 3. Informal geologic time unit corresponding to any stratigraphic unit.

age ratio The ratio of daughter to parent isotope. Often used to indicate a ratio that is perturbed by some factor and therefore not indicative of the absolute age of the mineral.

agglomerate Contemporaneous pyroclastic rock containing a predominance of rounded or subangular fragments greater than 32 mm. in diameter.

agglutinate A pyroclastic deposit consisting of an accumulation of originally plastic ejecta (chiefly volcanic bombs and driblet) and formed by the coherence of the fragments upon solidification. The cement is the glossy skin of the fragments at their point of contact. Distinguished from agglomerate by the presence of a glassy cement, by the occurrence of fragments of spalled-off scoria in the interstices between the blocks, and by the general absence of an ash or tuff matrix.

aggradation 1. The process of building up a surface by deposition. 2. The growth of a permafrost area. In both senses, the opposite of degradation.

aggrade 1. To build up the grade or slope (of the earth) by deposition of sediment. 2. It is sug-

gested, in accordance with Davis' original proposal, that "graded" be used specifically for the stream in which equilibrium is maintained and that "degrading" and "aggrading" be restricted to cases of the shifting equilibrium. "Degrading" is down-cutting approximately at grade, in contradistinction to such self-explanatory terms as trench or incise. "Aggrading" is upbuilding approximately at grade.

There is no need for using either "aggrade" or "degrade" to describe short-period variations in steam activity, i.e., as synonyms for filling or scouring of a channel, or for the more general terms erosion and deposition.

aggregate 1. To bring together; to collect or unite into a mass. 2. Composed of a mixture of substances, separable by mechanical means. 3. The mineral material, such as sand, gravel, shells, slag, or broken stone, with which cement or bituminous material is mixed to form a mortar or concrete. Fine aggregate may be considered as the material that will pass a 1/4-inch screen, and coarse aggregate as the material that will not pass a 1/4-inch screen.

aggregate structure A mass of separate little crystals, scales, or grains which extinguish under the polarizing microscope at different intervals during the rotation of the stage.

aggressive or invasive magmas Those magmas which force their way into place.

Agnatha Class of vertebrates; jawless fishes, e.g., lampreys. Ord.-Rec.

agonic line A line passing through points on the earth's surface at which the direction of the magnetic needle is truly north and south; a line of no magnetic declination.

A-horizon Zone of eluviation. The uppermost zone in the soil profile, from which soluble salts and colloids have been leached, and in which organic matter has accumulated. *See* B-HORIZON

airborne magnetometer A device used to measure variations in the earth's magnetic field while being transported by an aircraft. Same as aerial magnetometer.

airborne scintillation counter Any scintillation counter especially designed to measure the ambient radioactivity from an aircraft in flight. The instrument measures gamma radiation by employing a phosphor which emits a minute flash of light on absorbing a gamma ray. A photomultiplier tube converts the light flashes into an electrical current or voltage variation which is proportional to the intensity of gamma radiation.

air damping The use of air, usually in condenser microphone detectors and in inductive geophones where the coil mass is small, to establish friction against the moving mass, causing decay of motion with time following application of impulse.

air drill A drill for boring holes in the earth employing air rather than water to remove cuttings from the hole.

air mass A widespread body of air which approximates horizontal homogeneity, i.e., its physical properties, level for level, are about the same over a wide area. It is possible to distinguish four main types of air masses, depending upon the geographical positions of their sources: (1) Equatorial air masses (E), origi-

nating in the equatorial part of the trade-wind zone; (2) Tropical air masses (T), formed in the subtropical anticyclones; (3) Polar air masses (P), typical of the subpolar anticyclones; (4) Arctic air masses (A), formed over the arctic fields of ice and snow. This main classification is further refined by subdividing the air masses into maritime (m) or continental (c) masses, depending on whether the source is oceanic or continental. In addition, monsoon air (M) is a transition form between cP and E, and superior air (S) is unique in that it is formed in the free atmosphere.

air shooting The act or action of applying a seismic pulse to the earth by detonating a charge or charges in the air above the surface of the earth; the process of exploration by the use of such detonations.

air wave The acoustic energy pulse transmitted through the air as a result of the detonation of a seismic shot.

airy isostasy That hypothesis of equilibrium for the earth's solid outer crust in which the crustal density is supposed constant so that mountains are compensated by "roots" analogous to the underwater extensions of icebergs floating in the ocean.

A K F diagram Triangular diagram showing the chemical character of a metamorphic rock in which the three components plotted are: $A=Al_2O_3+Fe_2O_3-(CaO+Na_2O)$, $K=K_2O$, $F=FeO+MgO+MnO$.

alabaster Terra alba. Compact fine-grained gypsum, white or delicately shaded. Used for ornamental vessels, figures, and other carvings.

alaskan bands A type of ogive,

q.v., formed by the exposure of dirt bands, *q.v.*

alaskite A plutonic rock consisting of orthoclase, microcline, and subordinate quartz, with few or no mafic constituents. Plagioclase may or may not be present. A leucocratic variety of granite.

alb Flat or gently inclined narrow shelf separating the nearly vertical side of an alpine glacial trough from the mountain slope above.

albedo The percentage of the incoming radiation that is reflected by a natural surface such as the ground, ice, snow, or water.

Albers conical equal-area map projection A map projection on which geographic meridians are represented by straight lines which meet at a common point; this common point serves as the center of a series of arcs of circles which represent the geographic parallels. Meridians and parallels intersect in right angles. Along two selected parallels, called standard parallels, the scale is held exact; along the other parallels, the scale varies with the latitude, but is constant along any given parallel. Between the standard parallels, the meridional scale is too great; beyond them, too small. At any point on the projection, the departure from exact scale along a parallel is of the opposite sign from the departure from exact scale along the meridian, and the two are so related as to produce an equal-area map projection. Passing through every point are two lines of true-length scale which intersect in right angles; these are called isoperimetric curves.

Albertan Middle Cambrian.

Albian *1.* Uppermost Lower Cretaceous. *2.* In the United States, Lower Silurian (not recommended). *See* ALBIONIAN

Albionian Lower Silurian.

albite *See* PLAGIOCLASE

albite-epidote-amphibolite facies Metamorphic rocks produced under intermediate temperature and pressure conditions by regional metamorphism or in the outer contact metamorphic zone.

albitite A coarse-grained dike rock consisting almost wholly of albite. Common accessory minerals are muscovite, garnet, apatite, quartz, and opaque oxides.

Alexandrian Lower Silurian.

alexandrite A variety of the mineral chrysoberyl which may appear to be either green or red, depending on the nature of the light by which it is examined.

Algae Class of thallophytes, includes single-celled plants and common seaweeds. Precamb.-Rec.

algal, *adj.* Of, pertaining to, or composed of algae.

algal limestone A limestone composed largely of remains of calcium-secreting algae or in which such algae serve to bind together the fragments of other lime-secreting forms.

algal structure A deposit, usually calcareous, which shows banding, irregular concentric structures, crusts, pseudopisolites or pseudoconcretionary forms, resulting from organic, colonial secretion and precipitation. Some so-called algal structures may be of inorganic origin.

Algoman orogeny Post-Archian diastrophism.

Algonkian Formerly, in the nomenclature of the United States Geological Survey, the second in order of age of the systems into which the stratified rocks of the earth's crust were divided; also the corresponding period of geologic time. Some authorities use Proterozoic in the same sense. As physical age measurements accumulate, the use of this term is changing. The American Commission on Stratigraphic Nomenclature (1954) suggests substitution of Late Precambrian for Algonkian.

alidade *1.* The part of surveying instrument consisting of a sighting device, index, and reading or recording devices. *2.* A straightedge ruler carrying a sighting device, such as slot sights or a telescope mounted parallel to the ruler.

alignment; alinement The placing or existence of points along a straight line. Also, the location of points with reference to a straight line or system of straight lines.

alkali *1.* Sodium carbonate or potassium carbonate, or more generally any bitter-tasting salt found at or near the surface in arid and semiarid regions. *2.* A strong base, e.g., $NaOH$ or KOH. *3.* An alkali metal.

alkalic Refers to: (1) solution containing alkali metal ions; (2) igneous rock with more alkali metals than are contained in feldspars, therefore such minerals as feldspathoids are present; (3) igneous rock with more alkali metals than average for its clan; (4) igneous rock with alkali-lime index less than 51; (5) igneous rocks of Atlantic series. *Obs.*

alkalic-calcic series Those igneous rock series having alkali-lime indices in the range 51–55.

alkalic igneous rocks *Petrol:* A term rather loosely used, generally meaning one of the following: *1.* More than average alkali (K_2O+Na_2O) for that clan in

which they occur. *2.* Containing feldspathoids or other minerals, such as acmite, so that the molecular ratio of alkali to silica is greater than 1:6. *3.* The term is sometimes defined also as embracing those rock series having a low alkali-lime index (51 or less).

alkali feldspar The alkali-rich feldspars microcline, orthoclase, albite, and anorthoclase.

alkali flat A level lakelike plain formed in low depressions where accumulated water evaporates depositing fine sediment and dissolved minerals which form a hard surface if mechanical sediments prevail or a crumbly powdered surface if efflorescent salts are abundant.

alkali-lime index The weight percentage of silica, in a sequence of igneous rocks on a variation diagram, where the weight percentages of CaO and of (K_2O+Na_2O) are equal, i.e., the point of crossing of the curves for CaO and (K_2O+Na_2O).

alkali metal Any metal of the alkali group, as lithium, sodium, potassium, rubidium, or caesium.

alkaline, *adj.* *1.* Having the qualities of a base. *Syn:* BASIC. *2.* Containing sodium and/or potassium in excess of the amount needed to form feldspar with the available silica, e.g., an alkaline rock—in this sense sometimes written alkalic. *3.* Containing ions of one or more alkali metals, e.g., an alkaline ore solution. *4.* Containing cations of the strong bases in excess of the anions of strong acids, e.g., an alkaline ore solution. (Note that geologic usage gives "alkaline solution" so many different meanings that it is ambiguous without further qualification; it is therefore recommended that alkalic be used when definitions *2* or *3* are meant.)

alkali rocks Igneous rocks in which the abundance of alkalies in relation to other constituents has impressed a distinctive mineralogical character; generally indicated by the presence of soda pyroxenes, soda amphiboles, and/or feldspathoids. *Cf.* CALC-ALKALIC SERIES

alkemade line A line connecting the composition points of two primary phases whose phase areas are adjacent and meet to form a boundary curve.

allanite Orthite. A mineral, a monoclinic member of the epidote group. Composition variable, formula $(Ca,Ce,La)_2(Al,Fe,Mg)_3(SiO_4)_3(OH)$. Commonly contains a little thorium and may be metamict.

Alleghenyan Lower Middle Pennsylvanian.

Alleghenyan orogeny Late Permian diastrophism.

Allen's rule Warm-blooded animals generally have shorter legs, tails, and ears in cold than in warm regions.

alliaceous Applied to minerals having the odor of garlic when rubbed, scratched, or heated; e.g., arsenical minerals.

Alling scale A system of classifying size grades of sediments, for use with thin and polished sections, with subdivisions based on the fourth root of 10.

allo A combining form signifying variation, departure from normal, reversal.

allochem Sediment formed by chemical or biochemical precipitation within a depositional basin; includes intraclasts, oolites, fossils, and pellets; *cf.* PSEUDOALLOCHEM

allochemical metamorphism Metamorphism accompanied by addition or removal of material so that bulk chemical composition of rock is changed.

allochthon Rocks that have been moved a long distance from their original place of deposition by some tectonic process, generally related to overthrusting or recumbent folding, or perhaps gravity sliding. Used in contrast to AUTOCHTHON, *q.v.*

allochthonous A term applied to rocks of which the dominant constituents have not been formed *in situ*. *Cf.* AUTOCHTHONOUS

allogene; allothigene A mineral or rock which has been transported to the site of deposition from without.

allogenic Term meaning generated elsewhere, applied to those constituents that came into existence outside of, and previously to, the rock of which they now constitute a part, e.g., the pebbles of a conglomerate. *Cf.* AUTHIGENIC

allophane An amorphous hydrated aluminosilicate gel of highly variable composition; P_2O_5 may be present in appreciable amounts.

Allotheria Subclass of mammals; consists of extinct primitive forms.

allotropic Term applied by J. J. Berzelius to those substances which may exist in two or more forms, as diamond and graphite.

alluvial *1.* Pertaining to alluvium. *2.* Formerly used as a term for recent unconsolidated sediments.

alluvial dam Sedimentary deposit built by an overloaded stream which dams its channel, especially characteristic of distributaries on alluvial fans.

alluvial fan A cone-shaped deposit of alluvium made by a stream where it runs out onto a level plain or meets a slower stream. The fans generally form where streams issue from mountains upon the lowland.

alluvial plain *1.* Flood plains produced by the filling of a valley bottom are alluvial plains and consist of fine mud, sand, or gravel. *2.* A plain resulting from the deposition of alluvium by water. In the southwestern United States most alluvial plains are formed by streams having a considerable grade, and hence they are generally referred to as alluvial slopes.

alluviation The deposition of mechanical sediments by rivers anywhere along their courses.

alluvium *1.* A general term for all detrital deposits resulting from the operations of modern rivers, thus including the sediments laid down in river beds, flood plains, lakes, fans at the foot of mountain slopes, and estuaries. *2.* The rather consistent usage of the term throughout its history makes it quite clear that alluvium is intended to apply to stream deposits of comparatively recent time, that the subaqueous deposits of seas and lakes are not intended to be included, and that permanent submergence is not a criterion. Alluvium may become lithified, as has happened frequently in the past, and then may be termed ancient alluvium.

almandine, almandite *See* GARNET

alnöite A lamprophyre consisting of biotite, augite, olivine, and melilite. Apatite, perovskite, nepheline, and opaque oxides are common accessories. *See* LAMPROPHYRE

alp Topographic shoulder located high on the side of a glaciated trough.

alpha particle A helium atom lacking two electrons and therefore having a double positive charge.

alpha rays; alpha radiation Radiation consisting of alpha particles emitted during the decay of some radioactive elements.

Alpides Great east-west structural belt including Alps of Europe and Himalayas and related mountains of Asia mostly folded in Tertiary time.

alpine Of, pertaining to, or like the Alps or any lofty mountain. Resembling a great mountain range of southern Europe called the Alps. Implies high elevation, particularly above tree line, and cold climate.

alpine glacier A glacier occupying a depression within or lying on mountainous terrain. *Syn:* MOUNTAIN GLACIER

alpine orogeny Series of diastrophic movements beginning perhaps in the late Triassic and continuing until the present. *Cf.* LARAMIDIAN

alpine range Signifies a range possessing the rugged peak-and-sierra form and the internal structures incidental to intense crumpling, metamorphism, and igneous intrusion as exemplified in the Swiss Alps.

alteration Change in the mineralogical composition of a rock, typically brought about by the action of hydrothermal solutions. Sometimes classed as a phase of metamorphism but usually distinguished from it because milder and more localized. Also applied to secondary (supergene) changes in rocks or minerals.

alternation of generations *1.* The orderly succession of sexual and asexual types of reproduction in the life cycle of many species of Foraminifera, resulting in the production of different kinds of tests; found also in other animals. *2.* The alternation of a spore-producing phase and a gamete-producing phase in the life cycle of a plant.

altimeter An aneroid barometer used for determining elevations.

altiplanation A special phase of solifluction that, under certain conditions, expresses itself in terracelike forms and flattened summits and passes that are essentially accumulations of loose rock materials.

altithermal, *n.* Period of high temperature, particularly the postglacial thermal optimum.

altitude *1.* The vertical angle between the plane of the horizon and the line to the observed point, as a star. *2.* The vertical distance between a point and a datum surface or plane, such as mean sea level. *See* ELEVATION

alumina Aluminum oxide, Al_2O_3.

alunite A mineral, $KAl_3(SO_4)_2(OH)_6$, hexagonal rhombohedral, usually in white, gray, or pink masses in hydrothermally altered feldspathic rocks.

alunitization Introduction of, or replacement by, alunite.

alunogen A mineral, $Al_2(SO_4)_3\cdot16H_2O$, triclinic, usually found as fibrous masses formed by the action of acid sulfate waters on rocks.

alveolar Having small cellular structures like a honeycomb.

amalgam *1.* A mineral, an alloy of silver and mercury. *2.* An alloy of mercury with another metal.

amazonite; Amazonstone A green variety of microcline. Used as a gem.

amber A fossil resin from prehistoric coniferous trees.

amblygonite A mineral, $LiAlPO_4(F,OH)$. Triclinic. An ore of lithium found in pegmatites.

amblypod An extinct hoofed mammal distinguished by stout pillarlike limbs ending in short, blunt feet like those of an elephant, and by the archaic nature of the teeth and skull.

ambulacrum Area or ray in echinoderms that marks a branch of the water vascular system and generally bears numerous tube feet.

amethyst A purple or bluish-violet variety of quartz, SiO_2. Used as a gem.

Ammanian Middle Upper Cretaceous.

ammonite One of a large extinct group of mollusks related to the living chambered nautilus. The sutures are complex and angular, whereas they are straight or simply curved in the nautilus and its relatives.

ammonoid An inclusive term for GONIATITES, CERATITES, and AMMONITES, *q.v.*

Ammonoidea Division of tetrabranchiate cephalopods, mostly coiled, whose septa meet the external shell to form folded sutures. Dev.-Cret.

Amniota Subphylum of vertebrates that are exclusively air-breathing. Includes reptiles, birds, and mammals.

amorphous Without form; applied to rocks and minerals having no definite crystalline structure.

amosite An asbestos mineral with iron content higher than anthophyllite.

Amphibia Class of vertebrates, air-breathing tetrapods that develop from a water-breathing larval tadpole stage. Dev.-Rec.

amphibian A cold-blooded animal with legs, feet, and lungs, that breathes by means of gills in the early stages and by means of lungs in the later stages of life. One of the Amphibia.

amphibole A mineral group, general formula $A_{2-3}B_5(Si,Al_4)O_{11}$-$(OH)_2$, where A is mainly Mg, Fe″, Ca, and Na; B is mainly Mg, Fe″, Al, and Fe‴. The amphiboles are common rock-forming minerals. Following are the most important amphiboles: anthophyllite, $(Mg,Fe)_7Si_8O_{22}$-$(OH)_2$, orthorhombic; the cummingtonite-grunerite series, $(Mg,-Fe)_7Si_8O_{22}(OH)_2$, monoclinic; the tremolite-actinolite series, $Ca_2(Mg,Fe″)_5Si_8O_{22}(OH)_2$, monoclinic; the glaucophane, riebeckite series, $Na_2(Mg,Fe″,Al,Fe‴)_5$-$Si_8O_{22}(OH)_2$, monoclinic; hornblende, $(Ca,Na)_3Mg,Fe″,Al,-Ti)_5(Si,Al)_8O_{22}(OH,F)_2$, monoclinic; crocidolite, nearly Na_2-$Fe_4‴Si_8O_{22}(OH)_2$, monoclinic.

amphibolite A crystalloblastic rock consisting mainly of amphibole and plagioclase. Quartz is absent, or present in small amounts only. When quartz is more abundant there is a gradation to hornblende-plagioclase gneiss. *See* FEATHER AMPHIBOLITE; GARBENSCHIEFER; OLLENITE

amphibolite facies Rocks produced by medium- to high-grade regional metamorphism.

Amphineura Class of mollusks whose flattened body is covered by eight articulated dorsal plates, exclusively marine; chitons. Ord.-Rec.

amphoteric Having both basic and acidic properties.

amplitude The elevation of the crest of a wave or ripple above the adjacent troughs. *Hydrodyn:* One-half the wave height.

amygdale A gas cavity or vesicle in volcanic and occasionally in intrusive rocks which has become filled with secondary (usually late magmatic or deuteric) products such as zeolites, calcite, chalcedony, or quartz. *Adj:* AMYGDALAR *Syn:* (Rare): AMYGDULE

amygdaloid A general name for volcanic rocks (ordinarily basalts or andesites) that contain numerous gas cavities (vesicles) filled with secondary minerals such as zeolites, calcite, chalcedony, or quartz. The filled cavities are called amygdules or amygdales. *Adj:* AMYGDALOIDAL

amygdule *1.* Small gas bubble in lava or other igneous rock filled with a secondary mineral such as zeolite, calcite, quartz, etc. *2.* An agate pebble.

An Abbreviation for anorthite. *See* PLAGIOCLASE

anaerobic, *adj.* *1.* Living or active in the absence of free oxygen. *2.* Pertaining to or induced by organisms that can live in the absence of free oxygen.

analbite High temperature albite; inversion occurs at about 700° C.

analcime; analcite A mineral, $NaAlSi_2O_6.H_2O$, an isometric zeolite, commonly found in diabase and in alkali-rich basalts.

analytic group Rock stratigraphic unit formerly a formation but up-graded because subdivisions of the unit are now considered to be formations.

analyzer That part of a polariscope that receives the light after polarization and exhibits its properties. In a petrographic microscope, the polarizing mechanism (Nicol prism, Polaroid, etc.) which intersects the light after it has passed through the object.

Anamnia Subphylum of vertebrates that are aquatic and breathe with gills during some part of their life histories; includes fish and amphibians.

anamorphic zone The zone of rock-flowage, especially characterized by silicatization involving decarbonation, dehydration, and deoxidation. *See* KATAMORPHIC ZONE

anaplasis A condition of progressive ontogenetic development. Evolutionary state characterized by increasing vigor and diversification of organisms; considered to be the first stage in an evolutionary cycle. *Cf.* METAPLASIS; CATAPLASIS

anastomosing *1.* As anastomosing stream (braided stream, *q.v.*) branching, interlacing, intercommunicating, thereby producing a netlike or braided appearance. *2.* netted; intervened; said of leaves marked by cross veins forming a network; sometimes the vein branches meet only at the margin.

anatase Octahedrite. A mineral, TiO_2. Tetragonal, trimorphous with rutile and brookite.

anatexis *1.* A high-temperature metamorphic process by which plutonic rock in the deeper levels of the crust is dissolved and regenerated as a magma. *Cf.* SYNTEXIS. *2.* The complete melting of crustal rocks to form granitic magma, as opposed to rheomorphism or mobilization, which implies merely the development of sufficient liquid to permit movement. Some include both processes under the term anatexis.

anatexites Metamorphic rocks, formed by the process of anatexis. They show only faint schistose structure and are granitelike in composition.

anatomy The phase of morphology which treats of the internal structure of organisms.

anauxite A clay mineral near kaolinite, but containing excess silica, probably as interlayered sheets.

anchi Combining form, meaning "almost," and used as a prefix in petrologic terms.

anchored dune Sand dune stabilized by growth of vegetation.

anchor ice Ice that forms in the bottom of rivers when the rest of the water is not frozen. *Syn:* GROUND ICE; BOTTOM ICE

andalusite A mineral, Al_2SiO_5, trimorphous with kyanite and sillimanite. Orthorhombic. Commonly occurs in schists and gneisses.

andesine *See* PLAGIOCLASE

andesite A volcanic rock composed essentially of andesine and one or more mafic constituents. The plagioclase is usually strongly zoned and may range in composition from about An_{35} to An_{70}, but the average composition usually falls within the range of andesine. When the rock is porphyritic, the phenocrystic plagioclase is usually more calcic than the groundmass plagioclase, and in addition the groundmass may contain small amounts of microcrystalline or occult potassic feldspar and cristobalite. Pyroxene, hornblende, or biotite, or all three in various proportions may constitute the mafic constituents.

andesite line The geographic boundary between the circum-Pacific rock province (the andesite-dacite-rhyolite association of the Pacific margin) and the intro-Pacific rock province (the olivine basalt-trachyte association of the islands lying within the Pacific Basin). It is based primarily on petrographic data and runs from Alaska via Japan, the Marianas, Palau Islands, Bismarck Archipelago, and the Fiji and Tonga groups to the east of New Zealand and Chatham Islands. Along the eastern side of the Pacific the position of the line is less clearly defined, but probably it runs along the coasts of North and South America. In the South Pacific it has not yet been traced.

andradite *See* GARNET

Angara Stable shield region in northern Asia.

Angiospermae Class of Spermatophyta or Pteropsida; plants with highly specialized flowers and seeds. Jur.-Rec.

angle of dip A synonym for dip.

angle of incidence In optics, the angle between the incident ray of light and the normal to the surface.

angle of repose The maximum slope or angle at which a material such as soil or loose rock remains stable. When exceeded, mass movement by slipping as well as by water erosion may be expected. *Syn:* CRITICAL SLOPE

anglesite A mineral, $PbSO_4$, orthorhombic. A common alteration product of lead sulfide ores.

Angoumian Upper Turonian.

Angström unit (Often anglicized to Angstrom; abbreviated A. or Å.) A unit of length, 10^{-8} cm., commonly used in structural crystallography. *See* kX

angular, *adj.* A roundness grade showing very little or no evidence of wear, with edges and corners sharp. Secondary corners, *q.v.,* numerous (15 to 30) and sharp. Class limits 0 to 0.15.

angularity *1.* Sharpness of edges and corners of grains. A grain is angular if most of the edges or corners are sharp, and rounded if most are smooth. Not to be confused with sphericity, *q.v.* A nearly spherical particle may have sharp corners and be angular, while a flat pebble may be not spherical in shape but still be well rounded as to its corners. *Cf.* SHAPE. *2. Geophys:*

Stepout-moveout or moveout time, *q.v.*

angular unconformity An unconformity in which the older strata dip at a different angle (generally steeper) than the younger strata. *See* DISCONFORMITY

anhedral Xenomorphic; allotriomorphic, *q.v.*

anhedron A term proposed by L. V. Pirsson for an individual mineral component of an igneous rock that lacks crystal boundaries. *Obs.* The adjectives allotriomorphic, xenomorphic, and anhedral imply the same concept.

anhydrite A mineral, anhydrous calcium sulfate, $CaSO_4$. Orthorhombic, commonly massive in evaporite beds.

anhydrous Completely or essentially without water, as anhydrous magma.

animal Organism that is sensitive, capable of voluntary movement, and requires organic matter for its food. *Cf.* PLANT; PROTIST

Animalia The animal kingdom.

anion An ion that moves, or that would move, toward an anode; hence nearly always synonymous with NEGATIVE ION. (In voltaic cells postive ions move toward the anode, and are sometimes called anions.)

Anisian Lower Middle Triassic.

anisotropic Having physical properties that vary in different directions; specifically in crystal optics, showing double refraction. Characteristic of all crystalline substances except those belonging to the isometric system. *See* ISOTROPIC

anisotropy Condition of having different properties in different directions; example: the state of geologic strata of transmitting sound waves with different velocities in the vertical and in the horizontal directions.

ankerite A mineral, a ferroan variety of dolomite, $CaCO_3 \cdot (Mg,Fe,Mn)CO_3$.

annabergite Nickel bloom. A mineral, $Ni_3(AsO_4)_2 \cdot 8H_2O$; monoclinic, usually found as green incrustations as an alteration product of nickel arsenides.

Annelida The phylum of invertebrate animals which includes the segmented worms.

annual layer 1. Sedimentary layer deposited or presumed to have been deposited during the course of a year, e.g., glacial varve. 2. Dark layer in stratified salt deposit containing disseminated anhydrite.

annual ring The layer of xylem (wood) formed by one year's growth of cambium.

annular drainage pattern Annular drainage, as the name implies, is ringlike in pattern. It is subsequent in origin and associated with maturely dissected dome or basin structures.

anomaly 1. A deviation from uniformity; a local feature distinguishable in a geophysical, geochemical, or geobotanical measurement over a larger area; a feature considered capable of being associated with commercially valuable petroleum or other mineral deposits; an area or restricted portion of a geophysical survey, such as magnetic or gravitational, which is different in appearance from the survey in general; specifically, an area within which it appears that successful drilling or other search for hydrocarbons or minerals may be conducted. In seismic usage anomaly is generally synonymous with structure, but it is also used for spurious or unexplainable seismic events or for

local deviations of potential functions which can be conclusively attributed to no unique cause. 2. The departure of the local mean value of a meteorological element from the mean value for the latitude. 3. (Gravity) In comparing any set of observational data with a computed theoretical curve, the difference of an observed value and the corresponding computed value (observed minus computed).

anorogenic A geological feature that forms during a period of tectonic quiescence between orogenic periods.

anorthite See PLAGIOCLASE

anorthoclase Triclinic alkali feldspars containing more sodium than $Ab_{63}Or_{37}$ (see PLAGIOCLASE) which invert to monoclinic symmetry when heated and reinvert to triclinic when cooled.

anorthosite A plutonic rock composed almost wholly of plagioclase.

antecedent platform A postulated submarine platform 50 meters or more below sea level from which barrier reefs and atolls grow upward to the water surface. The formation of the platform predates its colonization by corals. Hence, it is termed an antecedent platform.

antecedent valley A valley which was established before orogenic movement occurred.

antediluvial Formerly referred to time or deposits antedating Noah's flood.

anterior 1. The front. 2. In brachiopods, the side opposite the beak. 3. In pelecypods, the end opposite the pallial sinus or outlet of the siphons. 4. In gastropods, the end with the aperture.

anthophyllite See AMPHIBOLE

Anthozoa Class of coelenterates

represented by polyps that build solitary or colonial calareous external skeletons; corals. Ord.-Rec.

anthracite *1.* Generally a hard, black lustrous coal containing a high percentage of fixed carbon and a low percentage of volatile matter, commonly referred to as "hard coal" and mined in the United States, mostly in eastern Pennsylvania, although in small quantities in other states. *2.* Non-agglomerating anthracitic coal having 92% or more, and less than 98% of fixed carbon (dry, mineral-matter-free) and 8% or less, and more than 2% of volatile matter (dry, mineral-matter-free).

anthraxolite Refers to a highly graphitic coal—an example quoted having a percentage of 97.72 fixed carbon—such as anthracite-like asphaltic material occurring in veins in Precambrian slate of the Sudbury district.

anthraxylon [<*Gr. anthrax* coal + *xylon* wood] The vitreous-appearing components of coal, which in thin section are shown to be derived from the woody tissues of plants, such as stems, limbs, branches, twigs, roots, including both wood and cortex, changed and broken up in fragments of greatly varying sizes through biological decomposition and weathering during the peat stage, and later flattened and transformed into coal through the coalification process, but still present as definite units.

anticlinal *1. Geol:* inclined toward each other, as, the ridge tiles of the roof of a house. *2.* Of, or pertaining to, an anticline.

anticlinal axis The plane or surface that divides an anticline as symmetrically as possible.

anticlinal bend An upwardly convex flexure in which one limb dips gently toward the apex and the other limb dips more steeply away from it. *Cf.* MONOCLINAL FLEXURE; UNICLINE; MONOCLINE

anticlinal mountain A mountain formed by an anticlinal fold.

anticlinal theory The theory that water, oil, and gas accumulate in the order named, in up-bowed strata, provided such a structure contains reservoir rocks in proper relation to source rocks and an impervious barrier.

anticlinal valleys Those which follow anticlinal axes.

anticline A fold that is convex upward or had such an attitude at some stage of development. In simple anticlines the beds are oppositely inclined, whereas in more complex types the limbs may dip in the same direction. Some anticlines are of such complicated form that no simple definition can be given. Anticlines may also be defined as folds with older rocks toward the center of curvature, providing the structural history has not been unusually complex.

anticlinorium A series of anticlines and synclines so arranged structurally that together they form a general arch or anticline.

anticyclone An area of relatively high pressure with closed isobars, the pressure gradient being directed from the center so that the wind blows spirally outward in a clockwise direction in the northern hemisphere, counterclockwise in the southern.

antidune A transient form of ripple on the stream bed analogous to a sand dune. An antidune progressively moves upstream.

antigorite *See* SERPENTINE

antimonite *1.* The native sulfide of antimony; stibnite. *2.* A salt or ester of antimonous acid; a compound containing the radical $SbO_3{}^{-3}$ of $SbO_2{}^-$. *See* STIBNITE

antimony A mineral, the native element, occurring in tin-white masses. Hexagonal rhombohedral.

antiperthite An intergrowth of sodic and potassic feldspar generally thought to have formed during slow cooling by unmixing of sodium and potassium ions in an originally homogeneous alkalic feldspar. In the antiperthites the potassic member (usually orthoclase) forms thin films, lamellae, strings, or irregular veinlets within the sodic member (usually albite). *See* PERTHITE

anti-root Theoretical upward projection of a vitreous zone underlying the earth's solid crust. It is supposed to rise beneath the thick sial of continents or mountain chains and contributes to isostatic balance.

antistress minerals Minerals such as leucite, nepheline, alkalic feldspar, andalusite, and cordierite which cannot form or are unstable in an environment of high shearing stress, and hence are not found in highly deformed rocks.

antithetic faults Faults that dip in the opposite direction from that in which the associated sediments dip. Opposite of synthetic faults.

Ao horizon That portion of the A horizon of a soil profile which is composed of pure humus.

Aoo horizon Uppermost portion of the A horizon of soil profile which consists of undecomposed vegetable litter.

Ap Abbreviation for apatite in normative rock calculations.

apatite A mineral group, consisting of fluorapatite, $Ca_5(PO_4)_3F$, very common; chlorapatite, Ca_5-

$(PO_4)_3Cl$, rare; hydroxylapatite, $Ca_5(PO_4)_3(OH)$, rare. Hexagonal. The principal mineral of phosphorites is a carbonate-containing variety of fluorapatite, called collophane or francolite.

aperiodic motion Any nonperiodic motion; any motion with a continuous frequency spectrum. Example: a pulse from a shot in a shot hole.

apex *1*. The tip, point, or angular summit of anything, as, the apex of a mountain. The end, edge, or crest of a vein nearest the surface. *2*. The highest point of a stratum, as, a coal seam. *3*. *Geol:* The top of an anticlinal fold of strata. This term, as used in United States Revised Statutes, has been the occasion of much litigation. It is supposed to mean something nearly equivalent to outcrop. *4*. *Paleontol:* The pointed, initial end of an elongate or conical form (as in a coral, gastropod, foraminifer, etc.). *5*. In a conodont, the point where two limbs join. *6*. In a brachiopod, the place of initial growth.

aphanite A general term applied to dense, homogeneous rocks whose constituents are too small to be distinguished by the unaided eye. The adjective form aphanitic is currently used more frequently than the noun.

aphanitic Pertaining to a texture of rocks in which the crystalline constituents are too small to be distinguished with the unaided eye. It includes both microcrystalline and cryptocrystalline textures.

A.P.I. American Petroleum Institute, a cooperative trade organization devoted to advancement of the petroleum industry.

API gravity The standard American Petroleum Institute method for specifying the density of crude petroleum. The density in degrees API is equal $\dfrac{141.5}{P} -131.5$ where P is the specific gravity of the oil measured at 60° F. Note: This is one of several so-called Baumé scales for comparing lighter liquids with water.

aplite A dike rock consisting almost entirely of light-colored mineral constituents and having a characteristic fine-grained granitic texture. Aplites may range in composition from granitic to gabbroic, but when the term is used with no modifier it is generally understood to be granitic, i.e., consisting essentially of quartz and orthoclase.

apo- [*Gr.*] Prefix implying the derivation of one kind of rock from another. Applied to volcanic rocks, it indicates they have devitrified; to sedimentary rocks, that they have undergone metamorphism without destruction of original texture.

apophyllite A mineral, KCa₄(Si₂O₅)₄F.8H₂O. Tetragonal.

apophysis *1.* A branch from a vein or dike to which it is attached; an epiphesis is the same, but not attached. *2.* A small dike or sill injected from a larger intrusive body into adjacent rocks.

Appalachian orogeny Late Paleozoic diastrophism beginning perhaps in the Late Devonian and continuing until end of Permian.

apparent dip The dip of a rock layer as exposed in any section not at a right angle to the strike. It is a component of and hence always less than the true dip.

apparent movement of faults The apparent movement observed in any chance section across a fault is a function of several variables:

(1) The attitude of the fault; (2) the attitude of the disrupted strata; (3) the attitude of the surface upon which the fault is observed; and (4) the true movement (net slip) along the fault.

apparent plunge Inclination of a normal projection of lineation in the plane of a vertical cross section.

apparent velocity The velocity with which a fixed phase of a seismic wave, usually its front or beginning, passes an observer.

applanation All physiographic processes which tend to reduce the relief of a district and, dominantly, by adding material to the area or areas affected, cause the topography to become more and more plainlike.

appraisal curve A curve or plotted relationship showing, for oil or gas wells operating under similar conditions, the production for a given time or period as compared to the ultimate production. Usually the abscissae of the curve express barrels (or gas volumes) produced during the year, and the ordinates indicate the ultimate production.

apron Outwash plain, *q.v.*

Aptian Lower Cretaceous, between Barremian and Albian.

aquamarine A transparent, light bluish-green variety of beryl. Used as a gem.

aqueous *1.* Pertaining to water. *2.* Pertaining to sediment deposited by water.

aqueous ripple marks Ripple marks made by waves and water currents as distinguished from ripple marks made by the wind, called aeolian ripple marks.

aquiclude A formation which, although porous and capable of absorbing water slowly, will not transmit it fast enough to furnish an appreciable supply for a well or spring.

aquifer Stratum or zone below the surface of the earth capable of producing water as from a well.

aquifuge A rock which contains no interconnected openings or interstices and therefore neither absorbs nor transmits water.

Aquitanian Lower lower Miocene or uppermost Oligocene.

Arachnida A large and varied group of specialized arthropods among which spiders, mites, ticks, scorpions, and Merostomata are living examples.

Arachnoidea Class of arthropods; includes Arachnida and Merostomata.

aragonite A mineral, orthorhombic $CaCO_3$, dimorphous with calcite.

arborescent Descriptive of large treelike plants. Syn: DENDRITIC, q.v.

Arbuckle orogeny Mid-Pennsylvanian diastrophism.

arc Islands or mountains arranged in a great curve.

arch 1. An anticline. 2. In plutonic rocks, the planar or linear flow structures may form a dome that extends across the whole pluton. In an arch the flow structures are confined to the borders of the pluton.

archaeocyathid One of an extinct group of calcareous cup-shaped spongelike organisms found in the Lower and Middle Cambrian; world-wide in distribution.

arch-bend The place of maximum curvature on a fold, especially a recumbent fold.

Archean; Archaean 1. The term, meaning ancient, has been generally applied to the oldest rocks of the Precambrian. As more physical measurements of geo-

logic time are made, the usage is changing. The Am. Comm. Strat. Nomenclature now recommends substitution of the term Early Precambrian. 2. Older of two Precambrian systems or periods. Obs. Syn: ARCHEOZOIC

Archeocyathea Pleospongia.

Archeozoic 1. The era during which, or during the later part of which, the oldest system of rocks was made. 2. Belonging to the last of three subdivisions of Archean time, when the lowest forms of life probably existed. As more physical measurements of geologic time are made, this term becomes more obsolete. It is now considered part of the Early Precambrian. 3. Older of two Precambrian eras; not recognized by U. S. Geological Survey.

archipelago Any sea or broad sheet of water interspersed with many islands or with a group of islands; also, such a group of islands.

Arctic 1. The region within the Arctic Circle (66°30′ N.). 2. Geog: Lands north of the 50° F. July isotherm (or that of whichever month is warmest) provided the mean temperature for the coldest month is not higher than 32° F.

Arctic pack 1. The drifting ice floes of the Arctic Ocean. 2. A synonym for "polar ice."

arcuate Curved or bowed.

Ardenian orogeny Silurian-Devonian diastrophism.

areal eruption Volcanic eruption resulting from collapse of the roof of a batholith; the volcanic rocks grade into parent plutonic rocks.

areal geology That branch of geology which pertains to the distribution, position, and form of the areas of the earth's surface occupied by different kinds of rock or different geologic units, and to the making of geologic maps.

areal map A geologic map showing the horizontal area or extent of rock units exposed at the surface.

arenaceous, *adj.* Applied to rocks that have been derived from sand or that contain sand. Not to be confounded with siliceous.

Arenigian Upper Lower Ordovician.

arenite; arenyte Consolidated rock of the texture of sand irrespective of composition. *Syn:* PSAMMITE

arête [*Fr.*] An acute and rugged crest of a mountain range, or a subsidiary ridge between two mountains or of a mountain spur such as that between two cirques. *See* MATTERHORN

argentiferous Containing silver.

argentite A mineral, Ag_2S. Monoclinic, pseudo-isometric. An important ore of silver. *Syn:* SILVER GLANCE

argillaceous Applied to all rocks or substances composed of clay, or having a notable proportion of clay in their composition, as roofing slate, shale, etc. Argillaceous rock are readily distinguished by the peculiar odor they emit when breathed on—known in mineralogy as the "argillaceous odor."

An adjective descriptive of a rock containing appreciable clay. *Cf.* PELITIC, LUTACEOUS

argillation Development of clay minerals by weathering of aluminum silicates.

argillite An argillite is defined as a rock derived either from siltstone, claystone, or shale, that has undergone a somewhat higher degree of induration than is present in those rocks. Argillite

holds an intermediate position between the rocks named and slate. Cleavage is approximately parallel to bedding in which it differs from slate. An argillite may be argillaceous, bituminous, calcareous, carbonaceous, ferruginous, siliceous, etc.

Argovian Lower Lusitanian.

arid, *adj.* A climate in which the rainfall is insufficient to support vegetation.

Wladimir Köppen and R. Geiger in their *Klimakarte der Erde* (Justus Perthes Gotta, 1928) use the following formulas for the limits of rainfall for arid and semiarid climates:

Rainfall mainly in cold season . . .
$$R=2t$$
Rainfall evenly distributed throughout the year . . .
$$R=2t+14$$
Rainfall mainly in hot season . . .
$$R=2t+28$$
where t is the mean annual temperature in °C. If the annual rainfall in centimeters is less than R and greater than 1/2R the climate is desert or arid.

aridity, *n.* The state of a region in respect to its dryness or lack of moisture. The amount of rainfall is not a sure index, for the aridity of a region depends in part on temperature.

Various attempts have been made to formulate an index of the degree of aridity for purposes of climatic classification, but none have been generally accepted. The difficulty in part is the insufficiency of data, principally data concerning evaporation. Therefore, the most usable indices are those that use temperature and precipitation data.

Arikareean Lower Miocene.

arithmetic mean particle diameter A measure of average particle size obtained by summing the products of the size grade mid-points times the frequency of particles in each class, and dividing by the total frequency.

Arkansas stone A true novaculite, *q.v.*, used as an oilstone for sharpening tools or instruments. Found in the Ozark Mountains of Arkansas.

arkose A sandstone containing 25% or more of feldspars usually derived from the disintegration of acid igneous rocks of granitoid texture. The minerals of an arkose may accumulate in place or be transported.

arkosic Having wholly or in part the character of arkose.

arkosic sandstone A sandstone in which much feldspar is present. This may range from unassorted products of granular disintegration of fine- or medium-grained granite to a partly sorted river-laid or even marine arkosic sandstone. Has been used for various other kinds of rock, including graywacke.

arm An inlet of water from the sea or other body of water.

armored mud ball Rounded pebble or boulder originally composed of a mud core which became studded with small pebbles as the mass of mud rolled along.

arrival (first, secondary, etc.) *Seis. explor:* Refers to the appearance of energy on a record traveling by way of some path under consideration. "First arrivals" indicates energy arriving with the earliest possible travel-time. "Secondary arrivals" refers to weaker or later energy returns by some other path. *Syn:* BREAK; KICK

arroyo *1.* The channel of an ephemeral or intermittent stream, usually with vertical banks of unconsolidated material 2 feet or more high. *Syn:* WADY; BAR-

RANCA. *2.* Vertical-walled, flat-floored channel of ephemeral stream of the semiarid Southwest.

arsenate A salt or ester of arsenic acid; a compound containing the radical AsO_4^{-3} or AsO_3^{-}.

arsenic A mineral, the native element, occurring in gray masses. Hexagonal rhombohedral.

arsenide A compound of arsenic with one other more positive element or radical.

arsenolite A mineral, arsenious oxide, As_2O_3. Cubic.

arsenopyrite A mineral, FeAsS, tin-white. Monoclinic, pseudo-orthorhombic. *Syn:* MISPICKEL

arterite A veined gneiss in which the vein-material was injected from a magma. Venite is a veined gneiss of similar aspect and composition, but differs from arterite in that the vein-material has been derived by secretion from the rock itself. Where it is impossible to discriminate between arterite and venite, the term phlebite is used.

artesian Refers to ground water under sufficient hydrostatic head to rise above the aquifer containing it.

artesian aquifer One that contains artesian water.

artesian basin A geologic structural feature or combination of such features in which water is confined under artesian pressure.

artesian spring One whose water issues under artesian pressure, generally through some fissure or other opening in the confining bed that overlies the aquifer.

artesian water Ground water that is under sufficient pressure to rise above the level at which it is encountered by a well, but which does not necessarily rise to or above the surface of the ground.

artesian well One in which the

water level rises above the top of the aquifer, whether or not the water flows at the land surface.

Arthrodiran One of a group of extinct fish that were abundant in the Devonian, with heavily armored heads which are movably jointed to similar armor covering the anterior part of the body.

Arthrophyta Equisetineae.

Arthropoda Phylum of segmented animals encased in an external chitinous skeleton with jointed legs.

Articulata Class of brachiopods whose shells generally have well-developed articulating teeth and sockets; shells calcareous. Camb.-Rec.

articulate *1.* Jointed; provided with nodes or joints, or places where separation may naturally take place. *Paleontol: 2.* One of a subclass of the crinoids (the Articulata) in which the calyx is relatively flexible; *3.* One of a class of Brachiopoda (the Articulata) in which the shells are held together along the hinge line by means of articulating devices of various kinds.

articulation *1.* Movable joint. *2.* Manner of joining of adjacent mineral grains in a rock; contact may be smooth and plane, curved or sinuous, angularly interlocked or sutured, or one mineral may completely enclose another.

artifacts Man-made objects of prehistoric age, such as weapons or tools of flint.

Artinskian Upper lower Permian.

asar *See* OSAR

asbestos *1.* White, gray, green-gray, or blue-gray fibrous variety of amphibole, usually tremolite or actinolite, or of chrysotile. Blue asbestos is crocidolite. *2.* Highly fibrous minerals used for commercial purposes, especially those varieties resistant to heat and chemical attack.

ascension, infiltration by The theory of infiltration by ascension in solution from below considers that orebearing solutions come from the heated zones of the earth and that they rise through cavities and at diminished temperatures and pressures deposit their burdens.

aschistic Pertains to rocks of minor igneous intrusions that have not been differentiated into light and dark portions but that have essentially the same composition as the larger intrusions with which they are associated.

asexual Refers to any type of reproduction which does not involve the union of sex cells (gametes).

asexual reproduction Reproduction of organisms without sexual combination; generally accomplished by budding from or fragmentation of a mature individual.

ash *1.* Inorganic residue remaining after ignition of combustible substances, quantitatively determined by definite prescribed methods. In the case of coal and coke, the methods employed shall be those prescribed in the Standard Methods of Laboratory Sampling of Coal and Coke, A. S. T. M. Designation: D 271 of the American Society for Testing Materials. *2.* Volcanic dust and particles less than 4 mm. in diameter.

ash, volcanic Uncemented pyroclastic material consisting of fragments mostly under 4 mm. in diameter. Coarse ash is from 1/4 to 4 mm. in grain size; fine ash is below 1/4 mm. Without a qualifying adjective, the term should be applied only to essential ejecta.

ash cone A volcanic cone built primarily of unconsolidated ash and generally shaped something like a saucer, with a rim in the form of a wide circle and a broad central depression often nearly at the same elevation as the surrounding country. They usually show maximum growth on the leeward side. Individual ash beds forming the cone dip both inward and outward, those in the high part of the rim approaching the angle of repose. Ash cones are believed to be the result of violent hydro-explosions caused when lava erupts under water or water-saturated rocks close to the surface. In form, ash cones bear a general resemblance to maars. Consolidated ash cones are called tuff cones or tuff rings.

ash fall *1*. A rain of airborne volcanic ash falling from an eruption cloud. Characteristic of vulcanian eruptions. *2*. A deposit of volcanic ash resulting from such a fall and lying on the ground surface.

ash flow *1*. An avalanche of volcanic ash, generally a highly heated mixture of volcanic gases and ash, traveling down the flanks of a volcano or along the surface of the ground and produced by the explosive disintegration of viscous lava in a volcanic crater or by the explosive emission of gas-charged ash from a fissure or group of fissures. Ash flows of the type described at Mount Pelée are considered to represent the feeblest type of the nuée ardente. The solid materials contained in a typical ash flow are generally unsorted and ordinarily include volcanic dust, pumice, scoria, and blocks in addition to ash. *2*. A deposit of volcanic ash and other debris resulting from such a flow and lying on the ground surface. *Syn:* IGNIMBRITE

Ashgillian Upper Upper Ordovician.

ash shower A rain of airborne volcanic ash falling from an eruption cloud, generally of short duration. *See* ASH FALL

Aso lava A type of indurated pyroclastic deposit produced during the explosive eruptions that formed the Aso Caldera of Kyushu, Japan. Chiefly a lavalike tuff consisting of lenses or spindles of black and gray obsidian lying in a duffaceous matrix that displays a streaky, varicolored banding or eutaxitic structure. Possibly erupted as extremely hot, gas-rich dust and ash carrying large clots of molten, vesiculated volcanic glass. Similar to deposits variously described as welded tuff, welded pumice, ignimbrite, and tuff-lava.

aspect (of facies) Appearance, composition, or inferred environmental implications of a particular rock body or fossil assemblage.

asphalt A brown-to-black solid or semisolid bituminous substance, occurring in nature, but also obtained as the residue from the refining of certain petroleums and then known as artificial asphalt. Asphalt melts between 150° and 200° F. and is soluble in carbon disulfide. Belongs to the group of solid and semisolid hydrocarbons, the others being asphaltites and asphaltic pyrobitumens. *See* ALBERTITE; ELATERITE; GILSONITE; GRAHAMITE; IMPSONITE; NIGRITE; WURTZILITE. *Syn:* MINERAL PITCH; ASPHALTUM

asphalt-base petroleum Crude oils which, upon processing, yield relatively large amounts of asphaltic residues.

asphaltic sand Natural mixtures of asphalts with varying proportions of loose sand grains. The quantity of bituminous cementing material extracted from the sand may run as high as 10% and this bitumen is composed of a soft asphalt which rarely has a penetration as low as 60°.

asphaltite *1.* A dark-colored, solid, difficultly fusible, naturally occurring hydrocarbon complex, insoluble in water, but more or less completely soluble in carbon disulfide, benzol, etc. *2.* One of the harder of the solid hydrocarbons with melting points between 250° and 600° F. Examples are gilsonite and grahamite.

aspites Volcanoes characterized by bases that are wide in proportion to their height. They usually have a crater on the summit, and the material is generally rheumatitic. Mauna Loa is an example. Vesuvius is pseudo-aspite.

assay *1.* To test ores or minerals by chemical or blowpipe examination. To determine the proportion of metals in ores by smelting in the way appropriate to each. Gold and silver require an additional process called cupelling, for the purpose of separating them from the base metals. *See* FIRE ASSAY. *2.* An examination of a mineral, an ore, or alloy differing from a complete analysis in that it determines only certain ingredients in the substance examined, whereas an analysis determines everything it contains.

assay foot The assay value multiplied by the number of feet across which the sample is taken.

assay inch The assay value multiplied by the number of inches over which the sample was taken.

assay limit The limits of an ore body determined by the amount of valuable material shown by assays.

assay ton A weight of 29.166+ grams used in assaying, for convenience. Since it bears the same relation to the milligram that a ton of 2000 pounds does to the troy ounce the weight in milligrams of precious metal obtained from the assay of an ore gives directly the number of ounces to the ton.

assay value The amount of the gold or silver, in ounces per ton of ore, as shown by assay of any given sample. Average assay value. The weighted result obtained from a number of samples, by multiplying the assay value of each sample by the width or thickness of the ore face over which it is taken, and then dividing the sum of these products by the total width of cross section sampled. The result obtained would represent an average face sample.

assemblage zone Biostratigraphic unit defined and identified by a group of associated fossils rather than by a single index fossil. *Syn:* CENOZONE. *Cf.* RANGE ZONE, FAUNIZONE, FLORIZONE

assimilation The incorporation into a magma, of material originally present in the wall rock. The term does not specify the exact mechanism or results; the "assimilated" material may be present as crystals from the original wall rocks, newly formed crystals including wall rock elements, or as a true solution in the liquid phase of the magma. The resulting rock is called hybrid. Also termed magmatic assimilation.

association *1.* A climax community that is the largest subdivision of a climax, biome, or formation. 2. Loosely, any stable community.

associations of igneous rocks Kindreds. Groups of rocks having chemical and petrographic characteristics in common, and usually occurring together. *See* PETROGRAPHIC PROVINCE

Astartian Sequanian.

asterism *Mineral:* A starlike effect seen either by transmitted or reflected light.

asteroid A free-moving, star-shaped echinoderm usually with five arms or rays radiating from a central disk, the rays being fairly thick and not sharply separated from the central disk.

Asteroidea A subclass of invertebrate animals, belonging to the phylum Echinodermata; the starfish.

asteroplankton Tiny primitive organisms supposed to have reached the earth from outer space.

asthenolith 1. Body of magma locally melted anywhere at any time within any solid portion of the earth. 2. Local radiogenic magma pocket. 3. Accumulation of sialic magma of low viscosity and very small residual strength at the upper surface of the salsima layer.

asthenosphere The shell within the earth, some tens of kilometers below the surface and of undefined thickness, which is a shell of weakness where plastic movements take place to permit isostatic adjustments.

Astian Upper Pliocene. *Syn:* PIACENZIAN

astogeny Asexual reproduction by budding of new individuals from old ones as in corals and bryozoans.

astrolabe Instrument for measuring altitudes of celestial objects. Three general types used in surveying: pendulum, planespheric, prismatic.

Asturian orogeny Mid-Upper Carboniferous diastrophism.

asymmetrical 1. Without proper proportion of parts; unsymmetrical. 2. *Crystallog:* Having no center, plane, or axis of symmetry.

asymmetrical ripple mark The normal form of ripple mark, with short downstream slopes and comparatively long gentle upstream slopes. *See* WATER CURRENT RIPPLE MARK

asymmetric fold A fold in which one limb dips more steeply than the other. If one limb becomes overturned, the term overfold or overturned fold is used.

atacamite A mineral, $Cu_4Cl_2(OH)_6$, orthorhombic, blackish green.

atectonic An adjective to describe an event that occurs when orogeny is not taking place. *Syn:* NONTECTONIC

Atlantic series, province, or **suite** One of two great groups of igneous rocks (along with the Pacific group), based on their tectonic setting. The Atlantic series are found in nonorogenic areas, often associated with block sinking and great crustal instability, and erupted along faults and fissures or through explosion vents. The Atlantic series was originally described as occurring in the coastal districts of the Atlantic basin. Later it became evident that there was no intrinsic connection with the Atlantic Ocean, the Hawaiian lavas, for example, being of "Atlantic" type, and hence the name intra-Pacific province is synonymous with Atlantic province.

The exact connotation varies with different authors, but in

general, the term Atlantic is used to include those (alkalic) magma series having low alkali-lime indices and yielding undersaturated residuums, whereas the term Pacific is used for those more calcic magmas, associated with folded mountains such as those of the circum-Pacific orogeny, which trend toward more calcic, oversaturated residuums, e.g., rhyolites and dacites. A third group, the Mediterranean series, has also been proposed. The terms Atlantic and Pacific as applied to rock kindreds have generally been abandoned.

"Atlantic" type of coast line Trend of folded belts is transverse to the coast. Contrasts with "Pacific" type of coast line, *q.v.*

atmometer An instrument for measuring the rate of evaporation; an atmidometer or evaporimeter. Four main classes of atmometers may be distinguished: (1) large evaporation tanks sunk in the ground or floating on protected waters; (2) small open evaporation pans; (3) porous porcelain bodies; (4) atmometers with wet paper surfaces, represented by the Piché evaporimeter.

atmophile elements *1.* The most typical elements of the atmosphere (H, C, N, O, I, Hg, and inert gases). *2.* Elements which occur either in the uncombined state, or which, as volatile compounds, will concentrate in the gaseous primordial atmosphere.

atmosphere *1.* The gaseous envelope surrounding the earth. The atmosphere is odorless, colorless, tasteless; very mobile, flowing readily under even a slight pressure gradient; elastic, compressible, capable of unlimited expansion, a poor conductor of heat, but able to transmit vibrations with considerable velocity. Its weight has been calculated as 5.9×10^{15} tons. One-half the mass of the atmosphere lies below 3.46 miles. The ordinary term for the mixture of gases comprising the atmosphere is air, which also includes water vapor and solid and liquid particles. *2.* A unit of pressure: A normal atmosphere is equal to the pressure exerted by a vertical column of mercury 760 mm. in height, at 0° C., and with gravity taken at 980. 665 cm./sec.^{2}, equal to about 14.7 pounds per square inch.

atmospheric pressure The force per unit area exerted by the atmosphere in any part of the atmospheric envelope. Some of the expressions for the normal value of the atmospheric pressure at sea level are: 76.0 centimeters of mercury; 29.92 inches of mercury; 1033.3 centimeters of water; 33.9 feet of water; 1033.3 grams per square centimeter; 1,013,250.0 dynes per square centimeter; 14.66 pounds per square inch; 1.01325 bars (1 bar = 1,000,000 dynes/cm.^{2}); 1013.25 millibars.

atmospheric radiation The radiation emitted by the atmosphere in two directions, upward to space and downward to the earth, and consisting mainly of the long-wave terrestrial radiation plus the small amount of short-wave solar radiation absorbed in the atmosphere. Figuring on the basis of a year and using a heat unit of 10^{22} calories it has been calculated that of the 201 heat units absorbed in the atmosphere 134 are returned to the earth as the so-called back radiation, and 67 are lost to space. In summer this back radiation equals or exceeds one-half of the incoming solar radiation in all northern latitudes; in winter, it exceeds the total incoming solar radiation at all latitudes above 15° N.

atmospheric water Water which exists in the atmosphere in gaseous, liquid, or solid state.

Atokan Lower Pennsylvanian, above Morrowan.

atoll A ringlike "coral" island or islands encircling or nearly encircling a lagoon. It should be noted that the term "coral" island for most of these tropical islands is incorrect as calcareous algae (Lithothamnion) often forms much more than 50% of them.

atoll reef A ring-shaped, coral reef, often carrying low sand islands, enclosing a body of water.

atoll texture A ring of one mineral with another mineral or minerals within and without the ring.

atomic bond Attraction exerted between atoms and ions. Four types are: metallic, ionic or polar, homopolar or co-ordinate, residual or van der Waals. Bonding may be intermediate between these types.

atomic mass Variously but not commonly used as a synonym for atomic weight, mass number, or the mass of an individual atom.

atomic number The number of positive charges on the nucleus of an atom; the number of protons in the nucleus.

atomic proportions or **ratios** The ratios or proportions in which the various atomic species occur in a substance, obtained by dividing weight per cent of each substance by the atomic weight of the substance. When recalculated to atoms per 100 atoms total, the values are atom per cent.

atomic radius The radius of an atom (average distance from the center to the outermost electron of the neutral atom), commonly expressed in Angstrom units (10^{-8} cm.).

atomic weight Average relative weight of the atoms of an element referred to an arbitrary standard of 16.0000 for the atomic weight of oxygen. The atomic weight scale used by chemists takes 16.0000 as the average atomic weight of oxygen atoms as they occur in nature; the scale used by physicists takes 16.00435 as the atomic weight of the most abundant oxygen isotope. Division by a factor of 1.000272 converts an atomic weight on the physicists' scale to the weight on the chemists' scale.

atom per cent *See* ATOMIC PROPORTIONS

attapulgite *See* PALYGORSKITE

attenuation constant A term used to describe a mathematical parameter in a material where a physical quantity of value x_0 is changed to a value x_1 by virtue of traveling a unit distance through a medium, or by virtue of the elapse of a unit time, and x_0 and x_1 are related by the equation $x_1 = x_0 e^{-p}$ where $p = \alpha + j\beta$; $\alpha : \beta$ are real and $j = \sqrt{-1}$; α is the attenuation constant; β is the phase shift or unit phase angle. A more specific geophysical definition is given in Dobrin. The relation between the initial amplitude I_0 of a seismic disturbance and the amplitude I at a distance r is given by $I = \dfrac{I_0 e^{-qr}}{r}$ where q is the attenuation constant.

Atterberg scale A proposed grade scale for the classification of sediments based on a decimal system beginning with 2 mm. The limits of the subclass are found by taking the square root of the product of the larger grade limits. The subdivision thus made follows the logarithmic rule. This has become the accepted European standard for classification of particle size.

Attican orogeny Late Miocene diastrophism.

attitude A general term to describe the relation of some directional feature in a rock to a horizontal plane. The attitude of planar features (bedding, foliation, joints, etc.) is described by giving the strike and dip. The attitude of a linear feature (fold axis, lineation, etc.) is described by giving the strike of the horizontal projection of the linear feature and its plunge.

attraction, gravitational A reciprocal attractive force existing between two point masses or particles of matter. The gravitational force between two bodies is directly proportional to the product of their masses and inversely proportional to the square of the distance between their centers of gravity (true of spheres of special type). Einstein's theory modifies this simple relationship expressed by Newton.

attrition 1. Wearing away by friction. 2. The wear and tear that rock particles in transit undergo through mutual rubbing, grinding, knocking, scraping, and bumping with resulting comminution in size.

aufeis [*Ger.*] A sheet of ice formed on a river flood plain in winter when shoals in the river freeze solid or are otherwise dammed so that water spreads over the flood plain and freezes.

augen [*Ger.* eyes] *Petrol:* Applied to large, lenticular mineral grains or aggregates of minerals which in cross section have the shape of an eye. They usually occur in metamorphic rocks, especially gneisses, where they are commonly formed of potassium feldspar.

augen gneiss A general term for gneissose rocks containing phacoidal crystals or aggregates. The augen ("eyes") may represent uncrushed fragments, or porphyroblasts.

augen schist A mylonitic rock characterized by the presence of recrystallized minerals in schistose streaks and lenticles.

augen structure A structure found in some gneisses and granites in which certain of the constituents are squeezed into elliptical or lens-shaped forms and, especially if surrounded by parallel flakes of mica, resemble eyes.

auger Any drilling device in which the cuttings are mechanically continuously removed from the bottom of the bore during the drilling operation without the use of fluids. A rotary drilling device used to drill shot holes or geophone holes in which the cuttings are removed by the device itself without the use of fluids.

augite *See* PYROXENE

Auluroidea Subclass of primitive stelleroids resembling ophiuroids in some respects. Ord.-Carb.

aureole *Geol:* A zone surrounding an igneous intrusion in which contact metamorphism of the country rock has taken place. *Syn:* CONTACT AUREOLE; CONTACT ZONE

auri-argentiferous Containing both gold and silver; applied to minerals.

auric Of, pertaining to, or containing gold, especially when combined in its highest or triad valency, as auric chloride. $AuCl_3$.

auriferous Containing gold.

austral Southern.

Austrian orogeny Mid-cretaceous diastrophism.

authigenic *1.* Generated on the spot. A term applied to growth in place of occurrence. It includes secondary enlargement. *2.* Pertaining to minerals formed on the spot where they are now found, before burial and consolidation of the sediment. They are the products of chemical and biochemical action.

auto- [*Gr.*] A combining form meaning self.

autochthon *1. Alpine geol:* A succession of beds that have been moved comparatively little from their original site of formation, although they may be intensely folded and faulted. *2.* A fossil now occurring where the organism once lived; not transported.

autochthonous, *adj.* A term applied to rocks of which the dominant constituents have been formed *in situ,* e.g., rock salt. *Cf.* ALLOCHTHONOUS

autoclastic A term applied to rocks that have been brecciated in place by mechanical processes, e.g., brush breccias. *Syn:* PROTOCLASTIC. *See* CRUSH CONGLOMERATE

autogeosyncline A parageosyncline that subsides as an elliptical basin or trough but without associated highlands.

autointrusion A process wherein the residual liquid of a differentiating magma is drawn into rifts formed in the crystal mesh at a late stage by deformation of unspecified origin.

autolith Cognate xenolith. An inclusion or fragment of older igneous rock that is genetically related to the rock including it.

autometamorphism; automorphism *1.* A type of metamorphism caused by decrease in temperature in newly congealed igneous rock in which residual hydrothermal solutions are able to react with the igneous minerals, e.g., the albitization of basalt to form spilite. *2.* The alteration of an igneous rock by its own residual liquors.

autometasomatism Process of alteration of newly crystallized igneous rock by its own last, water-rich, liquid fraction which is trapped within the rock generally by an impervious chilled border.

automorphic A term applied to those minerals of igneous rocks that are bounded by their own crystal faces. Rocks that consist predominantly of an automorphic mineral assemblage are said to have an automorphic-granular or panidiomorphic-granular texture. *Syn:* IDIOMORPHIC; EUHEDRAL. *Cf.* ALLOTRIOMORPHIC; XENOMORPHIC; ANHEDRAL

autotype *1.* Hypotype illustrated later by the author of a species. *2.* Genotype species by original designation.

Autunian Lower Permian.

autunite A mineral, $Ca(UO_2)_2$-$(PO_4)_2.8$-$12H_2O$, a common secondary mineral occurring in yellow plates. Tetragonal. Fluorescent.

Auversian Ledian.

auxiliary fault Branch fault; minor fault ending against a major one.

auxiliary minerals In the Johannsen classification of igneous rocks, those light-colored, relatively rare or unimportant minerals such as apatite, muscovite, corundum, fluorite, and topaz.

available moisture Moisture in soil that is available for use by plants.

available relief The vertical distance between the altitude of the original surface, after uplift, and the level at which grade is first attained.

avalanche A large mass of snow or ice, sometimes accompanied by other material, moving rapidly down a mountain slope. Avalanches are usually classified by the type of snow involved as climax, combination, damp snow, delayed action, direct action, dry snow, hangfire, and windslab avalanche.

aven A vertical shaft leading upward from a cave passage, at times connecting with passages above.

aventurine *1.* A kind of glass containing gold-colored inclusions. *2. Adj:* Having the appearance of such glass, applied especially to transparent or translucent quartz or feldspar containing shiny inclusions.

average igneous rock A theoretical rock whose chemical composition is believed to be similar to the average composition of the outermost shell of the earth extending to a depth of about ten miles. This composition is calculated in different ways and there is not complete agreement as to how an average should be reached or its significance.

average velocity *Seismol:* The ratio of the distance traversed along a ray by a seismic pulse to the time required for that traverse. The average velocity is usually measured or expressed for a ray perpendicular to the reference datum plane.

aves Class of vertebrates; birds. Jur.-Rec.

Avonian Dinantian.

Axes, Beta *Struct. petrol:* An axis defined on a Schmidt net by the intersection of a group of great circles representing foliation surfaces. It may or may not coincide with a lineation.

axes, fabric *Struct. petrol:* Three mutually perpendicular directions in tectonites, usually denoted *a*, *b*, and *c*, which refer to the movement pattern.

axes, tectonic A general term for the a, b, c, fabric coordinates used by structural geologists and petrologists.

axial angle *1.* The acute angle between the two optic axes of a biaxial crystal (symbol 2V). *2.* Axial angle in air (symbol 2E) is the larger angle between the optic axes after being refracted on leaving the crystal.

axial compression *See* COMPRESSION, AXIAL

axial elements The axial ratio and the angles between the axes of a crystal.

axial plane *1.* A crystallographic plane that includes two of the crystallographic axes. *2.* As applied to folds, it is a plane that intersects the crest or trough in such a manner that the limbs or sides of the fold are more or less symmetrically arranged with reference to it. *3.* The plane of the optic axes of an optically biaxial crystal.

axial plane cleavage Rock cleavage essentially parallel to the axial plane of a fold.

axial-plane folding Large-scale secondary folding of pre-existing folds in response to movements which varied considerably from those which caused the original folding. Thus the axial planes have been folded.

axial plane foliation Foliation developed in rocks parallel to the axial plane of a fold and perpendicular to the chief deformational pressure.

axial plane schistosity Schistosity developed parallel to the axial planes of folds.

axial plane separation Distance between axial planes of adjacent anticline and syncline.

axial ratio The ratio obtained by comparing the length of a crystallographic axis with one of the lateral axes taken as unity.

axial symmetry Spheroidal symmetry. *Struct. petrol:* Refers to symmetry of fabric or symmetry of movement. Spheroidal symmetry of fabric is characterized by an axis of symmetry, like an oblate or prolate spheroid. Axial symmetry of movement is typified by the settling of sediments in a body of stagnant water or the deformation of a sphere into an oblate spheroid.

axial trace The intersection of the axial plane of a fold with the surface of the earth or any other specified surface. Sometimes such a line is loosely and incorrectly called the axis.

axial trough Distortion of a fold axis downward into a form similar to a syncline.

axinite A mineral, $H(Ca,Fe,Mn)_3$-$Al_2B(SiO_4)_3$, in brown, violet, or green triclinic crystals.

axis *1.* A straight line, real or imaginary, passing through a body, on which it revolves or may be supposed to revolve; a line passing through a body or system around which the parts are symmetrically arranged. *2. Crystallog:* One of the imaginary lines in a crystal which are used as co-ordinate axes of reference in determining the positions and symbols of the crystal planes. *3.* A line where a folded bed shows the maximum curvature. Also defined as the line formed by the intersection of the axial plane of a fold with a bedding surface. Also loosely used for line on a map that divides a fold as symmetrically as possible. *4.* The central or dominating region of a mountain chain, or the line of which follows the crest of a range and thus indicates the position of the most conspicuous part of the uplift. *5.* The line made by the intersection of the axial plane with the beds; the trend of the crest of an anticline or the trough of a syncline. *6.* Nearest approximation to a line which, when moved parallel to itself, describes a folded s-surface. *7.* Loosely applied to a long narrow anticline or syncline.

axis of a fold The line following the apex of an anticline or the lowest part of a syncline.

axis of rotation The imaginary line about which all the parts of a rotating body turn.

axis of symmetry An imaginary line in a crystal, about which it may be rotated so as to occupy the same position in space 2, 3, 4, or 6 times in a complete 360° revolution.

azeotropic mixtures A special case of gas-liquid equilibria, in binary or higher systems in which certain mixtures, upon boiling or condensation, have gas and liquid phases of identical compositions.

azimuth *1. of a body:* That arc of the horizon that is included between the meridian circle at the given place and a vertical plane passing through the body. It is measured, in surveying, from due north around to the right. *2.* The horizontal direction reckoned clockwise from the meridian plane. In this country the basic control surveys measure azimuths from the south. This is not true for all countries or all surveys. *3. of a line:* The angle which a line forms with the true meridian as measured on an imaginary horizontal circle.

azimuthal or **zenithal map projection** A map projection on which the azimuths or directions of all lines radiating from a central point or pole are the same as the azimuths or directions of the corresponding lines on the sphere.

azimuth compass A magnetic compass supplied with sights, for measuring the angle that a line on the earth's surface, or the vertical circle through a heavenly body, makes with the magnetic meridian.

azoic Formerly that part of geologic time represented by the Precambrian stratified rocks; also, the rocks formed during that time. Later restricted to the period and system called Archean, which is now called Early Precambrian. Azoic now is practically obsolete.

Azonal soils Any group of soils without well-developed profile characteristics, owing to their youth, conditions of parent material, or relief that prevents development of normal soil-profile characteristics.

azurite A mineral, $Cu_2(CO_3)(OH)_2$. Monoclinic. Deep blue. A common secondary mineral.

B

b- (direction) *Struct. petrol:* That direction in the plane of movement at right angles to the direction of tectonic transport. In a slickensided surface, b lies in this surface but is at right angles to the striae.

back *Min: 1.* The top or roof of an underground passage; *2.* That part of a lode which is nearest the surface in relation to any portion of the workings of the mine; thus the back of the level or stope is that part of the unstoped lode which is above. *3. Meteor.* (*verb*): To change direction counterclockwise; applied to the wind when it so changes, as for example from the north to the northwest, east to northeast, etc., in the Northern Hemisphere; opposite in meaning to veer, *q.v.*, which signifies clockwise change, as from north to northeast in the Northern Hemisphere. In the Southern Hemisphere the meanings of these words in terms of the cardinal directions are exactly reversed.

backdeep An oceanic depression on the concave side of an island arc.

back-folding; backward folding Folding in which the folds are overturned toward the interior of an orogenic belt. In the Alps the backward folds are overturned toward the south, whereas most of the folds are overturned toward the north.

background *1.* The normal slight radioactivity shown by a counter, not due to abnormal amounts of radioactive elements in adjacent rocks, soils, or waters. The background count is contributed from three sources: cosmic rays, radioactive impurities in the counter, and the usual trace amounts of radioactivity in the vicinity of the counter. *2.* In geochemical prospecting it refers to the range in values representing the normal concentration of a given element in a given material under investigation such as rock, soil, plants, and water.

back limb More gently dipping side of an asymmetrical anticline produced by lateral thrusting.

back reef Area behind the reef, between it and the land. Used with different meanings by different authors for: the reef flat, the lagoonal deposits, or for areas of deposits of sediments of land origin connecting the land with the reef.

backrush The seaward return of the water following the uprush of the waves. For any given tide stage the point of farthest return seaward of the backrush is known as the limit of backrush or limit of backwash.

backset eddy The ocean circulation is made up of great eddies, which in turn set up smaller eddies between the main current and the coastal border. These smaller currents revolve in the reverse direction to that of the great circulation. Eddies of this kind are appropriately called backset eddies.

backshore *1.* Upper shore zone beyond the reach of ordinary waves and tides. *2.* One or more nearly horizontal surfaces called berms formed landward from the beach crest; may slope inland.

backsight *1.* Backsight method (plane table). A method in plane table traversing wherein orientation of the table is effected by aligning the alidade on an established map line and then rotating the table until the line of sight is coincident with the corresponding ground line. *2.* A sight on a previously established survey point. In leveling: a reading on a rod held on a point whose elevation is known and which is not the closing sight of a circuit. In traversing, a sight on a previously established point which is not the closing sight of a circuit.

back-slope *Geol:* The less-sloping side of a ridge. Contrasted with escarpment, the steeper slope. *Syn:* STRUCTURAL PLAIN

back-thrusting Thrusting toward the interior of an orogenic belt. In the Appalachian Valley and Ridge Province the relative direction of thrusting has generally been northwest. Thrusts in which the relative direction of thrusting has been southeast are back-thrusts.

backwash Return flow of water on a beach after the advance of a wave. *See* BACKRUSH

backwater *1.* A creek or series of connected lagoons parallel to a coast, separated narrowly from the sea, and communicating with it by barred outlets. *2.* A currentless body of water of the same trend as a river and fed

from it at the lower end by a back-flow; usually in the plural.

baddeleyite A mineral, ZrO_2. Monoclinic.

badlands A region nearly devoid of vegetation where erosion, instead of carving hills and valleys of the ordinary type, has cut the land into an intricate maze of narrow ravines and sharp crests and pinnacles. Travel across such a region is almost impossible, hence the name. Specifically, the Badlands of the Dakotas. Termed mauvais terres.

bahamite Consolidated limestone composed of sediment similar to that now accumulating in the Bahamas; high purity, generally fine-grained, massively bedded, widely extensive, without abundant fossils.

bail *1.* To dip or throw out; as, to bail water. *2.* To clear of water by dipping or throwing it out; as, to bail a boat. *3.* The handle of a bucket used for hoisting ore, rock, water, etc., from a mine.

bailer *1.* A long cylindrical container with a valve at the bottom, used in cable tool drilling for removing water, cuttings, mud, and oil from a well. *2.* A person who removes water from a mine by dipping it up with a bucket. *3.* A metal tank, or skip, with a valve in the bottom, used for unwatering a mine.

bajada *1.* The nearly flat surface of a continuous apron consisting of confluent alluvial fans which, together with the pediment, make up the piedmont slope in a basin. Anglicized spelling is bahada. *2.* A series of confluent alluvial fans along the base of a mountain range. It is underlain entirely by gravelly detritus that is ill sorted and poorly stratified. The convexities of the component fans impart to the bajada an undulating surface. *Syn:* COMPOUND ALLUVIAL FAN; ALLUVIAL SLOPE, *q.v.*

Bajocian Middle Middle or lower Middle Jurassic, above Aalenian.

balanced forces A system of forces in which all forces are balanced so that no acceleration occurs. Unbalanced forces cause acceleration.

balas A rose-red variety of spinel. Corruption of Badakhshan, a locality in Afghanistan, where it is found.

bald A high rounded knob or mountain top, bare of forest. Local in southern states.

ballas A hard globular variety of diamond.

ballast Broken stone, gravel, sand, etc., used for keeping railroad ties in place.

ball clay; pipe clay A plastic white-burning clay used as a bond in chinaware.

banco An oxbow lake or meander cut off from a river by an alteration in its course. Local in Texas.

band A stratum or lamina conspicuous because it differs in color from adjacent layers. A group of layers displaying color differences is described as being banded.

banded The texture of rocks having thin and nearly parallel bands of different textures, colors, or minerals. Eutaxitic.

banded ore Banded texture. Ore composed of bands as layers that may be composed of the same minerals differing in color or textures or proportions, or they may be composed of different minerals.

banded structure A term applied to veins having distinct layers or bands. This may be due to successive periods of deposition, or replacement of some earlier rock.

banded textures Banded ores, *q.v.*

banded vein A vein made up of layers of different minerals parallel with the walls. Also called ribbon vein.

bank *1.* The rising ground bordering a lake, river, or sea; on a river, designated as right or left as it would appear facing downstream. *2.* An elevation of the sea floor of large area, surrounded by deeper water, but safe for surface navigation; a submerged plateau or shelf, a shoal, or shallow.

bank deposits Shoal water, local mounds, ridges and terraces of sediments, rising above the surrounding sea bottom and of more limited extent than the blanket deposits of shelf areas.

bankfull or **bankfull stage** The water surface elevation attained by the stream when flowing at capacity, i.e., stage above which banks are overflowed.

bar *1.* A mass of sand, gravel, or alluvium deposited on the bed of a stream, sea, or lake, or at the mouth of a stream forming an obstruction to water navigation. *2.* A term used in a generic sense to include various types of submerged or emergent embankments of sand and gravel built on the sea floor by waves and currents. *3.* An offshore ridge or mound of sand, gravel, or other unconsolidated material submerged at least at high tide, especially at the mouth of a river or estuary, or lying a short distance from and usually parallel to, the beach. *4. Meteor:* A unit of pressure equal to 10^6 dynes/cm.^{2}; equivalent to a mercurial barometer reading of 750.076 mm. at $0°$ C. (or 29.5306 inches at 32° F.), gravity being equal to 980.616 cm./sec.². It is equal to the mean atmospheric pressure at about 100 meters above mean sea level. The standard atmospheric pressure of 760 mm. or 29.921 inches is equal to 1,013,250.1444 dynes/cm.² or 1,013.3 millibar. *5. Paleontol:* Any conodont with one usually large denticle at one end above main part of escutcheon, with discrete denticles and generally with an anticusp, anterior process or lateral process. That portion of the conodont which holds the denticles.

Barbados earth A deposit consisting of fossil radiolarians. *See* TRIPOLI

barchan *1.* A dune having crescentic ground plan, with the convex side facing the wind; the profile is asymmetric, with the gentler slope on the convex side, and the steeper slope on the concave or leeward side. *2.* The crescent or barchan type is most characteristic of the inland desert regions. It presents a gently convex surface to the wind, while the lee side is steep and abrupt. The horns of the crescent mark the lateral advance of the sand. Its wide distribution and all but universal presence in the sandy deserts of all continents make this type the normal one for sand hills formed on an open area.

barite; baryte A mineral, BaSO₄. Orthorhombic. Sp. gr. 4.5. The principal ore of barium, also used in paints and drilling muds.

barite dollar Rounded disk-shaped masses of barite formed in a sandstone or sandy shale. *Cf.* BARITE ROSE; PETRIFIED ROSE

barite rose; barite rosette Petrified rose, *q.v.*

barnacle Member of the Cirripedia; a sessile mollusk.

barograph A barometer which makes a continuous record of barometric changes. Barographs may be of the mercurial or aneroid variety, but are generally of the latter type.

barometer An instrument for measuring atmospheric pressure. There are two general types: *1.* Mercury—A U-shaped tube containing a liquid (commonly mercury), one end closed, the other exposed to the air. Displacement of the mercury in the tube is a measure of atmospheric pressure. *2.* Aneroid—Without liquid. A corrugated vacuum box sensitive to external pressure whose expansion or contraction is indicated on a graduated dial by means of mechanical devices. The dial may be graduated in terms of inches of mercury or elevation in feet or meters, or both.

barometric elevation In surveying, an elevation above mean sea level established by the use of instruments which involve measuring the difference in air pressure between the point in question and some reference base of known value, whose elevation is based on a more precise type of data. May involve repeat measurements and a check for variation of local pressure with time and weather.

barometric pressure Atmospheric pressure as indicated or measured by a barometer.

barred basin A marine basin or depression which is partially or wholly isolated or cut off from other basins of the main marine area.

barrel, oil A volumetric unit of measurement equivalent to 42 U.S. gallons.

Barremian Lower Cretaceous, between Hauterivian and Aptian.

barrens An area relatively barren of vegetation in comparison with adjacent areas because of adverse soil or climatic conditions, or wind, or other adverse environmental factors—for example, sand barrens or rock barrens.

barrier *1.* A continuous offshore ridge built by the shore drift. The barrier follows the line of breakers instead of the shore line. *Cf.* BARRIER BEACH, *q.v.* 2. Ice shelf. *3.* Ice shelf in some particular locality, e.g., Ross Barrier. Barrier is no longer used in official British publications and maps, being replaced by ice shelf and ice front.

barrier bar Barrier bars are ridges usually composed of water-worn gravel, deposited by currents in shallow water at some distance from land. Their crests are horizontal, and mark the storm limit of the waves and currents that built them. In cross section they exhibit anticlinals of deposition. Aberrant forms are V-bars, J-bars, looped bars, etc.

barrier beach Offshore bar. This term refers to a single elongate sand ridge rising slightly above the high-tide level and extending generally parallel with the coast, but separated from it by a lagoon. The term should apply to islands and spits. *Cf.* BARRIER ISLAND

barrier flat The relatively flat area, often occupied by pools of water, separating the exposed or seaward edge of a barrier and the lagoon behind the barrier.

barrier ice Shelf ice, *1.*

barrier iceberg Tabular iceberg broken off from an ice shelf or piedmont ice afloat.

barrier island Preferred by some to offshore bar. *1.* Similar to a barrier beach but consisting of multiple instead of single ridges and commonly having dunes, vegetated zones, and swampy terraces extending lagoonward from the beach. *2.* A detached portion of a barrier beach between two inlets.

barrier reef A coral reef that is separated from the coast by a lagoon that is too deep for coral growth. Generally, barrier reefs follow the coasts for long distances, often with short interruptions, termed passes.

Barrovian metamorphism Regional metamorphism that can be zoned into metamorphic facies.

Barstovian Upper Miocene.

bar theory A theory advanced by Ochsenius in 1877 to account for thick deposits of salt, gypsum, and other evaporites. The theory assumes a lagoon separated from the ocean proper by a bar. As water is lost by evaporation and evaporites are formed in the lagoon, additional water of normal salinity flows from the ocean. Because some water in the lagoon is evaporating, the salinity there constantly increases, and finally reaches a point where gypsum, salt, and other evaporites are deposited.

Bartonian Upper upper Eocene.

barysphere Centrosphere, *q.v.*

basal conglomerate A coarse, usually well-sorted and lithologically homogeneous sedimentary deposit which is found just above an erosional break. The initial stratigraphic unit overlying an unconformity, formed by a rising sea level or encroaching sea.

basal pinacoid *Crystallog:* A form consisting of two parallel plane faces on a crystal, so oriented as to cut only the vertical axis *c*, and to be parallel with the plane of the lateral axes *a* and *b*.

basal plane Basal pinacoid, *q.v.*

basalt *1.* An extrusive rock composed primarily of calcic plagioclase and pyroxene, with or without olivine. The plagioclase is normally zoned and usually ranges in composition from bytownite to labradorite, but less calcic varieties are known. Augite, pigeonite and hypersthene or bronzite are the common pyroxenes. Apatite and magnetite are almost always present as accessories. Basalts rich in olivine and calcic augite are generally classified as olivine basalts; those poor in olivine and containing orthopyroxene and/or pigeonite are generally classified as tholeiitic basalts or tholeiites. The groundmass of tholeiitic basalts is commonly glassy, or if crystallized, usually contains quartz and alkalic feldspar. *2.* More generally, any fine-grained, dark-colored igneous rock.

basaltic crystal layer or shell An inner layer of worldwide extent, composed of basalt, underlying the oceans, and the granitic continents.

basal till Till carried at or deposited from the under surface of a glacier.

basanite An extrusive rock composed of calcic plagioclase, augite, olivine, and a feldspathoid (nepheline, leucite, or analcime). Essentially a feldspathoidal olivine basalt.

base *1.* A substance whose water solution has a bitter taste and a soapy feel and changes the color of certain organic dyes. *2.* A substance containing the OH radical which dissociates to form OH^- ions when dissolved in water. *3.* A substance capable of accepting protons from a donor. *4.* A cation (e.g., base exchange). *5.* A base metal or a base metal oxide (e.g., a rock with a high content of bases). *6.* A substance with basic properties. *7.* A substance capable of combining with silica in a rock, such as lime, potash, etc.

base correction In exploration, particularly in magnetics or gravity or barometric surveys, where a base station is used, the base correction is the adjustment required to reduce measurements made in the field so that they can be expressed with reference to the base station values.

base exchange Ion exchange. The clay particle with its cations may be regarded as a kind of salt in which the colloidal clay particle is the anion. Certin cations may replace others making the clay more flocculent. The cation replacement is known as the "base exchange."

base level *1.* The level below which a land surface cannot be reduced by running water. Sea level is considered the principal base level. Principal streams serve as local or temporary base levels for their tributaries. *2. V:* To reduce by erosion to or toward a base level.

base line *1.* A surveyed line established with more than usual care, to which surveys are referred for co-ordination and correlation. *2.* Triangulation: The side of one of a series of connected triangles, the length of which is measured with prescribed accuracy and precision, and from which the lengths of the other triangle sides are obtained by computation or (by plane table) by graphic methods. The base line is the initial measurement in triangulation. *3.* Land surveys: An east-west surveyed line along the astronomic parallel passing through the initial point. Townships are numbered north and south from the base line. *4.* Aeromagnetic: An aeromagnetic profile flown at least twice in opposite directions and at the same level in order to establish a line of reference of magnetic intensities on which to base an aeromagnetic survey.

base map A map on which information may be placed for purposes of comparison or geographical correlation.

The term base map was at one time applied to a class of maps now known as outline maps. It may be applied to topographic maps, also termed mother maps, which are used in the construction of many types of maps by the addition of particular data.

basement *1.* Complex, generally of igneous and metamorphic rocks, overlain unconformably by sedimentary strata. *2.* Crustal layer beneath a sedimentary layer and above the Mohorovičić discontinuity.

basement complex A series of rocks generally with complex structure beneath the dominantly sedimentary rocks. In many places they are igneous and metamorphic rocks of either Early or Late Precambrian, but in some places may be much younger, as Paleozoic, Mesozoic, or even Cenozoic.

base metal *1.* A metal inferior in value to gold and silver (commonly restricted to the ore metals). *2.* A metal more chemically active than gold, silver, and the platinum metals.

base net (triangulation) The triangle formed by sighting a third point from the two ends of a base line; or two adjacent triangles with the base line being a common side to each. The base net is the initial figure in a triangulation system.

base of weathering In seismic interpretation, the boundary between the low-velocity surface layer and an underlying comparatively high-velocity layer. This may correspond to the geologic base of weathering, but not necessarily. The boundary may vary with time. The boundary is considered in deriving time corrections for seismic records.

base station In exploration, particularly magnetic or gravity or barometric surveys, a reference station where quantities under investigation have known values or may be under repeated or continuous measurement in order to establish additional stations in relation to it.

basic *1. Chem:* Performing the office of a base in a salt; having the base in excess. *2.* Having more than one equivalent of the base for each equivalent of acid. *3. Geol:* A general descriptive term for those igneous rocks that are comparatively low in silica. About 55% or 50% is the superior limit. *Cf.* ACIDIC. *4.* In furnace practice, a slag in which the earthy bases are in excess of the amount required to form a "neutral" slag with the silica present. *5.* In water solutions, having a pH greater than 7 (not necessarily identical with *2* above).

basic borders in igneous rocks Refers to the occurrence of more basic rocks at the margins of igneous intrusions. Variously interpreted as chilled zones, basic fronts, etc.

basic front In granitization, an advancing zone enriched in calcium, magnesium and iron, which is said to represent those elements in the sediments being granitized, over and above those necessary to form granite. During the granitization process these are displaced and move through the rock ahead of the granitization front, usually as a zone enriched in hornblende or pyroxene.

basic rock A term rather loosely used in lithology to mean generally one of the following: *1.* An igneous rock containing 45% to 52% of silica, free or combined. *2.* An igneous rock in which minerals comparatively low in silica and rich in the metallic bases, such as the amphiboles, the pyroxenes, biotite, and olivine are dominant. *3.* Very loosely, an igneous rock composed dominantly of dark-colored minerals. In all three senses contrasted with acid.

The term is misleading and undesirable and is going out of use. As used in the first sense above it is being replaced by subsilicic and as used in the second sense it should be replaced by mafic or by some term denoting the dominant mineral or minerals. *See* BASIC. *2.* As used in the third sense it should be replaced by melanocratic.

basic types Primary types.

basification The development of a more basic rock, commonly richer in hornblende, biotite, and oligoclase, presumably by the contamination of a granitic magma by assimilation of country rock. This phenomenon occurs chiefly at the margins of the granite mass.

basin *1.* An amphitheater, cirque, or corrie. Local in Rocky Mountains. *2.* An extensive depressed area into which the adjacent land drains, and having no surface outlet. Use confined almost wholly to the arid West. *3.* The drainage or catchment area of a stream or lake. *4. Struct. geol:* A syncline that is circular or elliptical in plan; i.e., the outcrop of each formation is essentially circular or elliptical, and the beds dip inward.

basin, sedimentary A segment of the earth's crust which has been downwarped, usually for a considerable time, but with intermittent risings and sinkings. The sediments in such basins increase in thickness toward the center of the basin.

basin, starved A depositional basin which received a thinner section of deposits than adjoining areas because the rate of subsidence was materially greater than the rate of deposition.

basin, structural A synclinal tract or area in which the rocks dip generally toward a central point, and in which folding occurred subsequent to deposition.

basin and range landscape Landscape consisting of fault-block mountains and intervening basins.

basin and range structure Regional structure dominated by fault-block mountains separated by sediment-filled basins.

basin folds Anticlinal and synclinal folds occurring in structural basins and regarded by some as due to differential settling.

basining *Geol:* A settlement of the ground in the form of basins, in many cases, at least, due to the solution and transportation of underground deposits of salt and gypsum. Such basining produces numerous depressions, from those of a few square yards to those 50 square miles in area, in the high-plains region east of the Rocky Mountains.

basin order *Geomorph:* A first order basin contains all of the drainage area of a first order stream; a second order basin contains all of the drainage area of a second order stream, etc. *See* STREAM ORDER

basin range A kind of mountain range characteristic of the Great Basin province and formed by a faulted and tilted block of strata.

bastard quartz A miner's term for a white, glassy quartz without other mineralization.

batholith *1.* Originally defined in 1895 as a stock-shaped or shield-shaped mass of igneous rock intruded as the fusion of older formations. On removal of its rock cover and on continued denudation, this mass holds its diameter or grows broader to unknown depths. *2.* A body of intrusive rock, with the general characteristics of stocks, but of much larger size than is generally attributed to stocks or bosses.

bathometer An instrument for measuring depths of water.

Bathonian Upper Jurassic, below Callovian.

bathy- Combining form meaning depth, usually applied to oceans or lakes.

bathyal *1.* Pertaining to the benthonic environment on the continental slope, ranging in depth from 200 to 2000 meters. *2.* Pertaining to the bottom and overlying waters between 100 and 1000 fathoms (600 and 6000 feet). *3.* Of, or pertaining to, the deeper parts of the ocean; deep sea.

bathymetric Relating to measurement of depths; usually applied to the ocean.

bathymetric chart A topographic map of the bed of the ocean.

bathypelagic Referring to that portion of the deep waters of the ocean which lie between depths of 200 and 2000 meters.

bathyplankton The plankton of the greater depths, especially the abyssal zone.

battery ore Manganese oxide ore suitable for use in dry cells.

batture Elevated river bed, as where a river is confined by natural levees above flood-plain level.

Baumé gravity *See* GRAVITY, BAUMÉ

bauxite *1.* Hydrated alumina. Essentially $Al_2O_3.2H_2O$. The principal ore of aluminum; also used collectively for lateritic aluminous ores. *2.* A rock composed of aluminum hydroxides and impurities in the form of free silica, clay, silt, and iron hydroxides. It is seemingly formed in tropical and subtropical latitudes under conditions of good surface drainage. A clay containing much bauxite should be termed bauxitic.

bauxitization Development of bauxite from either primary aluminum silicates or secondary clay minerals.

Baveno law *See* TWIN LAW

b-axis *Struct. petrol:* A fabric axis normal to the direction of movement or a-axis. It lies in the foliation surface (ab), if such is developed, and in many instances coincides with a lineation, as along fold-axes or intersections of s-planes. In a slickensided surface, b is at right angles to the striae (lineation).

bay *1.* A recess in the shore or an inlet of a sea or lake between two capes or headlands, not as large as a gulf but larger than a cove. *Cf.* BIGHT; EMBAYMENT. *2.* A swampy area, usually oval-shaped and covered with brush;

local on South Atlantic Coast.
3. Min: An open space for waste
between two packs in a longwall
working.

bay bar *See* BAYMOUTH BAR

bay head Southern United States.
A swamp at the head of a bay.

bay-head bar A bar built a short
distance out from the shore at
the head of a bay.

baymouth bar A bar extending
partially or entirely across the
mouth of a bay.

bayou A lake, or small sluggish
secondary stream, often in an
abandoned channel or a river
delta. Local on Gulf Coast. One
of the half-closed channels of a
river delta. Local on Mississippi
Delta.

bc-fracture *Struct. petrol:* A tension fracture parallel with the
bc fabric plane and normal to a.
The orientation of these fractures
subnormal to fabric axis a affords a criterion for direction
sense of shear.

bc-plane *Struct. petrol:* A plane
that is perpendicular to the plane
of movement and parallel to the
b-direction in that plane, i.e., it
is perpendicular to a, the direction of tectonic transport.

Bé° Abbreviation for Baumé degree.

beach The gently sloping shore
of a body of water which is
washed by waves or tides, especially the parts covered by
sand or pebbles.

beach berm Nearly horizontal
bench or narrow terrace formed
by wave action in unconsolidated
material on the backshore of a
beach with surface rising behind it and sloping off in front.
Some beaches have no berm,
others have more than one.

beach cusp Cuspate deposits of
beach material built by wave action along the foreshore. Sand,

gravel, or coarse cobblestones
are heaped together in rather uniformly spaced ridges which trend
at right angles to the sea margin,
tapering out to a point near the
water's edge.

beach face The section of the
beach normally exposed to the
action of the wave uprush. The
foreshore zone of a beach. *See*
SHORE FACE

beach placers Placer deposits
either on a present or ancient
sea beach. There are a series of
these at Nome, Alaska, known as
first, second, or third beach, etc.,
due to change of shore line.

beach plain An irregular surface
consisting of successive embankments added to a growing compound spit by longshore currents. The embankments may
be closely spaced or widespread
with lagoons between them.

beach profile of equilibrium A
profile normal to the length of
a beach and concave upward.
The slope is steep above normal
high water and more gentle seaward. Equilibrium is attained
when the slope is so steep that
the backwash aided by gravity
can just return all the material
which the larger swash can drive
upward against the pull of gravity.

beach ridge An essentially continuous mound of beach material
behind the beach that has been
heaped up by wave or other action. Ridges may occur singly or
as a series of approximately parallel deposits. In England they
are called fulls.

beach scarp An almost vertical
slope along the beach caused by
erosion by wave action. It may
vary in height from a few inches
to several feet, depending on
wave action and the nature and
composition of the beach.

bead *1.* The globule of precious metal obtained by the cupellation process. *2.* A glassy drop of flux, as borax, used as a solvent for a color test for various elements before the blowpipe.

beaded drainage Pattern of short minor streams connecting small pools, characteristic of an area underlain by permafrost.

beak *Paleontol: 1.* The generally pointed extremity of a brachiopod or pelecypod shell which marks the beginning of shell growth; *2.* The prolongation of certain univalve shells containing the canal (as in a gastropod). (Not in general usage in this sense by paleontologists.) *3. Bot:* A long, prominent, and substantial point; applied particularly to prolongations of fruits and pistils.

Beaman stadia arc; Beaman arc An auxiliary attachment on an alidade consisting of a stadia arc, mounted on the outer side of the ordinary vertical arc, and enabling the observer to determine differences in elevation of the instrument and the stadia rod without use of vertical angles.

bean ore A name for limonite, when found in lenticular aggregations. Called also pea ore, when found in small, rounded masses. A coarse-grained pisolitic iron ore.

bearing The direction of a line with reference to the cardinal points of the compass. True bearing: The horizontal angle between a ground line and a geography meridian. A bearing may be referred to either the south or north point. (N. 30° E., or S. 30° W.) Magnetic bearing: The horizontal angle between a ground line and the magnetic meridian. A magnetic bearing differs from a true bearing by the exact angle of magnetic declination of the locality.

beat A periodic pulsation caused by the simultaneous occurrence of two waves, currents, or sounds of slightly different frequency; to cause two waves of slightly different frequency to be opposed; "beat frequency," that frequency which is the difference of two different frequencies.

Beaufort wind scale A system of estimating wind velocities, originally based (1806) by its inventor, Admiral Sir Francis Beaufort of the British Navy, on the

Beaufort Code Number	Beaufort's Description of Wind	Limits of Speed Miles per hour	Knots
0	Calm	0 - 1	0 - 1
1	Light air	1 - 3	1 - 3
2	Light breeze	4 - 7	4 - 6
3	Gentle breeze	8 - 12	7 - 10
4	Moderate breeze	13 - 18	11 - 16
5	Fresh breeze	19 - 24	17 - 21
6	Strong breeze	25 - 31	22 - 27
7	Moderate gale	32 - 38	28 - 33
8	Fresh gale	39 - 46	34 - 40
9	Strong gale	47 - 54	41 - 47
10	Whole gale	55 - 63	48 - 55
11	Storm	64 - 75	56 - 65
12	Hurricane	75 +	65 +

effects of various wind speeds on the amount of canvas which a full-rigged frigate of the early 19th century could carry; since modified and widely used in international meteorology.

Probable equivalents of the wind scale for an anemometer 10 meters above a level surface are: (see table on page 46)

Becke test *Opt. mineral:* A test used under the microscope for comparing indices of refraction. The so-called Becke line appears to move toward the material (i.e., mineral or immersion liquid) of higher refractivity as the tube of the microscope is raised.

bed *1.* The smallest division of a stratified series, and marked by a more or less well-defined divisional plane from its neighbors above and below. *2.* A seam or deposit of mineral, later in origin than the rock below and older than the rock above, i.e., a regular member of the series of formations, and not an intrusion. A deposit, as of ore (or coal), parallel to the stratification. *3.* That portion of an outcrop or face of a quarry which occurs between two bedding planes. *4.* The level surface of rock upon which a curb or crib is laid. *5.* *Geophys:* A rock mass usually of large horizontal extent compared to vertical or near-vertical thickness, bounded, especially on its upper side, by material with different physical properties. *6.* The floor or bottom on which any body of water rests.

bedded Applied to rocks resulting from consolidated sediments, and accordingly exhibiting planes of separation designated bedding planes.

bedded deposit *1.* Any stratified deposit. *2.* *Econ. geol:* Blanket deposit.

bedding Collective term signifying existence of beds or laminae. Planes dividing sedimentary rocks of the same or different lithology. Structure occurring in granite and similar rocks evident in a tendency to split more or less horizontally or parallel to the land surface.

bedding cleavage Cleavage that is parallel to the bedding.

bedding fault A fault that is parallel to the bedding.

bedding fissility A term generally restricted to primary foliation parallel to the bedding of sedimentary rocks, i.e., it forms while the sediment is being deposited and compacted. It is the result of the parallelism of the platy minerals to the bedding plane, partly because they were deposited that way and partly because they were rotated into this position during compaction.

bedding joint Joint parallel to bedding.

bedding plane In sedimentary or stratified rocks, the division planes which separate the individual layers, beds, or strata.

bedding schistosity Schistosity that is parallel to the bedding.

Bedford stone Mississippian limestone quarried extensively near Bedford, Indiana, for building purposes.

bed load *1.* Soil, rock particles, or other debris rolled along the bottom of a stream by the moving water, as contrasted with the "silt load" carried in suspension. *2.* That part of the total sediment load of a stream composed of all particles greater than a limiting size whether moving on the bed or in suspension; includes all bed material in movement.

bed material The material of which the bed is composed, and may be the result of either suspended or bed-load movement, or both, or, in some cases, may be even residual.

Bedoulian Lower Aptian.

bedrock *1.* The solid rock underlying auriferous gravel, sand, clay, etc., and upon which the alluvial gold rests. *2.* Any solid rock exposed at the surface of the earth or overlain by unconsolidated material.

beekite *1.* A concretionary form of calcite, occurring commonly in small rings on the surface of a fossil shell (coral, sponge, etc.), which has weathered out of its matrix. *2.* Chalcedony occurring in the form of subspherical discoid, rosettelike or doughnut-shaped accretions, generally intervoluted as bands or layers and commonly found on silicified fossils and on joint planes.

behead *Geol:* To cut off and capture by erosion the upper portion of a watercourse. Said of the encroachment of a stronger stream upon a weaker one.

beheaded stream In stream piracy the stream from which water has been diverted.

beidellite An aluminian montmorillonite.

belemnite An exinct type of cephalopod known from cigar-shaped fossils.

belt A zone or band of a particular kind of rock strata exposed on the surface. *Cf.* ZONE. An elongated area of mineralization.

belted plain A coastal plain feature found in an area of essentially horizontal or slightly dipping strata where differential erosion causes the durable strata to form belts of hilly land a few feet higher than the lower surface. Such a land surface, found both on recent coastal plains, as in eastern United States, and on older plains, as in interior New York, and in the Paris Basin, France, is known as a belted plain.

bench *1.* A strip of relatively level earth or rock, raised and narrow. A small terrace or comparatively level platform breaking the continuity of a declivity. *2.* A level or gently sloping erosion plane inclined seaward. *3.* A nearly horizontal area at about the level of maximum high water on the sea side of a dike. *4.* One of two or more divisions of a coal seam, separated by slate, etc., or simply separated by the process of cutting the coal, one bench or layer being cut before the adjacent one. *5.* A level layer worked separately in a mine. *6.* An elongated area of mineralization, usually marked by a characteristic mineralogy or structure.

bench mark A relatively permanent material object, natural or artificial, bearing a marked point whose elevation above or below an adopted datum (such as sea level) is known. The usual designation is B.M. or P.B.M. (permanent bench mark). A temporary or supplemental bench mark (T.B.M.) is of a less permanent nature, and the elevation may be less precise.

bench placers Placers in ancient stream deposits from 50 to 300 feet above present streams.

bend *1.* A curve in a river channel whose lateral changes involve a decrease in radius. Bends generally grow into meanders. *2.* In Cornwall, indurated clay; a term applied by the miner to any hardened argillaceous substance.

beneficiate To improve the grade or ore by milling, sintering, etc.

benthic Benthonic. Includes all of the bottom terrain from the shore line to the greatest deeps.

benthonic 1. Refers to the bottom of a body of standing water. *Cf.* PELAGIC. 2. Of or pertaining to sea-floor types of life or marine bottom-dwelling forms of life. Pertaining to the benthos, *q.v.*

benthos 1. The life dwelling on the bottom of the sea. Also applied to deepest part of a sea or ocean. 2. Bottom-dwelling forms of marine life, either in fixed position or in attachment to the substratum, or capable of crawling, burrowing, or swimming on, in, or above the substratum. 3. The bottom of the sea, especially of the deep oceans.

bentonite Taylorite. Bentonite is a clay formed from the decomposition of volcanic ash and is largely composed of the clay minerals montmorillonite and beidellite. The rock must be produced by decomposition of volcanic ash and not from the decomposition of other substances. The color ranges from white to light green and light blue when fresh. On exposure the color frequently becomes a light cream and gradually changes to yellow and in some cases to red or brown. The rock commonly has great ability to absorb or adsorb water and to swell accordingly.

berg 1. A hill or mountain. Local in Hudson River Valley. 2. An iceberg.

bergschrund The crevasse occurring at the head of a mountain glacier, which separates the moving snow and ice of the glacier from the relatively immobile snow and ice adhering to the headwall of the valley. It commonly penetrates to the rock face of the headwall.

berg till A glacial deposit having the resemblance of both till and lacustrine clays which formed from materials rafted into ice border lakes by icebergs.

berm 1. Terraces which originate from the interruption of an erosion cycle with rejuvenation of a stream in the mature stage of its development and renewed dissection, leaving remnants of the earlier valley floor above flood level. 2. A nearly horizontal portion of the beach or backshore formed by the deposit of material by wave action. Some beaches have no berms, others have one or several.

berm crest The seaward limit and generally the highest point of a marine berm. *Syn:* BERM EDGE

Berriasian Equal to part of or underlies Valanginian at base of Cretaceous.

beryl A mineral, composition $Be_3Al_2Si_6O_{18}$, but commonly containing up to 6% total Na_2O, Li_2O, and Cs_2O, and about 2% H_2O. Hexagonal. Occurs mainly in granitic pegmatites. Emerald and aquamarine are gem varieties.

beta axes *See* AXES, BETA

beta particle An electron.

beta quartz Quartz formed at a temperature between 573° C. and 870° C. The commonest examples are the pipyramidal quartz crystals found as phenocrysts in quartz porphyries.

beta radiation The emission of either an electron or a positron by an atomic nucleus. If the particle emitted is an electron, the emission is said to be β-emission; if a positron, it is said to be $\beta+$ emission. That portion of radiation from a radioactive source which could be strongly deflected by a perpendicular magnetic field.

bev Abbreviation for billion electric volts.

beveling The planing by erosion of the outcropping edges of strata. When the observer travels in the direction of dip, he crosses successively younger beds.

B-girdle Circular pattern in petrofabric diagrams indicating a b-axis

B-horizon Illuvial horizon. The lower soil zone which is enriched by the deposition or precipitation of material from the overlying zone or A-horizon.

bi Abbreviation for biotite in normative calculations of metamorphic rocks and in diagrams.

biaxial Having two optic axes or lines of no double refraction. Typical of crystals in the orthorhombic, monoclinic, and triclinic systems.

biaxial indicatrix Ellipsoid whose three axes at right angles to each other are proportional in length to the indices of refraction of a biaxial crystal.

bicarbonate A salt containing a metal and the radical HCO_3, e.g., $NaHCO_3$.

bichromate Dichromate.

bifid, *adj.* Two-cleft, as apices of some petals or leaves.

bifurcate, *adj.* Forked, as some Y-shaped hairs, stigmas, or styles.

bight A bend or curve, as in a river or mountain chain; a bend in a coast forming an open bay; also the bay itself.

bilateral symmetry With the individual parts arranged symmetrically along the two sides of an elongate axis, as in the earthworm, cat, etc.

billow A wave, especially a great wave or surge of water.

binary, *adj.* Composed of two elements, of an element and a radical that acts like an element, or of two such radicals. Thus $NaCl, Na_2O, Na_2SO_4$, and $(NH_4)_2-SO_4$ are all binary compounds.

binary granite *1.* A granite consisting of quartz and feldspar only. *2.* A granite containing both biotite and muscovite mica.

binary system A system consisting of two components, e.g., the system $MgO-SiO_2$.

binomen Name consisting of two words such as the name of a species, first a generic name and second a specific name.

binomial Irrespective of the nature of the concept by which species are circumscribed, the unit must fit into the binomial system of nomenclature. It must have a Latin name and that Latin name, composed of two words —the generic name and the specific name—is the binomial.

binomial system System by which organisms are known by first a generic name and second a specific or trivial name; subspecies or varieties receive a third name.

biochemical Refers to chemical processes or substances related to or produced by the activity of living organisms.

biochemical deposit A precipitated deposit resulting directly or indirectly from vital activities of an organism, such as bacterial iron ores and limestones.

biochron Geologic time unit corresponding to biostratigraphic range zone.

biochronology *1.* Geologic time scale based on fossils. *2.* Study and relations between geologic time and organic evolution. *3.* Dating of geologic events by biostratigraphic evidence.

bioclastic Refers to rocks consisting of fragmental organic remains.

biocoenose An assemblage of organisms that live together as an interrelated community. A natural ecological unit.

biofacies *1.* Lateral variations in the biologic aspect of a stratigraphic unit. *2.* Assemblages of animals or plants formed at the same time under different conditions.

biogenesis *1.* Formation by the action of organisms. *2.* The doctrine that all life has been derived from previously living organisms.

biogenetic law Ontogeny. The so-called "law" of recapitulation: Ontogeny recapitulates phylogeny.

biogenic Pertaining to a deposit resulting from the physiological activities of organisms. The rock thus formed is designated a biolith.

bioherm *1.* A moundlike or circumscribed mass built exclusively or mainly by sedentary organisms such as corals, stromatoporoids, algae, etc., and enclosed in normal rock of different lithological character. *2.* An organic reef or mound built by corals, stromatoporoids, gastropods, echinoderms, Foraminifera, mollusks, and other organisms.

biologic facies *1.* Particular association of organisms. *2.* Paleontologic nature of a stratigraphic unit. *3.* Rocks or sediments characterized by their biologic content.

biologic species Species whose recognition is based on biologic relations, particularly the willingness or ability of individuals to interbreed.

biology The study of all organisms; includes neontology and paleontology.

biomass Total mass of living organisms.

biome A major climax community composed of plants and animals. Equivalent to climax or formation. A major ecologic zone or region corresponding to a climatic zone or region.

biomechanical deposit A deposit due to the detrital accumulation of organic material, as in the cases of limestones and coal.

biometrics The application of measurement and statistics to biologic studies.

biophile An element which is required by or is found in the bodies of living organisms. The list of such elements includes C, H, O, N, P, S, Cl, I, Br, Ca, Mg, K, Na, V, Fe, Mn, and Cu. All may belong also to the chalcophile or lithophile groups.

biospecies *1.* A species living at the present time all of whose characters, relations, reactions, and activities can be observed. *2.* Group of gamodemes capable of interbreeding.

biosphere *1.* Zone at and adjacent to the earth's surface where all life exists. *2.* All living organisms of the earth. *3.* All living things on the earth's surface as distinguished from those occurring in the atmosphere, hydrosphere, and lithosphere.

biostratigraphic Pertaining to that which is characterized by its contained fossil assemblage.

biostratigraphic unit Rock stratigraphic unit defined and identified by contained fossils without regard to lithologic or other physical features or relations; *cf.* LITHOSTRATIGRAPHIC UNIT

biostratigraphic zone Bed or group of beds identified by their fossils.

biostratigraphy The paleontological aspects of stratigraphy. The separation and differentiation of rock units on the basis of assemblages of fossils which they contain.

biostrome A bedded structure composed of shell beds, crinoid beds, coral beds, etc., which was built by sedentary organisms. In contrast to bioherms, they lack moundlike or lenslike form.

biota The animal and plant life of a region; flora and fauna collectively.

biotite A mineral, a member of the mica group. Formula $K(Mg,Fe'')_3(Al,Fe''')Si_3O_{10}(OH)_2$. A common rock-forming mineral. Monoclinic, perfect basal cleavage. Dark brown to green.

biotope 1. A term used by ecologists and biologists to designate an area of uniform ecology and organic adaptation. 2. An ecological term matching "biofacies," and which signifies organic environment. 3. Faunal or floral unit which may be interpreted environmentally, and which reflects the influence of the environment of the biota. 4. An area inhabited by a uniform community adapted to its environment.

biozone 1. Biostratigraphic unit including all strata deposited during the existence of a particular kind of fossil; cf. TEILZONE. 2. Biostratigraphic unit identified by the actual occurrence of a particular kind of fossil (not recommended). Syn: RANGE ZONE. 3. Originally proposed as a geologic time unit corresponding to 1 above (obsolete). Syn: BIOCHRON

bipartite oölite Oölite whose central portion is divided into two more or less distinct fractions of different texture so that it has an asymmetrical appearance.

Birch discontinuity Seismic discontinuity within the earth's mantle at a depth of about 900 km. caused perhaps by phase or chemical change or both.

bird 1. Those parts of the airborne magnetometer, including the case but excluding the cables, which are streamed behind an aircraft. Also, the bomb used in air seismic shooting. 2. Member of the vertebrate class Aves.

birdfoot delta A delta formed by the outgrowth of fingers or pairs of natural levees at the mouths of river distributaries making the digitate or "birdfoot" form typified by the Mississippi delta.

birdseye limestone Very fine grained limestone containing spots or tubes of crystalline calcite.

birefringence Double refraction. The property possessed by crystals belonging to other than the isometric system of splitting a beam of ordinary light into two beams which traverse the crystal at different speeds, and as they pass out of it produce characteristic optical effects that are recognizable with the proper instruments or, in some cases, by the eye alone. Mineral: Generally defined as the difference between the greatest and the least indices of refraction.

biscuit-board topography Topography characterized by a rolling upland out of which cirques have been cut like big bites, and which represents an early or partial stage in glaciation.

bisector A plane or line of symmetry.

bisectrix A line bisecting the angle between the two optic axes of a biaxial crystal, designated acute or obtuse depending on which of the complementary angles is being referred to.

biserial Consisting of a double series as with the plates of cystoid brachioles and some crinoid arms.

bisexual Describing an organism which produces both eggs and sperms, and a flower which bears both stamens and pistil(s).

bismuthinite; bismuth glance A mineral, Bi_2S_3. Orthorhombic.

bisphenoid A crystal form similar to a tetrahedron which has been elongated parallel to one of the crystal axes.

bit, drilling The cutting device at the lower end of cable drilling tools or rotary drill pipe, the function of which is to accomplish the actual boring or cutting.

bitter lakes Lakes rich in sulfates and alkaline carbonates, as distinct from salt lakes.

bittern *1.* The bitter mother liquor that remains in saltworks after the salt has crystallized out. *2.* Natural solutions in evaporite basins which resemble saltwork liquors, especially in their high magnesium content.

bitumen *1.* A general name for various solid and semisolid hydrocarbons. In 1912 the term was used by the American Society for Testing Materials to include all those hydrocarbons which are soluble in carbon bisulfide, whether gases, easily mobile liquids, viscous liquids, or solids. *See* ASPHALT. *2.* Originally, native mineral pitch, tar, or asphalt. The term is generally applied to any of the flammable, viscid, liquid, or solid hydrocarbon mixtures soluble in carbon disulfide; often used interchangeably with hydrocarbons.

bituminous *1.* Yielding bitumen, or holding bitumen in composition. This term is also commonly used for certain varieties of coal which burn freely with flame, although they really contain no bitumen. *2.* Containing much organic or at least carbonaceous matter, mostly in the form of the tarry hydrocarbons which are usually described as bitumen. *3.* Having the odor of bitumen. Often applied to minerals. *4.* Yielding volatile bituminous matter on heating (e.g., bituminous coal). *See* HUMIC

bivalve Common term for the pelecypods, *q.v.*

bivariant equilibrium Said of a system having two degrees of freedom.

Bk Abbreviation for barkevikite in normative calculations of metamorphic rocks.

black body An ideal body, the surface of which absorbs all the radiation that falls upon it; i.e., it neither reflects nor transmits any of the incident radiation. The nearest approach to such a body among natural substances is soot, though the sun is often considered as a black body in meteorological studies of its radiation.

black damp Gas containing carbon monoxide that escapes from coal in coal mines; it is deadly.

black diamond Carbonado. *See* DIAMOND

blackjack *1.* A dark variety of zinc-blend or sulfide of zinc. It has a resinous luster and yields a light-colored streak or powder. *Cf.* BLENDE; SPHALERITE. *2.* Crude black oil used to lubricate mine-car wheels. *3.* Soft black, carbonaceous clay or earth associated with coal. *4.* In Derbyshire, a kind of cannel coal. *5.* In Illinois, a thin stratum of coal interbedded with layers of slate. A poor, bony coal.

black mud A mud, formed in lagoons, sounds, or bays, in which there is poor circulation or weak tides. The color is generally due to black sulfides of iron, and to organic matter.

Blackriverian Lower Mohawkian.

black sands Local deposits of heavy minerals concentrated by wave and current action on beaches. The heavy minerals consist largely of magnetite, ilmenite, and hematite associated with other minerals such as garnet, rutile, zircon, chromite, amphiboles, and pyroxenes.

black shale Biopelite. A type of shale usually very thin-bedded, rich in sulphides (especially pyrite which may have replaced fossils) and rich in organic material, deposited under barred basin conditions causing anaerobic accumulation.

Blancan Upper Pliocene or lowermost Pleistocene.

blanket deposit *1*. A flat deposit of ore of which the length and breadth are relatively great as compared with the thickness. The term is current among miners, but it has no very exact scientific meaning. More or less synonymous terms are flat sheets, bedded veins, beds, or flat masses. *2*. Sedimentary deposit of great lateral extent and relatively uniform thickness, particularly a sandstone.

blanket sand A body of sand or sandstone that covers a considerable two-dimensional area. Often called a sheet sand.

blastetrix In an anisotropic medium, any surface perpendicular to which is a direction of greatest ease of growth.

blasting Abrasion effected by the movement of fine particles against a stationary fragment. In a sandblast or dry blasting the carrying agent is air; in wet blasting it is a current of water.

blasto- [*Gr.*] Prefix denoting presence in a rock of residual structures, more or less modified by metamorphism, but still recognized, e.g., blastoporphyritic.

Blastoidea Class of stemmed budlike echinoderms with body enclosed by 13 plates regularly arranged in 3 circlets, and ambulacral areas borne on the body surface. Ord.-Perm.

blastophitic A metamorphosed rock which originally contained lath-shaped crystals partly or wholly enclosed in augite and in which part of the original texture remains.

blastoporphyritic A term applied to the textures of metamorphic rocks derived from porphyritic rocks, and in which the porphyritic character still remains as a relict feature, veiled but not obliterated by subsequent recrystallization.

blastopsammite A relict fragment of sandstone contained in a metamorphosed conglomerate.

bleaching clay As used in the oil industries refers to clays that in their natural state, or after chemical activation, have capacity for adsorbing coloring matter from oil.

bleach spot Deoxidation sphere. A greenish or yellowish area in red-colored rocks developed by the reduction of ferric oxide around an organic particle.

bleb A small, usually rounded inclusion of one material in another, as blebs of olivene, poikilitically enclosed in pyroxene.

bleed In England, to give off water or gas, as from coal or other stratum.

bleeding core In oil-field usage, one which shows little or no evidence of petroleum when first removed from the core barrel, but after a short time turns brown and exudes a film or drops of oil.

blende Sphalerite, *q.v.*

blind valley *1.* A feature in karst areas where a stream flows or disappears into a tunnel at the closed end of a valley. *2.* A type of valley in which a spring emerges from an underground channel to form a surface stream whose valley is enclosed at the head by steep and possibly precipitous walls.

blister cone A domelike cone on a lava flow which formed when the cooling crust buckled over caves resulting from the flow of molten lava beneath the hardening crust.

block An angular fragment over 256 mm. in diameter showing little or no modification in form due to transportation; similar in size to a boulder.

block caving A method of mining ore from the top down in successive layers of much greater thickness than characteristic of top slicing. Each block is undercut over the greater part of its bottom area and the supporting pillars blasted out. As the block caves and settles, the cover follows. The method might be considered as involving many of the features of top slicing combined with ore caving, but also on a larger scale. Also called "caving system" and "Cumberland method of mining."

block diagram Three-dimensional perspective representation of geologic or topographic features showing a surface area and generally two vertical cross sections.

block folding Folding in an uplifted block bounded by steep faults that results from lateral spreading over lower blocks.

block mountains Mountains carved by erosion from large uplifted earth-blocks bounded on one side or both by fault-scarps. *See* FAULT BLOCK MOUNTAINS

blocks, volcanic Essential, accessory, or accidental volcanic ejecta, usually angular and larger than 32 mm. in diameter, erupted in a solid state.

blockstripes Forms transitional to stone stripes but containing material coarser and of less uniform size than in stone stripes.

bloom *1.* An earthy mineral that is frequently found as an efflorescence, as cobalt bloom. Also called blossom. *2.* The fluorescence of petroleum. *3. V:* To form an efflorescence; as salts with which alkali soils are impregnated bloom out on the surface of the earth in dry weather, after a rain or irrigation.

blowhole *1.* A hole in a sea cliff from which columns of spray often accompanied with noise are forced upward. Blowholes are formed by wave erosion which extends sea caves along joints or other cracks to the surface. The expansion of air in the hole when the wave subsides creates the driving force to eject water out of the blowhole. *2.* Blowholes are the minute craters formed on the surfaces of thick lava flows. They are often visible on driblet cones.

blown or **eolian sands** Those produced by the action of windborne particles of rocks; chemical composition of blown sands depends to a large extent on the original rocks from which they have been derived. The sorting is not good.

blowout *1.* A general term for various saucer-, cup-, or trough-shaped hollows formed by wind erosion on a pre-existing dune or other sand deposit; the adjoining accumulation of sand derived from the depression, where readily recognizable, is commonly included. *See* BLOWOUT DUNE. *2.* A term much used by prospectors and miners for any surface exposure of strongly altered, discolored rock associated, or thought to be associated, with a mineral deposit. *3.* In drilling a well by the rotary method an unexpected volume of gas under pressure sometimes "blows" the mud-laden drilling fluid from the hole, thus putting an end to drilling until controlled. The term is also used in standard-tool drilling when the flow of gas is sufficient to interfere with drilling operation.

blowout dune A term sometimes applied to the accumulations of sand derived from blowout troughs or basins, particularly where the accumulation is of large size and rises to considerable height above the source area.

blowpipe A tube through which air is forced into a flame, to direct it and increase its intensity. In the compound blowpipe, two jets of gas (one of which may be air) are united at the point of combustion.

blue asbestos *See* CROCIDOLITE.

blue band *1.* A layer of dense, bubble-free ice in a glacier. *2.* The dark ribbon effect produced on the surface of the glacier by the exposure of these layers. *3.* A thin but persistent bed of bluish clay that is found near base of No. 6 coal throughout the Illinois-Indiana coal basin.

blue ground A term applied to the slaty-blue or blue-green kimberlite breccia of the diamond pipes of South Africa, occurring beneath a superficial oxidized covering known as yellow ground.

blue mud *1.* An ocean-bottom deposit containing up to 75% of terrigenous materials, of dimensions below 0.03 mm. The depth-range of occurrence is about 750 to 16,800 feet. Colors range from reddish to brownish at the surface, but beneath the surface the colors of the wet muds are gray to blue. *2.* A common variety of deep-sea mud having a bluish-gray color due to presence of organic matter and finely divided iron sulfides. Calcium carbonate is present in variable amounts up to 35%.

blue vitriol Chalcanthite.

bluff *1.* Any high headland, or bank presenting a precipitous front. *2.* In America, the name given to the high vertical banks of certain rivers. *3.* A high steep bank or cliff. *4.* Altered country rock filling a lode. Analogous to mullock of Australia.

board coal In England, coal having a fibrous or woody appearance.

bodily tides Tides or tilts of the surface of the earth caused by the gravitational field of the sun and moon.

body waves Either transverse or longitudinal seismic waves transmitted in the interior of an elastic solid or fluid and not related to a boundary surface. A perfectly sharp distinction between body waves and surface waves is difficult to make unless the waves are plane or spherical.

boehmite A mineral, AlO(OH), dimorph of diaspore. Orthorhombic. A major constituent of some bauxites.

bog Morass; swamp. *1.* Common name in Scotland and Ireland for a wet spongy morass, chiefly composed of decaying vegetable matter or peat. *2.* A swamp or tract of wet land, covered in many cases with peat.

Bogs called morasses in Scotland and swamps in America often contain well-preserved trunks of trees, especially of the oak in Ireland and of the cypress in America.

bogaz Deep and narrow chasms in a karst country that are caused by water penetrating a line of weakness such as a fault or bedding plane or joint.

bog burst Refers to a bog built up into a low dome higher than the surrounding land and dammed by the organic material growing around the margin of the bogs. This dam ultimately breaks under conditions of great rainfall and the escaping flood transports black organic matter over considerable distances.

boghead coal *1.* A variety of bituminous or subbituminous coal resembling cannel coal in appearance and in behavior during combustion. It is characterized by a high percentage of algal remains and volatile matter. Upon distillation it gives exceptionally high yields of tar and oil. *Cf.* KEROSENE SHALE. *2.* A non-banded coal with the translucent attritus consisting predominately of algae, and having less than 5% of anthraxylon.

bog iron A spongy variety of hydrated oxide of iron or limonite. Found in layers and lumps on level sandy soils which have been covered with swamp or bog. *Cf.* BROWN IRON ORE

bog manganese Wad.

bog ore A spongy variety of hydrated oxide of iron or limonite. Found in layers and lumps on level sandy soils which have been covered with swamp or bog. Includes bog iron ore, bog manganese ore, bog lime, a calcareous deposit of similar origin.

bogue Bayou.

Bohemian ruby A jeweler's name for rose quartz when cut as a gem. Also pyrope garnet.

Bohemian topaz A jeweler's name for yellow quartz when cut as a gem.

boiling point *1.* The temperature at which a liquid begins to boil, or to be converted into vapor by bubbles forming within its mass. It varies with the pressure. *2.* The temperature at which crude oil on being heated begins to give forth its different distillates. The boiling point of crude oils and the amounts of distillates obtained at specified temperatures differ considerably.

boiling spring *1.* A spring or fountain which gives out water at the boiling point or at a high temperature. *2.* A spring rising from the bottom of residual clay basins at the head of interior valleys. (Jamaica)

bojite *1.* Hornblende gabbro with primary hornblende. *2.* Hornblende diorite.

bolson In Southwest: *1.* A basin; a depression or valley having no outlet. *2.* A large basin or depression; a wide valley drained by a stream flowing through canyons at each end.

bombs, volcanic Pyroclastic ejecta consisting of fragments of lava that were liquid, or plastic at the time of ejection, and having forms, surface markings, or internal structures acquired during flight through the air or at the time of landing after flight. They range from a few millimeters to several feet in length. Bombs less than 4 mm. in diameter are better classed as volcanic ash or dust.

bonanza [*Sp.* fair weather] In miners' phrase, good luck, or a body of rich ore. A mine is in bonanza when it is profitably producing ore. A body of rich ore.

bond, covalent A linkage between two atoms in a molecule, with no difference in electric charge on the two atoms; a linkage formed by the sharing of electron pairs.

bond, homopolar Covalent bond.

bond, ionic A linkage between two atoms, with a separation of electric charge on the two atoms; a linkage formed by the transfer or shift of electrons from one atom to the other.

bond, metallic The linkage between atoms in metals, characterized by fairly mobile electrons not firmly held to particular atoms.

bond, polar Ionic bond.

bond, van der Waals See VAN DER WAALS FORCES

bone bed In England, a term applied to several thin strata or layers, from their containing innumerable fragments of fossil bones, scales, teeth, coprolites, and also organic remains.

bone phosphate The calcium phosphate obtained from bones; also in commerce, applied to calcium phosphate obtained from phosphatic rocks, e.g., those of North Carolina.

Bononian Lower Portlandian.

book structure 1. A peculiar rock structure resulting from numerous parallel sheets of slate alternating with quartz. 2. Alternation of parallel slabs or slivers of rock with quartz or other gangue mineral in a vein.

boracite A mineral, $Mg_6Cl_2B_{14}O_{26}$, found in evaporites. Orthorhombic, pseudocubic.

borate A salt or ester of boric acid; a compound containing the radical BO_3^{-3}.

borax A mineral, $Na_2B_4O_7.10H_2O$, an ore of boron. Monoclinic.

borax bead In blowpipe analysis, a drop of borax, which, fused with a small quantity of a metallic oxide, will show the characteristic color of the element; as, a blue borax bead indicates the presence of cobalt.

border facies of igneous rocks See BASIC BORDERS IN IGNEOUS ROCKS

borderland Long relatively narrow land mass adjacent to a continental border that contributed sediment to a geosyncline or confined an epicontinental sea. See CONTINENTAL SHELF, CONTINENTAL BORDERLAND

bore Egre; Eager. 1. A violent rush of tidal water; the advancing edge or front of the tidal wave as it ascends a river or estuary. 2. A tidal flood with a high, abrupt front (such as occurs in the Amazon in South America, the Hugli in India, and the Bay of Fundy). 3. Submarine sand ridge in very shallow water that may rise to intertidal level. 4. A borehole or boring.

boreal Northern.

borehole A hole drilled into the earth, often to a great depth, as a prospective oil well or for exploratory purposes.

bornhardt An inselberg, q.v., of large size.

bornite Peacock copper ore. A mineral, Cu_5FeS_4, characterized by a reddish-brown color on fresh fracture, tarnishing to iridescent purple. Isometric. An important ore of copper.

bort 1. A trade name for diamonds too badly flawed or too off-color to be used in jewelry. 2. Carbonado or black diamond. Useful for abrasion.

boss 1. A mass of intrusive rock which forms at the surface rounded, craggy, or variously shaped eminences, having a circular, elliptical, or irregular ground plan, and descending into the earth with vertical or steeply inclined sides. *Syn:* STOCK. 2. In Foraminifera, a round and raised or knoblike structure. 3. Coarse, short nodules occurring on the spire of a gastropod. 4. The cone which supports the spheroidal summit of a tubercle on an echinoid plate.

botryoidal Having the form of a bunch of grapes. Said usually of minerals.

bottom 1. Bottom is a word frequently heard in the Mississippi Valley and farther west, and used to designate the alluvial tracts along the river courses, which are sometimes called bottom lands, and sometimes simply bottoms. 2. The bed of a body of still or running water. 3. The floor of an underground passage; also sometimes referred to as the sill of a level. 4. Bottom flow= underflow. A density current denser than any part of the surrounding fluid and which flows along the bottom of the body of water.

bottom-hole pressure The hydraulic pressure existing at the bottom or test position in a borehole as determined by one of several geophysical devices.

bottom land Lowland formed by alluvial deposit along a stream or in a lake basin; a flood plain.

bottom load Material rolled, pushed, or bounced along the bottom of a stream. *Cf.* BED LOAD; TRACTIONAL LOAD

bottom-set beds The layers of finer material carried out and deposited on the bottom of the sea or a lake in front of a delta. As the delta grows forward they are covered by the fore-set beds. *See* FORE-SET BEDS; TOP-SET BEDS

boudin One of a series of sausage-shaped segments occurring in a boudinage structure.

boudinage A structure in which beds set in a yielding matrix are divided by cross-fractures into pillowlike segments. The cross-fractures are not sharp, but rather rounded, and may be compared with the "necks" that develop in ductile metal test-pieces under tension. The name is derived from the word boudin [*Fr.* sausage] because in section the structure resembles a string of link sausages.

Bouguer anomaly The gravity value existing after the Bouguer corrections to a level datum have been applied.

Bouguer reduction Bouguer correction. A correction made in gravity work to take account of the altitude of the station and the rock between the station and sea level.

boulangerite A mineral, $Pb_5Sb_4S_{11}$. Monoclinic.

boulder; bowlder 1. A term for large rounded blocks of stone lying on the surface of the ground, or sometimes embedded in loose soil, different in composition from the rocks in the vicinity, and which have been therefore transported from a distance. 2. A fragment of rock brought by natural means from a distance (though this notion of transportation from a distance is not always, in later usage, involved) and usually large and rounded in shape. Cobblestones taken from river beds are, in some American localities, called boulders. About 256 mm. (Wentworth scale).

boulder barricade A belt of boulders along a shore line

visible between low and half tides.

boulder clay Till; drift clay; drift. Boulder clay is an unstratified or little stratified and unassorted deposit of silty and clayey materials in which are embedded particles in the size range from sands to boulders.

boulder pavement *1.* Surface of boulder-rich till abraded to flatness by glacier movement. *2.* Boulders in till, when grouped in an approximately horizontal plane and striated on their upper surfaces in a common direction constitute a boulder pavement according to the usage of the Scottish geologists.

boulder rampart A narrow ridge of boulders thrown up along part of the edge of a reef flat, especially on the side from which the prevailing winds blow. The rampart, which seldom exceeds 1 or 2 m. in height, occurs close behind the lithothamnion ridge where it is present.

boulder train Boulder trains take their origin from knobs or prominences of rock which lay in the path of glacial advance and gave off boulders readily and abundantly to the overriding ice. Such trains lie in the line of glacial movement, but the boulders are not carried forward in strictly parallel lines. They may therefore appropriately be called boulder fans. The boulders are of a single kind, or at least of the few kinds represented by the parent knob. They usually grow smaller and more worn as traced away from it. They mingle with the underlying drift, and in this respect differ from the boulder belts.

boundary *1.* A line between areas of the earth's surface occupied by rocks or formations of different type and age; especially used in connection with geologic mapping, hence, also, a line between two formations or cartographic units on a geologic map. *2.* That which indicates or fixes a limit or extent or marks a bound, as of territory. *3.* A plane separating two formations or other rock units.

boundary monument A material object placed on or near a boundary line to preserve and identify the location of the boundary line on the ground.

boundary tension A general term used to designate all surface and interfacial tensions at boundary surfaces, such as liquid-gas, liquid-liquid, and liquid-solid.

boundary waves Seismic waves which are propagated along free surfaces or acoustic interfaces, and which depend on layering for their existence.

bournonite Cog-wheel ore. A mineral, $PbCuSbS_3$. Orthorhombic.

Bowen's reaction series A series of minerals, wherein any early formed mineral phase tends to react with the melt, later in the differentiation, to yield a new mineral further down in the series. Thus early formed crystals of olivine react with later liquids to form pyroxene crystals; these in turn may further react with still later liquids to form amphiboles. There are two different series, a continuous reaction series, *q.v.*, and a discontinuous reaction series, *q.v.*

box canyon A canyon having steep rock sides and a zigzag course, presenting a view from its bottom of four almost vertical walls.

box folds A fold in which the broad flat top of an anticline (or the broad flat bottom of a syncline) is bordered on either side by steeply dipping limbs.

box work Limonite and other minerals which originally formed as blades or plates along cleavage or fracture planes and then the intervening material dissolved leaving the intersecting blades or plates as a network. Usually found on the ceilings of caves.

brachiole Armlike appendage of cystoids that arises in the vicinity of the mouth.

Brachiopoda A phylum of marine, shelled animals with two unequal shells or valves each of which normally is bilaterally symmetrical. Also called lamp shells.

brachyanticline A term used in the U.S.S.R. to designate a long, narrow anticline.

brachy axis The shorter lateral axis in the crystals of the orthorhombic and triclinic systems. *Obs.*

brachydome Side dome. *Crystallog:* A dome parallel to the shorter lateral axis. *Obs.*

brachyhaline Polyhaline. *See* BRACKISH

brachypinacoid Side pinacoid. A pinacoid parallel to the vertical and the shorter lateral axis.

brachysyncline Short broad syncline.

brackish *1.* Slightly salty. *2.* Term applied to waters whose saline content is intermediate between that of streams and sea water; neither fresh nor salty, but in between. *3.* Salty, generally less so than sea water, variously defined as less than 30 to 15 parts per thousand salinity. Different degrees of brackishness may be recognized in decreasing order of salinity: polyhaline, pliohaline, mesohaline, miohaline, and oligohaline.

Bradfordian Uppermost Devo-

nian, may be transitional to Mississippian.

Bradygenesis Retardation of development of a group of organisms which may progressively diminish the rate so that certain individuals in some or all of their characters may fall more and more behind the normal rate of progress.

Bragg's law The angle at which X rays are reflected from a crystal depends upon the interval between planes or layers in the crystal and on the wave length of the X rays, according to the following formula: $n\lambda = 2d \sin\theta$ where λ is the wave length, d the crystal spacing, and θ is the reflection angle.

braid To branch and rejoin producing a netlike pattern, as with some streams.

braided stream *1.* A braided stream is one flowing in several dividing and reuniting channels resembling the strands of a braid, the cause of division being the obstruction by sediment deposited by the stream. *2.* Where more sediment is being brought to any part of a stream than it can remove, the building of bars becomes excessive, and the stream develops an intricate network of interlacing channels, and is said to be braided. *See* ANASTOMOSING

brammallite Sodium-illite A clay mineral related to illites, but containing Na$>$K.

branch *1.* A creek or brook, as used locally in southern states. Also used to designate one of the bifurcations of a stream, as, a fork. *2.* Subdivision of an igneous rock series.

branch fault Auxiliary fault.

Branchiopoda Class of crustaceans with leaflike appendages, many with bivalved shells. Camb.-Rec.

braunite A mineral, $3Mn_2O_3$.-$MnSiO_3$. Tetragonal, commonly in brownish-black masses.

Bravais lattice Simple crystal lattice; 14 varieties occur.

breached anticline An anticline that has been more deeply eroded in the center. Consequently, erosional scarps face inward toward the center of the anticline.

breached cone A cinder cone in which lava has broken through the sides and carried away the broken materials.

breached crater Volcanic craters have generally a complete rim, but in some cases the heavy lava rises in the crater until its weight is so great that it bursts through one wall of the crater and flows out through the breach. Such craters are known as breached craters.

breadcrust bomb A volcanic bomb with a checkered and cracked exterior resulting from the shrinkage of the skin upon congealing. *See* BOMBS, VOLCANIC

break Arrival; event; kick. *1.* On a seismogram trace, a sudden displacement indicating the arrival of energy over some path of interest, used especially for near surface paths, as "first breaks" of energy refracted along the "weathered layer" base in exploration seismic operations. *2.* Abrupt change in surface slope.

breaker A wave breaking on the shore, over a reef, etc. Breakers may be (roughly) classified into three kinds although there is much overlapping. Spilling breakers break gradually over quite a distance; plunging breakers tend to curl over and break with a crash; and surging breakers peak up, but then instead of spilling or plunging they surge up the beach face.

breaker depth Breaking depth. The still-water depth at the point where the wave breaks.

breaker height Average height of breaking waves from trough to crest.

breaker terrace In glacial or artificial lakes where water rises against a bank of kame gravels, a characteristic terrace develops, composed of the heaviest stones handled by the waves. The front has a steep slope and has no admixture of fine gravels. Similar forms are built of lighter gravels by moderate waves, but these are destroyed in heavy storms. Those built by the heaviest cobbles which can be moved are persistent forms and are very characteristic of lakes in the glacial drift, especially of those in the kame areas.

breaks *1.* The broken land at the border of an upland that is dissected by ravines. *2.* An area in rolling land eroded by small ravines and gullies; also used to indicate any sudden change in topography, as from a plain to hilly country.

break thrust A thrust fault that cuts across one limb of a fold.

breccia [*It.*] *1.* Fragmental rock whose components are angular and therefore, as distinguished from conglomerates, are not waterworn. There are friction or fault breccias, talus breccias, and eruptive breccias. *2.* A rock made up of highly angular coarse fragments. May be sedimentary or formed by crushing or grinding along faults.

breccia, volcanic *See* VOLCANIC BRECCIA

Bretonian Upper Cambrian.

Bretonian orogeny Post-Devonian diastrophism.

bridal-veil fall A cataract of great height and such small volume that the falling water is dissipated in spray before reaching the lower stream bed.

bridge *1.* A solutional remnant forming a rock span across a cave inclined less than 45° from the horizontal. *2.* Collapsed walls or large fragments of rock falling and lodging in a drill hole in such a way as to obstruct passage of drilling tools. Also a mechanical obstruction placed intentionally to obstruct a drill hole. *3.* A circuit composed of four or more elements connected in a loop, usually having a source of electrical power connected across at least two elements of the loop, and used for measuring electrical impedance. Also, a jumper or wire connector used to short-circuit or to offer a path of negligible impedance around an electrical circuit or circuit element. Also, a plug or obstruction in a shot hole above the bottom of the hole, usually formed by caving or an exploding charge whether accidentally or intentionally. *V:* To form a bridge or to be bridged.

bright coal *1.* Anthraxylon. The constituent of banded coal which is of a jet-black pitchy appearance, more compact than dull coal, and breaking with a conchoidal fracture when viewed macroscopically, and which in thin section always shows preserved cell structure of woody plant tissue, either of stem, branch, or root. *2.* A coal composed of anthraxylon and attritus, in which the translucent cell-wall degradation matter or translucent humic matter predominates. *3.* A banded coal containing less than 20% opaque attritus and more than 5% anthraxylon.

4. A type of banded coal containing from 100% to 81% pure bright ingredients (vitrain, clarain, and fusain), the remainder consisting of claro-durain and durain.

brine Water strongly impregnated with salt.

British thermal unit Abbreviated B. t. u. A unit of heat which is 1/180 part of that required to raise the temperature of one pound of water from 32° F. to 212° F. at sea level. Usually considered as that amount of heat required to raise the temperature of one pound of water from 63° F. to 64° F.

brittleness Property of material that ruptures easily with little or no plastic flow.

brochantite A mineral, $Cu_4(SO_4)(OH)_6$, common in the oxidation zone of copper sulfide deposits. Monoclinic, emerald to dark green.

brodel *1.* A bulbous mass of silt, without horizontal continuity and completely enclosed by clay except through "necks" by which they are connected with overlying silt beds. *2.* Highly irregular, aimlessly contorted interpenetrating structures in Pleistocene sediments. *Cf.* INVOLUTION; CRYOTURBATION

bromide A compound of bromine with one other more positive element or radical.

bromoform $CHBr_3$, tribromomethane, m.p. 5° C., sp.gr. 2.9; a colorless liquid, of narcotic odor. Used especially in mineral separation.

bronzite A variety of the enstatite-hypersthene series. *See* PYROXENE

brook A stream of less length and volume than a creek, as used locally in the Northeast. Generally, one of the smallest branches or ultimate ramifications of a drainage system.

brookite A mineral, TiO_2. Orthorhombic, trimorphous with rutile and anatase.

brow *1.* The edge of the top of a hill or mountain; the point at which a gentle slope changes to an abrupt one; the top of a bluff or cliff. *2.* The frontal portion of a nappe, in which the strata commonly are overrolled.

brown coal Lignite. A low rank coal which is brown, brownish black, but rarely black. It commonly retains the structures of the original wood. It is high in moisture, low in heat value, and checks badly upon drying.

brown iron ore Its approximate formula is $2Fe_2O_3.3H_2O$, equivalent to about 59.8% iron. Probably a mixture of hydrous iron oxides. Residual and replacement limonite, mainly at erosion surfaces. *Syn:* BROWN HEMATITE; LIMONITE

brown soils A zonal group of soils having a brown surface horizon which grades below into lighter colored soil, and finally into a layer of carbonate accumulation, developed under short grasses, bunch grasses, and shrubs in a temperate to cool, semiarid climate.

brownstone Ferruginous sandstone in which the grains are generally coated with iron oxide. Applied almost exclusively to a dark brown sandstone derived from the Triassic of the Connecticut River Valley.

brucite A mineral, $Mg(OH)_2$. Commonly in foliated masses. Hexagonal rhombohedral.

Brunton A small pocket compass with sights and a reflector attached, used in sketching mine workings, as in mine examinations, or in preliminary surveys.

Bruxellian Lower middle Eocene.

Bryophyta Division of non-vascular plants that may have differentiated stems and leaves but no true roots; includes liverworts and mosses.

Bryozoa Phylum of tiny colonial animals equipped with a lophophore that build calcareous structures of many kinds, mostly marine. Ord.-Rec. The phylum of invertebrate animals which are popularly called "moss animals." (Called Polyzoa by some zoologists.)

B-tectonite *1.* Tectonite whose fabric indicates an axial direction rather than a slip surface. *2. Struct. Petrol:* A tectonite is a deformed rock the fabric of which is the result of the systematic movement of the individual units under a common external force. In a B-tectonite a lineation is prominent and s-planes may be absent. The point diagram commonly shows a girdle about the b-axis.

B.t.u. An abbreviation for British thermal unit.

bubble point A state of fluids characterized by the coexistence of a liquid phase with an infinitesimal quantity of gas phase in equilibrium.

bubble train (in lava) A string or strings of vesicles, marking the path followed by the rising gas escaping from a lava flow.

bubble trend Planar or linear bubble zone as in glacial ice.

bucking plate; bucking iron An iron plate on which ore is ground by hand by means of a muller. Extensively used for the final reduction of ore samples for assaying.

buffalo wallow These are the minor, very shallow depressions on the upland surface. They may be from a few feet to a few rods in diameter and from a fraction of a foot to several feet in depth.

buffer solution A solution to which large amounts of acid or base may be added with only a very small resultant change in the hydrogen ion concentration.

Buffonism The theory, proposed by G. L. L. de Buffon in 1766, that the direct action of external conditions is a factor in the volutionary modification of species.

buhrstone; burrstone; burstone A silicified fossiliferous limestone, with abundant cavities which were formerly occupied by fossil shells. Its cellular character and toughness occasioned its extensive use as a millstone in former years.

building stone Any stone used in masonry construction, generally stone of superior quality that is quarried and trimmed or cut to form regular blocks.

bulb glacier Where valley glaciers descend to the foot of a mountain and out upon an open slope, as in a broad valley or upon a plain, the glacier ends spread into an ice fan, or bulb glacier, or piedmont bulb. If two or more such bulbs coalesce a broad-spreading glacier end is formed, to which the name piedmont glacier is applied.

bulk modulus Volume elasticity; incompressibility modulus. Under increasing force per unit area a body will decrease in size but increase in density.

bulk sample A large sample consisting of tons or hundreds of tons which is then milled and the grade computed from the results.

bullion *1.* Concretion found in some types of coal; composed of carbonate or silica stained by brown humic derivatives; often

well-preserved plant structures form the nuclei. *2.* Nodules of clay, ironstone, pyrite, shale, etc., which generally enclose a fossil.

bull quartz A miner's or prospector's term for white, coarse-grained, barren quartz.

Bunter Lower Triassic.

Buntsandstein Bunter.

buoyancy The resultant of upward forces, exerted by the water on a submerged or floating body, equal to the weight of the water displaced by this body.

Burdigalian Upper lower Miocene.

buried hill Hills consisting of resistant older rock over which later sediments were deposited. The sedimentary beds have the form of an anticline as the result of original dip, unequal compaction, and other causes.

buried placers Old placer deposits which have become buried beneath lava flows or other strata.

burrow Boring. *1.* A cylindrical tube, often filled with clay or sand, which may lie along the bedding plane or penetrate the rock, made by a mud-eating worm or a mollusk. *2.* A hole in the ground, rock, or wood, etc., made by certain animals for shelter.

butane A gaseous hydrocarbon of the paraffin series, formula C_4H_{10}.

butte [*Fr.*] Mesa. A conspicuous isolated hill or small mountain, especially one with very steep or precipitous sides, or a turretlike formation such as those found in the bad lands.

button The globule of metal remaining on an assay-cupel or in a crucible, at the end of the fusion.

buttress *1.* A ridge on the inner surface of a valve of a pelecypod which serves as a support for part of the hinge. 2. Aboral extension of apical denticle, generally on inner and outer sides in a conodont.

b.y. Billion years.

bysmalith A more or less vertical cylindrical body of igneous rock that crosscuts the adjacent sediments and has been injected by pushing up the overlying strata along steep faults. The term was introduced by J. P. Iddings.

bytownite *See* PLAGIOCLASE

c

c Abbreviation for corundum in normative rock calculations.

cable tools The equipment used in the standard, percussion, or cable tool method of drilling. It consists essentially of a steel bit fastened below drill stem and jars, all suspended on a wire line. The whole can be lowered or raised by controlling machinery near the mouth of the hole. In drilling, the tools are alternately lifted and dropped, the rock being cut by the repeated blows of the bit.

cadastral map A map showing the boundaries of subdivisions of land, usually with the bearings and lengths thereof and the areas of individual tracts, for purposes of describing and recording ownership.

cadastral survey A survey relating to land boundaries and subdivisions, made to create units suitable for transfer or to define limitations of title, for example, the surveys of city or town lots.

cafemic A mnemonic term used collectively for the calcium, ferrous-ferric, and magnesium constituents of rocks or magmas; an extension of the CIPW (1902) term "femic."

Cainozoic Cenozoic.

Calabrian Lower Pleistocene.

calamine Hemimorphite. Sometimes used in Europe for smithsonite.

calaverite A mineral, $AuTe_2$, which commonly contains some Ag. Monoclinic.

calc- [*Lat.*] Prefix meaning limy, i.e., containing calcium carbonate.

calc-alkalic series Those igneous rock series having an alkali-lime index of 55 to 61.

Calcarea Calcispongiae. A group of sponges (Porifera) in which the spicules are composed of calcium carbonate.

calcarenite A name suggested by A. W. Grabau for a "limestone or dolomite composed of coral or shell sand or of sand derived from the erosion of older limestones." The name is derived from the Latin for lime and sand. Size of particles ranges from 1/16 to 2 mm.

calcareous Containing calcium carbonate.

calcareous alga A seaweed that builds a more or less solid structure of calcium carbonate.

calcareous ooze *See* OOZE, CALCAREOUS

calcareous tufa *See* TUFA

calcarinate Cemented with calcium carbonate.

calcic *1.* Containing calcium, as, calcic plagioclase, calcic pyroxene. Also said of igneous rocks containing such minerals. *2.* Refers to igneous rocks having an alkali-lime index of more than 61.

calcic series Those igneous rock series having an alkali-lime index of 61 or greater.

calcify To make or become hard or stony by the deposit of calcium salts.

calcilutite *1.* A name suggested by A. W. Grabau for a limestone or dolomite made up of calcareous rock flour, the composition of which is typically nonsiliceous, though many calcilutites have an intermixture of clayey material. *2.* A calcium carbonate rock made up of grains or crystals with an average diameter less than 1/16 mm.

calcirudite A name suggested by A. W. Grabau for a "limestone or dolomite composed of broken or worn fragments of coral or shells or of limestone fragments, the interstices filled with calcite, sand, or mud, and with a calcareous cement." The word is derived from the Latin for lime and rubble.

calcisiltite Limestone composed of calcareous sediment of silt size.

Calcispongia Class of sponges with skeletons composed of separate or fused calcareous spicules. Dev.-Rec.

calcite A mineral, calcium carbonate, $CaCO_3$. Hexagonal-rhombohedral, dimorphous with aragonite. One of the commonest minerals; the principal constituent of limestone.

calcitic dolomite A carbonate rock in which the percentage of calcite is between 10 and 50, and the percentage of dolomite between 50 and 90.

calcitization Alteration of aragonite to calcite.

calcium carbonate A solid, $CaCO_3$, occurring in nature, as calcite, etc.

calcrete Caliche.

calc-schist A marble with a more or less distinct schistosity due to the parallelism of platy crystals of calcite. *See* MARBLE; SCHIST.

calc-silicate hornfels A fine-grained metamorphic rock rich in calc-silicate minerals.

calc-silicate marble A marble with conspicuous calcium and/or magnesium silicate minerals.

calc-sinter Stalactitic or stalagmitic carbonate of lime. This is so called from the German *Kalk* (lime) and *sintern* (to drop). It is deposited from thermal springs holding carbonate of lime in solution.

calcspar Calcite.

calc-tufa Where evaporation goes on steadily at the surface, while water is brought up by capillary action from below, calcium carbonate may form a cement to the soil, or to the crumbling rock near the surface, and a solid calc-tufa may arise by continued transference of matter in solution from lower levels.

caldera A large basin-shaped volcanic depression, more or less circular or cirquelike in form, the diameter of which is many times greater than that of the included volcanic vent or vents, no matter what the steepness of the walls or form of the floor. Three major types: explosion, collapse, erosion.

caldera complex The diverse rock assemblage underlying a caldera, comprising dikes, sills, stocks, and vents breccias; craterfills of lava; talus beds of tuff, cinder, and agglomerate; fault gouge and fault breccias; talus fans along fault escarpments; cinder cones; and other products laid down in a caldera.

Caledonian orogeny *1.* Post-Silurian diastrophism. *2.* In a broad sense, series of diastrophic movements beginning perhaps in Early

Ordovician and continuing through Silurian.

Caledonides Mountain system raised in late Silurian to early Devonian time, particularly that occurring in Scandinavia and Scotland.

calf A piece of floating ice which has broken away from a larger piece of sea ice or land ice; specifically, such a piece which rises to the surface after breaking away from the submerged portion of its parent body.

caliche *1.* In Chile and Peru, impure native nitrate of soda. *2.* In Uco, Peru, a thin layer of clayey soil capping auriferous veins. *3.* In Chile, whitish clay in the selvage of veins. In Mexico: *4.* Feldspar; a white clay; *5.* A compact transition limestone. In Colombia: *6.* A mineral vein recently discovered; *7.* In placer mining, a bank composed of clay, sand, and gravel. *8.* In Mexico and southwest U.S., gravel, sand, or desert debris cemented by porous calcium carbonate; also the calcium carbonate itself. *See* DURICRUST

californite A compact, massive vesuvianite. Used as an ornamental stone.

caliper log A graphic record which shows, to scale, the diameter of a drilled hole. The caliper is lowered in the hole and arms are sprung outward, gauging the varying width of the hole as the device is drawn upward, recording the diameter of the hole on quadrille paper.

Callovian Uppermost Middle or lowermost Upper Jurassic.

calomel Horn quicksilver; mercurial horn ore. Mercurous chloride, Hg_2Cl_2.

calving Breaking off and floating away as icebergs of large masses of a glacier that reaches the sea.

calyx *1.* Upper part of a corallite in which a coral polyp sits. *2.* Plated structure of a crinoid body; excludes stem and arms.

camber *1.* A convex terminal shoulder of the continental shelf. *2.* A structure that forms in areas of flat-lying rocks. A plastic clay beneath a more competent bed flows toward a valley so that the competent bed sags downward and appears to be draped over the sides of the valley.

Cambrian The oldest of the systems into which the Paleozoic stratified rocks are divided; also, the corresponding geologic period.

camouflage Substitution in a crystal lattice of a trace element for a common element of the same valence, e.g., Ga^{+3} for Al^{+3}. The trace element is said to be camouflaged by the common element.

Campanian Upper middle Senonian.

Campbell's law Where two streams that head opposite to each other are affected by an even lengthwise tilting movement, that one whose declivity is increased cuts down vigorously and grows in length headward at the expense of the other. If the tilting that affects them is part of a general warping, the divide migrates toward an axis of upwarping. The general law that axes of upwarping become divides is subject to exception where such axes are crossed by antecedent rivers.

camptonite A lamprophyre having pyroxene, sodic hornblende and olivine as dark constituents and labradorite as its light constituent. Sodic orthoclase may also be present.

Canada balsam A yellowish, transparent balsam yielded by a North American species of silver fir; used for mounting microscopic preparations and as an adhesive for glass in optical instruments. When exposed to the air, it becomes brittle and discolored, and its refractive index gradually increases. The average values for the index of refraction are 1.524 (uncooked), 1.538 (slightly undercooked), and 1.543 (overcooked). For normally cooked balsam the refractive index is between 1.534 and 1.540.

Canadian 1. Lower Ordovician. 2. System between Ozarkian and Ordovician. *Obs.*

canal 1. An artificial watercourse cut through a land area for navigation, irrigation. 2. A long narrow arm of the sea extending far inland. 3. On the Atlantic Coast, a sluggish coastal stream. 4. A long, fairly straight natural channel with steeply sloping sides, generally a mile or more in width. 5. A cave passage partly filled with water. 6. A hollow, gutterlike extension of the lower (anterior) end of a gastropod shell which carries within it the siphon. 7. The tubes which run lengthwise of the walls of the test as in the foraminiferal family the Camerinidae.

Canastotan Lower Upper Silurian.

cancrinite A hexagonal mineral; $(Na_2Ca)_4[(CO_3H_2O)_{0-3}(AlSiO_4)_6]$. Occurs in nepheline syenites.

candle ice Elongate prismatic crystals of ice arranged perpendicular to the surface. These separate during the thawing of sea, lake, or other layered ice.

cannel coal A variety of bituminous coal of uniform and compact fine-grained texture with a general absence of banded structure. It is dark gray to black in color, has a greasy luster, and is noticeably of conchoidal or shell-like fracture. It is noncaking, yields a high percentage of volatile matter, ignites easily, and burns with a luminous smoky flame.

cannel shale A black shale formed by the accumulation of sapropels accompanied by a considerable quantity of inorganic material, chiefly silt and clay.

canyon 1. A steep-walled chasm, gorge, or ravine; a channel cut by running water in the surface of the earth, the sides of which are composed of cliffs or series of cliffs rising from its bed. Sometimes spelled cañon. 2. *Oceanog:* A deep submarine depression of valley form with relatively steep sides.

capacitance Electrical capacity. That property of a pair of electrical conductors whereby an electrical charge is stored when a difference of potential is applied to the conductors.

capacity The ability of a water or wind current to transport detritus, as measured by the quantity it can carry past a given point in a unit of time.

cape 1. A point of land extending into the sea or a lake; a headland. 2. A relatively extensive land area jutting seaward from a continent or large island which prominently marks a change in, or interrupts notably, the coastal trend; a prominent feature.

capillarity The attractive force between two unlike molecules, illustrated by the rising of water in capillary tubes of hairlike diameters or the drawing-up of water in small interstices, as those between the grains of a rock.

capillary Resembling a hair; fine, minute; having a very small bore.

capillary conductivity (soil water) 1. Physical property related to the readiness with which unsaturated soil transmits water. 2. Ratio of water flow velocity to driving force in unsaturated soil.

capillary fringe A zone, in which the pressure is less than atmospheric, overlying the zone of saturation and containing capillary interstices some or all of which are filled with water that is continuous with the water in the zone of saturation but is held above that zone by capillarity acting against gravity.

capillary interstice 1. An opening small enough for water to be held in it by capillarity at a considerable height above the level at which it is held by hydrostatic pressure. 2. An opening or void small enough to produce appreciable capillary rise.

capillary migration Movement of liquid water produced by the molecular attraction of the rock material for the water.

capillary pressure 1. The difference in pressure existing between two phases, air-fluid, gas-fluid or between fluids, measured at points of the interface and occurring in the interconnected phases in a rock. 2. The difference in pressure across the interface between two immiscible fluid phases jointly occupying the pores of a rock. It is caused by the tension in the interfacial surface, and its value depends on the curvature of the interfacial surface.

capillary water (soils) The portion of soil water which is held by cohesion as a continuous film around the particles and in the capillary spaces. Most of this water is available to plants.

cap rock 1. A disklike plate over all or part of the top of most salt domes in the Gulf Coast states, and some in Germany, composed of anhydrite, gypsum, limestone, and occasionally sulfur. 2. A comparatively impervious stratum immediately overlying an oil- or gas-bearing rock. 3. See CALICHE

capture 1. Piracy, q.v. 2. Substitution in a crystal lattice of a trace element for a common element of lower valence, e.g., Pb^{++} for K^+

Caradocian Lower Upper Ordovician.

carapace 1. Paleontol: A bony or chitinous case covering the dorsal part of an animal. 2. Structure: Upper normal limb of a recumbent fold.

carat [Fr.] 1. A unit employed in weighing diamonds, and equal to 3 1/6 troy grains (205 mg.). A carat-grain is one-fourth of a carat. The international metric carat (C.M.) of 200 mg. has been made the standard in Great Britain, France, Germany, Holland, and the United States. 2. A term employed to distinguish the fineness of a gold alloy, and meaning one-twenty-fourth. Fine gold is 24-carat gold. Goldsmiths' standard is 22 carats fine, i.e., contains 22 parts gold, 1 copper, and 1 silver. Symbol: k.

carbide A compound of carbon with one other more positive element or radical.

carboid General name for a group of pyrobitumens that are insoluble in carbon disulfide.

carbonaceous 1. Coaly. 2. Pertaining to, or composed largely of, carbon. 3. The carbonaceous sediments include original organic tissues and subsequently produced derivatives of which the composition is chemically organic.

carbonaceous shale Dark colored shale containing carbonaceous matter.

carbonado *See* DIAMOND

carbonate A salt or ester of carbonic acid; a compound containing the radical CO_3^-

carbonation *1.* The process of introduction of carbon dioxide into a fluid. *2.* A process of chemical weathering by which minerals that contain lime, soda, potash, or other basic oxides are changed to carbonates by the action of carbonic acid in water or air.

carbonatite The term is not synonymous with limestone. Carbonatites are intrusive carbonate rocks which are associated with alkaline igneous intrusive activity in many localities. They have been regarded as: *1.* Surely intrusive and just as surely not igneous. *2.* Rocks formed as a phase of a magma that was rich both in soda and lime, as well as being in a highly carbonated condition. *3.* Mobilized or hydrothermally redistributed sedimentary limestones. *4.* Almost pure carbonate rocks, which appear to have been formed by reaction of basic magma with walls of limestone and dolomite.

carbon 14 A radioactive isotope of carbon with atomic weight 14, produced by collisions between neutrons and atmospheric nitrogen. Useful in determining the age of carbonaceous material younger than 30,000 years. Half-life 5700 years.

Carboniferous *1.* Period or system of the Paleozoic younger than Devonian and older than Permian; equivalent to combined Mississippian and Pennsylvanian.

2. Formerly considered by US-GS to be last Paleozoic division consisting of Mississippian, Pennsylvanian, and Permian. *Obs.*

carbonitization The replacement of minerals in a rock by carbonates frequently results from the activity of carbon dioxide in aqueous solution.

carbonization *1.* In the coalification process, carbonization characterizes the progressive changes undergone by the preserved organic matter and biochemical decomposition products between the death of the plant or animal and the stage of essentially complete reduction to residual carbon, *in situ*. *2.* The slow decay under water of organic material, plant or animal, resulting in a concentration of carbon as a film of carbon showing more or less distinctly the form and structure of the original tissue. *3.* The process of converting to carbon, by removing other ingredients, a substance containing carbon, as in the charring of wood or the natural formation of anthracite.

carbon ratio *1.* The ratio of the fixed carbon in any coal to the fixed carbon plus the volatile hydrocarbons; expressed in percentage. *2.* The ratio of the most common carbon isotope (C^{12}) to either of the less common isotopes (C^{13} or C^{14}), or the reciprocal of one of these ratios. If unspecified, the term generally refers to the ratio (C^{12}/C^{13}).

carbon ratio theory The theory that in any area the gravity of the oil varies inversely as the carbon ratio of the coal. As temperatures and pressures increase, the percentage of fixed carbon in coal increases, the grade of the coals rises, and the oils become lighter. Increase in metamorphic processes results in elimination of volatile constituents from coal but increases the lighter and more volatile hydrocarbons in oil.

Carbo-Permian Permo-Carboniferous.

carborundum A crystalline compound, SiC, consisting of silicon and carbon. It is produced in an electric furnace and used as an abrasive. Silicon carbide.

cardinal 1. Pertains to the hinge in brachiopods and pelecypods. 2. In corals, pertains to the generally longer of the two septa which develop from the single axial septum of the early growth stages (located opposite the counter septum).

cardinal points The four principal points of the compass: North, South, East, and West.

carina (nae) 1. A raised ridge or keel. 2. In some corals, one of the vertical strengthening plates which extend a short distance from the septa; these appear in cross section as septal spines. 3. In a barnacle, one of the two unpaired plates of the fixed tubular portion of the shell which adjoins the terga. 4. A keel or flange as found around the edge of some foraminiferal tests. 5. In conodonts, the central denticulated, nodose, or smooth ridge extending down the middle of the platform or blade.

Carlsbad twin *See* TWIN LAW

carnallite A mineral, KMgCl₃.6H₂O. Orthorhombic. An ore of potassium.

Carnian Lower Upper Triassic.

carnotite A mineral, K(UO₂)-(VO₄)₂.1-3H₂O. Monoclinic. Usually occurs as a fine-grained canary-yellow incrustation. An ore of U and V.

Carolina bay Ovate depression, generally marshy, of a type occurring abundantly on the coastal plain from New Jersey to Florida; origin attributed to fallen meteorites, upwelling springs, eddy currents, etc.

Carpoidea Class of unsymmetrical echinoderms with flattened body and tail-like stem. Camb.-Dev.

carpospore Spores produced by the carpogonium of red algae.

Carrara marble A general name given to all the marbles quarried near Carrara, Italy. The prevailing colors are white to bluish, or white with blue veins; a fine grade of statuary marble is here included.

carrier bed Deep, porous, and permeable beds, such as coarse sheet sands, through which oil can migrate for long distances. The concept of migration in this manner has not been widely accepted.

cartography 1. The science and art of expressing graphically, by means of maps and charts, the visible physical features of the earth's surface, both natural and man-made. 2. The science and art of map construction.

cascade 1. A waterfall, usually a small waterfall; especially one of a series of small falls, formed by water in its descent over rocks. 2. A gravity-collapse structure. A bed that buckles into a series of recumbent folds as it slides down the flanks of an anticline. 3. Series of small closely spaced waterfalls or very steep rapids.

Cascadian orogeny Post-Tertiary diastrophism.

cascalho Alluvial material including gravel and ferruginous sand in which Brazilian diamonds are found.

case-hardening The process by which the surface of a porous rock, especially sandstone or tuff is coated by a cement, or desert varnish, *q.v.*, formed by evaporation of mineral-bearing solutions.

casing-head gas Unprocessed natural gas produced from a reservoir containing oil. Such gas contains gasoline vapors and is so called because it is usually produced under low pressure through the casing head of an oil well.

Caspian Masses of salt water included in the dry land; so called from the Caspian Sea, the largest of them.

Cassadagan Middle Upper Devonian above Chemungian.

Casselian Chattian.

cassiterite Tin-stone. A mineral, SnO_2. Tetragonal. The most important ore of tin.

cast *1.* The mineral or other substance that fills a hole in a rock which has been formed by the solution of the original hard material of which the shell or skeleton consisted. *2.* A natural mold which has been filled naturally with some mineral substance. (This is usage as opposed to artificial cast.) *3.* Restricted to casts in which the filling is of an uncrystallized substance, as opposed to pseudomorphs in which the replacing matter is a crystallized mineral. *4.* A second type of plant fossil that is closely related to the compression is the cast. A cast results from the filling of a cavity formed by the decay of some or all of the tissues of a plant part.

castings Fecal pellets; coprolite, *q.v.*

cata- [<*Gr. kata*] Prefix used to denote that the rock belongs to the "deepest" zone of metamorphism, characterized by very high temperature and hydrostatic pressure and relatively low shearing stress. *See* APO-; KATA-; EPI-; META-; MESO-

cataclasis Rock deformation accomplished by fracture and rotation of mineral grains or aggregates; granulation.

cataclasite A rock that has been formed by shattering (cataclasis) which has been less extreme than in the case of a mylonite. *See* AUGEN GNEISS; AUGEN SCHIST; CRUSH BRECCIA; CRUSH CONGLOMERATE; FLASER GABBRO; MYLONITE; PROTOCLASTIC

cataclastic *1.* Pertaining to a texture found in metamorphic rocks in which brittle minerals have been broken and flattened in a direction at a right angle to the pressure stress. *2.* Refers to coarse fragmentation of rock in transit, e.g., glacial action.

cataclysm *1.* Any overwhelming flood of water; especially, the Noachian deluge. *2.* Any violent and extensive subversion of the ordinary phenomena of nature; an extensive stratigraphic catastrophe. *3.* Any violent flood or inundation that overspreads or sweeps over a country. *Syn:* DELUGE; DEBACLE. The term is now obsolete but is found in many early geological works.

catagenesis Evolutionary process resulting in decadence and decreased vigor. *Cf.* ANAGENESIS

catalysis Acceleration or deceleration of a reaction produced by a substance which may be recovered practically unchanged after the reaction.

catalyst The agent causing catalysis, *q.v.*

cataract A waterfall, usually of great volume; a cascade in which the vertical fall has been concentrated in one sheer drop or overflow.

catastrophe *1. Geol:* A sudden, violent change in the physical conditions of the earth's surface; a cataclysm. *2. Min:* A disaster in which many lives are lost or much property damaged, as by a mine fire, explosion, inrush of water, etc.

catastrophism The doctrine that explained the differences between fossils in successive stratigraphic horizons by assuming a general catastrophe followed by creation of the different organisms found in the next younger beds.

catazone The deepest zone of rock metamorphism where very high pressures and temperatures both prevail.

catchment area As applied to an aquifer the term includes its intake area and all areas that contribute surface water to the intake area.

catchment basin Drainage basin.

cathode Electronegative pole.

cathode rays Rays that, when a Crookes's tube is excited by an alternating high potential current of electricity, or by a series of spark discharges, pass in straight lines from the cathode to the opposite wall of the tube, producing a fluorescent area.

cation An ion that moves, or that would move, toward a cathode; hence nearly always synonymous with positive ion. In voltaic cells negative ions move toward the cathode, and are sometimes called cations.

cation exchange Base exchange.

catlinite Pipestone. Catlinite is an indurated clay used by the Dakota Indians for the making of pipes.

catoctin Monadnock; residual; inselberg. Erosional knobs and ridges found on the Piedmont plain.

catogene A general term for sedimentary rocks, since they were formed by deposition from above, as of suspended material. *Cf.* HYPOGENE

cat's-eye A greenish, chatoyant variety of chrysoberyl.

catstep Narrow, generally backward tilted terrace on steep hillside produced by slumping.

cauldron subsidence *1.* A structure resulting from the lowering along a steep ring fracture of a more or less cylindrical block, usually 1 to 10 miles in diameter, into a magma chamber. Usually associated with ring-dikes. In surface cauldron subsidence the ring fracture penetrates the surface of the earth, as a result of which volcanic rocks are lowered. In underground cauldron subsidence, the ring fracture does not penetrate the surface. *2.* The process of forming a cauldron subsidence.

caustic metamorphism Metamorphism in contact rock produced by the heat of lava flows and small dikes.

cave *1.* A natural cavity, recess, chamber, or series of chambers and galleries beneath the surface of the earth, within a mountain, a ledge of rocks, etc.; sometimes a similar cavity artificially excavated. *2.* Any hollow cavity. *3.* A cellar or underground room. *4.* The ash pit in a glass furnace. *5.* The partial or complete falling in of a mine; called also cave-in. *6.* Underground opening generally produced by solution of limestone large enough to be entered by a man.

cave breccia Angular fragments of limestone forming a fill.

cave coral A rough, knobby growth of calcite resembling coral in shape. *Syn:* CORAL FORMATION

cave earth *1.* Deposits of clay, silt, sand, or gravel flooring or filling a cave passage. In a more restricted sense cave earth includes only the finer fractions, i.e., clay, silt, and fine sand deposits. *Syn:* FILL. *2.* Cave earth is a term that has been applied to the deposits of sand, clay, etc., washed into caves. The term should have no standing in scientific terminology.

cave ice Ice formed in a cave by natural processes. Loosely but incorrectly applied to dripstone and flowstone.

cave marble Cryptocrystalline banded deposit of calcite or aragonite capable of taking a high polish. *Syn:* CAVE ONYX

cave pearl Smooth, rounded concretion of calcite or aragonite formed by concentric precipitation around a nucleus. Usually found in caves. *Syn:* PISOLITE

cavern A subterranean hollow; an underground cavity; a cave. Often used, as distinguished from cave, with the implication of largeness or indefinite extent.

cavernous Containing cavities or caverns, sometimes quite large. Most frequent in limestones and dolomites.

cave system The underground network of passages, chambers, etc., or of caves in a given area whether continuous or discontinuous from a single opening.

caving system A method of mining in which the ore, the support of a great block being removed, is allowed to cave or fall, and in falling is broken sufficiently to be handled; the overlying strata subside as the ore is withdrawn. There are several varieties of the system. *See* BLOCK CAVING

cavitation *1.* Corrasive and corrosive effect of collapsing of bubbles produced by decrease of pressure due to increase of velocity (Bernoulli effect) at point where pressure is increased due

to decrease of velocity. *2. Geophys:* The formation of a bubble by a charge detonated in water.

cavity Solutional concavity in limestone caves, the outline of which is determined by a joint or joints. Also applied to small hollows in cavernous lava.

c-axis *Struct. petrol:* The reference axis that is at right angles to the plane of movement. That is, in a pack of sliding cards, it is the direction perpendicular to the cards.

cay *1.* A flat mound of sand built up on a reef flat slightly above high tide level. In some such mounds there is a large admixture of coral fragments, and the surfaces of the mounds may show a number of concentric ridges formed by successive additions along the peripheries of the mounds. *2.* A key; a comparatively small and low coastal island of sand or coral. Pronounced "key." The spelling "kay" is common in the West Indies. *3.* A low insular bank of sand, coral, etc., awash or drying at low water.

Cayugan Upper Silurian.

Cazenovian Lower Middle Devonian.

Cc Abbreviation for calcite in normative rock calculations.

celadonite A green member of the mica group of high iron content, generally occurring in cavities in basaltic rocks.

celestite A mineral, $SrSO_4$. Orthorhombic. The principal ore of strontium.

cell The unit of structure of plants and animals; the essential feature of a cell is its living protoplasm, surrounded in plant cells by a wall.

cellular *1.* Characterized by small openings or cells which may or may not be connected. *Cf.* VE-SICULAR; POROUS. *2. Petrol:* Applied to igneous rocks, especially lavas, containing numerous gas cavities. *Syn:* VESICULAR; SCORI-ACEOUS

Celsius scale A thermometric scale, proposed in 1742 by Anders Celsius with 0° as the boiling point of water and 100° as the melting point of ice, just the reverse of the centigrade scale, *q.v.*

The present system whereby the freezing point is marked 0 and the boiling point 100 was introduced by Chistin, of Lyons, in 1743. This particular scale is now generally referred to as the centigrade scale or the Celsius scale, and sometimes the centesimal scale.

cement *1.* Chemically precipitated material occurring in the interstices between allogenic particles of clastic rocks. Silica, carbonates, iron oxides and hydroxides, gypsum, and barite are the most common. Clay minerals and other fine clastic particles should not be considered cement. *2.* The word is also used in gold-mining regions to describe various consolidated, fragmental aggregates, such as breccia, conglomerate, and the like, that are auriferous. *3.* A finely divided metal obtained by precipitation. *Cf.* PORT-LAND CEMENT

cementation The process of precipitation of a binding material around grains or minerals in rocks. Quartz, calcite, dolomite, siderite, and iron oxide are common cementing materials.

cement deposits The Cambrian conglomerates occupying supposed old beaches or channels. Gold bearing in the Black Hills.

cement rock An argillaceous limestone used in the manufacture of natural hydraulic cement. Contains lime, silica, and alumina in varying proportions, and usually more or less magnesia.

cement texture A result of the replacement of cementing matter of sandstones by ore minerals.

Cenomanian Lower Upper Cretaceous.

cenote *1.* Cenotes are a natural draining shallow well or hole in Yucatan into which inhabitants descend to draw spring water. *2.* A type of sink developed in limestone areas by the collapse of caverns which cuts off natural channels of circulation and allows water to fill the depression.

Cenozoic The latest of the four eras into which geologic time, as recorded by the stratified rocks of the earth's crust, is divided; it extends from the close of the Mesozoic era to and including the present. Also the whole group of stratified rocks deposited during the Cenozoic era. The Cenozoic era includes the periods called Tertiary and Quaternary in the nomenclature of the U. S. Geological Survey; some European authorities divide it, on a different basis, into the Paleogene and Neogene periods, and still others extend the Tertiary period to include the whole.

center counter *Struct. petrol:* A circular hole in a piece of cardboard or plastic, used to count the number or percentage of points on a point diagram. The area of the hole is ordinarily 1% of the area of the larger projection and is usually 1 cm. in radius.

center line In U.S. public land surveys, the line connecting opposite quarter-section or sixteenth-section corners.

center of gravity That point in a body or system of bodies through which the resultant attraction of gravity acts when the body or system of bodies is in any position; that point from which the body can be suspended or poised in equilibrium in any position.

center of instrument The point on the vertical axis of rotation at the same elevation as the axis of collimation when that axis is in a horizontal position. A point at, or near, the intersection of the horizontal and vertical axes of a transit.

center of symmetry Point in an object any straight line through which encounters exactly similar points on opposite sides.

centigrade scale A modification of the thermometric scale introduced by Anders Celsius. It has its zero at the melting point of ice, while 100° represents the boiling point of pure water at a pressure of 760 mm. of mercury. A centigrade degree is 9/5 of a Fahrenheit degree. The centigrade scale and the absolute scale are alike to the extent that on both the interval between the freezing and boiling points of water is divided into a hundred degrees.

centipoise Unit for measuring viscosity, which is the tendency of a fluid to resist change of form. The centipoise is 1/100 poise. *See* POISE; VISCOSITY, ABSOLUTE

central tendency The tendency of individuals in a variable population to cluster morphologically around some more or less mean type.

centrifugal force The upward component of the kinetic reaction mv^2/ρ, where m is the mass, v the velocity, and ρ is the radius of curvature of the path of a moving particle, from Newton's second law of motion. This force is equal to a balancing component, F sin θ, called the centripetal force, or acceleration, where the vector F is the resultant of applied forces and θ is the angular motion in polar coordinates.

centrifugal replacement Replacement of a mineral which begins in the central part of the host mineral and works outward.

centripetal force The component F sin θ of an applied force which balances the centrifugal force acting on a moving particle changing direction. The vector F is the resultant of applied forces and θ is the angular motion in polar coordinates.

centripetal replacement Replacement of a mineral from the periphery inward.

centrosphere Barysphere. The central core of the earth, composed of heavy material and making up most of its mass.

cephalon Dorsal head shield of some arthropods consisting of several fused segments.

cephalopod One of the Cephalopoda. A marine invertebrate characterized by a head surrounded by tentacles and, in most fossil forms, by the presence of a straight or spirally coiled, calcareous shell divided into numerous interior chambers.

Cephalopoda Most highly developed class of mollusks that swam by ejecting a jet of water from the mantle cavity through a muscular funnel. Most of those preserved as fossils had straight to symmetrically coiled shells divided into chambers by transverse septa. Camb.-Rec.

ceramic Of or pertaining to pottery—including porcelain and terra cotta—or its manufacture, fictile art, or ceramics in general. Now often taken to include all products made by the use of heat such as pottery, chinaware, glass, cement, etc.

cerargyrite Horn silver. A mineral AgCl. Isometric. A secondary mineral; an ore of silver.

ceratite A type of ammonoid with sutures in which the lobes are subdivided into subordinate crenulations although the saddles remain smoothly rounded, and undivided.

cerussite A mineral, $PbCO_3$, a member of the aragonite group. Orthorhombic. An ore of lead.

cf [*Lat.* conferre] To compare. Used in paleontology to indicate that a specimen or specimens are closely comparable to but not the same as a named species.

chain *1.* The legal unit of length for the survey of public lands of the United States. The chain is the equivalent of 66 feet. The name is derived from Edmund Gunter's chain, which was a series of links connected by rings. Advantage in measuring in chains is that 10 sq. chains = 1 acre. *2.* Any series of related, interconnected, or similar natural features, e.g., chain of mountains, islands, lakes.

chain coral A colonial coral found commonly in the Silurian; the name refers to the chainlike appearance of the upper surface of the colony.

chaining The operation of measuring a distance on the earth by means of a tape, commonly called a chain.

chain structure *See* INOSILICATES

chalcanthite Blue vitriol. A mineral, $CuSO_4.5H_2O$. Triclinic.

chalcedony Cryptocrystalline quartz and much chert, commonly microscopically fibrous. The material of agate.

chalcocite A mineral, Cu_2S. Orthorhombic. An important ore of copper, common in the zone of secondary enrichment.

chalcophile elements Elements which show a strong affinity for sulfur, and which are readily soluble in molten iron monosulfide; elements commonly found in sulfide ores.

chalcopyrite Copper pyrites. A mineral, $CuFeS_2$. Tetragonal. An important ore of copper.

chalk A very soft, white to light gray, unindurated limestone composed of the tests of floating microorganisms and some bottom-dwelling forms (ammonoids and pelecypods) in a matrix of finely crystalline calcite; some chalk may be almost devoid of organic remains.

chalybite Siderite.

chamber *1.* An enlargement of a cave passage forming a cavity of relatively large size. *Syn:* HALL. *2.* In Foraminifera, the unit of which all foraminiferal tests are composed, consisting of a cavity and the wall surrounding it. *3.* The internal divisions of a cephalopod shell formed by septa which partition off the inner part of the cephalopod shell.

chamosite A mineral, a member of the chlorite group, composition approximately (Fe″,Mg,Al,Fe‴)$_6$(AlSi$_3$)O$_{10}$(OH)$_8$. Monoclinic. An important constituent of many oölitic Fe ores.

Champlainian *1.* Middle Ordovician. *2.* Ordovician. *Obs.*

chance packing A random combination of systematically packed grain colonies surrounded by, or alternating with, colonies packed haphazardly. The average porosity of chance-packed aggregates of uniform spheres is slightly less than 40%.

Chandler wobble Movement of the earth's axis that completes a cycle in about 420 days.

channel 1. The deepest portion of a stream, bay, or strait through which the main volume or current of water flows. 2. The part of a body of water deep enough to be used for navigation through an area otherwise too shallow for navigation. 3. A large strait, as the English Channel. 4. *Metal:* A sow or runner. 5. A cut along the line where rock or stone is to be split. 6. *Paleontol:* A groove, such as the groove that winds down the columella near its base in some shells and terminates in the siphonal notch or in the canal.

channel capacity The maximum flow which a given channel is capable of transmitting without overtopping its banks. *See* BANKFULL STAGE

channeled upland Grooved upland.

channel-fill deposit Deposit which has accumulated in a stream channel where the transporting capacity of the stream has been insufficient to remove the sand and detritus as rapidly as it has been delivered.

channel-lag deposit Relatively coarse materials that have been sorted out and left as a residual accumulation in the normal processes of a stream.

channel-mouth bar Bar built where a stream enters a body of standing water, resulting from decrease in velocity.

channel recording A system, chain, or cascade of interconnected devices through which

geophysical data may flow from source to recorder, e.g., geophone, amplifier (with filters and gain control), galvanometer, and optical system.

channel sample A sample taken at a given spot but covering a relatively long distance and narrow width. It yields an average value and masks details. A composite collection, which is usually taken across the face of a formation or vein to give an average sample.

channel sands Sandstone deposited in a stream bed or other channel eroded into the underlying bed. Frequently contain oil, gold, or other valuable minerals.

channel storage The volume of water in definite stream channels above a given measuring point or "outlet" at a given time during the progress of runoff.

channel wave Any elastic wave which is propagated in a sound channel due to a low-velocity layer in the solid earth, the ocean, or the atmosphere.

channel width *Geomorph:* Width of a channel or stream near bankfull stage. *Symbol:* w.

c h a o s An exceedingly coarse breccia in which many blocks are 200 feet long, some are 1/4 mile long, and a few more than 1/2 mile long. Found in the Death Valley area of California and in adjacent areas, it has been interpreted by some as a gigantic fault breccia.

chaos structure Imbricated series of relatively minor lenticular thrust blocks occurring beneath a major thrust block.

character In seismic work, a recognizable appearance of an event or reflection on records which serves to identify it or permit its correlation—often indefinable and without basis.

characteristic radiation A spectrum of definite wave lengths of electromagnetic radiation characteristic of the atomic number of the emitting element.

charge In seismic work, the explosive combination employed for a shot defined by the quantity and type of explosive used.

Charmouthian Middle Lower Jurassic.

charnockite 1. A quartzo-feldspathic gneiss or granulite with hypersthene. Regarded by some petrologists as igneous. 2. A granitic rock with hypersthene as its chief mafic constituent. Originally applied to the granitic member of a series of hypersthene-bearing rocks ranging in composition from granite through norite to hypersthene pyroxenite. Some petrographers regard charnockites as the product of deep-seated metamorphism. 3. Granulites characterized by the mineral assemblage quartz-orthoclase-hypersthene with or without garnet and plagioclase feldspar.

chart datum The plane or level to which soundings on a chart are referred, usually taken to correspond to a low water stage of the tide. Cf. DATUM PLANE

chasm 1. A deep breach in the earth's surface; an abyss; a gorge; a deep canyon. 2. A deep recess extending below the floor of a cave.

chat 1. An oil-field term applied to a chert conglomerate at the base of the Pennsylvanian in parts of Kansas. Also applied to the upper and cherty part of the underlying Mississippian limestone. 2. The finely crushed gangue remaining after the extraction of lead and zinc minerals.

chatoyant Having a luster resembling the changing luster of the eye of a cat. Chatoyancy is generally a property of translucent materials containing parallel fibrous structures capable of scattering light.

chattermark A scar made by vibratory chipping of a bedrock surface by drift carried in the base of a glacier.

Chattian Upper Oligocene

Chautauquan Upper Upper Devonian, below Bradfordian.

Chazyan Lower Ordovician.

chelation Decomposition or disintegration of rocks or minerals resulting from the action of organisms or organic substances.

chemical activity See ACTIVITY, CHEMICAL

chemical equilibrium A state of balance between two opposing chemical reactions. The amount of any substance being built up is exactly counterbalanced by the amount being used up in the other reaction, so that concentrations of all participating substances remain constant.

chemical limestone A rock composed predominantly of calcite, formed by direct chemical precipitation.

chemical potential 1. The chemical potential of a component i in a system is equal to the change of the Gibbs free energy of the system with the change in the number of moles m_i, the temperature, pressure, and number of moles of all other components being kept constant. The chemical potential is an intensive quantity, and the chemical potential of a component is defined at each point of the system. See GIBBS FREE ENERGY; INTENSIVE VARIABLE. 2. Partial molal free energy. If to a given system in a given state, an infinitesimal amount of a chemical species (element or compound) is added in such a way that the thermal and mechanical energies are not affected, the increase in energy of the system divided by the amount of the chemical species added is the chemical potential of that species.

chemical precipitate A sediment formed of material precipitated from solution or colloidal suspension, as distinguished from material transported and deposited as detrital particles, which is clastic.

chemosphere Atmospheric zone about 25 to 100 km. above the earth's surface containing a concentration of ozone.

Chemungian Middle Upper Devonian below Cassadagan.

chenier Beach ridge built upon swamp deposits.

chernozem; tchornozem; tschernosem [*Russ.* black mold] Very black soil rich in humus and carbonates that forms under cool to temperate, semiarid conditions; first distinguished in Russia where it covers most of the Aralo-Caspian plain and much of European Russia. It has a close resemblance to the regur or cotton soil of India.

chert *1.* Insoluble residue. Cryptocrystalline varieties of silica regardless of color, composed mainly of petrographically microscopic chalcedony and/or quartz particles whose outlines range from easily resolvable to nonresolvable with binocular microscope at magnifications ordinarily used. Particles rarely exceed 0.5 mm. in diameter. *2. Mineral:* A compact, siliceous rock formed of chalcedonic or opaline silica, one or both, and of organic or precipitated origin. Chert occurs distributed through

limestone, affording cherty limestones. Flint is a variety of chert.

chertification Essentially silicification, especially by fine-grained quartz or chalcedony, used mainly in the descriptions of the Mississippi Valley lead-zinc deposits.

chessylite Azurite.

Chesterian Upper Mississippian.

chevron fold Very sharp, V-shaped fold in layered rocks, generally small.

chiastolite A variety of andalusite, in which carbonaceous impurities are arranged in a regular manner along the longer axis of the crystal, in some varieties like the X (Greek "chi"), whence the name.

Chideruan Uppermost Permian.

Chile saltpeter Sodium nitrate.

chilled contact That part of an igneous rock that is finer grained nearer the contact than the rest of the igneous rock. It is believed to have cooled more rapidly than the main body of igneous rock and hence to be finer grained.

chimney *1.* An ore shoot. *Cf.* CHUTE. *2.* A natural vent or opening in the earth as a volcano. *3.* A vertical shaft in the roof of a cave passage, smaller than an aven.

chimney rock *1.* An erosional feature formed where waves wear away materials on all sides, particularly along joint planes leaving angular steep-sided remnants. *Cf.* CHIMNEY

china clay Clay derived from decomposition of feldspar and suitable for the manufacture of chinaware or porcelain. *See* KAOLIN

chip A flat fragment with maximum dimension between 4 and 64 mm.

chip sample A series of chips

of ore or rock taken either in a continuous line across an exposure or at uniformly distributed intervals.

chi-square test Statistical test that measures the probability of randomness in a distribution.

chitin A nitrogenous substance similar to fingernails.

Chitinozoa An extinct order of rhizopod protozoans; black, sporelike bodies with pseudochitinous tests, ranging from Ordovician to Devonian.

chiton Popularly called "coat-of-mail" shells. Invertebrate marine molluscan animals which have a flexible dorsal shield that consists of eight overlapping calcareous valves or plates.

chloanthite A mineral, $(Ni,Co)As_{2-3}$. Isometric. An ore of nickel.

chloride A compound of chlorine with one other more positive element or radical.

chlorides A common term for ores containing chloride of silver.

chlorinity Originally defined as the total amount of chlorine, bromine, and iodine in grams contained in one kilogram of sea water, assuming that the bromine and iodine have been replaced by chlorine. Now defined as identical with the mass in grams of "atomic weight silver" just necessary to precipitate the halogens in 0.3285233 kg. of sea water.

chlorite group A term used for a group of platyhydrous silicates of aluminum, ferrous iron, and magnesium which are closely related to the micas. Ferric iron and chromium may replace aluminum, and manganese, ferrous iron. Monoclinic, generally of a greenish color. Common in low-grade metamorphic rocks.

chloritization The replacement by, conversion into, or introduction of chlorite.

chloritoid A dark-green, brittle mica found in metamorphic rocks. $(Fe'',Mg)_2Al_4Si_2O_{10}(OH)_4$.

chlorophaeite A mineral closely related to chlorite in composition and found in the groundmass of tholeitic basalts where it occupies spaces between feldspar laths, forms pseudomorphs after olivine, or occurs in veinlets and amygdules. The fresh substance is pale green, but in weathered rocks it may be dark green, brown, or red.

Chondrichthyes Class of vertebrates consisting of fish with skeletons of cartilage rather than bone; sharks. Dev.-Rec.

chondrite Stony meteorite containing chondrules embedded in a fine-grained matrix of pyroxene, olivine, and nickel-iron with or without glass.

chondrodite A mineral, $Mg_5(SiO_4)_2(OH,F)_2$. Monoclinic. Commonly occurs in contact-metamorphosed dolomites.

chondrule A small rounded body of various materials, though chiefly olivine or enstatite, found embedded in a usually fragmental base in certain of the stony meteorites.

chonolith An intrusive body of igneous rock, so irregular in form, and in its relation to the invaded formations so obscure, that it cannot be properly designated as a dike, sill, or laccolith.

Chordata Phylum of animals with a notochord which in most is replaced by a bony spinal column. Vertebrata. May or may not be considered to include the Protochordata which do not develop a spinal column.

C-horizon A layer of unconsolidated material, relatively little affected by the influence of organisms and presumed to be similar in chemical, physical, and mineralogical composition to the material from which at least a portion of the overlying solum has developed. Any slight alteration of the upper part of the C, such as reduction of calcium carbonate content in glacial till, unaccompanied by other changes, is designated as C_1.

chromate A salt or ester of chromic acid; a compound containing the radical CrO_4^{--}.

chromatography Method of qualitative chemical analysis in which a solution is tested by applying it to treated porous paper and identifications made on the basis of the nature and location of resulting colored spots.

chromite A mineral of the spinel group, formula (Mg,Fe'')-$(Cr,Al,Fe''')_2O_4$. Isometric. The principal ore of chromium.

chron A term originally introduced designating an indefinite division of geologic time. More recently proposed as the time unit equivalent to the stratigraphic unit, "subseries," and geologic name, "Mohawkian."

chronofauna Geographically restricted natural assemblage of interacting animal populations that maintained its basic structure over a geologically significant period of time.

chronolithologic unit Time-rock unit.

chronometer A portable timekeeper or clock of high precision.

chronostratigraphic unit Geologic time unit; in order of decreasing magnitude: era, period, stage, epoch, age.

chronotaxis Similarity in age. *Cf.* HOMOTAXIS

chrysoberyl Alexandrite, *q.v.* A mineral, $BeAl_2O_4$. Orthorhombic. Used as a gem.

chrysocolla A mineral, $CuSiO_3$.-$2H_2O$. Usually in green to blue-green masses.

chrysolite Olivine.

chrysoprase An apple-green chalcedony, used as a gem.

chrysotile asbestos A highly fibrous variety of serpentine.

chrystocrene A mass of ice formed in the interstices of a talus by the freezing of the waters of a subjacent stream.

chunk mineral In Wisconsin, applied to masses of galena as broken out of the mine.

churn drill *See* CABLE TOOLS

chute *1.* Chutes are the narrow passages of water between an island and the mainland. *2.* Of water, a fall; a quick descent, as in a river, or a steep channel, or narrow sloping passage by which water falls to a lower level; a rapid, a shoot. *3.* A channel or shaft underground, or an inclined trough above ground, through which ore falls or is "shot" by gravity from a higher to a lower level. *4.* In Pennsylvania, a crosscut connecting a gangway with a heading. *5.* An inclined watercourse, natural or artificial, especially one through which boats or timber are carried, as in a dam. *6.* A narrow channel with a free current, especially on the lower Mississippi River. *7.* A body of ore, usually of elongated form, extending downward within a vein.

chute cutoff Chute, *q.v.*

cienaga *1.* An area where the water table is at or near the surface of the ground. Standing water occurs in depressions in the area, and it is covered with grass or sometimes with heavy vegetation. The term is usually applied to areas ranging in size from several hundred square feet to several hundred or more acres. Sometimes springs or small streams originate in the cienaga and flow from it for short distances. 2. An elevated or hillside marsh containing springs. Local in Southwest.

cilium Tiny hairlike structure. Bands of cilia vibrate rhythmically and produce water currents or serve to move tiny organisms through the water.

Cincinnatian Upper Ordovician.

cinder Scoriaceous lava from a volcano; volcanic scoria.

cinder coal 1. In England, coal altered by heat from an intrusion of lava. 2. In Australia, a very inferior natural coke, little better than ash.

cinder cone A conical elevation formed by the accumulation of volcanic ash or clinkerlike material around a vent. Possesses steeper slopes and may attain larger size than an ash cone. Also called ash cone.

cinders, volcanic Primarily uncemented, essential, glassy, and vesicular volcanic ejecta ranging chiefly from 4 to 3 mm. in diameter.

cinnabar A mineral, HgS. Hexagonal rhombohedral. Color vermilion. The principal ore of mercury.

C.I.P.W. classification Norm system, q.v. From the initial letters of the names of the men who originated it: Cross, Iddings, Pirsson, and Washington.

circular sections Although most sections through ellipsoids are ellipses, two sections that contain the intermediate axis and are symmetrical, disposed relative to the long and short axes, are circles. The circular sections are often referred to in discussing rock deformation in terms of the strain ellipsoid.

circulation In rotary drilling, the process of pumping mud-laden or other fluid down drill pipe, through the drilling bit, and upward to the surface through the annulus between drill-hole walls and drill pipe.

circumferential wave Seismic wave that travels parallel to the earth's surface.

Circum-Pacific province See PACIFIC SERIES

cirque 1. A hollow, shaped like a Roman armchair. It is bowl-like, open in front, and its back and sides are formed by arêtes which rise like arms. In the bowl of the cirque there is commonly a small round lake or tarn. 2. A deep, steep-walled recess in a mountain, caused by glacial erosion. Syn: CWM (Wales); CORRIE (Scotland); BOTN (Sweden); KAR (Germany)

cirque glacier A small glacier occupying a cirque or resting on the headwall of a cirque.

cirque lake Small body of water occupying a cirque depression, dammed by a rock lip, small moraine, or both. See TARN

cirriform Resembling cirrus clouds, wispy.

Cirripeda Class of crustaceans which become permanently attached and are covered by a group of overlapping calcareous plates. Barnacles. Ord.-Rec.

citrine See QUARTZ

cladogenesis 1. Phyletic splitting or branching; speciation. 2. Progressive evolutionary specialization.

Claibornian Middle Eocene.

claim 1. The portion of mining ground held under the Federal and local laws by one claimant or association, by virtue of one location and record. Lode claims, maximum size 600 by 1500 feet. Placer claims 660 by 1320 feet. A claim is sometimes called a "location." *See* MINING CLAIMS. 2. In South Africa, the portion of land upon a goldfield to which a miner is legally entitled. A Transvaal claim has an area equal to 64,025 English square feet, and is about 155 feet along the strike of the reef, and 413 feet across the line of reef.

clam A pelecypod, generally one that is not attached like an oyster.

clan *Petrog:* A clan of rocks is one bound by resemblances in composition.

Clapeyron's equation As usually used, this is an expression developed by R. J. E. Clausius (1850) relating the pressure and temperature of a phase transition in a closed system (such as melting) when the two modifications of the same substance coexist in equilibrium. It includes the heat of the transformation and the volume change of the transformation. It is sometimes also referred to as the Clausius-Clapeyron equation or the Clapeyron-Clausius equation.

clarain That ingredient of banded coal which appears megascopically as thin or very thick bands, intrinsically stratified parallel to the bedding plane; most often has a silky luster and scattered or diffuse reflection markedly less intense than the specular reflection of vitrain under the same illumination. It has no conchoidal fracture, but splits in sheets or irregular directions. Less friable than vitrain.

Accepted by Heerlen Congress of 1935 as applicable to coal consisting mainly of vitrinite admixed with exinite. Adopted as "clarite," spelled "clarit" in German but retaining "ain" ending in English and French usage.

Clarendonian Lower Pliocene or upper Miocene.

clarke The average percentage of an element in the earth's crust.

clarke of concentration Measure of the amount of an element present in a particular deposit or mineral.

class A biologic unit; a subdivision of a phylum.

classification *Biol.* and *Paleontol:* The formal arrangement of organisms in the groups of a hierarchy of taxonomic categories.

clast An individual constituent of detrital sediment or sedimentary rock produced by the physical disintegration of a larger mass.

clastation The act or method or means of disrupting rocks to form clastic sediments.

clastic Consisting of fragments of rocks or of organic structures that have been moved individually from their places of origin. *Cf.* DETRITAL, FRAGMENTAL

clastic dike A tabular body of clastic material transecting the bedding of a sedimentary formation, representing extraneous material that has invaded the containing formation along a crack either from below or from above. Sandstone dike, *q.v.*

clasticity index Measure of the maximum apparent grain size of a sediment.

clastic ratio The statistical relationship of the percentage of clastic rocks in a given geologic section compared with the percentage of nonclastic rocks in the same section.

clay 1. The term clay as used today carries with it three implications: a natural material with plastic properties, an essential composition of particles of very fine size grades, and an essential composition of crystalline fragments of minerals that are essentially hydrous aluminum silicates or occasionally hydrous magnesium silicates. The term implies nothing regarding origin but is based on properties, texture, and composition, which are, of course, interrelated—e.g., the plastic properties are the result of the constituent minerals and their small grain size. 2. A natural substance of soft rock which, when finely ground and mixed with water, forms a pasty, moldable mass that preserves its shape when air dried; the particles soften and coalesce upon being highly heated and form a stony mass upon cooling. Clays differ greatly mineralogically and chemically and consequently in their physical properties. Most of them contain many impurities, but ordinarily their base is hydrous aluminum silicate. 3. Soil consisting of inorganic material, the grains of which have diameters smaller than .005 millimeters. 4. Fine-grained soil that has a high plasticity index in relation to the liquid limit and consists mainly of particles less than 0.074 mm. (passing No. 200 sieve) in diameter. Cf. SILT

clay gall A dry, curled "clay-shaving" resulting from the drying and cracking of mud which is later embedded and flattened in a sand stratum.

clay gouge A thin seam of clay separating ore, or ore and rock.

clay ironstone 1. A clayey rock heavily charged with iron oxide, usually limonite; commonly in concretionary form. 2. Clayey carbonate of iron. A heavy compact or fine-grained clayey-looking stone, occurring in nodules

and uneven beds among carboniferous and other rocks. It contains only 20 to 30% of iron, and yet much of the iron produced by Great Britain is made from it.

clay mineral The clay minerals are finely crystalline, hydrous silicates with a crystal structure of the two-layer type (e.g., kaolinite) or three-layer type (e.g., montmorillonite) in which silicon and aluminum ions have tetrahedral coordination with respect to oxygen, while aluminum, ferrous and ferric iron, magnesium, chromium, lithium, manganese and other ions have octahedral coordination with respect to oxygen or hydroxyl. Exchangeable cations may be on the surfaces of the silicate layers, in an amount determined by the excess negative charge within the composite layer. These cations usually are calcium, and sodium, but may also be potassium, magnesium, hydrogen, aluminum, etc. The most common clay minerals belong to the kaolinite, montmorillonite, attapulgite, and illite or hydromica groups. Mixed-layer clay minerals are either randomly or regularly interstratified intergrowths of two or more clay minerals.

clay pan A stratum of stiff, compact, relatively impervious clay which is not cemented and if immersed in water may be worked into a soft plastic mass. It differs from hardpan, q.v.

clay plug Sediment with much organic muck deposited in a cutoff river meander.

clay shale Shale composed wholly or chiefly of argillaceous material, which again becomes clay on weathering.

clayslate 1. Slate derived from

shale. 2. Very hard consolidated shale.

claystone 1. Arthur Holmes states that claystone is an obsolete term for an altered feldspathic igneous rock in which the groundmass or even the entire rock has been reduced to clay minerals. A. H. Fay defines the term as representing a concretionary mass of clay found in alluvial deposits in the form of flat rounded disks of various shapes and he also states that it is a soft, earthy feldspathic rock occurring in veins and having the appearance of indurated clay.

In spite of the several meanings, the term is a good one and should be retained as applicable to indurated clay in the same sense as sandstone is applicable to indurated or cemented sand. The application of the term to concretionary bodies should be abandoned and these things given the correct name. The application to a partially weathered feldspathic igneous rock should also be given up. 2. Rocks in which much clay is present or which are largely composed of clay sometimes bound together by iron carbonate.

clay vein A body of clay, usually roughly tabular in form like an ore vein, which fills a crevice in a coal seam. It is believed to originate where pressure has been sufficient to force clay from the roof or floor into small fissures and in many cases to alter and enlarge them.

cleavage 1. *Crystallog:* The splitting, or tendency to split, along planes determined by the crystal structure. Cleavage is always parallel to a possible crystal face, i.e., to a rational lattice plane of the crystal, and is generally designated by the name of the face or form, as basal, pinacoidal, cubic, etc. 2. *Petrol:* A tendency to cleave or split along definite, parallel, closely spaced planes, which may be highly inclined to the bedding planes. It is a secondary structure, commonly confined to bedded rocks, is developed by pressure, and ordinarily is accompanied by at least some recrystallization of the rocks.

cleavelandite A white lamellar variety of albite.

clerici solution A solution having a specific gravity of 4.25, used for separating heavy and light minerals. The double formatemalonate.

cliachite Amorphous generally brownish material that constitutes most so-called bauxite.

cliff A high, steep face of rock; a precipice. *Cf.* SEA CLIFF

Cliftonian Middle Middle Silurian.

climate The sum total of the meteorological elements that characterize the average and extreme condition of the atmosphere over a long period of time at any one place or region of the earth's surface. These elements are temperature (including radiation); moisture (including humidity, precipitation, and cloudiness); wind (including storms); pressure; evaporation; and also, but of less importance, the composition and the chemical, optical, and electrical phenomena of the atmosphere. The characteristics of each of these so-called climatic elements are set forth in a standard series of numerical values, based on careful, systematic, and long-continued meteorological records, corrected and compared by well-known methods.

climate, continental The type of

climate characteristic of land areas separated from the moderating influence of oceans by distance or mountain barriers. It is marked by relatively large daily and seasonal changes in temperature.

climate, oceanic The type of climate characteristic of land areas near oceans which contribute to the humidity and at the same time have a moderating influence on temperature and range of temperature variation. *Syn:* MARINE CLIMATE

climate-stratigraphic unit Non-uniform time unit (geochron) corresponding to an important climatic interval in an alternating or changing series.

climatic classification Classification of the climates of the different regions of the earth's surface, based on one or more of the climatic elements such as (1) temperature, (2) rainfall, (3) humidity, (4) wind, (5) temperature and rainfall, (6) nearness to land and sea, and many others. Classifications may also be based on the distribution of vegetation, on physiological effects, or may be on any basis suitable for the particular purpose or investigation.

Wladimir Köppen in 1918 classified the world's climate into twenty-four climatic types according to annual monthly means of temperature and precipitation and also according to the distribution of the latter. His system has become standard among certain climatologists and geographers.

C. W. Thornthwaite's classification, announced in 1931, instead of employing simple temperature and precipitation values as limiting boundaries, introduces two new concepts, temperature

efficiency and precipitation effectiveness.

climatic cycles Actual or supposed recurrences of such weather phenomena as wet and dry years, hot and cold years, at more or less regular intervals in response to long-range terrestrial and solar influences, such as volcanic dust and sunspots. The best known of these cycles, which have been discovered in great numbers, are the Brückner Cycle, *q.v.*, and the glacial-interglacial periods.

climatic factors Certain physical conditions—other than the climatic elements—which currently control climate, or may by their changes over long periods cause climatic changes.

The current factors which exercise immediate control are latitude, altitude, distribution of land and sea, and topography. In addition to the above, some climatologists include many other factors, such as ocean currents, the semipermanent high- and low-pressure areas, prevailing wind, etc.

Some of the long-range factors are: obliquity of the ecliptic, extent and composition of the atmosphere, land elevation, land and water distribution, ocean circulation, etc.

climatic optimum Period of relatively high temperature since retreat of last Pleistocene glacier, maximum about 4000 B.C.

climatic province An area of the earth which has a definite climatological character, according to a certain climatic classification, *q.v.*

climax The terminal community of a sere which is in dynamic equilibrium with the prevailing climate. The major world climaxes are equivalent to formations and biomes. The term is also used in connection with any subdivision, such as climax association.

climbing bog In regions characterized by a short summer and a considerable amount of rainfall this plant sphagnum frequently extends upward from the original level of the swamp, carrying the marsh conditions to higher land.

climbing dune An active dune capable of moving over obstructions.

cline Group of organisms varying from place to place or from time to time that show no breaks in morphology or ability to interbreed.

clinker *1.* Burnt-looking, vitrified or slaggy material thrown out by a volcano. *2.* Rough, jagged lava, generally basic, typically occurring at the surface of lava flows. *3.* Slaggy or vitreous masses of coal ash.

clinker, volcanic Rough, jagged, scoriaceous, spinose fragments of lava, usually of basic composition and typically found on the surface of lava flows.

clinkstone An extrusive rock which is sonorous when struck with a hammer. *See* PHONOLITE

clino A term proposed by J. L. Rich for the environment of the sloping part of the floor of the sea which extends from wave base down to the more or less level deeper parts.

clinoaxis The inclined lateral axis in the monoclinic system, designated a.

clinochlore A mineral, a member of the chlorite group, composition approximately $(Mg,Fe'')_4Al_2$ $(Al_2Si_2)O_{10}(OH)_8$. Monoclinic.

clinodome Monoclinic crystal form whose faces are parallel to the inclined a-axis and intersect the other two.

clinoenstatite *See* PYROXENE

clinoferrosilite *See* PYROXENE

clinoform The subaqueous land form, analogous to the well-known "continental slope" of the oceans or to the fore-set beds of a delta.

clinometer A simple apparatus for measuring vertical angles, particularly dips, by means of a pendulum or spirit level and circular scale.

clinopinacoid Monoclinic crystal form whose faces are parallel to plane of a- and c-axis.

clinothem A term proposed by J. L. Rich for a rock unit formed in a clino environment.

clinozoisite A mineral, a member of the epidote group, Ca_2Al_3 $(SiO_4)_3(OH)$. Monoclinic.

Clintonian Lower Middle Silurian.

Clinton ore A red, fossiliferous, iron ore of the Clinton formation of the United States, with lenticular grains. *Syn:* OYESTONE ORE; FOSSIL ORE; FLAXSEED ORE

clod A term applied by miners to loosely consolidated shale commonly found in close conjunction with a coal bed.

closed basin A district draining to some depression or lake within its area, from which water escapes only by evaporation.

closed fold A fold in which compressive stress was sufficient to bring the opposing sides in contact. *See* TIGHT FOLD

closed form *Crystallog:* A crystal form that encloses a finite volume of space.

closed system A system is closed if during the process under consideration no transfer of matter either into or out of the system takes place.

close-grained Having fine and

closely arranged fibers, crystals, or texture. Usually said of rocks.

close-jointed A term applied to joints that are very near together.

close packing A pattern of stacking of equal spheres, each in contact with 12 others, such that the porosity is exactly $(1-\pi/3\sqrt{2})$ —about 26%. There are many such patterns, but the two most generally known and usually referred to are the face-centered cubic lattice and the hexagonal close-packed structure with an axial ratio $c/a = \sqrt{8/3}$ —about 1.633.

closure 1. A closed anticlinal structure. 2. Vertical distance between top of an anticlinal structure and lowest level at which a continuous encircling contour can be drawn. 3. Vertical distance between bottom of a depression and the lowest point in its rim. 4. Junction of the lateral limbs of a fold at its hinge; a fold closes in the direction toward which its limbs converge.

cloudburst A rainstorm in which the rate of fall is 100 mm. (3.94 inches) per hour. This is more than ten times the rate used by the U. S. Weather Bureau in defining a heavy rainfall.

It is generally thought to occur when something interferes with the uprushing vertical currents which support the great mass of water (estimated at 300,000 tons) in a cumulonimbus cloud and so causes it to be suddenly and almost totally released. In mountainous regions, where a moderately heavy fall of rain may strike a small watershed, the entire fall often converges in a narrow gorge and causes great loss of life and property.

coal The general name for natu-rally occurring, commonly stratified, rocklike, black to brown derivatives of forest-type vegetation that accumulated in peat beds which, by burial and dynamochemical processes, was compressed and altered to material with increasing carbon content and that does not contain so much incombustible material as to be unfit for fuel. In American terminology the rank varieties are lignitic coal (brown coal, lignite), bituminous coal (sub-bituminous, bituminous, semi-bituminous), and anthracite coal (semi-anthracite, anthracite, meta-anthracite). The coal series begins with peat and ends with graphite.

coal ball 1. A concretionary body consisting mainly of calcium carbonate, magnesium carbonate, iron carbonate, or iron oxide, with varying amounts of clay, shale, or sand. They occur in the coal beds or in adjacent rocks. 2. Accumulation of fossil plant material that has been impregnated with calcium or magnesium carbonate, iron sulfides, and minor amounts of other mineral constituents.

coal basin Depressions in the older rock formations, in which coal-bearing strata have been deposited.

coalescent Joined together; running together.

coalescing pediment The result of the coalescence of individual pediments which results in a continuous pediment surrounding a mountain range.

coal field A region in which deposits of coal occur. Also called coal basin when of basinlike structure.

coalification Those processes involved in the genetic and metamorphic history of coal beds. The plant materials that form coal may be, in part, simply incorporated, or they may be present in vitrinized or fusinized form. Materials contributing to coal differ in their response to diagenetic and metamorphic agencies, and the three essential processes of coalification are called incorporation, vitrinization, and fusinization.

coal land Land of the public domain which contains coal beds.

coal measures 1. Strata containing coal beds, particularly those of the Carboniferous. 2. Capitalized and used as a proper name for a stratigraphic unit more or less equivalent to the Pennsylvanian or Upper Carboniferous.

coal types Those differences due to variations in the kind of plant material of which the coal is composed, whereby such varieties as common banded coal, cannel coal, algal coal, and splint coal are produced.

coarse sand Sand with a diameter between 1/2 and 1 mm.

coarse topography An incompletely dissected surface, or one in which the erosional features are on a large scale.

coast A strip of land of indefinite width (may be several miles) that extends from the seashore inland to the first major change in terrain features.

coastal comb Sea ice thrown on the coast by high tide, surf, or compression.

coastal current One of the offshore currents flowing generally parallel to the shore line with a relatively uniform velocity (as compared to the littoral currents). They are not related genetically to waves and resulting surf but may be composed of currents related to distribution of mass in ocean waters or local eddies,

wind-driven currents and/or tidal currents.

coastal plains Any plain which has its margin on the shore of a large body of water, particularly the sea, and generally represents a strip of recently emerged sea bottom.

Coast and Geodetic Survey A bureau of the United States Government charged with the topographic and hydrographic survey of the coast and the execution of belts of primary triangulation, and lines of precise leveling in the interior.

coast line 1. Technically, the line that forms the boundary between the coast and the shore. 2. Commonly, the line that forms the boundary between the land and the water.

coast of emergence Shore line of emergence. Made by an elevation of the sea bottom, which is added to the land, causing the sea to withdraw correspondingly; the new shore line is determined by the amount of upheaval and the slope of the sea bottom.

A coast of emergence has its character determined by an elevation of the land, even though that elevation should have been followed by a downward movement of much smaller amount.

coast of submergence Shore line of submergence. Produced by a depression of the land and invasion by the sea, which fills the lower valleys. A coast of submergence is one of the principal features which are due to depression of the land, though depression may have been followed by a slight re-elevation.

coast shelf Submerged coastal plain. A wide submerged shelf with the gentle slope and low relief of the coastal plain which extends between the shore and the continental slope.

coaxial cable Electrical cable consisting of an inner conductor covered by concentric cylindrical layers composed alternately of insulating and conducting material. The term is often used in a restricted sense which limits the definition to a cable employing insulating material which exhibits the property of low loss at high frequencies.

cobble Boulderet; cobblestone. A rock fragment between 64 and 256 mm. in diameter, thus larger than a pebble and smaller than a boulder, rounded or otherwise abraded in the course of aqueous, eolian or glacial transport.

cobblestone *1.* Cobble. *2.* A rounded stone suitable for paving a street or road.

Coblanzian Coblentzian.

Coblentzian Upper Lower Devonian.

coccolith Very tiny calcareous plates, generally oval and perforated, borne on the surfaces of some marine flagellate organisms.

coccolithophore Flagellate organism that produces coccoliths.

cockade structure *1.* Concentric rings of different sulfides (and gangue?) surrounding inclusions. *2.* A term applied to successive crusts of unlike minerals deposited upon breccia fragments in a vein.

codeclination The complement of the declination (astronomic), 90° minus the declination. Same as polar distance.

coefficient A number indicating the degree of a quality possessed by a substance.

coelacanth One of the ancient (Devonian to Cretaceous as fossils, and one recent species) group of true or bony fishes, belonging to the Crossopterygii, allies of the lungfishes and near the ancestry of the amphibians.

Coelenterata *1.* Cnidaria. *2.* Phylum of solitary or colonial animals whose bodies consist of ectodermal and endodermal layers but lack a mesoderm; two forms, polyps and medusae, occur and may characterize alternate generations.

coelome A body cavity separate from the enteron occurring in multicelled animals other than the sponges and coelenterates.

cognate Term applied to a block of solidified lava which had been broken by later eruptions.

cognate inclusion Cognate xenolith; autolith, *q.v.* A term applied to a xenocryst or xenolith occurring in an igneous rock to which it is genetically related.

coherent Descriptive of two or more similar parts or organs of the same series touching one another more or less adhesively but not fused.

cohesion *1.* The resistance of a material, rock, or sediment against shear along a surface which is under no pressure. *2.* The capacity of sticking or adhering together. In effect the cohesion of soil or rock is that part of its shear strength which does not depend upon interparticle friction.

coincidence error In the recording of random events, the error which results from the finite resolving time of counting circuits. The number of impulses recorded by the circuit will be less than the number of impulses received if two or more impulses follow in a time shorter than the resolving time: $N = m(1-n_{\tau})$, where N is the true number of impulses, n is the recorded number, and τ is the resolving time.

coke Bituminous coal from

which the volatile constituents have been driven off by heat, so that the fixed carbon and the ash are fused together. Commonly artificial, but natural coke is also known.

coking coal Coal which can be converted into useful coke that must be strong enough to withstand handling. There is no direct relation between the elementary composition of coal and coking quality but generally coals with 80 to 90% carbon on a dry, ash-free basis are most satisfactory.

col [*Fr.*] A saddle or gap across a ridge or between two peaks; also, in a valley in which streams flow both ways from a divide, that part of the valley at the divide, especially if the valley slopes rather steeply away from the divide. *See* PASS

colatitude The complement of the latitude, or 90° minus the latitude.

cold avalanche The cold avalanche involves the movement of dry snow; it takes place in winter, most often during the time of greatest cold, and almost always coincides with a drop in temperature.

cold front The boundary line between advancing cold air and a mass of warm air under which the cold air pushes like a wedge. The surface of separation is called the frontal surface and this meets the earth in the cold front. Its passage is normally accompanied by a rise of pressure, a fall of temperature, a veer of wind, a heavy shower, and sometimes a line squall, perhaps with thunder.

The normal direction of slope of the frontal surface is at about 1 in 50 back from the cold front, but the point of the wedge may

become rounded owing to friction holding back the advance of the cold air on the surface so that the direction of slope is reversed below about 2000 feet.

colemanite A mineral, $Ca_2B_6O_{11}.5H_2O$. Monoclinic.

Coleoidea Subclass of cephalopods; Dibranchiata.

collapse breccia Founder breccia, *q.v.*

collapse caldera A caldera resulting primarily from collapse occasioned by the withdrawal of magmatic support at depth or, more rarely, by the internal solution of a volcanic cone. *See* CALDERA

collapse sink Caverns may become so enlarged by solution and erosion that they may locally collapse, thus giving rise to another class of sinkholes which may be called collapse sinks.

collapse structures Gravity-collapse structures. Structures resulting from the downhill sliding of rocks under the influence of gravity to produce small klippe or folds.

collective diagram *Struct. petrol:* A point or contour diagram prepared by collecting onto one diagram the data from two or more other diagrams.

collenchyma A strengthening tissue, composed of cells with walls usually thickened at the angles of the walls.

collimate *1.* To bring into line, as, the axes of two lenses or of two telescopes. Also to make parallel, as, refracted or reflected rays. *2.* To determine or correct the direction of the line of sight of a telescope by use of a collimator, or by vertical reflection from the surface of a basin of mercury.

collimation axis The straight line

passing through the optical center of the object glass of a transit and the horizontal rotation axis perpendicular to the latter.

collimation error The angle between the line of collimation (line of sight) of a telescope and its collimation axis.

collimation line The line through the nodal point of the objective lens of a telescope and the center of the reticle (intersection of the crosshairs).

collimation plane The plane described by the collimation axis during the revolution of a transit.

collimator A fixed telescope with spider lines in its focus, used to adjust a second telescope by looking through it in a reverse direction with the latter, so that images of the spider lines are formed in the focus of the second telescope, as if they originated in a distant point.

colloform Rounded reniform masses of mineral which result from colloidal precipitation.

colloid A substance that, when apparently dissolved in water, diffuses not at all or very slowly through a membrane and usually has little effect on freezing point, boiling point, or osmotic pressure of the solution; a substance in a state of fine subdivision, with particles ranging from 10^{-5} to 10^{-7} cm. in diameter.

colloidal dispersion A sol, or colloidal solution; a suspension of particles of colloidal size (the dispersed phase) in a medium, usually liquid (the continuous phase or dispersion medium).

collophane $Ca_8P_2O_8$. *See* APATITE

collophanite Collophane. A dull, colorless or snow-white hydrous, calcium phosphate. $Ca_8P_2O_8 + H_2O$.

colluvial Consisting of alluvium in part and also containing an-

gular fragments of the original rocks. Contrasted with alluvial and diluvial. Also, talus and cliff debris; material of avalanches.

colluvium A general term applied to loose and incoherent deposits, usually at the foot of a slope or cliff and brought there chiefly by gravity. Talus and cliff debris are included in such deposits.

colonial coral *See* CORAL, COLONIAL

colony 1. A group of similar organisms living together in close association; more specifically, a group of associated unicellular organisms among which there are no marked structural differences and little or no division of labor. 2. A group of individuals of a given species of animal or plant which is organized together so that the independence of individual members is partly or wholly lost.

Coloradan Middle Upper Cretaceous.

color index *Petrol:* The sum of the dark or colored minerals in a rock expressed in percentages. It is especially applied in the classification of igneous rocks. According to this index, rocks may be divided into leucocratic (color index, 0–30), mesotype or mesocratic (color index, 30–60), and melanocratic (color index, 60–100). Shand recognizes a fourth subdivision, namely hypermelanic (color index, 90–100).

color ratio Color index, *q.v.*

columbite A mineral, the part with Nb$>$Ta of the orthorhombic columbite-tantalite series, $(Fe,Mn)(Nb,Ta)_2O_6$. The principal ore of niobium (columbium).

columella A dome-shaped structure in the sporangia of bread mold and related fungi; also, a central mass of sterile tissue in

sporophytes of mosses and liverworts.

columnar jointing That variety
of jointing that breaks the rock
into columns. Usually the joints
form a more or less clearly defined hexagonal pattern. Most
characteristic of basaltic rocks.
Generally considered to be
shrinkage cracks because of
cooling.

columnar section A graphic expression of the sequence and
stratigraphic relations of rock
units in a region. In a vertical
column, lithology is shown by
standard symbols and thicknesses of rock units are drawn
to scale.

columnar structure *1.* A mineralogical structure in which the
unit is made up of slender columns, as in some amphiboles.
2. Columnar jointing, *q.v.*

comagmatic A term applied to
igneous rocks (or to the region
in which they occur) having a
common set of chemical, mineralogical, and textural features,
and hence regarded as having
been derived from a common
parent magma. Essentially synonymous with consanguineous.

Comanchean Lower Cretaceous.

comb; combed vein (comb structure) The place, in a fissure
which has been filled by successive depositions of mineral on
the walls, where the two sets of
layers thus deposited approach
most nearly or meet, closing
the fissure and exhibiting either
a drusy central cavity, or an
interlocking of crystals.

comber *1.* A deep-water wave
whose crest is pushed forward
by a strong wind, much larger
than a whitecap. *2.* A long-
period spilling breaker.

combustible shale Tasmanite.

Comleyan Lower Cambrian.

commensal Said of an organism
which lives with another as a
tenant or as a coinhabitant, but
not as a parasite.

commensalism The growth together of different species of
organisms in a manner which
is helpful to one without hurt
to its host.

comminution The reduction of
a substance to a fine powder;
pulverization; trituration.

common lead Lead having four
isotopes (mass numbers 204,
206, 207, 208) in the proportions generally obtained by analyzing lead from rocks and
lead minerals which are associated with little or no radioactive
material; commonly considered
to be the lead present at the time
of the earth's formation, as distinguished from lead produced
later by radioactive decay.

community An organized group
of plants or animals, or both. The
term is employed when it is not
necessary or desirable to use a
more specific designation such as
association, associates, etc.

comorphism Occurrence in more
than one state of coordination in
a crystal, e.g., aluminum in four-
or six-fold coordination in silicates.

compactability Property of sedimentary material permitting decrease in volume or thickness
under load accomplished by
closer crowding of constituent
particles and accompanied by decrease in porosity and increase
in density.

compaction Decrease in volume
of sediments, as a result of compressive stress, usually resulting
from continued deposition above
them, but also from drying and
other causes.

compaction shale Shale that owes

its strength to compaction rather than to cementation.

compass *1.* An instrument for determining directions, usually by the pointing of a magnetic needle free to turn in a horizontal plane, as, the ordinary surveyor's compass though sometimes having a clinometer attached. Also, a dip compass, for tracing magnetic iron ore, having a needle hung to move in a vertical plane. *2.* An instrument for describing circles, transferring measurements, etc.

ompensation, isostatic A theory of equilibrium of the earth's crust assuming that columns of rock and water standing on bases of equal area have equal weights irrespective of the elevation and configuration of their upper surfaces.

ompensation point Point at which the color of a mineral in thin section between crossed Nicols is compensated (becomes dark gray) by the introduction of a quartz wedge.

ompetency; competence *Hydraul:* Refers to the maximum size of particles of given specific gravity, which, at a given velocity, the stream will move. Thus, a small, rapid stream can move a relatively large particle, and while its competence is great the amount of material transported is small. Conversely a large, slow-moving stream may carry in suspension a great quantity of small particles, its competence being small, but its capacity great.

ompetent *1. Hydraul:* See COMPETENCY. *2.* Applied to beds or groups of beds which, during folding, are able to lift not only their own weight but that of the overlying beds without appreciable internal flowage.

ompetent beds Those beds or strata which, because of massiveness or inherent strength, are able to lift not only their own weight but also that of overlying rock.

complementary Refers to (1) rock-types differentiated from a common magma; (2) associated dikes or other minor intrusions regarded as leucocratic and melanocratic differentiates of a common magma; (3) small differentiated igneous bodies whose compositions if mixed would approximate composition of presumed source magma.

complementary rocks A term suggested by W. C. Brögger for the basic rocks, which, usually in the form of dikes, accompany larger intrusions of more acidic types and complement them in a chemical sense. The diverse differentiation products of one common magma. *Cf.* LAMPROPHYRE

complete glacier A complete glacier consists of two parts, the reservoir, where there is accumulation, and the dissipator, where there is wastage; these regions are separated by the névé line, and there is continual flow from the first to the second.

complex *1. Mineral:* Containing many ingredients; compound or composite. *2.* An assemblage of rocks of any age or origin that has been folded together, intricately mixed, involved, or otherwise complicated. *3.* Stratigraphic equivalent of the geologic time-unit eon.

complex ion Any ion consisting of several atoms, other than the common radicals like SO_4^{--} or NO_3^-. Examples are $Cu(NH_3)_4^{++}$, HgS_2^{--}, $AgCl_2^-$, $Au(CN)_2^-$.

complex ripple mark An interference ripple pattern of any kind.

complex spit A large spit with minor or secondary spits developed on the ends or points of the large spit.

component One of the independent substances present in each phase of a heterogeneous equilibrium. The number of components in a system is the minimum number of chemical constituents which must be specified in order to describe the composition of each phase present.

componental movement Mechanical deformation that is composed of many movements of component parts in such a way that the continuity of the rock is not impaired.

components The smallest number of independently variable chemical individuals (gaseous, liquid, or solid elements or compounds) by means of which the composition of each phase present may be quantitatively expressed.

composite coast An initial coast resulting from upwarping and subsidence of coastal blocks along lines transverse to the coast. Upwarping produces coastal salients, whereas downwarping produces embayments.

composite cone A volcanic cone, usually of large dimension, built of alternating layers of lava and pyroclastic material. *Syn:* STRATIFIED CONE; STRATO-VOLCANO. *See* VOLCANIC CONE

composite dike A dike composed of two or more intrusions of different chemical and mineralogical compositions.

composite fault scarp A scarp whose height is due partly to differential erosion and partly to fault movement.

composite fold A fold with small folds on its limbs, regardless of dimensions.

composite gneiss A banded rock resulting from intimate penetration of magma, usually granitic, into country rocks. *See* INJECTION GNEISS; MIGMATITE

composite mobile belt Mobile belt including two or more parallel geosynclinal troughs.

composite sample A sample of a type such that more than a single set of characteristics inherent in the original material may be combined.

composite sill A sill composed of two or more intrusions of different chemical and mineralogical compositions.

composite stream A river may be composite when drainage areas of different structure are included in the basin of a single stream.

composite topography The combination of topographic features from an earlier incomplete cycle of denudation with those of the current cycle of denudation.

composite vein A large fracture zone, up to many tens of feet in width, consisting of several parallel ore-filled fissures and converging diagonals, whose walls and intervening country rock have undergone some replacement.

composition 1. An aggregate, mixture, mass, or body formed by combining two or more substances; a composite substance. 2. The chemical constitution of a rock or mineral. 3. The mineralogical constitution of a rock.

composition plane Composition face; composition surface. A plane by which the two individuals of a contact twin are united. *See* TWIN

composition point In any plot of phase equilibria, that point whose coordinates represent the chemical composition of a phase or mixture.

composition triangle In ternary

systems, used in several connotations: *1*. The triangle formed by connecting the composition points of any three phases that may be in equilibrium with each other. *2*. The triangle formed by connecting the composition points of any three primary phases whose liquidus surfaces meet at a point. *3*. The triangle formed by connecting the composition points of any three phases in equilibrium at the liquidus, e.g., two solid solutions and a liquid solution.

compound alluvial fan Bajada; piedmont alluvial plain, *q.v.* The fans made by neighboring streams often grow laterally until they merge. The union of several such fans makes a compound alluvial fan, or a piedmont alluvial plain.

compound coral *See* CORAL, COMPOUND

compound ripple mark Complex ripple mark consisting of one set of ripples modified by another differently oriented set.

compound sample A mixture of a number of spot samples to form an aggregate single sample. Spot samples usually are taken according to some plan and some fixed number. They may be close together or scattered. The result is an average sample or composite sample. Four spot samples will reduce the sampling error by about one-half, as compared with a single sample.

compound twins *See* TWIN

compound valley A valley in which part of its course belongs to one class or stage of development and in the other part to another class.

compound valley glacier One composed of two or more individual ice streams coming from different tributary valleys.

compound vein *1*. A vein or lode consisting of a number of parallel fissures united by cross fissures, usually diagonally. *2*. A vein composed of several minerals.

compound volcano A volcano that consists of a complex of two or more cones, or a volcano that has an associated volcanic dome, either in its crater or on its flanks. Examples are Vesuvius and Mount Pelée.

compressibility The change of specific volume and density under hydrostatic pressure; reciprocal of bulk modulus, *q.v.*

compression A system of forces or stresses that tends to decrease the volume or shorten a substance, or the change of volume produced by such a system of forces.

compression, axial In experimental work with cylinders, a compression applied parallel with the cylinder axis; in interpretation of deformed rocks to be used in an appropriate sense only.

compressional wave Longitudinal wave; dilatational wave; P-wave; pressure wave; irrotational wave. A traveling disturbance in an elastic medium characterized by volume changes (and hence density changes) and by particle motion in line with the direction of travel of the wave.

compressive strength The load per unit of area under which a block fails by shear or splitting.

compressive stress A stress that tends to push together the material on opposite sides of a real or imaginary plane.

concentrate *1*. To increase the strength by diminishing the bulk as of a liquid or an ore; to intensify or purify by getting rid of useless material. *2*. To separate metal or ore from the gangue or associated rock.

concentric faults Faults that are concentrically arranged in plan.

concentric fold See PARALLEL FOLD

concentric fractures A system of fractures more or less concentrically disposed about a center.

concentric weathering Spheroidal weathering, q.v.

conch 1. A large gastropod shell, often of genus Strombus. 2. Any of various marine shells including bivalves. Obs. 3. In the cephalopods, the entire shell, exclusive of the protoconch, that is developed after the embryonal shell.

conchiolin A nitrogenous substance constituting the organic basis of most molluscan shells.

conchoidal A term used in descriptive mineralogy to describe the shell-like form of surface produced by the fracture of a brittle substance.

concordant A term used to describe those intrusive igneous bodies in which the contacts are parallel to the bedding (or foliation) of the country rock.

concordant injected body Concordant injection. Syn: CONCORDANT PLUTON

concordant injection Concordant injected body.

concordant pluton An intrusive igneous body, the contacts of which are parallel to the bedding (or foliation) of the country rock.

concretion A nodular or irregular concentration of certain authigenic constituents of sedimentary rocks and tuffs; developed by the localized deposition of material from solution, generally about a central nucleus. Harder than enclosing rock.

concretionary Tending to grow together. Particles of like chemical composition, when free to move, come together and form nodules of various sizes and shapes which are called concretions. Clay and ironstone nodules, balls of iron pyrite, turtle stones, etc., are good examples. Some greenstones exhibit concretionary structure.

concyclothem Cyclic sequence of strata resulting from the coalescence of two or more cyclothems.

condensate Known sometimes as distillate. A heavier hydrocarbon occurring usually in gas reservoirs of great depth and high pressure. It is normally in the vapor phase but condenses as reservoir pressure is reduced by production of gas. Cf. RETROGRADE CONDENSATION

condensation Hydrol: The process by which water changes from the gaseous state into the liquid or solid state. It is the reverse of evaporation.

condensed system 1. A system in which the vapor pressure is negligibly small and hence can be ignored. 2. A system in which the pressure maintained on the system is greater than the vapor pressure of any portion.

conduction Transmission through or by means of a conductor. Distinguished, in the case of heat, from convection and radiation.

conductivity A property of an electrical conductor defined as the electrical current per unit area divided by the voltage drop per unit length.

conductometry Measurement of conductivity to determine some property or behavior of electrolytes, e.g., concentration, ionization, reaction rate.

conduit 1. A passage, generally small, that is filled with water under hydrostatic head. 2. The vertical, cylindrical passageway through which magma moves upward in a volcano.

cone 1. Steep-sided pile of sand, gravel, and perhaps boulders with fanlike outwash base deposited against the melting front of a glacier. 2. Volcanic cone. 3. *Bot:* Specialized branch bearing an aggregate of sporophylls.

cone-in-cone structure A concretionary structure occurring in marls, ironstones, coals, etc., characterized by the development of a succession of cones one within another.

Conemaughian Upper Middle Pennsylvanian.

cone of depression The depression, roughly conical in shape, produced in a water table or piezometric surface by pumping or artesian flow.

cone sheet Funnel-shaped zone of fissures or dikes generally surrounding an igneous intrusion. *Cf.* RING DIKE

Conewangoan Upper Upper Devonian.

configuration The relative position of all electrodes as they are placed in electrical prospecting. In the Wenner configuration, four electrodes are placed in a straight line, the outer two being power electrodes and the inner potential electrodes, with equal spacing between electrodes. The Lee configuration is the same as the Wenner, with the addition of a center electrode.

confined ground water Artesian water, *q.v.*

confining bed One which, because of its position and its impermeability or low permeability relative to that of the aquifer, gives the water in the aquifer artesian head.

confining pressure An equal, all-sided pressure. In the crust of the earth the confining pressure is lithostatic pressure resulting from the load of overlying rocks. In experimental work, the confining pressure is a hydrostatic pressure, generally produced by liquids.

confluence The point where two streams meet.

confluence plain Plain formed by the merging of the valley floors of two or more streams.

confluence step The floors of main glaciated valleys often have giant steps which are evidently due to differential glacial erosion. Where two glaciated valleys of about the same size come together there may be a step up to the mouth of each one. This is called a confluence step.

conformability; conformity The mutual relation of conformable beds.

conformable 1. Strata or groups of strata lying one above another in parallel order are said to be conformable. 2. When beds or strata lie upon one another in unbroken and parallel order, and this arrangement shows that no disturbance or denudation has taken place at the locality while their deposition was going on, they are said to be conformable. But if one set of beds rests upon the eroded or the upturned edges of another, showing a change of conditions or a break between the formations of the two sets of rocks, they are said to be unconformable.

conformal map projection A map projection on which the shape of any small area of the surface mapped is preserved unchanged.

Conformal map projections are sometimes termed orthomorphic map projections, "orthomorphic" meaning "right-shape"; this is misleading because, if the area mapped is large, its shape will not be preserved, but only the shape of each small section of it. The exact condition for a conformal map projection is that the scale at any point be the same in all directions: the scale may change from point to point, but at each point it will be independent of the azimuth. Among the more important conformal map projections are the Mercator, the stereographic, the transverse Mercator, and the Lambert conformal map projections; the latter two are used in the state coordinate systems.

conformity *1. Stratig:* The relations of adjacent beds not separated by a sedimentary discontinuity. *2.* In dikes, relations of flow structure parallel to walls.

congelifluction Progressive a n d literal earth flow occurring under conditions of perennially frozen ground.

congelifraction Frost splitting.

congeliturbation Frost action in soil including heaving, solifluction, sludging, etc.

congeneric Belonging to the same genus.

conglomerate Puddingstone. *1.* Rounded waterworn fragments of rock or pebbles, cemented together by another mineral substance. *2.* A cemented clastic rock containing rounded fragments corresponding in their grade sizes to gravel or pebbles. Monogenetic and polygenetic types are recognized, according to the uniformity or variability of the composition and source of the pebbles.

conglomerate, volcanic *See* VOL-CANIC CONGLOMERATE

congruent melting point The temperature at a specified pressure at which a solid phase changes to a liquid phase of the same composition as the solid phase.

congruous drag folds Drag folds that bear a distinctive relationship to the major folds: (1) the axis of the drag fold is approximately parallel to the axis of the major fold; (2) the axial plane of the drag fold is approximately parallel to the axial plane of the major fold; and (3) the relative movement shown by the drag folds indicates that the beds nearer the major synclinal axis were moving upward relative to the beds nearer the anticlinal axis. Contrasts with incongruous drag folds, *q.v.*

Coniacian Lower Senonian.

conic map projection A map projection produced by projecting the geographic meridians and parallels onto a cone which is tangent to, or intersects the surface of a sphere, and then developing the cone into a plane.

Coniferales Subclass or order of gymnosperms; plants, many of them large trees, with needle- or scalelike leaves and seeds borne in cones.

coniferous Having cones as a reproductive structure.

conjugated fractures or veins *1.* Two sets of veins or joints occur which have the same strike, but dip in opposite directions. *2.* Any two sets of perpendicular sets of joints.

conjugate joint system A system of joints consisting of two sets that are symmetrically disposed about some other structural feature or about an inferred stress axis.

conjugate liquids Any two liquids which are immiscible in each other but are in equilibrium. The line connecting their composition points is a conjugation line.

conjugation line A special case of the line connecting the composition points of two immiscible liquids which are in equilibrium with each other. Sometimes used incorrectly as synonymous with alkemade line or with join.

connate *1.* Born, produced or originated together; connascent. *2.* United or joined; in particular, said of like or similar structures joined as one body or organ.

connate water *1.* Water entrapped in the interstices of a sedimentary rock at the time the rock was deposited. *2.* Interstitial water, *q.v.* *3.* Water adsorbed on mineral grains of reservoir rock and not produced with oil or gas. *4.* Water that has got into a rock formation by being entrapped in the interstices of the rock material (either sedimentary or extrusive igneous) at the time the material was deposited. It may be derived from either ocean water or land water.

conodont Tiny tooth- or jawlike fossil composed of calcium phosphate of uncertain zoological affinity; may have been derived from an annelid worm or fish. Ord.-Trias.

Conodontophorida Group of small jawlike fossils of uncertain zoological affinities. Ord.-Trias.

Conrad discontinuity Seismic discontinuity where velocity increases from 6.1 to 6.4–6.7 km. per second; occurs at various depths and is supposed to mark contact of "granitic" and "basaltic" layers.

consanguineous association Natural group of sediments or rocks of related origin.

consanguinity *Petrol:* Denotes a genetic relationship between igneous rocks which are presum-

ably derived from a common parent magma. Such rocks are closely associated in space and time and ordinarily they show a likeness with respect to chemical, mineralogical, and textural features and geological occurrence. Rock series which show consanguineous characteristics are also called kindreds, series, suites, tribes, or clans. *See* COMAGMATIC

consecutive calderas Nested calderas.

consequent *1.* Pertaining to or characterizing the earth movements which result from the external transfer of material in the process of gradation. *Cf.* ANTECEDENT. *2.* Having a course or direction dependent on, or controlled by, the geologic structure or by the form and slope of the surface. Said chiefly of streams and drainage.

consequent fault scarp The face of an initial scarp is rapidly changed into a young consequent scarp by the loss of waste, which slips, creeps, and washes down to the scarp base, there accumulating in landslides, talus slopes, and alluvial fans, which bury the fault line.

consequent stream One which follows a course that is a direct consequence of the original slope of the surface on which it developed.

consertal A textural term applied to igneous rocks in which irregularly shaped crystals in juxtaposition are closely fitted together, or conserted. *Obs.*

consolidation *1. Geol:* Any or all of the processes whereby loose, soft, or liquid earth materials become firm and coherent. *2. Soil Mech:* The adjustment of a saturated soil in response to increased load. Involves the squeezing of water from the pores and decrease in void ratio.

consortium A group of individuals of different species, generally belonging to different phyla, which live together in close association.

conspecific Belonging to the same species.

constructional *Geol:* Owing its form, position, direction, or general character to building-up processes, such as accumulation by deposition or by volcanic extrusion.

contact *1.* The place or surface where two different kinds of rocks come together. Although used for sedimentary rocks, as the contact between a limestone and sandstone, it is yet more especially employed as between igneous intrusions and their walls. The word is of wide use in western mining regions on account of the frequent occurrence of ore bodies along contacts. *2.* In South Africa, a lode of great length and between two kinds of rocks, one of which is generally an igneous intrusive. *3.* The surface between two fluids in a reservoir, as gas-oil contact; water-oil contact. *4.* The bedding plane bounding a formation, often called "top" in petroleum geology. *5.* As a prefix, used to qualify an igneous rock name by implying that the texture is poikiloblastic.

contact deposit A mineral deposit found between two unlike rocks, usually applied to an ore body at the contact between a sedimentary rock and an igneous rock. A contact lode or vein.

contact metamorphism Metamorphism genetically related to the intrusion (or extrusion) of magmas and taking place in rocks at or near their contact with a body of igneous rock. *See* THERMAL METAMORPHISM

contact metasomatism A mass change in the composition of the rock other than the elimination of gases involved in simple metamorphism.

contact minerals Minerals formed by contact metamorphism.

contact twin *See* TWIN

contact vein A variety of fissure vein, between different kinds of rock occupying a typical fracture from faulting, or it may be a replacement vein formed by mineralized solutions percolating along the surface of the contact where the rock is usually more permeable and there replacing one or both of the walls by metasomatic process. Contact deposit.

contact zone *See* AUREOLE

contamination *Petrol:* Usually applied to magmas and denoting the addition of foreign rock material, as by assimilation of wall rock.

contemporaneous deformation Deformation, especially folding and faulting, that takes place while the rocks are being deposited. Used in contrast to folding and faulting that takes place long after the sedimentation.

contiguous Touching without fusion; used irrespective of whether the parts are like or unlike.

continent Large land mass rising more or less abruptly above the deep ocean floor; includes marginal areas that are shallowly submerged. At present continents constitute about one-third of the earth's surface.

continental apron The gentle incline at the base of the continental slope leading to the deep oceanic basins.

continental basin A region in

the interior of a continent comprising one or several closed basins.

continental borderland *1.* Zone bordering a continent, below sea level, which is highly irregular and includes depths well in excess of those typical of a continental shelf. *2.* Terraced area or submerged plateau adjacent to a continental shelf but at greater depth. *3.* Borderland.

continental deposits Sedimentary deposits laid down within a general land area and deposited in lakes or streams or by the wind, as contrasted with marine deposits, laid down in the sea.

continental drift The concept that the continents can drift on the surface of the earth because of the weakness of the suboceanic crust, much as ice can drift through water.

continental glacier An ice sheet covering a large part of a continent, e.g., the Antarctic ice sheet.

continental island *1.* An island which is near and geologically related to a continent, as are the British Isles. *2.* Continental islands are merely detached fragments of the continent near which they stand and from which they are separated, in almost all cases, by shoal water. The limit between deep and shallow water is drawn at the 100-fathom line, and nearly all continental islands rest upon submarine platforms which are under water less than 100 fathoms deep and run into the submerged continental shelf.

continental margin Zone separating the emergent continents from the deep sea bottom; generally consists of continental shelf, continental slope and continental rise.

continental nuclei Craton, *q.v.*

continental ocean That part of the deep ocean overlying a layer of sial as contrasted with "true" ocean floored by sima.

continental plate Thick crust underlying a continent.

continental platform Platform-like mass of a continent that stands above the surrounding oceanic basins. The continental shelf is part of the continental platform.

continental rise Submarine surface beyond base of continental slope, generally with gradient less than 1 to 1000, occurring at depths from about 4500 to 17,000 feet and leading down to abyssal plains.

continental rock A rock unit laid down on land as opposed to one laid down in marine water. It may be lacustrine, palustrine, eolian, fluvial, or volcanic.

continental shelf Gently sloping, shallowly submerged marginal zone of the continents extending from the shore to an abrupt increase in bottom inclination; greatest average depth less than 600 feet, slope generally less than 1 to 1000, local relief less than 60 feet, width ranging from very narrow to more than 200 miles.

continental slope Continuously sloping portion of the continental margin with gradient of more than 1 to 40, beginning at the outer edge of the continental shelf and bounded on the outside by a rather abrupt decrease in slope where the continental rise begins at depths ranging from about 4500 to 10,000 feet; formerly considered to extend to abyssal plains.

continuous deformation Deformation accomplished by flowage rather than by rupture.

continuous permafrost zone Regional zone predominantly underlain by permafrost, with no permafrost at widely scattered sites.

continuous profiling A seismic method of shooting in which seismometer stations are placed uniformly along the length of a line and shot from holes also spaced along the line so that each hole records seismic ray paths identical geometrically with those from immediately adjacent holes, so that events may be carried continuously by equal time comparisons.

continuous reaction series That branch of Bowen's reaction series, q.v., comprising the plagioclase group of minerals, in which reaction of early formed crystals with later liquids takes place without abrupt phase changes, i.e., continuously.

contorted Bent or twisted together. Used where strata are very much folded or crumpled on a considerable scale. If on a small scale they are said to be corrugated.

contour 1. Outline of an object. 2. Line connecting points of equal value on a map or diagram, most commonly points of equal elevation on a map.

contour diagram A type of petrofabric diagram prepared by contouring of a point diagram; its purpose is to obtain easier visualization of the results of the petrofabric study.

contour interval The difference in value between two adjacent contour lines. Generally, it refers to the difference in elevation between two adjacent contour lines.

contour line 1. A line on a map representing a contour. Present usage makes contour and contour line synonymous. 2. A line connecting points of equal value

(generally elevation) above or below some reference value such as a datum plane. Contour lines are commonly used to depict topographic or structural shapes. The quantified properties of sediments or other phenomena can be recorded by contour lines.

contour map A map showing by contour lines, q.v., topographic or structural or thickness or facies differences in the area mapped.

contour, structural An imaginary line of equal elevation on a selected stratigraphic horizon, called the structural datum.

contour, topographic An imaginary line on the ground, all points of which are at the same elevation above (or below) a specified datum surface.

contraction Shrinking. Rocks in passing from a vitreous to a crystalline texture shrink considerably, which may account for the subsidence of certain areas. The whole globe of the earth has shrunk by cooling.

contraction hypothesis Theory that compression causing folding and thrusting is a result of a shrinking of the earth. The crust must decrease in size to accommodate itself to the shrinking interior of the earth.

controlled mosaic A mosaic fitted to a control plot by rephotographing the component vertical photographs to compensate for scale variations resulting from tilt and for variations in flight altitude.

control station A point on the ground whose position (horizontal, vertical) is used as a base for a dependent survey. *Geol:* Any surveyed point (side shot, rod shot, etc.) used for vertical or horizontal control for geologic features.

Conularida Group of four-sided more or less chitinous fossils of elongated pyramidal form with flaplike folds closing the large terminal opening; of uncertain zoologic affinities. Camb.-Trias.

conulariid *1.* A group of extinct marine animals that had chitinous, pyramidal, or flattened conical shells with marked quadrilateral symmetry. Formerly considered to be extinct mollusks, and prior to 1937 usually grouped with the gastropods. *2.* Conulariids may be a type of worm. *3.* Considered since 1937 a subordinate division of the coelenterates.

convection A process of mass movement of portions of any fluid medium (liquid or gas) in a gravitational field as a consequence of different temperatures in the medium and hence different densities. The process thus moves both the medium and the heat, and the term convection is used to signify either or both.

convection cell Space occupied by a single convection current.

convection currents Transfer of material due to differences in density, generally brought about by heating. Characteristic of the atmosphere and bodies of water. Drag along the base of the crust by convection currents generated within the interior of the earth has been suggested to be a cause of orogeny.

convective flow A type of postulated slow movement deep within the earth depending upon differences in temperature and resulting differences in density within large-scale "cells" with material rising in the cells of higher temperature and falling in the cells of lower temperature. Such convective movement has

been postulated to explain large-scale tectonic features, such as island arcs.

convergence *1.* A term applied to the diminishing interval between geologic horizons, in some cases due to unconformable relationship and in others to variable rates of deposition, the latter applying especially to basin deposits. *See* ISOPACH. *2.* The line of demarcation between turbid river water and clear lake water, which denotes a downstream movement of water on the lake bottom and an upstream movement of water at the surface. *3.* In refraction phenomena, the decreasing of the distance between orthogonals in the direction of wave travel. This denotes an area of increasing wave height and energy concentration. *4.* In wind-setup phenomena, the increase in setup observed over that which would occur in an equivalent rectangular basin of uniform depth, caused by changes in planform or depth; also the decrease in basin width or depth causing such increase in setup. *5. Paleontol:* Resemblance which is not due to direct relationship or genetic affinity. *See* CONVERGENT EVOLUTION

convergence map *See* ISOCHORE MAP

convergent evolution Adaptive convergence. *1.* The process whereby phylogenetic stocks that are not closely related produce similar-appearing forms. Such forms are not as closely related genetically as they seem to be. *2.* The evolution toward a common adaptation when it occurs in forms which have independently developed similar adaptations and are far removed from each other in the scale of relationship.

coordinate bond Covalent bond.

coordinates Linear or angular quantities (usually two-dimensional) which designate the position which a point occupies in a given reference plane or system.

coordination number The number of atoms, ions, groups, or molecules that can be directly attached to a central atom. *Geol:* Refers most commonly to the number of oxygen atoms that can surround a central cation.

copepod One of the Copepoda. A minute crustacean without any distinct sort of carapace; none known as fossils.

Copepoda A subclass of the Crustacea in the phylum Arthropoda.

copper A mineral, native copper. Isometric. A minor but formerly important ore of the metal.

copperas Melanterite, *q.v.*

copper glance Chalcocite. *Obs.*

coprecipitation The carrying down by a precipitate of substances normally soluble under the conditions of precipitation.

coprolite Fecal pellets; castings. The undigestible residue that has been eaten and passed through the alimentary canal of some animal. Petrified excrement.

copropel Dark-brown or gray coprogenic ooze, containing chitinous exoskeletons of benthonic arthropods in addition to reworked organic matter. *Cf.* GYTTJA

coquina Soft porous limestone composed of broken shells, corals, and other organic debris.

coral A bottom-dwelling, sessile, marine coelenterate; some are solitary individuals, but the majority grow in colonies; they secrete external skeletons of calcium carbonate. Calcareous skeleton of a coral or group of corals.

coral, colonial A coral in which the individuals are attached together as a unit and do not exist as separate animals.

coral, compound Skeleton of a colonial coral.

coral formation A formation, generally developed on cave walls, nodular in form with a rough or granular surface resembling coral. *Syn:* CAVE CORAL

coralgal Refers to carbonate sediment derived from corals and algae.

Corallian Lusitanian.

coralline *1.* Pertaining to, composed of, or having the structure of corals, as, coralline limestone. *2.* Pertaining to the lime-secreting types of red algae. *Syn:* NULLIPORES. *3.* Applied to Bryozoa before their true nature was discovered. *Syn:* ZOOPHYTES; BRYOZOA; POLYZOA

corallite *1.* Skeleton of an individual coral animal. *2.* Skeleton of an individual coral in a colony.

corallum The calcareous exoskeleton of an individual or compound coral.

coral mud and sand Deposits formed around coral islands and coasts bordered by coral reefs, containing abundant fragments of corals. Near the reefs the grade sizes are relatively coarse and the deposit is described as coral sand whereas further out the grades become gradually finer until the material is a coral mud.

coral reef *1.* A reef formed by the action of reef-building coral polyps, which separate carbonate of lime from the waters of the sea to form their internal skeleton. *3.* Coral reef signifies the usual complex of skeletal and shell growths, of which the framework is true coral *in situ*, though a large part may be composed of nullipore or other algal material, molluscan or other debris of littoral species, shells of the plankton, and chemically precipitated carbonates of calcium and magnesium. The corals themselves may make up less than one-half of a reef, yet its existence and increase depends on the successful growth of these animals in spite of a constant battle with the surf. 4. A coral reef is a ridge or mound of limestone, the upper surface of which lies, or lay at the time of its formation, near the level of the sea, and is predominantly composed of calcium carbonate secreted by organisms, of which the most important are corals. 5. The modern definition includes the idea that the deposit must be firm enough to resist erosion by waves.

coral rock Reef limestone differs from the majority of fragmental and organic deposits in the fact that it is largely built up in a solid coherent form from the first, and therefore constitutes a rock mass in the strict sense, without any process of cementation.

Coral sea The tropical region of the western Pacific Ocean where luxuriant reef corals grow.

coral zone The depth of the sea at which corals abound.

Cordaitales Subclass or order of gymnosperms; large plants and trees with much central pith, long straplike leaves, and seeds borne in bunches among the leaves. Dev.-Trias.

cordate Heart-shaped; with a sinus and rounded lobes at the base, and ovate in general outline; often restricted to the basal portion rather than to the outline of the entire organ.

cordierite A mineral, $Mg_2Al_4Si_5O_{18}$. Orthorhombic. A common mineral of metamorphic rocks.

cordillera [Sp.] A group of mountain ranges including valleys, plains, rivers, lakes, etc.; its component ranges may have various trends by the cordillera will have one general direction. A mountain range or system in some cases the main mountain axis of a continent; specifically the great mountain region of western North America between the Central Lowland and the Pacific Ocean.

core 1. Central part of the earth beginning at a depth of about 2900 km., probably consisting of iron-nickel alloy; divisible into an outer core that may be liquid and an inner core about 1300 km. in radius that may be solid. 2. Sample of rock obtained in core drilling. 3. The central part of something, especially the filling of a hollow object.

core barrel A hollow cylinder attached to a specially designed bit and used to obtain and preserve a continuous section or core of the rocks penetrated in drilling.

core drilling Drilling with a hollow bit and core barrel in order to obtain a rock core.

core test A hole drilled with a core drill, usually for the purpose of securing geological information, and sometimes with the purpose of investigating geological structure.

Coriolis force The apparent force caused by the earth's rotation which serves to deflect a moving body on the surface of the earth to the right in the northern hemisphere, but to the left in the southern hemisphere.

The French mathematician Gaspard Gustave de Coriolis discussed the effects of rotation coordinate systems in 1844, but the first complete explanation of this apparent force was by William Ferrel in 1859, hence Ferrel's law, *q.v.*

corner A point on a land boundary at which two or more boundary lines meet. Not the same as monument, which refers to the physical evidence of the corner's location on the ground.

cornice An overhanging ledge of snow formed downwind from some obstruction, commonly a snow-covered ridge or a large drift.

corona A zone of minerals, usually radial around another mineral, or at the contact between two minerals. The term has been applied to reaction rims, corrosion rims, and originally crystallized minerals. *Syn:* KELYPHITE

corrading stream When the debris supplied to a stream is less than its capacity for carrying load the stream abrades its bed and is said to be a corrading, downcutting, or degrading stream.

corrasion Mechanical erosion performed by moving agents such as wear by glacial ice, wind, running water, etc.

correlation *1.* The determination of the equivalence in geologic age and stratigraphic position of two formations or other stratigraphic units in separated areas; or, more broadly, the determination of the contemporaneity of events in the geologic histories of two areas. Correlations may be based on paleontologic or physical evidence. *2.* In seismic interpretation, the picking of corresponding phases, obtained at two or more separated seismometer spreads, of those seismic events which appear to originate at the same geologic formation boundary.

corrosion Most commonly used for chemical erosion, whether accomplished by motionless or moving agents.

corrosion rim or border A modification of the outlines of phenocrysts due to the corrosive action of a magma upon minerals which under different conditions were previously stable. A special case of the reaction rim, *q.v. Cf.* CORONA

corry Cirque in Scotland.

cortlandtite A peridotite composed of large hornblende crystals with poikilitically included olivine crystals.

corundolite A rock consisting of corundum and iron oxides. *See* EMERY ROCK

corundum A mineral, Al_2O_3. Hexagonal. Sapphire and ruby are gem varieties.

cosmic dust Fine particles of cosmic or meteoric origin, or the remains of small meteorites which have been decomposed on passing through the earth's atmosphere.

cosmochemistry Study of the distribution of elements in the universe.

cosmogony Speculation regarding origin of the universe including origin of the earth.

cosmology Science of the universe.

cosmopolitan species An organism distributed widely throughout the world and occurring in various geographic provinces.

cospecific Conspecific.

coteau [*Fr.*] A small hill or hillock. In the northern part of the United States it was generally applied by early French travelers to a range of hills or to an escarpment forming the edge of a plateau. Such an escarpment is usually dissected, so that at a distance it resembles a range of hills. The Coteau des Prairies and Coteau du Missouri are escarpments of this character.

cotectic surface A curved surface in a quaternary system, representing the intersection of two primary phase volumes, one or both of which are solid solution series. It is the bivariant equivalent of the univariant cotectic line in ternary systems.

cotype *1.* Used sometimes as equivalent to syntype, *q.v.* *2.* Used sometimes as equivalent to paratype, *q.v.* Not recommended for usage in either sense. *3.* Cotypes are plants that were in a different collection from that which contained the type specimens but were also used in writing the description. The term is not a proper synonym for isotypes.

coulee [*Fr.*] *1.* A short, blocky, steep-sided lava flow, generally of glassy rhyolite or obsidian, issuing from the flank of a volcanic dome or from the summit crater of a volcano. *2.* The term coulee is generally applied throughout the northern tier of states to any steep-sided gulch or water channel and at times even to a stream valley of considerable length. A solidified stream or sheet of lava.

coulee lake A lake formed when a lava flow acts as a dam across some stream valley.

couloir A deep gorge; a gully on a mountainside, especially in the Swiss Alps.

Coulomb attraction Attraction between ions of opposite electric charges.

country rock A general term applied to the rock surrounding and penetrated by mineral veins; in a wider sense applied to the rocks invaded by and surrounding an igneous intrusion.

couple Consists of two equal forces acting in opposite directions in the same plane but not along the same line.

coupled wave C-wave. A surface seismic wave of complex motion in an elastic medium, described only by mathematical explanation.

Couvinian Lower Middle Devonian.

covalent bond *See* BOND, COVALENT

cove *1.* A small bay or open harbor; it is also popularly applied to small areas of plain or valley that extend into mountains or plateaus. In New Mexico and Arizona the re-entrants in the borders of mesas and plateaus are also called rincons [*Sp.* an inner corner]. *2.* Precipitously walled, cirquelike opening at the head of a small steep valley produced by erosion of shale below a thick massive sandstone.

covellite A mineral, CuS, of indigo-blue color. Hexagonal. A common secondary mineral; an ore of copper.

cracking Process of breaking down large complex molecules, particularly hydrocarbons, to produce smaller simpler ones.

crag *1.* A fossiliferous sandy marl of marine origin; generally used, capitalized, as part of the names of several formations of Pliocene age in eastern England. *2.* A steep, rugged rock; a rough broken cliff or projecting point of rock. *3.* A detached fragment of rock.

crag-and-tail *1.* A streamline hill or ridge, resulting from glaciation and consisting of a knob of resistant bedrock (the "crag"), with an elongate body (the "tail") of more erodible bedrock, or till, or both, on its lee side.

crater *1.* Bowl-shaped topographic depression with steep slopes, generally of considerable size. *2.* Volcanic orifice.

crater cone A cone built up around a volcanic vent by lava which reached the surface through that vent, either in a molten state or in fragmental condition.

crater lake A lake, generally of fresh water, formed by the accumulation of rain and ground water in a volcanic crater or caldera with relatively impermeable floor and walls. An example is Crater Lake, Oregon.

craterlet A small crater.

crater, volcanic A steep-walled depression at the top of a volcanic cone or on the flanks of a volcano, directly above a pipe or vent that feeds the volcano, and out of which volcanic materials are ejected. In its simplest form, usually a flat-bottomed or pointed, inverted cone more or less circular in plan. The diameter of the floor is seldom over 1000 feet; the depth may be as much as several hundred feet. Primarily the result of explosions or collapse at the top of a volcanic conduit. *See* EXPLOSION CRATER

cratogenic *1.* Formed in or in relation to a craton. *2.* Of or pertaining to a craton.

craton A relatively immobile part of the earth, generally of large size.

cratonic shelf Zone lying between more positive and negative areas of a craton.

creek *Topog:* *1.* A stream of less volume than a river. *2.* A small tidal channel through a coastal marsh. *3.* In Maryland and Virginia, a wide arm of a river or bay. *4.* A long shallow stream

of intermittent flow or an arroyo in southwestern United States.

creekology An ironical term for unscientific methods of choosing drilling sites or prospective oil or gas acreage and particularly applied to selection based on the general appearance of outcrops, topography, drainage, etc.

creep *1.* An imperceptibly slow, more or less continuous downward and outward movement of slope-forming soil or rock. The movement is essentially viscous, under shear stresses sufficient to produce permanent deformation but too small to produce shear failure, as in a landslide. *2.* Slow deformation that results from long application of a stress. By many it is limited to stresses below the elastic limit. Part of the creep is a permanent deformation. Part of the deformation is elastic; and from this part the specimen recovers.

creep recovery Elastic aftereffect; elastic afterworking. Gradual recovery of elastic creep strain upon release of applied stress as distinguished from "forward" creep.

crenulations Wrinkles. Small folds, with a wave length of a few millimeters, chiefly in metamorphic rocks.

crescent beaches Crescent-shaped beaches concave toward the sea which form at the heads of bays and at the mouths of streams entering these bays along hilly and mountainous coasts.

crest *1. Topog:* The summit land of any eminence; the highest natural projection which crowns a hill or mountain, from which the surface dips downward in opposite directions. *2.* The highest point on an anticline. *See* CREST LINE. *3.* The line connecting the highest points on the same bed in an infinite number of cross sections across a fold.

crestal plane The plane formed by joining the crests of all beds in an anticline.

crest length The length of a wave along its crest.

crest line In an anticline the line connecting the highest points on the same bed in an infinite number of cross sections. Not necessarily the same as the axis of a fold.

crest of wave *1.* The highest part of a wave. *2.* That part of the wave above still-water level.

cretaceous *1.* Of the nature of chalk; relating to chalk. *2.* The third and latest of the periods included in the Mesozoic era; also the system of strata deposited in the Cretaceous period.

crevasse *1.* A fissure in the ice formed under the influence of various strains. *2.* A nearly vertical fissure in a glacier. *3.* *Topog:* A break in a levee or other stream embankment.

crevasse hoar Depth hoar, *q.v.*, found in crevasses or other open spaces below the surface of a snow field or glacier.

crevice *1.* A shallow fissure in the bedrock under a gold placer, in which small but highly concentrated deposits of gold are found. *2.* The fissure containing a vein. As employed in the Colorado statute relative to a discovery shaft, a crevice is a mineral-bearing vein. *3.* Narrow, deep opening in a cavern floor. A narrow, high passageway. *4.* An enlarged joint whether mineralized or not. *5.* Corruption of crevasse.

crinoid One of the Crinoidea.

crinoidal limestone A rock composed in great part of crystalline joints of encrinites, with Foraminifera, corals, and mollusks.

Crinoidea A type of echinoderm consisting of a cup or "head" containing the vital organs, numerous radiating arms, an elongate, jointed stem, and roots by which it is attached to the sea bottom while the body, stem, and arms float.

criquina Limestones composed very largely of fragments of crinoids.

cristobalite A mineral, SiO_2. Tetragonal, trimorphous with quartz and tridymite. A high-temperature form is isometric.

critical angle Angle of incidence at which refracted light just grazes the surface of contact between two different media.

critical density The density of a substance at its critical temperature and under its critical pressure.

critical materials Those materials vital to the national defense, the main source of which is within the continental limits of the United States, which may not be produced in quality and quantity sufficient to meet requirements.

critical point The point at which the properties of a liquid and its vapor become indistinguishable. *Syn:* CRITICAL TEMPERATURE

critical pressure The pressure required to condense a gas at the critical temperature, above which, regardless of pressure, the gas cannot be liquefied.

critical slope Angle of repose.

critical temperature That temperature above which a substance can exist only in the gaseous state, no matter what pressure is exerted.

critical velocity That rate of flow, in a pipe, at which laminar or streamline changes to turbulent flow. In the latter, particles move in sinuous and erratic courses. *See* REYNOLDS NUMBER

crocidolite Blue asbestos. *See* AMPHIBOLE

crocoite A mineral, $PbCrO_4$, orange. Monoclinic.

Croixan Upper Cambrian.

crop out To be exposed at the surface; referring to strata. *See* OUTCROP

cross-bedding *1.* The arrangement of laminations of strata transverse or oblique to the main planes of stratification of the strata concerned; inclined, often lenticular, beds between the main bedding planes; found only in granular sediments. *2.* Term should be applied to inclined bedding found only in profiles at right angles to the current direction.

cross-bedding, torrential Fine, horizontally laminated strata alternating with uniformly cross-bedded strata composed of coarser materials. Believed to originate under desert conditions of concentrated rainfall, abundant wind action, and playa lake deposition.

crosscut *1.* A small passageway driven at right angles to the main entry to connect it with a parallel entry or air course. Also used in Arkansas instead of "breaking through." *2.* A level, driven across the course of a vein or in general across the direction of the main workings or across the "grain of coal."

crossed Nicols Two Nicol prisms placed so that their vibration planes are mutually at right angles. *Opt. mineral:* An anisotropic crystal is interposed between the Nicol prisms in order to observe optical interference effects. The petrographic microscope is normally used with nicol prisms (or equivalent polarizing devices) in the crossed position.

crossed twinning Repeated twinning after two laws. Shown in microcline.

cross fault A fault that strikes diagonally or perpendicularly to the strike of a strata.

cross-lamination Crossbedding; false bedding. The structure commonly present in granular sedimentary rocks, which consists of tabular, irregularly lenticular, or wedge-shaped bodies lying essentially parallel to the general stratification and which themselves show a pronounced laminated structure in which the laminae are steeply inclined to the general bedding.

Crossopterygii A large group of true fishes, Devonian to Recent (only one known living species) including among others the coelacanths, the early members ancestral to amphibians and related to lungfishes.

cross section A profile portraying an interpretation of a vertical section of the earth explored by geophysical and/or geological methods.

cross-stratification The arrangement of layers at one or more angles to the dip of the formation. A cross-stratified unit is one with layers deposited at an angle to the original dip of the formation. Many authors have used "cross-bedding" and "cross-lamination" as synonymous with cross-stratification, but it is proposed to restrict the terms cross-bedding and cross-lamination to a quantitative meaning depending on the thickness of the individual layers, or cross-strata.

crude oil A bitumen of liquid consistency comparatively volatile composed principally of hydrocarbon, usually with traces of sulfur, nitrogen, or oxygen compounds.

crush breccia A breccia formed

essentially *in situ* by cataclasis. *See* CATACLASITE; CRUSH CONGLOMERATE

crush conglomerate *1.* These beds are very much faulted, crushed, and folded and every stage can be traced between a continuous limestone-band and one which has been broken up into small rounded fragments, so as to present precisely the appearance of conglomerate. *2.* Similar to a fault breccia except that the fragments are more rounded in a crush conglomerate. *3.* Tectonic conglomerate, *q.v.*

crushing strength The compressive stress necessary to cause a solid to fail by fracture.

crust *1.* A hard layer at the surface of softer material. *2.* Outer layer of the earth, originally considered to overlie a molten interior, now defined in various ways: lithosphere; sial; material above Mohorovičić discontinuity (favored); tectonosphere; etc. Commonly used in a figurative and imprecise sense. *3.* A layer of hard snow lying upon a soft layer.

Crustacea Subphylum of arthropods with two pairs of antennae and generally some biramous appendages. Camb.-Rec.

crustal plate Portion of the earth's crust beneath an oceanic or continental region.

crustification Those deposits of minerals and ores that are in layers or crusts and that, therefore, have been distinctively deposited from solution.

cryergic Periglacial in broad sense; refers to processes or deposits that are not actually peripheral to glaciated regions.

cryogenic lake Lake in a region of permanently frozen ground produced by local thawing.

cryogenic period Informal designation for a time interval in geologic history during which large bodies of ice occurred at or near the poles and climate was generally suitable for growth of continental glaciers.

cryolite A mineral, Na_3AlF_6. Monoclinic.

cryology *1.* In the United States, the study of refrigeration. *2.* In Europe, a synonym for glaciology. *3.* The study of ice and snow. *4.* The study of sea ice.

cryoluminescence Low temperature increase of weak luminescence or its production in normally non-fluorescent material.

cryopedology The science of intensive frost action and permanently frozen ground including studies of the processes and their occurrence and also the engineering devices which may be invented to avoid or overcome difficulties induced by them.

cryoplanation Reduction of land surfaces by processes associated with frost action.

cryosphere All of the earth's surface that is permanently frozen.

cryoturbation Frost action including frost heaving.

crypto- [<*Gr.* kryptos] A combining form meaning hidden, covered, secret.

cryptobatholithic The first of six stages in the erosion of a batholith; it is not exposed, but its presence is indicated by dikes, sills, and mineral veins in the roof, or by areas of alteration in the overlying rock.

cryptobatholithic stage The batholith is not exposed. Dikes, sills, and veins are found in the roof of the supposed batholith.

cryptocrystalline Crystalline, but so fine-grained that the individual components cannot be seen with a magnifying lens.

cryptoexplosion structure Cryptovolcanic structure. May be result of meteoric impact.

Cryptogamia Plants that do not reproduce by seeds. Includes thallophytes, bryophytes, and pteridophytes.

cryptomelane A mineral, K-$(Mn,^{+4}Mn^{+2})_8O_{16}$. Monoclinic, usually massive.

cryptoperthite An extremely fine-grained intergrowth of potassic and sodic feldspar detectable only by means of X rays; not visible either with the naked eye or with the aid of the microscope. *See* PERTHITE

cryptovolcanic (structure) A small, nearly circular area of highly disturbed strata in which there is no trace of volcanic materials to confirm a volcanic origin. Hence the name "crypto," meaning hidden.

Cryptozoic Precambrian; eon of hidden life.

cryptozoon Problematical Cambrian and Ordovician fossils, probably algae; reef-forming, hemispherical, irregular, or spreading structures made of concentric laminae of calcite.

crystal The regular polyhedral form, bounded by plane surfaces, which is the outward expression of a periodic or regularly repeating internal arrangement of atoms.

crystal axis A reference axis used for the description of the vectorial properties of a crystal. There are generally three noncoplanar axes, chosen parallel to the edges of the unit cell of the crystal structure so as to be parallel to symmetry directions if possible.

crystal chemistry A study of the factors that determine the forms in which solids crystallize, and the relations between the properties of solids and their structures.

crystal class One of the 32 crystallographically possible combinations or groups of symmetry operations that operate so as to leave one point, or origin, fixed.

crystal flotation *Petrol:* The act or process of floating of light crystals in a body of magma. Contrasted with crystal settling.

crystal fractionation Magmatic differentiation resulting from the settling out of crystals from a melt.

crystal gliding Translation gliding.

crystal lattice The regular and repeated three-dimensional arrangement of atoms or ions in a crystal.

crystalline Of or pertaining to the nature of a crystal, having regular molecular structure. Contrasted with amorphous.

crystalline rock *1.* Rock consisting of minerals in an obviously crystalline state. *2.* An inexact general term for igneous and metamorphic rocks as opposed to sedimentary.

crystallinity *Petrol:* The degree of crystallization exhibited by an igneous rock; expressed by terms such as holocrystalline, hypocrystalline, holohyaline.

crystallization The process through which crystalline phases separate from a fluid, viscous, or dispersed state (gas, liquid solution, or rigid solution).

crystallization, heat of *See* HEAT OF CRYSTALLIZATION

crystallization interval *1.* The interval of temperature (or less frequently, pressure), between the formation of the first crystal and the disappearance of the last drop of liquid from a magma upon cooling, usually excluding late stage aqueous fluids. *2.* More specifically, when referring to a given mineral, the range or ranges of temperatures over which that particular phase is in equilibrium with liquid. In the case of equilibria along reaction lines or reaction surfaces, crystallization intervals as thus defined include temperature ranges where certain solid phases are actually decreasing in amount with decrease in temperature.

crystallization magnetization Chemical magnetization.

crystallization nuclei Small particles of any kind around which ice crystals begin to form when a substance freezes.

crystallization schistosity Fissility resulting from the preferred orientation of crystals that grew in the easiest direction.

crystallizing force *1.* Potentiality of minerals to develop crystal form within a solid medium. *2.* Expansive force of minerals growing in a solid medium; force is different in different crystallographic directions. *3.* Tendency of minerals to grow more rapidly in one crystallographic direction than in another.

crystalloblastesis Deformation accomplished by metamorphic recrystallization.

crystalloblastic A crystalline texture due to metamorphic recrystallization. A characteristic of this texture is that the essential constituents are simultaneous crystallizations and are not formed in sequence, so that each may be found as inclusions in all the others.

crystallography The science of the interatomic arrangement of solid matter, its causes, its nature, and its consequences.

crystalloluminescence Emission of light from a substance during crystallization.

crystal mush Partially crystallized magma.

crystal optics The science which treats of the transmission of light in crystals.

crystal sedimentation Settling of crystals in a liquid magma.

crystal seeding *See* NUCLEATION

crystal settling Gravitative sinking of crystals from the liquid in which they formed, by virtue of their greater density. The settling may be aided by convection currents carrying the crystal-laden magma down.

crystal structure The periodic or repeating arrangement of atoms in a crystal.

crystal systems The 32 possible crystal classes, distinguished from one another by their point-group symmetry, are classified under six systems, each characterized by the relative lengths and inclinations of the assumed crystallographic axes, or more accurately, by certain characteristic symmetry elements. These are: (1) isometric; (2) tetragonal; (3) hexagonal; (4) orthorhombic; (5) monoclinic; (6) triclinic.

crystal tuff *1.* Tuff that consists dominantly of ejected volcanic crystals and single crystal fragments. The fragments show typical volcanic ash structures. *2.* The crystals usually are broken euhedra of the common phenocrysts of lava, and may be sheathed in an envelope of glass. *3.* An indurated deposit of volcanic ash dominantly composed of intratelluric crystals blown out during a volcanic eruption. The term should properly be restricted to tuffs containing more than 75% by volume of crystals.

cubanite A mineral, $CuFe_2S_3$. Orthorhombic.

cube *Crystallog:* A form in the isometric system enclosed by six symmetrically equivalent faces at right angles to one another.

cubic packing The manner of arrangement of solid units in a sediment in which the unit cell is a cube, the eight corners of which are the centers of the spheres or solids involved. This is the loosest, or most open type of systematic packing.

cubic system Isometric system, q.v.

cuesta [Sp.] 1. Used in the southwestern United States for a sloping plain which is terminated on one side by a steep slope. It seems to have no relation to the structure, but only to topographic form, and while the long slope of a wold, or dip slope, is a cuesta, a cuesta is not always a dip slope. 2. A Spanish term which means the flank or slope of a hill. As used by many American geographers it means an unsymmetrical ridge with one slope long and gentle and generally agreeing with the dip of the resistant bed or beds that form it and the other slope steep or even precipitous on the cut edges of the beds that form the gentle slope. Hogback, q.v.

Cuisian Bruxellian.

cul-de-sac Partially filled, abandoned swallow hole. A cavern passage that connects with another passage at only one point and ends abruptly in a rock wall or is blocked by cave fill or debris.

culm A vernacular term variously applied, according to the locality, to carbonaceous shale, or to fissile varieties of anthracite coal.

culmination 1. Term applied to the highest point on the crown of a nappe. Syn: AXIS CULMINATION. 2. Portion of a fold system,

generally more or less at right angles to the folds, away from which the folds plunge. 3. The position of a heavenly body which is continually above the horizon, the position of lowest apparent altitude. 4. The highest or lowest altitude attained by a heavenly body as it crosses the meridian.

cumberlandite An ultramafic rock composed largely of magnetite, ilmenite, and olivine with minor plagioclase.

cummingtonite See AMPHIBOLE

cumuliform Resembling cumulus clouds; billowy.

cumulo dome Protrusion of viscous lava from a volcanic vent with little lateral spreading.

cumulo-volcano Cumulo dome.

cup coral A solitary coral, as opposed to a colonial coral. Syn: FOSSIL COW'S HORN; FOUR-PART CORAL; HORN CORAL; SIMPLE CORAL; SOLITARY CORAL

cupel Small cup made of bone ash used in gold or silver assaying with lead.

cupellation Process of assaying for precious metals with a cupel.

cupola 1. An isolated body of plutonic rock that lies near a bigger body. Both bodies are presumed to enlarge downward and join at depth to form a single mass. 2. A large vaulted dome in the Radiolaria.

cupriferous Copper bearing. The Nipigon or Keweenawan formation.

cuprite A mineral, Cu_2O. Isometric. Red.

cuprous Of, pertaining to, or containing copper. Especially compounds in which copper is monovalent.

curie Unit of radioactive disintegration, 3.70×10^{10} disintegrations per second.

Curie point or **temperature** Temperature below which a substance ceases to be paramagnetic.

Curie's law The law, established by Pierre Curie, that magnetic susceptibility is inversely proportional to the absolute temperature.

current *1.* The flowing of water, or other liquid or gas. *2.* The vertical component of air motion; an air current is thus distinguished from the wind, which is the horizontal component. *3.* A large-scale horizontal motion of air. *4.* A large stream of ocean water moving continuously in about the same path, and distinguished from the water through which it flows mainly by temperature and salinity differences.

current base Maximum depth in standing water below which currents are ineffective in moving sediment.

current bedding Crossbedding, *q.v.*

current, coastal *See* COASTAL CURRENT

current cross-ripples Ripples which result from the interference of a current with a pre-existing set of ripples, if the action of the current is sufficiently weak and only of very short duration. As there is no oscillation of the current, there is no reason for a transformation into the hexagonal pattern, and the two sets of ripples may be found intersecting at any angle.

current mark An irregular structure produced by erosion on tidal flats where the falling tidal waters erode numerous channels and leave uneroded areas as flat "plateaus" between channels. Channel fillings made on burial of such surfaces may resemble casts of logs. Current marks are also made in the beach zone on

the lee side of obstructions. A small depression begins at the obstruction and extends downward toward the water. They are common on beaches in the tidal zone on the downshore side of pebbles, shells, etc.

current ripple A ripple mark produced by the action of a current flowing steadily in one direction over a bed of sand. These "current ripples" have a long, gentle slope toward the direction from which the current comes, and a shorter steeper slope on the lee side. Sand grains removed from the gentle slope are carried to the crest and dropped down the steeper slope, causing the ripples to migrate slowly with the current, much as sand dunes migrate with the wind.

curvature, earth (correction for) An adjustment applied to a long line of sight in the computation of difference in elevation. Atmospheric refraction partially compensates for earth curvature; hence, correction tables take both curvature and refraction into account.

cusp *1.* One of a series of naturally formed low mounds of beach material separated by crescent-shaped troughs spaced at more or less regular intervals along the beach face. *Also* BEACH CUSP. *2.* In conodonts, the large main denticle which is ordinarily above the aboral attachment scar or escutcheon, sometimes called the superior fang or main cusp.

cuspidate, *adj.* With an apex somewhat abruptly and sharply concavely constricted into an elongated, sharply pointed tip.

cut-and-fill *1.* During the development of the meanders the lateral planation on the one side is accompanied by deposition on the other. *2.* A structure resulting from the removal of a small portion of a bed or lamina prior to deposition of an overlying bed or lamina.

cutbank The concave wall of a meandering stream that is maintained as a steep or even overhanging cliff by the impinging of water at its base.

cutoff A new and relatively short channel formed when a stream cuts through the neck of an oxbow or horseshoe bend.

cutoff grade The lowest grade of mineralized material that qualifies as ore in a given deposit, i.e., material of the lowest assay that is included in an ore estimate.

cutoff spur When along the course of an entrenched river lateral erosion becomes predominant, a spur projecting into a loop may ultimately be worn away at the root, so that the river breaks through at this point and, abandoning its curved course, leaves an elevation isolated from the high ground on either bank which is known as a cutoff spur.

cut terrace Shelves carved in the shores of lakes by the action of waves and currents; they are bounded on both their shoreward and lakeward margins by steeper slopes; the former inclines upward and forms a sea cliff, the latter slopes downward and forms a terrace scarp. Their upper limit is a horizontal line marking the level of the water at the time they were formed, their surface slopes gently lakeward.

cuttings The fragmental rock samples broken or torn from the penetrated rock during the course of drilling.

Cuvier's principle Some very different characters of complex organisms are commonly as-

sociated, e.g., kinds of feet and teeth among the vertebrates.

C-wave Coupled wave, *q.v.*

cyanite *See* KYANITE

cycad Member of the Cycadophytes.

Cycadophytes Subclass or order of gymnosperms; plants with compound leaves consisting of simple leaflets arranged on both sides of a common stem and naked seeds borne in simple cones. Perm.-Rec.

cycle This is the period in which a continent or any part of it would be reduced from its initial form of uplift to base level.

cycle in the life of a river The lapse of time for which the land mass, on which an original river has begun its work, stands perfectly still after its first elevation or deformation, and so remains until the river has completed its task of carrying away all the mass of rocks that rise above its base level.

cycle of denudation The alternate upheaval and wearing down, together constitute a cycle of denudation, from base level back to base level. *Cf.* CYCLE OF EROSION

cycle of development The whole region presents the most emphatic expression not only of its structure, but also of the more recent cycles of development through which it has passed.

cycle of erosion The time involved in the reduction of a recently uplifted land area to a base level. Geographical cycle, *q.v.*

cycle of sedimentation 1. A sequence of related processes and conditions repeated in the same order that is recorded in a sedimentary deposit. 2. The cycle of sediment formation, transportation, and deposition.

cycle of shore development The progressive changes from the time when the water first assumes its level and rests against the new shore to the time when it has brought its boundaries into harmony with its movements so that no more work can be done.

cycle of topographical development Each cycle begins with the uplift of an area approximately at base level, the processes of denudation working with minimum efficiency and extreme slowness. The movement of upheaval revivifies the destructive agencies, and the work of carving out a surface of relief begins afresh, only to terminate, unless interrupted by renewed elevation, in once more base-leveling the region. A complete cycle is thus from base level back to base level, though, as it is a cycle, a beginning may be selected in any part of it.

cycle of underground drainage It begins with surface drainage and in its youth develops subterranean drainage near the points of easy escape for the water. In its maturity there is the maximum of subterranean drainage and the lower parts of the caverns have begun to retreat by collapse while in the uppermost reaches of the stream the transformation from surface to subsurface drainage may still be in progress. Old age is shown by the more general condition of collapse and the return to surface drainage. Briefly, it may be stated that the cycle is: surface drainage, partial subterranean drainage, and a return to surface drainage. The final state is peneplanation or base leveling.

cycles, igneous Refers to the usual sequence of events in which there are flows first, then large intrusions, and finally dikes.

cyclic evolution Evolution, supposed by some to have occurred in many lineages, involving successively (1) initial rapid and vigorous expansion, (2) long stable or slowly changing phase, and (3) final short episode in which overspecialized, degenerate, or inadaptive forms led to extinction.

cyclic twinning Repeated twinning of three or more individuals according to the same twin law but with the twinning axes not parallel. Often simulates high symmetry as fourfold, fivefold, sixfold, or eightfold axes, some of which are impossible in an untwinned crystal.

cyclone A circular or nearly circular area of low atmospheric pressure around which the winds blow counterclockwise in the northern hemisphere and clockwise in the southern. It may cause precipitation and cloudiness over many thousands of square miles.

cyclosilicates See SILICATES, CLASSIFICATION

cyclothem The "ideal" cyclothem consists of ten members, but because of extremely variable development a cyclothem cannot be defined rigidly in terms of the members actually present at any locality.

cylindrical map projection A map projection produced by projecting the geographic meridians and parallels onto a cylinder which is tangent to (or intersects) the surface of a sphere, and then developing the cylinder into a plane.

cymoid structure Vein-shaped like a reverse curve. Cymoid loop: splitting of a vein on its dip or strike into two branches, both of which curve away from the general trend and then unite to resume a direction parallel to but not in line with the original trend.

Cystoidea Mostly stemmed echinoderms with irregularly to regularly arranged body plates pierced by pores and biserial brachioles that appear to be outgrowths of structures originating at the mouth. Ord.-Dev. Blastoids are included by some in this class.

D

d The spacing between successive identical planes in a crystal structure. The list of d's obtained by X-ray methods is characteristic of each substance and is widely used for mineral identification.

Dacian Lower upper Pliocene.

dacite The extrusive equivalent of quartz diorite (tonalite). The principal minerals are plagioclase (andesine and oligoclase), quartz, pyroxene or hornblende or both with minor biotite and sanidine. All of these minerals may occur as phenocrysts in a glassy or finely crystalline groundmass of alkalic feldspar and silica minerals. Biotite, sanidine, and hornblende are more prominent in rocks transitional into quartz latite and rhyodacite.

dahlite A carbonate-apatite mineral or association occurring as concretionary spherulites.

daily mean *1.* The average value of any meteorological element, such as temperature, pressure, humidity, etc., over a period of 24 hours. *2.* The average values of any meteorological element for each day of the year obtained from a record of many years in which case they are sometimes called normal daily values.

daily retardation (of tides) The amount of time by which corresponding tidal phases grow later day by day (averages approximately 50 minutes).

Dakotan Lower Upper Cretaceous.

dale A vale or small valley.

dalles [*Fr.*] In the Northwest, the nearly vertical walls of a canyon or gorge, usually containing a rapid. *Also* DELLS

Danian Lowermost Paleocene or uppermost Cretaceous.

darcy A standard unit of permeability. One darcy is equivalent to the passage of one cubic centimeter of fluid of one centipoise viscosity flowing in one second under a pressure differential of one atmosphere through a porous medium having an area of cross section of one square centimeter and a length of one centimeter. A millidarcy is one one-thousandth.

Darcy's law A derived formula for the flow of fluids on the assumption that the flow is laminar and that inertia can be neglected. The numerical formulation of this law is used generally in studies of gas, oil, and water production from underground formations. For example, in gas flow, the velocity of the flow is proportional to the pressure gradient multiplied by the ratio of permeability times density, divided by the viscosity of the gas.

dark-colored mineral Dark mineral.

dark mineral Any one of a group of rock-forming minerals that are dark-colored even in thin section. Mafite.

dark ruby silver *See* PYRARGYRITE

Darwinism Doctrine that organic evolution resulted from variation and the selection of favored individuals through natural selection.

datolite A mineral, $CaBSiO_4$ (OH). Monoclinic. Commonly occurs in cavities in diabase or basalt.

datum Any numerical or geometrical quantity or set of such quantities which may serve as a reference or base for other quantities.

For a group of statistical references, the plural form is data, as, geographic data for a list of latitudes and longitudes. Where the concept is geometrical and particular, rather than statistical and inclusive, the plural form is datums, as, two geodetic datums have been used in this country in recent years.

datum elevation A level reference elevation used in mapping, usually sea level. In seismic mapping, the time datum used is near the surface.

datum level The level (usually sea level or mean level of nearest considerable body of water) from which altitudes are measured in surveys.

datum plane *1.* The horizontal plane to which soundings, ground elevations, or water surface elevations are referred. *Also* REFERENCE PLANE. *2.* An arbitrary reference surface, used in seismic mapping to minimize or eliminate local topographic effects, to which seismic times and velocity determinations are referred.

datum water level The level at which water is first struck in a shaft.

daughter element An element formed from another by radioactive decay; e.g., radon is the daughter element of radium.

D-coal Coal material that predominates in durain; occurs as microscopic particles in the lungs of miners.

dead cave A cave wherein the formations are dry; a cave in which deposition and excavation have ceased.

dead coral reef A coral reef or part of a coral reef with no living corals.

dead ground Rock in a mine, which, although producing no ore, requires to be removed in order to get at productive ground.

dead line Base of barren core of a metalliferous batholith, exposed during epibatholithic, *q.v.*, stage of erosion.

debouchure *1.* The mouth of a river or channel; the point from which a spring bursts. *2.* Point at which tubular passages connect with larger passages or chambers. Point of issuance of an underground stream.

debris *1.* [*Fr.*] Wreck, ruins, remains. *Geol:* Applied to a collection of the larger fragments of rocks and strata, to distinguish them from detritus, or those which are pulverized. *2.* The material resulting from the decay and disintegration of rocks. It may occur in the place where it was produced, or it may be transported by streams of water or ice and deposited in other localities. Rock waste. *3. Glaciol:* Rocks, earth, and other material lying on the surface of a glacier.

debris avalanche The sudden movement downslope of the soil mantle on steep slopes caused by its complete saturation through protracted heavy rains.

debris cone A fan-shaped deposit of soil, sand, gravel, and boulders up at the point where a mountain stream meets a valley, or otherwise where its velocity is reduced sufficiently to cause such deposits. Similar to alluvial fan, but consists of coarser material lying on steeper slopes.

debris fall The relatively free falling of predominantly unconsolidated earth or debris from a vertical or overhanging cliff, cave, or arch.

debris flow A general designation for all types of rapid flowage involving debris of various kinds and conditions.

debris line Landward limit of debris washed upon a beach by storm waves.

debris slide The rapid downward movement of predominantly unconsolidated and incoherent earth and debris in which the mass does not show backward rotation but slides or rolls forward, forming an irregular hummocky deposit which may resemble morainal topography.

debyeogram X-ray powder pattern; Debye-Scherrer diagram. The photographic film record of the directions in which a powdered crystal selectively scatters X rays of a single wave length. The film is arranged in a cylinder about the specimen and the X-ray beam passes through the specimen at right angles to the axis of this cylinder. *See* POWDER METHOD; BRAGG'S LAW

Debye-Scherrer diagram *See* DEBYEOGRAM

decapod A lobsterlike crustacean.

decay constant The fraction of a large number of atoms of a radioactive element which decays per unit time; generally denoted by the symbol λ.

decay of waves When waves leave a generating area (fetch) and pass through a calm (or region of lighter winds), they undergo a change. The significant wave length increases and the significant wave height decreases.

deccan basalt; deccan trap Fine-grained, nonporphyritic, tholeiitic basaltic lava, covering an area of about 200,000 square miles in the Deccan region of southeast India and consisting essentially of labradorite, clinopyroxene, and iron ore. Olivine is generally absent, or is present in minor amount, usually near the bottom of flows. Corresponds to the plateau basalt of the Pacific Northwest and the Thulean province of western Scotland, northeast Ireland, and Iceland.

decibel A unit used to express power or intensity ratios in electrical and acoustical technology as well as seismic work. $DB = 10 \log_{10} I_1/I_2$, where I is intensity. Used in seismic studies to express intensity ratios, particularly in discussions of absorption and dissipation of wave energy.

deciduous Referring to plant parts which fall off within a year of time of their production; refers also to plants which lose their leaves regularly each year, as opposed to evergreens, the leaves of which remain on the stems longer than a year.

decimillimeter 1/100 mm.; abbreviation $D\mu$.

decke [*Ger.*] Nappe [*Fr.*], *q.v.*

decken structure Nappe structure. A series of large recumbent folds or overthrust sheets, or both, lying one above the other.

declination The angle, variable with geographic position, between the direction in which the magnetic needle points and the true meridian.

declination arc A graduated arc attached to the alidade of a surveyor's compass or transit, on which the magnetic declination is set off.

decline curve A graphic representation of the decline in production of an oil or gas well or group of wells. Production rates (ordinates) are plotted against time (abscissae) and the curve drawn approximately through the points. The projected curve is integrated to predict ultimate future production.

declinometer An instrument, often self-registering, for measuring or recording the declination of the magnetic needle.

declivity A descending slope, as opposed to acclivity.

declivity, law of In homogeneous material and with equal quantities of water, the rate of erosion of slopes is dependent on their declivities, the steeper being degraded the faster.

décollation Décollement.

décollement The independent disruption by folding or faulting of sedimentary beds by sliding over the underlying rocks.

decomposition The breaking down of minerals by themselves or in rocks through chemical processes, usually related to weathering.

decrepitation The breaking up, usually violent and with a crackling noise, of mineral substances when exposed to heat, as when common salt is thrown upon the fire.

decussate structure A microstructure in which the axes of contiguous crystals lie in diverse directions. This crisscross structure is most noticeable in rocks composed dominantly of minerals with a columnar habit.

dedolomitization The destruction of dolomite to form calcite and periclase, the latter usually hydrating to form brucite as in brucite marble or predazzite. Presumably this takes place by contact metamorphism at rather low pressures.

deep Oceanic areas of exceptional depth, representing depressions in the ocean floor, often troughlike or synclinal in form. The term is generally understood to be restricted to depths greater than 18,000 feet (3000 fathoms). Secondary and smaller bounded areas within the great ocean basins with depths exceeding 5000 to 6000 meters.

deep inland seas Adjacent seas in restricted communication with the open ocean. Depths are greater than 200 meters; the floors are commonly 2000 to 5000 meters below sea level. The Mediterranean, East and West Indian basins, the Red Sea, and the Black Sea are examples. *Also* MEDITERRANEAN SEAS; DEEP-SEA BASINS

deep marginal seas Adjacent seas with depths exceeding 200 meters. Deep marginal seas are widely open to the oceans at the water surface but are restricted at depth by submarine ridges with or without islands. Examples are the eastern Asiatic marginal seas.

deep-sea furrow Geotectocline.

deep-sea plain A broad and nearly level area forming by far the greater part of the ocean floor. Its depth varies from about 2000 to 3000 fathoms, but its slopes are always very gentle.

deep-sea terrace A benchlike feature bordering an elevation of the deep-sea floor at depths greater than 300 fathoms.

Deerparkian Middle Lower Devonian.

defect lattice Crystal lattice from which some atoms are missing leaving vacant spaces.

deflation The removal of material from a beach or other land surface by wind action.

deflation basin Topographic basin resulting from wind erosion.

deflection *1.* One type of pattern shown by maps of mountain ranges; it is a sudden change in the trend of one or more branches of the mountain range. *2. Geophys:* Applied to the vertical direction, the angle between the geoid and the spheroid, or the angle between the vertical and the normal to the spheroid; more properly, the deviation of the vertical.

deflocculate To break up from a flocculated state; to convert into very fine particles. *Syn:* PEPTIZE

deflocculating agent An agent which produces deflocculation, as for example the alkalis in certain concentration, and which therefore hinders settling.

deformation ellipsoid *See* STRAIN ELLIPSOID

deformation fabric *1.* The orientation in space of the elements of a rock produced by external stress on the rock. It results from a rotation or movement of the constituent elements under stress, or from growth of new elements in a common orientation controlled by the stress conditions. *2. Struct. petrol:* A deformation fabric results where the components of the rock owe their orientation to the operation of stress which has produced a penetrative differential movement of the components.

deformation of rocks Any change in the original form or volume of rock masses produced by tectonic forces; folding, faulting, and solid flow are common modes of deformation.

deformation plane Plane normal to flow surface and parallel to direction of movement; the a-c plane of structural petrology.

deformation twinning Twinning produced by deformation and gliding within a pre-existing crystal.

degenerate Having lost some of the structures, or the symmetry of structure, of the ancestral condition.

deglaciation The uncovering of an area from beneath glacier ice as a result of shrinkage of a glacier.

degradation The general lowering of the surface of the land by erosive processes, especially by the removal of material through erosion and transportation by flowing water.

degree day A departure of one degree per day in the mean daily temperature, from an adopted standard reference temperature, usually 65° F. When the mean temperature on a given day is 65° F., or higher, that day is not considered in making the monthly total. 65° F. was chosen the standard because, according to heating engineers, the minimum temperature of bodily comfort in the home is reached when the mean daily temperature falls below that value.

degree of freedom Capability of variation of a system. The number of degrees of freedom in a system is the number of independent variables, temperature, pressure, and concentration in the different phases, which must be specified in order to define the system completely. Alternatively, the number of degrees of freedom is the number of variables which may be changed independently without causing the appearance or disappearance of a phase. *See* VARIANCE OF A SYSTEM

degrees of frost A phrase used in England; it means the number of degrees that the temperature falls below the freezing point: thus, a day with a temperature of 27° F. may be designated as a day of 5 degrees of frost.

dehydrate To render free from water.

dehydration water Chemically combined water released during mineral reactions or transformations.

delayed runoff Most of that rain water which sinks into the ground eventually returns to the surface by slow seepage and from springs; it is the delayed runoff.

delay time Intercept time. Additional time for any segment of a ray path over the time which would be required to traverse the horizontal component of that segment at highest velocity encountered on the trajectory. For a layer of velocity V_0 and thickness L overlying a substratum of velocity V_1, the delay time, $D=2$ L cos i/V_0 where $i=\sin^{-1}V_0/V_1$.

deliquescent Capable of becoming liquid by the absorption of water from the air.

dellenite A variety of rhyolite transitional into quartz latite.

Delmontian Uppermost Miocene or lower Pliocene.

delta *1*. An alluvial deposit, usually triangular, at the mouth of a river. *2*. A tidal delta is a similar deposit at the mouth of a tidal inlet, put there by tidal currents. *3*. A wave delta is a deposit made by large waves

which run over the top of a spit or bar beach and down the landward side. *4*. A deposit of sediment formed at the mouth of a river either in the ocean or a lake which results in progradation of the shore line. The name delta [<*Gr.* capital letter "delta," which is triangular] has been applied because of the triangular shape assumed by the salients formed by deltas built out from straight coast.

deltageosyncline *See* EXOGEOSYNCLINE

delta lake Rivers are partly or wholly responsible for a class of lakes which may be called delta lakes. Lake Pontchartrain in Louisiana is an example. Here detritus brought down by the river was deposited around an area of shallow water, converting the latter into a basin.

delta plain Plains formed by the accumulation of silt at the mouths of streams, or by overflow along their lower courses.

deltohedron Deltoid dodecahedron. An isometric crystal form with 12 quadrilateral faces distributed as determined by tetrahedral symmetry; the Miller symbol is $\{hhl\}$ with $h<l$.

deltoid Triangular; deltalike.

deluge The term applied by early writers to the Noachian flood.

demersal Refers to fish and other nektonic animals that live on or adjacent to the seabottom and feed on benthonic organisms.

dendrite *1*. A branching figure resembling a shrub or tree, produced on or in a mineral or rock by the crystallization of a foreign mineral, usually an oxide of manganese, as in the moss agate; also the mineral or rock so marked. *2*. A crystallized arborescent form, as of gold or silver; an arborization.

dendritic drainage pattern The dendritic drainage pattern is characterized by irregular branching in all directions with the tributaries joining the main stream at all angles.

dendrochronology Study and matching of tree rings with the object of dating events in the recent past.

dense, *adj.* *1.* Having its parts massed or crowded together; close; compact. *2. Petrol:* A textural term applied to fine-grained, aphanitic rocks in which the grain size generally averages less than 0.05 to 0.1 mm.

densilog Record of the varying density of rocks penetrated in drilling.

density *1.* The mass or quantity of a substance in grams per cubic centimeter. *2.* The quality of being dense, close, or compact. *3.* The quantity of electricity per unit of volume at a point in space, or the quantity of electricity per unit of area at a point on a surface.

density current Turbidity current. A highly turbid and relatively dense current which moves along the bottom slope of a body of standing water. It may also occur as an underflow in a lake or reservoir, a dust storm, or a descending cloud of volcanic dust.

dentate, *adj.* With sharp, spreading, rather coarse indentations or teeth that are perpendicular to the margin.

denudation *1.* A laying bare; the process of washing away of the covering of strata. *2.* That process which, if continued far enough, would reduce all surface inequalities of the globe to a uniform base level.

denude To wear away or remove overlying matter from underlying rocks, exposing them to view.

deoxidation spheres Bleach spots, *q.v.*

departure (plane surveying) The orthographic projection of a line on an east-west axis of reference. The departure (dep.) of a line is the difference of the meridian distances or longitudes of the ends of the line. It is east or positive, and sometimes called the easting, for a line whose azimuth or bearing is in the northeast or southeast quadrant; it is west or negative, and sometimes called the westing, for a line whose azimuth or bearing is in the southwest or northwest quadrant.

depauperate fauna Dwarf fauna, *q.v.*

depergelation The act or process of thawing permanently frozen ground.

deplanation A term that includes all physiographic processes which tend to reduce the relief of a district, and so cause the topography eventually to become more and more plainlike in contour, dominantly by subtracting material from the area or areas affected.

depletion *1.* The act of emptying, reducing, or exhausting, as the depletion of natural resources. *Min:* Specifically said of ore reserves. *2.* The loss sustained by its owner through the progressive exhaustion of a mineral deposit.

depletion allowance A proportion of income derived from mining or oil production that is considered to be a return of capital not subject to income tax.

depocenter An area or site of maximum deposition.

deposit *1.* Anything laid down.

Formerly applied to suspended matter left by the agency of water, but now made to include also mineral matter in any form, and precipitated by chemical or other agencies, as the ores, etc., in veins. 2. The term mineral deposit or ore deposit is arbitrarily used to designate a natural occurrence of a useful mineral or ore in sufficient extent and degree of concentration to invite exploitation.

deposition 1. The laying down of potential rock-forming material; sedimentation. 2. The precipitation of mineral matter from solution as the deposition of agate, vein quartz, etc.

depositional magnetization Remanent magnetization of sedimentary rock resulting from the depositional alinement of previously magnetized grains.

depreciation The waste of assets due to exhaustion, wear and tear, and obsolescence of property. Not to be confused with depletion, *q.v.*

depression A low place of any size on a plain surface, with drainage underground or by evaporation; a hollow completely surrounded by higher ground and having no natural outlet for surface drainage.

depth 1. The vertical distance from the still-water level (or datum as specified) to the bottom. 2. A term which may be used for a few of the deepest soundings.

depth ice 1. Bottom ice. 2. Small particles of ice formed below the surface of the sea when it is churned by wave action.

Depth of compensation, isostatic The depth at which major density differences of the earth's crust are compensated, isostatically. This depth is variously cal-

culated to lie between 100 and 113.7 km.

depth zone within the earth Zones giving rise to different metamorphic assemblages. *See* EPIZONE; MESOZONE; KATAZONE

dermal gliding Extensive horizontal shearing and displacement within the earth's crust.

de-roofing Foundering of part of the roof of a batholith resulting in the extrusion of magma onto the earth's surface.

derrick 1. The framework or tower over a deep drill hole, such as that of an oil well, for supporting the tackle for boring, hoisting, or lowering. 2. Any of various hoisting apparatus employing a tackle rigged at the end of a spar or beam.

descriptive mineralogy That branch of mineralogy devoted to the description of the physical and chemical properties and occurrences and uses of minerals.

desert A region so devoid of vegetation as to be incapable of supporting any considerable population. Four kinds of deserts, may be distinguished: (1) the polar ice and snow deserts, marked by perpetual snow cover and intense cold; (2) the middle latitude deserts, in the basinlike interiors of the continents, such as the Gobi, characterized by scant rainfall and high summer temperatures; (3) the trade wind deserts, notably the Sahara, the distinguishing features of which are negligible precipitation and large daily temperature range; and (4) coastal deserts where there is a cold current on the western coast of a large land mass such as occurs in Peru. *See* ARID for a formula used by Wladimir Köppen to determine the limit of rainfall which constitutes a desert climate.

desert crust *See* DESERT PAVEMENT

desert dome Convex-upward rock surface representing penultimate stage in desert erosion of a granitic mountain mass.

desert pavement Desert crust. When loose material containing pebbles or larger stones is exposed to wind action the finer dust and sand are blown away and the pebbles gradually accumulate on the surface, forming a sort of mosaic which protects the finer material underneath from attack. This is the desert pavement. *See* PEBBLE MOSAICS

desert polish A smooth and shining surface imparted to rocks or other hard substances by the wind-blown sand and dust of desert regions.

desert topography In arid regions the rain and frost do relatively little work, and rock destruction is almost entirely mechanical and carried on by the wind, and by the heating of the rocks by a desert sun followed by a swift chill that comes after sunset. As a result of this difference in the effective agents of destruction, the topographic forms in arid regions are entirely different from those in regions of normal rainfall.

desert varnish A surface stain or crust of manganese or iron oxide, of brown or black color and usually with a glistening luster, which characterizes many exposed rock surfaces in the desert. It coats not only ledges of rock in place, but also boulders and pebbles that are scattered over the surface of the ground.

desiccate To dry up; to deprive or exhaust of moisture; to preserve by drying.

desiccation breccia *1.* Dried, mud-cracked polygons which have broken into fragments and then have been deposited with other sediments. *2.* A type of intraformational breccia, *q.v. See* EDGEWISE CONGLOMERATE

desiccation conglomerate A deposit of coarse rounded fragments formed by the fragmentation, erosion, and transportation of the plates of a mud-cracked (desiccation-cracked) layer of sediment.

desiccation crack Crack formed by shrinkage of clay or clayey beds in the course of drying under the influence of the sun's heat.

desiccation polygons Nonsorted polygons produced by drying.

desilication *1.* The removal of silica from a rock; freeing of silica by the breakdown of silicates is particularly important. *2.* Removal of silica from a magma by reaction with wall rock, as with limestone, to form solid lime silicates.

Desmoinesian Lower Middle Pennsylvanian.

Desmospongia Class of sponges with skeletons composed of siliceous or horny spicules of many forms other than hexactinellid. Camb.-Rec.

desorption Removal of adsorbed material.

destructional Pertaining to destruction or shaped by destructive forces; as in geology, a plain which has been formed by erosion.

detached core In some tight folds the beds in the center of a fold are so squeezed that only detached remnants of the bed remain in the center of the fold.

detail log An electric log of a well bore with a scale expanded beyond the conventional 1 inch per 100 feet of depth, made in order to portray more clearly minor variations in the formations penetrated by the hole.

detector *See* SEISMOMETER

detector spread In seismic work, the layout of detectors or seismometers to obtain information by shooting.

determinative mineralogy That branch of mineralogy which comprises the determination of the nature, composition, and classification of minerals, by all or any means available, as physical tests, blowpipe or wet analyses, and the crystallographic and the optical properties.

detrital Clastic; allogenic, *q.v.* Said of minerals occurring in sedimentary rocks, which were derived from pre-existing igneous, sedimentary, or metamorphic rocks.

detrital ratio Clastic ratio.

detritus *1.* Material produced by the disintegration and weathering of rocks that has been moved from its site of origin. *2.* A deposit of such material.

deuteric A term applied to alterations in an igneous rock produced during the later stages of, and as a direct consequence of, the consolidation of the magma or lava. The term discriminates such alterations from the more strictly secondary changes due to a later period of alteration. *Syn:* PAULOPOST

deuteric effects Metasomatic effects which have taken place in direct continuation of the magma of the rock itself.

deuterium A hydrogen isotope containing a neutron in addition to the proton in its nucleus. The hydrogen in "heavy water."

development *1. Geol:* Applied to those progressive changes in fossil genera, and species, which have followed one another during the deposition of the strata of the earth. *2.* Work done in a mine to open up ore bodies, as sinking shafts and driving levels, etc.

development well *See* FIELD DEVELOPMENT WELL

development work Work undertaken to open up ore bodies as distinguished from the work of actual ore extraction. Sometimes development work is distinguished from exploratory work on the one hand and from stope preparation on the other.

deviation Applied to the vertical direction, the angle between the geoid and the spheroid of the earth, or the angle between the vertical and the normal to the spheroid. *Syn:* DEFLECTION

devitrification The process by which glassy rocks break up into definite minerals. The latter are usually excessively minute crystals of quartz and feldspar. The change from a glassy to a crystalline state after solidification.

Devonian In the ordinarily accepted classification, the fourth in order of age of the periods comprised in the Paleozoic era, following the Silurian and succeeded by the Mississippian. Also the system of strata deposited at that time. Sometimes called the Age of Fishes.

dew Water condensed onto objects near the ground whose temperatures have fallen below the dew point of the adjacent air due to radiational cooling during the night, but are still above freezing; frost occurs when the temperatures are below freezing. Dew does not fall from the sky, as older theories taught and as is still popularly believed.

dew point The temperature to which air must be cooled, at constant pressure and constant water vapor content, in order for saturation to occur. Since the pressure of the water vapor content of the air then becomes the saturation pressure, the dew point may also be defined as the temperature at which the saturation pressure is the same as the existing vapor pressure.

dextral drag fold A drag fold such that the trace of a given bed on the surface is displaced to the right by the drag folds.

dextral fault Fault in which the block on the far side appears to be offset to the right. Right-lateral fault.

dextral fold Asymmetric fold in which the long limb is apparently offset to the right by the short limb as one looks along the long limb (i.e., offset in the same manner as in a right-hand fault, *q.v.*).

Di Abbreviation for diopside in normative rock calculations and diagrams.

dia- [*Gr.*] A prefix denoting through; also between, apart, across.

diabase A rock of basaltic composition, consisting essentially of labradorite and pyroxene, and characterized by ophitic texture. Rocks containing significant amounts of olivine are olivine diabases. In Great Britain basaltic rocks with ophitic texture are called dolerites, and the term diabase is restricted to altered dolerites.

diabase amphibolite Amphibolite formed by dynamic metamorphism of diabase.

diabasic A textural term applied to igneous rocks in which discrete crystals or grains of pyroxene (usually augite) fill the interstices between lath-shaped feldspar (usually plagioclase) crystals. Characteristic of dia-

bases and some gabbros. *Syn:* OPHITIC

diadochy Replacement or replaceability of one atom or ion in a crystal lattice by another.

diagenesis Process involving physical and chemical changes in sediment after deposition that converts it to consolidated rock; includes compaction, cementation, recrystallization, and perhaps replacement as in the development of dolomite.

diagnostic minerals Symptomatic minerals. Those minerals, such as olivine, quartz, etc., which indicate a rock to be under- or over-saturated.

diagonal fault Oblique fault. A fault that strikes diagonally to the strike of the adjacent strata.

diagonal joint Joint in igneous rock crossing flow lines or layers at angle of about 45°, corresponding to shear planes.

diagonal-slip fault Oblique-slip fault. A fault in which the net slip is diagonal down or up the fault plane; that is, a fault which is neither a strike-slip nor a dip-slip fault.

diagram, orientation *Struct. petrol:* A diagram, usually on a Schmidt net, which shows the degree of concentration or dispersion of selected features of rock fabric such as lineation, crystal axes, cleavage or twinning planes, etc.

diagram, scatter *Struct. petrol:* An orientation diagram which has not been contoured; lineations, axes, or poles of planes are represented by points.

diallage The variety of monoclinic pyroxene characterized by conspicuous parting parallel to the front pinacoid a $\{100\}$.

dialysis Separation of a colloid from ions and molecules in true solution, by permitting the latter to diffuse through a membrane which is impervious to the colloidal particles.

diamagnetic Pertaining to substances having a permeability less than that of a vacuum, i.e., less than 1. Such materials are repelled by a magnetic field, e.g., metallic bismuth. *Ant:* PARAMAGNETIC

diamond A mineral, the element carbon, the hardest substance known. Isometric. Used as a gem and industrially in cutting tools. Bort and carbonado (black diamond) are black or dark-colored diamond aggregates.

diamond bit A rotary drilling bit studded with borts-type diamonds.

diaphanous Permitting the light to shine through.

diaphthoresis Retrogressive metamorphism; retrograde metamorphism, *q.v.*

diapir Piercement fold.

diapir fold Piercing fold. Anticlines in which a mobile core, such as salt, has injected the more brittle overlying rock.

diaspore A mineral, AlO(OH). Orthorhombic. A constituent of some bauxites.

diastem *1.* A depositional break of less magnitude than a disconformity, *q.v.*, which is represented elsewhere by a group of strata of less than formation value. *2.* A deposition break or hiatus of assumed minor duration. A diastem represents an intraformational break and is therefore represented by deposits of less than formation rank elsewhere. No faunal or floral change.

diastrophism The process or processes by which the crust of the earth is deformed, producing continents and ocean basins, plateaus and mountains, flexures and folds of strata, and faults.

Also the results of these processes.

diathermic Allowing a free passage of heat.

diatom Microscopic, single-celled plant growing in marine or fresh water. Diatoms secrete siliceous frustules in a great variety of forms that may accumulate in sediments in enormous numbers.

diatomaceous earth A friable earthy deposit composed of nearly pure silica and consisting essentially of the frustules of the microscopic plants called diatoms. Diatomite, *q.v.* Sometimes wrongly called infusorial earth, *q.v.*

diatomite The silica of diatoms dried to a fine powder and used in the manufacture of dynamite, pottery glaze, etc.

diatom ooze A soft siliceous deposit found on the bottom of the deep sea made largely or partly of the shells of diatoms; similar deposits are formed from the shells of Radiolaria.

diatreme A general term for a volcanic vent or pipe drilled through enclosing rocks (usually flat-lying sedimentary rocks) by the explosive energy of gas-charged magmas. The diamond-bearing kimberlite pipes of South Africa are diatremes.

Dibranchiata Subclass of cephalopods with internal shells or none; includes belemnites, squids, and octopods. Miss.-Rec.

dichroism *See* PLEOCHROISM

dichromate A salt or ester of dichromic acid; a compound containing the radical $Cr_2O_7^{--}$.

dichroscope An instrument for observing pleochroism in minerals.

dickite A clay mineral of the kaolin group. It has the same composition, $Al_2Si_2O_5(OH)_4$, as kaolinite and nacrite, but is structurally distinct. Usually occurs in hydrothermal veins.

didodecahedron Diploid.

differential compaction The relative change in thickness of mud and sand (or limestone) after burial due to reduction in pore space. Under loading, the mud compacts more than the sand (or limestone), accentuating initial dip of the beds and developing conformable sections which thicken and thin locally. In addition to physical compression, the forcing out of water and drying of sediments are important.

differential erosion The more rapid erosion of one portion of the earth's surface as compared with another.

differential forces Forces that are not equal on all sides of a body and hence produce distortion. In contrast to hydrostatic pressure which is equal on all sides of the body and causes dilation.

differential melting A partial melting process, in which a portion of the material remains as solid crystals.

differential pressure The difference in pressure between the two sides of an orifice; the difference between reservoir and sand-face pressure; between pressure at the bottom of a well and at the wellhead; between flowing pressure at the wellhead and that in the gathering line. Any difference in pressure between that upstream and downstream where a restriction to flow exists.

differential thermal analysis A method of analysis by determining the temperature at which thermal reactions take place in a material when it is heated continuously to an elevated temperature, and also the intensity and general character of such reactions. Generally the apparatus is arranged to record the difference in temperature between an inert, nonreacting substance and the reacting material. Especially useful in the analysis of clay minerals.

differential weathering When rocks are not uniform in character but are softer or more soluble in some places than in others, an uneven surface may be developed; in deserts by the action of the wind and in moist regions by solution. Columns of rock which have been isolated in any way show the effect of differential weathering.

differentiated dike A dike that consists of more than one kind of rock because of magmatic differentiation of an originally homogeneous magma into two or more fractions.

differentiated sill A sill that consists of more than one kind of rock because of magmatic differentiation of an originally homogeneous magma into two or more fractions.

differentiation, gravitational Differentiation accomplished through the existence of a gravitational field, as by sinking of a heavy phase (liquid or crystals), or the rising of a light phase (liquid, crystals, or gases) through the magma.

diffraction *1.* Term applied to the bending of rays not in accord with Snell's law, as, for example, the bending of rays around obstacles. *2.* The interference of light or other forms of radiant energy, such as X rays, electrons, and neutrons, produced by scattering due to edges or points of material objects. The essential feature in each case is that the scattering centers be separated by distances that are comparable to the wave length of the radiation. 3. *Seismol:* A seismic pulse emanating from an upper edge of a faulted reflecting horizon, or from a convex upward sudden change in dip of a reflecting horizon having the appearance and some of the properties of a reflection pulse.

diffraction of water waves The phenomenon by which energy is transmitted laterally along a wave crest. When a portion of a train of waves is interrupted by a barrier such as a breakwater, the effect of diffraction is manifested by propagation of waves into the sheltered region within the barrier's geometric shadow.

diffraction spacing Spacing of diffraction lines or points in the X-ray photograph of a mineral.

diffusion The spreading out of molecules, atoms, or ions into a vacuum, a fluid, or a porous medium, in a direction tending to equalize concentrations in all parts of a system.

diffusion coefficient A parameter in diffusion calculations, having the dimensions distance-squared divided by time. It varies with the nature of the particles diffusing, the nature of the diffusion medium, and temperature. It is expressed by the formula: $[l^2\ t^{-1}]$ where l=length, t=time.

diffusivity, thermal Coefficient of thermal diffusion. A thermal property of matter, with the dimensions of area per unit time.

diggings Applicable to all mineral deposits and mining camps, but in usage in the United States applied to placer mining only.

digitation A subsidiary recumbent anticline emanating from a much larger recumbent anticline. Where several such smaller folds are associated, they resemble the fingers of a hand.

dike *1.* A tabular body of igneous rock that cuts across the structure of adjacent rocks or cuts massive rocks. Although most dikes result from the intrusion of magma, some are the result of metasomatic replacement. *2.* A wall or mound built around a low-lying area to prevent flooding.

dikelet A small offshoot or apophysis from a dike.

dike set A group of parallel dikes.

dike swarm A set of parallel dikes, but more numerous than in a dike set.

dike wall Sometimes crevices in the rocks are filled with lavas from below; then the lavas cool into rocks of a firmer texture than those of the adjacent formations; afterward, by degradation, the softer rocks on either side are carried away, and the lava rocks stand in walls. Lavas intruded in this manner are called dikes, and dike walls are common in volcanic regions.

dilatational wave P-wave, *q.v.*

dilation *1.* The expansion of ice from the freezing of water in fissures. *2.* Dilatation. Deformation that is change in volume, but not in shape. *3. Volcanol:* The process of widening of an initial fissure concomitant with the injection of magma.

dilation dike Dike resulting from the intrusion of magma into a fracture whose walls moved away from each other.

dilation veins Fat lenses in schists thought to be caused by bulging of schistose rocks due to pressure transmitted by mineralizing solutions.

diluvial *1.* Pertaining to floods. *2.* Related to or consisting of diluvium.

diluvium *Obs.* *1.* Masses of waste which are now recognized as the result of glacial action, but which, when the term was applied, were supposed to be due to great floods. *2.* Name given to all coarse superficial accumulations which were formerly supposed to have resulted from a general deluge; now employed as a general term for all the glacial and fluvio-glacial deposits of the Ice age.

dimensional orientation *Struct. petrol:* A preferred orientation that is shown by the shape of the individual grains.

dimension stone Stone that is quarried or cut in accordance with required dimensions.

dimorph One of the two forms of a dimorphic crystalline chemical compound or organism.

dimorphism *1. Paleontol:* The characteristic of having two distinct forms in the same species, as male and female, megaspheric and microspheric stages. *2. Mineral:* The crystallization in two crystal forms of the same chemical compound, e.g., pyrite and marcasite.

Dinantian Lower Carboniferous.

dioctahedral Refers to the structure of layered clay minerals in which only two-thirds of the possible octahedral positions of aluminum are occupied by other cations.

diopside *See* PYROXENE

diorite A plutonic rock composed essentially of sodic plagioclase (usually andesine) and hornblende, biotite, or pyroxene. Small amounts of quartz and orthoclase may be present.

dioxide An oxide containing two atoms of oxygen per molecule, e.g., MnO_2, ZrO_2.

dip, *n.* *1.* The angle at which a stratum or any planar feature is inclined from the horizontal. The dip is at a right angle to the strike. *2.* In England, a heading or other underground way driven to the deep. *3.* A dip entry, dip room, etc. A heading driven to the full rise in steep mines.

dip-and-fault structure A structure in which an inclined series of beds, dipping in one direction, is cut by gravity (normal) faults dipping in the opposite direction. Sometimes the result of superficial movements under gravity.

dip calculation Any of a number of methods of converting observed seismic arrival time values to the dip of a reflector; most commonly the conversion of delta T values to dip values by a conversion factor based upon the geometry of the seismic array and approximate seismic propagational velocity.

dip compass Dipping compass; dip needle, *q.v.*

dip fault A fault that strikes approximately perpendicularly to the strike of the bedding or cleavage.

dip joint A joint that strikes approximately perpendicularly to the strike of the bedding or cleavage.

diploblastic Refers to structure of animals consisting of ectodermal and endodermal layers but without true mesoderm.

dip logging Any of several methods, electrical and caliper, of measuring the dip of formations traversed by boreholes.

diploid *1.* Isometric crystal form composed of 24 faces each meeting the axes at unequal distances. *2.* Refers to cells furnished with two sets of chromosomes.

diploidy Condition of having two of each kind of chromosome; normal in all but sex cells.

dip needle A magnetized needle suspended on a horizontal pivot and provided with a counter arm so that both the sensitivity and position of the needle may be controlled.

dipole Any object that is oppositely charged at two points. Most commonly refers to a molecule that has concentrations of positive and negative charge at two different points.

dip separation In faulting, the distance between two parts of a disrupted index plane (bed, dike, vein, etc.) measured in the fault plane parallel to its dip.

dip shift Dip slip, q.v.

dip shooting Any system of seismic surveying where the primary concern, both instrumental and computational, is the registration and computation of reflections for dip values, with minor emphasis on correlation of records from shot point to shot point.

dip slip The component of the slip parallel with the fault dip, or its projection on a line in the fault surface perpendicular to the fault strike.

dip-slip fault A fault in which the net slip is practically in the line of the fault dip.

dip slope A slope of the land surface which conforms approximately to the dip of the underlying rocks.

dip-strike symbol The symbol used on geological maps to show the strike and dip of some planar feature, such as bedding, foliation, joints, etc.

dip throw The component of the slip measured parallel with the dip of the strata.

dipyramid Crystal form consisting of two pyramids meeting at a plane of symmetry.

directional drilling The art of drilling a borehole wherein the course of the hole is planned before drilling. Such holes are usually drilled with rotary equipment, and are useful in drilling divergent tests from one location, tests which otherwise might be inaccessible, as, controls for fire and wild wells, etc.

directional structure All those sedimentary structures which have directional significance, and including crossbedding, flow markings, and ripple marks.

direct runoff That part of the runoff which consists of water that has not passed beneath the surface since it was last precipitated out of the atmosphere.

dirt-band ogive Alaskan band, q.v.

dirt cone Debris cone, q.v. *1.* Protecting as it does the ice below, a local ice hillock rises upon its dirt patch site as the surrounding surface is lowered, and as this grows in height its declivities increase and a portion of the dirt slides down the side. The first product of this shaping is an almost perfectly conical ice hill encased in dirt and known as a debris, sand, or dirt cone. *2.* A cone of ice or snow formed through the protection from ablation afforded by a thin veneer of dirt or debris.

disappearing stream A surface stream that disappears underground in a sink.

discharge Rate of flow at a given instant in terms of volume per unit of time.

discoidal Having the form of a disk.

discolith A discoidal coccolith.

disconformity *1.* Unconformity between parallel strata: *cf.* ANGULAR UNCONFORMITY. *2.* Such an unconformity marked by appreciable erosional relief; *cf.* PARA-

CONFORMITY. 3. Local contact plane in dike where flow structures are discordant.

discontinuities in earth structure Sudden or rapid changes with depth in one or more of the physical properties of the materials constituting the earth, as evidenced by seismic data.

discontinuous deformation Deformation of rocks accomplished by rupture rather than by flowage.

discontinuous permafrost zone Regional zone, intermediate between continuous permafrost zone and sporadic permafrost zone, underlain by permafrost in some areas and free of permafrost in other areas.

discontinuous reaction series That branch of Bowen's reaction series, q.v., including the minerals olivine, pyroxene, amphibole, and biotite, each change in the series representing an abrupt phase change.

discordance Geol: A lack of parallelism between contiguous strata; an unconformity.

discordant A term used to describe an igneous contact that cuts across the bedding or foliation of adjacent rocks.

discordant basin A shallow negative area in an island arc region which cuts across the other structural trends.

discovery claim The first claim in which a mineral deposit is found, and when this is within a gulch or on a stream the claims are simply marked or numbered from the discovery claim either by letters or figures up or down the gulch or stream.

discovery well A well discovering oil or gas in a pool hitherto unknown and unproductive.

disequilibrium assemblage As-sociated minerals not in thermodynamic equilibrium.

disharmonic fold 1. A fold in which abrupt changes in geometric relations occur in passing from one bed to another, especially where alternations of plastic and rigid beds occur. 2. A fold that changes in form with depth.

disharmonic relations Deviation from parallelism in beds or planes as inclinations vary.

disintegration 1. A term often applied to the natural mechanical breaking down of a rock on weathering. 2. That stage in the decomposition of vegetable and animal substances which takes place in the presence of oxygen and moisture and which may be regarded as a slow combustion of organic substance, leaving no solid carbon compounds and producing only volatile substances, namely carbon dioxide and water. Cf. MOLDERING; PEAT FORMATION; PUTREFACTION. 3. The breaking down of striae in a brachiopod.

disjunctive folds Folds in which brittle beds, interbedded with more plastic beds, pull apart to become separate blocks.

disk The shape of a solid which is notably flat, and elongated in two directions, classified by Theodore Zingg as one in which the ratio of breadth to length is greater than 2/3, and the ratio of thickness to breadth is less than 2/3.

dislocation 1. Displacement of rocks on opposite sides of a fracture relative to each other. Sometimes used synonymously with fault. 2. Crystallog. and Metal: A structural defect on a crystal.

dismembered river system A river system consisting of a trunk river and tributaries, the lower part of which has been flooded by the sea. As a result of flooding, the streams which were formerly tributaries of the trunk river enter the sea by separate mouths.

disorder In crystals, a statistical randomness in the filling of certain available sites by given atoms, or in the choice of between two or more atomic varieties for a given site.

dispersal pattern *Geochem. prospecting:* Pattern of distribution of metal content of soil, rock, water, or vegetation.

dispersed phase Material in the form of colloidal particles suspended in another substance called the continuous phase or dispersion medium.

dispersion *1. Opt. mineral:* The optical constants for different parts of the spectrum. The indices of refraction of a substance vary with the wave length of the transmitted light in crystals of low symmetry (monoclinic and triclinic). The principal optical directions within the crystal vary with the wave length of light. *2. Seismol:* A sorting of wave trains of different wave lengths due to a variation of speed with wave length in the medium.

dispersion halo A region surrounding an ore deposit in which the ore-metal concentration is intermediate between that of the ore and that of the country rock.

displacement *1.* The word "displacement" should receive no technical meaning, but is reserved for general use; it may be applied to a relative movement of the two sides of the fault, measured in any direction, when that direction is specified; for instance, the displacement of a stratum along a drift in a mine would be the distance between the two sections of the stratum

measured along the drift. The word "dislocation" will also be most useful in a general sense. *2. Chem.* A reaction in which an elementary substance displaces and sets free a constituent element from a compound.

displacement plane The a-b fabric plane of structural petrology.

displacement pressure The minimum pressure required to force the entry of a nonwetting fluid into a porous medium saturated with a wetting liquid.

disposal well A well drilled or used for disposal of brines or other fluids in order to prevent contamination of the surface by such wastes.

disrupted gouge Similar to chattermarks, but of more striking character. They mark the action of a large mass of rock carried forcibly over a rock surface whose nature favors a coarse, rough breakage rather than a smooth gouge.

dissected *1.* Cut by erosion into hills and valleys or into flat upland areas separated by valleys. Applicable especially to plains or peneplains in process of erosion after an uplift. *2. Paleobot:* Divided into many slender segments.

dissection *Geol:* The work of erosion in destroying the continuity of a relatively even surface by cutting ravines or valleys into it.

disseminated ore Ore carrying fine particles of minerals, usually sulfides, scattered through rock or gangue matter, and without genetic significance.

dissociation The breakdown of a substance into several others, as $CaCO_3 \rightarrow CaO + CO_2$ by heat, or $NaCl \rightarrow Na^+ + Cl^-$ by solution in water.

dissociation constant The equilibrium constant for a dissociation reaction; the product of activities (or less accurately, of concentrations) of the products of dissociation divided by the activity (or concentration) of the original substance. Commonly used for ionization reactions, in which case it is synonymous with ionization constant. The dissociation constant of a very slightly soluble compound is called its solubility product.

dissociation point The temperature at which a compound breaks up reversibly to form two or more other substances, e.g., $CaCO_3 \rightarrow CaO + CO_2$. To define the point precisely, all variables should be stated, such as pressure and composition of any gaseous or liquid phase surrounding the compound itself. "Dissociation" refers to the breakup itself, and covers a wide variety of types, such as the breakup of molecular groupings in gases or liquids.

dissociation temperature A presumed fixed temperature "point" at which a given dissociation occurs; actually, it is usually a range due to the compositional or pressure variance, and may refer merely to the temperature at which the rate of a given dissociation becomes appreciable, under stated conditions.

dissolution The process of dissolving or, more rarely, of melting.

distal; distalis, *adj.* Ventral. That part of a pollen grain or spore which is turned outward in its tetrad. In monopored or monocolpate grains, it is the side upon which the pore or furrow is borne. In other grains, the distal and proximal sides are generally not distinguishable from each other after the tetrad has been broken up into individual grains. In pores, the distal side is opposite the tetrad scar.

distaxy Unlike crystallographic orientation in a mineral grain and overgrowth.

disthene *Syn:* KYANITE

distillation The process of decomposition whereby the original chitinous material of certain fossils has lost its nitrogen, oxygen, and hydrogen, and is now represented by a film of carbonaceous material.

distortion Change in shape.

distortional waves Equivolumnar waves; secondary waves; shear waves; transverse waves; S-waves, *q.v.*

distributary *1.* An outflowing branch of a river, such as occurs characteristically on a delta. *2.* A river branch flowing away from the main stream and not rejoining it. Contrasted with tributary.

distribution scatter Graphic representation of relations of specimens with respect to chosen variable characters. *Cf.* SCATTER DIAGRAM

distributive province The environment embracing all rocks that contribute to the formation of a contemporaneous sedimentary deposit and the agents responsible for their distribution.

disturbance *1.* The bending or faulting of rock or stratum from its original position. *2.* Folding and/or faulting that affects a large area but is not extensive enough to be called a revolution. The distinction between a disturbance and a revolution is very arbitrary.

diurnal Daily. Applied to many meteorological phenomena having a distinctive daily behavior. For instance, there exist two types of well-defined diurnal pressure changes. One obtains at places of considerable elevation and is marked by a barometric maximum during the warmest hours and minimum during the coldest. The other applies to low, especially sea level, stations and is the reverse of the above, the maximum occurring during the coldest hours and the minimum during the warmest.

divergence *1.* Adaptive radiation, *q.v.* *2.* In refraction phenomena, the spreading of orthogonals in the direction of wave travel. This denotes an area of decreasing wave height and energy concentration. *3.* In wind-setup phenomena, the decrease in setup observed under that which would occur in an equivalent rectangular basin of uniform depth, caused by changes in planform or depth. Also the increase in basin width or depth causing such decrease in setup.

diverted stream In stream piracy the stream that was diverted from the beheaded stream to the pirate stream. *See* PIRACY

divide The line of separation between drainage systems; the summit of an interfluve. The highest summit of a pass or gap.

diviner One who purportedly divines the location of oil, gas, water, or ore deposits in the earth; a dowser.

divining rod Dowsing rod; wiggle stick. Forked twig considered by some to have magic properties when held in the hands of a dowser. Twig is supposed to dip when held over ore, oil, or water deposits, depending upon the specialty of the dowser.

Djulfian Upper upper Permian.

D layer Atmospheric zone within the chemosphere at height of about 50 km. that reflects low frequency radio waves.

DNA Deoxyribonucleic acid concentrated mainly in the nuclear structures of organisms.

do- *Petrol:* A prefix indicating that one factor dominates over another within the ratios 7/1 and 5/3 (7 and 1.67); e.g., docrystalline, docalcic, etc.

doab [*Hind.*] *1.* The name given in India to the tongue of land that lies between the confluence of two or more rivers, as the doabs of the Punjab, or plains that lie between the rivers of that regions. *2.* A dark sandy clay found in the vicinity of many Irish bogs.

dodecahedron *1.* The isometric crystal form composed of twelve rhombic faces, each parallel to one crystallographic axis and intersecting the other two at equal distances; specifically called the rhombic dodecahedron. *2.* Any isometric form consisting of twelve congruent faces, as the pentagonal dodecahedron or pyritohedron, the tetrahedral pentagonal dodecahedron or tetartoid, etc.

Dogger Middle Jurassic.

dogtooth spar A variety of calcite with sharp-pointed crystals.

dolarenite Dolomite rock consisting of sand sized grains.

doldrums The equatorial belt of calms or light fitful winds, lying between the northeast winds of the Northern Hemisphere and the southeast trades of the Southern. The doldrums are variable in position, and tend to move north and south with the sun, with a lag of about six weeks, though they are more often north than south of the equator. In addition to the absence of sustained wind, the doldrums are subject to heavy downpours, thunderstorms, and squalls.

dolerite Applied in Great Britain to fresh basaltic rocks with ophitic texture. Used in the same sense as diabase in used in the U.S.A.

doleritic *See* OPHITIC; DIABASIC

dolimorphic A term applied to rocks in which released minerals are prominent. An example is a lamprophyre from Madagascar consisting essentially of biotite and quartz with a little hornblende.

dolinen; doline; dolina *1.* The dolinen (called by English writers swallow holes, sinkholes, or cockpits) are rounded hollows varying from 30 to 3000 feet in diameter, and from 6 to 330 feet in depth. They may be either dish-, funnel-, or well-shaped. *2.* [*It.*] Name given to the funnel-shaped cavities which communicate with the underground drainage-system in limestone regions. Similar cavities are known in this country as sinks and swallow holes.

dolomite *1.* A mineral, CaMg-$(CO_3)_2$, commonly with some Fe replacing Mg (ankerite). Hexagonal rhombohedral. A common rock-forming mineral. *2.* A term applied to those rocks that approximate the mineral dolomite in composition. *Syn:* MAGNESIAN LIMESTONE. It occurs in a great many crystalline and noncrystalline forms the same as pure limestone, and among rocks of all geological ages. When the carbonate of magnesia is not present in the above proportion the rock may still be called a magnesian limestone, but not a dolomite, strictly speaking.

dolomite limestone Term applied to a carbonate rock composed predominantly of dolomite. (Not recommended.)

dolomitization The process whereby limestone becomes dolomite by the substitution of magnesium carbonate for a portion of the original calcium carbonate.

dolomold (*Insol. residue*) Originally called dolocast. *Obs.* Rhombohedral cavities of any size left in chert, pyrite, shale, limonite, glauconite, etc., by the solution of dolomite (or calcite) crystals.

dolomorphic In an insoluble residue a condition in which calcite or dolomite has been replaced by an insoluble mineral which fills the rhombohedral dolomoldic cavity in chert or other matrix.

dolostone A term proposed by R. R. Shrock for a sedimentary rock composed of fragmental, concretionary, or precipitated dolomite of organic or inorganic origin.

domain By domain is meant the areal extent of a given lithology or environment. Thus the domain of a facies of sedimentation refers to the area wherein a given set of physical controls combined to produce a distinctive facies.

dome *1.* A roughly symmetrical upfold, the beds dipping in all directions, more or less equally, from a point. *2.* A smoothly rounded, rock-capped mountain summit, roughly resembling the dome or cupola of a building. *3.* An open crystal form consisting of two faces astride a symmetry plane. *4.* A prism parallel to one of the lateral axes a or b. *Obs. 5.* A pinacoid cutting the vertical axis c and one of the lateral axes $\overline{a}$ or b. *Obs. 6.* (Oceanic) The dome [*Ger.* Kuppe; *Fr.* dome], an elevation of small area, but rising with a steep angle to a depth more than 200 meters from the surface. *7.* Any structural deformation characterized by local uplift approximately circular in outline, e.g., the salt domes of Louisiana and Texas.

domed mountain Mountain formed from pressure below rather than from lateral compression.

Domerian Upper Charmouthian.

dominant vitrain A field term to denote, in accordance with an arbitrary scale established for use in describing banded coal, a frequency of occurrence of vitrain bands comprising more than 60% of the total coal layer.

doodlebug Any one of a large number of unscientific devices with which it is claimed minerals and oil deposits can be located.

Dordonian Maestrichtian.

dornick; dornock In the United States, a small rock or boulder; specifically a boulder of iron ore found in limonite mines.

dorsal, *adj.* Back; relating to the back or outer surface of a part or organ, as, the lower side of a leaf; the opposite of ventral.

dorsiventral, *adj.* Refers to plant structures which have structurally different upper and lower surfaces, e.g., many leaves, fern prothalli, liverwort thalli.

dot chart *1.* Graphical aid used in correction of station gravity for terrain effect, or computing gravity effects of irregular masses; can be used also in magnetic interpretation. A graticule. *2.* A graphical, transparent chart used in the calculation of the gravity effects of various structures; dots on the chart represent unit areas.

double layer Ionic atmosphere containing enough ions of one charge to equal the opposite charge of a surrounded particle.

double refraction *See* BIREFRINGENCE

doubly plunging fold A fold that

plunges in opposite directions from a central point. In a doubly plunging anticline, the plunge is away from this point; in a doubly plunging syncline, the plunge is toward this point.

douse; douce; dowse *1.* To beat out or to extinguish an ignited jet of fire damp. To search for deposits of ore, for lodes, or water, by aid of the dousing or divining rod.

downbuckle Abrupt downward bending of the earth's crust.

down-cutting stream *See* CORRADING STREAM

down-dip block Block on the down-dip side of a strike fault.

downdrift The direction of predominant movement of littoral materials.

downs *1.* A term usually applied to hillocks of sand thrown up by the sea, or the wind along the seacoast. It is also a general name for any undulating tract of upland too light for cultivation and covered with short grass. *2.* A hill; especially a bank or hillock of sand thrown up by the wind in or near the shore; a flattish-topped hill. A tract of open upland, often undulating and covered with a fine turf which serves chiefly for the grazing of sheep.

downthrow The wall of a fault that has moved relatively downward. "Downthrown" is preferred by USGS.

Downtonian Uppermost Silurian or lowermost Devonian.

down-valley migration (meanders) As soon as the initial bends are developed in a young river into somewhat systematic curves or meanders, it not only deepens its valley, but also widens the meander belt, and pushes the whole system of curves down valley.

downward enrichment A term which is synonymous with "secondary enrichment" as the latter has applied to enrichment of ore bodies by the downward percolation of waters.

downwarp Term meaning opposite of upwarp, *q.v.*

downwasting The diminishing of glacier ice in thickness during ablation.

dowser One who operates a divining rod, *q.v.*

dowsing Searching for water, oil, or minerals with a dowsing rod.

dowsing rod Divining rod, *q.v.* Wiggle stick.

drag *1.* Minor folding or strata along the walls of a fault in in which the "drag" of displacement has produced flexures in the beds on either side. *2.* Fragments of ore torn from a lode by faulting and remaining in the fault zone. *3.* A name applied to occurrences of roof shale penetrating downward into a coal seam. They are associated with boulders in the coal, and their form clearly demonstrates that they result from the sinking of the boulders through the soft peat.

drag folds In the narrow sense, minor folds that form in an incompetent bed when the competent beds on either side of it move in such a way as to subject it to a couple. The axes of the minor folds are perpendicular to the direction in which the beds slip; the acute angle between the main bedding and the axial planes of the drag folds indicate the direction of the shear. In a broad sense, used for any fold that is a subsidiary part of a larger fold.

drag mark *1.* Long even mark commonly with longitudinal striations produced by current drag of an object across a sedimentary surface. *2.* Impression or cast of such a mark on the under surface of an overlying bed.

dragon's skin In England, a familiar term among miners and quarrymen for the stems of Lepidodendron, whose rhomboidal leaf scars somewhat resemble the scales of reptiles.

drainage *1.* The processes of discharge of water from an area by stream or sheet flow and removal of excess water from soil by downward flow. *2.* The means for effecting the removal of water.

drainage area A term applied to that area of a reservoir contributing oil or gas to a well. It is a poor descriptive term because it suggests gravity rather than pressure as the agent of movement. It is inexact because any such "area" is affected by thickness, porosity, permeability, and pressure.

drainage basin *Hydrol:* A part of the surface of the lithosphere that is occupied by a drainage system or contributes surface water to that system.

drainage characteristics The hydrology and related features of streams, lakes, swamps, marshes, and canals within an area. Includes consideration, in their seasonal aspects, of depths, widths, banks, bottom conditions, velocities, gradients, turbidity, sedimentation, temperatures, ice conditions, and other pertinent related items.

drainage density *Geomorph:* Symbol D, D_d. Ratio of total length of all channels within a drainage basin to the area of that basin; a measure of topographic scale or texture.

drainage divide A drainage divide is the rim of a drainage basin. It is the boundary between adjacent drainage basins. The term watershed has been used to mean both drainage basin and drainage divide, and the uncertainty of meaning entailed by this double usage makes the term undesirable.

drainage pattern Arrangement of natural drainage lines within an area; patterns are related to local geology and geologic history.

drainage system A stream and its tributaries constitute a drainage system, and the area drained by a river system through a valley system is a drainage basin.

drapery Curtainlike forms of travertine, usually formed through the union of a row of stalactites.

draw 1. In the United States, a ravine, usually dry, but forming a watercourse in a freshet, furrowed vertically by torrents. 2. A valley or basin readily convertible into an irrigation reservoir by constructing a dam across its outlet. 3. A natural depression or swale; a small natural drainageway.

drawdown The lowering of the water table or piezometric surface caused by pumping (or artesian flow).

draw works In rotary drilling, that part of the equipment functioning as a hoist to raise or lower drill pipe, and in some types to transmit power to the rotary table.

dreikanter Pebble shaped by eolian sandblasting with plane faces bounded by three sharp edges or angles.

Dresbachian Lower Croixan.

drewite Drewite is a title proposed for the calcareous ooze consisting of impalpable calcareous material, most of which is probably precipitated through the agency of denitrifying bacteria. Formed of minute aragonite needles.

drift 1. A horizontal passage underground. A drift follows the vein, as distinguished from a crosscut, which intersects it, or a level or gallery, which may do either. 2. *Coal min:* A gangway or entry above water level, driven from the surface in the seam. 3. Any rock material, such as boulders, till, gravel, sand, or clay, transported by a glacier and deposited by or from the ice or by or in water derived from the melting of the ice. Generally used of the glacial deposits of the Pleistocene epoch. Detrital deposits. 4. Detrital material washed into a cave from a sink or vertical entrance. 5. Floating material deposited on a beach. Driftwood. 6. The motion, of sea, ice or of vessels, resulting from ocean currents and wind stress. 7. Wind-driven snow in motion along the surface, sometimes rising to heights of 100 feet or more. 8. Snow lodged in the lee of surface irregularities under the influence of the wind. 9. *Geophys:* A time variation common to nearly all sensitive gravimeters, due to slow changes occurring in the springs or mountings of the instrumental systems; this variation is corrected by repeated observations at a base station and in other ways.

drift-barrier lake *See* MORAINAL LAKE

drift current A broad, shallow, slow-moving ocean or lake current.

drift curve Graph of a series of gravity values read at the same station at different times and plotted in terms of instrument reading versus time.

drift deposit Any accumulation of glacial origin; glacial or fluvio-glacial deposit.

drift glaciers Small glaciers nourished by blown snow.

drift ice *1.* Floating ice. *2.* Any ice that has drifted from its place of origin.

drifting Opening a drift; driving a drift. *See* DRIFT, *1, 2*

drift map A map showing the distribution of various glacial and fluvio-glacial deposits, generally called drift.

drift mine A mine opened by a drift.

drift sheet A sheetlike body of glacial drift, continuous or discontinuous, deposited during a single glaciation (e.g., Cary drift sheet) or during a closely related succession of glaciations (e.g., Wisconsin drift sheet).

drift theory That theory of the origin of coal which holds that the plant matter constituting coal was washed from its original place of growth and deposited in another locality where coalification then came about.

drilling mud A suspension, generally aqueous, used in rotary drilling and pumped down through the drill pipe to seal off porous zones and to counterbalance the pressure of oil and gas; consists of various substances in a finely divided state among which bentonite and barite are common. Oil may be used as a base instead of water.

drill-stem test A test of the productive capacity of a well when still full of drilling mud. The testing tool is lowered into the hole attached to the drill pipe and placed opposite the formation to be tested. Packers are set to shut off the weight of the drilling mud, and the tool is opened to permit the flow of any formation fluid into the drill pipe, where it can be measured.

driphole *1.* A small hole or niche in clay or rock beneath a point where water drips. *2.* The center hole in a formation built up beneath a water drip.

dripstone Material deposited by dripping solution. A single term to replace stalactite and stalagmite.

driven well A well which is sunk by driving a casing, at the end of which there is a drive point, without the aid of any drilling, boring, or jetting device.

drive pipe *1.* A pipe which is driven or forced into a bored hole, to shut off water, or prevent caving. *2.* A thick type of casing fitted at its lower end with a sharp steel shoe, which is employed when heavy driving has to be resorted to for inserting the casing.

drive shoe A protecting end attached to the bottom of drive pipe and casing.

drought Dryness due to lack of rain. An absolute drought is a period of at least 15 consecutive days to none of which is credited 0.01 inches of rain or more. A partial drought is a period of at least 29 consecutive days, the mean daily rainfall of which does not exceed 0.01 inches. A dry spell is a period of at least 15 consecutive days to none of which is credited 0.04 inches or more.

drown To submerge land with water, whether by a rise in the level of a lake, ocean, or river, or by a sinking of the land, as the lowering of a coastal region drowns the lower courses of the rivers and connects their valleys into estuaries.

drowned coast The presence of certain long, narrow channels which are largely free from islands suggests that a subsidence of the coast has transformed the lower portions of the old river valleys into tidal estuaries, thus changing a hilly land surface into an archipelago of small islands. A shore line exhibiting these characteristics is termed a "drowned coast."

drowned glacial erosion coast A coast having deep estuaries with basin depressions. Fiords and wide glacial troughs like the St. Lawrence, Bay of Fundy, the Skaggerack, and the White Sea are examples.

drowned river mouth When a section of the coast line sinks with reference to the sea, the water invades all the near shore valleys, thus "drowning" them and yielding a drowned river mouth or estuary.

drowned topography Depression whereby the lower courses of most of the rivers are submerged beneath the sea hastens the reduction of what is left above sea level, and by decreasing the slope of the lower courses often causes the building of flood plains at these points. The coasts of Maine, Norway, and Maryland afford excellent examples of such topography.

drum; drumlin [<*Ir., Gael.* druim; also druman, the back, a ridge, summit] *1.* Gravel hills that have an elongated form, are generally steepest toward one side, and rise in every other direction by much more gentle acclivities. *2.* Till is sometimes accumulated in hills of elliptical base and arched profile, known as drumlins, the longer axis often measuring half a mile or more and standing parallel to the direction in which the ice sheet moved, the height reaching 100

to 200 feet. *3.* A streamlined hill or ridge of glacial drift with long axis paralleling direction of flow of former glacier.

druse *1.* A crust of small crystals lining the sides of a cavity, usually the same minerals as those that constitute the enclosing rock. *2.* A cavity of this sort. *3.* (*Insol. residue*) Clusters or aggregates of subhedral crystals with definitely developed faces, commonly incrusted. May be microgeodic. Applied to chert, quartz, oölites, and others. *4.* A hole or bubble in glacial ice filled with a mixture of air and ice crystals.

drusy, *adj.* *1.* A term applied to rocks containing numerous druses. Miarolitic, *q.v.* *2.* A term used to express the appearance or habit of a crystalline aggregate whose surface is covered with a layer of small crystals.

drusy mosaic Crystalline mosaic produced by the deposition of minerals from solution in cavities other than the pores between sedimentary particles.

dry (state of ground, *q.v.*) Condition in which pore space of ground to depths of 3 inches or more is essentially free of water (moisture content is less than permanent wilting percentage, *q.v.*).

dry basin If an interior basin exists in a climate so arid that the superficial flow of water, which constitutes drainage, is only potential and not actual, or else is occasional only and not continuous, it contains no perennial lake and is called a dry basin.

dry-bone ore A miner's term for an earthy, friable carbonate of zinc. Smithsonite, *q.v.* Frequently applied to the hydrated silicate, so-called calamine. Usually found associated in veins or beds is stratified calcareous rocks accompanying sulfides of zinc, iron, and lead. Locally applied to zinc silicate ore.

dry bulk density Natural density.

dry delta Alluvial fan, alluvial cone.

dry firn A dry granular snow which has been compacted by the combined action of sun, wind, and fluctuations in air temperature; also called "dry old snow."

dry hole Somewhat loosely used in oil and gas development, but in general any well that does not produce oil or gas in commercial quantity. A dry hole may flow water, a minor quantity of gas, or may even yield some oil, the oil or gas being in volumes too small to be profitable.

dry ice 1. Solid CO_2 2. Bare glacier ice with no standing water or slush. 3. Ice with temperature below the freezing point.

dry ore An argentiferous ore that does not contain enough lead for smelting purposes.

dry pergelisol Soil material having the requisite mean temperature to be permanently frozen but lacking water.

dry permafrost Ground having the requisite mean temperature to be permanently frozen but lacking ice content, or "dry."

dry snow In the International Snow Classification, snow with a temperature at below the freezing point.

dry valley In England, a valley which, although originally carved out by running water, is now streamless. In the United States, such a valley is referred to as a wind gap.

DTA Abbreviation for Differential Thermal Analysis.

ductile 1. Capable of being drawn through the opening of a die without breaking and with a reduction of the cross-sectional area, as a ductile wire. 2. *Mineral:* Capable of considerable deformation, especially stretching, without breaking; said of several native metals and occasionally said of some tellurides and sulfides. 3. Pertaining to a substance that readily deforms plastically.

ductility Property of solid material that undergoes more or less plastic deformation before it ruptures.

dug well Well sunk by manual digging, shallow and of large diameter.

Duhem's theorem The state of any closed system is completely defined by the values of any two independent variables, extensive or intensive, provided the initial masses of each component are given. The choice of variables, however, must not conflict with the phase rule.

dull A surface texture of a pebble or grain that lacks luster. This lack is caused by numerous minute irregularities so that reflected light is diffused and scattered.

dumortierite A mineral, $Al_8BSi_3O_{19}(OH)$. Orthorhombic; blue, lavender, to greenish-blue. Used as raw material in the manufacture of mullite refractories.

dumpy level A leveling instrument in which the telescope is permanently attached to the leveling base, either rigidly or by a hinge that can be manipulated by means of a micrometer screw.

The dumpy level takes its name from the dumpy appearance of the early type of this instrument, the telescope of which was short and has a large object glass.

dune *1. Geol:* A low hill, or bank, of drifted sand. *2.* Mounds and ridges of wind-blown or eolian sand are dunes. Once started, a dune becomes an obstacle to blowing sand, and the lodgment of more sand causes the dune to grow. In this way, mounds and ridges of sand, scores and sometimes even hundreds of feet high are built by the wind. *3.* A mound, ridge, or hill of wind-blown sand, either bare or covered with vegetation. The term has been applied also to subaqueous features, but unless a suitable modifier is used with the term, an eolian denotation is assumed.

dune complex A group of wandering dunes which make up the moving landscape.

dune lake Lake formed as a result of blocking of the mouths of streams by sand transported along the shore by combined action of winds and waves.

dune ridge A series of parallel foredunes built along the shore of a retreating sea.

dunite A peridotite consisting almost wholly of olivine and containing accessory pyroxene and chromite.

durability index Term applied by C. K. Wentworth to the relative resistance to abrasion exhibited by a sedimentary particle in the course of transportation.

durain Material occurring in megascopic bands in coal characterized by gray to brownish-black color, rough surface, and faintly greasy luster; consists mainly of exinite and inertite.

duration In wave forecasting, the length of time the wind blows in essentially the same direction over the fetch (generating area).

duricrust The case-hardened crust of soil formed in semiarid climates by the precipitation of salts at the surface of the ground as the ground water evaporates. It contains aluminous, ferruginous, siliceous, and calcareous material.

durite *See* DURAIN

dust Dust consists of dry organic and inorganic matter so finely divided that it may be picked up and carried away by the atmosphere without difficulty.

dust, volcanic Pyroclastic detritus consisting mostly of particles less than 1/4 mm. in diameter, i.e., fine volcanic ash. It may be composed of essential, accessory, or accidental material.

dust avalanche Avalanche, *q.v.*, of dry, loose snow.

Dust Bowl Region in southwestern plains states subject to periodic severe drought.

dust hole Dust well.

dust storm *1.* A strong wind carrying large clouds of dust (or silt), common in desert and plain regions; its influence may be felt thousands of miles from the source. China, the United States, Egypt, the Sahara, the Gobi, and numerous other parts of the world are subject to dust storms. *2.* For the development of a dust storm, there are three essentials: (1) an ample supply of fine dust or dry silt, (2) relatively strong winds to stir it up, and (3) a steep lapse rate of temperature in the dust-carrying air. There is a marked distinction between dust storms and sandstorms, *q.v.*

dust tuff An indurated deposit of volcanic dust. Essentially a fine-grained tuff.

dust well *1.* A pit in glacier ice or sea ice produced when small dark particles on the ice surface are heated by sunlight and sink down into the ice. *2.* Cylindrical tubes generally penetrating the ice to a depth of six or eight inches. They range in size from less than one quarter inch to larger than a foot in diameter. *Syn:* CRYOCONITE HOLES, *q.v.;* DUST HOLES

dwarf fauna Depauperate fauna. A fauna characterized by fossils of stunted size.

dy A sapropel, composed of organic matter brought into a lake in colloidal form and precipitated there.

Dyas Permian.

dyke English spelling of dike.

dyke swarm *See* DIKE SWARM

dynamic breccia Tectonic breccia. An autoclastic rock clearly showing that it was formed as a result of tectonic movements which crushed and broke the formation. It usually is found in brittle rocks where loading has not been sufficient to render the rocks plastic.

dynamic climatology The explanation of climate according to the effects of atmospheric circulation.

dynamic geology Deals with the causes and processes of geological change.

dynamic metamorphism Dynamometamorphism. Metamorphism produced exclusively or largely by rock deformation, principally folding and faulting.

dynamochemical Refers to chemical activity induced by pressure and heat, particularly within the earth.

dynamometamorphism *See* DYNAMIC METAMORPHISM

dyne That force which produces an acceleration of 1 centimeter per second when acting upon a mass of 1 gram.

E

e-; ex- In Latin-formed words usually denotes that parts are missing, as: exstipulate, without stipules; estriate, without strips.

earth *1.* The solid matter of the globe in distinction from water and air. The ground. The firm land of the earth's surface. *2.* Loose material of the earth's surface; the disintegrated particles of solid matter in distinction from rock; soil. *3. Chem:* A name formerly given to certain inodorous, dry, and uninflammable substances which are metallic oxides but were formerly regarded as elementary bodies. *4.* A term used for soft shaly or clayey ground when sinking through the coal measures. *5.* Material which can be removed and handled economically with pick and shovel or by hand, or which can be loosened and removed with a power shovel.

earth current *1.* Telluric current. Natural electrical currents circulating in the crust of the earth, constituting a world-wide system subject both to spasmodic and periodic variations in intensity and direction which are consistently related to changes noted in other cosmic phenomena, such as the earth's magnetic field, the aurora and solar activity. *2.* A current flowing through a wire the extremities of which are grounded at points on the earth differing in electrical potential. The earth current is due to this difference, which is very generally temporary and often very large.

earth curvature *See* CURVATURE, EARTH

earth fall A landslide.

earth-flow A slow flow of earth lubricated with water, occurring as either a low-angle terrace flow or a somewhat steeper but slow hillside flow.

earth hummocks Patterned ground with an essentially circular mesh, a nonsorted appearance, and a form characterized by its three-dimensional, knoblike shape and cover of vegetation.

earth movement Differential movement of the earth's crust; local elevation or subsidence of the land.

earthquake Groups of elastic waves propagating in the earth, set up by a transient disturbance of the elastic equilibrium of a portion of the earth. Perceptible trembling to violent shaking of the ground, produced by the sudden displacement of rocks below the earth's surface.

earth's crust The external part of the earth, accessible to geological investigation. The use of this term does not necessarily imply that the rest of the earth is not also solid.

earth slide Earth slides are those which most nearly resemble snow slides. When a mass of earth begins to slide and still retains a certain cohesion it moves as a block or blocks without other apparent deformation than the change in level: this is the foirage (landslip) of the French authors and resembles the planche (board) of snow, the initial stage of the snowy avalanche. If the earth continues to slide a sufficient distance the mass breaks up, becomes pulverized, and then moves as a fluid substance; a phenomenon analogous to the course pursued by the ground avalanche.

earth temperature The temperature of the surface of the earth. Heat is received by direct radiation from the sun, by radiation and conduction from the atmosphere, and by conduction from below; heat is lost by radiation and conduction; the net balance between gain and loss determines the temperature.

The surface soils exhibit diurnal and seasonal changes in temperature. The diurnal changes are not usually noticeable below about 12 inches, but the seasonal changes extend to about 50 feet.

earth tilting A slight movement or displacement of the surface of the ground as in some forms of earthquakes.

earth tremor A slight earthquake.

earthy manganese Wad, *q.v.*

easement An incorporeal right existing distinct from the ownership of the soil, consisting of a liberty, privilege, or use of another's land without profit or compensation; a right of way.

ebb current The movement of the tidal current away from shore or down a tidal stream.

ebb tide A nontechnical term referring to that period of tide between a high water and the succeeding low water; falling tide.

echelon faults Separate faults having parallel but steplike trends; the group having one more or less general direction but with the individuals parallel to each other and at an angle to that direction. Thought to be the result of torsion in a region of differential diastrophism. From term en echelon, the original derivation of which was the Latin *scala,* ladder.

Echinodermata A phylum of exclusively marine, invertebrate animals, nearly all of whom have a radial and five-rayed symmetry, a skeleton made of calcium carbonate plates. Many spines, hence the popular name: spiny-skinned animals.

echinoid One of a group of invertebrates; a class of the Echinodermata which includes the sea urchins and their close allies.

Echinoidea Class of free-moving echinoderms mostly with rigidly plated bodies of spherical to flattened disklike forms; sea urchins, sand dollars. Ord.-Rec.

echo sounder A survey instrument that determines the depth of water by measuring the time required for a sound signal to travel to the bottom and return. It may be either "sonic" or "supersonic" depending on the frequency of sound wave, the "sonic" being generally within the audible ranges (under 15,000 cycles per sec.).

eclogite A granular rock composed essentially of garnet (almandine-pyrope) and pyroxene (omphacite).

eclogite facies Metamorphic rocks of gabbroid composition consisting mainly of omphacite (pyroxene) and garnet.

ecologic facies Facies determined by nature of environment.

ecology The study of the mutual

relationships between organisms and their environments.

E concept Approximately the contribution of a single ion to lattice energy, but also taken into account are surrounding ions and structural differences.

economic geology Deals with geological materials of practical utility and the application of geology to engineering. Generally used today in the narrow sense to include only the application of geology to mineral materials.

economic mineral Any mineral having a commercial value. *See* ORE

ecosystem Ecologic system; an organic community and its physical environment.

ecoulement A downhill gliding of a large mass of rock under the influence of gravity, during or as a result of tectonic deformation. Such a movement resulting from ordinary agents of erosion constitutes a landslide, *q.v.*

ectoderm The outer body layer of organisms.

Ectoprocta True bryozoans with anus outside of the lophophore circle. Ord.-Rec.

edaphic Pertaining to the soil, especially with respect to its influence on organisms; soil factors.

eddy A current of air or water running contrary to the main current, especially one moving in a circle; a whirlpool.

eddy current A circular movement of water of comparatively limited area formed on the side of a main current.

Edenian Lower Cincinnatian.

edge water The water surrounding or bordering oil or gas in a pool. Edge water usually encroaches on a field after much of the oil and gas has been recovered and the pressure has become greatly reduced.

edge-water drive A process whereby energy for the production of oil is derived principally from the pressure of edge water in the formation.

edgewise conglomerate A conglomerate consisting of small flat pieces of (usually calcareous) rocks packed in such a manner as to lie steeply inclined with reference to the bedding plane of the stratum.

Edrioasteroidea Class of discoidal echinoderms attached by their lower surfaces and bearing on their upper surfaces five ambulacral areas that resemble starfish. Camb.-Miss.

edrioasteroids Extinct Paleozoic echinoderms that combined some of characteristics of cystoids and starfish; flourished in the Ordovician.

effective permeability The observed permeability of a porous medium to one fluid phase under conditions of physical interaction between this phase and other fluid phases present.

effective porosity *1. Hydrol:* Often used in same sense as specific yield. It is the ratio of the volume of water, oil, or other liquid, which after being saturated with that liquid, it will yield under any specified hydraulic conditions to its own volume. *2.* The property of rock or soil containing intercommunicating interstices, expressed as a per cent of bulk volume occupied by such interstices.

effective size *Soil mech:* The maximum diameter of the smallest 10 per cent of the particles of a sediment. Equals the grain diameter at the 90 percentile in sedimentary petrography.

effective size of grain *Hydrol:* The diameter of the grains in an assumed rock or soil that would transmit water at the same rate as the rock or soil under consideration and that is composed of spherical grains of equal size and arranged in a specified manner.

effervesce To bubble and hiss, as limestone on which acid is poured.

effloresce To change on the surface or throughout to a powder from the loss of water of crystallization on exposure to the air. Efflorescent, *adj.*

efflorescence Surface encrustation, commonly powdery, produced by evaporation.

effluent [<*Lat.* ex, out; fluo, flow] *1.* Flowing forth out of. *Geol:* Flowing out, as lava through fissures in the side of a volcano, as a river from a lake. *2.* Anything that flows forth. *Geog:* A stream flowing out of another or forming the outlet of a lake.

effluent seepage Seepage out of the lithosphere.

effusion *1.* The act or process of effusing or pouring out; that which is effused or poured out. *2. Volcanol:* An emission of liquid lava or pyroclastic material from a vent or fissure.

effusive *1.* Pouring out; pouring forth freely. *2. Geol:* A term applied to that class of igneous rocks derived from magmas or magmatic materials poured out or ejected at the earth's surface (i.e., volcanic rocks), as distinct from the so-called intrusive or plutonic rocks that are injected at depth. *See* EXTRUSIVE ROCKS

Eh *See* OXIDATION-REDUCTION POTENTIAL

Eifelian Couvinian.

einkanter A ventifact upon which only one facet has been cut by wind-blown sand. *See* DREIKANTER; VENTIFACT

ejecta; ejectamenta Material thrown out by a volcano, such as ash, lapilli, bombs.

elastic aftereffect Creep recovery, *q.v.*

elastic afterworking Creep recovery, *q.v.*

elastic bitumen *See* ELATERITE

elastic constants Certain mathematical constants that serve to describe the elastic properties of matter.

elastic deformation A nonpermanent deformation, after which a body returns to its original shape when the load is released. Often limited to that deformation in which stress and strain are linearly related in accordance with Hooke's law.

elastic discontinuity Boundary between strata that reflects seismic waves.

elastic flow The part of the deformation from which the specimen recovers is called "elastic flow."

elasticity The property or quality of being elastic, i.e., an elastic body returns to its original form or condition after a displacing force is removed.

elastic limit The maximum stress that a specimen can withstand without undergoing permanent deformation either by solid flow or by rupture. *Syn:* YIELD POINT

elastic medium A material which returns to its original from or condition after a displacing force is removed.

elasticoviscous Liquivitreous.

elastic rebound The recovery of elastic strain.

elastic rebound theory Faulting arises from the sudden release of elastic energy which has slowly accumulated in the earth. Just before the rupture, the energy released by the faulting is entirely potential energy stored as elastic strain in the rocks. At the time of rupture the rocks on either side of the fault spring back to a position of little or no strain.

elaterite A massive amorphous dark-brown hydrocarbon ranging from soft and elastic to hard and brittle. It melts in a candle flame without decrepitation, has a conchoidal fracture, and gives a brown streak.

E layer Irregular atmospheric zone within ionosphere at height of about 150 km., intensely ionized; reflects medium frequency radio waves.

electrical well logging The process of recording the formations traversed by a drill hole, based on the measurements of two basic parameters observable in uncased holes; namely, the spontaneous potential (S.P.) and the resistivity of the formations to the flow of electric currents. The detailed study *in situ* of the formations penetrated by a drill hole, based on measurements made systematically by lowering an apparatus in the hole responding to the following physical factors or parameters: (1) the resistivities of the rocks; (2) their porosity, (3) their electrical anisotropy, (4) their temperature, (5) the resistivity of the drilling muds.

electric log The log of a well or borehole obtained by lowering electrodes in the hole and measuring various electrical properties of the geological formations traversed. Electrical current is introduced by a number of methods.

electric potential Force required to bring a unit charge from infinity to a charged point of the same sign or energy released by opposite movement.

electrochemical series Electromotive force series.

electrode Either terminal of an electric source; either of the conductors by which the current enters and leaves an electrolyte. May be a wire, a plate, or other conducting object.

electrode reaction The chemical reaction taking place at an electrode in contact with a solution; the reaction consists of the addition of electrons from the electrode to a substance in the solution, or the removal of electrons by the electrode from a substance in solution. *Syn:* HALF REACTION

electrojet Electromagnetic current flowing in the ionosphere; one follows the magnetic equator, two others occur at the poles.

electrokinetics Electric properties of moving substances.

electrolyte An electric conductor in which passage of current is accompanied by liberation of substances at the electrodes; also a substance which becomes such a conductor when dissolved in water. Electrolytes include acids, bases, and salts.

electromagnetic damping Commonly found in seismometers of the induction type. It may be used in mechanical seismographs by employing a copper plate moving between two permanent magnets. Induction seismometers depend upon voltage generated by motion of coil in the magnetic field.

electromagnetic prospecting A geophysical method employing the generation of electromagnetic waves at the earth's surface; when the waves penetrate the earth and impinge on a conducting formation or ore body they induce currents in the conductors which are the source of new waves radiated from the conductors and detected by instruments at the surface.

lectromotive force series Metallic elements arranged in the order of their standard electrode potentials and their ability to replace each other in solutions of their salts. In order of decreasing potential they are: K, Na, Ca, Mg, Fe++, Zn, Fe+++, Cu.

lectron The elementary particle of mass 9×10^{-28} grams and unit electrical charge (4.80×10^{-10} e.s.u.).

lectron capture A type of radioactive transformation in which an electron from one of the inner shells of an atom is captured by the nucleus; especially important in the transformation K^{40}—A^{40}.

lectronegativity Strength of the ionic bond of a cation. *See* ELECTROMOTIVE FORCE SERIES

lectron shell A group of electrons in an atom, all having approximately the same average distance from the nucleus and approximately the same energy.

lectron volt The kinetic energy acquired by an electron falling through a potential difference of 1 volt. It is equal to 1.6×10^{-12} erg.

lectro-osmosis Press of a solution against electric potential.

lectrostatic valence The quotient of the charge on a simple ion divided by its coordination number.

lectroviscosity Viscosity of fluids as influenced by electric properties. Viscosity generally increases more in low-conductivity solutions flowing through narrow capillaries than in high-conductivity fluids.

lectrum Argentian gold (Au, Ag), deep to pale yellow. *See* GOLD

element *1.* A substance which cannot be decomposed into other substances. *2.* A substance all of whose atoms have the same atomic number. The first definition was accepted until the discovery of radioactivity (1896), and is still useful in a qualitative sense. It is no longer strictly correct, because (a) natural radioactive decay involves the decomposition of one element into others, (b) one element may be converted into another by bombardment with high-speed particles, (c) an element can be separated into its isotopes. The second definition is accurate, but it has little relevance to ordinary chemical reactions or to geologic processes.

element, equant *Struct. petrol:* A fabric element of approximately equal dimensions.

element, fabric *Struct. petrol:* A single crystal or group of crystals which behaves as a unit with respect to the applied forces.

element, linear *Struct. petrol:* A fabric element of rodlike form where one dimension is much greater than the other two.

element, planar *Struct. petrol:* A fabric element having two dimensions conspicuously in excess of the third is described as planar.

Eleutherozoa Subphylum of echinoderms including all free-moving forms. Ord.-Rec.

elevation *1.* A particular height or altitude above a general level, as, the height of a locality above the level of the sea; of a building, etc.: above the level of the ground. *2.* In U.S., term generally refers to height in feet above mean sea level. *See* ALTITUDE, 2

elevation correction In gravity measurements, the corrections applied to observed gravity values because of differences of station elevation to reduce them to any arbitrary reference or datum level, usually sea level. The corrections consist of (1) the free-air correction, to take care of the vertical decrease of gravity with increase of elevation, and (2) the Bougeur correction, to take care of the attraction of the material between the reference datum and that of the individual station. *Seismol:* In seismic measurements, the corrections applied to observed reflection time values due to differences of station elevation in order to reduce the observations to an arbitrary reference datum or fiducial plane.

ellipsoidal lavas; ellipsoidal basalts *Syn:* PILLOW LAVAS

elutriation Purification by washing and pouring off the lighter matter suspended in water, leaving the heavier portions behind.

eluvial *1.* Formed by the rotting of rock in place to a greater or less depth. *2.* A term applied to materials carried to lower depths by descending vadose waters.

eluviated horizon The A-horizon of soil profile.

eluviation The movement of soil material from one place to another within the soil, in solution or in suspension, when there is an excess of rainfall over evaporation. Horizons that have lost material through eluviation are referred to as eluvial and those that have received material as illuvial. Eluviation may take place downward or sidewise according to the direction of water movement. As used, the term refers especially, but not exclusively, to the movement of colloids, whereas leaching refers to the complete removal of material in solution.

eluvium Atmospheric accumulations *in situ,* or at least only shifted by wind, in distinction to alluvium, which requires the action of water.

emanations, magmatic A combination of volatile and nonvolatile materials given off by a magma at various stages in its history, and with various compositions and densities. The term usually includes both aqueous liquids and gases, and both the pegmatitic and the hydrothermal fluids. *See* MINERALIZER

emanations, volcanic Volatile or nonvolatile materials emitted from volcanoes, fumaroles, or lavas at the earth's surface, usually consisting of a mixture of water vapor and one or more of the other volcanic gases, *q.v.*

emarginate, *adj.* With a shallow notch at the apex.

embankment *1.* When the combined action of waves and currents extends a barrier into deep water, an embankment is formed, which in many cases becomes of very grand proportions. In the formation of embankments the debris of which they are composed is swept along the surface of the barrier or terrace leading to them, and deposited when deep water is reached. This process continues until the embankment has been built up to the water surface. *2.* Artificial ridge of earth or broken rocks such as a dike or railroad grade across a valley.

embayed Formed into a bay or bays, as an embayed shore.

embayed crystal Crystal penetrated by another generally euhedral crystal.

embayment *1.* An identation in a shore line forming an open bay. *2.* The formation of a bay. *3.* Term describing a continental border area that has sagged concurrently with deposition so that an unusually thick section of sediment results. An embayment is similar to a basin of sedimentation or a geosyncline, and some embayments may be one flank of a larger subsiding feature. *4.* Used in a structural sense to designate a re-entrant of sedimentary rocks into a crystalline massif.

embouchure [*Fr.*] The mouth of a river, or that part where it enters the sea. *See* DEBOUCHURE

emerald A bright emerald-green variety of beryl, the color being due to the presence of chromium. Used as a gem.

emergence *1.* A term which implies that part of the ocean floor has become dry land but does not imply whether the sea receded or the land rose. *2.* Point at which an underground stream comes to the surface. *Syn:* RESURGENCE; RISE. *3. Paleobot:* An outgrowth, consisting of epidermal and cortical tissues lacking vascular tissues; e.g., rose prickles.

emergent form Emergent forms of topography are those built up partly beneath the water, but gradually rising above it. Deltas built into dry land, lakes filled up with silts, turned into marshes, and later into dry land, are examples of this kind.

emery *1.* An abrasive consisting mainly of pulverized corundum. *2.* A granular rock composed of corundum, magnetite, and spinel with or without margarite, chloritoid, etc., resulting from metamorphism of highly aluminous sediments.

emery rock A rock that contains

corundum and iron ores. *See* CORUNDOLITE

eminence A mass of high land; a high ground or place.

emplace *1.* To move to a particular position; said of intrusive rocks. *2.* To develop in a particular place; said of ore deposits.

Emscherian Coniacian.

Emsian Upper Lower Devonian.

emulsion A colloidal dispersion of one liquid in another.

en Abbreviation for enstatite.

enantiomorphous *Crystallog:* Similar in form but not superposable; related to each other as the right hand is to the left, hence, one the mirror image of the other.

enantiotropic forms Polymorphic forms which possess an inversion point at which they are in equilibrium, i.e., they are interconvertible. In such cases, the vapor-pressure curves intersect below the melting point of the highest temperature polymorphic form.

enantiotropy Polymorphism in minerals that is reversible at a definite temperature and pressure.

enargite A mineral, Cu_3AsS_4. Orthorhombic. An ore of copper.

encroachment The advancement of water, replacing withdrawn oil or gas in a reservoir.

endellite Hydrated halloysite. A clay mineral, $Al_2Si_2O_5(OH)_4 \cdot 2H_2O$, which readily dehydrates to halloysite.

endemic, *adj.* Native or confined naturally to a particular and unusually restricted area or region; biologically a relic of once wide distribution.

end member *1.* One of two or more relatively simple compounds or substances occurring in a mixture. *2.* One of two or more distinctive forms between which more or less gradual and continuous variation occurs.

end moraine *1.* Moraine marking the terminal position of a valley glacier. *2.* Terminal moraine.

endo- [<*Gr.* endon] A combining form meaning within.

endoderm Inner body layer of organisms that lines the digestive tract.

endogene effects Internal effects upon the margin of an intrusive body itself.

endogenetic *1.* Pertaining to rocks resulting from physical and chemical reactions, their origin being due to forces within the material. In general, they are nonclastic, chemical precipitates formed by "solidification, precipitation, or extraction of the mineral matter from the states of igneous fusion, aqueous solution or vaporization." *Cf.* AUTHIGENIC. *2.* Endogenic. A term applied to processes that originate within the earth and to rocks, ore deposits, and land forms which owe their origin to such processes. Contrasted with exogenetic.

endogenous Produced from within; originating from or due to internal causes. *Syn:* ENDOGENETIC; ENDOGENIC. Contrasted with exogenous.

endometamorphism; endomorphism The modification produced in an igneous rock due to the partial or complete assimilation of portions of the rocks invaded by its magma; a phase of contact metamorphism in which attention is directed to the changes suffered by the intrusive body instead of to those produced in the invaded formations. *Adj:* ENDOMETAMORPHIC, ENDOMORPHIC

endoskeleton The foreign material, frequently calcium carbonate, secreted by an animal to form a rigid internal support for its soft parts.

endothermic Designating, or pertaining to, a reaction which occurs with an absorption of heat. Opposed to exothermic.

endothermic reaction A reaction that proceeds with the absorption of heat.

end product Stable element resulting from radioactive decay.

endrumpf *Cf.* PRIMÄRRUMPF; PENEPLAIN

endurance limit Fatigue limit. Limiting stress below which specimens can withstand hundreds of millions of repetitions of stress without fracturing. Considerably less than the rupture strength.

en echelon Parallel structural features that are offset like the edges of shingles on a roof when viewed from the side.

energy coefficient The ratio of the energy in a wave per unit crest length transmitted forward with the wave at a point in shallow water to the energy in a wave per unit crest length transmitted forward with the wave in deep water. On refraction diagrams this is equal to the ratio of the distance between a pair of orthogonals at a selected point to the distance between the same pair of orthogonals in deep water. Also the square of the refraction coefficient.

engineering geology The application of the geological sciences to engineering practice for the purpose of assuring that the geologic factors affecting the location, design, construction, operation, and maintenance of engineering works are recognized and adequately provided for.

englacial Pertaining to the inside of a glacier.

englacial drift *1.* This is regarded as having been the material embraced within the glacial ice, or borne on its surface, and by its melting let loosely down upon the true till, formed beneath the ice. 2. May be applied to any erratic material that, at any time during its transportation, may be enclosed within the ice even though it be essentially at the bottom of the glacier and may have been actually at the bottom a little while before and may again be at the base a little later on; or it may be applied, less technically but more significantly, to that only which is embedded in the heart of the ice and borne passively along with it free from basal influence until it is at length brought out to the surface of the terminal slope by the agency of ablation.

engulfment If a great reservoir of molten lava, underlying a cone, should be drawn off through a side fissure instead of through the central vent, as sometimes happens, the upper part of the cone might fall by its own weight. This process is known as engulfment.

enormous quantities of water More than 150,000,000 gallons per day. *Cf.* VERY LARGE; LARGE; MODERATE; SMALL; VERY SMALL; MEAGER

enrichment The action of natural agencies which increases the metallic content of an ore. Secondary sulfide enrichment refers to the formation of new sulfide minerals which contain a larger percentage of the metals.

enstatite *See* PYROXENE

enterolithic structure Small folds resulting from changes in volume due to chemical changes in a rock.

enteron Digestive cavity of animals, generally consists of esophagus, stomach, and intestine.

Enterozoa Animals with true digestive cavity or enteron. Eumetazoa; includes all phyla except Protozoa and Porifera.

enthalpy Heat content per unit mass.

entrenched meander A meander eroded below the surface of the valley in which it was formed; may result from either uplift of a region without tilting or lowering of base level.

entrenched meander valley One whose stream, having inherited a meandering course from a previous erosion cycle, has sunk itself into the rock with little modification of its original course.

entrenched stream A narrow, meandering trench cut in a wide-open, flat-bottomed trough, the trough being sunk well beneath the general surface of the adjacent upland. *See* INTRENCHED STREAM

entropy *1.* A measure of the unavailable energy in a system, i.e., energy that cannot be converted into another form of energy. *2.* A measure of the mixing of different kinds of sediment; high entropy is approach to unmixed sediment of one kind.

entropy function facies map Map showing areal relations of facies based on degrees of intermixing of three end members; does not distinguish between end members.

entry *1. Coal min:* A haulage road, gangway, or airway to the surface. *2.* An underground passage used for haulage or ventilation, or as a manway. If it is driven directly down a steep dip it becomes a slope. *See* PORTAL

entry pressure The minimum capillary pressure that will force the entry of a nonwetting fluid into capillary openings saturated with a wetting fluid. *Syn:* DISPLACEMENT PRESSURE; FOREFRONT PRESSURE

envelope *1.* The outer part of a recumbent fold; especially used to contrast the sedimentary cover of a recumbent anticline with the crystalline cone. *2.* Metamorphic rocks surrounding an igneous intrusion.

environment The sum total of all the external conditions which may act upon an organism or community, to influence its development or existence. For example, the surrounding air, light, moisture, temperature, wind, soil, and other organisms are parts of the environment, or environmental factors.

Eocene *1.* Epoch of the Tertiary between the Paleocene and Oligocene and strata of that age; considered by some to be the oldest Tertiary and to include the Paleocene. *2.* Originally, the older Tertiary, included Oligocene. *Obs. Syn:* EOGENE

Eocrinoidea Class of stemmed echinoderms with body enclosed by four circlets of regularly arranged plates and arms like the biserial brachioles of cystoids; formerly included in the Cystoidea. Camb.-Ord.

Eocryptozoic Early Precambrian.

Eogene Lower of two Cenozoic subdivisions, consisting of Paleocene, Eocone, and Oligocene. *Cf.* NEOGENE

eolian Aeolian, *Obs. 1.* Applied to deposits arranged by the wind, as the sands and other loose materials along shores, etc. (From Eolus, the god of winds.) Subaerial is often used in much the same sense. *2.* Applied to the erosive action of the wind, and to deposits which are due to the transporting action of the wind.

eolith The most primitive type of man-made stone implements.

eon; aeon A period of existence; an age; an infinite space of time. The term is used by some geologists to denote any one of the grand divisions of geological time.

Eotvos torsion balance A gravity instrument consisting of a pair of masses suspended by a sensitive torsion fiber and so supported that they are displaced both horizontally and vertically from each other. A measurement is made of the rotation of the suspended system about the fiber caused by slight differences in the direction of gravitational force on the two weights.

Eotvos unit The unit of measurement in work with Eotvos torsion balance having the dimensions of acceleration divided by length, for the gradient and differential curvature values. For the gradient, 1 Eotvos unit (1E.)$= 1 \times 10^{-9}$ gal. per horizontal centimeter.

epeirogenesis Epeirogeny.

epeirogenic movement [$<Gr.$ epeiros, a continent] The broad uplift or depression of areas of the land or of the sea bottom, in which the strata are not folded or crumpled, but may be tilted or may retain their original horizontal attitude.

epeirogeny The broad movements of uplift and subsidence which affect the whole or large portions of continental areas or of the oceanic basins.

ephemeral stream A stream or portion of a stream which flows only in direct response to precipitation. It receives little or no water from springs and no long-continued supply from melting snow or other sources. Its channel is at all times above the water table. The term may be arbitrarily restricted to streams which do not flow continuously during periods of one month.

ephemeris A statement presenting positions and related data for a celestial body for given epochs (dates) at uniform intervals of time. Also a publication containing such data for a number of celestial bodies.

ephemeris time Time as measured by relative changes in the positions of the earth, moon, and stars.

epi- [Gr.] 1. A prefix indicating alternation. 2. A prefix indicating that the rock belongs in the "uppermost zone" of metamorphism, i.e., it originated under moderate temperature, low hydrostatic pressure, and powerful stress. See APO-; CATA-; KATA-; MESO-; META-. 3. A Greek prefix signifying on or upon.

epibole Biostratigraphic unit corresponding to a hemeral.

epicenter The point on the earth's surface directly above the focus of an earthquake.

epiclastic Textural term applied to mechanically deposited sediments (gravel, sand, mud) consisting of weathered products of older rocks. Detrital material from pre-existent rocks.

epicontinental Situated upon a continental plateau or platform, as, an epicontinental sea.

epicontinental geosyncline Geosyncline developed within the boundaries of a continent.

epicontinental marginal sea That part of the ocean, generally less than 7500 feet deep, overlying a portion of the continental margin beyond the continental shelf; commonly partly enclosed by shallow banks, extensions of the land or islands.

epicontinental sea 1. Those shallow portions of the sea which lie upon the continental shelf, and those portions which extend into the interior of the continent with like shallow depths, such as the Baltic Sea and Hudson Bay, may be called epicontinental seas. 2. Independent intercontinental seas with an abyssal area are mediterraneans (*Mittelmeere*), while the shallow type, without the abyssal area, constitute the true epicontinental sea.

epidote A mineral, $Ca_2(Al,Fe''')_3$-$(SiO_4)_3(OH)$. Monoclinic. A common mineral in metamorphic rocks.

epieugeosyncline Deeply subsiding troughs with limited volcanism associated with rather narrow uplifts and overlying a deformed and intruded eugeosyncline.

epigene 1. Geological processes originating at or near the surface of the earth. 2. A group name for volcanic and sedimentary classes of rocks, i.e., rocks formed at or near the surface of the earth. Cf. HYPOGENE. 3. Foreign. Said of forms of crystals not natural to the substances in which they are found. Cf. PSEUDOMORPH

epineritic That portion of the marine environment extending from low tide to a depth of water of less than 120 feet.

epinorm Theoretical calculation of minerals in metamorphic rocks of the epizone as indicated by chemical analyses.

epiplankton Those organisms which habitually live upon a floating object to which they are attached or on which they move freely.

Epiric Upper Permian and Triassic.

epithermal A term applied to those ore deposits formed in and along fissures or other openings in rocks by deposition at shallow depths from ascending hot solutions. They are distinguished from mesothermal and hypothermal lodes by the minerals they contain, by their textures, and by the character of the alteration of their wall rocks.

epithermal deposit Deposit formed in and along fissures or other openings in rocks by deposition at shallow depths from ascending hot solutions.

epizone 1. The "upper zone" of metamorphism. In this zone the distinctive physical conditions are moderate temperature, lower hydrostatic pressure, and powerful stress, and the rocks characteristically produced include mylonites, and cataclastic rocks generally, phyllites, chlorite schists, talc-schists, porphyroids, and in part marbles and quartzites. 2. Metamorphic environment characterized by low temperature and hydrostatic pressure, with or without high stress, resulting in chemical and mechanical metamorphism; characterized by hydrous silicates.

epoch Geologic time unit corresponding to a series; subdivision of a period; formerly used also for other smaller divisions of geologic time.

epsomite Epsom salt. A mineral, $MgSO_4.7H_2O$. Orthorhombic.

equal-area net A type of projection of points on a sphere to a flat surface (circle). The areas of every square degree on the projection are equal.

equant, *adj.* A term applied to crystals that have the same or nearly the same diameter in every direction. *Syn:* EQUIDIMENSIONAL

equant element *See* ELEMENT, EQUANT

equator The great circle midway between the two poles and dividing the grain into two polar hemispheres.

equatorial ridge An interlacunar ridge extending from pore to pore along the equator in lophate grains. It may be continuous, as in the grains of Taraxacum, or interrupted to admit the equatorial lacunae when these are present, as in the grains of Scorzonera hispanica and Tragopogon pratensis.

equi- [<*Lat.* aequi-] A prefix meaning having equal, equally.

equiareal projection Projection from the center of a sphere through a point on its surface to a plane tangent at the south pole so constructed that areas between meridians and parallels on the plane are equal to corresponding ones on the surface of the sphere.

equigranular, *adj.* A textural term applied to rocks whose essential minerals are all of one order of size.

equilibrium Equilibrium exists in any system when the phases of the system do not undergo any change of properties with the passage of time and provided the phases have the same properties when the same conditions, with respect to the variants, are again reached by a different procedure.

equilibrium constant The equilibrium constant of a chemical reaction is the quotient formed by multiplying together the activities of the products, each raised to a power indicated by its coefficient in the equation, and dividing by a similar product of the activities of the reactants. The number obtained by using concentrations instead of activities is often nearly the same; it is commonly called the "classical" equilibrium constant, as opposed to the "thermodynamic" equilibrium constant in terms of activities.

equinox The time when the center of the sun crosses the equator.

equiplanation [<*Lat.* aequus, equal, planus, a plain] All physiographic processes which tend to reduce the relief of a region and so cause the topography eventually to become more plain-like in contour, without involving any loss or gain of material, i.e., the amounts of material remain apparently equal, or are not increased or decreased by the plain-producing process or processes. Material may be exported from certain districts during the time equiplanation is in progress, but this export takes place quite independent of the equiplanating.

equipotential surface A surface on which the potential is everywhere constant for the attractive forces concerned.

equivalent *1. Geol:* Corresponding in geologic age or stratigraphic position; said of formations, etc. *2.* Applied to grains of ore or vein-stuff of varying diameters and density, which fall through water at an equal velocity. Usually used in the plural.

equivalent grade In textural classification, refers to arithmetic mean size.

equivalent molecular unit In the Niggli calculation of the molecular norm, the sum of all cations in the formula of a given mineral; thus $Na_2O.Al_2O_3.2SiO = 6$ nepheline equivalent units, as there are 6 cations in the formula.

equivalent radius The radius of a spherical particle of density 2.65 (quartz) which would have the same settling rate as the given particle.

equivalent weight Equals the molecular weight of the substance or a submultiple of it, chosen according to some convention.

equivolumnar waves Distortional waves; secondary waves; shear waves; transverse waves; S-waves, *q.v.*

era *Geol:* In general, a large division of geologic time; specifically, a division of geologic time of the highest order, comprising one or more periods. The eras now generally recognized are the Archeozoic, Proterozoic, Paleozoic, Mesozoic, and Cenozoic.

E-ray *See* EXTRAORDINARY RAY

erg A term used in the Sahara, and applicable elsewhere, for a vast region covered deeply with pure sand and occupied by dunes.

Erian Middle Devonian.

Erian orogeny Early Devonian diastrophism.

erodible Capable of being eroded.

erosion The group of processes whereby earthy or rock material is loosened or dissolved and removed from any part of the earth's surface. It includes the processes of weathering, solution, corrasion, and transportation. The mechanical wear and transportation are effected by running water, waves, moving ice, or winds, which use rock fragments to pound or grind other rocks to powder or sand.

erosion scarp A scarp produced by the agents of erosion.

erosion surface A land surface shaped by the disintegrating, dissolving, and wearing action of streams, ice, rain, winds, and other land and atmospheric agencies.

erosion thrust A thrust fault along which the hanging wall moved across an erosion surface.

erratic *1.* Those large water-worn and ice-borne blocks (boulders) which are scattered so generally over the higher and middle latitudes of the Northern Hemisphere. *2.* A transported rock fragment different from the bedrock on which it lies, either free or as part of a sediment. The term is generally applied to fragments transported by glacier ice or by floating ice.

error, average The mean of all the errors taken without regard to sign.

error, constant A systematic error which is the same in both magnitude and sign through a given series of observations.

error, personal A systematic error caused by an observer's personal habits in making observations, or due to his tendency to react mentally and physically in the same way under similar conditions.

error, systematic An error whose algebraic sign and, to some extent, magnitude bear a fixed relation to some condition or set of conditions.

In its broadest sense, the term systematic error includes constant errors. Under similar conditions systematic errors tend to be repeated; if the conditions do not change, the error will be constant. The inclusive definition is preferred.

Systematic errors are regular, and therefore are subject to *a priori* determination.

eruption, volcanic The emission or ejection of volcanic materials at the earth's surface from a crater of pipe or from a fissure. Central eruptions are those in which volcanic materials are emitted from a central vent or pipe and ordinarily result in the formation of a volcanic cone; fissure eruptions are those in which lava or pyroclastic materials emanate from a relatively narrow fissure or group of fissures, commonly building lava plains and lava plateaus. The character of volcanic eruptions varies from relatively quiet out-pourings of fluid lava, as in most Hawaiian eruptions, to violent explosions accompanied by showers of volcanic ash, like that of Krakatau in 1883.

eruption cloud A convoluted, rolling mass of partly condensed water vapor, dust, and ash, generally highly charged with electricity, emitted from a volcano during an explosive eruption. It may rise to great heights (several miles) above the volcano.

eruptive *1.* Descriptive of igneous rocks that reach the surface of the earth in a molten condition. *2.* Refers to material thrown out by a volcano. *3.* Applies to any igneous rock (not recommended).

erythrite Cobalt bloom. A mineral, $Co_3(AsO_4)_2.8H_2O$. Monoclinic. A secondary mineral.

Erzgebirgian orogeny Early Late Carboniferous diastrophism.

escape velocity That minimum velocity which any particle or mass must have in order to escape from the gravitational attraction of a body. If the movement of the particle is not vertical, the vertical component of the movement must be equal to or greater than the escape velocity. For the earth it is 11.2 km./sec. if resistance of air is neglected.

escarpment *1.* [<*Fr.* escarper, to cut steeply] A steep face terminating high lands abruptly. *2.* A slope; a steep descent; a declivity. *Geol:* The steep face frequently presented by the abrupt termination of stratified rocks.

eschar Esker, *q.v.*

escutcheon A diamond-shaped basal expansion, pit, or cavity seen on the aboral surface (of a conodont).

eskar Esker, *q.v.*

eskar delta Osar delta, *q.v.*

eskar terrace Osar terrace, *q.v.*

eskar Osar; asar; eschar; eskar; serpent kame. *1.* Eskers or kames, unlike the drumlins, are rudely stratified accumulations of gravel, sand, and waterworn stones. They are of rough fluvial or torrential origin, and occur in long tortuous ridges (serpent kames), mounds, and hummocks. They have the general direction of the drainage, though sometimes not according with the present course of drainage. *2.* Serpentine ridges of gravel and sand. These are often associated with kames, and are taken to mark channels in the decaying ice sheet, through which streams washed much of the finer drift, leaving the coarser gravel between the ice walls.

esker fan Small plains of gravel and sand built at the mouth of sub-glacial tunnels and channels in the ice; associated with an esker or eskerlike chain of deposits made in the ice sheet at the same time.

essential ejecta *1.* Pyroclastic detritus, whether loose or indurated, which is of immediate, juvenile, magmatic origin. *2.* Juvenile ejecta. Fresh magmatic material thrown out in liquid form by a volcano.

essential element An element whose absence in an organism

causes functional disturbances in the organism.

essential minerals Those mineral constituents of a rock that are necessary to its classification and nomenclature. An essential constituent is not necessarily a major constituent, for the presence in a rock of minor amounts of such minerals as nepheline, olivine, or quartz may affect its classification. *See* ACCESSORY MINERALS

essexite A plutonic rock composed essentially of plagioclase hornblende, biotite, and titanaugite with subordinate alkali feldspar and nepheline. An alkalic gabbro.

estuarine Of, pertaining to, or formed in an estuary.

estuary Drainage channel adjacent to the sea in which the tide ebbs and flows. Some estuaries are the lower courses of rivers or smaller streams, others are no more than drainage ways that lead seawater into and out of coastal swamps.

etched *1.* Term applied to a rough frosted surface, as of minerals or sand grains. *2.* Pitted or corroded in such manner that a pattern of pits or lines is produced which is related to the crystal or tectonic structure. *See* FROSTING

etch figure A marking, usually minute pits, produced by a solvent on a crystal surface; the form varies with the species and solvent but conforms to the symmetry of the crystal, hence revealing its crystal structure.

etching A roughening of the surface of a sand grain or crystal as a result of a solvent.

ethane A colorless, gaseous compound (C_2H_6), of the paraffin series contained in the gases given off by petroleum and in illuminating gas.

Etroeungtian Strunian.

eu- [<*Gr.* eu, well; originally the neuter of eys, good] A prefix meaning good, advantageous.

eucrystalline, *adj.* A textural term relating to igneous rocks, such as granites, which are well crystallized.

eugeosyncline An orthogeosyncline in which volcanic rocks are abundant.

euhedral Idiomorphic; automorphic, *q.v.*

Eumetazoa Animals whose cells are organized into tissues and organs. Enterozoa; includes all phyla except Protozoa and Porifera.

eupelagic Having purely pelagic qualities.

euryhaline Tolerant of considerable difference in salinity; generally refers to marine organisms.

eurypterid One of a group of very large, extinct arthropods, closely related to the trilobites.

eustasy World-wide simultaneous change in sea level.

eustatic Pertaining to simultaneous, world-wide changes in sea level.

eutaxitic Applied to a structure of certain volcanic rocks with a streaked or blotched appearance due to the alternation of bands or elongated lenses of different color, composition, or texture; the bands, etc., having been originally ejected as individual portions of magma which were drawn out together in a viscous state and formed a heterogeneous mass by welding. The term is most appropriately used in describing the structure of a majority of welded tuffs.

eutectic Pertaining to a mixture of substances that do not form solid solutions, having its components in such proportions that its melting point is the lowest possible with those components.

eutectic point or **eutectic temperature** The lowest melting temperature obtainable with mixtures of given components, provided that the components do not form solid solutions.

eutectic ratio The ratio of solid phases forming from the eutectic liquid at the eutectic point; it is such as to yield a gross composition for the crystal mixture that is identical with that of the liquid. Most frequently stated in terms of weight per cent.

eutectic texture; eutectoid texture Intergrowths of minerals, either along crystallographic or bleb boundaries, similar to those precipitated from eutectic solutions.

Eutheria Infraclass of mammals. Monodelphia or placentals.

eutrophic Refers to lakes with little oxygen in the bottom waters and much nutrient matter.

euxinic Term applied to a restricted circulation (barred basin) environment, or the sediments deposited in such an environment.

ev Abbreviation for one electron volt.

evaporite One of the sediments which are deposited from aqueous solution as a result of extensive or total evaporation of the solvent.

evaporite-solution breccia A breccia formed by a removal of the evaporites.

evapo-transpiration A term embracing that portion of the precipitation returned to the air through direct evaporation or by transpiration of vegetation, no attempt being made to distinguish between the two.

event, seismic Applied to any definite phase change or amplitude difference on a seismic record; it may be a reflection, a refraction, a diffraction, or a random signal.

everglade A tract of swampy land covered mostly with tall grass; a swamp or inundated tract of low land. Local in the South.

evolution *1.* The theory that life on earth has developed gradually, generally from simple to complex, all by change and branching of species. *2.* Phylogyny; the development of a race with regard to the structural changes which took place from generation to generation.

evolutionary momentum The idea that organic function is activity and activity is motion led to the notion that evolution may continue to inadaptive lengths and result in extinction.

exfoliation The breaking- or peeling-off of scales, lamellae, as concentric sheets from bare rock surfaces by the action of either physical or chemical forces.

exhaustion *Min:* The complete removal of ore reserves.

exhumed topography Monadnocks, mountains, or other topographic forms buried under younger rocks and exposed again by erosion. *Cf.* MENDIP

exo- *[Gr.]* A prefix signifying out of, outside, outer layer.

exogene Organism or fossil introduced into a biologic or paleontological association from another place.

exogene effects Effects upon the rocks invaded by igneous masses.

exogenetic *1.* Pertaining to a rock made up of fragments of older rocks and owing its origin chiefly to agents acting from without. *2.* Applied to processes originating at or near the surface of the earth, such as weathering and denudation, and to

rocks, ore deposits, and land forms which owe their origin to such processes. *Contr. with* ENDOGENETIC; ENDOGENIC

exogenic differentiation Chemical differentiation during a cycle of rock weathering and sediment transportation and deposition.

exogeosyncline A parageosyncline that lies along the cratonal border and obtains its sediments from erosion of complementing highlands in the orthogeosynclinal belt that lies outside the craton.

exoskeleton The protection surrounding the soft body of an animal, as the shell of brachiopods and pelecypods, etc.

exosphere Space beyond the earth's atmosphere; begins at a height of about 1000 km.

exothermic Designating, or pertaining to, a reaction which occurs with a liberation of heat. *Ant:* ENDOTHERMIC

exothermic reaction A reaction that proceeds with the evolution of heat.

exotic That which has been introduced from other regions.

expansion fissures *Petrog:* A system of irregularly radiating fissures which ramify through feldspars and other minerals adjacent to olivine crystals that have been replaced by serpentine. Characteristic of norites and gabbros. The alteration of olivine to serpentine involves a considerable increase in volume, and the stresses so produced are relieved by the fissuring of the surrounding minerals.

exploit *1.* To make complete use of; to utilize. *2.* To make research or experiment; to explore.

exploration *1.* The work involved in looking for ore. Often confused with exploitation. *2.* In the petroleum industry, the search for natural accumulations of oil and gas by any geological, geophysical, or other suitable means.

exploratory well A well drilled either in search of a new and as yet undiscovered pool of oil or gas, or with the hope of greatly extending the limits of a pool already partly developed.

explorer's alidade *See* GALE ALIDADE

explosion breccia A deposit of coarse, indurated volcanic debris containing blocks torn from the walls of a volcanic vent and lying in a matrix of comminuted rock. The absence of magmatic ejecta indicates that the explosions which give rise to this type of rock are of phreatic origin.

explosion caldera A caldera resulting primarily from a violent volcanic explosion which blows out a huge mass of rock, leaving a broad, deep basin in its place. Relatively rare and small in size compared to collapse calderas. An example is Bandaisan in Japan, where phreatic eruptions were followed by enormous avalanches that left an amphitheaterlike basin.

explosion crater A volcanic crater formed by a violent explosion commonly developed along rift zones on the flanks of large volcanoes and occasionally at the summit of volcanoes. Distinguished from ordinary craters at the top of volcanic cones and from pit craters, which are produced largely by collapse. *Syn:* EXPLOSION PIT

explosion tuff A tuff of which the constituent ash particles have been dropped directly into place after being ejected from a volcanic vent, the term thus distinguishing such tuffs from the more ordinary types which are washed into place.

explosive evolution Relatively rapid splitting of a group of animals into numerous different lines of descent within a period of time geologically short.

explosive index Percentage of pyroclastic ejecta among the total products of a volcanic eruption.

explosive radiation Explosive evolution.

exposure *Geol:* The condition or fact of being exposed to view, either naturally or artificially; that part of a rock, bed, or formation which is so exposed; an outcrop.

exsolution Unmixing. Solid solutions of some pairs of minerals form only at high temperatures and become unstable at lower temperatures. When these cool slowly, one mineral may separate out of the other at a certain point in the cooling-temperature curve. This is known as unmixing, or exsolution.

exsolved *See* EXSOLUTION

exsudation The scaling off of rock surfaces through growth of salines by capillary action has been called exsudation. It probably has only local importance as a weathering process.

extended consequent stream *1.* Extended consequents are streams of an older type which become extended across the newly emerged coastal plain. These streams do not differ from those originating on the coastal plain, except in their greater volume of water and hence greater erosive power. They will, therefore, cut deeper than the others, becoming the master streams of their respective regions, and directing to a large extent the further development of their drainage system. Streams extended across a dry delta may also be classed here, as are those extended across a plain of glacial deposition.

extension fractures Fractures that form parallel to a compressive force. In a sense they are tension fractures.

extension joints Joints that form parallel to a compressive force. In a sense they are tension fractures.

extensive quantity Thermodynamic quantities such as volume or mass that depend on the total quantity of matter in the system.

extensive variables Any variable whose value is dependent upon the total amount of the phase, for example the total volume, total free energy, etc. *Syn:* EXTERNAL VARIABLE

external mold The impression, in adjoining rock, of the outer sides of the hard parts of an organism.

external rotation Rotation of small mineral aggregates in metamorphic rocks whose internal relationships are little disturbed.

extinction *1.* A position at which a birefringent substance on the stage of a polarizing microscope with crossed Nicols is dark, even though the line of sight is not parallel to an optic axis; also the darkness so obtained. *2.* The disappearance of species or larger units of animals or plants because they succumb to changed conditions of environment, etc.

extinction angle The angle through which a section of an anistropic crystal must be revolved from a known crystallographic plane or direction to the position of maximum darkness (extinction) under the petrographic microscope. Commonly

diagnostic in the identification of a crystal.

extinction direction One of two directions in a crystal parallel to the vibration planes of crossed Nicols.

extracontinental geosyncline Geosyncline situated outside of and marginal to a continent.

extralateral right In U.S. mining law, one who locates on the public domain a claim in which a vein comes to an apex is entitled to extralateral rights which pertain to parts of the vein beyond the planes passed through the side lines of his claim, but lying within vertical cross planes passed through the end lines.

extraordinary ray; E-ray In optically uniaxial crystals, the ray of polarized light that vibrates at an angle to the basal pinacoid and whose refraction varies with that angle.

extreme *1. Adj:* Applied to the highest and the lowest temperatures (or other meteorological element) which had occurred over a very long record for each month and for the year. *2. Adj; N:* Sometimes applied to the extremes of temperatures in individual months; and again to the average of the highest and the lowest temperatures, as the so-called "mean monthly extremes and mean annual extremes."

extrusion *1.* The act or process of thrusting or pushing out; also a form produced by the process; a protrusion. *2. Geol:* The emission of magmatic material (generally said of lavas) at the earth's surface; also the structure or form produced by the process, such as a lava flow, volcanic dome, or certain pyroclastic rocks.

extrusion flow hypothesis A theory which explains the movement of glacier ice out of a basin-shaped bed or down a gentle gradient by assuming that the differential pressures caused by weight of the overlying ice forces the basal portion of the glacier to flow like a plastic substance. In this theory, extrusion flow depends on the thickness of the ice and the steepness of the surface slope. *See* GRAVITY FLOW

extrusive rocks Applied to those igneous rocks derived from magmas or magmatic materials poured out or ejected at the earth's surface, as distinct from the intrusive or plutonic igneous rocks which have solidified from magmas that have been injected into older rocks at depth without reaching the surface. *Syn:* EFFUSIVE ROCKS; VOLCANIC ROCKS

exudation basin A spoon-shaped depression found at the heads of outlet glaciers of the Greenland ice cap.

eyed structure Augen structure, *q.v.*

F

fa Abbreviation for fayalite. *See* OLIVINE

fabric *1.* The orientation in space of the elements of which a rock is composed. *2. Petrol:* That factor of the texture of a crystalline rock which depends on the relative sizes, the shapes, and the arrangement of the component crystals.

fabric, depositional *Struct. petrol:* A depositional fabric results from deposition of unconsolidated rock components from a fluid medium, as in undeformed, unmetamorphosed sediments or igneous rock gravity differentiates.

fabric, growth *Struct. petrol:* A growth fabric results where the orientation of the fabric elements is independent of stress and resultant movement (e.g., growth from the walls of a fissure, growth in a pressure shadow, etc.).

fabric element A rock component, ranging from an atom or ion to a mineral grain or group of grains in pebbles, lenses, layers, etc., that acts as a unit in response to deformative forces.

fabric habit Relations between the shape of a mineral grain and its lattice structure.

face *V: 1.* To be directed toward, to turn toward; *2.* To be directed toward younger rocks, e.g., overturned strata and structures face downward. *N: 3. Min:* End or surface where work is being or was last done in any level or gently inclined part of a mining operation; *cf.* BACK; *4. Coal min:* Surface of principal jointing in a coal bed. *5.* In structure, original upper surface of a stratum, especially if it has been raised to a vertical or steeply inclined position. *6. Crystallog:* Plane surface of a crystal.

facet *1.* The polished surface of a cut gemstone. *2.* Any nearly plane surface abraded on a rock fragment, e.g., by glaciation. *3.* Asymmetrically scalloped rock surfaces. *Syn:* FLUTE; SOLUTION RIPPLE

faceted spur *1.* In a river valley the spurs between ravines run down and die out at, or near, the river; in a glaciated valley, these are ground away by the longitudinal erosion up to the level of the ice and after its recession terminate in more or less well-defined inverted V-shapes in the wall of the main valley; these spurs are said to be faceted. *2.* The end of a ridge which has been truncated or steeply beveled by stream erosion, glaciation, or faulting.

facies *Petrog: 1.* General appearance or nature of one part of a rock body as contrasted with other parts; *2.* Part of a rock body as differentiated from other parts by appearance or composition; *3.* A kind of rock distinguished from other more or less related kinds. *Stratig:* 4. A stratigraphic body as distinguished from other bodies of different appearance or composition. 5. A lateral subdivision of a stratigraphic unit; *cf.* LITHOFACIES; BIOFACIES; TECTOFACIES

facies, igneous A variety of igneous rock. Especially applied to an igneous rock that in some respects is a departure from the normal or typical rock of the mass to which it belongs. Thus a mass of granite may grade into a porphyritic facies near its borders.

facies contour Line indicating equivalence in lithofacies development, e.g., a particular value of the sand-shale ratio.

facies departure map Map showing areal relations of facies based on degree of similarity to some particular sedimentary composition.

facies evolution Gradual change in the nature of facies and their relations with a particular area.

facies family Group of closely related and associated facies, e.g., different parts of an organic reef.

facies fauna A group of animals adapted to life on a restricted type of sea floor or other environment.

facies fossil A fossil, usually a species, which is adapted to life in a restricted environment.

facies map A map showing the distribution of different types of sedimentary facies occurring within a designated geologic unit.

facies sequence Succession of vertically related facies.

facies strike Direction indicated by facies contours.

facies suite All broadly related facies, e.g., all marine deposits.

facies tract System of different but genetically interconnected

facies; originally included areas of erosion which furnished sediments to areas of deposition.

facing Applied to the original direction of a layer.

factor, conversion That factor by which the numerical value of a measurement made in one system of units must be multiplied to arrive at the numerical value of the same measurement in another system of units.

faecal pellets Excreta, mainly of invertebrates, present especially in modern marine deposits but also as fossils in sedimentary rocks. Most are of simple ovoid form and 1 mm. or less in size. More rarely they are rod-shaped with either longitudinal or transverse sculpturing. Coprolites, *q.v.,* are of similar origin but much larger.

Fahrenheit The name of one of the most widely used temperature scales. Named after Gabriel Daniel Fahrenheit (1686–1736), a physicist and maker of scientific instruments, who introduced this scale of temperature through his interest in meteorology and was the first to use mercury in a thermometer.

fall; falls A cascade, waterfall, or cataract. The flow or descent of one body of water into another.

falling dune Sand blown off a mesa top into a valley or canyon may form a solid wall, sloping at the angle of rest of dry sand, or a fan extending downward from a re-entrant in the mesa wall.

fall line *1.* A line characterized by numerous waterfalls, as the edge of a plateau in passing which the streams make a sudden descent. *2.* A large river whose valley is extended across a coastal plain often has low falls or rapids near the inner margin of the plain, which determine the "head of navigation" or uppermost point that can be reached by vessels from the river mouth. A line drawn through the falls on successive rivers is called the fall line. The falls occur when the river passes from a steeper slope on the resistant rocks of the older land to a nearly level channel excavated in the weak strata of the plain.

false anticline Anticlinelike structure produced by compaction of sediment over a resistant mass such as a buried hill or reef.

false equilibria Growth of a metastable or monotropic phase under conditions apparently indicating true equilibria, as in the development of andalusite crystals where sillimanite actually represents the stable phase.

false topaz A yellow variety of quartz resembling topaz.

Famennian Upper Upper Devonian, below Strunian.

families of igneous rocks Subgroups, under clans, in the classification of igneous rocks, e.g., the syenite family.

family A taxonomic division used in the classification of animals and plants; a group of closely related genera.

fan *1.* An accumulation of debris brought down by a stream descending through a steep ravine and debouching in the plain beneath, where the detrital material spreads out in the shape of a fan, forming a section of a very low cone. See ALLUVIAL FAN. *2.* In worms, the modified appendage used to draw in water containing oxygen and microscopic organism.

fan bay The head of an alluvial fan which extends a consider-

able distance into a mountain canyon.

fan fold An anticlinal fold in which the two limbs dip toward one another, or a syncline in which the two limbs dip away from one another.

fanglomerate A fanglomerate is composed of heterogeneous materials which were originally deposited in an alluvial fan but which since deposition have been cemented into solid rock.

fan shooting A refraction type of seismic shooting in which a fan of detectors is laid out from a single shot point. Arrival times of refraction impulses at the detectors, when less than normal, may indicate presence of relatively shallow salt masses (salt domes) encountered by seismic ray paths.

farad The electrical unit of capacity in the practical system, or 9×10^{11} stat-farads, where the stat-farad is a stat-coulomb per stat-volt.

fast electron Electron traveling at high velocity; physically equivalent to a beta ray.

fast ice A floe of ice extending from the land and fast to it. *Syn:* LAND FLOE; SHORE FLOE; ICE FOOT

fat clay Clay of relatively high plasticity. *Cf.* LEAN CLAY

fathogram A continuous profile of the depth obtained by echo soundings.

fathom A unit of measurement used for soundings. It is equal to 6 feet (1.83 meters).

fathometer The copyrighted trade name for a type of echo sounder.

fatigue limit *See* ENDURANCE LIMIT

fault A fracture or fracture zone along which there has been displacement of the sides relative to one another parallel to the fracture. The displacement may be a few inches or many miles.

fault basin A region depressed relative to the surrounding regions and separated from them by faults.

fault block *1.* A mass bounded on at least two opposite sides by faults; it may be elevated or depressed relatively to the adjoining region, or it may be elevated relatively to the region on one side and depressed relatively to that on the other. *2.* A body of rock bounded by one or more faults.

fault breccia The assembly of broken fragments frequently found along faults.

fault complex Intricate system of interconnecting and intersecting faults of the same or different ages.

fault dip The vertical inclination of the fault surface or shear zone, measured from a horizontal plane.

fault embayment A depressed region in a fault zone or between two faults invaded by the sea. The Red Sea and Tomales Bay on the San Andreas fault are examples.

faulting The movement which produces relative displacement of adjacent rock masses along a fracture.

fault line The intersection of a fault surface with the surface of the earth or with any artificial surface of reference.

fault-line scarp A scarp that is the result of differential erosion along a fault line rather than the direct result of the movement along the fault. *See* OBSEQUENT and RESEQUENT FAULT-LINE SCARPS

fault plane A fault surface, *q.v.,* without notable curvature.

fault scarp The cliff formed by a fault. Most fault scarps have been modified by erosion since the faulting.

fault set Two or more parallel faults within an area constitute a fault set.

fault strike The direction of the intersection of the fault surface, or the shear zone, with a horizontal plane.

fault surface The surface along which dislocation has taken place. *Cf.* FAULT PLANE

fault system Consists of two or more fault sets that were formed at the same time.

fault trap A trap whose closure results from the presence of one or more faults.

fault trellis drainage pattern A variety of trellis pattern found where a series of parallel faults have brought together alternating bands of strong and weak rock.

fault wedge Wedge-shaped block between two faults.

fault zone A fault, instead of being a single clean fracture, may be a zone hundreds or thousands of feet wide; the fault zone consists of numerous interlacing small faults or a confused zone of gouge, breccia, or mylonite.

fauna The animals of any place or time that lived in association with each other. The limitations of any fauna are relative. They may be interpreted broadly as of the fauna of a continent or of a geologic period, or restrictively as of the fauna of a small area of the sea bottom during a single season. A paleontologic fauna consists only of those animals whose remains are preserved as fossils.

faunal Pertaining to a natural assemblage of animals.

faunal province Region characterized by occurrence more or less wide-distributed within it of a specified assemblage of animals (fauna).

faunal realm Same as faunal province but more inclusive in that it may be divisible into two or more parts classed as subrealms or provinces.

faunizone 1. Biostratigraphic unit characterized by the presence of a particular fauna that may have either time or environmental significance. *Cf.* ASSEMBLAGE ZONE. 2. Biostratigraphic unit consisting of various more or less overlapping biozones; has dominantly time-stratigraphic significance.

faunule A diminutive fauna. *Paleontol:* An association of animals found in a single stratum or a succession of strata of limited thickness.

f-axis *Struct. petrol:* Axis of rotation, normal to t, around which a gliding plane may be bent.

fayalite *See* OLIVINE

feather joints A series of joints that branch diagonally from a larger joint or fault.

fecal pellets *See* FAECAL PELLETS

feeder 1. Small vein joining a larger vein. 2. A spring or stream. 3. A blower of gas, as in a coal mine.

feeder channels Channels parallel to shore along which feeder currents flow before converging and forming the neck of a rip current.

feldspar; felspar A group of abundant rock-forming minerals. *See* MICROCLINE; ORTHOCLASE; PLAGIOCLASE; ANORTHOCLASE

feldspathic Containing feldspar as a principal ingredient.

feldspathic or felspathic sandstone A sandstone containing from 10 to 25% feldspar intermediate between a pure quartzose sandstone and an arkose. *Cf.* ARKOSIC SANDSTONE

feldspathoids Name given to several minerals, aluminosilicates of Na, K, or Ca, that are similar in composition to the feldspars, but contain less silica than the corresponding feldspar. Leucite and nepheline are the most common; others are melilite and sodalite. The German equivalent, feldspatvertreter, indicates the chief occurrence of these minerals; they take the place of feldspars in igneous rocks that are too low in silica for feldspar to form or that contain more alkalies and aluminum than can be accommodated in the feldspars.

felsenmeer [*Ger.* sea of rock] Above the limit of the growth of trees (tree or timberline) rock destruction goes on with great rapidity, as is indicated by the wild and chaotic confusion of rock pieces. It is pre-eminently characteristic of lofty mountain slopes. There is no English term for it.

felsic A mnemonic term derived from (fe) for feldspar, (l) for lenads or feldspathoids, and (s) for silica and applied to light-colored rocks containing an abundance of one or all of these constituents. Also applied to the minerals themselves, the chief felsic minerals being quartz, feldspars, feldspathoids, and muscovite. *Syn:* ACID, *4, q.v.;* MAFIC, *q.v.;* SILICIC, *q.v.*

felsite An igneous rock with or without phenocrysts, in which either the whole or the groundmass consists of a cryptocrystalline aggregate of felsic minerals, quartz and potassium feldspar being those characteristically developed. When phenocrysts of quartz are present the rock is termed a quartz felsite or, more commonly, a quartz porphyry.

felsitic, *adj.* A textural term

ordinarily applied to dense, light-colored igneous rocks made up of crystals that are too small to be readily distinguished with the unaided eye. In this sense the term is essentially synonymous with microcrystalline. Occasionally the term is used as a microscopic term, and is applied to the groundmass of porphyritic rocks which are not glassy but are rather too fine-grained for the constituents to be determined with the use of the microscope. In this sense the term is synonymous with cryptocrystalline. The terms microcrystalline and cryptocrystalline are preferred.

felty; felted A textural term applied to dense, holocrystalline igneous rocks or to the dense, holocrystalline groundmass of porphyritic igneous rocks consisting of tightly appressed microlites, generally of feldspar, interwoven in irregular, unoriented fashion. If, as is characteristic of many andesites and trachytes, the crowded microlites of feldspar are disposed in a subparallel manner as a result of flow, and their interstices are occupied by micro- or cryptocrystalline material, the texture is called pilotaxitic or trachytic.

femic A mnemonic term derived from (fe) for iron and (m) for magnesium and applied to the group of standard normative minerals in which these elements are an essential component, including the pyroxene and olivine molecules and most of the normative accessory minerals (magnetite, ilmenite, hematite). The corresponding term for the ferromagnesian minerals actually present in a rock is MAFIC, *q.v.*

fence diagram Three or more geologic sections showing the relationship of wells to subsurface formations. To give proper perspective, scales diminish with distance from the foreground. When several sections are used together, they form a fencelike enclosure, hence the name. Similar in some respects to a block diagram, but having the advantage of transparency, which is not possible in a block diagram.

Fenoscandia Ancient stable region in northwestern Europe.

fenster Window. An erosional break through an overthrust sheet or through a large recumbent anticline whereby the rocks beneath the thrust sheet are exposed. The term "window" has sometimes been erroneously used in the United States for areas in which the normal stratigraphic succession has not been disturbed by faulting, but where older strata are exposed along the crest of an anticline.

ferberite *See* WOLFRAMITE

Fermat's principle The ray (which is perpendicular to the wave front) reaching a given point by a "minimum time" path between the source and the point. If the intervening medium contains parts having different rates of propagation, the path will in general not be straight but will be that which has the minimum over-all propagation time between the two points.

Ferrel's law Coriolis force, *q.v.* A statement of the fact that currents of air or water are deflected by the rotation of the earth to the right in the Northern Hemisphere and to the left in the Southern Hemisphere.

ferreto zone Reddish brown or reddish zone in permeable near-surface material produced under conditions of free subsurface drainage by the deposition of secondary iron oxide.

ferricrete Soil zone more or less cemented with iron oxide.

ferride A member of a group of elements related to iron, including Ti, V, Cr, Mn, Fe, Co, Ni.

ferroan-dolomite Dolomite in which not more than half of the magnesium has been replaced by iron.

ferrogabbro A gabbroic rock in which the pyroxene or olivine or both are exceptionally rich in iron.

ferromagnesian *Petrol:* Containing iron and magnesium. Applied to certain dark silicate minerals, especially amphibole, pyroxene, biotite, and olivine, and to igneous rocks containing them as dominant constituents.

ferromagnetic Refers to those paramagnetic materials having a magnetic permeability considerably greater than one. They are attracted by a magnet.

ferrosilite *See* PYROXENE

ferruginate *1. Adj:* Cemented with iron minerals generally limonite. *2. V:* To stain with iron.

ferruginous Containing iron. Descriptive of rocks of red color but not necessarily abnormal iron content.

festoon A type of cross-lamination resulting from (1) the erosion of plunging troughs having the shape of a quadrant of an elongate ellipsoid, (2) the filling of the troughs by sets of thin laminae conforming in general to the shape of the trough floors, and (3) the partial destruction of the filling laminae by subsequent erosion, producing younger troughs.

fetch *1.* In wave forecasting, the continuous area of water over which the wind blows in essentially a constant direction. Sometimes used synonymously with fetch length. *Also* GENERATING AREA. *2.* In wind setup phenomena, for inclosed bodies of water, the distance between the points of maximum and minimum water surface elevations. This would usually coincide with the longest axis in the general wind direction.

fetid Having a disagreeable odor caused by the occurrence of certain bituminous substances or hydrogen sulfide. Such an odor is apparent when some varieties of limestone and quartz are broken or rubbed vigorously.

fiard [*Sw.*] *1.* Sea-drowned valleys which are not river estuaries, occur in lowland countries, and are composed of hard rocks. *2.* A glaciated re-entrant of the sea with low glaciated sides. Fiards are shorter and shallower than fiords. For example, Norway is a fiord country, while Sweden has few fiords but many fiards.

fibroblastic Nematoblastic.

fiducial mark *1.* An index line or point. A line or point used as a basis of reference. *2. Photogrammetry:* Index marks rigidly connected with the camera lens through the camera body and forming images on the negative which defines the principal point of the photograph.

fiducial time A time on a seismograph record which may be marked to correspond, by employing necessary corrections, to a datum plane in space.

field *1.* A large tract or area of many square miles containing valuable minerals. *See* COAL FIELD. *2.* A colliery, or firm of colliery proprietors. *3.* The immediate locality and surroundings of a mine explosion. *4.* A region or space traversed by lines of force, as, gravitational, magnetic, or electric.

field capacity The amount of water held in a soil by capillary action after gravitational water has percolated downward and drained away; expressed as the ratio of the weight of water retained to the weight of dry soil.

field development well Any well drilled within the presently known or proved productive area of a pool (reservoir) as indicated by reasonable interpretation of subsurface data, with the objective of obtaining oil or gas from that pool.

field focus The total area or volume which the source of an earthquake occupied. If a fault is the source, the focus is the local fault surface, and is called the "field" because it is inferred from the area of shaking as observed in the field.

field ice Sea ice, *q.v.*

field intensity Magnetic field strength (H), *q.v.*

figure of the earth The sea-level surface of the earth, the geoid, or a modified surface, the cogeoid, related to the geoid in a defined manner.

filament The stalk of a stamen, with an anther at its apex; also, a threadlike row of cells.

filiform texture Threadlike forms consisting of one mineral embedded in another mineral.

fill *1.* The withdrawal of the river current from the outer side of the curve, leaves that bank bordered by quiet water, in which deposition will probably result. Such deposition may be called a fill. *2.* Material deposited or washed into a cave passageway. Fill is generally prefixed by a word describing its dominant grain size—sand fill, silt fill, clay fill, gravel fill. *3.* Any sediment deposited by any agent so as to fill or partly fill a valley, sink, or other depression. *4.* Material used to raise the surface of the land generally in a low area.

fillers Mineral and other minerals used for a specific purpose in a manufactured product but not as essential constituents.

fill terrace A term to comprise the series of terms—alluvial terrace, glacial terrace, and others—which are formed after the rejuvenation of a stream-filled valley or a valley surface made by aggregation.

filltop terrace Fill terrace whose surface is the original depositional surface.

film, intergranular *See* INTERGRANULAR FILM

filter pressing *1. Geol:* The process of the straining out of liquid when an igneous rock has partly crystallized and then is subjected to pressure by earth movements, etc. *2.* A process of magmatic differentiation wherein a magma having crystallized to a "mush" of interlocking crystals in liquid becomes compressed, permitting the liquid to move toward regions of lower pressure and hence become separated from the crystals.

filter sand Sand suitable for use in filtering the suspended matter from water.

find, *n. 1.* That which is found, particularly something valuable or interesting. *2.* Meteorite found but not observed to fall.

fine gold Almost pure gold. The value of bullion gold depends on its percentage of fineness. *See* FINENESS; FLOAT GOLD

fine-grained soil Soil consisting mostly of clay and silt, more than 50% by weight smaller than 0.074 mm. in diameter.

fineness The proportion of pure silver or gold in jewelry, bullion, or coin, often expressed in parts per thousand. The fineness of United States coin is nine-tenths, or 900 fine; that of English gold coin is eleven-twelfths or 917 fine, and English silver coin is 925 fine.

fineness factor A measure of average particle size obtained by summing the products of the reciprocal of the size grade midpoints times the frequency of particles in each class expressed as a decimal part of the total frequency.

fines *1.* The fine fraction of a sediment or the product of rock crushing, particularly that which passes through a grading sieve. *2.* The fraction of sand and gravel finer than 0.074 mm. in particle diameter.

fine sand All grains between .25 mm. and .125 mm. in diameter.

finger Minor structure radiating from a major one.

finger lake Long narrow rock basins occupied by lakes.

Fingerlakesian Lower Upper Devonian.

fiord; fjord A long, deep arm of the sea, occupying a portion of a channel having high steep walls, a bottom made uneven by bosses and sills, and with side streams entering from high-level valleys by cascades or steep rapids.

fire assay The assaying of metallic ores, usually gold and silver, by methods requiring a furnace heat. It commonly involves the processes of scorification, cupellation, etc.

fire clay *1.* Any clay capable of resisting very high heat without passing into a glassy clay, no alkaline substance being present to form a flux. *2.* Formerly used for almost any soft non-bedded clay immediately underlying a carboniferous coal bed, many of which are not refractory. *Cf.* UNTERCLAY

fire-clay mineral Mellorite. A poorly crystallized (partly disordered) kaolinite.

firefountaining The rhythmic eruption of gas-charged lava (normally basaltic) from a volcanic vent, either a localized central vent or a fissure, forming a fountain of molten rock. Lava fountains are a common type of eruption in Hawaii, issuing from fissures along rift zones on the flanks of Mauna Loa and commonly reaching heights of 300 feet and even 1000 feet in extreme cases. The coalescing of lava fountains along a fissure produces the so-called curtain of fire.

fire opal A transparent hyacinth-red opal which may or may not show play of colors.

firn *1.* A name given to snow above the glaciers which is partly consolidated by alternate thawing and freezing, but has not yet become glacier ice. *See* NÉVÉ. *2.* Compacted, granular but still pervious snow with a density usually greater than 0.4 but less than 0.82. By some workers considered to be any snow that has survived one or more ablation seasons. Firn may later become glacial ice. *Syn:* ACCUMULATION AREA. Névé is used as a synonym for firn in both senses.

firn basin Accumulation area of a glacier.

firn field *1.* A mass of firn which is not part of a glacier. *2.* The accumulation areas of a glacier.

firn limit The highest level on a glacier to which the snow cover recedes during the ablation season. Firn limit is preferable to firn line, for a zone of snow patches usually marks the transition from bare ice to a solid snow cover.

firn snow *See* FIRN, 2

first arrival The primary or first impulse recorded by seismographs. In the refraction method of seismic prospecting quantity observed is the time between the initiation of the seismic wave by an explosion and the first disturbance indicated by a seismic detector at a measured distance from the shot point. Since first arrivals only are considered, the wave causing the disturbance is that which has traveled the minimum time path between shot point and detector. *See* FERMAT'S PRINCIPLE

first law of thermodynamics The first law of thermodynamics introduces the concept of internal energy of a system and expresses the fact that the change of energy of the system is equal to the amount of energy received from the external world. The energy received from the external world is equal to the heat taken in by the system and the work done on the system.

first order geosyncline Extensive belt of major geosynclines such as that of the Alpine system.

first order nappe Overturned generally recumbent anticlinal fold in which the middle part of the overturned limb is replaced by a thrust fault.

firth A narrow arm of the sea; also the opening of a river into the sea. *Syn:* ESTUARY; FRITH

fishing The operation of attempting to recover a piece of drilling or other equipment broken off or lost from the drilling tools and left in the hole.

fishtail bit A rotary bit used to drill soft formations. The blade is flattened and divided, the divided ends curving away from the direction of rotation. Resembling a fishtail, hence the name.

fissile bedding Term applied to bedding which consists of laminae less than 2 mm. in thickness.

fissility A property of splitting easily along closely spaced parallel planes.

fission *1.* The splitting of an atomic nucleus into at least two parts of comparable size, accompanied by ejection of two or three neutrons (and occasionally other particles). *2.* Separation of calyx of coral by cleavage. *3.* Reproduction of the asexual type in which one polyp divides to form two new ones, as in coelenterates.

fissionable Capable of undergoing fission, usually by the action of neutrons, but also of protons, deuterons, alpha particles, electrons, and gamma radiation.

fissure *1.* An extensive crack, break, or fracture in the rocks. A mere joint or crack persisting only for a few inches or a few feet is not usually termed a fissure by geologists or miners, although in a strict physical sense it is one. *2.* Where there are well-defined boundaries, very slight evidence of ore within such boundaries is sufficient to prove the existence of a lode. Such boundaries constitute the sides of a fissure.

fissure eruption *See* ERUPTION, VOLCANIC

fissure polygons Nonsorted polygons.

fissure vein *1.* A cleft or crack in the rock material of the earth's crust, filled with mineral matter different from the walls and precipitated therein from aqueous solution, or introduced by sublimation or pneumatolysis. *2.* A mineral mass, tabular in form, as a whole, although frequently irregular in detail, occupying or accompanying a fracture or set of fractures in the inclosing rock; this mineral mass has been formed later than the country rock, either through the filling of open spaces along the latter or through chemical alteration of the adjoining rock.

fiveling Crystal formed by five-fold cyclic twinning.

fix The position on a map of a point of observation obtained by surveying processes. Also, the act of determining such a position.

fixed carbon In the case of coal, coke, and bituminous materials, the solid residue other than ash, obtained by destructive distillation, determined by definite prescribed methods.

fixed ground water Ground water held in saturated material with interstices so small that it is attached to the pore walls, and is usually not available as a source of water for pumping.

Flagellata Class of protozoans consisting of single-celled organisms of fixed shape with one or more long whiplike structures used for locomotion.

flagging *Geophys:* The use by surveyors of flags of cloth or paper to mark instrumental or shot locations.

flaggy Strata from 10 to 100 mm. thick.

flags Thin-bedded hard sandstone that can be used for flagstones.

flagstone A rock that splits readily into slabs suitable for flagging.

flake A flat fragment with maximum dimension of less than 4 mm.

flamboyant structure The optical continuity of the crystals or grains as disturbed by a divergent structure caused by slight differences in orientation.

flame photometry Spectrum measurement of a substance heated to incandescence in a flame.

flame struture *1.* Load cast showing evidence of some horizontal slip. *2.* Load cast in which part of an underlying layer has been squeezed irregularly upward into the overlying layer.

flame test The use of the characteristic coloration imparted to a flame to detect the presence of certain elements.

flammable Capable of being easily ignited. Preferred for technical use to inflammable because of ambiguity of the "in-" prefix. This usage is general in the petroleum industry.

flanking moraine The sidelong or flanking moraines left by lobations or tonguelike projections of an ice sheet.

flanks The limbs of folds. *Syn:* LEGS; SHANKS; BRANCHES; SLOPES

flap A gravity-collapse structure. A bed that has slid down the side of an anticline and bent over so that it is now upside down.

flaser gabbro A cataclastic gabbro in which are preserved lenses (phacoids, augen) of undeformed rock. *See* MYLONITE

flaser structure A structure developed in gneisses, gabbros, etc., by dynamic metamorphism. Small lenses of granular material are separated by wavy ribbons and streaks of finely crystalline, foliated material, usually aggregates of parallel scales in wavy or bent lines.

flash box A box in which a light source, electromagnet, and telescope are all mounted in the pendulum apparatus of gravitational recording.

flat *1.* A general term meaning smooth, or even; a surface of low relief. *See* TIDAL FLAT; VALLEY FLAT, etc. *2.* [*Derbyshire; N. Wales*] A horizontal vein or ore deposit; auxiliary to a main vein; also any horizontal portion of a vein elsewhere not horizontal.

flatiron A triangular-shaped sloping-mesa type of hogback ridge, often occurring in series on the flank of a mountain.

flat joint In igneous rocks, joint dipping at an angle of 45° or less, randomly oriented with respect to others.

flat lode A lode which varies in inclination from the horizontal to about 15°. *See* FLAT

flatness *1.* A measure of the shape of a pebble given by the sum of the long and intermediate diameters of the pebble divided by twice the short diameter. *2.* A measure of the shape of a pebble given by the ratio of the radius of curvature of the most convex portion of the flattest face to the mean radius of the pebble.

flat of ore A horizontal ore deposit occupying a bedding plane in the rock. *See* FLAT

flats and pitches *1.* In the Upper Mississippi lead and zinc district the term is applied to the near horizontal solution openings in the galena dolomite (flats) and the interconnecting inclined joints or fractures (pitches) in which the ore has been deposited. *2.* Applied to certain ore bodies of characteristic form that occur in regions of bedded sedimentary rocks. Such ore bodies have a steplike form with

the "flats" following nearly horizontal bedding planes and the "pitches" following steeply dipping joint planes or fractures.

flattening, plane of *Struct. petrol:* The pebbles or grains are flat and perpendicular to the greatest principal stress axis. The plane of schistosity is called a plane of flattening.

flaw Blatt [*Ger.*]. A steep, transverse fault along which the displacement has been parallel to the strike of the fault. That is, a steep, transverse strike-slip fault. *Cf.* TEAR FAULT

flaxseed ore An oölitic iron ore in which the oölites have been somewhat flattened parallel to the bedding plane so that they are disk-shaped rather than spherical.

F layer Atmospheric zone within the ionosphere at a height of about 225 km. that reflects high frequency radio waves.

fleckshiefer An argillaceous rock in which there has been incipient production of new minerals as a result of low-grade metamorphism. *See* SPOTTED SLATE

flexible Bends without breaking and without a tendency to return to its original form.

flexible sandstone Itacolumite, *q.v.*

flexural slip Movement in relatively competent rocks in which bending of layers dominates over slip between them.

flexure *1. Syn:* FOLD. *2.* A broad domical structure.

flexure correction A correction necessary in pendulum observations of gravity. The vibrating pendulum produces oscillations of the receiver case, of the pillar, and of the surface soil. Rather complex coupled vibration phenomena arise and the period of the pendulum itself changes.

Numerous methods have been suggested to correct for this influence or to eliminate it. Since the correction is of the order of 10- to 40 × 10^{-7} sec. on solid rock or cemented and may increase to as much as 500 × 10^{-7} sec. on marshy ground, it must be determined accurately.

flexure-slip folding Movement in a layered rock in which competent bands are folded but slipping occurs along deformed s-planes in incompetent bands; most common type of deformation.

flint A dense fine-grained form of silica which is very tough and breaks with a conchoidal fracture and cutting edges. Of various colors, white, yellow, gray, and black. *See* CHERT

flint clay A flintlike fire clay which when ground up develops no plasticity.

flint crush rock A black flinty product of dynamic metamorphism associated with mylonite, and representing a fritted or partly fused variety of the latter; generally structureless, but occasionally showing incipient traces of crystallization.

float; floater; float mineral; float ore Terms much used among miners and geologists for pieces of ore or rock which have fallen from veins or strata, or have been separated from the parent vein or strata by weathering agencies. Not usually applied to stream gravels.

float copper *1.* In the Lake Superior region, fine scales of metallic copper (especially produced by abrasion in stamping) which do not readily settle in water. *2.* Native copper found away from its original rock. *Cf.* FLOAT ORE

float gold; flour gold Particles

of gold so small and thin that they float on and are liable to be carried off by the water.

floating *1.* Relations of large sedimentary particles not in contact with each other contained in much finer grained matrix. *2.* Relations of quartz sand grains more or less sparingly disseminated in limestone.

floating sand grain Isolated sand grain, particularly in limestone, not in contact with other scattered grains.

float ore Fragments of vein material found on the surface, and usually downstream or downhill from the outcrop.

flocculant A substance that induces or promotes flocculation.

flocculate To aggregate into small lumps; said especially of soils and colloids.

floe Mass of floating ice some 100 feet to 5 miles across not fast to any shore, formed by breaking up of the frozen surface of a large body of water.

floe-berg A thick mass of floe ice heaped together by the collision of floes with each other or with the shore.

floe ice Floating ice of much greater thickness is sometimes seen, but it is doubtful if these great thicknesses represent the ice formed by freezing of undisturbed sea water. At any rate, the ice formed in winter is often broken up in summer into floating pieces, floe ice, and the floe ice is sometimes crowded together in ice packs.

floe till *See* TILL

floetz The name given by A. G. Werner to certain rocks which were flat, horizontal, and parallel to each other.

flood *1.* Any relatively high streamflow which overtops the natural or artificial banks in any reach of a stream. *2. Sedimentary petrol:* A term implying the occurrence of a particular species so far in excess of all others as to constitute almost a pure concentrate.

flood basalt *See* PLATEAU BASALT

flood basin The flood basins can be defined either as the tracts actually covered by water during the highest known floods or as the flat areas between the sloping low plains on one side and the river lands on the other, occupied by heavy soils and commonly having either no vegetation or a strictly swampy vegetation.

flood current The movement of the tidal current toward the shore or up a tidal stream.

flood frequency Over a period of years, the average number of times a flood of a given magnitude is likely to occur.

flooding A term used for the drowning out of a well by water, often resulting from drilling too deeply into the sand.

flood peak The maximum rate of flow attained at a given point during a flood event.

flood plain That portion of a river valley, adjacent to the river channel, which is built of sediments during the present regimen of the stream and which is covered with water when the river overflows its banks at flood stages.

flood-plain meander scar A class of scars which includes any and all features on a flood plain that mark the former course of a stream meander.

flood-plain scrolls Patches of material having curved crescentic shapes originating from deposition along the inside curve of river meanders, and incorporated

in large numbers into the flood plain.

flood tide *1.* The flow, or rising toward the shore, is called flood tide, and the falling away, ebb tide. *2.* A nontechnical term referring to that period of tide between low water and the succeeding high water; a rising tide.

floor *1.* The bed or bottom of the ocean. A comparatively level valley bottom; any low-lying ground surface. *2.* That part of any subterranean gallery upon which you walk or upon which a tramway is laid.

flora The plants collectively of a given formation, age, or region. *Cf.* FAUNA

flos ferri An arborescent variety of aragonite.

flotation Method of mineral separation whereby a froth created in water by a variety of reagents floats some finely crushed minerals whereas others sink.

flour copper Very fine scaly native copper that floats on water and is very difficult to save in milling. *See* FLOAT COPPER

flour gold The finest gold dust, much of which will float on water. *See* FLOAT GOLD

flow *1.* The movement of a fluid such as air, water, or magma. *2.* The plastic deformation of solids. *Syn:* SOLID FLOW; ROCK FLOWAGE; PLASTIC FLOW. *3.* A tabular-shaped body of lava that consolidated from magma on the surface of the earth.

flow, gliding That type of solid flow which takes place by the combined mechanisms of translation- and twin-gliding.

flow, pseudoviscous Load recrystallization. The type of solid flow which takes place under a strain and a stress too low to produce gliding flow, producing instead intergranular movement and dimensional orientation for the most part.

flowage folds *1.* Minor folds that are the result of the flowage of rocks toward a synclinal axis, toward which the minor folds are overturned. *2.* Folds in which layers of rock are thinned at crest and thickened at trough.

flow banding A structure of igneous rocks, especially common to silicic lava flows, due to the movement or flow of magmas or lavas and evidenced by the alternation of mineralogically unlike layers.

flow breccia A type of lava flow, usually of silicic composition, in which fragments of solidified or partly solidified lava, produced by explosion or flowage, have become welded together or cemented by the still fluid parts of the same flow.

flow cast A "roll," lobate ridge, or other raised feature produced on the underside of a sand layer by the sand's flowing into a depression in underlying soft hydroplastic sediment. The underlying rock, typically coal or mudstone, preserves no diagnostic structure.

flow cleavage That variety of rock cleavage that is the result of solid flow of the rock. *See* FOLIATION

flow-duration curve A curve secured from an arrangement of daily streamflows in the order of their magnitudes.

flow earth Material on a slope characterized by local derivation and lack of sorting. *Syn:* SOLIFLUCTION MANTLE

flow folding Ptygmatic folding. Folding in beds which offer so little resistance to deformation that they assume any shape impressed upon them by more rigid

rocks surrounding them or by the general stress pattern of the deformed zone.

flow gneiss Gneiss whose structure was produced by flowage in an igneous mass before complete solidification.

flowing well Well from which water or oil flows without pumping.

flow layer Rock layer differing mineralogically or structurally from adjacent layers produced by flowage before the complete consolidation of magma.

flow lines *See* FLOW STRUCTURE; FLOW TEXTURE

flow stage That stage in the consolidation of a magma when it is still sufficiently fluid to flow as a liquid.

flowstone Deposits of calcium carbonate have also accumulated against the walls in many places where water trickles from the rock. Here and there these accumulations assume forms that closely resemble masses of ice, and some of the "cascades frozen in stone" are large and impressive. To distinguish this material from that deposited by dripping water, it has been called flowstone.

flow stretching Orientation and possible deformation of crystals with long axes in direction of plastic flow in metamorphic rocks.

flow structure Fluidal structure. A structure of igneous rocks, generally but not necessarily restricted to volcanic rocks, in which the stream or flow lines of the magma are revealed by alternating bands or layers of differing composition, crystallinity, or texture, or by a subparallel arrangement of prismatic or tabular crystals.

flow surface Plane separating adjacent flow layers.

flow symmetry Symmetry of movement comparable to the symmetry of equal and interchangeable parts located with reference to a center or one or more axes or planes. *See* AXIAL, ISOTROPIC, MONOCLINIC, ORTHO- RHOMBIC, POLAR, TETRAGONAL and TRICLINIC SYMMETRY

flow texture Fluidal texture. A texture common to the glassy groundmass of extrusive rocks; especially lavas, in which the stream or flow lines of the once molten material are revealed by a subparallel arrangement of prismatic or tabular crystals or microlites.

flow units The nearly contemporaneous subdivisions of a lava flow (usually basaltic) which consists of two or more parts poured one over the other during the course of a single eruption. In cross section, a typical flow unit has a lenticular form, ranging from about 100 to 300 feet in width and from 10 to 30 feet in thickness. In the longitudinal direction the unit may be as much as a half mile long.

fluid *1.* Having particles which move easily and change their relative position without a separation of the mass, and which yield easily to pressure; capable of flowing; liquid or gaseous. *2.* A substance in which the constituent particles are in disordered array, permitting deformation when subjected to stress. The distinction between plastic and fluid is generally in degree of deformation under a given stress. *3.* A substance of properties intermediate between those of a gas and a liquid, *q.v.* The specific definition of fluid in phase equilibrium studies in-

cludes all noncrystalline phases, with the exception of the special limiting cases of a liquid and a gas phase, when in equilibrium with each other.

fluid contact The surface in a reservoir separating two regions characterized by predominant differences in fluid saturation. Because of capillary and other phenomena, fluid-saturization change is not necessarily abrupt or complete, nor is the surface necessarily horizontal.

fluid inclusions *See* INCLUSIONS, FLUID

fluidity factor Relation between the densities of a fluid and suspended solid particles which in part determines the sorting of transported sediment.

fluidization Process in which gas passes through loose fine-grained material, mixes with it, and causes it to flow like a liquid; may occur at the time of volcanic eruption as in a glowing avalanche.

fluid pressure Pressure exerted by fluid contained in rock.

flume A deep, narrow ravine or gorge, with nearly perpendicular walls and a stream forming a series of cascades.

fluorapatite *See* APATITE

fluorbarite Trade name for a fluorite-barite mixture used in glassmaking.

fluorescence Emission of visible light by a substance exposed to ultraviolet light, useful in examining well cuttings for oil shows and in prospecting for some minerals.

fluoride A compound of fluorine with one other element or radical.

fluorite Fluorspar. A mineral, CaF_2. Isometric. The principal ore of fluorine.

fluorographic method A method

involving exposing soil samples to ultraviolet light and recording the emitted light on a light-sensitive medium. The densities of the recorded sample images are measured by a transmission photometer.

fluorologging A logging technique based on the principle that the rocks overlying an oil accumulation are characterized by anomalously high fluorescent intensities. This technique involves the preparation of logs by plotting the fluorescent intensity of well cuttings against depth.

fluorspar Fluorite.

flushing The driving of oil or gas from a trap through the agency of ground water. Flushing may occur wherever there is sufficient water in motion, but particularly near the rim of artesian basins.

flute Asymmetrical scalloped rock surfaces. Drapes of drip or flowstone (commercial cave). *Syn:* FACET; SOLUTION RIPPLE

flute casts Sharp, subconical welts occurring on bottom surfaces of sandstone layers, in which one end is rounded or bulbous and the other flares out to merge gradually with the striated bottom of the sandstone layer.

fluting *1.* Smooth gutterlike channels or deep smooth furrows worn in the surface of rocks by glacial action. *2.* Fluting is a peculiar method of surface decay by which granite or gneisses are left with a corrugated or fluted surface.

fluvial Of, or pertaining to, rivers; growing or living in streams or ponds; produced by river action, as, a fluvial plain.

fluvial geomorphic cycle The normal cycle of erosion by streams, leading to the formation of a peneplain.

fluviatile Belonging to a river; produced by river action; growing or living in fresh-water rivers.

fluviatile dam Dam formed in a valley of sediment deposited by a tributary.

fluviation All of the numerous activities engaged in and the various processes employed by streams are grouped under fluviation. Hence, gradation is carried on or achieved principally by the process of fluviation.

fluvioglacial Glaciofluvial. Pertaining to streams flowing from glaciers or to the deposits made by such streams.

flux *1.* Substance that reduces the melting point of a mixture. *2.* Passage across a physical boundary such as CO_2 from atmosphere to hydrosphere, or across a chemical boundary as CO_2 from atmosphere to organic matter. *3.* State of change.

fluxing ore An ore containing an appreciable amount of valuable metal, but smelted mainly because it contains fluxing agents required in the reduction of richer ores.

flux stone Limestone, dolomite, or other rock used in metallurgical processes to lower the fusion temperature of ore.

flysch The widespread deposits of sandstones, marls, shales, and clays, which lie on the northern and southern borders of the Alps. Although largely consisting of sandy and calcareous shales (hence the name—in reference to their fissile character) the flysch also contains beds of sandstone and conglomerate.

fo Abbreviation for forsterite. *See* OLIVINE

foam crust An ablation feature on snow which has the appearance of small overlapping waves like sea foam on a beach. Foam crust is the result of evaporation by the sun's rays. Foam crust may develop into ploughshares.

focal sphere Theoretical sphere enclosing the focal region of an earthquake.

focus *Seismol:* The source of a given set of elastic waves. The true center of an earthquake, within which the strain energy is first converted to elastic wave energy.

foehn A warm, dry wind which blows down the slopes on the leeward of a ridge of mountains. Owing to its warmth and dryness it melts the snow very quickly and causes a considerable rise in temperature.

The air when coming against the ridge of mountains ascends and dynamic cooling takes place with condensation and precipitation. The temperature of the air falls at the adiabatic rate for wet air, that is at about 1° C. for every 200 meters of ascent. When the air descends the slopes on the other side of the mountain, having lost its moisture, it is dynamically warmed at the "dry adiabatic" rate of 1° C. for every 100 meters and reaches the valleys as a warm, dry wind.

The foehn is likely to occur wherever cyclonic systems pass over mountainous regions; it frequently occurs on the coast of Greenland.

fog A cloud formed at the surface of the earth by the condensation of atmospheric water vapor into a multitude of minute water droplets (average diameter about 40 microns) or, less frequently, tiny ice crystals, which interferes to varying degrees with the horizontal visibility at the surface. The types of fog may be classified as follows:

(a) Air-mass fogs, in which the principal factor of formation is the cooling of the air to its dew point. They consist of three main types, advection fog, radiation fog, and upslope fog.

(b) Frontal fogs, in which the evaporation of water vapor into the air from falling precipitation, acts to raise the dew point while other factors lower the temperature so that condensation results. Frontal fogs are subdivided into the prefrontal, frontal passage, and postfrontal types.

fold *1.* A bend in strata or any planar structure. *2.* A broad median external undulation or plica that may be situated on either the dorsal or ventral valve of a brachiopod. *3.* Major rounded elevation of a brachiopod shell along longitudinal mid-line, affecting both outer and inner shell surfaces; generally on brachial valve.

fold, flexure A type of fold, in size microscopic to orogenic, in which movement took place normal to the axial line and parallel with the limbs, producing notable shortening. The thickness of the sliding prisms forming the limbs directly with the amplitude of the resulting fold.

fold-fault Fault formed in causal connection with folding.

fold nappe A recumbent fold, of which the reversed middle limb has been completely sheared out as a result of the great horizontal translation.

fold system Group of folds showing common characteristics and trends and, presumably, of common origin.

foliate A general term for any foliated rock. *See* GNEISS; SCHIST

foliation *1.* The laminated

structure resulting from segregation of different minerals into layers parallel to the schistosity. 2. Foliation is considered synonymous with "flow cleavage," "slaty cleavage," and schistosity by many writers to describe parallel fabrics in metamorphic rocks. Considerable ambiguity attends their current use. 3. In addition to its rude stratification, the ice of the deeper portions of a glacier often acquires a stratiform structure which may perhaps best be called foliation to distinguish it from stratification which arises from deposition. The foliation appears to result mainly from the shearing of one part over another in the course of movements to which the ice is subjected.

foliation, axial-plane *See* AXIAL-PLANE FOLDING

fondo The environment represented by all of the ocean floor not encompassed by unda and clino, *q.v.*

fondoform The subaqueous land form constituting the main floor of the water body.

fondothem A rock unit formed in a fondo, *q.v.*, environment.

fool's gold Pyrite, a sulfide of iron, FeS_2.

foot The bottom of a slope, grade, or declivity. A term for the lower part of any elevated land form.

foothill One of the lower subsidiary hills at the foot of a mountain, or of higher hills. Commonly used in the plural.

footwall The mass of rock beneath a fault plane, vein, lode, or bed of ore.

foram Abbreviated name for foraminifer.

Foraminifera Subclass of the Sarcodina; unicellular animals mostly of microscopic size that secrete tests, composed of calcium carbonate, or build them of cemented sedimentary grains, consisting of one to many chambers arranged in a great variety of ways. Most are marine. Ord.-Rec.

force That which changes or tends to produce a change in the state of rest or motion of a body.

ford Passage across a stream where water is not too deep for wading or the movement of land vehicles.

foredeep A long, narrow, crustal depression, or furrow, bordering a folded orogenic belt or island arc on the convex side, commonly on the oceanward side.

foredune Dune developed along the shoreward face of a beach ridge.

foreland *1.* A promontory; a jutting of high land into the sea. At the beginning of a cycle the waves attack the coast at all points, cutting or nipping back the initial form of the land into a cliff; at a later stage, transportation of material alongshore begins, and the waste from the edge and bottom of the land, together with the river sediment, is built out at certain points in front of the older mainland in deposits of various shapes, which are appropriately grouped together under the general term forelands. *2.* In folded mountain ranges three zones may be distinguished: (1) a rigid, unyielding mass which is not folded, (2) the zone of folding, (3) the zone of diminishing action, where the folding gradually dies away or ends in a fault. The side of the range toward which the overturned folds incline is called the foreland, and may be either the unfolded mass or the zone of diminishing action. *3.* The relatively stable area, lying in shallower water, represented by the continental platform. *4.* The resistant block toward which the geosynclinal sediments move when compressed. *5.* In its structural sense: The region in front of a series of overthrust sheets.

foreland shelf Part of the relatively stable continental region that extends inward from the hingebelt of a geosyncline.

fore limb Steeper dipping side of an asymmetrical anticline produced by lateral thrusting.

fore reef The steeply dipping talus slope commonly found on the seaward side of an organic reef.

fore-set beds The series of inclined layers accumulated as sediment rolls down the steep frontal slope of a delta. *See* BOTTOM-SET BEDS; TOP-SET BEDS

foreshock An earthquake which precedes a larger earthquake within a fairly short time interval (of the order of a few days or weeks), and which originates at or near the focus of the larger earthquake.

foreshore Lower shore zone, between ordinary low and high water levels. *Cf.* BACKSHORE

foresight A sight on a new survey point, made in connection with its determination; or a sight on a previously established point, to close a circuit.

foreslope Slope extending from the outer margin of an organic reef to an arbitrary depth of 6 fathoms.

forest bed Interglacial deposit containing woody remains of trees and other vegetation.

form All the faces of a crystal that have a like position relative to the elements (planes, axes, etc.) of symmetry.

format Informal rock stratigraphic unit bounded by marker horizons believed to be isochronous surfaces that can be traced across facies changes, particularly in the subsurface, and useful for correlations between areas where the stratigraphic section is divided into different formations that do not correspond in time value.

formation *1.* Something naturally formed, commonly differing conspicuously from adjacent objects or material, or being noteworthy for some other reason. *2. Stratig:* The primary unit in lithostratigraphy consisting of a succession of strata useful for mapping or description. Most formations possess certain distinctive lithologic features that may indicate genetic relationships. Ordinarily the upper and lower boundaries of a formation are determined lithologically, but they may be unconformities or be determined by the occurrence of guide fossils. The age or time value of a formation is not necessarily the same wherever it is recognized. Formations may be combined in groups or subdivided into members. *3. Speleol:* Secondary deposit in a cave forming stalactites, stalagmites, etc. *4. Paleobot:* Biome; climax.

formation factor The electrical resistance of a rock saturated with an electrolyte, divided by the resistivity of the electrolyte. There is an inverse linear relationship between the formation factor and the porosity and permeability of the rock. Known also as formation resistivity factor.

formation water Water naturally occurring in sedimentary strata. *Cf.* CONNATE WATER

form contour Topographic contour determined by stereoscopic study of aerial photographs without ground control or by other means not involving conventional surveying.

form energy Potentiality of minerals to develop crystal form within a solid medium.

form genus *1.* A series of related genera which have resulted from the splitting up of an old familiar genus, as, Fusulina, Productus, etc. *2.* A complex of genera which are known to be distinct but which have not as yet been named because all have the same general habit. Examples are Tetragraptus and Monograptus. *3.* A general designation for the residuum after a genus has been partly revised. Examples are Zaphrentis, Orthoceras, and Calymene. *4.* Fossil plants are named according to the same set of rules that governs the naming of living plants, but the names usually refer to parts rather than complete organisms. Since the generic name may apply to only a leaf, a seed, or some other part, the genus is called a form genus or artificial genus, as contrasted with a natural genus.

form species *1.* A group of closely related species, all of which possess essentially similar characteristics but vary each from the other in features now considered to be of about varietal value. *2.* A morphotypic species.

forsterite *See* OLIVINE

fosse *1.* Depression or unfilled area often found between the terraced ice contact of glacial sand plains and morainal mounds forming a belt within the ice-covered field, as on Nantucket. *2.* A ditch, moat, or trench, specifically between a glacier and a moraine or rock wall.

fossil *1.* The remains or traces of animals or plants which have

been preserved by natural causes in the earth's crust exclusive of organisms which have been buried since the beginning of historic time. *2.* Anything dug from the earth. *Obs.*

fossil assemblage Fossils naturally associated in a stratum; they possibly were derived from more than a single fossil community.

fossil community Fossils that in life were ecologically related among themselves.

fossil cow's horn Horn coral, *q.v.*

fossil fuel Coal and petroleum.

fossiliferous Containing organic remains.

fossilize To convert into a fossil; to petrify.

fossil ore Fossiliferous red hematite.

fossil soil A soil developed upon an old land surface and later covered by younger formations.

fossil wax *See* OZOCERITE

founder To sink deeply, generally beneath the sea.

foundry sand Includes those siliceous sands that are used to make the forms for casting metals.

Four Corners Region General region where Utah, Colorado, Arizona, and New Mexico meet. This is the only place in the United States where four states have a common corner.

foveolate, *adj.* Pitted. The pit (foveola) may be solitary or not.

fractional crystallization Separation of a magma into two phases, crystals and liquid, possibly followed by a gross separation of the two phases from each other by other processes such as filter pressing, etc.

fractionation Separation of a substance from a mixture, e.g., one isotope from another of the same element.

fracture *1.* The manner of breaking and appearance of a mineral when broken, which is distinctive for certain minerals, as conchoidal fracture. 2. Breaks in rocks due to intense folding or faulting. 3. The process of breaking oil-, gas-, or water-bearing strata by injecting a fluid under such pressure as to cause partings in the rock.

fracture cleavage Fracture cleavage is a capacity to part along closely spaced parallel surfaces of fracture or near-fracture, commonly in a single set, but occasionally in intersecting sets. It is closely related to joint structure, but the joints are so closely spaced as to give the rock a distinctive structure not ordinarily to be described in terms of joints. Where the fracture cleavage is in a single direction the rock is rendered minutely fissile parallel to a single surface. When in intersecting sets, the rock breaks in polygonal blocks or in parallelopipeds. Fracture cleavage differs from ordinary flow cleavage or schistosity in that the surfaces of breaking are not determined by a parallel arrangement of mineral particles but are independent of any such arrangement. Also it does not pervade the entire mass and affect all particles, as does flow cleavage.

fractured Fissured. Broken by interconnecting cracks. A common structure in limestone oil reservoirs (Ellenburger, W. Tex.; Hunton, Okla.). Reported to exist in certain shale reservoirs (Mancos, Col.; Monterey, Calif.).

fracture porosity Porosity resulting from presence of openings produced by the breaking or shattering of an otherwise less pervious rock.

fracturing See HYDROFRACTURING

fragmental Consisting of broken material, particularly that which has been moved from its place of origin.

fragmental rocks Clastics.

fragmental texture A general term applied to that of rocks composed of fine materials and including sandy, conglomeratic, bouldery, and brecciated materials. A texture of clastic rocks.

fragmentary 1. Geol: Applied to rock masses composed of the fragments or debris of other rocks; rocks not homogeneous in texture; nearly synonymous with breccias or breccioconglomerates, q.v. 2. Rocks consisting of a congeries of particles which have not grown together but are fragments which have been broken off their parent masses and brought together by some external agency, their coherence being caused either by mechanical compression or by a cement of some other substance.

francolite See APATITE

Franconian Middle Croixan.

frangible Capable of being broken; breakable; brittle; fragile.

franklinite A mineral, (Fe,″Zn,- Mn″)(Fe,‴Mn‴)$_2$O$_4$, a member of the spinel group. Isometric. An ore of zinc.

Frasch process A process for mining sulfur in which superheated water is forced into the sulfur deposits for the purpose of melting the sulfur. The molten sulfur is then pumped to the surface. Used extensively in Louisiana and Texas.

Frasnian Lower Upper Devonian.

Fredericksburgian Upper Lower Cretaceous.

free 1. Native; uncombined with other substances, as, free gold or silver. 2. Coal is said to be "free" when it is loose and easily mined, or when it will "run" without mining.

free-air anomaly The difference at any point on the earth between the measured gravity and the gravity calculated for the theoretical gravity at sea level and a "free-air" coefficient determined only by the elevation of the station with respect to sea level.

free-air correction See FREE-AIR ANOMALY

free coal In Scotland, coal easily broken or which burns freely.

free energy The capacity of a system to perform work, a change in free energy being measured by the maximum work obtainable from a given process.

free-milling Applied to ores which contain free gold or silver, and can be reduced by crushing and amalgamation, without roasting or other chemical treatment.

free period (of a seismograph) The time for one complete swing of the seismograph mass when all damping is removed and the earth is quiet.

freeze The condition which exists when over a widespread area the surface temperature of a whole air mass remains below 0° C. or 32° F. for a sufficient time to constitute the characteristic feature of the weather. It differs from the "dry freeze" or "black frost," purely local freezing due to chilling of the surface air by rapid radiation from a restricted portion of the earth.

freezing index Number of degree-days between highest and lowest points on a curve of cumulative degree-days versus time for one freezing season; a measure of combined duration and magnitude of below-freezing temperature during a freezing season.

freezing interval That temperature interval between the solidus and the liquidus for a given composition. Syn: CRYSTALLIZATION INTERVAL

freezing point The temperature at which a liquid solidifies; especially applied to pure water which has its freezing point at 0° C. or 32° F. under normal atmospheric pressure.

freibergite A silver-rich variety of tetrahedrite.

frequency The number of complete waves which pass a given point per second, or the number of complete vibrations per second, or revolutions per second, made by a vibrating particle.

frequency distribution The numerical or quantitative distribution of objects or material in a series of closely related classes generally selected on the basis of some progressively variable physical character.

fresh water Water with less than 0.2 per cent salinity.

fresh-water limestone Underclay limestone. 1. A limestone formed by direct precipitation in fresh water. 2. A thin dense nodular, relatively unfossiliferous limestone underlying the coals and closely related to the underclay in the Central Interior Coal Basin.

Fresnel ellipsoid Ellipsoid the lengths of whose axes are proportional to the velocities of light vibrating parallel to X, Y, and Z.

friable Easily crumbled, as would be the case with rock that is poorly cemented.

frigid climate Climate of a region in which there is a more or less permanent cover of snow and ice and material a little below the ground surface is permanently frozen.

fringe water Water occurring in the capillary fringe.

fringing reef *1.* The coral reefs around other lands or islands rest on the bottom along the shores. They are either fringing or barrier reefs, according to their position. Fringing reefs are attached directly to the shore, while barrier reefs, like artificial moles, are separated from the shore by a channel of water. *2.* A reef whose inner margin is composed of a belt of materials which have become subaerial through wind and waves; the outer margin consists of submerged coral rock and living corals.

frit *N: 1.* Material of which glass is composed; *2.* Semifused stony mass. *V: 3.* To partly fuse.

frith Estuary; fiord; firth, *q.v.*

front *1. Petrol:* A metamorphic zone of changing mineralization developed outward from a large expanding igneous intrusion; *cf.* BASIC FRONT. *2. Meteor:* The contact between two different air masses, commonly cold and warm, that generally moves in an easterly direction. *3. Topog:* More or less linear outer slope of a mountain range that rises above a plain or plateau.

frontal moraine Terminal moraine.

frontland Foreland.

front pinacoid Orthopinacoid. *See* PINACOID

frost *1.* A light, feathery deposit of ice caused by the condensation of water vapor, directly in the crystalline form, on terrestrial objects whose temperatures are below freezing, the process being the same as that by which dew is formed, except that the latter occurs only when the temperature of the bedewed object is above freezing. Frost is designated as "light," "heavy," or "killing" by the U. S. Weather

Bureau. *2.* The occurrence of temperatures below freezing.

frost action The weathering process caused by repeated cycles of freezing and thawing.

frost circles Circular cracks developed by freezing in horizontal thin bedded limestone cut by two sets of joints meeting at right angles; commonly 15 to 25 feet in diameter.

frost crack Opening in soil produced by the development of an ice wedge.

frost-crack polygon Nonsorted polygon produced by low temperature contraction of frozen ground.

frost creep Soil creep resulting from frost action.

frost-heaved mound Stone ring, *q.v.*

frost heaving The lifting of a surface by the internal action of frost. It generally occurs after a thaw, when the soil is filled with water droplets and when a sudden drop of the temperature below freezing changes the droplets into ice crystals, which involves expansion, and consequently causes an upward movement of the soil.

frost hillocks The marked upward bulging sometimes present in the center of each polygon in cellular soils.

frosting A lusterless, ground-glass, or mat surface imposed on the surface of rounded quartz grains because of innumerable close contacts with other similar grains. Generally believed to be caused by wind action.

frost line The maximum depth to which the ground becomes frozen; it may be given for a particular winter, for the average of several winters, or for the extreme depth ever reached. In the United States, frost penetrates on the average to about an inch in the south up to over 60 inches in Minnesota and Maine.

frost mound General term for knolls, hummocks, and hills associated with frozen ground; includes earth hummocks, falsen, pinges.

frost polygons *See* POLYGON GROUND

frost splitting Breaking of rock by water freezing in its cracks.

frost stirring Frost heaving and thrusting in surface zone of annual freeze and thaw; does not involve mass movement.

frost thrusting Lateral soil movement resulting from freezing.

frost weathering The mechanical disintegration of earth materials brought about by frost action. Frost wedging.

frost wedging Frost weathering.

frozen Said of vein material which adheres closely to the inclosing walls.

frozen ground Tjäle. Ground that has a temperature 0° or lower and generally contains a variable amount of water in the form of ice.

frustule The siliceous shell of a diatom, consisting of two valves, one overlapping the other.

Fs Abbreviation for ferrosilite.

fucoid A term commonly applied in the past to any indefinite marking found on a sediment which could not be referred to a described genus. The term was derived from the marine alga, fucus, which it was supposed might leave such a marking if buried under favorable conditions.

fugitive constituents Those substances which were present in the magma before crystallization set in, but were for the greater part lost during the process of crystallization, so that they do not commonly appear as rock constituents.

fulcrum The intersection of the end of a recurved spit with the next succeeding stage in development of a compound recurved spit.

fulgurite [<*Lat.* fulgur, lightning] Little tubes of glassy rock that have been fused from all sorts of other rocks by lightning strokes. They are especially frequent in exposed crags on mountain tops.

Fuller's earth A fine earth resembling clay, but lacking plasticity. It is much the same chemically as clay, but has a decidedly higher percentage of water. It is high in magnesia and possesses the property of decolorizing oils and fats by retaining the coloring matter.

fumarole A hole or vent from which fumes or vapors issue; a spring or geyser which emits steam or gaseous vapor; found usually in volcanic areas.

fundamental form Unit form.

fundamental strength The maximum stress that a substance can withstand, regardless of time, under given physical conditions without rupturing or plastically deforming continuously.

Fungi Class of thallophytes, probably polyphyletic, multicelled plants that feed on organic matter rather than performing photosynthesis. Dev-Rec.

funnel pluton Pluton having the general shape of an inverted cone; most consist of layered gabbroic rocks.

furcate Forked.

furrow *1.* [*Ger.* Furche; *Fr.* sillon] A valley or channel-like hollow in the continental border, and more or less at right angles to it. *2.* An elongated depression in the earth's crust of a depth excessive in comparison to the ordinary, more or less equidimensional depressions of the ocean floors and the continental platforms.

furrow cast Impression on the lower side of a sedimentary layer of a furrow in the surface of its underlying bed.

fusain Coal material with the appearance and structure of charcoal; friable, sooty, and generally high in ash; consists mainly of fusite.

fusibility scale A list of minerals arranged in the order of their fusibility; von Kobell's scale of fusibility follows: (1) stibnite, (2) natrolite, (3) almandine garnet, (4) actinolite, (5) orthoclase, (6) bronzite.

fusiform, *adj.* Spindle-shaped; narrowed both ways from a swollen middle.

fusion *1.* Act or operation of melting or rendering liquid by heat. *2.* State of being melted or dissolved by heat. *3.* Union or blending of things as if melted together.

fusion-pressure curve; fusion curve A pressure vs. temperature plot of the univariant equilibrium crystal liquid in a unary system; sometimes incorrectly assumed to represent the behavior of the same substance in the earth (not a unary system).

fusulinid Any fossil belonging to one of the several genera of the Fusulinidae; a foraminifer shaped like a grain of wheat. Fusulinids are important guide fossils in the Pennsylvanian and Permian systems.

future ore A class of ore whose existence is a reasonable possibility in view of the strength and continuity of geologic-mineralogic relationships and extent of ore bodies already developed, a measure of whose continuity is available as a criterion of what may be expected as mining operations progress. *Syn:* POSSIBLE ORE

G

g *1. Earthquake seismol:* A phase designation applied to Love waves of very long period (25 sec. to several minutes), which, when detectable, are the first (fastest) surface waves on seismograms of distant earthquakes. *2.* Designation for gravity in formulas.

gabbro *1.* A plutonic rock consisting of calcic plagioclase (commonly labradorite) and clinopyroxene, with or without orthopyroxene and olivine. Apatite and magnetite or ilmenite are common accessories. *2.* Loosely used for any coarse-grained dark igneous rock.

gage height The water-surface elevation referred to some arbitrary datum.

gahnite A mineral, $(Zn,Fe,''Mg)-Al_2O_4$, a member of the spinel group. Isometric.

gal An acceleration of one centimeter per second per second. A milligal is 0.001 gal. The term gal is not an abbreviation: it was invented to honor the memory of Galileo.

gale In general, a wind with a velocity exceeding 30 miles an hour; the precise limiting velocities vary among the different meteorological services. In both British and American practice, however, it is a wind of force 8 or 9 in the original Beaufort wind scale, *q.v.,* i.e., the velocity is from 39 to 54 miles an hour.

Gale alidade Explorer's alidade.

A light compact alidade, with a low pillar and a reflecting prism through which the ocular may be viewed from above. As used by petroleum geologists it is commonly equipped with the Stebinger drum, *q.v.*

galena Galenite. Lead glance. A mineral, PbS. Isometric. The principal ore of lead.

gallery *1.* A subsidiary passage in a cave at a higher level than the main passage. *2.* A horizontal or nearly horizontal underground passage either natural or artificial.

galvanometer An instrument for measuring a small electric current or for detecting its presence or direction by means of the movement of a magnetic needle or of a wire or coil in a magnetic field. String (wire) or mirror galvanometers are used in oscillographs and other instruments of applied geophysics.

Gamachian Upper Cincinnatian.

gamete A sex cell which fuses with another sex cell in sexual reproduction.

gamma Common unit of magnetic intensity, equal to 10^{-5} oersted.

gamma radiation Emission by radioactive substances of quanta of energy corresponding to X rays and visible light but with a much shorter wave length than light; may be detected by gamma-ray Geiger counters.

gamma ray Rays or quanta of

energy emitted by radioactive substances corresponding to X rays and visible light but having a much shorter wave length than light.

gamma-ray log Record of radioactive intensity in strata penetrated in a well.

gamma-ray well logging A method of logging boreholes by observing the natural radioactivity of rocks through which the hole passes. It was developed for logging holes which can not be logged electrically because they are cased.

gamma structure 1. Thrust sheet with underlying low-angle thrust plane steepening abruptly downward. 2. Overthrusting or overfolding in one direction only.

gangue The nonmetalliferous or nonvaluable metalliferous minerals in the ore; veinstone or lode filling. The mineral associated with the ore in a vein.

ganister 1. A highly refractory siliceous sedimentary rock used for furnace linings. 2. A mixture of ground quartz and fire clay, used in lining Bessemer converters. 3. A local name for a fine close-grained siliceous clay that occurs under certain coal beds in Derbyshire, Yorkshire, and the North of England.

gap 1. In Pennsylvania, any deep sharp notch in a mountain ridge. Water gaps are those notches or passes which penetrate to the bases of the mountains, and give passage to the larger streams. 2. Any deep notch, ravine, or opening between hills or in a ridge or mountain chain. 3. In faulting, the horizontal separation, q.v., can be measured parallel to the strike of the fault. Gap is that component of this separation measured parallel to the strike of the disrupted index

plane (bed, vein, dike, etc.). Overlap is defined in the same way; however, gap is used when it is possible to walk at right angles to the strike of the disrupted index plane and miss it completely. Overlap is used when under similar conditions one would cross the index plane twice in certain places. 4. A steep-sided furrow which cuts transversely across a ridge or rise.

Gargasian Upper Aptian.

garnet A mineral group, formula $A_3B_2(SiO_4)_3$, where $A=Ca,Mg,Fe^{++}$, and Mn^{++}; and $B=Al$, Fe^{++}, Mn^{++} and Cr. Isometric. The principal end members are almandine ($Fe''Al$), pyrope (Mg-Al), spessartite (MnAl), grossularite (CaAl), andradite (Ca-Fe'''), and uvarovite (CaCr). Garnet from contact metamorphosed limestones is usually grossularite-andradite, from pegmatites usually spessartite, from schists usually almandine-pyrope, from kimberlites usually pyrope. Used as a gem and as an abrasive.

garnierite Name given to various poorly defined hydrated magnesium nickel silicates. An ore of nickel.

gas 1. A fluid having neither independent shape nor volume, but tending to expand indefinitely. 2. As generally used, a fluid of low density and high compressibility. The specific recognition of a gas as distinct from a liquid of the same composition requires the simultaneous presence of both phases at equilibrium. See LIQUID; VAPOR; FLUID. 3. Gas is considered as a mineral and while *in situ* is a part of the land.

gas cap Free gas occurring above oil in a reservoir, and present whenever more gas is available than will dissolve in the associated oil under existing pressure and temperature.

gas-cap drive The force exerted by the energy of expanding gas of a gas cap, used to produce oil from the reservoir.

gas cycling (recycling) A secondary-recovery process involving injection into the reservoir of the gas or a portion of the gas produced with the oil from that reservoir. When pressure is maintained, gas cycling may be one of the means employed.

gaseous transfer The process whereby a magma differentiates by separation of a gaseous phase which then moves relative to the magma.

gas field A tract or district yielding natural gas.

gash fractures Open gashes diagonal to the fault or fault zone; they are tension fractures.

gas phase Any chemical substance in the form of gas as contrasted with liquid or solid form is said to be in the gas phase.

gas storage, underground Underground reservoirs used for the storage of natural gas which has been transported from its original location and is stored for the primary purposes of conservation, fuller utilization of pipe line facilities, and more effective delivery to markets, rather than for pressure maintenance.

gas streaming A process of differentiation in which the formation of a gas phase at a late stage in the crystallization results in partial expulsion, by the escaping gas bubbles, of residual liquid from among the network of crystals.

gastrolith Stomach stone. Highly polished, well-rounded pebbles associated with Saurian skeletons. Believed to have been stomach stones.

gastropod A member of the phylum Mollusca, class Gastropoda; usually with a calcareous exoskeleton or shell, which is asymmetrically coiled and without internal chambers or partitions. *Syn:* SNAIL

Gastropoda A class of the phylum Mollusca; commonly known as gastropods, *q.v.,* or snails.

gas well *1.* A deep boring, from which natural gas is discharged. *2.* As used in oil and gas leases, a well having such a pressure and volume of gas, and, taking into account its proximity to market, as can be utilized commercially.

gauge pressure The pressure as read on an ordinary spring or Bourdon type gauge, usually expressed in pounds per square inch. It is the absolute pressure less that exerted by the atmosphere. Abbreviation: psig.

Gault Albian.

gauss The unit of magnetic field intensity, equal to 1 dyne per unit pole. The preferred term for this unit is the oersted.

Gaussian curve Normal distribution curve.

geanticline A broad uplift, generally referring to the land mass from which sediments in a geosyncline are derived. Originally used as a synonym of anticlinorium and the opposite of synclinorium.

Gedinnian Lower Lower Devonian.

geest Material derived from rock decay *in situ*.

Geiger counter An instrument which detects gamma rays given off by radioactive substances, consisting of a discharge tube which responds to the ionization produced by the rays in a gas which fills the tube. A Geiger-Mueller counter.

Geiger-Mueller counter An ionization chamber with its vacuum and applied potential so adjusted that a gamma ray or other ionizing particle through it causes a momentary current to flow. The surges of current can be amplified and counted so as to measure the intensity of radioactivity in the neighborhood of the chamber.

gel A jellylike material formed by coagulation of a colloidal dispersion.

gem A general term for any precious or semiprecious stone, as, diamond, ruby, topaz, etc., especially when cut or polished for ornamental purposes.

gemology [*Am.*] **gemmology** [*Eng.*] The study of gems.

gene The fundamental unit governing hereditary characters that with others constitutes a chromosome. Genes are believed to be very complex molecules.

gene complex The interacting system of all the genetic factors of an organism.

genera Plural of genus, *q.v.*

generating area In wave forecasting, the continuous area of water surface over which the wind blows in essentially a constant direction. Sometimes used synonymously with fetch length. *Also* FETCH

generation of waves 1. The creation of waves by natural or mechanical means. 2. In wave forecasting, the creation and growth of waves caused by a wind blowing over a water surface for a certain period of time. The area involved is called the generating area or fetch.

generative folds Folds that increase in amplitude in successive beds with the accompaniment of an increase in stratigraphic thickness towards the axial region.

generic Pertaining to a genus.

generic name Name of a genus, consisting of one word that is capitalized; in contrast, a specific name generally is not capitalized.

genetic Pertaining to relationships due to a common origin.

genetic drift Gradual change with time in the genetic composition of a continuing population resulting from the elimination of some genetic features and the appearance of others.

genetics The science which deals with the process of heredity of the transmission of characters from generation to generation.

genetic species Species based upon genetic relations or closeness of kinship.

genomorph 1. Individual of a genus which differs from the genotype in expressing some common orthogenetic trend. 2. A form genus; group of superficially similar, but not closely related, species.

genosyntype One of several species upon which a genus was based if no genotype was designated.

genotype 1. Type species of a genus. 2. Holotype of the type species of genus. 3. Any specimen of the type species of a genus. 4. In genetics, the genetic constitution of an organism or a species in contrast to its observable physical characteristics.

genus A group of species believed to have descended from a common direct ancestor that are similar enough to constitute a useful unit at this level of taxonomy.

geo 1. In Iceland, a narrow inlet walled in by steep cliffs. 2. An element in many compound words of Greek origin, meaning the earth.

geocentric Pertaining to, or measured from, the earth's center; having or relating to the earth as a center.

geocentric latitude Latitude measured in angle between equatorial plane and a line connecting the earth's center with a point on its surface. *Cf.* GEOGRAPHIC LATITUDE

geochemical anomaly A concentration of one or more elements in rock, soil, sediment, vegetation, or water markedly different from the normal concentration in the surroundings. Sometimes applied also to abnormal concentrations of hydrocarbons in soils.

geochemical cycle The sequence of stages in the migration of elements during geologic changes. Rankama and Sahama distinguish a major cycle, proceeding from magma to igneous rocks to sediments to sedimentary rocks to metamorphic rocks and possibly through migmatites back to magma, and a minor or exogenic cycle proceeding from sediments to sedimentary rocks to weathered material and back to sediments again.

geochemical exploration Exploration or prospecting methods depending on chemical analysis of the rocks or soil, or of soil gas, or of plants.

geochemical facies *1.* Area characterized by particular physiochemical conditions influencing the production and accumulation of sediment; *2.* Facies defined on the basis of trace element occurrences, associations and ratios.

geochemical prospecting *1.* The search for concealed deposits of metallic ores by analyzing soils, surface waters, and/or organisms for abnormal concentrations of metals. *2.* The search for petroleum accumulations by analyzing soil gases for hydrocarbons.

geochemistry The study of (a) the relative and absolute abundances of the elements and of the atomic species (isotopes) in the earth, and (b) the distribution and migration of the individual elements in the various parts of the earth (the atmosphere, hydrosphere, crust, etc.), and in minerals and rocks, with the object of discovering principles governing this distribution and migration. Geochemistry may be defined very broadly to include all parts of geology that involve chemical changes or may be focused more narrowly on the distribution of the elements, as in Brian Mason's definition; the latter is commonly understood if the term is used without qualification.

geochron Time interval corresponding to a rock stratigraphic unit; may vary from place to place depending on age of rock unit.

geochronologic sequence The placing of the rocks of the earth's crust in a systematic framework of variously ranked time-stratigraphic units to show their relative position and age with respect to earth history as a whole.

geochronologic unit Unit of geologic time, e.g., period, epoch.

geochronology The study of time in relationship to the history of the earth, or a system of dating developed for this purpose. Absolute chronology (sometimes called absolute age) involves dating of geologic events in years. Relative chronology involves the system of successive eras, periods, and epochs used in geology and paleontology. Literally the science of earth time.

geochronometry Measurement of geologic time.

geode Hollow, globular bodies, varying in size from an inch to a foot or more in size, and characteristic of certain limestone beds, while rarely found in shales. Significant features are (1) subspherical shape, (2) a hollow interior, (3) a clay film between the geode wall and the enclosing limestone matrix, (4) an outer chalcedonic layer, (5) an interior drusy lining of inward projecting crystals, and (6) evidence of expansion or growth.

geodepression A long, narrow depression, not necessarily filled by sediments.

geodesic coordinates Coordinates used in the study of the geometry of metric curved spaces in the neighborhood of a point O, called the origin, any point in the neighborhood of which may be identified by the geodesic through it and O and by the arc distance along the geodesic.

geodesic line A line of shortest distance between any two points on any mathematically defined surface. Also termed a geodesic.

geodesy; geodetics The investigation of any scientific questions connected with the shape and dimensions of the earth. This is the function of a geodetic survey.

geodetic coordinates *See* GEO-DESIC COORDINATES

geodetic datum A datum consisting of 5 quantities: the latitude and the longitude of an initial point, the azimuth of a line from this point, and two constants necessary to define the terrestrial spheroid.

It forms the basis for the computation of horizontal con-

trol surveys in which the curvature of the earth is considered.

geodetic line The shortest-distance line between any two given points on the surface of the spheroid.

geofracture Master fracture of great age, separating blocks of the earth's crust, that has influenced later tectonic activity.

geognosy *1.* The science which treats of the solid body of the earth as a whole and of the different occurrences of minerals and rocks of which it is composed and of the origin of these and their relations to one another. *2.* A term invented to express absolute knowledge of the earth, in contradistinction to geology, which embraces both the facts and our reasonings respecting them. That part of geology treating of the materials of the earth and its general exterior and interior constitution.

geographical cycle Cycle of erosion, *q.v.* Every land form passes through a comparatively systematic series of changes from its youth, when its form is defined chiefly by constructional processes, past its maturity, when the processes of subaerial sculpture have carved a great variety of mouldings and channelings, toward its old age, in which the accomplishment of the full measure of denudation reduces the mass essentially to base level, however high it may have been originally. *See* GEOMORPHIC CYCLE

geographic center The geographic center of an area on the earth has been defined as that point on which the area would balance if it were a plate of uniform thickness. In other words, it is the center of gravity of that plate.

geographic latitude Latitude measured in angle between axis of the earth and plane of the horizon at a point on the earth's surface. *Cf.* GEOCENTRIC LATITUDE

geographic province Large region characterized by similar geographic features.

geography The science that treats of the surface of the earth, including its form and development, the phenomena that take place thereon, and the plants, animals, and peoples that inhabit it, considered in relation to the earth's surface; also a book or treatise on the above subject.

geoid The figure of the earth considered as a mean sea-level surface extended continuously through the continents.

geologic; geological The generally preferred usage is as follows: geologic data; geologic investigation or survey; geological organization, survey, or society; geological era; geological time.

geological horizon This term denotes merely position. A horizon has no thickness, being merely a stratigraphic level, or plane. The deposit of a particular time usually identified by distinctive fossils.

geological thermometry Measurement or estimation, by direct or indirect methods, of the maximum, minimum, or actual temperatures at which geological processes occur or have occurred in the past.

geologic high Sometimes used in oil fields to indicate a later geological formation regardless of elevation; opposed to geologic low, which refers to earlier formations. *Cf.* TOPOGRAPHIC HIGH

geologic province Large region characterized by similar geologic history and development.

geologic thermometer A term applied to known temperature limits within which certain minerals or mineral aggregates must have formed; based on the thermal data relating to the fusion points of rocks and minerals, and the inversion- or transition-points of allotropic modifications of rock-forming compounds, and in general to the equilibrium conditions and stability ranges under different conditions of pressure for various minerals, allotropes, solid-solutions, eutectics, and other mineral aggregates.

geologic time *See* TIME-STRATIGRAPHIC

geologic time unit Time unit corresponding with a time-stratigraphic unit, e.g., period, epoch, age.

geologist One versed in geology, or engaged in geological study or investigation.

geology *1.* The science which treats of the earth, the rocks of which it is composed, and the changes which it has undergone or is undergoing. *2.* Earth science including physical geology and geophysics; the history of the earth, stratigraphy, and paleontology; mineralogy, petrology; and engineering, mining, and petroleum geology.

geomagnetic Pertaining to the magnetic field of the earth.

geomagnetic poles Poles of the earth's magnetic field located about 4000 miles above its surface. One pole is at 78 1/2° N., 69° W., and the other pole at 78 1/2° S., 111° E. They do not correspond to the surface magnetic poles.

geomorphic Of, or pertaining to, the figure of the earth or the form of its surface; resembling the earth.

geomorphic cycle Geographical cycle; cycle of erosion, *q.v.*

geomorphogeny That part of geomorphology which treats of the origin and development of the earth's surface features.

geomorphology That branch of both physiography and geology which deals with the form of the earth, the general configuration of its surface, and the changes that take place in the evolution of land forms.

geopetal Indicating top to bottom relations in rocks at time of formation.

geopetal fabric Internal structure or organization of a rock indicating original orientation such as top and bottom of strata.

geophone A detector, placed on or in the ground in seismic work, which responds to the ground motion at the point of its location. *Syn:* SEISMOMETER; SEISMOGRAPH; GEOTECTOR; PICKUP; JUG; TORTUGA

geophysical The form geophysical is used to the exclusion of any other that might be derived from the term geophysics.

geophysical survey The exploration of an area in which geophysical properties and relationships unique to the area are mapped by one or more geophysical methods.

geophysicist One who studies or practices the science of the physics of the earth.

geophysics The science of the earth with respect to its structure, composition, and development.

Geophysics is a branch of experimental physics dealing with the earth, including its atmosphere and hydrosphere. It includes the sciences of dynamical geology and physical geography, and makes use of geodesy, geol-ogy, seismology, meteorology, oceanography, magnetism, and other earth sciences in collecting and interpreting earth data. Geophysical methods have been applied successfully to the identification of underground structures in the earth and to the search for structures of a particular type, as for example, those associated with oil-bearing sands.

geophysics, applied Geologic exploration or prospecting using the instruments and applying the methods of physics and engineering; exploration by observation of seismic or electrical phenomena or of the earth's gravitational or magnetic fields or thermal distribution.

Georgian Lower Cambrian.

geosphere *1.* The solid portion of the earth, synonymous with the lithosphere. *2.* Inclusive term for the earth and its hydrosphere and atmosphere. *3.* Any one of the so-called spheres which occur as concentric layers within the earth.

geostrophic Pertaining to deflective force due to rotation of the earth.

geosynclinal *See* GEOSYNCLINE

geosynclinal cycle Progression of events characteristic of a geosynclinal region including subsidence, sediment filling, compression, uplift, erosion, and attainment of stability.

geosynclinal prism The load of sediments which accumulates in the downwarped area of a geosyncline.

geosynclinal sediment Associated sediments or rocks presumed to be characteristic of geosynclinal deposition; consist of great thickness of intimately intermixed sandstone and shale with abundant conglomerate near borders and commonly showing graded bedding.

geosyncline *1.* Large generally linear trough that subsided deeply throughout a long period of time in which a thick succession of stratified sediments and possibly extrusive volcanic rocks commonly accumulated. The strata of many geosynclines have been folded into mountains. Many different kinds have been differentiated and named. *2.* The area of such a trough. *3.* A stratigraphic surface that subsided in such a trough.

geotectocline A tectocline filled with sediment. *Syn:* GEOSYNCLINE

geotectogene *See* TECTOGENE

geotectonic Pertaining to the form, arrangement, and structure of the rock masses composing the earth's crust. Structural.

geothermal gradient The change in temperature of the earth with depth, expressed either in degrees per unit depth, or in units of depth per degree.

geothermic; geothermal Of, or pertaining to, the heat of the earth's interior.

geothermic degree The average depth within the earth's crust corresponding to an increase of one degree in temperature.

gerontic Pertaining to the old-age stage in the life history of an individual animal.

geyser Literally, a roarer; intermittent hot springs or fountains. Columns of water are thrown out at intervals with great force, often rising to between 100 and 200 feet; and after the jet of water ceases, a column of steam rushes out with a thundering roar, and the eruption then ceases for an interval.

geyser basin A broad topographic basin in which a number of geysers are grouped together.

geyserite Siliceous sinter, *q.v.* A general term for siliceous deposits, usually opaline silica, formed around thermal springs and geysers, whether loose, compact, or concretionary.

geyser pipe The narrow tube or well of a geyser extending downward from the surface pool, which is ordinarily contained in the top of a sinter mound.

geyser pool The comparatively shallow pool of heated water ordinarily contained in a sinter crater or sinter mound at the top of a geyser pipe or orifice.

ghost Faint indication of a structure such as a crystal or fossil more or less obliterated by diagenesis or replacement.

Ghyben-Herzberg lens Lens-shaped body of fresh ground water that floats on salt water beneath small oceanic islands and in the sediments of marine coastal areas.

giantism *See* GIGANTISM

Gibbs free energy A thermodynamic potential, associated with the variables pressure and temperature. In an irreversible thermodynamic process at constant temperature and pressure the Gibbs free energy of a system decreases; in a reversible process the Gibbs free energy remains constant.

gibbsite A mineral, $Al(OH)_3$. Monoclinic. A principal constituent of many bauxites.

gigantism A type of phylogerontism in which overspecialization is shown as an increase in the size of the animal.

gilgai soil Soil developed in part of Australia with local surface relief up to 8 feet, consisting of mounds or ridges known as puffs composed of calcareous soil with lime nodules, and depressions or valleys termed shelves underlain by noncalcareous soil.

gilsonite One of the varieties of asphalt having a black color, brilliant luster, brown streak, and conchoidal fracture.

girdle *1. Struct. petrol:* The pattern shown by many petrofabric diagrams whereby the points are concentrated in a band of varying width, commonly normal to a fabric axis. *2.* A marginal band (in a chiton) of uniform width, differentiated from the central area which, on the back of the animal, consists of eight articulating plates or valves.

girdle, ac (also **ab, bc**) *Struct. petrol:* A girdle of points in a petrofabric diagram having a trend parallel with the plane of the a and c fabric axes (or with the $\overline{a}$ and $\overline{c}$ axes, or with the b and $\overline{c}$ axes). *Syn:* GIRDLE MAXIMUM

girdle diagram Fabric diagram on polar coordinates showing concentration of points in a great circle band.

girdle maximum Concentration of poles along a great circle in a fabric diagram generally indicating an axis of rotation.

Gish-Rooney method An artificial-current conductive direct-current method of measuring ground resistivity which avoids polarization by continually reversing the current with a set of commutators.

Givetian Upper Middle Devonian.

gizzard stone Gastrolith.

glacial *Geol:* Pertaining to, characteristic of, produced or deposited by, or derived from a glacier.

glacial advance *1.* Increase in the area and thickness of a glacier. *2.* A time interval marked by such increase.

glacial anticyclone A semipermanent high-pressure area capping a continental glacier. Although W. H. Hobbs postulated that snow falling from such an anticyclone provided the important snow source for glacier formation, present-day meteorological thought indicates the most important source to be snowfall from migratory cyclones.

glacial boulder A boulder that has been transported by a glacier.

glacial canyon Glacial canyons are characterized by several peculiar features: (1) They are U-shaped rather than V-shaped in cross profile; (2) small tributary gorges usually enter at levels considerably above the canyon bottoms; (3) in longitudinal profile the canyon bottoms are irregularly terraced; (4) the canyons are sometimes locally expanded into amphitheaters; (5) the canyon bottom is not always obdurate rock.

glacial cycle The phrase glacial cycle is here reserved for the ideal case of so long a continuance of glaciation under fixed climatic conditions, except for changes of climate with change of altitude due to degradation, that glacial erosion would be carried to its completion, truncating all the higher mountains at the snow line, and therefore causing snowfall to replace rainfall, and normal erosion to replace glacial erosion.

glacial drift Sediment (a) in transport in glaciers, (b) deposited by glaciers, and (c) predominantly of glacial origin, made in the sea or in bodies of glacial meltwater. *See* DRIFT

glacial epoch The Pleistocene epoch, the earlier of the two epochs comprised in the Quaternary period; characterized by the extensive glaciation of regions now free from ice.

glacial erosion Reduction of the earth's surface as a result of the presence or passage of a glacier.

glacial erratic Erratic.

glacial flow Glacier flow.

glacial geology The study of features resulting from glacial erosion and deposition. Contrast with glaciology, the study of the physics, form, and regimens of glaciers.

glacial groove A large furrow cut by the abrading action of rock fragments contained in a glacier.

glacial ice Ice that is flowing or that shows evidence of having flowed.

glacial lake 1. A sheet of water owing its existence to the effects of the glacial period. They are of two classes, those excavated in the rock, and those produced by the irregular deposit of heaps of drift. 2. Lake fed by glacial meltwater. 3. Lake lying against or on a glacier.

glacial lobe 1. One of the lobate protrusions of the margin of an ice sheet, sometimes a score or more miles in width, as where the ice has been free to spread out in depressions along its margin. 2. A tonguelike projection from the main mass of a continental glacier.

glacial markings Small features, etched in rock as the result of glacial abrasion, such as chattermarks and striations.

glacial maximum 1. The position of greatest advance of a glacier. 2. The time of greatest advance of a glacier.

glacial milk Glacial meltwater containing suspended light-colored rock particles of silt or clay size. *See* ROCK FLOUR

glacial mill A vertical or steeply inclined opening in glacial ice through which melt water can pour. Water may have a vertical motion. *Syn:* MOULIN

glacial plain Plains constructed by the direct action of the ice itself.

glacial recession Reduction in area and thickness of a glacier. A time interval marked by such reduction. Glacial retreat, *q.v.*, is not a synonym, because it refers only to reduction in area.

glacial retreat A glacier is said to retreat when its front recedes. The ice may be actually moving forward toward this front, but the rate of backward melting at the front, if it exceeds the rate of forward movement, will cause the position of the front to recede.

glacial scour lake *See* FINGER LAKE

glacial scratches *See* GLACIAL STRIAE

glacial stairway Glaciated valley whose floor rises in a series of irregular steplike benches.

glacial striae (*sing.* **stria**) 1. Usually straight, more or less regular scratches, commonly parallel in sets, on smoothed surfaces of rocks, due to glacial abrasion; glacial scratches. 2. Curved, crooked, and intermittent gouges, of irregular depth and width, and rough definition, or certain rock surfaces, sometimes due to abrasion by icebergs. *See* GLACIAL STRIATION

glacial striation 1. Fine-cut lines on the surface of the bedrock which were inscribed by the over-riding ice. 2. A scratch or small groove cut into a surface of the bedrock or mantle by rock fragments carried in a glacier.

glacial theory The theory that large elevated portions of the temperate and frigid zones were covered during the early Quaternary, and perhaps during some earlier epochs, by slowly moving ice sheets and glaciers, that transported vast masses of drift to lower latitudes, assisted by icebergs drifting along the coast. No longer a theory, but accepted as fact.

glaciate *1.* To cover with glacier ice. *2.* To subject to the action of a glacier.

glaciated *1.* Said of a country which has been scoured and worn down by glacial action, or strewn with ice-laid drift. *2.* Covered by and subjected to the action of a glacier.

glaciation Alteration of the earth's solid surface through erosion and deposition by glacier ice.

glaciation limit The lowest level at which glaciers can develop.

glacier A mass of ice with definite lateral limits, with motion in a definite direction, and originating from the compacting of snow by pressure. Moraines are not diagnostic, and the definition should not include those masses of arctic ice which, by reason of their low temperature, are fixed in position. In Alaska, flood-plain icing or masses of ground ice.

glacier bands *1.* Any of several phenomena which appear to the observer as a series of bands on a glacier surface. See ALASKAN BANDS; ICE BANDS; OGIVES; PARALLEL BANDS. *2.* The ice layers or lenses causing this banded appearance.

glacier burst The sudden release of a reservoir of water which has been impounded within or by a glacier.

glacieret; hanging glacier *1.* Small alpine glaciers are sometimes called glacierets, or, if

visible high in the sides of mountain valleys, hanging glaciers. *2.* A very small glacier on a mountain slope or in a cirque. Sometimes called cirque glacier.

glacier flood The sudden forward rush of a glacier, accompanied by pronounced thickening and extensive surface breakage, may be called a glacier flood. The resemblance to a river flood is noteworthy. A river flood passes from the source to the mouth of a river in a few hours or a few days and its effects are soon past; but the far less mobile ice requires several years for the transmission of the glacier flood, and its duration is months long, while years are required to bring the ice surface back to its preflood state.

glacier flow The motion that exists within the body of a glacier. Glacier flow may exist without movement of the glacier front. See EXTRUSION FLOW HYPOTHESIS; GRAVITY FLOW; STREAMING FLOW

glacier ice A body of ice developed from snow which becomes large enough to move from its place of accumulation.

glacierization *1.* In the United States, the inundation of the land by ice. *2.* In British usage, approximately equivalent to glaciation.

glacier lake A lake formed between the margin of a glacier and an encircling rim of hills, due to the damming of the natural drainage; a glacial lake.

glacier-lobe lake A lake whose basin was excavated by the eroding of a glacier lobe over the drainage basin of a former river. Examples are the Great Lakes of the Laurentian River system.

glacier reservoir Region of accumulation.

glacier table A large block of stone supported by a column or pedestal of ice on the surface of a glacier. Glacier tables occur when the general level of the ice is lowered by evaporation and melting, while the ice under the rock, insulated from the sun's rays, stays at the former level.

glacier tongue 1. An outlet glacier of an ice sheet or ice cap. 2. The lower part of a valley glacier.

glacier well Moulin; glacier mill. All streams on the surface of a glacier eventually encounter the marginal crevasses and plunge down in foaming cascades, producing well-known "glacier wells" or "glacier mills."

glacier wind 1. A cold wind blowing out of apertures in a glacier front. This wind is caused by the difference in density between the cold air inside the ice caves and the warmer outside air. 2. Any wind blowing off a glacier, usually a katabatic wind, *q.v.*

glacio A combining form frequently used with other words to denote formation by or relationship to glaciers. The usage is self-evident in such words as glacioaqueous, glaciofluvial, glaciomarine, and glaciolacustrine.

glaciofluvial Fluvioglacial. Pertaining to streams flowing from glaciers or to the deposits made by such streams.

glacio-isostacy Balance and level in areas influenced by the weight of glacial ice.

glaciology The science of existing glaciers.

glance A term used to designate various minerals having a splendent luster, as silver glance, lead glance, etc.

glance copper Chalcocite.

glass A state of matter intermediate between the close-packed, highly ordered array of a crystal, and the poorly packed, highly disordered array of a gas. Most glasses are supercooled liquids, i.e., metastable, but there is no break in the change in properties between the metastable and stable states. The distinction between glass and liquid is solely on the basis of viscosity, and is not necessarily related, except indirectly, to the difference between metastable and stable states.

glass, volcanic *See* VOLCANIC GLASS

glass sand An extremely pure silica sand useful for making glass and pottery.

glass sponge Popular term for a class of Porifera (sponges) in which the skeletal framework consists of six-rayed spicules of silica.

glauberite A mineral, $Na_2Ca(SO_4)_2$. Monoclinic.

glauconite A green mineral, closely related to the micas and essentially a hydrous potassium iron silicate. Commonly occurs in sedimentary rocks of marine origin. Also used as a name for a rock of high glauconite content.

glauconitic sandstone A quartz sandstone or an arkosic sandstone rich in glauconite grains.

glaucophane *See* AMPHIBOLE

glei; gley A soil horizon in which the material is bluish gray or blue-gray, more or less sticky, compact, and often structureless. It is developed under the influence of excessive moisture.

glide direction The direction of gliding along glide planes in a mineral.

glide line *Struct. petrol:* In single-crystal deformation, the possible direction, or directions, of movement in a glide plane; in a tectonite the direction of movement in an s-surface indicated either from field observation or from interpretation of preferred orientation of the fabric.

glide plane; slip plane *Struct. geol:* In single-crystal deformation, a lattice plane on which translation- or twin-gliding takes place in a tectonite, an s-surface characterized (in a statistical sense) by a preferred orientation of one or more fabric elements which indicate movement in the s-surface.

gliding, *n.* Slip or movement along certain lattice planes in crystalline substances, produced by deformation and characterized either as translation-gliding or twin-gliding, *q.v.*

glimmer [*Ger.*] Mica.

glint In Norway, a boundary. An escarpment, particularly one produced by the outcrop of a dipping resistant formation.

glint lake A lake whose basin is excavated in hard rock where a glacier is held in check by an escarpment. An illustration is Torne Träsk in northern Lapland.

globigerina ooze A calcareous marine deposit formed in deep water (but less than 12,000 feet) consisting chiefly of calcareous shells of Foraminifera, especially Globigerina spp. These are surface-dwelling forms, which reach the bottom only after death.

Globigerina ooze contains more than 30% $CaCO_3$, of which the greater part consists of pelagic Foraminifera. The carbonate content averages 64% but ranges from 30 to 97%.

globular *Petrol:* A textural term synonymous with spherulitic, *q.v.*

globular map projection A map projection representing a hemisphere, on which the equator and a central geographic meridian are represented by straight lines intersecting at right angles; these lines are divided into equal parts. All meridians, except the central one, are represented by circular arcs connecting points of equal division on the equator with the poles. The parallels, except the equator, are circular arcs dividing the central and extreme outer meridians into equal parts. The extreme outer meridian limits the projection and is a full circle.

glory hole *1.* A large open pit from which ore is or has been extracted. *See* MILLING. *2.* An opening through which to observe the interior of a furnace.

glowing avalanche Volcanic eruption feature similar to a glowing cloud (nuée ardente) but propelled by gravity rather than by the auto-explosion of magma.

glowing avalanche deposit Chaotically brecciated material that should not be confused with welded tuff.

glowing cloud Nuée ardente.

gneiss A coarse-grained rock in which bands rich in granular minerals alternate with bands in which schistose minerals predominate. *See* AUGEN GNEISS; CHARNOCKITE; COMPOSITE GNEISS; GRANITE GNEISS; GRANULITE; INJECTION GNEISS; ORTHOGNEISS; PARAGNEISS; SCHIST

gneissic; gneissoid, *adj.* Having the appearance or character of gneiss, *q.v.*

gneissose *1.* Resembling gneiss. *2.* Having composite structure of alternating schistose and granulose bands and lenses which differ in mineral composition and texture.

goethite A mineral, FeO(OH). Orthorhombic. Most limonite is impure goethite.

gold The native metal, commonly alloyed with silver and to a lesser extent with copper in natural occurrences. Isometric. Sp. gr. 19.3 pure, down to 15.0 with increase in Ag content.

gold dust Fine particles of gold, such as are obtained in placer mining. An impure dust is sometimes called commercial dust.

Goldschmidt's mineralogical phase rule Under natural rock-forming conditions, the probability of finding a system with a variance (degrees of freedom) of less than two (temperature and pressure) is small. Any given natural mineral assemblage, igneous or metamorphic, seems to be the stable one over a range of temperature and pressure. Thus, with a variance of two, the phase rule is reduced to a special case, $P=C$, in which the maximum number of phases possible is equal to the number of components.

goldstone See AVENTURINE

gondwana; gondwanaland Theoretical ancient continent including India, Australia, Antarctica and parts of southern Africa and South America supposed to have fragmented and drifted apart in post-Carboniferous time.

goniatite An ammonoid cephalopod, characteristic of Devonian and Carboniferous, in which the sutures have developed lobes and saddles which give an angular appearance to the suture line.

goniometer An instrument for measuring the angles between crystal faces.

gorge [Fr.] 1. As most generally used in English, the word gorge means a narrow passage, with precipitous, rocky sides, enclosed among the mountains. A ravine need not be enclosed; and this word would hardly be applied to a mere depression in the soil, as ravine might be. 2. A canyon; a rugged and deep ravine or gulch. 3. A jam; as an ice gorge.

gossan; gozzan A ferruginous deposit filling the upper parts of mineral veins or forming a superficial cover on masses of pyrite. It consists principally of hydrated oxide of iron and has resulted from the oxidation and removal of the sulfur as well as the copper, etc. Syn: IRON HAT

Gotlandian Silurian (restricted).

gouge N: 1. A layer of soft material along the wall of a vein, favoring the miner, by enabling him after "gouging" it out with a pick, to attack the solid vein from the side; 2. Finely abraded material occurring between the walls of a fault, the result of grinding movement; 3. In Nova Scotia, a narrow band of gold-bearing slate next the vein, which can be extracted by a thin, long-pointed stick. V: 4. To work a mine without plan or system; 5. To contract the face of a mine working by neglecting to keep the sides cut away.

graben A block, generally long compared to its width, that has been downthrown along faults relative to the rocks on either side.

grab sample 1. Sample of rock or sediment taken more or less indiscriminately at any place. 2. Subaqueous sample of bottom sediment obtained by an instrument with moveable jaws that close after being dropped to the bottom.

gradation Geol: The bringing of a surface or a stream bed to grade, through erosion, transportation, and deposition by running water. *See* AGGRADATION; DEGRADATION

grade *1.* Continuous descending curve of a stream channel just steep enough for current to flow and transport its load of sediment. *2.* Measure of inclination expressed in per cent. *3.* Varying inclination, e.g., of a road. *4.* Expression of relative quality, e.g., high grade or low grade.

graded *Geol:* Brought to or established at grade, through the action of running water carrying a load of sediment, by eroding or degrading at some places and depositing or aggrading in other places.

graded bedding Diadactic structure, *q.v.* A type of stratification each stratum of which displays a gradation in grain size from coarse below to fine above.

graded profile *See* PROFILE OF EQUILIBRIUM

graded sediment *Geol:* A sediment consisting chiefly of grains of the same size range. *Engin:* A sediment having a uniform or equable distribution of particles from coarse to fine.

graded shore line A shore line that has been straightened by the building of bars across embayments and by the cutting back of headlands. The coast consists of alternately steep and low reaches.

graded slope Unbroken slopes worn or built to the least inclination at which the waste supplied by weathering can be urged onward.

graded stream A graded stream is one in which, over a period of years, slope is delicately adjusted to provide, with available discharge and with prevailing channel characteristics, just the velocity required for the transporta-

tion of the load supplied from the drainage basin. The graded stream is a system in equilibrium; its diagnostic characteristic is that any change in any of the controlling factors will cause a displacement of the equilibrium in a direction that will tend to absorb the effect of the change.

grade level Where the slopes are steep, erosion will occur; and near the sea, where the gradients are gentle, deposition of the water-borne sediments will take place, so that eventually the whole course of the stream will be reduced to a uniform gradient. When this condition is reached the stream is said to have found its grade level. If the volume of the water and the rate of erosion were uniform throughout the whole course of the stream, the profile of the river bed would be a straight line.

grade scale A subdivision of an essentially continuous scale of particle sizes into a series of size classes. *See* WENTWORTH SCALE

grade scale, Atterberg A decimal grade scale for particle size, with 2 mm. as the reference unit, and involving the fixed ratio 10. Subdivisions are the geometric means of the grade limits: 0.2, 0.6, 2.0, 6.3, 20.0.

grade scale, Phi A logarithmic transformation of the Wentworth grade scale based on the negative logarithm to the base 2 of the particle diameter.

grade scale, Tyler standard A scale for sizing particles based on the square root of 2 used as specifications for sieve mesh. Alternate class limits closely approximate the class limits on the Udden grade scale, and the intermediate limits are the geometric means of the Udden scale values: 0.50, 0.71, 1.00, 1.41, 2.00.

grade scale, Udden A grade scale for particle size, with 1 mm. as the reference point, and involving the fixed ratio 2 to 1/2, depending on whether the scale is increasing or decreasing, as 1/4, 1/2, 1, 2, 4.

grade scale, Wentworth An extended version of the Udden grade scale with descriptive class terms for various sizes of sedimentary particles.

gradient *1.* Slope, particularly of a stream or a land surface. Measurements are expressed in per cent, feet per mile or degrees. *2.* Change in value of one variable with respect to another variable, especially vertical or horizontal distance, e.g., gravity, temperature, magnetic intensity, electric potential, etc.

grading Degree of mixing of size classes in sedimentary material. Well graded implies more or less uniform distribution from coarse to fine; poorly graded implies uniformity in size or lack of continuous distribution. *Cf.* SORTING

grading factor The coefficient of sorting of a clastic sediment. Perfect sorting has a grading factor of 1.0.

gradiometer Any instrument that measures grades or slopes. An instrument for measuring the gradient of any physical quantity, such as the magnetic or gravitational field. A form of torsion balance with 3 weights sensitive to gravity gradients but not to curvatures.

graduation Division, *q.v.*

grahamite A hydrocarbon resembling albertite in its jet-black luster. It is soluble in carbon disulfide and chloroform but not in alcohol, and is fusible. Occurs in veinlike masses. Specific gravity 1.145. Has conchoidal fracture and is brittle.

grain *Geol: 1.* The particles or discrete crystals which comprise a rock or sediment; *2.* The individual particles which form settled snow, firn, and glacier ice. Glacier grains are single crystals of ice, but snow and firn grains are agglomerations of many snow crystals; *3.* A direction of splitting in rock, less pronounced than the rift and usually at right angles to it. *4. Coal min:* In England, the lines of structure or parting in the rocks parallel with the main gangways and hence crossing the breasts. *5.* A unit of weight equal to 0.0648 part of a gram, 0.000143 part of an avoirdupois pound, and 0.04167 part of a pennyweight. Derived from the weight of a grain of wheat.

grain growth Solid state enlargement of some crystals at the expense of others producing a coarser texture in an essentially monomineralic rock like limestone; commonly termed recrystallization.

grain plane A plane of parting in metamorphic rocks at right angles to the cleavage.

grain size A term relating to the size of mineral particles that make up a rock or sediment.

gram-atom The atomic weight, in grams, of a substance.

gram formula weight *See* MOLECULAR WEIGHT

gram molecular weight *See* MOLECULAR WEIGHT

granite *1.* A plutonic rock consisting essentially of alkalic feldspar and quartz. Sodic plagioclase, usually oligoclase is commonly present in small amounts and muscovite, biotite, hornblende, or rarely pyroxene may be mafic constituents. *2. Seismol:* A rock in which velocity of the compressional wave lies somewhat between 5.5 and 6.2 km./sec. *3.* Loosely used for any light-colored, coarse-grained igneous rock.

granite gneiss *1.* A coarsely crystalline, banded metamorphic rock of granitic composition. *2.* A primary igneous gneiss of granitic composition. *See* AUGEN GNEISS; GNEISS; ORTHOGNEISS

granite porphyry *See* QUARTZ PORPHYRY

granite tectonics The structural features of plutons and the relationship between them.

granitic *1.* Of, pertaining to, or composed of, granite or granite-like rock. *2.* A textural term applied to coarse- and medium-grained, granular igneous rocks in which all or nearly all of the mineral constituents are anhedral (xenomorphic) and of approximately the same size. In this sense the term is synonymous with hypidiomorphic-granular or hypautomorphic-granular. *See* HYPIDIOMORPHIC

granitization; granitisation A term used in somewhat different connotations by different authors, but in general, referring to the production of a granitic rock from sediments by an unspecified process. Some would limit the term to the production of granite in place, without the formation of a "notable" amount of liquids; others would include all granitic rocks formed from sediments by any process, regardless of the amount of liquid formed or any evidence of movement. The precise mechanism, frequency, and magnitude of the process are still in dispute.

granitoid A term applied to the texture of holocrystalline igneous

or metasomatic rocks such as granites in which the constituents are mostly anhedral or xenomorphic and of uniform size.

granoblastic *1.* The texture of metamorphic rocks composed of equidimensional elements. *2.* A term applied to secondary texture due to diagenetic change either by crystallization or recrystallization in the solid state, in which the grains are of equal size (equigranular).

granodiorite A plutonic rock consisting of quartz, calcic oligoclase or andesine, and orthoclase, with biotite, hornblende, or pyroxene as mafic constituents. Granodiorite is intermediate between quartz monzonite and quartz diorite and contains at least twice as much plagioclase as orthoclase.

granophyre A quartz porphyry or fine-grained porphyritic granite characterized by a groundmass with micrographic (granophyric) texture.

granophyric A texture in igneous rocks characterized by the irregular intergrowth of blebs, patches, and threads of quartz in a base of feldspar. It is similar to graphic and micrographic but differs from these textures in that the intergrowth of quartz and feldspar is more irregular.

granular *1.* A textural term applied to holocrystalline rocks in which most of the mineral grains are equant or equidimensional. *2.* Also applied to sedimentary rock made up of grains or granules. *3. Paleobot:* Covered with very small grains; minutely or finely mealy.

granular disintegration A type of mechanical weathering, in regions of great extremes of temperature, involving the breaking of rock into small fragments or into the component crystal units without chemical decay, due to varying coefficients of expansion.

granularity *Petrol:* The feature of rock texture relating to the size of the constituent grains or crystals. Expressed by such terms as fine-, medium-, or coarse-grained; phanerocrystalline, microcrystalline, etc. Essentially synonymous with grain size.

granule *1.* Rounded rock fragments larger than very coarse sand grains but smaller than pebbles. *2.* Granular mineral products used primarily to form a protective and decorative coating on composition roofing.

granulite *1.* A metamorphic rock composed of even-sized, interlocking granular minerals. *2.* A metamorphic belonging to a high-temperature facies characterized by the presence of mica and hornblende. Coarse and fine bands alternate and produce a regular planar schistosity. *3.* In French literature, the term has been used as a synonym for muscovite granite. *See* CHARNOCKITE; GNEISS; QUARTZITE

granulite facies Gneissic rocks produced by deep-seated high-grade regional metamorphism.

granulometric Refers to size measurements of sedimentary particles.

granulose Having very small granules on the surface as on the test of some foraminifers or on epitheca or tabulae in some corals.

graphic A rock texture resulting from the regular intergrowth of quartz and feldspar. The quartz is commonly cuneiform, resembling runic inscriptions on the background of feldspar. Less commonly, other pairs of minerals are thus intergrown. When this kind of intergrowth is reduced to microscopic dimensions the texture becomes micrographic, and the material is called micropegmatite. *See* GRANOPHYRIC

graphic log A graphic record, usually in the form of a strip, on which the formations penetrated in drilling are drawn to a uniform vertical scale. In addition to lithology, such logs usually indicate the points at which oil, gas, or water was found, and the lengths of casing used. Usually, also, conventional colors and symbols are used in order to abbreviate the record.

graphite Plumbago; black lead. A mineral, native carbon, dimorphous with diamond. Hexagonal. Black to steel-gray, very soft (H=1).

graptolite Extinct colonial organism that produced chitinous enclosing and supporting structures, generally considered a hydrozoan but supposed by some paleontologists to be related to the primitive chordates.

Graptolithina Class of extinct colonial animals of uncertain zoologic affinity, referred to coelenterates or hemichordates, that constructed variously formed and arranged series of tiny chitinous thecae. Camb.-Dev.

graticule *1.* A network of lines representing geographic parallels and meridians forming a map projection. *2.* A template, divided into appropriately designed blocks or cells, for graphically integrating a quantity such as gravity. Graticules are much used in computing terrain corrections and the gravitational or magnetic attraction of irregular masses.

grating *Opt:* A system of close equidistant and parallel lines or bars, used for producing spectra by diffraction. *Applied geophys:* A graticule.

gravel *1.* Accumulation of rounded waterworn pebbles. The word gravel is generally applied when the size of the pebbles does not much exceed that of an ordinary hen's egg. The finer varieties are called sand while the coarser varieties are called shingle. *2.* An accumulation of rounded rock or mineral pieces larger than 2 mm. in diameter. Divided into granule, pebble, cobble, and boulder gravel. *3.* Consists of rock grains or fragments with a diameter range of from 76 mm. (3 in.) to 4.76 mm. (retention on a No. 4 sieve). The individual grains are usually more or less rounded. *4.* Accumulation of uncemented pebbles. Pebble gravel. May or may not include interstitial sand ranging from 50 to 70% of total mass. *Cf.* BOULDER, COBBLE, and GRANULE GRAVEL

gravimeter *1.* An instrument for measuring variations in the magnitude of the earth's gravitational field; a gravity meter. *2.* An instrument for determining specific gravities, particularly of liquids. *See* HYDROMETER

gravitational constant The constant γ in the law of universal gravitation. Its value is $6.673\pm.033 \times 10^{-8}$ cm.^{8}/gm. sec.^{2}.

gravitational gliding Extensive sliding of strata down the slope of an uplifted area producing low angle overthrust faults, recumbent folds, or nappes.

gravitational separation The separation of oil, gas, and water in a reservoir rock in accordance with their relative gravities.

gravitational theory One of the migration theories which assume oil and gas to move because of their buoyancy or lower specific gravities relative to that of the associated water.

gravitational water Water which exists in the large pores of the soil and which the force of gravity will remove from the soil when conditions for free drainage exist.

gravity; gravitation *1.* The resultant effect upon any body of matter in the universe of the inverse square law attraction between it and all other matter lying within the frame of reference and of any centrifugal force which may act on the body because of its motion in any orbit. *2.* The resultant force on any body of matter at or near the earth's surface due to the attraction by the earth and to its rotation about its axis. *3.* The force exerted by the earth and by its rotation on unit mass or the acceleration imparted to a freely falling body in the absence of frictional forces.

gravity, Baumé Specific gravity of a fluid in the relation which the weight of a unit volume of the fluid bears to that of the same volume of water. Antoine Baumé devised a system in which fluids with a specific gravity of 1.00 (that of water) were at 10°. The Baumé scale for oil was replaced in 1921 by the API Gravity scale. The Baumé scale is defined by the equation:

$$\text{Degrees Baumé} = \frac{140}{\text{Sp. Gr. } 60° \text{ F}} -130.$$

See API GRAVITY

gravity anomaly Difference between theoretical calculated and observed terrestrial gravity; excess observed gravity is positive and deficiency is negatively anomalous. *See* BOUGUER, FREE-AIR, and ISOSTATIC ANOMALY

gravity compaction Compaction of sediment resulting from over-burden pressure.

gravity fault *1.* A fault along which the hanging wall has moved down relative to the foot-wall. See NORMAL FAULT. *2.* Sometimes restricted to those faults that are the result of with-drawal of support, either below or on the side.

gravity flow A type of glacier movement in which the flow of the ice is caused by the down-slope component of gravity in an ice mass resting on a sloping floor.

gravity gradiometer An instru-ment for measuring the gradient of gravity.

gravity instruments Devices for measuring the differences in the gravity force or acceleration at two or more points. They are of three principal types (a) A stat-ic type in which a linear or angular displacement is observed or nulled by an opposing force (see GRAVIMETERS); (b) A dy-namic type in which the period of oscillation is a function of gravity and is the quantity di-rectly observed; (c) A gradient measuring type, e.g., Eotvos torsion balance.

gravity meter See GRAVIMETER

gravity of oils Specific gravity, expressed usually in degrees API. See API GRAVITY

gravity sliding Downslope shear-ing movement of part of the earth's crust on the flank of a large uplifted area.

gravity unit; G unit One-tenth of a milligal (prospecting but not scientific usage).

gravity wave A wave whose ve-locity of propagation is con-trolled primarily by gravity. Wa-ter waves of a length greater than 2 inches are considered gravity waves.

gray copper ore Tetrahedrite; tennantite, *q.v.*

gray hematite Specularite, *q.v.*

graywacke; greywacke A type of sandstone marked by: (1) large detrital quartz and feldspars (phenocysts) set in a (2) prom-inent to dominant "clay" matrix (and hence absence of infiltra-tion or mineral cement) which may on low-grade metamorphism (diagenesis) be converted to chlorite and sericite and partially replaced by carbonate, (3) a dark color, (4) generally tough and well indurated, (5) extreme angularity of the detrital compo-nents (microbreccia), (6) pres-ence in smaller or larger quan-tities of rock fragments, mainly chert, quartzite, slate or phyllite, and (7) certain macroscopic structures (graded bedding, intra-formational conglomerates of shale or slate chips, slip bedding, etc.) and (8) certain rock as-sociations.

greasy Applied to the luster of minerals. Having the luster of oily glass, as nepheline.

great circle The line of inter-section of the surface of a sphere and any plane which passes through the center of the sphere. The shortest distance between any two points on a sphere is along the arc of a great circle connecting the two points.

green earth *1.* Glauconite, found in cavities of amygdaloids and other eruptive rocks, and used as a pigment by artists. *2.* Chlo-rite; a variety of talc.

greenhouse effect The thermal result of the fact that compara-tively short wave length solar radiation penetrates the atmos-phere rather freely, only to be largely absorbed near and at the earth's surface, whereas the long wave length terrestrial radiation passes upward with great difficulty. This effect is due to the fact that the absorption bands of water vapor, ozone, and carbon dioxide are more prominent in the wave lengths occupied by terrestrial radiation than in the short wave lengths of solar radiation. Hence the lower atmosphere is almost perfectly transparent to incoming radiation, but partially opaque to outgoing longwave radiation.

green marble A commercial term for serpentine.

Green Mountains disturbance Vermontian orogeny.

green mud A fine-grained terrigenous mud or oceanic ooze found near the edge of the continental shelf, and similar to other terrigenous muds except for the greenish color and, perhaps, less organic matter. It occurs at depths of 300 to 7500 feet. A deep-sea terrigenous deposit characterized by the presence of a considerable proportion of glauconite and $CaCO_3$ in variable amounts up to 50%.

greensand Glauconitic sand; less commonly, any glauconitic sediment.

greenschist A metamorphosed basic igneous rock which owes its color and schistosity to abundant chlorite. *See* GREENSTONE; OPHIOLITE.

greenschist facies Metamorphic rocks produced under low temperature conditions.

greenstone An old field term applied to altered basic igneous rocks which owe their color to the presence of chlorite, hornblende, and epidote. *See* GREENSCHIST; OPHIOLITE

greisen *1.* A pneumatolytically altered granitic rock composed largely of quartz, mica, and topaz. The mica is usually muscovite or lithium mica, and tourmaline, fluorite, rutile, cassiterite, and wolframite are common accessories. *2.* A granitoid but often somewhat cellular rock composed of quartz and muscovite or some related mica, rich in fluorine. It is the characteristic mother rock of the ore of tin, cassiterite, and is in most cases a result of the contact action of granite and its evolved mineralizers. *3.* A coarse-grained tin-bearing rock which contains muscovite, quartz, topaz, or tourmaline.

grid *1.* A systematic array of points or lines: (a) At or along which field observations are made. (b) For which computations are made. *2.* The control electrode in thermionic tubes.

gridiron twinning *See* CROSSED TWINNING

grinding The crushing of small grains through the effect of continued contact and pressure by larger pebbles.

grinding pebbles Pebbles, usually of chert or quartz, used for grinding in ball mills, etc., where contamination with iron must be avoided.

grindstone *1.* A tough sandstone of fine and even grain, composed almost entirely of quartz, mostly in angular grains. It must have sufficient cementing material to hold the grains together but not enough to fill the pores and cause the surface to wear smooth. *2.* A large circular stone made from sandstone and used quite extensively for the sharpening of many different tools and instruments.

grit *1.* Sand, especially coarse sand. *2.* Coarse-grained sandstone. *3.* Sandstone with angular grains. *4.* Sandstone with grains of varying size producing a rough surface. *5.* Sandstone suitable for grindstones.

groin; groyne A shore-protection and improvement structure (built usually to trap littoral drift or retard erosion of the shore). It is narrow in width (measured parallel to the shore line), and its length may vary from less than one hundred to several hundred feet (extending from a point landward of the shore line out into the water).

groove casts Rounded or sharp crested rectilinear ridges, a few mm. high and many cm. long, occurring on undersurfaces of sandstone layers lying on mudstone.

grossularite *See* GARNET

grotto A hole eroded in the wall of a cave by seepage or lateral stream erosion. A small cave.

ground fog A shallow but often dense fog, *q.v.*, of the radiation type, through which the stars may be observed at night and the sun in the daytime. It appears first at the ground and remains there even after it thickens.

ground ice Anchor ice. *1.* Ice formed about stones over the bottoms of streams or lakes. *2.* Bodies of more or less clear ice in permanently frozen ground. Deposits which are evidently only temporary features are excluded under this definition, and the term is not applied to deposits which seem to be on top of the ground. Stagnant earth-covered glaciers appear to fall about in the dividing line of this definition. If their glacial origin is evident, they would be excluded.

ground-ice mound Pingo.

ground-ice wedges Ground ice occurring chiefly in a network of more or less vertical wedges, surrounding isolated bodies of frozen ground.

ground magnetometer A magnetometer primarily suitable for making observations of magnetic field intensity on the surface of the earth.

groundmass The material between the phenocrysts in a porphyritic igneous rock. It includes the basis or base as well as the smaller crystals of the rock. *Syn:* MATRIX

ground moraine The material deposited from a glacier on the ground surface over which the glacier has moved. It is bordered by lateral and/or end moraines.

ground motion The displacement of the ground due to the passage of elastic waves arising from earthquakes, explosions, seismic shots, machinery, wind, traffic, and other causes.

ground resistivity The resistivity of soil and rock materials. *See* RESISTIVITY

ground swell A long high ocean swell. Also, this swell as it rises to prominent height in shallow water. Not usually so high or dangerous as blind rollers.

ground water Phreatic water, *q.v.* That part of the subsurface water which is in the zone of saturation.

ground-water dam A body of material which is impermeable or has only low permeability and which occurs below the surface in such a position that it impedes the horizontal movement of ground water and consequently causes a pronounced difference in the level of the water table on opposite sides of it.

ground-water decrement *See* DECREMENT, GROUND-WATER

ground-water discharge Discharge

of water from the zone of saturation.

ground-water divide A line on a water table on each side of which the water table slopes downward in a direction away from the line.

ground-water flow That portion of the precipitation which has been absorbed by the ground and has become part of the ground water, alternately being discharged as spring and seepage water into the stream channels and leaving no drainage as runoff.

ground-water level Ground-water surface.

ground-water reservoir Aquifer, *q.v.*

ground-water runoff That part of the runoff which consists of water that since its last precipitation has existed as ground water.

ground-water surface This level, below which the rock and subsoil (down to unknown depths) are full of water, is known as the ground-water level, ground-water surface, or water table.

group *1. General:* An association of any kind based upon some feature of similarity or relationship. *Stratig:* 2. Lithostratigraphic unit consisting of two or more formations; *3.* More or less informally recognized succession of strata too thick or inclusive to be considered a formation; *4.* Subdivision of a series. *Obs. Cf.* STAGE

group velocity *1. Oceanog:* The velocity at which a wave group travels. In deep water, it is equal to half the velocity of the individual waves within the group. *2. Geophys:* The velocity of individual wave crests in a dispersive, continuous medium in which several frequencies are apparent.

In a medium in which the velocity varies with frequency the wave train changes its shape as it progresses, in which case the group velocity may differ materially from the phase velocity.

growth fabric Crystal arrangement determined by growth from a plane surface such as the wall of a vein.

growth twinning Twinning resulting from change in lattice orientation during the growth of a crystal. *Cf.* DEFORMATION TWINNING

groyne *See* GROIN

grunerite *See* AMPHIBOLE

grus An accumulation of fragmental products derived locally from the decomposition of granite. *Cf.* ARKOSE; SAPROLITE

Gshelian Upper Upper Carboniferous below Uralian.

Guadalupian Middle Permian.

guano *1.* Applied to deposits of the excrement of bats or other animals. *2.* A substance found in great abundance on some coasts or islands frequented by sea fowls and composed chiefly of their excrement. It is rich in phosphates and nitrogenous matter.

guide fossil Any kind of category (species, genus, etc.) of fossil useful in the identification of a stratigraphic unit. The best guide fossil of a time-stratigraphic unit should have short stratigraphic range, wide geographic distribution, broad ecologic tolerance, and occur abundantly. Some of the most satisfactory ones were planktonic or pelagic organisms whose distribution was not influenced by benthonic conditions. *Syn:* INDEX FOSSIL

gulch A small ravine; a small, shallow canyon with smoothly inclined slopes and steep sides. Local in Far West.

gulf *1.* (1) A portion of the sea
partially enclosed by a more or
less extensive sweep of the coast.
The distinction between gulf and
bay is not always clearly marked,
but in general a bay is wider in
proportion to its amount of
recession than a gulf; the latter
term is applied to long landlocked portions of sea opening
through a strait, which are never
called bays. (2) A deep hollow,
chasm, abyss. (3) A profound
depth (in river or ocean); the
deep. *2.* A large deposit of ore
in a lode. *3.* Elongated karst valley, steep sided, level floor of
alluvium; a "window" of an
underground drainage system,
generally formed by the merging of several collapse sinks.
Syn: UVALA (in a limited sense)

Gulfian Upper Cretaceous.

gulf type (Hoyt) gravimeter A
meter consisting of a mass suspended at the end of a spring,
the latter so designed that its
extension will cause the mass to
rotate. By this means the linear
displacement of the spring is
converted into an angular deflection which is more easily
measured. The design also mini-
mizes the sensitivity to seismic
disturbances and the basic instrument is therefore well suited
for underwater observations.

gulf type (Vacquier) magnetometer
A flux-gate or saturable reactor
type of recording magnetometer.
Used primarily in aircraft and
there includes means for keeping
the measuring element aligned
in the direction of maximum intensity (i.e., total field). In this
case it records variations in the
total field regardless of variations
in its direction. Sometimes used
in the sense of including the
equipment for establishing the

position of the aircraft as well
as the magnetometer itself.

gully *1.* A small ravine. *2.* Any
erosion channel so deep that it
cannot be crossed by a wheeled
vehicle or eliminated by plowing.
3. (Oceanic) The extension of a
trough or basin which penetrates
the land or a submarine elevation, either with a uniform or a
gradually diminishing depth, or
which is bounded on one side
by land and on the other by a
submarine elevation, may be
called a gully [*Ger:* Rinne; *Fr:*
chenal], if long and narrow.

gully erosion Removal of soil by
running water, with formation of
channels that cannot be smoothed
out completely by normal cultivation.

gully gravure A process or more
exactly a recurrent cycle of processes by which the steep slopes
of hills and mountains retreat;
in the cycle, gullying is recurrent
in time but shifts laterally in
place. The slope retreats by repeated scoring or graving. Each
groove is a gully, and each new
groove is parallel to earlier
grooves. In time all parts of the
slope are grooved. The slope retreats by repeated incisions, each
of about the same depth and so
disposed as to reduce rather than
emphasize inequalities.

gumbo *1.* A name current in
western and southern states for
those soils that yield a sticky
mud when wet. In southwest
Missouri, a puttylike clay associated with lead and zinc deposits. In Texas, a clay encountered in drilling for oil and sulfur. *2.* The stratified portion of
the lower till of the Mississippi
Valley.

gumbotil *1.* Leached deoxidized
clay containing siliceous stones;
the product of thorough chemi-

cal decomposition of clay-rich till. *2.* Gray to dark-colored, thoroughly leached, nonlaminated, deoxidized clay, very sticky and breaking with starchlike fracture when wet, very hard and tenacious when dry. Chiefly the result of weathering of drift.

G unit Gravity unit, *q.v.*

Günz First Pleistocene glaciation.

gut *1.* A narrow passage such as a strait or inlet. *2.* A channel in otherwise shallower water, generally formed by water in motion.

guyot (gē'yō) Tablemount, *q.v.*

Gymnospermae Class of the Spermatophyta or Pteropsida; plants whose seeds are not enclosed in an ovary.

gyprock *1.* A rock composed chiefly of gypsum. *2.* A driller's term for a rock of any kind in which he has trouble in making holes.

gypsum Alabaster; selenite; satin spar. A mineral, $CaSO_4.2H_2O$. Monoclinic. A common mineral of evaporities. Used in the manufacture of plaster of Paris.

gypsum flower Curved, twisted crystal growths of gypsum resembling flowers.

gypsum test plate An accessory to the polarizing microscope which gives a full wave-length path difference (retardation).

gyttja *1.* A sapropelic black mud in which the organic matter is more or less determinable, characteristic of eutrophic and oligotrophic lakes. *2.* A natural solid hydrocarbon, tasmanite.

H

Haanel depth rule A rule of thumb for estimating the depth of a magnetic body, valid if the body may be regarded as magnetically equivalent to a single pole. The depth of such a pole is equal to the horizontal distance from the point of maximum vertical magnetic intensity to the points where the intensity is one-third the maximum value.

habit *Crystallog:* The characteristic shape, as determined by the crystal faces developed and their shapes and relative proportions.

habitat The environment in which the life needs of a plant or animal are supplied.

hachure A short line used in drawing and engraving, especially in shading and denoting different surfaces as in map drawing to represent slopes of the ground.

hackly Showing jagged points in fracture.

hade *1.* The angle of inclination of a vein, fault, or lode measured from the vertical. *2.* To deviate from the vertical; said of a vein, fault, or lode.

hailstone imprint A small crater formed by a hailstone falling on a soft sediment surface. The hailstone imprint is generally larger, deeper, and more irregular than a raindrop imprint.

hair zeolite A synonym for fibrous zeolite, which may be natrolite, scolecite, or mesolite.

haldenhang An explanatory translation of haldenhang is: undertalus rock slope of degradation.

half life The time period in which half the initial number of atoms of a radioactive element disintegrate into atoms of the element into which they change directly.

half reaction Electrode reaction.

halide A general term including chloride, bromide, and iodide.

Halimeda Green calcareous algae which occur on the sea floor at shallow depths and as dense growths on the floors of some coral-reef lagoons.

halite Rock salt. A mineral, NaCl. Isometric. A common mineral of evaporites.

Halliburton contact log A trade name used by the Halliburton Oil Well Cementing Company for a log recorded with an electrode system which is a replica of the Schlumberger Microlog tool.

halloysite Metahalloysite. A common clay mineral, composition $Al_2Si_2O_5(OH)_4$ like kaolinite, but structurally distinct.

halmyrolysis; halmyrosis *1.* A group name for the processes by which ions are removed from solution in sea water. *2.* The chemical rearrangements and replacements that occur while the sediment is still on the sea floor. *3.* Submarine weathering of sediment or rock.

halo A crescent or ring partly or entirely surrounding a central area characterized by values of opposite sign. Encountered principally in magnetic and geochemical surveys.

halogen Any one of the elements in Group VIIb of the periodic table (F, Cl, Br, I).

Hamiltonian Erian.

hammada Plateau in a desert region whose rocky surface has been denuded by wind erosion.

hammock A hummock. Local in Southeast and on the Gulf Coast.

hand level A small leveling instrument in which the spirit level is so mounted that the observer may view the bubble at the same time that he observes an object through the telescope.

hand specimen *Petrol:* A piece of rock trimmed to a size, usually $1 \times 3 \times 4$ inches, for megascopic study and for preservation in a reference or study collection.

hang *1.* In Bristol, the hade of a fault. *2.* To have its charge choked up or arched in one part, while the part underneath falls away so as to leave a gap; said of a blast furnace.

hanging *1.* The hanging wall; the rock on the upper side of a mineral vein or deposit. *2.* Sticking or wedging of part of the charge in a blast furace. *See* HANG, 2

hanging glacier *1.* A comparatively small glacier on an incline so steep that the forefoot of the ice constantly breaks off and falls downward. *2.* A small glacier terminating on a steep slope or at the lower end of a hanging valley. *See* GLACIERET

hanging side; hanging wall; hanger The wall or side above the ore body.

hanging valley *1.* A valley the floor of which is notably higher than the level of the valley or shore to which it leads. *2.* A

tributary valley whose floor is higher than the floor of the trunk valley in the area of junction.

hanging wall The mass of rock above a fault plane, vein, lode, or bed of ore.

haplo- [*Gr.*] A combining form meaning single or simple, as haplogranite, etc.

hard *1.* Containing certain mineral salts in solution, especially calcium carbonate; said of water having more than eight or ten grains of such matter to the gallon. *2.* In ceramics, requiring great heat: said of muffle colors in porcelain decoration. *3.* Solid, compact, difficult to break or scratch: *See* HARDNESS SCALE

hard coal Anthracite.

hardness *1.* Resistance to scratching or abrasion. The brittle hardness of the mineralogist differs from the penetration (ductile) hardness of the metallurgist. *2.* Quality of water that prevents lathering because of calcium and magnesium salts which form insoluble soaps.

hardness scale The empirical scale by which the hardness of a mineral is determined as compared with a standard. The Mohs scale is as follows: 1. Talc; 2. Gypsum; 3. Calcite; 4. Fluorite; 5. Apatite; 6. Orthoclase; 7. Quartz; 8. Topaz; 9. Corundum; 10. Diamond.

hardpan *1.* A hard impervious layer, composed chiefly of clay, cemented by relatively insoluble materials, does not become plastic when mixed with water, and definitely limits the downward movement of water and roots. It can be shattered by explosives. *2. Placer min:* Applied to layers of gravel occurring a few feet below the surface and cemented by limonite.

hard radiation Radiation of high energy.

hard rock Rock which requires drilling and blasting for its economical removal. Loosely used to distinguish igneous and metamorphic from sedimentary rock.

hard rock geology Geology of igneous and metamorphic rocks.

hard water Water containing dissolved salts of calcium and magnesium that produce insoluble soaps and prevent lathering.

hardway In quarrying, especially in the quarrying of granite. The rift is the direction of easiest parting, the grain is a second direction of parting, and the hardway is the third and most difficult direction along which parting takes place.

Harker diagram See VARIATION DIAGRAM

Harlechian Lower Cambrian.

harmonic folding Folding in which, with depth, there are no sudden changes in the form of the folds. Contrasts with disharmonic folding, q.v.

harmonic relations Parallelism in beds or planes as inclinations vary.

harpolith Large, sickle-shaped intrusions injected into previously deformed strata, then, with the host rocks, stretched horizontally in the direction of maximum orogenic displacement.

Hartman's law The acute angle between two sets of intersecting shear planes is bisected by the greatest principal stress axis, whereas the obtuse angle is bisected by the least principal stress axis.

harzburgite A peridotite composed of olivine and subordinate orthopyroxene with accessory opaque oxides. Syn: SAXONITE

haulageway The gangway, entry, or tunnel through which loaded or empty mine cars are hauled by animal or mechanical power.

hausmannite A mineral, Mn_3O_4.

Hauterivian Lower Cretaceous between Valanginian and Barremian.

Hawaiian eruption A type of volcanic eruption in which great quantities of extremely fluid basaltic lava are poured out, mainly issuing in lava fountains from fissures on the flanks of a volcano. Explosive phenomena are rare, but much spatter and scoria are piled into cones and mounds along the vents. Characteristic of shield volcanoes.

Hawaiian-type bomb Pancake-shaped bomb.

haystack Rounded, conical-shaped hill developed as a result of solution. Syn: COCKPIT; HUM; PEPINO; MOGOTES

head 1. A comparatively high promontory with either a cliff or steep face. It extends into a large body of water, such as a sea or lake. An unnamed head is usually called a headland. 2. Pressure of a fluid upon a unit area due to the height at which the surface of the fluid stands above the point where the pressure is determined. Usually expressed as pounds per square inch, and sometimes as actual feet of head or fluid column. 3. The section of surf rip current which has widened out seaward of the breakers. 4. Those features and structures in consolidated and unconsolidated soils which are clearly the result of slow flow, from higher to lower ground, while oversaturated with water from melting snow or ice, rain, or lines of springs or seepages.

head erosion Headward erosion; headwater erosion, q.v.

headframe Structure above a

mine shaft supporting the pulley over which the hoisting cable passes.

headland 1. Any projection of the land into the sea; generally applied to a cape or promontory of some boldness and elevation. See CAPE; HEAD; PROMONTORY; TONGUE. 2. In soil conservation: (1) The source of a stream. (2) The water upstream from a structure.

headwall The steep, wall-like cliff at the back of a cirque.

headward erosion Head erosion; headwater erosion. A valley is lengthened at its upper end and is cut back by the water which flows in at its head, the direction being determined by the greatest column of water which enters it. This is called headward erosion.

headwater erosion Head erosion; headward erosion, q.v.

heat budget Amount of heat seasonally absorbed and given off by a body of water.

heat budget, annual (of a lake) The amount of heat necessary to raise its water from the minimum temperature of winter to the maximum summer temperature.

heat capacity The amount of heat required to raise the temperature of the system one degree absolute. Heat capacity at constant pressure refers to the heat required to raise the system one degree with the system held at a constant pressure. Heat capacity is an extensive quantity.

heat conductivity Thermal conductivity, q.v.

heat content Enthalpy, q.v.

heat flow Dissipation of heat coming from within the earth by conduction or radiation at the surface; average about 1.2×10^{-6} cal./cm.^{2}/sec.

heat gradient Change in temperature of the earth with depth; approximately 30° C. per kilometer in the upper part of the crust.

heat of crystallization or **melting** The heat energy released upon crystallization or absorbed upon melting under isothermal conditions in a unary system. Sometimes loosely and incorrectly used as equivalent to the heat of solution of the same phase in a binary or higher system.

heat of dissociation The heat energy released or absorbed upon the breakup or dissociation of a phase into two or more simpler phases, as $CaCO_3 \rightarrow CaO + CO_2$. Sometimes used to indicate the heat effects upon ionization during solution.

heat of melting Heat of crystallization.

heat of solution The heat energy absorbed or released upon dissolving a solid in a liquid. It is equal to the heat of melting only for unary systems. The magnitude, and even the sign, of the value is dependent upon the concentration in the solution; there is no general relationship between the values for the heat of solution in the pure solvent and in the saturated solution. The identical amount of heat, but opposite in sign, is released or absorbed upon crystallization.

heave 1. In faulting, the horizontal component of the dip separation; that is, the apparent horizontal component of displacement of a disrupted index plane on a vertical cross section, the strike of which is perpendicular to the strike of the fault. 2. A rising of the floor of a mine caused by its being too soft to resist the weight on the pillars.

heaving shale A condition in which shale squeezes into a drill hole. Often this occurs adjacent to faulted traps where the shale is under considerable pressure, though gas pressure within the formation and the nature of clay minerals in the shale have an important contributing effect.

heavy liquids *Petrol:* A general term applied to a group of heavy organic liquids, inorganic solutions, and fused salts (heavy melts) used for the determination of the specific gravity of mineral particles, or for the separation of minerals having, respectively, lower and higher specific gravities (or densities) than the liquid used. Examples are bromoform, methylene iodide, and clerici solution.

heavy minerals The accessory detrital minerals of a sedimentary rock, of high specific gravity, which are separated in the laboratory from minerals of lesser specific gravity by means of liquids of high density, such as bromoform. *Igneous petrol:* Mafic minerals.

heavy spar Barite.

hectare Metric unit of land measure, 10,000 square meters; 2.471 acres.

hectorite A clay mineral. *See* MONTMORILLONITE

hedenbergite *See* PYROXENE

hedreocraton Persistent craton that strongly influenced later continental development.

height of instrument (H.I.) *1.* In spirit leveling: The height of the line of sight of a leveling instrument above the adopted datum. *2.* Stadia surveying: The height of the center of the telescope (horizontal axis) of transit or telescopic alidade above the ground or station mark. *3.* Trigonometrical leveling: The height of the center of the theodolite (horizontal axis) above the ground or station mark. *4.* The elevation of the center of the surveying telescope.

height of wave The vertical distance between a crest and the preceding trough. *See* SIGNIFICANT WAVE HEIGHT

Helderbergian Lower Lower Devonian.

helictite A distorted twiglike lateral projection of calcium carbonate, found in caves, etc. *Cf.* STALACTITE; STALAGMITE

heliotrope An instrument composed of one or more plane mirrors, so mounted and arranged that a beam of sunlight may be reflected by it in any desired direction.

Placed over a survey station, a heliotrope is used to direct a beam of sunlight toward a distant survey station, where it can be observed with a theodolite. It provides an excellent target in observing horizontal directions, such targets having been observed on at distances of over 150 miles and approaching 200 miles.

Helmholtz free energy A thermodynamic potential that is a function of temperature and volume. This potential is useful in determining the course of constant volume isothermal processes.

Helvetian Lower middle Miocene.

hematite A mineral, Fe_2O_3. Hexagonal rhombohedral. The principal ore of iron.

hemera The time interval corresponding to the acme of an organism. This is not a good time-stratigraphic unit because an acme may be expected to vary in time value from place to place.

hemi- [*Gr.*] A combining form meaning half.

Hemichordata Subdivision of the Protochordata or Chordata consisting of animals with a notochord only in the preoral region and with three primary segments of the coelom in the adult.

hemidome That form in a crystal composed of two parallel domatic planes in the triclinic, or of two parallel orthodomatic planes in the monoclinic system of crystallization. *Obs.*

hemihedral *Crystallog:* Having a lower grade of symmetry than, and only half as many faces as, the corresponding form of full or normal symmetry for the system. HEMIMORPHIC; TETARTO-HEDRAL

hemimorphic *Crystallog:* Having no transverse plane of symmetry and no center of symmetry, and composed of forms belonging to only one end of the axis of symmetry.

hemimorphite Calamine. A mineral, $Zn_4Si_2O_7(OH).H_2O$. Orthorhombic. A common secondary mineral; an ore of zinc.

Hemingfordian Middle Miocene.

hemiprism A form produced by two parallel planes cutting the two lateral axes in the triclinic system of crystallization. *Obs.*

Hemphillian Middle Pliocene.

henry The electromagnetic unit of self- or mutual induction in the practical c.g.s. system. It is that inductance of a circuit which gives rise to an induced e.m.f. of one volt for a current variation rate of one ampere per second.

Henry's law The amount of a gas absorbed by a given volume of a liquid at a given temperature is directly proportional to the pressure of the gas. It is applicable only to dilute solutions.

heptane A liquid hydrocarbon of the paraffin series, formula C_7H_{16}.

Hercynian orogeny Variscan diastrophism.

hercynite A mineral, a member of the spinel group, $(Fe,Mg)Al_2O_4$. Isometric.

heredity *1.* The transmission of characters from parents to offspring; the science which deals with this process is genetics. *2.* The organic relation between successive generations with secures persistence of characteristics and yet allows new ones to emerge. *3.* Inherited endogenic factors that control the development of an individual organism.

herringbone cross-lamination Under conditions of frequently shifting current direction, as along the littoral zone, thin layers of sand are cross-laminated in opposite direction in alternating layers, giving rise to a "herringbone structure" if viewed in transverse section.

herringbone texture A long narrow spine, with more or less symmetrically arranged parallel zones of different composition on either side of it.

hetero- [*Gr.*] Signifies various, or of more than one kind of form, as, heterophyllous, with more than one kind or form of leaf.

heteroblastic A term applied by Friedrich Becke to designate rocks in which the essential constituents are of two distinct orders of magnitude.

heterodesmic Bonded in more than one way; said of atoms in crystals.

heterogeneous *1.* A characteristic of a medium or a field of force which signifies that the medium has properties which vary with position within it. *Ant:*

HOMOGENEOUS. *2.* Differing in kind; having unlike qualities; possessed of different characteristics; opposed to homogeneous. *3. Paleobot:* Lacking uniformity in kind of part or organ.

heterogeneous equilibria More than one homogeneous system interacting. *Syn:* PHASE EQUILIBRIA, *q.v.,* each phase being a homogeneous system within itself.

heterogony Allometry.

heteromorphism The phenomenon whereby two magmas of identical chemical composition may crystallize into two different mineral aggregates as a result of different cooling histories.

heterozygous Having differently constituted paired chromosomes; a heterozygous individual will not exhibit recessive characters.

Hettangian Lowermost Lower Jurassic.

heulandite A mineral, $CaAl_2Si_6O_{16}.5H_2O$. A zeolite. Monoclinic.

hexacoral Coral with hexagonal symmetry. Meso.-Rec.

Hexacorrallia *1.* A subclass of corals distinguished by their hexameral symmetry. *2.* One of the three chief types of corals for geologists and paleontologists. *Syn:* HEXACORALLA

hexagonal system The crystal system that has three equal axes intersecting at 120° and lying in one plane, and a fourth unequal axis perpendicular to the other three.

hexahedron The cube.

hexane A liquid hydrocarbon of the paraffin series, formula C_6H_{14}.

hexoctahedron Isometric crystal form bounded by 48 faces each cutting the three crystallographic axes at different distances.

H.F.W. An abbreviation signifying "hole full of water," and used in drilling reports and on well logs.

hiatus *1.* Literally, the "gap" in rock sequence represented by geological formations which normally would be present, but are missing, due either to the fact that they were never deposited, or were eroded prior to deposition of the immediately overlying beds. *2.* Time value of strata missing at a physical break or unconformity in a stratigraphic sequence. *Cf.* LACUNA. *3.* Time value of an episode of nondeposition that is only part of the time value of an unconformity.

high, structural A term applied to the upper or higher part of a dome or other anticlinal structure. *See* STRUCTURE

high-angle fault A fault with a dip greater than 45°.

high energy environment Environment characterized by considerable current and/or wave action that prevents the settling of fine-grained sediment.

higher high water The higher of the two high waters of any tidal day. The single high water occurring daily during periods when the tide is diurnal is considered to be a higher high water.

higher low water The higher of two low waters of any tidal day.

high-grade *1.* Rich ore. *2.* To steal or pilfer ore or gold, as from a mine by a miner. *See* HIGH-GRADING

high-grade ore Rich ore. *Cf.* LOW-GRADE ORE

high-grading Larceny of small particles of ore or gold by employees in a mine.

highland *1.* Includes all mountains, the heights of the land which are greater than hills, and all elevated masses of land, which are called plateaus, or tablelands. *2.* Elevated or mountainous land; an elevated region or country.

high-oblique photograph An oblique photograph which shows the horizon.

high plain *1.* An extensive area of relatively level land not situated near sea level. *2.* (Plural) In the United States, plains extending along the east side of the Rocky Mountains.

high-quartz Quartz formed at temperatures of more than 573° consisting of SiO_4 tetrahedra arranged in a more symmetrical lattice than those formed at lower temperatures; inversion is reversible.

high-rank graywacke Feldspathic graywacke.

high-rank metamorphism Metamorphism accomplished under conditions of high temperature and pressure. *See* METAMORPHIC GRADE

high-speed layer A layer, usually sedimentary, in which the speed of wave propagation is greater than it is in at least one adjacent layer.

high tide; high water Maximum height reached by each rising tide.

high-volatile A bituminous coal Nonagglomerating bituminous coal having less than 69% of fixed carbon (dry, mineral-matter-free) and more than 31% of volatile matter (dry, mineral-matter-free) and 14,000 or more B.t.u. (moist, mineral-matter-free).

high-volatile B bituminous coal Nonagglomerating bituminous coal having 13,000 or more, and less than 14,000 B.t.u. (moist, mineral-matter-free).

high-volatile C bituminous coal Either agglomerating or non-weathering bituminous coal having 11,000 or more, and less than 13,000 B.t.u. (moist, mineral-matter-free).

high-water line In strictness, the intersection of the plane of mean high water with the shore. The shore line delineated on the nautical charts of the Coast and Geodetic Survey is an approximation of the high-water line.

hill *1.* A prominence smaller than a mountain. Some hills, like some mountains, are volcanic heaps, and many, like mountains, are produced by dissection of plateaus and plains; but none are the direct result of uplift. *2.* In general, the term hill is properly restricted to more or less abrupt elevations of less than 1000 feet, all altitudes exceeding this being mountains. *3.* A mass of material rising above the level of the surrounding country and culminating in a well-marked crest or summit. *4.* An arch or high place in a mine. *5.* In Scotland, the surface at a mine. *6.* In the North of England and the Midlands, an underground inclined plane.

hill creep; hillside creep Soil and any superficial material may move slowly downhill under the influence of gravity. Near the surface, the dip of strata may be modified by this creep.

hillock A small hill.

hinge Line along which maximum curvature of a fold occurs; it lies at the intersection of the axial plane and an s-surface.

hingebelt Zone of downfolding separating a frontal geosyncline from the continental foreland.

hinge fault *1.* A fault in which the movement is an angular or rotational one on one side of an axis normal to the fault plane. *2.* A fault along one side of which the wall rocks have rotated as a block with respect to the rocks on the other wall.

hinge line *1.* The line which separates the region in which a beach has been upwarped from that in which it is still horizontal. First use in this sense attributed to Frank Leverett. *2.* A node line drawn from an extinct outlet through points where a beach splits vertically because of uplifts of the outlet. *3.* A line in the plane of a hinge fault separating the part of the fault along which thrust or reverse movement has occurred from that showing normal movement. *4.* A line of abrupt flexure, usually applied to relatively gentle tiltings due to loading attending advance and retreat of continental glaciers. *5.* The line along which articulation takes place in a brachiopod.

hinterland *1.* That zone containing the beach flanks and the area inland from the coast line to a distance of five miles. *2.* The region lying behind the coast district. *3.* A subjective term referring to the relatively undisturbed terrain on the back of a folded mountain range, i.e., the side away from which the thrusting and recumbent folding appears to have taken place. *4.* The actively moving block which forces the geosynclinal sediments toward the foreland. If both blocks move equally, the distinction between foreland and hinterland breaks down. *5. Geog:* The land which lies behind a seaport or seaboard and supplies the bulk of the exports, and in which are distributed the bulk of the imports of that seaport or seaboard.

histogram Multiple-bar diagram showing relative abundances of specimens, materials, or other

quantitative determinations divided into a number of regularly arranged classes.

histology The microscopic study of tissues.

Hm Abbreviation for hematite in normative rock calculations.

Ho Abbreviation for hornblende in normative calculations of metamorphic rocks.

hoar An ice-crystal deposit formed by the sublimation of water vapor onto a solid body at temperatures below freezing.

hogback *1.* A sharp anticlinal, ridge, decreasing in height at both ends until it runs out. *2.* A ridge produced by highly tilted strata. *3.* A name applied in the Rocky Mountain region to a sharp-crested ridge formed by a hard bed of rock that dips rather steeply downward. *4.* In England, a sharp rise in the floor of a coal seam.

hog wallow Faintly billowing surface with low coalescent mounds 6 to 10 inches higher than the depressions.

holarctic Refers to arctic regions as a whole.

holdfast Basal portion of thalli which anchors them to solid objects in water.

hollow *1.* A small ravine; a low tract of land encompassed by hills or mountains. *2.* A large sink. (Colloquial)

Holmes' classification A classification of igneous rocks based primarily upon the degree of saturation, and secondarily on other aspects of the mineralogical composition.

holo- [*Gr.*] A combining form meaning whole, entire.

holoblast Newly grown minerals.

Holocene Recent.

holocrystalline Applied to rocks consisting entirely of crystallized minerals and no glass. The minerals may or may not have crystal boundaries, and the rocks may be granular or porphyritic.

holocrystalline-porphyritic, *adj.* A term originated by Harry Rosenbusch for the texture of porphyritic rocks with a holocrystalline groundmass.

holohedral *Crystallog:* Belonging to the highest symmetry class of its crystal system.

holohyaline, *adj.* Applied to rocks consisting entirely of glass.

holoplankton Animals which live their complete life cycle in the floating state. *Syn:* PERMANENT PLANKTON

holosome Intertongued stratigraphic unit that may be either depositional (one or more holostromes) or hiatal (one or more hiatuses).

holostrome Stratigraphic unit consisting of beds laid down in a complete transgressive-regressive sequence including strata that may later have been removed by erosion.

holosymmetric Holohedral.

Holothuroidea One of a subdivision of the phylum Echinodermata; a free living animal with elongated, more or less cylindrical body. *Syn:* SEA CUCUMBER

holotype *1.* Single specimen chosen by the original author of a species which is the name-bearer and with which comparison must be made in typological taxonomy. *2.* Such a specimen chosen later. *Obs. Syn:* LECTOTYPE. *3.* Type species of a genus. *Obs.*

homeoblastic A term used instead of equigranular and applied to metamorphic rocks to indicate that the texture so described is due to recrystallization.

homeomorphs; homoeomorphs *1.* Specimens, species, or genera

which are very similar to each other because they are related. *2.* Two convergent species, so similar as hardly to be distinguished on superficial characters. *3.* Two organisms of different ancestry which have similarity of form. *Syn:* ISOMORPH

homeomorphy *1.* The tendency of different genetic stocks to pass, quite independently, through similar stages of development. *2.* Similarity of form in organisms of related ancestries. *3.* Similarity in the derivation of comparable structures in organisms that may or may not be closely related, resulting from parallel or convergent evolution. *See* HOMEOMORPHS

Hommel's classification A chemicomineralogical classification of igneous rocks proposed by W. Hommel (1919).

homo- [*Gr.*] A combining form denoting one and the same; common, joint, like. Usually the opposite of hetero-.

homoaxial folding Folding along parallel axes.

homoclinal shifting Because of the lack of homogeneity of structure in a cuesta or homoclinal ridge the law of equal declivities does not apply. Erosion is very slow on the gentle dip slope of resistant rock; but on the steeper obsequent slope, or escarpment, it is rapid. The divide formed by the crest line of the cuesta or monoclinal ridge is thus forced to migrate towards the dip, and as the general level of the surface is lowered the subsequent streams and the valley lowlands migrate also in the same direction. The process is termed homoclinal shifting.

homoclinal valley Monoclinal valley, *q.v.*

homocline *1. Geol:* A group of

inclined beds of the same dip, which may be either monoclinal, one limb of a fold, or isoclinal, but whose actual relations are not determinate. Used in a more restricted sense than a monocline in that it applies to small or fragmentary areas. 2. A structural condition in which the beds dip uniformly in one direction. Cf. MONOCLINE

homoeotype; homotype A specimen compared by a competent observer with the holotype, lectotype, or other primary type of a species.

homogeneous 1. Of the same kind or nature; consisting of similar parts, or of elements of a like nature, opposed to heterogeneous. 2. Geochem: Alike in all parts; consisting of a single phase; as, homogeneous system, homogeneous mixture, homogeneous equilibrium. 3. A characteristic of a medium which signifies that the physical property of every element of volume has the same value regardless of its location. 4. Consisting throughout of identical or closely similar material which may be a single substance or a mixture whose proportions and properties do not vary.

homogeneous deformation Affine deformation. Homogeneity or inhomogeneity of deformation is a mathematical concept expressed in terms of affinity or nonaffinity. Affinity means the relation between two figures in the same plane that correspond to each other, point to point, and straight line to straight line. Geometrically, an affine transformation is one in which similar figures remain similar figures, similarly situated. The mathematical expression for such a trans-

formation is: $y = ax + b$ where a is not equal to zero.

homogeneous equilibria Those equilibria between various atomic, ionic, or molecular species within a homogeneous phase, typically in liquid or gas phases.

homogeneous phase Any phase whose chemical composition and physical state are uniform throughout, neglecting irregularities on an atomic scale. It may be gaseous, liquid, or crystalline.

homogenous Homologous.

homonym Any one of two or more identical names used to identify different organisms or objects. In taxonomy, only the oldest is a valid name. Commonly used to identify a junior homonym.

homoplastic Similarly adapted through parallel but independent evolution.

homopolar bond See BOND, HOMOPOLAR

homopycnal inflow Homopycnal (equally dense) inflow occurs where a sediment-laden stream enters a basin filled with fluid of comparable density, as when a stream enters a fresh-water lake. The resulting delta is the classical type with top-, fore-, and bottom-set beds.

homoseism Lines drawn through all points simultaneously affected by an earthquake shock.

homotaxial A term proposed by Thomas Huxley to designate those strata, in regions more or less widely separated, that have apparently the same relative position in the geological series.

homotype Homoeotype, q.v.

homozygous Having similarly constituted paired chromosomes; a homozygous individual will exhibit recessive characters.

"honeycomb" coral A compound coral belonging to a Paleozoic

family which has prismatic corallites so arranged as to resemble the cells of a honeycomb.

hoodoos Pillars developed by erosion of horizontal strata of varying hardness in regions where most rainfall is concentrated during a short period of the year. *See* EARTH PILLARS; PILLAR

hook The end of a spit turned toward the shore, owing to a deflection of the current that built it, or to the opposing action of two or more currents. *See* RECURVED SPIT

Hooke's law Stress is proportional to strain.

hook valley Barbed tributaries, *q.v.*

horizon *1.* The surface separating two beds and hence having no thickness. *2.* The various layers, each of which is a few inches to a foot or more thick, that comprise a soil. *See* MARKER BED, *1* and *2*

horizontal Any direction at a point which lies in the plane tangent to the gravity equipotential surface at the point.

horizontal axis (theodolite or transit) The axis about which the telescope of a theodolite or transit rotates when moved vertically.

horizontal classification Taxonomic classification that emphasizes similarity in evolutionary development; is more likely to create polyphyletic groups than is vertical classification.

horizontal couple Two equal parallel forces acting in opposite directions and not on the same straight line. The plane containing these two forces is essentially horizontal.

horizontal displacement A term used by C. F. Tolman to designate strike slip, *q.v.*

horizontal fault A fault with no vertical displacement.

horizontal separation In faulting the distance between the two parts of a disrupted index plane (bed, vein, dike, etc.) measured in any specified horizontal direction.

horizontal slip In faulting the horizontal component of the net slip.

horn A high pyramidal peak with steep sides formed by the intersecting walls of three or more cirques, as, the Matterhorn.

hornblende *See* AMPHIBOLE

hornblendite A plutonic rock composed essentially of hornblende.

horn coral A solitary coral, conical in shape, and generally belonging to the subclass Rugosa. *Syn:* CUP CORAL; FOSSIL COW'S HORN; SIMPLE CORAL; SOLITARY CORAL

hornfels A fine-grained, nonschistose metamorphic rock resulting from contact metamorphism. Large crystals may be present and may represent either porphyroblasts or relic phenocrysts. This word, however, is often employed in so wide a sense as to lose any precise meaning, and some writers have affronted the English language by using hornfels as a verb. *See* CALC-SILICATE HORNFELS; FLECK-SCHIEFER; MACULOSE; PORCELANITE; SPILOSITE; SPOTTED SLATE

hornfels facies Pyroxene-hornfels facies.

hornito A small mound of driblet or spatter built on the back of a lava flow (generally pahoehoe) and formed by the gradual accumulation of clots of lava ejected through an opening in the roof of an underlying lava tube. The typical hornito is a rounded, more or less beehive-shaped mound. Driblet spires are a type of hornito shaped like a thin column or spine. *Syn:* DRIBLET CONE

horn quicksilver Mercurial horn ore; calomel, *q.v.*

horn silver Cerargyrite.

horse *Min: 1.* A large block of unmineralized rock included in a vein. *2.* Rock occupying a channel cut into a coal bed. *3.* Ridge of limestone rising from beneath residual phosphate deposit in Tennessee. *4.* In structure, a large block of displaced wall rock caught along a fault, particularly a high-angle normal fault.

horse latitudes The belts of calms, light winds and fine, clear weather between the trade wind belts and the prevailing westerly winds of higher latitudes. The belts move north and south after the sun in a similar way to the doldrums. The name arose from the old practice of throwing overboard horses which were being transported to America or the West Indies when the ship's passage was unduly prolonged. Some say they were named after Ross, a British explorer; in German atlases these latitudes appear as *Ross Breiten*. But Ross is an old German name for horse and when translated into English they may mistakenly have become the horse latitudes. •

horseshoe lake *See* OXBOW

horsetail ore Ore in fractures which diverge from a major fracture.

horst *1.* A mass of earth-crust which is limited by faults and which stands in relief with respect to its surroundings. *2.* A block of the earth's crust, generally long compared to its width that has been uplifted along

faults relative to the rocks on either side. *3.* A pendant with the connection portion smaller than the body. A knobby ledge of limestone beneath a thin mantle of soil.

host A mineral that contains an inclusion.

host rock The wall rock of an epigenetic ore deposit.

Hotchkiss superdip A modification of the dip needle which is used as a magnetometer. It measures variations in the total field. *See* DIPPING COMPASS; DIP NEEDLE

hot spring A thermal spring whose water has a higher temperature than that of the human body (above 98° F.).

hourglass valley A valley locally constricted, as where it cuts through a fault scarp or a former drainage divide, so that it is much narrower than on either side.

Hubble constant Relates the rate of nebular recession to distance from a center.

huebnerite *See* WOLFRAMITE

huerfano [*Sp.* Pronounced "ware-fa-no."] *1.* Tejon (disk-shaped) and huerfano (orphan) are used for circumscribed eminences. The latter is applied especially to solitary eminences standing far away from kindred masses. *2.* A hill or mountain of older rock, entirely surrounded, but not covered, by any kind of later sedimentary rock. Used occasionally in southwestern United States. *Syn:* LOST MOUNTAIN; ISLAND HILL

Hughes balance A low-frequency (500–2000 cycles) induction balance used in early treasure or pipe finders.

hum *1.* A residual standing above a recently eroded limestone surface. *2.* A rounded, conical-shaped hill resulting from solution. *Syn:* COCKPIT; HAYSTACK; PEPINO; MOGOTES

humic Derived from plants, carbonaceous. *Cf.* BITUMINOUS

humic acid *1.* A gelatinous material formed as a precipitate when organic matter is treated with a strong base and the resulting solution is acidified. *2.* Any of various complex organic acids supposedly formed by the partial decay of organic matter. An indefinite term of widely varying usage. Humic acid is generally agreed to be an effective adsorbent, but regarding its acid properties and its role in weathering and soil formation opinions differ widely.

humic gley soil Gumbotil.

humidity The condition of the atmosphere in respect to water vapor. When the word "humidity" is employed without a qualifying adjective the relative humidity is usually meant. However, humidity may be expressed in many different ways, such as by absolute humidity, mixing ratio, saturation deficit, specific humidity, etc.

humidity, absolute The actual quantity or mass of water vapor present in a given volume of air. Generally expressed in grains per cubic foot or in grams per cubic meter.

humidity, relative The ratio of the actual amount of water vapor present in the portion of the atmosphere under consideration to the quantity which would be there if it were saturated.

hummock *1.* A mound or knoll. Ice is said to be hummocky when it consists of the fragments and dislocated parts of a previously existing sheet, refrozen together, and thus producing a rugged surface. *2.* A small eleva-

tion; hillock. *3.* A pile or ridge of ice on an ice field. *4.* A more or less elevated piece of ground rising out of a swamp, often densely wooded; an area of deep, rich soil, usually covered by hardwood vegetation; a small elevation; a hillock.

hummocky moraine Area of glacial knob and kettle topography; may have been produced by either live or stagnant ice.

humus Substance of organic origin that is fairly but not entirely resistant to further bacterial decay. It is black, has a higher carbon content, commonly 52–58%, and lower nitrogen content than the original material. It may accumulate subaerially in soil or subaqueously in sediment.

humus layer The top portion of the soil which owes its characteristic features to its content of humus. The humus may be incorporated or unincorporated in the mineral soil.

Huronian *1.* Originally, schists and phyllites constituting the upper of two Precambrian systems. *Obs. 2.* Lower system of the restricted Proterozoic.

hurricane [<*Sp.* huracán] *1.* A name given primarily to the violent wind storms of the West Indies and Gulf of Mexico, which are cyclones with diameters of from 50 to 1000 miles, wherein the winds reach hurricane force near a central calm space; the whole system advances in a straight or curved track. Similar tropical storms off the coasts of Queensland are also known as hurricanes. *2.* In the Beaufort wind scale, *q.v.,* the name hurricane is given to a wind of force 12, and its velocity equivalent is put at a mean velocity exceeding 75 miles per hour.

Huygens' principle An important principle of wave propagation involving the concept that every point on an advancing wave front may be regarded as the source of a wavelet and that a later wave front is the envelope which may be drawn tangent to all the wavelets.

Hy Abbreviation for hypersthene in normative rock calculations.

hyacinth A transparent red, or brownish, variety of zircon, sometimes used as a gem.

hyaline Transparent, like glass.

hyalite A variety of opal which occurs in clear globular or botryoidal forms resembling drops of melted glass.

hyalo- [*Gr.*] A prefix meaning glass.

hyalocrystalline, *adj.* A textural term applied to porphyritic rocks in which phenocrysts and groundmass are equal or nearly equal in amount; the ratio of crystals to groundmass being between 5 to 3 and 3 to 5.

hyalo-ophitic, *adj.* An intersertal texture in which the basis is more abundant and not so much separated by the crystals as in the usual intersertal texture.

hyalopilitic, *adj.* A textural term applied to igneous rocks consisting of needlelike microlites in a glassy groundmass. Pilotaxitic is the same texture without glass. When the amount of glass is decreased and the number of crystals is increased, the texture becomes intersertal, although that texture includes also rocks in which the interstitial material is not glass.

hybrid *1.* A term originally applied to "intermediate" rocks at a time when they were regarded as the products of composite magmas derived from the admixture of the "trachytic" and "pyroxenic" magmas of R. W. E. von Bunsen. By Alfred Harker, 1904, the term is adopted for abnormal igneous rocks, of which marcasite is an example, formed by the mixture of two magmas, or by the assimilation of a rock already consolidated by the magma of a later intrusion. *2.* Individual organism descended from parents belonging to different species. *3.* In a much restricted sense, a heterozygous individual.

hybrid rocks Rocks of supposed heterogeneous origin. The term was originally used to refer to igneous rocks formed by the mixing of two compositionally contrasted primary world-wide magmas; it is now used in a more general sense to include all igneous rocks formed through the mixing of materials from several sources, as by assimilation of solid igneous rocks by later intrusions from the same source, or assimilation of country rocks. In this latter sense synonymous with contaminated rocks. Hybridization, *n.*

hydatogenic *Geol:* Derived from or modified by substances in a liquid condition. Said of the genesis of ores and other minerals. Contrasted with pneumatogenic.

hydrargillite Gibbsite, *q.v.*

hydrate A compound formed by the union of water with some other substance, and represented as actually containing water; e.g., gypsum, $CaSO_4.2H_2O$. Less properly, a hydroxide; e.g., calcium hydrate, $Ca(OH)_2$.

hydration The chemical combination of water with another substance.

hydraulic *1.* Of or pertaining to fluids in motion; conveying, or acting, by water; operated or moved by means of water, as, hydraulic mining. 2. Hardening or setting under water, as, hydraulic cement.

hydraulic cement Cement formerly produced by burning impure limestone (waterlime) which contains proper proportions of alumina and silica; now supplanted by Portland cement.

hydraulic conductivity Ratio of flow velocity to driving force for viscous flow under saturated conditions of a specified liquid in a porous medium.

hydraulic discharge Discharge of ground water in the liquid state directly from the zone of saturation upon the land or into a body of surface water through springs or artificial openings such as wells.

hydraulic fracturing A general term, for which there are numerous trade or service names, for the fracturing of rock in an oil or gas reservoir by pumping a fluid under high pressure into the well. The purpose is to produce artificial openings in the rock in order to increase permeability.

hydraulic gradient 1. Pressure gradient. As applied to an aquifer it is the rate of change of pressure head per unit of distance of flow at a given point and in a given direction. 2. As applied to streams, the slope of the energy grade line, or slope of line representing the sum of kinetic and potential energy along the channel length. It is equal to the slope of the water surface in steady, uniform flow. 3. A vector point function equal to the decrease in hydraulic head per unit distance in direction of greatest decrease in rate.

hydraulic jump 1. In fluid flow, a change in flow conditions ac-

companied by a stationary, abrupt turbulent rise in water level in the direction of flow. 2. A type of stationary wave.

hydraulic lime A variety of calcined limestone which, when pulverized, absorbs water without swelling or heating and affords a paste or cement that hardens under water.

hydraulic limestone A limestone which contains some silica and alumina, and which yields a quicklime that will set or form a firm, strong mass under water, as in hydraulic cements.

hydraulic mining A method of mining in which a bank of gold-bearing earth or gravel is washed away by a powerful jet of water and carried into sluices, where the gold separates from the earth by its specific gravity. Also used for other ores, earth, anthracite culm, etc. Hydraulic mining is made unlawful and prohibited in certain river systems where it obstructs navigation and injures adjoining landowners.

hydraulic profile The vertical section of the piezometric surface of an aquifer.

hydraulic radius *Hydraul.* and *Geomorph:* The ratio of the cross-sectional area of a stream to its wetted perimeter. *Symbol:* R. *Syn:* HYDRAULIC MEAN DEPTH

hydraulics That branch of science or of engineering which treats of water or other fluid in motion, its action in rivers and canals, the works and machinery for conducting or raising it, its use in driving machinery, etc.

hydro- [*Gr.*] A combining form meaning water, presence of hydrogen.

hydrobiotite A clay mineral composed of mixed layers of biotite and vermiculite.

hydrocarbon A compound containing only the two elements carbon and hydrogen.

hydrochemical prospecting Prospecting guided by the trace element content of ground and surface water.

hydroclastic Clastic through the agency of water; said of fragmental rocks deposited by water.

hydrodynamic Of or relating to the force or pressure of water or other fluids.

hydrodynamic wave H-wave. A surface seismic wave recognized by L. Don Leet similar to Rayleigh waves but moving in an opposite or counterclockwise sense, so that the wave is moving forward at its maximum "up" position.

hydroexplosion A general term for a volcanic explosion caused by the generation of steam from any body of water. It includes phreatic, phreatomagmatic, submarine, and littoral explosions.

hydrofracturing Process of increasing the permeability of strata near a well by pumping in water and sand under high pressure. Hydraulic pressure opens cracks and bedding planes and sand introduced into these serves to keep them open when pressure is reduced.

hydrogenation theory Because petroleum contains approximately 5% more hydrogen than is usually found in marine organic matter, one theory for the origin of petroleum is that hydrogen—given off by rocks through different agencies—combined with organic matter contained in beds relatively nearer the surface. The hydrogen might also have been of organic origin.

hydrogen bond Force uniting hydrogen atoms to other atoms of greater electronegativity.

hydrogenesis A process of nat-

ural condensation of moisture in the air spaces in the surface soil or rock.

hydrogen ion concentration (pH) A measure of the acidity of a solution. Usually given as the "pH" of the solution, which is the logarithm, to the base 10, of the reciprocal of the concentration of hydrogen ions in grams (H^+) per liter. The actual occurrence of the hydrogen ions as hydrated ("hydronium," H_3O^+) ions in the liquid is immaterial.

hydrogeochemistry Geochemistry of water.

hydrograph A graph showing stage, flow, velocity, or other property of water with respect to time.

hydrography 1. The description of the sea, lakes, rivers, and other aqueous portions of the earth's surface. 2. That branch of geography which treats of the waters that form part of the surface of the terraqueous globe, as, streams, rivers, lakes, seas, and the great oceans.

hydrolith Term proposed by A. W. Grabau for an aqueo-chemically precipitated rock (rock salt, gypsum, etc.).

hydrologic cycle The complete cycle of phenomena through which water passes, commencing as atmospheric water vapor, passing into liquid and solid form as precipitation, thence along or into the ground surface, and finally again returning to the form of atmospheric water vapor by means of evaporation and transpiration. *Syn:* WATER CYCLE

hydrology The science that relates to the water of the earth.

hydrolysate; hydrolyzate Sediments consisting partly of chemically undecomposed, finely ground rock powder and partly of insoluble matter derived from hydrolytic decomposition during weathering. Bauxites, clays, shales, etc., belong to this class.

hydrolysis Chemical process in which a salt combines with water to form an acid and a base. If one of the products is insoluble or if the base decomposes to an insoluble oxide, the process may continue to completion.

hydrolyzate Hydroxide resulting from hydrolysis; may be precipitated as sediment.

hydrometamorphism The alteration of rocks by the addition, subtraction, or exchange of material brought or carried in solution by water, without the influence of high temperature or pressure.

hydrometer A tubular device made of glass with the lower end weighted, graduated in specific gravity, degrees API, or other units, designed to determine the gravity of liquids by the depth to which the hydrometer sinks when immersed.

hydromica A term of rather loose usage applied to illite and sericite. *See* ILLITE

hydromuscovite Illite; hydromica.

hydrophilic Having strong affinity for water; said of colloids which swell in water and are not easily coagulated.

hydrophobic Lacking strong affinity for water; said of colloids whose particles are not highly hydrated and which coagulate easily.

hydrophone A pressure-sensitive detector designed for use in liquid or quasi-liquid elastic wave-propagating media.

hydroplasticity Plasticity that results from the presence of pore water in sediments.

hydroscope An instrument for detecting moisture, especially in the air.

hydrosol A colloidal system in which water is the dispersion medium.

hydrosphere *1.* The water portion of the earth, as distinguished from the solid part which is called the lithosphere, *q.v.* *2.* In a more inclusive sense, the water vapor in the atmosphere, the sea, the rivers and the ground waters. *3.* The liquid and solid water that rests on the lithosphere, including the solid, liquid, and gaseous materials that are suspended or dissolved in the water.

hydrostatic head The height of a vertical column of water, the weight of which, if of unit cross section, is equal to the hydrostatic pressure at a point.

hydrostatic level Static level. That level which for a given point in an aquifer, passes through the top of a column of water that can be supported by the hydrostatic pressure of the water at that point.

hydrostatic pressure The pressure exerted by the water at any given point in a body of water at rest. That of ground water is generally due to the weight of water at higher levels in the same zone of saturation.

hydrostatics That branch of physics which relates to the pressure and equilibrium of liquids, as, water, mercury, etc.; the principles of statics applied to water and other liquids.

hydrostatic stress State of stress in which all principal stresses are equal.

hydrothermal An adjective applied to heated or hot magmatic emanations rich in water, to the processes in which they are concerned, and to the rocks, ore deposits, alteration products, and springs produced by them.

hydrothermal alteration Those phase changes resulting from the interaction of hydrothermal stage fluids ("hydrothermal solutions") with pre-existing solid phases, such as kaolinization of feldspars, etc. Also used to cover changes in rocks brought about by the addition or removal of materials through the medium of hydrothermal fluids, e.g., silicification.

hydrothermal stage A stage in the normal sequence of crystallization of a magma containing volatiles, at which time the residual fluid is strongly enriched in water and other volatiles. The exact limits of the stage are variously defined by different authors, in terms of either phase assemblage (one vs. two liquids, gas vs. liquid), temperature, composition, or vapor pressure. Most definitions place it as the last stage of igneous activity, presumably coming at a later time (and hence lower temperature) than the pegmatitic stage.

hydrothermal synthesis Mineral synthesis in the presence of water at elevated temperatures.

hydrothermal water Warm water ascending from a deeper zone within the earth; needs not be exclusively magmatic.

hydroxide A compound of an element with the radical or ion, OH, as, sodium hydroxide, NaOH.

hydroxylapatite See APATITE

hydrozincite A basic zinc carbonate, perhaps $ZnCO_3 2Zn(OH)_2$. Massive, fibrous, earthy, or compact, as incrustations. Color white, grayish, or yellowish. Occurs at mines of zinc, as a result of alteration. Syn: ZINC BLOOM

Hydrozoa A class of Coelenter-

ata. An aquatic, usually marine, animal of small size, somewhat more highly specialized than the sponges; usually colonial; some build a skeletal deposit of calcium carbonate; rarely preserved as fossils.

hygrometer An instrument or apparatus for measuring the degree of moisture of the atmosphere.

hygroscopic Having the property of readily absorbing moisture from the atmosphere.

hygroscopicity coefficient The amount or percentage of water absorbed and held by a material in a saturated atmosphere.

hygroscopic water Water which is so tightly held by the attraction of soil particles that it cannot be removed except as a gas, by raising the temperature above the boiling point of water. This water is unavailable to plants.

hypabyssal A general adjective applied to minor intrusions such as sills and dikes, and to the rocks that compose them, which have crystallized under conditions intermediate between the plutonic and extrusive classes, being distinguished from these types in some cases by texture and in others only by mode of occurrence.

hypabyssal rocks Igneous rocks that have risen from the depths as magma but solidified mainly as minor intrusions such as dikes and sills before reaching the surface.

hyper- [Gr.] Over; above; abnormally great.

hyperfusible Any substance, such as water, occurring in the end-stage magmatic fluids that serves to lower melting ranges. Syn: HYPERFUSIBLE COMPONENT

hyperpycnal inflow Hyperpycnal (more dense) inflow occurs where the sediment-laden fluid flows down the side of the basin and then along the bottom as a turbidity current, with vertical mixing inhibited because the dense fluid seeks to remain at the lowest possible level. Delta formation by such flow is most frequent at the mouth of submarine canyons.

hypersthene *See* PYROXENE

hypidiomorphic *1.* A general term applied to those minerals of igneous rocks that are bounded only in part by their characteristic crystal faces, i.e., crystal forms intermediate between allotriomorphic (anhedral) and idiomorphic (euhedral). *Syn:* SUBHEDRAL; HYPAUTOMORPHIC. *2.* A textural term applied to granular plutonic rocks in which there are few idiomorphic minerals, most of the constituents being hypidiomorphic or subhedral. The texture of such rocks is said to be hypidiomorphic-granular or hypautomorphic-granular.

hypo- [*Gr.*] A prefix meaning under, beneath, down, less than the ordinary or norm.

hypocrystalline Applied to igneous rocks that consist partly of crystals and partly of glass. *Syn:* HYPOHYALINE

hypogene, *adj.* *1.* Used by Sir Charles Lyell and intended as a group name for plutonic and metamorphic classes of rocks, i.e., rocks formed within the earth. *2.* Used by Sir Archibald Geikie for geological processes originating within the earth. *3.* Applied to mineral or ore deposits formed by generally ascending waters. Contrasted with supergene, *q.v.*

hypolimnion The lower layer of water in a sea or lake.

hyponym When a name is first applied to a group, the group should be so described, or illustrated, or referred to preserved plants, that its identity can be recognized by other botanists. A name not so described or identified is a hyponym and nonvalid for the group for which it was intended.

hypopycnal inflow Hypopycnal (less dense) inflow occurs where sediment-laden fluid moves out over the surface of denser fluid filling the basin, as in the case of a stream discharging into the ocean. If the magnitude of discharge is small, a lunate bar forms off the outlet; if moderate to large, a cuspate, arcuate, or bird-foot type of delta will form.

hypothermal Originating at relatively high temperatures ($300°$–$500°$ C.).

hypothermal deposits Deposits formed at high temperatures and pressures in and along openings in rocks by deposition from fluids derived from consolidating igneous rocks.

hypotype A described or figured specimen, used in publication extending or correcting the knowledge of a previously defined species.

Hypozoic Precambrian; era of lowly life. *Obs.*

hypsithermal interval Postglacial warm interval extending from about 7000 to 600 B.C. responsible for the last 6-foot eustatic rise of sea level. *Syn:* POSTGLACIAL CLIMATIC OPTIMUM; THERMAL MAXIMUM

hypsographic map A topographic map on which elevations are referred to a sea-level datum.

hypsometric Relating to elevation above a datum, usually sea level.

hysteresis *1.* A lag in the return of an elastically deformed specimen to its original shape after the load has been released. 2. An effect, involving energy loss, found to varying degrees in magnetic, electric, and elastic media when they are subjected to variation by a cyclical applied force. In such media the polarization or stress is not a single valued function of the applied force, or, stated in another way, the state of the medium depends on its previous history as well as the instantaneous value of the applied force. May be visualized as resulting from some kind of internal friction.

-ic; -ical Suffixes employed to convert certain terms into adjective form, the two adjectives derived from the same root word sometimes having slightly different meanings, but often employed according to custom or personal preference without differentiation.

ice The solid state of water, specifically the dense substance formed by the freezing of liquid water or by the recrystallization of fallen snow. Ice formed by the sublimation of water vapor is usually known as snow or hoar, *q.v. See* GLACIER ICE; SEA ICE; GROUND ICE.

ice age The glacial period.

iceberg *1.* [*Dan.* berg, mountain] Large masses of ice broken off from the lower ends of the huge glaciers, which in high altitudes force their way down to and into the sea. They float nine-tenths in the water and one-tenth out, so that for every foot of ice above water there are nine feet below. *2.* A glacier on a seacoast often stretches out its icy foot into the ocean, and, when this part is finally broken off, by the movement of the sea or otherwise, it becomes an iceberg. *3.* A mass of land ice (including shelf ice) that has broken away from its parent formation on or near the coast and either floats in the sea or is stranded on a shoal.

icecap *1.* The ice which spreads with some approach to equality in all directions from a center is a glacier, is indeed the type of greatest glaciers, but is commonly called an icecap. The same name is applied to any glacier in which there is movement in all directions from the center, even though its shape departs widely from a circle. The glacier covering the larger part of Greenland is a good example of a large icecap, and the glaciers on some of the flat-topped peninsula promontories of the same island are good examples of small ones. If icecaps cover a large part of a continent, as some of those of the past have done, they are often called continental glaciers. *2.* A small ice sheet. *3.* Improperly used to designate the floating sea ice around the North Pole.

ice cascade When the slope of a glacier bed increases suddenly, an ice cascade is developed, but an ice cascade has little in common with the rapids or falls of rivers.

ice-contact forms Stratified drift bodies such as kames, kame terraces, and eskers, deposited in contact with melting glacier ice.

ice dam lake Whenever a continental glacier, either in advancing its front or in retiring, lies across the lines of drainage upon their downstream side, water is impounded along the ice front so as to form ice dam lakes.

iced firn A mixture of ice and firn.

ice drift Loose floating ice.

ice face Ice cliff.

ice fall That portion of a glacier which flows down a steep gradient, resulting in a zone of crevasses and seracs, *q.v.*

ice foot In polar seas the land is often bordered by a fringe of ice, called the ice foot. *See* FAST ICE

ice front 1. The terminus of a glacier. 2. The seaward-facing cliff of shelf ice.

ice island 1. A large tabular ice mass, several hundred feet thick and several square miles in area, floating in the Arctic ice pack. Ice islands may have an undulating surface, and streams and ponds in summer. 2. Any tabular iceberg. 3. Ice-island iceberg. 4. Floeberg. 5. An island completely covered by ice and snow.

ice jam 1. Fragments of broken river ice lodged in a narrow portion of the river channel. 2. Large fragments of lake ice thawed loose in early spring and shoved against the shore.

Iceland spar Transparent cleavage fragments of calcite, which, owing to its strong double refraction, are used for optical purposes.

ice layer 1. Approximately horizontal layer of ground ice, sometimes lenticular in form.

ice lobe Glacial or glacier lobe, *q.v.*

ice mountain An iceberg.

ice pack Pack ice. A term applied to a phenomenon which occurs in Arctic regions, when the ice first formed on the surface of the sea becomes broken up and separate portions piled or packed on top of each other, forming masses very difficult to navigate.

ice pan A large, flat piece of sea ice, protruding a few inches to three feet above the water, usually composed of winter ice up to one year old.

ice pillar Glacier table, *q.v.*

ice plateau 1. An ice-covered highland area whose upper surface is relatively level, and whose sides slope steeply to lowlands or the ocean. 2. Any ice sheet with a level or gently rounded surface.

ice pole The area around which the more consolidated part of the Arctic ice pack is located. In 1959 its location was about 84° N. Lat. and 160° W. Long. *Syn:* POLE OF INACCESSIBILITY

ice push The expansion ice formed on a lake or embayment of the sea which accompanies a rise in temperature. As the ice expands horizontally it pushes unconsolidated debris on the shore into ramparts or irregular ridges.

ice-push ridge Lake rampart; walled lake.

ice rafting Transport of rock particles and other materials by floating ice.

ice rampart Lake rampart, *q.v.*

ice-scoured plain A region reduced to the condition of a plain by actual ice scour.

ice sheet A glacier forming in continuous cover over a land surface, with the ice moving outward in many directions. Continental glaciers, icecaps, and some highland glaciers are examples of ice sheets.

ice shelf Floating ice permanently attached to a land mass, as the Ross Ice Shelf in the Antarctic. Now the preferred term for ice barrier, ice front, and shelf ice, *q.v.*

ice tongue 1. That portion of a valley glacier below the firn line.

2. Outlet glaciers from an ice-cap. *3.* Glacial lobes, *q.v.*

ice vein Ice wedge.

ice wedge; ground-ice wedge Vertical, wedge-shaped vein of ground ice.

ice-wedge polygon Large-scale polygonal feature commonly outlined by shallow trenches underlain by ice wedges.

ichnology Term proposed by F. T. Buckland prior to 1844. The study of fossil footprints. *Obs.*

ichor, *n.* A term proposed by J. J. Sederholm (1933) for a granitic juice or liquor, capable of granitizing rocks, and derived from a granitic magma. *Syn:* EMANATION; MINERALIZER; RESIDUAL MAGMA

icicle A pendant, somewhat conical, shaft of ice formed by the freezing of dripping water.

I.C.S.G The International Commission of Snow and Glaciers.

Iddings' classification A classification of igneous rocks by J. P. Iddings (1913) which attempts to correlate the mineralogical classifications of Harry Rosenbusch and Ferdinand Zirkel with the chemicomineralogical C.I.P.W. or norm classification system.

ideal gas Perfect gas. One which obeys the gas laws perfectly, particularly Boyle's law. The term implies infinitely small gas particles and no interactions between particles.

ideal solutions A solution in which the forces between molecules are identical throughout. In nonideal solutions (containing several different types of molecules or ions) the interactions between unlike types are different from that between identical types, and the behavior will be nonideal.

ideotype Specimen other than a topotype identified by the original author of a species.

idioblastic An idioblastic mineral is one which shows crystal faces against an adjacent mineral.

idiogenous Said of deposits contemporaneous in origin with the rocks in which they occur, i.e., primary deposits which are constituents of the rocks in which they occur.

idiogeosyncline *1.* An intermontane trough in which sediments accumulated. *2.* Marginal basin, short lived and weakly folded.

idiomorphic Euhedral; automorphic, *q.v.*

idocrase Vesuvianite. A mineral, $Ca_{10}Al_4(Mg,Fe)_2(SiO_4)_5(Si_2O_7)_2(OH)_4$. Tetragonal. Common in contact-metamorphosed limestones.

igneoaqueous Formed by the joint action of fire and water. Thus ashes thrown from a volcano into water and there deposited in a stratified form might properly be said to be of igneoaqueous origin.

igneous, *adj. Petrol:* Formed by solidification from a molten or partially molten state. Said of the rocks of one of the two great classes into which all rocks are divided, and contrasted with sedimentary. Rocks formed in this manner have also been called plutonic rocks, and are often divided for convenience into plutonic and volcanic rocks, but there is no clear line between the two.

igneous breccia *1.* Breccia consisting of igneous rock. *2.* Breccia produced by igneous action, includes pyroclastic, flow and contact breccias.

igneous complex Intimately associated and roughly contemporaneous igneous rocks.

igneous emanations Gases and liquids which are given off during igneous activity.

igneous facies *See* FACIES, IGNEOUS

igneous rocks Formed by solidification of hot mobile material termed magma.

igneous rock series A term originated by W. C. Brögger (1904) for an assemblage of igneous rocks in a single district and belonging to a single period of igneous activity, characterized by a certain community of chemical, mineralogical, and occasionally also textural properties. *See* CONSANGUINITY

ignimbrite *1.* A silicic volcanic rock forming thick, massive, compact, lavalike sheets that cover a wide area in the central part of North Island, New Zealand. The rock is chiefly a fine-grained rhyolitic tuff formed mainly of glass particles (shards) in which crystals of feldspar, quartz, and occasionally hypersthene or hornblende are embedded. The glass particles are firmly "welded" and bend around the crystals, and evidently were of a viscous nature when they were deposited. The deposits are believed to have been produced by the eruption of dense clouds of incandescent volcanic glass in a semimolten or viscous state from groups of fissures. *Syn:* WELDED TUFF. *2.* The deposit of a fiery cloud or pyroclastic flow, extensive and generally thick with well-developed prismatic jointing.

IGY International Geophysical Year, beginning July 1, 1957, ending December 31, 1958.

Il Abbreviation for ilmenite in normative rock calculations.

Illinoisan Third Pleistocene glaciation.

illite Glimmerton [*Ger.*]; hydromica. Names used for a group of clay minerals abundant in argillaceous sediments. They are intermediate in composition between muscovite and montmorillonite; recent studies have shown that many are made up of interlayered mica and montmorillonite.

illuvial horizon B-horizon of the soil profile.

illuviation The deposition in an underlying layer of soil (soil horizon B) of colloids, soluble salts, and small mineral particles which have been leached out of an overlying soil layer (soil horizon A). The action occurs in humid climates.

ilmenite A mineral, $FeTiO_3$. Hexagonal rhombohedral. The principal ore of titanium.

ilvaite Lievrite. A mineral, $Ca-Fe''_2Fe'''(SiO_4)_2(OH)$. Orthorhombic.

imbibition The tendency of granular rock or any porous medium to "imbibe" a fluid, usually water, under the force of capillary attraction, and in the absence of any pressure.

imbricate The shingling or overlapping effect of stream flow upon flat pebbles in the stream bed. The pebbles are inclined so that the upper edge of each individual is inclined in the direction of the current.

imbricate structure *1.* In general refers to tabular masses that overlap one another as shingles on a roof. *2. Struct. geol:* A series of thrust sheets dipping in the same direction, sometimes called shingle-block structure. Schuppen structure [*Ger.*].

immature lignite A more or less descriptive term commonly, and to some extent indiscriminately, used in coal literature to apply to low-rank types of lignite.

immature soil *1.* A soil in which erosion exceeds the rate at which the soil develops downward. *2.* Soil that has not reached maturity as shown by lack of zonation.

immiscibility or **miscibility gap** A break in an otherwise completely miscible series between two materials, either liquid or crystalline.

immiscible Said of two or more liquid or solid solutions that are not capable of being mixed, as oil and water. The two (or more) liquids can still be in equilibrium with each other.

impact The wearing away of smaller rocks or fragments through the effect of definite blows of relatively larger fragments on the relatively smaller rocks or fragments.

impact bomb Porous mass of impactite formed by splattering; may enclose pebbles, etc.

impactite Vesicular glassy to finely crystalline material produced where a meteor has struck the earth; consists of meteoric material and slag.

impact law A formula expressing the relationship of large particle diameter and fluid density to the settling velocity of large particles in a given liquid medium.

impact slag Glassy material produced mainly by the melting of local sediment or rock where a meteorite has struck the earth.

impedance In electric circuits or measurements, the generalized resistance or opposition to current flow in other than pure direct currents; commonly includes complex components of resistance, inductance, and capacity.

impermeable; impervious *Hydrol:* Having a texture that does not permit water to move through it perceptibly under the head differences ordinarily found in subsurface water.

impervious Impermeable, *q.v.* Impassable; applied to strata such as clays, shales, etc., which will not permit the penetration of water, petroleum, or natural gas.

impregnated Containing metallic minerals, scattered or diffused through the mass. Properly used in referring to country rock containing mineral similar to that in the vein.

impression *1.* The form or shape left on a soft surface by materials which have come in contact with it. Usually occurs as a negative or concave feature on the top of a bed. A cast of it will sometimes be found on the base of the overlying bed. *See* IMPRINT. *2.* Results from the burial of plant parts in soils which subsequently harden into rock, in much the same manner as an imprint is left when a leaf is pressed into the surface of wet cement which is allowed to "set." Impressions thus preserve the external structural features of plant parts.

imprint *1.* The impression made on a soft surface of mud or sand by organic or inorganic materials which have come in contact with it. *Syn:* IMPRESSION. *2.* Evidence of deformative movement within rocks.

impulse A short-period force or action; in seismograph prospecting, the effect of an explosive or mechanical source of seismic waves.

Inarticulata Class of brachiopods whose shells lack articulating teeth and sockets, mostly with chitino-phosphatic shells.

incidence, angle of The angle

between the normal to the wave front and the normal to a reflecting or refracting surface.

incise Cut down into, as a river cuts into a plateau.

incised or **entrenched meander** A deep tortuous valley cut by a rejuvenated stream, the meandering course having been acquired in a former cycle.

inclination 1. *Geol:* The dip of a bed, fault, vein, or other tabular body measured from the horizontal. 2. *Geophys:* The angle between any direction and the vertical. *See* DIP; MAGNETIC INCLINATION

inclined contact Applied to a contact plane of oil or gas with underlying water, in which the plane slopes or is inclined. Usually due to the fact that the water is in motion because of a hydraulic gradient across the bed.

inclined extinction Oblique extinction.

inclined fold Fold whose axial plane is not vertical.

inclinometer 1. A dipping compass. 2. An instrument for measuring inclination or slope, as of the ground or of an embankment; clinometer.

inclosed meanders Stream meanders that are more or less closely bordered or inclosed by the valley walls.

included gas Gases in isolated interstices in either the zone of aeration or the zone of saturation.

inclusion 1. *Petrol:* A crystal or fragment of another substance or a minute cavity filled with gas or liquid enclosed in a crystal. 2. A fragment of older rock enclosed in an igneous rock; a xenolith.

inclusions, fluid During the crystallization of minerals, or during recrystallization following fracturing, small portions of the fluids present may become trapped within the mineral grains. Most of these are small (0.001–0.01 mm.), and frequently contain a small bubble of a gaseous phase in addition to the liquid (usually hydrous) phase.

incompatible minerals Two or more minerals which, at the specified conditions, would at equilibrium react together to form a new phase or phases, until the eventual elimination of one or more of the original minerals, e.g., quartz and any unsaturated mineral.

incompetent bed 1. *Geol:* Not combining sufficient firmness and flexibility to transmit a thrust and to lift a load by bending; consequently, admitting only the deformation of flowage: said of strata and rock structure. *See* COMPETENT, 1. 2. Competent and incompetent are relative terms. An incompetent bed is one that is relatively weak and thus cannot transmit pressure for any distance. 3. A bed which, because it lacks strength or cohesiveness, is unable to lift its own or the weight above it without breaking, when it undergoes such movement as folding.

incompetent folding *See* FLOW FOLDING

incompressibility modulus Modulus of volume elasticity; modulus of elasticity, *q.v.*

incongruent melting Melting accompanied by decomposition or by reaction with the liquid, so that one solid phase is converted into another; melting to give a liquid different in composition from the original solid. For example, orthoclase melts incongruently to give leucite and a liquid richer in silica than the original orthoclase.

incongruent solution Dissolution accompanied by decomposition or by reaction with the liquid, so that one solid phase is converted into another; dissolution to give dissolved material in different proportions from those in the original solid.

incongruous drag folds Drag folds that do not have the characteristics of congruous drag folds, q.v.

incongruous folds Minor and drag folds that do not agree with Pumpelly's rule, q.v.

incretion Cylindrical concretions with a hollow core.

incrustation A crust or hard coating of anything upon or within a body, as, a deposit of lime inside a steam boiler.

index contour Certain contour lines (usually every fifth) accentuated by use of a line heavier than the intervening lines and whose elevation or other value is indicated by figures along its course.

index ellipsoid Ellipsoid whose axes are proportional to the indices of refraction in different directions.

index fossil 1. Guide fossil. 2. Fossil characteristic of an assemblage zone and so far as known restricted to it. 3. Fossil by whose name a biostratigraphic zone is known.

index map A map which shows the location of collections of related data, whether in the form of other maps, or statistical tables, or descriptions.

index mineral *Metamorph. petrol:* A mineral whose first appearance (in passing from low to higher grades of metamorphism) marks the outer limit of the zone in question.

index of refraction A character-izing number which expresses the ratio of the velocity of light *in vacuo* to the velocity of light in the substance. The conventional symbol is *n*.

index plane A surface of any bed, dike, or vein, which may be regarded as a plane and used as a base for measurement of fault movements.

index zone Zone recognizable by paleontologic or lithologic characters that can be traced laterally and identifies a reference position in a stratigraphic section.

Indian summer Any spell of warm, quiet, hazy weather that may occur in October or even in early November; in some years there may be only a few days of such weather or none at all, while in other years there may be one or more extended periods.

The term dates back to the eighteenth century in the United States. There are equivalents of Indian summer in the countries of Europe, but they are there known by other names.

indicated ore Ore for which tonnage and grade are computed partly from specific measurements and partly from projection for a reasonable distance on geologic evidence.

indicator, *n.* An erratic whose place of origin in the bedrock is known.

indicator plant *Geobot. prospecting:* Plant or tree that grows exclusively or preferentially on soil rich in a given metal or other element.

indicator vein A vein which is not metalliferous itself, but, if followed, leads to ore deposits.

indicatrix Index ellipsoid.

indigenous 1. Originating in a specific place; *in situ.* 2. Designating rocks, minerals, or ores originating in place, as opposed to those transported from a distance.

indigenous "limonite" "Limonite" precipitated within the same cavity or group of cavaties in which the sulfide source of the iron formerly existed.

induced magnetization Impermanent magnetization produced by an applied magnetic field; it is reversible like that in a soft iron magnet.

induction *1.* The process by which a magnetizable body becomes magnetized by merely placing it in a magnetic field. *2.* The process by which a body becomes electrified by merely placing it in an electric field. *3.* The process by which electric currents are initiated in a conductor by merely placing it in an electromagnetic field.

induction log A continuous record of the conductivity of strata traversed by a borehole as a function of depth.

indurated Rendered hard; confined in geological use to masses hardened by heat, baked, etc., as distinguished from hard or compact in natural structure.

In modern usage the term is applied to rocks hardened not only by heat, but also by pressure and cementation.

induration The process of hardening of sediments or other rock aggregates through cementation, pressure, heat, or other cause.

indusium The membranous cover of a fern sorus.

inequigranular A textural term applied to rocks whose essential minerals are of different orders of size, e.g., porphyries.

inert gas One of the chemically unreactive gases in Group O of the periodic system (He, Ne, A, Kr, Xe, Rn).

inertia That property of a body

by virtue of which it offers resistance to a change of its motion of translation.

infant stream A stream which has just begun the work of tearing down and carrying away the upland.

inferior Lower in position, as in the orientation of Foraminifera and other shelled invertebrates.

inferred ore *1.* Ore for which quantitative estimates are based largely on broad knowledge of the geologic character of the deposit and for which there are few if any samples or measurements. *2.* A term used in essentially the same sense as possible ore and extension ore, *q.v.*

infiltration *1.* The flow of a fluid into a substance through pores or small openings. It connotes flow into a substance in contradistinction to the word percolation, which connotes flow through a porous substance. *2.* The flow or movement of water through the soil surface into the ground. *3.* The deposition of mineral matter among the grains or pores of a rock by the permeation or percolation of water carrying it in solution. *4.* The material filling a vein as though deposited from a solution in water.

infiltration capacity The maximum rate at which the soil, when in a given condition, can absorb falling rain.

infiltration rate Maximum rate at which soil can absorb rain or shallow impounded water.

infiltration velocity Volume of water moving downward into soil per unit of area and time.

influent *1.* A tributary stream or river; affluent. *2.* A stream or stretch of a stream is influent with respect to ground water if it contributes water to the zone of saturation. The upper surface of such a stream stands higher than the water table or other piezometric surface of the aquifer to which it contributes.

infra- [*Lat.*] In combinations, signifies below.

infraglacial Applied to deposits formed and accumulated underneath or in the bottom parts of glaciers and ice sheets, and to the geological action of the ice upon rocks over which it flows.

infralittoral *Geol:* Below the region of littoral deposits.

infraneritic Pertaining to the marine environment in water from 120 to 600 feet deep.

infrastructure C. E. Wegmann's term for the migmatitic zone lying beneath the superstructure, *q.v.*, in an evolving granitic magma. The two zones fold in disharmonic fashion with the migmatite filling the arches in the superstructure.

infra-subspecific form Subdivision of an organic population.

Infusoria Ciliata.

infusorial earth An earthy substance or soft rock composed of the siliceous skeletons of small aquatic plants called diatoms. A former and common, but incorrect, usage; properly, diatomaceous earth. Useful as an absorbent of nitroglycerin. Called also infusorial silica and fossil flour, and in special forms rottenstone and electro-silicon; kieselguhr. *Syn:* TRIPOLITE

ingrown meander A meander deepened as a result of rejuvenation of a stream course, as, from down-valley tilting.

inherent ash Ash derived from mineral constituents of vegetable material in coal rather than from accompanying sediment.

initial dip The angle of slope of bedding surfaces at the time of deposition, the contacts between layers usually being approximately parallel with the surface of deposition unless subsequently altered by differential compaction or other deformational processes.

initial form The form at the beginning of any geographic cycle. Any dynamic process which produces a change in the relative position of land and sea may interrupt a cycle at any stage of development and cause the initial form of the new cycle. Later stages and forms may be called appropriately sequential.

initial open flow A term applied to the rate of flow of a gas well immediately following completion. The flow is gauged with a Pitot tube, or other instrument, with no restricting pressure other than atmospheric, and the rate is calculated in cubic feet per 24 hours.

initial production The volume or quantity of gas or oil initially produced by a well in a certain interval of time, usually 24 hours. Gas wells are rated in terms of cubic feet, and oil wells in barrels of 42 gallons. In the case of gas wells, the initial production is usually that volume produced and delivered into the gathering line against whatever pressure may exist in the latter, thus differing from initial open flow, which is that volume produced into the air, with no other restricting pressure.

injected igneous body An intrusive igneous body that is entirely inclosed by the invaded formations, except along the relatively narrow feeding channel. Examples are dikes, sills, laccoliths, phacoliths, etc. Contrasted with subjacent igneous body.

injection complex General term for ancient rocks, mostly plutonic, underlying the oldest sedimentary formations in the eastern United States.

injection folding Deformation in a plastic layer between more competent layers resulting from differential changes in thickness.

injection gneiss A gneiss whose banding is wholly or partly due to lit-par-lit injection of granitic magma. *See* COMPOSITE GNEISS; GNEISS; MIGMATITE

injection metamorphism Metamorphism accompanied by intimate injection of sheets and streaks of liquid magma in zones near plutonic rocks.

injection water Water forced into oil sands to promote secondary recovery.

injection well Well into which water or gas is pumped in an oil field to promote secondary recovery or to maintain subsurface pressure.

inland ice Informal designation for the interior zone of a large ice cap or continental glacier.

inland seas Adjacent seas that are largely surrounded by land or shallow waters so that communication with the open ocean is restricted to one or a few straits.

inlet A short, narrow waterway connecting a bay, lagoon, or similar body of water with a large parent body of water. An arm of the sea (or other body of water) that is long compared to its width and that may extend a considerable distance inland. *See* TIDAL INLET

inlier *1.* A more or less circular or elliptical area of older rocks surrounded by younger strata. Often the result of erosion of the crest of an anticline. *Ant:* OUTLIER

inner core Central part of earth's core beginning at depth of about 5000 km., probably solid.

inosilicate Metasilicate, *q.v.* Silicate structures in which the SiO_4 tetrahedra are joined together to produce chains of indefinite length, the ends being at the surfaces of the crystal. The amphiboles are an example.

in place Said of rock occupying, relative to surrounding masses, the position that it had when formed. If an ore body is continuous to the extent that it may maintain that character, then it is "in place." *See* IN SITU

Insecta Subphylum of arthropods with three pairs of legs, mostly terrestrial and winged. Dev.-Rec.

inselberg Prominent steep-sided residual hills and mountains rising abruptly from plains make a landscape type rather common in Africa. The residuals are generally bare and rocky, large and small, isolated and in hill and mountain groups, and they are surrounded by lowland surfaces of erosion that are generally true plains, as distinguished from peneplains.

insequent *Geol:* Developed on the present surface, but not consequent on nor controlled by the structure; said of streams, drainage, and dissection of a certain type. A type of drainage in which young streams flowing on a nearly level plain wander irregularly.

insequent stream *1.* Streams the courses of which are not due to (consequent upon) determinable factors are called insequent streams [in (con) sequent = insequent].

inshore In beach terminology, the zone of variable width extending from the shore face through the breaker zone.

inshore current Any current in or landward of the breaker zone.

in situ In its natural position or place. *Geol:* Said specifically of a rock, soil, or fossil when in the situation in which it was originally formed or deposited. *See* IN PLACE

insolation *Meteor:* Received solar radiation, as by the earth; also rate of delivery of all direct solar energy per unit of horizontal surface.

insoluble residue Siliceous residue. Material remaining after a specimen has been dissolved in hydrochloric or acetic acid, chiefly composed of shale, chert, quartz, other siliceous material and various insoluble detrital minerals.

instability *See* METASTABLE

instant *1.* Point in time. *2.* Time of beginning or ending of the deposition of a stratigraphic unit. *3.* Geologic time unit equivalent to a biostratigraphic zone. *4.* Smallest time interval distinguishable in the geologic record. *See* MOMENT

instar *1.* Moult stage of an insect. *2.* Immature moulted shell of an ostracod.

insulated stream A stream or reach of a stream is insulated with respect to ground water if it neither contributes water to the zone of saturation nor receives water from it. It is separated from the zone of saturation by an impermeable bed.

intake Recharge, *q.v.*

intake area (of an aquifer) An area where water is absorbed which eventually reaches a part of an aquifer that is in the zone of saturation.

integrated drainage The drainage of any initial surface becomes "integrated" as the local undrained depressions, common to all such surfaces, become incorporated into one master drainage system.

intensity (of an earthquake) A number describing the effects of an earthquake on man, on structures built by him, and on the earth's surface. The number is rated on the basis of an "earthquake intensity scale"; the scale in common use in the United States today is the Modified Mercalli Intensity Scale of 1931.

inter- [*Lat.*] In composition, signifies between closely related parts or organs.

interbedded Occurring between beds, or lying in a bed parallel to other beds of a different material; interstratified.

intercalate *v.* To insert among others, as, a bed or stratum of lava between layers of other material; to interstratify.

intercepts *Crystallog:* Distances cut off on axes of reference by planes.

intercept time Delay time, *q.v.*

interface Contact surface separating two different substances.

interfacial angle *Crystallog:* The angle between the normals to two crystal faces.

interfacial tension The force tending to reduce the area of contact between two liquids or between a liquid and a solid.

interference *1.* The masking of a desired signal by others arriving at very nearly the same time. *2.* The vector sum of the displacements (or velocities or accelerations) of wave trans-arriving at a point from the same source by different paths. Also used to describe the same result when waves arrive from two or more sources.

interference color Colors produced by the destruction or weakening of certain wave lengths of a composite beam of light by interference. An important element in the determination of minerals in thin section under the polarizing microscope.

interference figure A system of colored rings and curves combined with black bars and curves seen when a mineral grain is examined in a certain way under the microscope or other suitable optical instrument. The interference figure is due to birefringence, *q.v.*, and is one of the most useful optical aids in identifying minerals.

interference ripple mark *1.* Results when two sets of symmetrical ripples are formed by two systems of waves crossing nearly at right angles. The cell-like pattern of some interference ripple marks led Edward Hitchcock to regard them as "tadpole nests." *2.* Ripples formed during a single phase of current action by a complex current. *See* OSCILLATION CROSS RIPPLE MARK

interfinger To grade or pass from one material into another through a series of interlocking or overlapping wedge-shaped layers.

interfluve The district between adjacent streams flowing in the same general direction.

interfolding Simultaneous development of differently oriented folds that do not cross or interfere.

interformational conglomerate Those gravels and their indurated equivalents that often are present within a formation of which the constituents have a source external to the formation.

intergelisol *See* PERELTOK

interglacial Pertaining to the time between glaciations. An interglacial age.

intergranular A textural term proposed by J. W. Evans (1916) and applied to volcanic rocks in which there is an aggregation of grains of augite, not in parallel optical continuity (as in subophitic texture), between a network of feldspar laths which may be diverse, subradial, or subparallel. Distinguished from an intersertal texture by the absence of interstitial glass, or other substances which may fill the interstices between the feldspar laths. Characteristic of certain basaltic and doleritic rocks. *Cf.* GRANULITIC

intergranular film A film, of variable thickness and nature, occurring between the grains of a rock. It varies in thickness and composition, particularly with temperature. It is used more or less synonymously with interstitial fluid and pore fluid.

intergrowth *Petrol.* and *Mineral:* Commonly applied to a state of interlocking of different crystals due to simultaneous crystallization. An example of an intergrowth would be perthite. Rock textures such as graphic, micrographic, and granophyric are spoken of as intergrowth textures.

interior The country extending indefinitely inland of the hinterland.

interior basin Basin situated within the relatively stable area of a continent.

interior salt domes Domes in east Texas, northern Louisiana, southern Arkansas and Mississippi located at a distance from the Gulf Coast salt domes. Three general groupings are: (1) in the Tyler Basin, northeast Texas, (2) on the east flank of the Sabine arch in northern Louisiana, (3) in southern Alabama, eastern Louisiana, and south-central Mississippi. *See* SALT DOME; PIERCEMENT DOME

interior sea A body of water, usually marine, lying upon a continental platform and largely surrounded by land.

interior valley A large steep-sided isolated solution valley, generally floored with alluvium. (Jamaica.) *Syn:* POLJE

interlobate Situated between lobes. *Geol:* Lying between adjacent glacial lobes, as deposits.

intermediate focus earthquake Earthquake whose focus is at a depth of between 65 and 300 km.

intermediate rock An igneous rock containing between 52 and 66% SiO_2.

intermittent stream *1.* Stream which flows but part of the time, as, after a rainstorm, during wet weather, or during but part of the year. *See* PERENNIAL STREAMS. *2.* One which flows only at certain times when it receives water from springs (spring fed) or from some surface source (surface fed) such as melting snow in mountainous areas.

intermontane Lying between mountains.

intermontane area Structural and topographic basin enclosed by diverging and converging mountain ranges.

intermontane glaciers Glaciers produced by the confluence of several valley glaciers and occupying a trough between separate mountain ranges.

intermontane troughs Subsiding areas in an island arc region which lie among the positive elements of the area.

intermountain Area between mountains that mark the margins of an orogen. [*Ger.*] Zwischengebirge. *Syn:* INTERMONTANE AREA

internal energy *See* FIRST LAW OF THERMODYNAMICS

internal mold *See* MOLD, INTERNAL

internal rotation Rotation of individual small particles within a rock such as might be accomplished by flowage.

internal waves Waves that occur within a fluid whose density changes with depth, either abruptly at a sharp surface of discontinuity (an interface), or gradually. Their amplitude is greatest at the density discontinuity or, in the case of a gradual density change, somewhere in the interior of the fluid and not at the free upper surface where the surface waves have their maximum amplitude.

interpreter A person who deduces the geological significance of geophysical data.

interpretive log A sample log based on rotary cuttings in which the geologist has attempted to portray only the rock cut by the bit at the level indicated, ignoring the admixed material from a higher level.

interrupted profile The break or interruption in a normal stream profile where the head of the second-cycle valley after rejuvenation touches the first-cycle valley. Commonly considered as evidence of plural cycles of erosion but may be due to other causes. *See* NICKPOINT

interrupted stream *1.* One which contains (1) perennial reaches with intervening intermittent or ephemeral reaches or (2) intermittent reaches with intervening ephemeral reaches. *2.* An interrupted stream flows at some places and not at others; and an intermittent stream flows at some times and not at others. *See* LOST RIVER

interrrupted water table One that

has a pronounced descent along a ground-water dam.

intersertal A texture of igneous rocks wherein a base or mesostasis of glass and small crystals fills the interstices between unoriented feldspar laths, the base forming a relatively small proportion of the rock. When the amount of the base increases and the feldspar laths decrease, the texture becomes hyalo-ophitic, and with a still greater increase in the amount of the base the texture becomes hyalopilitic.

interstadial; interstade Refers to interglacial time or deposits.

interstice Pore, *1*. Void, *q.v.*

interstitial deposits Deposits that fill the pores of rocks. Frequently used in place of impregnation deposits.

interstitial fluid *See* INTERGRANULAR FILM

interstitial matrix Fine sedimentary material occurring between coarser grains; maximum size 0.02 mm.

interstitial solid solution Occurrence of foreign atoms or ions in the lattice interstices of a crystal.

interstratified Interbedded; strata laid between or alternating with others.

intertongued lithofacies Stratigraphic body, distinguished from others by its gross lithologic character, that intertongues with its neighbor rather than passing into it by gradual lithologic change. *Cf.* STATISTICAL LITHOFACIES; LITHOSOME

interval *1.* The vertical distance between strata or units of reference. *2.* Contour interval is the vertical distance between two successive contour lines on a topographic, structure, or other contour map.

interval velocity The ratio of any

distance interval to the corresponding time interval in: (1) a time distance curve in refraction shooting; (2) a well velocity survey (borehole survey).

interzonal soil Immature soil.

intra- [*Lat.*] A prefix meaning within, inside, into, intro-.

intracratonal geosyncline *See* PARAGEOSYNCLINE

intracratonic Situated within a stable continental region.

intracratonic basin Ovate structurally depressed area of considerable size within a continent; includes exogeosyncline, autogeosyncline, and zeugogeosyncline.

intracyclothem Cyclic sequence of strata resulting from the splitting of a cyclothem.

interfacies A minor stratigraphic facies occurring within a major one.

intraformational Formed by, existing in, or characterizing the interior of a geological formation.

intrageosyncline Geosyncline situated within a continent.

intragranular movements In rock deformation, displacements that take place within the individual crystals by movement along glide planes.

inframontane Situated or acting within a mountain.

intramontane trough Term introduced by J. H. F. Umbgrove and equivalent to epieugeosyncline.

Intra-Pacific province *See* ATLANTIC SERIES

intrastratal solution Chemical attrition which acts on the constituents of a rock after deposition.

intratelluric Applied to the period of crystallization of a magma prior to its effusion as a lava, and represented in many volcanic rocks by phenocrysts formed under comparatively deep-seated conditions. Crystals such as these, belonging to an earlier generation than the groundmass, are also described as intratelluric.

intrazonal soil One of the great group of soils with more or less well developed soil characteristics that reflect the dominating influence of some local factor of relief, parent material or age over the normal effect of climate and vegetation.

intrenched meander See EN-TRENCHED MEANDER

intrenched stream A stream flowing in a gorge or narrow valley that has been cut as a result of rejuvenation of the stream. See ENTRENCHED STREAM

intrinsic ash Inherent ash.

intrusion *1.* A body of igneous rock that invades older rock. The invading rock may be a plastic solid or magma that pushes its way into the older rock. Some magmas may be emplaced by magmatic stoping, *q.v.* Intrusion should not be used for bodies of igneous-looking rock that are the result of metasomatic replacement. *2.* The process of formation of an intrusion.

intrusion displacement Faulting coincident with the intrusion of an igneous rock.

intrusive *Petrol:* Having, while fluid, penetrated into or between other rocks, but solidifying before reaching the surface. Said of plutonic igneous rocks and contrasted with effusive or extrusive.

intrusive contact A contact between an igneous rock and some other rock indicating that the igneous rock is the younger. The younger rock may send dikes into the older rock, have inclu-

sions of the older rock, or be chilled against the older rock.

intrusive rock A rock that consolidated from magma beneath the surface of the earth.

invar An alloy of nickel and steel having a very low coefficient of thermal expansion.

Invar was discovered by C. E. Guillaume of the International Bureau of Weights and Measures, Paris. Having a coefficient of thermal expansion of about one twenty-fifth that of steel, it has replaced steel in the construction of tapes for measuring geodetic base lines, and is used in other places where a metal of that characteristic is desired. Invar is used in the construction of some leveling rods and first-order leveling instruments. Invar is also used in the construction of pendulums.

invariant equilibrium A phase assemblage having zero degrees of freedom, i.e., neither temperature, pressure, nor composition may be varied without loss of one or more phases.

inverse square law The law of nature which states that the force between elements of mass, of electrical charge, or between magnetic poles varies inversely as the square of the distance between them.

inverse zoning In plagioclase, the change by which crystals become more calcic in outer parts.

inversion *1.* The folding back of strata upon themselves, as by the overturning of a fold in such a manner that the order of succession appears to be reversed. *2.* A change of phase, generally from one solid to another of different structure, as quartz inverting to tridymite. In the strict sense both phases must have the same chemical composition (i.e., they are polymorphs), but the term is widely used in petrology for phase changes involving minor changes in composition, as, biotite "inverting" to chlorite. Transformation has a similar meaning.

inversion point *1.* The temperature at which one polymorphic form of a substance, in equilibrium with vapor, reversibly changes into another under invariant conditions. *2.* The temperature at which one polymorphic form of a substance inverts reversibly into another under univariant conditions, the pressure being specified. *3.* Loosely used to indicate the lowest temperature of which a monotropic phase inverts at an appreciable rate into a stable phase, or at which a given phase dissociates at an appreciable rate, under given conditions. *4.* A point of maximum or minimum on the curve expressing the variation of any physical quantity, such as volume, velocity, or electrical resistance with change of condition, or at which the quantity changes (algebraic) sign. *5.* A single point at which different phases are capable of existing together at equilibrium. *Syn:* TRANSITION POINT

invertebrate *1.* Without a backbone or spinal column. *2.* Of, or pertaining to, the Invertebrata. *3.* Of, or pertaining to, all the phyla of animals exclusive of the Chordata or animals with notochord or backbones.

inverted limb The overturned limb of a fold.

inverted plunge A plunge of a fold such that the younger rocks plunge beneath the older rocks.

involution *1. Struct. geol:* Refolding of large nappes such as those in the Alps. Two nappes

may be refolded together after they first formed; or one nappe may penetrate the underside or upper side of an older nappe thus causing the older nappe to wrap around the younger nappe. *2. Glacial geol:* Used as a synonym of brodel and cryoturbation, *q.v.*

iodate A salt or ester of iodic acid; a compound containing the radical IO_3.

iodide A compound of iodine with one other more positive element or radical.

ion An atom or group of atoms with an electric charge.

ion exchange Reversible exchange of ions contained in a crystal for different ions in solution without destruction of crystal structure or disturbance of electrical neutrality. The process is accomplished by diffusion and occurs typically in crystals possessing one or two dimensional channel-ways where ions are relatively weakly bonded. Also occurs in resins consisting of three dimensional hydrocarbon networks to which are attached many ionizable groups. *Syn:* BASE EXCHANGE

ionic atmosphere Diffused ions as in a solution surrounding a charged particle.

ionic bond *See* BOND, IONIC

ionic diffusion The movement, by diffusion in a concentration gradient, of charged ions.

ionic displacement Displacement of ions in a crystal.

ionic dissociation Dissociation of uncharged materials within a homogeneous phase, such as water or a silicate melt, into plus and minus charged ions.

ionic potential The positive charge on a cation divided by its radius in angstroms.

ionic radius The radius of an

ion, commonly expressed in angstrom units.

ionic substitution The partial or complete proxying of one or more types of ions for one or more other types of ions in a given structural site in a crystal lattice.

ionization Production of charged particles from neutral atoms by removal of electrons.

ionization constant See DISSOCIATION CONSTANT

ionization energy The energy required to remove an electron from an atom or molecule: the ionization potential multiplied by the charge on the electron.

ionization potential The voltage required to drive an electron completely out of an atom or molecule, leaving a positive ion but without imparting any kinetic energy to the electron.

ionogenic group Group of atoms constituting an ion.

ionosonde Radarlike instrument used to investigate the nature of the ionosphere.

ionosphere The highest layer of the earth's atmosphere in which ionization takes place. It lies above the stratosphere; its lower limit is about 35 miles high in daytime and about 60 miles during nights. The ionosphere reflects radio signals.

Iowan Early Wisconsin glaciation.

iridescence The exhibition of colored reflections from the surface of a mineral; a play of colors. Labradorite and some other feldspars show it. The tarnish on the surface of coal, chalcopyrite, etc., is iridescent.

iridosmine A natural alloy of iridium and osmium. Hexagonal.

iron bacteria Bacteria which cause the precipitation of iron oxide from solution either by

metabolizing chemically associated organic matter or oxidizing ferrous salts.

iron hat See GOSSAN

iron meteorite Meteorite consisting of iron and nickel.

iron pan A type of hardpan, q.v., in which a considerable amount of iron oxide is present.

ironstone Clay ironstone, q.v.

irradiation Exposure to rays of any kind, but term usually refers to alpha, beta, and gamma rays.

irreversible processes Any process which proceeds in one direction spontaneously, without external interference.

irrotational wave Compressional wave.

Irvingtonian Lower Pleistocene.

isallobar An imaginary line or a line upon a chart connecting the places of equal change of atmospheric pressure within a specified time.

isanomaly; isonomaly A line on a map connecting points of equal anomaly. Used especially for maps showing magnetic anomalies.

isinglass Mica in thin transparent sheets.

island 1. A tract of land, usually of moderate extent, surrounded by water; distinguished from a continent or the mainland, as, an island in the sea, an island in a river. 2. A body of land extending above and completely surrounded by water at the mean high-water stage. An area of dry land entirely surrounded by water or a swamp; an area of swamp entirely surrounded by open water.

island arc Curved chain of islands, like the Aleutians, generally convex toward the open ocean, margined by a deep submarine trench and enclosing a deep sea basin.

island shelf The zone around an island or island group, extending from the low-water line to the depths at which there is a marked increase of slope to greater depths. Conventionally its edge is taken at 100 fathoms (or 200 meters).

island slope The declivity from the outer edge of an island shelf into great depths.

iso- [*Gr.*] A prefix meaning equal, extensively used in conjunction with another word, to denote lines drawn on a map or chart to display the geographical distribution of any element, each line being drawn through the points at which the element has the same value.

In 1889 the tentative use of the word isogram was suggested by Sir Francis Galton as a generic term for all lines of this type. The name isopleth is literally applicable for this purpose and is so used by many writers.

Some of the more important examples of the use of iso are:

isobars—lines on a chart joining places of equal barometric pressure;

isotherms—lines showing equal temperatures;

isohyets—lines showing equal amounts of rainfall.

isoaxial Isotropic.

isobaric surface A surface in the atmosphere, every point of which has the same barometric pressure.

isobath *1*. Line on a marine map or chart joining points of equal depth usually in fathoms below mean sea level. *2*. A line on a land surface all points of which are the same vertical distance above the upper or lower surface of an aquifer may be called an isobath of the specified surface, or merely a line of equal depth to the surface.

isobed map Contour map showing the number of thickness of beds in a stratigraphic unit.

isobiolith Para-time-rock unit based on fossils.

isocal A line constructed on a map, somewhat similar to a contour line, but connecting points of equal calorific value of the coal in a bed.

isocarb *1*. A line constructed on a map, somewhat similar to a contour line, but connecting points of equal content of fixed carbon of coal in the bed. The fixed carbon is computed on ash- and moisture-free basis. *2*. A line passing through points whose carbon ratios, *q.v.*, are equal.

isochemical series A series of rocks having essentially identical chemical compositions.

isochore *1*. A line drawn through points of equal interval between two beds or other planes. *2*. A line connecting points of constant volume, as in P-V-T phase diagrams.

isochore map *1*. Convergence map. A map indicating by means of isochores, the varying interval (convergence) between two designated stratigraphic planes. Differs from isopach map in that it may express the variations in many units and the effects of one or more uncomformities, whereas the isopach map expresses variation within a single unit. Current usage shows little distinction between the terms. *2*. A map showing, by contours, the thickness of a pay section in a pool. The map is a basis for estimating reservoir content.

isochron *1*. A line on the surface of the earth connecting points at which a characteristic time or interval has the same value.

2. In seismic surveying, a contour line passing through points at which difference between arrival times from two reflecting surfaces is equal.

isochroneity Equivalent in time.

isochronous surface A time plane within a body of sediment or sedimentary rocks.

isoclinal *Geol:* Dipping in the same direction; hence, an isoclinal.

isoclinal fold Carinate fold. A fold the limbs of which have parallel dips; may be an anticline or a syncline. The fold may be vertical, overturned, or recumbent.

isocline *Geol:* A series of isoclinal strata. An anticline or syncline so closely folded that the rock beds of the two sides or limbs have the same dip. *See* ISOCLINAL FOLD. *Syn:* ISOCLINIC LINE

isoclinic line Isocline; isodip line. A line joining points at which the magnetic inclination (dip) is the same.

isocon Contour line indicating equal concentration, e.g., salinity.

isodimorphism Relations of two substances that are both similarly isomorphous and dimorphous.

isodip line Isocline; isoclinic line, *q.v.*

isodynamic line Any joining points of equal magnetic intensity. Applicable to the total intensity or the vertical, horizontal, north-south or east-west components. So used in terrestrial magnetism literature, especially in British and Canadian writings.

isofacial, *adj.* Isograde. Said of all rocks belonging to the same facies.

isofacies map A map showing, by suitable patterns, the distribution of one or more facies within a designated stratigraphic unit.

isogal In gravity prospecting, a contour line of equal gravity values (after gal, the common unit of gravity measurement; one gal=1 cm/sec/sec).

isogam In magnetic prospecting, a contour line of equal magnetic values (after gamma the common unit of magnetic measurements; one gamma=10^{-5} oersted).

isogeotherm A line or curved surface beneath the earth's surface through points having the same mean temperature. Also called isogeothermal lines.

isogonic line A line joining points of equal magnetic declination.

isograd *1.* A line connecting those rocks comprising the same facies. *2.* A line connecting similar temperature-pressure values. *3.* A line marking the boundary between two facies. *4.* A line of equal grade of metamorphism drawn on a map to distinguish metamorphic zones defined by index minerals.

isogram Contour line.

isohyetal Marking equality of rainfall.

isohyetal line A line on a land or water surface all points along which receive the same amount of precipitation.

isolated basin Autogeosyncline.

isoline map General term for any map on which some variable feature is contoured, e.g., isopach map.

isolithic lines Lines drawn on a paleolithologic map connecting points of similar lithology and separating rocks of differing characteristics.

isolith map One which portrays (by isolith lines) variations in aggregate thickness of a given lithologic facies as measured per pendicular to the bedding at selected points. These may be outcrops or drill holes.

isomagnetic Designating or pertaining to lines connecting points of equal magnetic force.

isomer One of two or more compounds containing the same elements united in the same proportion by weight, but differing in properties because of a difference in structure; usually applied to compounds having the same molecular weight, as distinguished from polymers.

isomeric Composed of the same elements united in the same proportion by weight, but differing in one or more properties owing to difference in structure.

isomesia The same medium, e.g., the environment of marine, lacustrian, or terrestrial deposition.

isometric projection A division of descriptive geometry in which a three-dimensional object is projected on to one plane. Cf. NORMAL PROJECTION

isometric system Crystallog: That system of crystals in which the forms are referred to three equal mutually perpendicular axes. See CUBIC SYSTEM

isomorphous Originally defined by E. A. Mitscherlich in 1819 as "having similar crystalline form," but now generally restricted to compounds that form solid solutions by isomorphous substitution, i.e., by the replacement of one ion for another in a crystal structure without alteration in the crystal form. Cf. ISOTYPIC

isonomaly Isanomaly, q.v.

isopach; isopachous line; isopachyte [Brit.] A line, on a map, drawn through points of equal thickness of a designated unit.

isopachous Of equal thickness. Said of maps, charts, etc., in which the shape of a body is indicated by lines drawn through points of equal thickness as projected onto any particular plane, and of the lines as drawn. Analogous to contour lines, but representing thickness. See ISOPACH

isopach strike Direction indicated by isopach contours.

isoperimetric curve A line on a map projection along which there is no variation from exact scale.

isopiestic level Level of uniform pressure at the base of isostatically balanced areas of the earth's crust; depth of compensation.

isopiestic line A contour of the piezometric surface of an aquifer. It is an imaginary line all points along which have the same static level.

isopleth 1. A line, on a map or chart, drawn through points of equal size or abundance. 2. A line of constant composition, as in a binary temperature vs. composition plot.

isoporic line A line drawn through points whose annual change in magnetic declination is equal.

isopycnic Of equal density.

isorads Lines joining points of equal radioactivity, drawn from Geiger- or scintillation-counter data to form an isorad map.

isoseismic line An imaginary line connecting all points on the surface of the earth where an earthquake shock is of the same intensity.

isostasy Theoretical balance of all large portions of the earth's crust as though they were floating on a denser underlying layer; thus areas of less dense crustal material rise topographically above areas of more dense material.

isostatic Subject to equal pressure from every side; being in hydrostatic equilibrium.

isostatic adjustment Isostatic compensation, q.v.

isostatic anomaly *1*. The difference between the observed value of gravity at a point after applying to it the isostatic correction and the normal value of gravity at the point. *2*. Anomaly on a map of observed gravity anomalies after applying the isostatic correction. Negative isostatic anomalies indicate undercompensation, implying a tendency to rise; positive isostatic anomalies connote overcompensation and a tendency to sink.

isostatic compensation Isostatic adjustment. *1*. An equilibrium condition in which elevated masses such as continents and mountains are compensated by a mass deficiency in the crust beneath them. The compensation for depressed areas is by a mass excess. *2*. The process in which lateral transport at the earth's surface by processes such as erosion and deposition is compensated by lateral movements in a subcrustal layer.

isostatic correction The adjustment made to values of gravity or to deflections of the vertical observed at a point to take account of the assumed mass deficiency under topographic features for which a topographic correction is also made.

isostratification map Contour map showing the number or thickness of beds in a stratigraphic unit.

isostructural Refers to minerals that are closely similar in crystallographic, physical, and chemical properties but have little tendency for isomorphous substitution; isotypic.

isotherm Any line connecting points of equal temperature. See ISOGEOTHERM

isothermal Having equal degrees of heat. Isothermal relationships between pressure and volume of a gas or other fluid are those resulting when the temperature is constant, and when heat is added or subtracted by an outside substance or body. See ADIABATIC

isothermal plane or **section** In ternary systems, a horizontal section cut through the solid temperature-composition model at a given temperature and showing phase relationships at that temperature.

isotope dilution An analytical technique involving addition of a known amount of an isotopic mixture of abnormal composition to the unknown amount of an element of normal or known isotopic composition. See SPIKE, ISOTOPIC

isotopes Elements having an identical number of protons in their nuclei, but differing in the number of their neutrons. Isotopes have the same atomic number, differing atomic weights and almost but not quite the same chemical properties.

isotopic *1*. Refers to chemical isotopes. *2*. Formed in the same sedimentary basin or geologic province.

isotopic fractionation Process resulting in the relative enrichment of one isotope in a mixture.

isotopic spike See SPIKE, ISOTOPIC

isotropic Having the same properties in all directions; most commonly used for optical properties. Typical of amorphous substances and of crystals of the isometric system. Contrast with anisotropic, q.v.

isotropic fabric Random orientation in space of the elements of which a rock is composed.

isotropic symmetry Symmetry in which parts are equal and interchangeable in all directions from a center, characterized by a sphere.

isotropy Condition of having the same properties in all directions. In an isotropic elastic medium, the velocities of propagation of elastic waves are independent of direction.

isthmus A narrow strip of land, bordered on both sides by water, that connects two larger bodies of land.

itabirite A hematite-quartz-schist. *See* ITACOLUMITE; JASPILITE; TACONITE

itacolumite Flexible sandstone; articulite. *1.* A fine-grained micaceous, thin-bedded sandstone, thin slabs of which have a certain degree of flexibility. *2.* A schistose and flexible quartzite containing mica, chlorite, and talc. *See* QUARTZITE

iteration Repeated occurrence of similar evolutionary trends in successive offshoots of a group.

iterative evolution *1.* Repeated development of new forms from a conservative stock. *2.* Repeated and independent evolution.

J

jack The receptacle counterpart of a plug in electrical connectors. *See* SPHALERITE

Jacksonian Upper Eocene.

Jacob's staff A single straight rod, pointed and iron shod at the bottom, and having a socket at the top; used instead of a tripod for supporting a compass.

jade; jadeite Nephrite. A hard and extremely tough material of varying composition, greenish white to deep green in color, used in making jewelry and carved ornaments. Both jadeite, a variety of pyroxene (nearly $NaAlSi_2O_6$), and nephrite, a variety of amphibole, are properly called jade.

jarosite A mineral, $KFe_3(SO_4)_2(OH)_6$. Hexagonal rhombohedral.

jars Accessories frequently used in standard drilling consisting of two heavy metal links free to pass one another to the limit of their length. The jars are part of the string of drilling tools and are used to jar the bit on the upward stroke, thus preventing the bit from sticking in a formation that might tend to hold it.

jasper Red, brown, green, impure, slightly translucent cryptocrystalline quartz with a dull fracture, abundant enough on Lake Superior and elsewhere to be a rock.

jasperoid *1.* A rock consisting essentially of cryptocrystalline, chalcedonic, or phenocrystalline silica, which has formed by the replacement of some other ma[terial], ordinarily calcite or dol[o]mite. *2.* Silicified limestone.

jaspilite A rock consisting es[s]entially of red jasper and iro[n] oxides in alternating bands. *Se[e]* ITABIRITE; TACONITE

Jeans and Jeffreys theory Tida[l] theory, *q.v.*

jellyfish A medusoid coelentera[te]; fossils are found which a[re] stomach casts of these animal[s]. True jellyfish are scyphozoan[s] but the sexual generation o[f] hydrozoans are tiny medusae.

jet *1.* A dense black lignite, tak[ing] a good polish. Sometime[s] used for jewelry. *2.* A blac[k] marble.

jet stream High-altitude swift a[ir] current.

jetty *1.* In the United States: O[n] open seacoasts, a structure e[x]tending into a body of wate[r] and designed to prevent shoa[l]ing of a channel by littoral ma[terials], and to direct and confin[e] the stream or tidal flow. Jetti[es] are built at the mouth of a rive[r] or tidal inlet to help deepe[n] and stabilize a channel. *2.* I[n] Great Britain, jetty is synon[y]mous with wharf or pier.

jig Device for concentrating mi[n]erals. Crushed ore is fed in[to] a box containing water who[se] level is rapidly raised and lowere[d] by action of a piston causin[g] heavier minerals to sink to th[e] bottom from which they a[re] drawn off.

Johannsen's classification A mineralogical classification of igneous rocks in which a rock is characterized by a number, the Johannsen number, consisting of three or four digits, each one of which has a specific mineralogical significance.

join The line (or plane) drawn between any two (or three) composition points. There is no special phase significance to a join; it need not be a limiting binary (or ternary) subsystem.

joint Fracture in rock, generally more or less vertical or transverse to bedding, along which no appreciable movement has occurred.

joint set A group of more or less parallel joints.

joint system Consists of two or more joint sets, q.v., or any group of joints with a characteristic pattern, such as a radiating pattern, a concentric pattern, etc.

jökull [Icel.] A type of glacier consisting of a large ice sheet.

jolly balance A toroidal spring balance used primarily for measuring specific gravity (density) by weighing a specimen when immersed in air and again when immersed in a liquid of known density (usually water, if the specimen is insoluble in H_2O).

jug A colloquial equivalent of detector, geophone, etc.

Jura Jurassic.

Jurassic Geol: The middle one of the three periods comprised in the Mesozoic era. Also the system of strata deposited during that period.

juvenile Coming to the surface for the first time; fresh, new in origin; applied chiefly to gases and waters.

juvenile gases Gases from the interior of the earth which are new and have never been at the surface of the earth.

juvenile water Water that is derived from the interior of the earth and has not previously existed as atmospheric or surface water.

K

K. Identifies Kelvin thermometric scale; $0°$ K. is absolute zero, $-273.13°$ C., or $-459.4°$ F.

K-A age Radioactive age based on determination of the potassium 40-argon 40 ratio.

kainite A mineral, $KCl.MgSO_4.-3H_2O$. Monoclinic.

kainozoic Cenozoic.

kame *1.* A conical hill or short irregular ridge of gravel or sand deposited in contact with glacier ice. *2.* Kames is a Scotch term applied to assemblages of short, conical, often steep hills, built of stratified materials and interlocking and blending in the most diversified manner. *3.* A mound composed chiefly of gravel or sand, whose form is the result of original deposition modified by settling during the melting of glacier ice against or upon which the sediment accumulated. *4.* A hill of stratified drift deposited, usually as a steep alluvial fan, against the edge of an ice sheet by debouching streams of sediment-laden meltwater. *5.* A low, steep-sided hill of stratified drift, formed in contact with glacier ice.

kame-and-kettle topography Surface formed by a kame complex interspersed with kettles. *Obs.*

kame complex A series of interconnecting kames.

kame field A group of kames, including in places kettles and eskers.

kame terrace *1.* A terracelike body of stratified drift deposited between a glacier and an adjacent valley wall. *2.* A terrace of glacial sand and gravel, deposited between a valley ice lobe (generally stagnant) and the bounding rock slope of the valley. *3.* Remnant of a depositional valley surface built in contact with glacial ice.

Kanawhan Upper Lower Pennsylvanian.

Kansan Second Pleistocene glaciation.

kaolin *1.* A rock composed essentially of clay minerals of the kaolinite group, most commonly kaolinite, but also halloysite, endellite, dickite, nacrite, etc. *2* China clay; porcelain clay. A clay, mainly hydrous aluminum silicate, from which porcelain may be made. *See* KAOLINITE

kaolinite A common clay mineral. Two-layer hydrous aluminum silicate having the general formula $Al_2(Si_2O_5)(OH)_4$. It consists of sheets of tetrahedrally coordinated silicon joined by an oxygen shared with octahedrally coordinated aluminum. Essentially, there is no isomorphous substitution. The mineral characteristic of the rock kaolin. *See* FIRE CLAY MINERAL

kar Cirque; corrie.

karat Carat.

Karnian Carnian.

karren *1.* Surface composed of blocks of limestone separated by narrow fissures. In calcareous districts the surface is sometimes quite bare and intersected by furrows, attaining a depth of several, sometimes as much as 30, feet. Such districts are known on the Continent as lapies or karren. 2. Fretted pinnacles or bands of limestone exposed as ridges or ledges; continuous over large areas as a system.

Karren results from differential solution of limestone and removal of residual limestone soil. *Syn:* LAPIES (in a limited sense); CLINT

karst *1.* Limestone, no matter how hard, is dissolved by rain or rivers, giving a more distinctive type of country, caves or even underground river channels being produced, into which the surface drainage sinks by rifts and swallow holes which have been similarly dissolved out, and the land is left dry and relatively barren. These features are so characteristic of the Karst district of the Adriatic coast that the name karst phenomena has been applied to them. 2. A limestone plateau marked by sinks, or karst holes, interspersed with abrupt ridges and irregular protuberant rocks; usually underlain by caverns and underground streams.

karsten Karren, *q.v.*

karstic, *adj.* Karst.

karst plain A plain on which sinkholes, uvala, subterranean drainage, and other karst features are developed.

karst topography In Karst, on the eastern side of the Adriatic Sea, the limestone rocks are so honeycombed by tunnels and openings dissolved out by ground waters, that much of the drainage is underground. Large sinks abound, some of them five or six hundred feet deep. Streamless

valleys are common, and valleys containing streams often end abruptly where the latter plunge into underground tunnels and caverns, sometimes to reappear as great springs elsewhere. Irregular topography of this kind, developed by the solution of surface and ground waters, is known as karst topography, after the type region in Yugoslavia and northeastern Italy.

kata [*Gr.*] A variant of cata-, *q.v.*

katabatic wind A wind that flows down slopes that are cooled by radiation, the direction of flow being controlled orographically. Such winds are the result of downward convection of cooled air. *Syn:* MOUNTAIN WIND, CANYON WIND; GRAVITY WIND

katamorphic zone *1.* The zone in which katamorphic processes are dominant. 2. The zone of katamorphism corresponds to the zone of rock fracture and is a zone of breaking down. It is especially characterized by solution, decrease of volume, and softening of the materials; the processes are destructive, resulting in degeneration. The zone is divided into the belt of weathering and the belt of cementation. *See* ANAMORPHIC ZONE

katamorphism Metamorphism at or near the surface of the lithosphere, forming simple minerals from complex ones.

kata-orogenic Refers to climax of orogenic movement.

katatectic Formed from the top downward.

katatectic layer Layer of solution residue, generally consisting of gypsum and/or anhydrite, in salt dome caprock.

katatectic surface Contact of two katatectic layers.

katazone *1.* The deepest zone in

the depth zone classification of metamorphic rocks. This zone would be characterized by high temperatures and pressures. The distinctive minerals include sillimanite, enstatite, hypersthene, orthoclase, cordierite, etc. Not to be confused with katamorphic zone, *q.v.*

kay *See* CAY; KEY

Kazanian Upper Permian.

K-bentonite Metabentonite with potassium occupying about 80% of exchangeable cation positions of the mica portion.

K-capture The capturing by an atomic nucleus of an orbital electron from the same atom. The electron usually captured is in the K-orbit. In geology significant only in K^{40}, of which about 10% decays by K-capture to A^{40}.

Keewatin According to the U.S. G.S., the oldest Precambrian series of rocks in the Lake Superior region. In the future, these will be placed in Early Precambrian.

kelephytic rims Zones or borders composed of microcrystalline aggregates of pyroxene or amphibole, which in some rocks are developed around olivine where it would otherwise be in contact with plagioclase, or around garnet where it would otherwise be in contact with olivine or other magnesium-rich minerals. Charles Bonney suggested that the term be restricted to occurrences of secondary origin, applying the term corona (reaction rim) to those that are primary.

Kelly; Kelly joint In rotary drilling, the square, grooved, or hexagonal member supported at the upper end by the swivel and passing through the rotary table, with the lower end screwed into and supporting the drill pipe. It transmits the rotary motion of the table to the drill pipe and can be raised or lowered through bushings in the table.

kelyphitic border Corona.

keratophyre A name originally applied to trachytic rocks containing highly sodic feldspars, but now more generally applied to all salic lavas and dike rocks characterized by containing albite or albite oligoclase, chlorite, epidote, and calcite. Originally the term was restricted to lavas of pre-Tertiary age but this distinction is not recognized in current usage. Some varieties of keratophyre contain sodic orthoclase, and sodic amphiboles and pyroxenes. Varieties containing quartz are known as quartz keratophyres. Keratophyres commonly are associated with spilitic rocks and interbedded with marine sediments.

kernite A mineral, $Na_2B_4O_7$.-$4H_2O$. Monoclinic. An important ore of boron.

kerogen *1.* The solid, bituminous mineraloid substance in oil shales which yields oil when the shales undergo destructive distillation. *2.* The bituminous matter in Scottish oil shale.

kerogen shale Oil shale.

kettle A depression in drift, made by the wasting away of a detached mass of glacier ice that had been either wholly or partly buried in the drift. Sölle [*Ger.*].

kettleback Horseback.

kettle basin; kettle hole *1.* Bowl-shaped depressions, usually 30 to 50 feet deep and 100 to 500 feet deep in larger diameter. Each depression, according to the accepted explanation, was the resting place, and often the burial place of a huge mass of ice that became detached during the melting; the final melting away of the ice left a hole where the ice lay. 2. A steep-sided hole or depression in rock, sand, or gravel, having a shape more or less like the interior of a kettle.

Keuper Upper Triassic.

Kewatinian 1. Archian. 2. Precambrian system older than Tamiskamian.

Keweenawan Younger of two Precambrian systems constituting the Proterozoic restricted.

key 1. A low island near the coast; used especially on the coasts of regions where Spanish is or formerly was spoken, as, the Florida Keys. 2. A low insular bank of sand, coral, etc., as one of the islets off the southern coast of Florida. *See* CAY

key bed 1. A bed with sufficiently distinctive characteristics to make it easily identifiable in correlation. 2. A bed the top or bottom of which is used as a datum in making structure contour maps. *See* MARKER BED, 1 and 2

key horizon The top or bottom of a bed or formation or a particular layer of fauna or flora that is so distinctive as to be of great help in stratigraphy and structure.

Keyseran Upper Upper Silurian.

Kf Abbreviation for potassic feldspar.

K-feldspar Potassium-bearing feldspar: orthoclase or microcline.

kick Arrival; break.

kidney ore A variety of hematite, occurring in compact kidney-shaped masses.

kieselguhr German name for diatomaceous earth, and more or less current in English. Used as an absorbent for nitroglycerin in dynamite. It is an inert substance or passive base whose only value lies in its capacity to absorb about three times its weight in

nitroglycerin. *See* INFUSORIAL EARTH

kieserite A mineral, $MgSO_4.H_2O$. Monoclinic.

Kilkenny coal Anthracite.

kill [*Du.* creek] A creek; stream; channel. Local in New York; little used in any other state.

Killarneyan orogeny Post-Proterozoic diastrophism.

kilometer A length of one thousand meters, equal to 3280.8 feet, or 0.621 of a mile. The chief unit for long distances in the metric system.

kimberlite A variety of mica peridotite consisting essentially of olivine, phlogopite, and subordinate melilite, with minor pyroxene, apatite, perovskite, and opaque oxides. Some examples contain diamonds.

Kimmerian orogeny Series of diastrophic movements beginning perhaps in Late Triassic and continuing to Early Cretaceous.

Kimmeridgian Middle Upper Jurassic.

Kinderhookian Lower Mississippian; may be transitional to Devonian.

kindred, *n. Petrol:* A group of igneous rocks which show consanguineous chemical and mineral characters, and which appear to be genetically related. *Cf.* SERIES; SUITE; CLAN; BRANCH. *See* CONSANGUINITY

kinematics Physics of motion.

kinetic metamorphism The deformation of rocks without accompanying chemical reconstitution.

kinetics Study of relations between forces and resultant movement.

kingdom The largest taxonomic division of organisms. Conventionally two kingdoms, plants and animals, are recognized.

Some biologists favor the recognition of one or more additional kingdoms for the reception of intermediate or ancestral organisms. *See* PROTISTA

klint A calcareous reef or bioherm, more resistant to erosion than the rocks that enclose it, and which thereby form ridges or hills. Plural is klintar.

klintite Biohermal limestone, particularly the massive core.

klippe An isolated block of rocks separated from the underlying rocks by a fault that normally, but not necessarily, has a gentle dip. Generally, the rocks above the fault are the older. A klippe may be an erosional remnant of an extensive overthrust sheet or it may have moved into place by gravity sliding.

knickpoint Points of abrupt change in the longitudinal profile of stream valleys.

knob A rounded hill or mountain, especially an isolated one. Local in the South.

knob-and-basin topography Knob-and-kettle topography; kame-and-kettle topography.

knoll *1.* A submerged elevation of rounded shape rising from the ocean floor, but less prominent than a seamount. *2.* A small rounded hill.

knot *1.* The unit of speed used in navigation. It is equal to 1 nautical mile (6,080.20 feet) per hour. *2.* The meeting point of two or more mountain chains.

knotty A term applied to rocks, usually slates or schists, so altered by contact metamorphism as to have new minerals developed, giving them a spotted or knotty appearance.

kopje In South Africa, a hillock; knob.

Kp Abbreviation for kaliophilite in normative rock calculations.

kratogen Craton, *q.v.* A term introduced by Leopold Kober, in 1921, for a relatively immobile part of the earth. It was modified to kraton by Hans Stille, and the preferred spelling is craton.

kratogenic area Craton.

kryoturbation Cryoturbation.

K section Circular cross section through a strain ellipsoid; there are two such sections, designated K_1 and K_2.

kugel [*Ger.* ball, sphere, globe, bulb] *Geol:* A general term applied to those igneous rocks characterized by spheroidal structures, such as orbicular granite, corsite, and especially kugelminette.

Kullenberg corer Device for sampling sediments of the deep sea bottom. Hydrostatic pressure forces the core barrel into the sediment as a piston is drawn upward through it. Cores up to 20 meters long have been obtained.

Kungurian Middle Permian.

kX *Struct. crystallog:* A unit of length. One kX=0.99798 Angstrom units.

kyanite Cyanite; disthene. A mineral, Al_2SiO_5, trimorphous with sillimanite and andalusite. Triclinic.

L

L *Earthquake seismol:* A phase designation referring to surface waves without respect to type (Love or Rayleigh). From "Undae longae," or "Long waves," as on early earthquake records, the surface waves were distinguished by their long periods relative to the preliminary waves (P and S). La and Lʀ refer to Love (Querwellen) waves and Rayleigh waves, respectively; in modern usage, Q and R are preferred to La and Lʀ.

labile Applied to particles in a rock that decompose easily.

labile constituent Feldspar and rock fragments in sediments and sedimentary rocks.

labile stage The temperature range in which nucleation and/or growth of crystals takes place readily.

labor A Spanish unit applied to a tract 1000 varas square and comprising 177.14 acres. Used in early land surveys in Texas.

labradorite *See* PLAGIOCLASE

laccolith A concordant, intrusive body that has domed up the overlying rocks and also has a floor that is generally horizontal but may be convex downward.

lacuna *1.* A cavity, hole, or gap. *2.* An unconformity. *3.* Unrecorded stratigraphic record at an unconformity, consists of (a) record destroyed by erosion, =erosional vacuity, and (b) record never represented by strata, = hiatus.

lacustrine *1.* Produced by or belonging to lakes. *2.* Of, or pertaining to, or formed or growing in, or inhabiting, lakes.

lacustrine plain Many former lakes have become extinct. Extinct lakes are recognized by various features. If a lake basin became extinct by having its basin filled, the former area of the lake is marked by a flat covered with deposits such as are formed in lakes. These deposits may be of gravel or sand along the shores, but the materials deposited far from shore are fine. Such a flat is a lacustrine plain. A lacustrine plain is a minor type of plain, and may lie in mountains, on plateaus, or on plains of a larger type.

ladder lode; ladder veins Roughly parallel fractures normal to the walls of a dike that have been filled with gangue or ore.

Ladinian Upper Middle Triassic.

ladu Avalanche of incandescent volcanic debris. *Cf.* GLOWING AVALANCHE

lag *1.* Any time delay. *2.* The phase angle by which the current is behind the e.m.f. in an induction circuit. *3.* The time delay between the breaking of the bridgewire in a detonating cap and the resulting explosion. Sufficiently small in modern caps to be negligible. *4.* The time delay between the arrival of a signal in a piece of equipment and the response, such as the making or breaking of a circuit by a relay.

lag gravel Residual accumulations of coarser particles from which the finer material has been blown away; similar to "desert pavement," but more restricted in its implications as to the extent and continuity of the accumulation. *See* DESERT PAVEMENT; PEBBLE ARMOR

lagoon *1.* Body of shallow water, particularly one possessing a restricted connection with the sea. *2.* Water body within an atoll or behind barrier reefs or islands.

lagoon cycle Refers to the filling of a lagoon by sediments from the land, atmosphere, and sea and the eventual erosion and destruction of these deposits by wave action. The sequence of events and the time required for this cycle are termed the lagoon cycle.

laguna [*Sp.*] *1.* Shallow ephemeral lakes, mostly found in the lower parts of the bolsons, and fed by streams whose sources are in the neighboring mountains, and which flow only during time of storm. *2.* A lake or pond. *3.* A pseudokarst feature; large shallow sinks with clay bottoms; developed in silts and sands of south-central United States.

lahar *1.* Landslide or mudflow of pyroclastic material on the flank of a volcano. *2.* Deposit produced by such a landslide. Lahars are described as wet if they are mixed with water derived from heavy rains, escaping from a crater lake or produced by melting snow. Dry lahera may result from tremors of a cone or by accumulating material becoming unstable on a steep slope. If the material retains much heat, they are termed hot lahars.

lake *1.* Any standing body of inland water, generally of considerable size. *2.* A pool of other more or less fluid substance, as oil or asphalt. *3.* A pigment formed by absorbing animal, vegetal, or coal-tar coloring matter from an aqueous solution by means of metallic bases.

lake-bottom plain In lakes very nearly the same kind of plains are made as those of the sea. Beaches made during these high-water levels were constructed along the shores of both Erie and Ontario. During this stand of the water, also, deltas were constructed which now exist as broad, level-topped areas of gravel. Over the bed of the lake, sand and clay were strewn, filling some of the depressions so that the surface, already quite level, was made into a more typical plain. Therefore, south of the beach-terraces and the ridges now forming on the present lake shore, and north of the ancient beaches, there are plains which were once lake bottom, and which owe some of their levelness to this fact.

lake pitch Asphalt from the Pitch Lake, Trinidad. It is richer than the land pitch in bituminous matter; soluble in petroleum spirit.

lake rampart A ridge of shore materials (sand, gravel, or driftwood) along a lake shore formed by the shoreward movement of lake ice, also called ice rampart.

lake terrace In small lakes, lowering of the lake level generally cuts short the shore-line cycle before it has reached an advanced stage. During an interval of stationary water level a map or line of low cliffs is cut, and in front of this there is a narrow shelf, partly cut and partly built, which remains as a lake terrace when the water level falls.

Lamarckism; Lamarckianism The idea that changes acquired or developed by individuals during their lifetimes are transmitted to their offspring; the inheritance of acquired characters.

Lambert conformal conic map projection A map projection on which all geographic meridians are represented by straight lines which meet in a common point outside the limits of the map, and the geographic parallels are represented by a series of arcs or circles having this common point for a center. Meridians and parallels intersect in right angles, and angles on the earth are correctly represented on the projection. This projection may have one standard parallel along which the scale is held exact, or there may be two such standard parallels, both maintaining exact scale. At any point on the map, the scale is the same in every direction. It changes along the meridians, and is constant along each parallel. Where there are two standard parallels, the scale between those parallels is too small; beyond them, too large.

The Lambert conformal conic map projection with two standard parallels is the base for the state coordinate systems devised by the U. S. Coast and Geodetic Survey for zones of limited north-south dimension, and indefinite east-west dimension. In those systems, the standard parallels are placed at distances of one-sixth the width (north-south) of the map from its upper and lower limits.

lamella One of the layers of a cell wall.

lamellar Composed of thin layers, plates, scales, or lamellae; disposed in layers like the leaves of a book.

lamellar flow Movement of liquid whereby successive layers glide over one another like cards in a sheared pack of playing cards. Contrasted with turbulent flow.

Lamellibranchiata Pelecypoda.

Lame's constants A pair of elastic constants which are mathematically convenient in the theory of elasticity. They are: $\lambda = \sigma E / (1+\sigma)(1-2\sigma)$ when $\sigma =$ Poisson's ratio and $E =$ Young's modulus, and $\mu = E/2(1 + \sigma) =$ the modulus of rigidity.

lamina 1. Unit layer or sheet of a sediment in which the stratification planes are one centimeter or less apart. Laminae need not be parallel to bedding. When they are at an angle to the bedding planes the term "cross-lamination" may be used. 2. A layer in a sedimentary rock less than 1 cm. in thickness that is visually separable from other layers above and below, the separation being determined by a discrete change in lithology, a sharp break in physical lithology, or by both. 3. *Paleontol:* In some corals the sheetlike structure formed by the juxtaposition of two layers of skeletal material in septa and the column, i.e., the axial structure. 4. A blade or expanded portion.

laminar flow 1. That type of flow in which the stream lines (or stream surfaces) remain distinct from one another (except for molecular mixing) over their entire length. Under laminar flow the head loss is proportional to the first power of the velocity. It is typical of groundwater movement under most conditions. 2. A flow of current without turbulence. A smooth flow at relatively slow velocity in which the fluid elements follow paths that are straight and are parallel to the channel walls. *See* LAMELLAR FLOW

laminated quartz Vein quartz characterized by slabs or films of other material. Laminated quartz is a general term including book structure and ribbon structure.

lamination *1.* The layering or bedding less than 1 cm. in thickness in a sedimentary rock. *2.* The more or less distinct alternation of material, which differ one from the other in grain size or composition.

Lampasan Upper Lower Pennsylvanian.

lamprophyre A group name applied to dark dike rocks in which dark minerals occur both as phenocrysts and in the groundmass and light minerals occur only in the groundmass. They differ from normal rocks in which light and dark minerals occur both as phenocrysts and in the groundmass. The essential constituents of lamprophyres are biotite, hornblende, or pyroxene or combinations of the three, and feldspar or feldspathoids. Olivine is present in some varieties. Apatite, perovskite, opaque oxides, and quartz are common accessories. Lamprophyres are commonly highly altered and contain much chlorite and calcite. They range in composition from syenitic to gabbroic and are transitional into ultramafics with increasing dark constituents. Usually they are rich in alkalies, especially potassium.

lamp shell *1.* Brachiopod, *q.v.* *2.* A terebratuloid brachiopod, the most characteristic Mesozoic brachiopod shell form, an ovate, curved hinge type which is aptly compared with an ancient Roman pottery lamp.

land bridge Land connection between continents that permitted the migration of organisms.

land chain A surveyor's chain of 100 links.

Landenian Upper Paleocene.

land form The term land form is applied by physiographers to each one of the multitudinous features that taken together make up the surface of the earth. It includes all broad features, such as plain, plateau, and mountain, and also all the minor features, such as hill, valley, slope, canyon, arroyo, and alluvial fan. Most of these features are the products of erosion, but the term includes also all forms due to sedimentation and to movements within the crust of the earth.

landslide Landslip, *q.v.* *1.* The perceptible downward sliding or falling of a relatively dry mass of earth, rock, or mixture of the two. *2.* Earth and rock which becomes loosened from a hillside by moisture or snow, and slides or falls down the slope. *See* SLIDE

landslip Landslide, *q.v.* *1.* A portion of land that has slid down in consequence of disturbance by an earthquake, or from being undermined by water washing away the lower beds which supported it. *2.* A portion of a hillside or sloping mass which becomes loosened or detached, and slips down. *3.* The slipping down of a considerable mass of earth or rock on a mountain or any steep slope; also the mass that slips down. Landslide is the word more common in the United States; landslip, the word usually used in England.

land-tied island *See* TOMBOLO

Lane-Wells micropetrograph Lane-Wells's version of the microlog (Schlumberger), *q.v.*

langbeinite A mineral, K_2Mg_2-

(SO₄)₃. Isometric. Occurs in potassium salt deposits; mined as a source of K_2SO_4.

lapidary A skilled workman who cuts and polishes gems or other stones.

lapidofacies Facies related to diagenesis.

lapies Certain parts of the Dinaric karst lands offer extraordinary difficulties of transit. These are regions of lapies, surfaces covered by a network of furrows and crests, well avoided by man and beast. Lapies are developed on surfaces of pure limestone and consist of narrow channels, or furrows, between which are ridges or crests, most often sharp, less frequently rounded in contour. The channels usually range from about 1 1/2 to 3 feet in depth but now and then reach 6 to 10 feet and even 16 to 20 feet; exceptionally there are lapies channels which are 30 to 40 feet deep. It was as far back as 1893 that appreciation of the association of lapies proper with limestone led to the classification of the lapies as karst forms. Lapies are found at all altitudes from sea level to lofty mountain summits. They were first observed and described in the limestone Alps in Switzerland, where in the cantons of German speech they are called Karren or Schratten and in districts of French speech lapiez or lapiaz or lapies, then rascles, esserts, and in the Jura, laissines.

lapilli Essential, accessory, and accidental volcanic ejecta ranging mostly from 4 mm. to 32 mm. in diameter.

lapis lazuli A translucent, rich Berlin-blue, azure-blue, violet-blue, or greenish-blue stone used for jewelry.

lap-out map Map showing the areal distribution of formations immediately overlying an unconformity.

lapse rate Temperature gradient, *q.v.*

Laramian Upper Upper Cretaceous above Montanan.

Laramidian orogeny 1. Post-Cretaceous diastrophism. 2. In broad sense, series of diastrophic movements beginning perhaps in Jurassic and continuing until present.

large quantities of water 1,500,-000 to 15,000,000 gallons per day. *Cf.* ENORMOUS; VERY LARGE; MODERATE; SMALL; VERY SMALL; MEAGER

Larsen variation diagram Weight per cent of each oxide constituent in a rock analysis is plotted as the ordinate against the "abscissa position," defined as $1/3$ $SiO_2 + K_2O \cdot FeO \cdot MgO \cdot CaO$; a smooth curve is drawn through the points representing a given constituent for a series of analyses.

larvikite A nepheline-bearing syenite with abundant rhombic phenocrysts of feldspar. Titanaugite, barkevikite, and lepidomelane are minor constituents and apatite, opaque oxides, zircon, and olivine are accessories.

late magmatic minerals Those formed during the later stages of magmatic activity, principally those formed between the main stage of crystallization and the pegmatitic stage. More or less synonymous with "reaction" minerals.

latent heat The amount of heat absorbed or emitted by a substance, under conditions of constant pressure and temperature, during a change of state. The numerical value of the latent heat is usually expressed in calories per gram. The various types of latent heat are as follows:

latent heat of evaporation for the change liquid-gas;

latent heat of sublimation for the change solid-gas;

latent heat of fusion for the change solid-liquid;

latent heat of crystallization for the change liquid-solid;

latent heat of solution for the change solute-solution;

latent heat of transition for the change solid-solid.

lateral accretion Wherever a stream meanders, it digs away its outer bank while the inner is building up the water level by the deposition of material brought there by rolling or pushing along the bottom. This is lateral accretion. If the stream be subject to overflow, sediment must settle from suspension in beds conforming to the surface. This is vertical accretion.

lateral erosion The action of the stream in impinging on one side of its channel and undermining the bank at that point, so that masses of material tumble down to be ultimately disintegrated; at the same time the channel keeps shifting toward the bank which is being undercut. The river therefore flows down the valley, cutting now into one bank and now into the other; this is known as lateral erosion or planation.

lateral migration Movement of oil or gas through permeable zones parallel to the stratification; a better term is parallel migration.

lateral moraine [<*Fr.* moraine laterale] *1.* Certain aggregations of drift which are left by a valley glacier after melting. *2.* An elongate body of drift, commonly thin, lying on the surface of a glacier in a valley, at or near the lateral margin of the glacier. *3.* An end moraine built along the lateral margin of a glacier lobe occupying a valley. First used by Louis Agassiz.

lateral planation The reduction of the land in interstream areas to a plane parallel to the stream profile, effected by the lateral swinging of the stream against its banks.

lateral secretion The theory that the contents of a vein or lode are derived from the adjacent wall rock.

laterite *1.* Red residual soil developed in humid tropical and subtropical regions of good drainage. It is leached of silica and contains concentrations particularly of iron and aluminum hydroxides. It may be an ore of iron, aluminum, manganese, or nickel. *2.* Altered basaltic rocks in India.

laterite profile Weathering profile up to 50 feet thick developed in some portions of the tropics consisting of A zone (Anreicherungszone), strongly leached iron-rich zone above water table; F zone (Fleckenzone), partly leached iron-stained zone at top of permanent water table; and Z zone (Zersatzzone), compact clay, zone of ion exchange.

laterolog (Schlumberger) A resistivity log in borehole surveying obtained with a current focusing system by the use of a multiple electrode arrangement. The current which tends to flow radially outward in all directions from a central electrode ring is "bucked" by the current emitted by two auxiliary electrodes symmetrically disposed above and below. The central current (called measuring current) is constrained to flow within a flat disk-shaped volume of rock perpendicular to the borehole. The beds outside this region have little influence on the measurement. *Cf.* GUARD ELECTRODE LOG. The proper amount of "bucking" current at any stage of the operation is regulated by a servo-mechanism which, in turn, is controlled by two pairs of so-called monitoring electrodes symmetrically located on either side of the central electrode between it and the outer "bucking" electrodes. (As soon as the potential of the electrodes of a pair in the monitoring system becomes unequal, the servo-mechanism increases or decreases the flow of current from the "bucking" electrodes, as the case requires, to re-establish the equal potential of the two monitors.) The spacing between the different electrodes is as shown:

```
            16"
X←——→11          X
Central  Monitor  Bucking
←————————40"————————→
```

late stage effects *See* LATE MAGMATIC MINERALS.

lath Long thin mineral crystal.

latite The extrusive equivalent of monzonite and a variety of trachyandesite in which potash feldspar and plagioclase are present either as normative or modal minerals in nearly equal amounts. Potash feldspar is often concealed in the fine-grained crystalline or glassy groundmass and thus a chemical analysis is often necessary for correct classification. Augite or hornblende is usually present and sometimes biotite plus accessory apatite and opaque oxides.

latitude *1.* Distance on the earth's surface from the equator, measured in degrees of the meridian. *2.* In plane surveying, the perpendicular distance in a

horizontal plane of a point from an east-west axis of reference. *See* DEPARTURE

latosol Laterite, *q.v.*

lattice drainage In the Adirondack Mountains the streams follow fault lines so generally that, when seen on a good map, the regularity of the system is extremely striking and has called forth the term lattice drainage. The term is seldom used and its equivalent "rectangular drainage" is preferred.

lattice energy For an ionic crystal, the energy absorbed when a mole of the crystal is dispersed into infinitely separated ions.

lattice orientation *Struct. petrol:* A preferred orientation that is shown by the lattice of the mineral. This is recognized by optical studies using the petrographic microscope or by X-ray studies.

Lattorfian Lower Oligocene.

Laué camera A single-crystal X-ray diffraction apparatus involving a stationary crystal and film and utilizing white X radiations.

Laué X-ray diffraction pattern produced by a single crystal with fixed orientation when exposed to a small unfiltered beam of radiation.

Laurasia Hypothetical continent in the Northern Hemisphere which supposedly broke up at about the end of the Carboniferous period to form the present northern continents.

laurdalite A variety of nepheline syenite with alkalic feldspar of rhombic form. Also contains biotite, pyroxene or amphibole and accessory apatite and sodalite.

Laurentian Gneissic granite constituting the older of two Precambrian systems. Archeozoic.

lava Fluid rock such as that which issues from a volcano or a fissure in the earth's surface; also the same material solidified by cooling.

lava blisters Small, hollow, steep-sided swellings raised on the surface of some pahoehoe lava flows and formed by gas bubbles puffing up the viscous crust of the flow. They are present on all types of pahoehoe but are most conspicuous on the type with a relatively smooth tachylite crust. *Syn:* TUMULUS

lava cascade A cascade of fluid, incandescent lava, formed when a lava river passes over a cliff or over a precipitous part of its course.

lava cave Lava cavern, *q.v.*

lava cavern In the production of an aa surface, if the crust is of sufficient strength not to be broken by the underflow the lava beneath may flow out and leave a cavern.

lava cone A volcanic cone built entirely or largely of lava flows, usually basaltic lavas that were very mobile at the time of eruption, and resembling a miniature shield volcano. Typical lava cones are about a mile in width, one to several hundred feet high, and have low angles of slope. They are formed mainly by fissure eruption, but at the summit some have small craters formed principally by collapse. Not to be confused with driblet or spatter cones.

lava delta A deltalike body of lava formed where a lava river flows into a lake or into the sea. Common in Hawaii.

lava dome; cumulo dome *1.* If the eruptions at a volcanic vent are exclusively of the explosive type, the material of the mountain which results is throughout tuff or cinder, and the volcano is described as a cinder cone. If,

on the other hand, the vent at every eruption exudes lava, a mountain of solid rock results which is a lava dome. 2. Lava domes are the greater masses of lava which, in the form of many individual flows, have issued from central vents in the proper directions to build a dome-shaped pile of lava. The world type is Mauna Loa.

lava field A wide expanse of lava flows, usually many square miles in extent, covering level or nearly level terrain and generally bearing clusters of cinder cones. Lava fields are commonly developed around the base of large, compound volcanoes or on the flanks of shield volcanoes such as those of the Hawaiian Islands.

lava flow *1.* A stream or river of fluid or viscous or solidified fragmented lava which issues from an individual volcanic cone or from a fissure in relatively quiet fashion, with little or no explosive activity. *2.* The solidified, stationary mass of rock formed when the lava stream congeals. Lava flows are generally tabular igneous bodies, thin compared to their horizontal extent, and elongated in the main direction of flow. Their form and internal structure depends chiefly on the fluidity of the lava, which, in turn, is a function of composition. Thus basic lava flows, such as basalt, are usually highly mobile, and flow for great distances, whereas silicic lavas, such as rhyolite and trachyte, are ordinarily sluggish in their flow, commonly fragmented, and remain heaped up, often in steep-sided volcanic domes or in short, steep-sided flows known as coulees.

lava fountain; fire fountain A

rhythmic jetlike eruption of lava issuing vertically from a central volcanic vent or from a fissure. Lava fountains are the common mode of eruption of basaltic lavas in Hawaii, where they emanate from fissures along rift zones developed on the flanks of the great volcanoes Mauna Loa and Kilauea, attaining heights of as much as 1000 feet. *See* FIRE-FOUNTAINING

lava lake A lake of fluid molten lava, usually basaltic, and ordinarily contained in a summit crater or in a pit crater on the flanks of a shield volcano. It may remain in existence for a long period of time (several years). The most famous lava lake is that of the fire pit of Halemaumau, lying in the caldera of Kilauea on the island of Hawaii.

lavanges Challanches; avalanches. Slow and gradual means are not the only causes of the diminution of the mountain snows; they also sink down in masses into the valleys, and thus expose themselves directly to the influence of heat. The masses which thus rush down the slopes are avalanches, likewise called in the Alps lavanges and challanches.

lava pit; fire pit A pit crater, usually developed at the summit or on the flanks of a shield volcano, or on the floor of a caldera containing an active or congealed lava lake. An example is Halemaumau crater, lying within the summit caldera of the volcano Kilauea on the island of Hawaii.

lava plain A broad stretch of level or nearly level land, usually many hundreds of square miles in extent, underlain by a relatively thin succession of lava flows, most of which are basaltic

and the product of fissure eruption. The flatness of the plain's surface is largely determined by the horizontal attitude of the underlying flows. An example is the Snake River basalt plain of southern Idaho.

lava plateau A broad, elevated tableland or flat-topped highland, usually many hundreds or thousands of square miles in extent, underlain by a thick succession of lava flows, most of which are tholeiitic basalts and the product of fissure eruption. An example is the Columbia Plateau of the northwestern United States.

lava shield Shield volcano.

lava tongue A short, tonguelike offshoot from a larger lava flow, ranging from a few feet to a mile or more in length.

lava tube Many lava flows develop hard crusts by the cooling and solidification of the upper surface. Later the supply of lava for the particular flow may cease and the liquid lava may drain out leaving a long tubular opening under the crust. *Cf.* LAVA CAVERN

lava tunnel A lava cavern or lava tube, *q.v.*, open at the ends.

law of priority The valid name of a genus or species can be only that name under which it was first designated.

law of reflection The angle between the reflected ray (normal to the wave front) and the normal to the reflecting surface is the same as the angle between this normal and the incident ray, provided the reflected wave is of the same type (travels with the same velocity) as the incident wave.

law of refraction Snell's law. When a wave crosses a boundary the wave normal changes direction in such a manner that the sine of the angle of incidence between wave normal and boundary normal divided by the velocity in the first medium equals the sine of the angle of refraction divided by the velocity in the second medium.

law of superposition The law that underlying strata must be older than overlying strata where there has been neither inversion nor overthrust. Upon this law all geological chronology is based.

law of universal gravitation Newton's law of gravitation. Every particle of mass attracts every other particle with a force inversely proportional to the square of the distance between them. $F = \gamma m_1.m_2/r^2$.

layer A bed or stratum of rock.

lazulite A mineral, $(Mg,Fe'')Al_2(PO_4)_2(OH)$. Monoclinic.

lazurite Lapis lazuli. A mineral, $3NaAlSiO_4.Na_2S$. Isometric.

Lc Abbreviation for leucite in normative rock calculations.

leach To wash or drain by percolation. To dissolve minerals or metals out of the ore, as by the use of cyanide or chlorine solutions, acids, or water.

lead glance Galena.

leadline A wire, or cord used in sounding. It is weighted at one end with a plummet (sounding lead). *Syn:* SOUNDING LINE

leads At other times, when the winds of widely separated areas blow away from each other, the pack is parted, with the formation of lanes or leads of open water.

lead-uranium ratio The ratio of amount of lead to amount of uranium in a rock or mineral, or of amounts of various isotopes of the two elements; used

in computing the geologic age of the rock or mineral.

leaf injections Paper-thin sheets of pegmatite alternating with thin sheets of schists. *See* LIT-PAR-LIT

league *1.* A unit of linear measure. A land league=3 statute miles, or 15,840 feet. A nautical league=3 geographical miles or 18,240.78 feet. *2.* An area embraced in a square 5000 varas on each side. It contains 4428.40 acres or 6.919 square miles. Term used chiefly in Texas land descriptions.

leakage halo An annular area of ground surface above a petroleum accumulation, supposedly characterized by an abnormal concentration in the soil gas of hydrocarbons which have leaked from the petroleum beneath. *Rare*

lean Applied to poor ores, or those containing a lower proportion of metal than is usually worked.

lean clay Clay of relatively low plasticity. *Cf.* FAT CLAY

lease Contract between landowner and another granting the latter right to search for and produce oil or mineral substances upon payment of an agreed rental, bonus, and/or royalty.

least squares *See* METHOD OF LEAST SQUARES

least-time path Minimum time path.

Le Chatelier's principle A general principle, having few exceptions, proposed by H. L. Le Chatelier. It is usually stated: If conditions of a system, initially at equilibrium, are changed, the equilibrium will shift in such a direction as to tend to restore the original conditions.

lectotype *1.* A syntype selected as the primary type of a species;

corresponds to holotype except that it was designated subsequent to the original description. 2. Genotype by subsequent designation.

ledge 1. A bed of several beds as in a quarry or natural outcrop, particularly those projecting in a steplike manner. 2. The surface of such a projecting bed. 3. *Min:* Projecting outcrop or vein, commonly quartz, that is supposed to be mineralized; also any narrow zone of mineralized rock. 4. In northern Michigan, bedrock.

Ledian Lower upper Eocene.

lee 1. Shelter, or the part or side sheltered or turned away from the wind. 2. Chiefly nautical: The quarter or region toward which the wind blows.

Leean Lower Lower Pennsylvanian

Lee configuration An electrical resistivity measuring method using two current electrodes and three equispaced potential electrodes.

lee side *Geol:* That side of glaciated rocks that looks away from the quarter whence the ice moves, or moved, as indicated by rough and weathered surfaces; opposed to shock side or stoss side. Also used for the lee sides of dunes.

leeward The direction toward which the prevailing wind is blowing; the direction toward which waves are traveling.

left-handed separation Where the horizontal separation along a fault is such that an observer walking along an index plane (bed, dike, vein, etc.) must, upon crossing the fault, turn to left to find the index plane on the opposite side of the fault. The actual movement along the fault can be a strike-slip move-

ment, a dip-slip movement, or a diagonal-slip movement.

left-lateral fault A strike-slip fault in which the movement is such that an observer walking toward the fault along an index plane (bed, dike, vein, etc.) must turn left to find the other part of the displaced index plane. *See* SINISTRAL FAULT

left-lateral separation Left-handed separation.

leg 1. A prop of timber supporting the end of a stull, or cap of a set of timber. 2. A single cycle in a wave train on a seismogram.

legend Explanation of the symbols and patterns shown on a map or diagram.

legitimacy Legitimacy refers only to whether or not a name has been accompanied by a suitable published description, or referred to a type specimen. If so, it is legitimate whether or not it conforms to the other rules. If not, it is illegitimate.

legua [*Sp.*] Land league used in the original surveys of the Philippines, California and Texas. It is equal to 2.63 miles or 4.24 kilometers. *See* LEAGUE

Lemberg solution An aqueous solution of logwood extract and $AlCl_6$ which produces a violet stain on calcite but leaves dolomite unchanged.

length of wave The horizontal distance between similar points on two successive waves measured perpendicularly to the crest.

lens A body of ore or rock thick in the middle and thin at the edges; similar to a double convex lens. *See* LENTICULAR

lens, sand A body of sand with the general form of a lens, thick in the central part and thinning toward the edges. *See* SAND WEDGE

lensing The thinning out of a stratum in one or more directions.

lenticular Shaped approximately like a double convex lens. When a mass of rock thins out from the center to a thin edge all around, it is said to be lenticular in form. *See* LENS

lenticular till *1.* This till may be of irregular thickness and distribution, but generally, where it is found plentifully, it is to a large extent massed in peculiar oblong or nearly round hills, which usually have quite steep sides and gently sloping, rounded tops, the whole presenting a very smooth and regular contour. Their outlines, as protracted upon a map, are lenticular in shape, whence the name. *2.* Shaped more or less like a lens; a short drumlin.

lentil *1.* Lens-shaped rock body. *2.* A minor rock-stratigraphic unit, a subdivision of a formation similar in rank to a member, having relatively small geographic extent and presumably wedging out in all directions.

lentille An isolated mass of rock containing fossils of a fauna older than the strata in which it occurs, though of contemporary age with those strata.

Leonardian Upper lower Permian.

Lepanto marble A trade name given to a gray marble enlivened by pink and white fossils; from the Lower Silurian, near Plattsburg, New York.

lepidoblastic A term applied to that type of flaky schistosity due to an abundance of minerals like micas and chlorites with a general parallel arrangement.

lepidolite A mineral of the mica group, $K(Mg,Li,Al)_3(AlSi_3)O_{10}$-

$(OH,F)_2$, rose, lilac, or gray. Monoclinic.

lepidomelane A variety of biotite, characterized by the presence of a large amount of ferric iron.

leptothermal Deposits intermediate between Waldemar Lindgren's mesothermal and epithermal zones.

leucite A mineral, $KAlSi_2O_6$. Pseudo-isometric. Found in K-rich volcanic rocks.

leucitohedron Trapezohedron.

leuco-; leuc- [<*Gr.* leuko-, leuk-] A combining form meaning: *1.* White, colorless; *2. Chem:* A colorless or weakly colored compound obtained by reduction of a dye, or closely related to a colored compound; *3. Mineral.* and *Petrol:* Light-colored.

leucocratic A term applied to light-colored rocks, especially igneous rocks, containing between 0 and 30% of dark minerals, i.e., rocks whose color index is between 0 and 30. *See* MESOCRATIC; MELANOCRATIC

Levantinian Upper upper Pliocene.

levee [*Fr.*] An artificial bank confining a stream channel or limiting areas subject to flooding; also a landing place, pier, or quay.

levee delta Deltas occasionally take the form of long narrow ridges upon one or both sides of a stream, resembling the natural levees in the "goosefoot" of the Mississippi. Normally the point where a tributary valley joins a larger one is marked by a notch in the wall of the latter, but in some cases a bisected spur appears instead.

level, circular A spirit level having the inside surface of its upper part ground to spherical shape, the outline of the bubble formed being circular and the graduations being concentric circles.

This form of spirit level is used where a high degree of precision is not required, as in plumbing a level rod or setting an instrument in approximate position. *Syn:* UNIVERSAL LEVEL; BULL'S-EYE LEVEL

level, spirit A small closed vessel of transparent material (glass), having the inside surface of its upper part curved (circular) in form; the vessel is nearly filled with a fluid of low viscosity (alcohol or ether), enough free space having been left for a bubble (blister) of air which will always assume a position at the top of the vessel.

leveling In surveying, the operation of ascertaining the comparative levels of different points of land, for the purpose of laying out a grade, etc., by sighting through a leveling instrument at one point to a leveling staff at another point.

leveling, direct The determination of differences of elevation by means of a continuous series of short horizontal lines, the vertical distances from which to adjacent ground marks are determined by direct observations on graduated rods with a leveling instrument equipped with a spirit level.

leveling, first-order Spirit leveling conforming to the following criteria: all first-order leveling to be divided into sections of 1 to 2 kilometers in length; each section to be leveled over in both forward and backward directions; the results of the two runnings over a section not to differ by more than 4.0 millimeters times the square root of the length of the section in kilometers (4.0 mm. $\sqrt{K}$), the equivalent of which is 0.017 foot times the square root of the length of the section in miles (0.017 ft. $\sqrt{M}$).

The above designation and criteria were recommended by the Federal Board of Surveys and Maps in May 1925.

leveling, indirect The determination of differences of elevation from (1) vertical angles and horizontal distances, as in trigonometric leveling; (2) comparative elevations derived from values of atmospheric pressure determined with a barometer, as in barometric leveling; and (3) elevations derived from values of the boiling point of water determined with a hypsometer, as in thermometric leveling.

leveling, second-order Spirit leveling which does not attain the quality of first-order leveling but does conform to the following criteria: lines between bench marks established by first-order leveling to be run in only one direction, using first-order instruments and methods; or other lines to be divided into sections, over which forward and backward runnings are to be made; the closure in either case not to exceed 8.4 millimeters times the square root of the length of the line (or section) in kilometers (8.4 mm. $\sqrt{K}$), the equivalent of which is 0.035 foot times the square root of the length of the line (or section) in miles (0.035 ft. $\sqrt{M}$).

The above designation and criteria were recommended by the Federal Board of Surveys and Maps in May 1925.

leveling, spirit The determination of elevations of points with respect to each other or with respect to a common datum by means of an instrument using a spirit level to establish a horizontal line of sight.

leveling, thermometric The determination of elevations above sea level from observed values of the boiling point of water.

The temperature at which water boils at any point on the earth depends upon the weight of the incumbent atmosphere at that point. *See* HYPSOMETER

leveling, third-order Leveling which does not attain the quality of second-order leveling, but does conform to the following criteria; lines of third-order leveling shall not be extended more than 30 miles from lines of first- or second-order leveling and must close upon lines of equal or a higher order of accuracy; closing errors must not exceed 12 millimeters times the square root of the length of the line in kilometers (12 mm. $\sqrt{K}$), the equivalent of which is 0.05 foot times the square root of the length of the line in miles (0.05 ft. $\sqrt{M}$).

The above designation and criteria were recommended by the Federal Board of Surveys and Maps in May 1925.

leveling datum A level surface to which heights are referred. The elevation of the datum is usually, but not always, zero (0). The generally adopted datum for leveling operations in the United States is mean sea level. For local surveys, where a sea-level connection is not available, an arbitrary datum may be adopted and defined in terms of an assumed elevation for some physical mark (bench mark). A datum for spirit leveling is not a plane, and the term datum plane is incorrectly used in such connection.

leveling instrument A surveyor's level bearing a telescope.

level of zero amplitude The level to which seasonal change of temperature extends into permafrost. Below this level the temperature gradient of permafrost is more or less stable the year around. An abbreviation of level of zero annual amplitude.

level rod A graduated rod used in measuring the distance between points on the ground and the line of sight of a leveling instrument.

level surface A surface which at every point is perpendicular to the plumb line or the direction in which gravity acts.

An equipotential surface, *q.v.* The surface of a body of still water. The surface of the ocean, if changes caused by tides, currents, winds, atmospheric pressure, etc., are not considered. The surface of the geoid. In a survey of a small area, sometimes treated as a plane surface. Level surfaces are approximately spheroidal in shape, the distance between any two level surfaces decreasing with increase of latitude, e.g., a level surface which is 1000 meters above the mean surface of the sea at the equator is 995 meters above that surface at the poles.

Lewistonian Upper Lower Silurian.

Lg *Earthquake seismol:* A phase designation given to a slow, short period Love wave which is found to travel only along nonoceanic paths. The subscript g refers to the possible importance of the granitic layer for their propagation.

Lias Liassic.

Liassic Lower Jurassic.

licks An American term given to boggy grounds affording salt springs, because the cattle go down to lick the salt there. In

Brazil these are called carrieros.

liesegang rings Rings or bands resulting from rhythmic precipitation in a gel.

Ligerian Lower Turonian.

light, polarized Light in which the vibrations are in one plane. Light is usually polarized with Nicol prisms (or modifications of them) or with manufactured materials such as Polaroid.

light-colored mineral Light mineral.

light minerals *Geol:* Applied to those rock-forming minerals that have a specific gravity less than 2.8, including such materials as quartz, calcite, feldspars, feldspathoids, and some micas. Also applied to the rock-forming minerals that are light in color, these minerals generally being the same as those that are classified as light on the basis of weight.

light ruby silver Proustite.

lignite *1.* A brownish-black coal in which the alteration of vegetal material has proceeded further than in peat but not so far as sub-bituminous coal. *2.* Consolidated lignitic coal having less than 8300 B.t.u. (moist, mineral-matter-free).

lily pond A terraced rimstone pool.

liman *1.* Shallow lagoon or embayment with muddy bottom. *2.* Area of mud or slime deposited near a river's mouth.

liman coast [<*Lat.* limus, mud] An alluvial coast usually with many lagoons.

limb *1.* One of the two parts of an anticline or syncline on either side of the axis. *2.* The graduated margin of an arc or circle in an instrument for measuring angles.

limburgite Glassy nepheline basalt. Phenocrysts of titanaugite, olivine, and opaque oxides in glassy groundmass.

lime Calcium oxide, CaO. Loosely used for calcium hydroxide, calcium carbonate, and even for calcium in deplorable expressions such as carbonate of lime or lime feldspar.

lime feldspar Misnomer for calcium feldspar. Anorthite. *See* PLAGIOCLASE

limestone *1.* A bedded sedimentary deposit consisting chiefly of calcium carbonate ($CaCO_3$) which yields lime when burned. Limestone is the most important and widely distributed of the carbonate rocks and is the consolidated equivalent of limy mud, calcareous sand, or shell fragments. *2.* A general term for that class of rocks which contain at least 80 per cent of the carbonates of calcium or magnesium. The suitability of the rock for the manufacture of lime is not an essential characteristic.

limestone reefs Aggregates of calcareous skeletons and other structures of plants and animals growing upward from submerged continental or island basements to the level of the ocean.

limnetic; limnic *1.* Pertaining to, or living in, fresh water. *2.* Restricted usage: Pertaining to communities of lake-dwelling organisms which are free from direct dependence on bottom or shore.

limnoblos Life of fresh water environment.

limnology *1.* The scientific study of fresh waters, especially that of ponds and lakes. In its broadest sense it deals with all physical, chemical, meteorological, and biological conditions pertaining to such a body of water. *2.* Since 1845 Friedrich Simony undertook the careful exploration of the depths and temperatures of all the lakes of the Salzkammergut. He continued his explorations for forty years, and thus became the founder of the special branch of the science termed by F. A. Forel, limnology, or the scientific study of lakes.

limonite A generic term for brown hydrous iron oxide, not specifically identified. Commonly consists mainly of goethite.

Lindgren's volume law A principle, pointed out by Waldemar Lindgren, that replacement occurs on approximately a volume-by-volume basis.

lineage 1. A series of genera and species which form an evolutionary series, each one being ancestral to its successor in the geological sequence; a line of evolution. 2. A broad belt of descent embracing series of communities each of which may include a wide range of forms that can be described as so many morphological species; a bundle of lines of descent. Syn: PLEXUS

lineament 1. Significant lines of landscapes which reveal the hidden architecture of the rock basement are described as lineaments. They are character lines of the earth's physiognomy. 2. An essentially rectilinear topographic feature resulting from a fault. 3. A topographic line that is structurally controlled. Lineaments are studied especially on aerial photographs. Sometimes inappropriately called a linear.

linear 1. N: A straight or gently curved physiographic feature on the earth's surface. 2. Adj: In paleobotany, long and narrow, the sides parallel or nearly so, as blades of most grasses.

linear cleavage A property of metamorphic rocks whereby they break in long pencil-like fragments; results from two intersecting cleavages or from linear parallelism of platy or prismatic minerals.

linear element See ELEMENT, LINEAR

lineation Any linear structure within or on a rock resulting from primary flowage in igneous rock or secondary flowage in metamorphic rock shown by rotation of mineral grains or other bodies, intersection of planes, slippage along gliding planes, and growth of crystals.

line of bearing The direction of the strike, or outcrop.

line of dip A line of greatest inclination of a stratum to the horizontal.

lingulid One of an ancient family of brachiopods with simple shells, dating from the Cambrian and persisting practically without change to the present.

linguoid One of the modifications of the simple normal type of current ripple shows a highly irregular pattern with a wide range in the variety of forms. The tonguelike outline of the unit forms of many examples of the pattern led W. H. Bucher to give it the name of linguoid. Negatives of these markings resemble small mud flows.

lining sight An instrument consisting essentially of a plate with a longitudinal slot in the middle and the means of suspending it vertically. It is used in conjunction with a plumb line for directing the courses of underground drifts, headings, etc.

link A unit of linear measure, one one-hundredth of a chain, and equivalent to 7.92 inches.

linked vein A steplike vein in which the ore follows one fissure for a short distance, then passes by a cross fissure to another nearly parallel, and so on.

Linnaean Conforming to the

principles of binomial nomenclature as advocated by Karl von Linné, who Latinized his name to Carolus Linnaeus.

Lipalian 1. A theoretical geologic period immediately antedating the Cambrian, unknown anywhere in the record of marine sedimentation. 2. The interval of time represented by a widespread unconformity separating Precambrian and Cambrian strata.

lipoid, *n.* Includes all materials extractable with petroleum solvents. Lipoids are fatlike substances of organic origin and complex chemical structure.

liquid 1. Flowing freely like water; fluid, not solid. 2. Characterized by free movement of the constituent molecules among themselves, but without the tendency to separate from one another characteristic of gases. 3. As generally used, a fluid of high density and low compressibility. The specific recognition of a liquid as distinct from a gas of the same composition requires the simultaneous presence of both phases at equilibrium. *See* GAS; FLUID; VAPOR

liquid flow Movement of a liquid, generally one of low viscosity, involving either or both laminar and turbulent flow.

liquid immiscibility A process of magmatic differentiation involving the separation of the magma into two or more immiscible liquid phases, which are then separated from each other by gravity or other processes.

liquid limit Water content of unconsolidated material at the point where it passes from a plastic solid to a turbid liquid as determined by standardized mechanical tests.

liquidus The locus of points in a temperature-composition diagram representing the maximum solubility (saturation) of a solid component or phase in the liquid phase. In a binary system it is a line, in a ternary system it is a curved surface, and in a quaternary system it is a volume. In an isoplethal study, at temperatures above the liquidus, the system is completely liquid, and at the intersection of the liquidus and the isopleth the liquid is in equilibrium with one crystalline phase.

list mill In gem cutting, a wheel covered with list or cloth, on which the gems are polished.

-lite Suffix from *Gr.* lithos (stone).

lith-; litho- [*Gr.*] 1. A prefix meaning stone or stonelike. 2. **-lith** A suffix meaning rock or rocklike.

lithic; lithologic Refers to sediments and rocks in which rock fragments are more important proportionally than feldspar grains.

lithic tuff 1. Tuffs that consist dominantly of crystalline rock fragments are called lithic tuffs. This is in contrast to the crystal tuff, *q.v.* Formed from quickly cooled volcanic materials, giving the rock a fine-grained structure and a crystal fabric. 2. An indurated deposit of volcanic ash in which the fragments are composed of previously formed rocks, e.g., accidental particles of sedimentary rock, accessory pieces of earlier rocks, or small bits of nes lava (essential ejecta) that first solidify in the vent and are then blown out.

lithification 1. That complex of processes that converts a newly deposited sediment into an indurated rock. It may occur shortly after deposition—may even be concurrent with it—or it may occur long after deposition. *Cf.* INDURATION; CEMENTATION. *2.* A type of coal-bed termination wherein the disappearance takes place because of a lateral increase in impurities resulting in a gradual change into bituminous shale or other rock.

lithify To turn to rock; to petrify; to crystallize as from a magma; to consolidate, such as the process of induration of a loose sediment. *Cf.* INDURATION

lithofacies The rock record of any sedimentary environment, including both physical and organic characters.

lithofacies map A map showing the areal variation in over-all aspect of the lithology of a stratigraphic unit. Emphasis may be placed on a dominant, average, or specific lithologic aspect of the unit in question.

lithofraction Breaking of rock fragments during transportation in streams or by wave action on beaches. *Cf.* SPLITTING

lithographic limestone; lithographic stone An exceedingly fine-grained, crystalline limestone. It is used for lithographic and not for structural work. The thin, impure layers overlying the lithographic rock in the Bavarian quarries are locally used as roofing tiles.

lithographic texture A term used to denote grain size in calcareous sedimentary rocks. The grain size corresponds to that of clay, or less than 1/256 mm.

lithoidal A term applied to dense, fine-grained, crystalline igneous rocks, to devitrified glasses, or to a groundmass of crystalline material as distinguished from glassy varieties. *Syn:* STONY. *See* FELSITIC

lithology *1.* The physical character of a rock, generally as

determined megascopically or with the aid of a low-power magnifier. *2.* The microscopic study and description of rocks. *Obs.* PETROGRAPHY

lithophile elements Elements enriched in the silicate crust. Elements with a greater free energy of oxidation, per gram atom of oxygen, than iron; they concentrate in the stony matter or slag crust of the earth, as oxides and more often as oxysalts, especially silicates.

lithophysae The large, hollow, bubblelike or roselike spherulites, usually with a radial and concentric structure, that occur in certain rhyolites, obsidians, and related rocks.

lithosol One of a group of azonal soils having no clearly expressed soil morphology and consisting of a freshly and imperfectly weathered mass of rock fragments; largely confined to steep hillsides.

lithosphere The solid portion of the earth, as contrasted with the atmosphere and hydrosphere. The earth's crust; the outermost portion or shell of the globe, as distinguished from the underlying barysphere or centrosphere.

lithostatic pressure The equal, all-sided pressure in the crust of the earth due to the weight of the overlying rocks.

lithostratigraphic unit Unit consisting of stratified, mainly sedimentary, rocks grouped on the basis of lithologic rather than biologic characters or time value. Rock-stratigraphic unit. *Cf.* BIO-STRATIGRAPHIC UNIT

lithostratigraphy *1.* Stratigraphy based only on the physical and petrographic features of rocks. *2.* Recognition and interpretation of the physical characters of sedimentary rocks.

lithotype *1.* Rock defined on the basis of certain selected physical characters. *2.* One of the four microscopically recognizable constituents of bonded coal; vitrain, clarain, durain, fusain.

lithozone *1.* Stratigraphic zone defined by lithology. *2.* Paratime-rock unit.

lit-par-lit [*Fr.* leaf-by-leaf] *Petrol:* Used to designate the intimate penetration of bedded, schistose, or other foliate rocks by innumerable narrow sheets and tongues of granitic rock, usually granitic igneous rocks.

littoral *1.* Belonging to, inhabiting, or taking place on or near the shore. *2.* The portion of the benthic which extends from the shore to approximately the 200-meter line. *3.* The benthonic environment between the limits of high and low tides.

littoral benthal The lighted sea bottom; this extends from the shore outward to depths of about 200 meters at the upper edge of the continental slope and is divided into the eulittoral and the sublittoral (or littoral proper).

littoral cone An adventive or accidental ash or tuff cone built on the stagnant surface of an aa lava flow and formed by the explosion of the lava when it runs into a body of water, usually the sea. Such cones are the result of steam explosions that hurl into the air large amounts of ash, lapilli, and small bombs derived from the new lava. In many ways littoral cones resemble the cinder-and-spatter cones built at central vents, but they lack craters and are generally better bedded than typical cinder cones. In Hawaii, littoral cones reach heights up to 300 feet and diameters up to half a mile.

littoral current Longshore current. Generated by waves breaking at an angle to the shore line, which move usually parallel to, and adjacent to the shore line within the surf zone.

littoral deposits Deposits of littoral drift located between high and low water lines.

littoral drift *1.* Applied to the movement along the coast of gravel, sand, and other material composing the bars and beaches. *2.* The material moved in the littoral zone under the influence of waves and currents.

littoral shelf Shallow, near shore, terracelike part of submerged lake bed produced by wave erosion and deposition.

littoral zone *1.* Strictly, zone bounded by high and low tide levels. *2.* Loosely, zone related to the shore, extending to some arbitrary shallow depth of water.

living fossil A modern animal that has descended from a very ancient stock with comparatively little change.

L-joints Primary flat joints. Horizontal or nearly horizontal joints that are found in igneous rocks and related to the intrusion of magma.

Llandeillian Llandellian.

Llandellian Upper Middle Ordovician.

Llandoverian Lower Silurian (restricted).

llano [*Sp.*] *Topog:* *1.* An extensive plain with or without vegetation. *2.* The term is an exact equivalent of the English word plain, and by Spanish-speaking persons is so used. Generally the term is applied to the vast treeless plains of South America.

Llanvirnian Lower Middle Ordovician.

load *1.* In erosion and corrasion the material which is transported

may be called the "load." The
load is transported by two methods: a portion floats with the water, and another portion is driven
along the bottom. 2. The sediment moved by a stream, whether in suspension or at the bottom,
is its load. 3. The quantity of
material actually transported by
a current. This is usually somewhat less than the actual capacity
of the current.

load cast Roll or other irregu-
larity at the base of an overlying
stratum, commonly sandstone,
projecting into an underlying
stratum, commonly shale or clay,
produced by differential settling
and compaction. Cf. FLOW CAST

loaded stream A stream is loaded
when it has all the sediment it
can carry; it is but partly loaded
when it is carrying less than it
might.

loam A soil composed of a mixture of clay, silt, sand, and organic matter.

lobe 1. The tongue of land within the meander. When the lobe
lies between two meanders and
is connected with the mainland
by a narrow passage, the narrow
passage is the neck. The cutting
action of the river narrows the
neck until finally the river breaks
through and forms a new channel or a cutoff. 2. A projection
of a glacial margin or of a body
of glacial drift beyond the main
mass of ice or drift. See GLACIAL
LOBE. 3. In a cephalopod, undu-
lations of the suture line which
are convex toward the apex and
concave toward the aperture of
the shell. 4. Paleobot: Any part
or segment of an organ; specifically a part of a petal or calyx
or leaf that represents a division
to about the middle.

local currents Natural earth currents of local origin such as those

arising from the oxidation of
sulfide deposits. A term used in
electrical prospecting.

local metamorphism Contact metamorphism.

local range-zone Teilzone.

local unconformity An unconformity on either side of which
the beds are parallel to one another but where the unconformity appears to be only of local
significance. A disconformity may
by similar in appearance but is
inferred to be of regional importance.

locate To mark out the boundaries of a mining claim and establish the right of possession.

loch; lock [Scot.] A lake; also
a bay or arm of the sea, especially when nearly landlocked.

Locke hand level Hand level
with fixed bubble tube that can
be used only for horizontal sighting.

Lockportian Upper Middle Silurian.

lode In Cornwall, strictly a fissure in the country rock filled
with mineral; usually applied to
metalliferous lodes. In general
miners' usage, a lode, vein, or
ledge is a tabular deposit of valuable mineral between definite
boundaries. Whether it is a fissure formation or not is not always known and does not affect
the legal title under the United
States Federal and local statutes
and customs relative to lodes.
But it must not be a placer, i.e.
it must consist of quartz or other
rock in place, and bear valuable
minerals.

As used by miners, before being defined by any authority, the
term "lode" simply meant that
formation by which the mine
could be led or guided. It is an
alteration of the verb "lead,"
and whatever the miner could

follow, expecting to find ore, was his lode. Some formation within which he could find ore, and out of which he could not expect to find ore, was his lode. Lode, as used by miners, is nearly synonymous with the term vein, as employed by geologists. The word should not be used for a flat or stratified mass. *See* LEDGE, *1;* LEAD, *1;* FISSURE; FISSURE VEIN; VEIN

A lode consists of several veins spaced closely enough so that all of them, together with the intervening rock, can be mined as a unit.

lode claim Vein claim.

lode mining claim A mining claim including a lode, fissure, or fissure vein. In the United States the maximum length along the lode or vein is 1500 feet and the maximum width is 600 feet.

A tract of land with defined surface boundaries, including all lodes, veins, and ledges throughout their entire depth, the top or apex of which lies inside of vertical planes extended downward through the surface boundary lines, although such veins in their downward course may extend outside of the vertical side planes of the surface location. The extension of inclined veins beyond the side lines has resulted in much litigation. In Mexico a claim is 100 meters square and is bounded by vertical planes through the surface lines. *See* CLAIM; MINING CLAIM

In some mining districts, as Bisbee, Arizona, the operating companies have entered into mutual contracts, specifically eliminating extralateral rights, and defining underground property rights by downward vertical planes through the surface boundaries.

lodestone; loadstone A piece of magnetite possessing polarity like a magnetic needle.

lode tin Tin ore (cassiterite) occurring in veins, as distinguished from stream tin or placer tin.

lodgement till Till deposited beneath a moving glacier, characterized by compact fissile structure and stones oriented with their long axes parallel to the direction of flow.

loess *1.* A homogeneous, nonstratified, unindurated deposit consisting predominantly of silt, with subordinate amounts of very fine sand and/or clay; a rude vertical parting is common at many places. For a majority of workers, the term has genetic implications in terms of eolian deposition. According to Alfred Scheidig, the term was first used in connection with deposits in the Rhine Valley, about 1821, and was introduced into English by Sir Charles Lyell in 1834. *2.* A sediment, commonly nonstratified and commonly unconsolidated, composed dominantly of silt-size particles, ordinarily with accessory clay and sand, deposited primarily by the wind. *3.* Thought by R. J. Russell to be colluvial rather than eolian in the Lower Mississippi Valley and to result from the reworking of older back-swamp deposits.

loess-doll Calcareous concretion occurring in loess.

loessification Development of loess from swampy terrace sediments by weathering and downslope creep.

loess kindchen A spheroidal or irregular nodule of calcium carbonate found in loess. *Syn:* LOESS PUPPEN; LOESS MÄNNCHEN

Loewinson-Lessing classification A chemical system of classification of igneous rocks.

log *1.* A graphic presentation of the lithologic and/or stratigraphic units traversed by a borehole. *2.* The similar presentation of the variation of some physical property in a borehole with depth, such as resistivity, self-potential, gamma-ray intensity or velocity. *3.* The record of formations penetrated, drilling progress, record of depth of water, oil, gas, or other minerals, the record of size and length of pipe used, and other written or recorded facts having to do with drilling a well.

logarithmic mean particle diameter A measure of average particle size obtained by taking the arithmetic mean of the particle size distribution in terms of logs of the class midpoints. *See* PHI MEAN PARTICLE DIAMETER

lognormal distribution A distribution in which the logarithm of a parameter is normally distributed.

log strip Long narrow paper strip on which a well log may be plotted.

longitude *1.* Distance east or west on the earth's surface, measured by the angle which the meridian through a place makes with some standard meridian, as, that of Greenwich or Paris. *2.* A coordinate distance, linear or angular, from a north-south reference line. *3. Geod:* The angle between the plane of the geodetic meridian and the plane of an initial meridian, arbitrarily chosen.

longitude correction The east-west corrections made to observed magnetic intensities by subtracting the earth's normal field.

longitudinal dune A very general term for various types of linear dune ridges, commonly more or less symmetrical in cross profile,

which are known or inferred to extend parallel to the direction of the dominant dune-building winds.

longitudinal fault A fault whose strike is parallel with the general structure.

longitudinal joint Joint extending parallel to flow lines in igneous rock, steeply dipping and best developed where flow lines are horizontal.

longitudinal stream A stream which runs parallel to the strike of the rocks.

longitudinal valley A valley having a direction the same as the strike. *See* SUBSEQUENT STREAM

longitudinal wave Primary wave; pressure wave; compressional wave; dilatational wave; irrotational wave. An elastic wave in which the displacements are in the direction of wave propagation.

long limb That side of an asymmetrical fold which extends farther than the other before inclination is reversed, generally the more gently dipping side.

long range order Orderliness of arrangement in crystal structure extending indefinitely beyond neighboring atoms or molecules; the normal or ideal state in a crystalline solid.

longshore bar Refers to slightly submerged sand ridges which extend generally parallel with the shore line and are submerged at least by high tides.

longshore drift The material transported by longshore drifting or longshore currents.

longwall A system of working seam of coal in which the whole seam is taken out and no pillar left, excepting the shaft pillars and sometimes the main-road pillars. Longwall advancing: mining the coal outward from the shaft pillar and maintaining roadways through the worked-out portion of the mine. Longwall retreating: first driving haulage road and airways to the boundary of a tract of coal and then mining it in a single face without pillars back toward the shaft. Longwork, Shropshire method. Combination longwall and Nottingham or Barry system.

loop A pattern of field observations which begin and end at the same point with a number of intervening observations. Such a pattern is useful in correcting for drift in gravity-meter observations, diurnal variation in magnetometer surveys, and to detect faults or other cause of misclosure in seismic dip shooting.

lophophore Circle or loop of tentacles surrounding the mouth of bryozoans and brachiopods.

lopolith A large floored intrusive that is centrally sunken into the form of a basin.

lorac A precision radio surveying technique in which two or more fixed transmitters emit continuous waves and in the resulting standing wave pattern the position of a mobile receiver is determined by measuring with it the phase difference of the waves emanating from two of the transmitters.

loran A pulse-type electronic navigation system for measuring distance differences with respect to fixed transmitters of known geographic position.

lost river *Geol:* A river that, by a secular increase in aridity, at first periodically in the driest season, and at last permanently, has lost its trunk, its detached tributaries losing themselves in the arid ground. River in a karst region which drains into an underground channel.

Lotharingian Uppermost lower Lower Jurassic.

louderback Outlier of lava flow forming dip slope in block faulted region; proves topography was produced by faulting rather than by erosion alone.

Love wave Q-wave. *1.* A transverse wave propagated along the boundary of two elastic media which both have rigidity, i.e., both media must be capable of propagating transverse waves. *2.* A surface seismic wave in which the particles of an elastic medium vibrate transverse to the direction of the wave's travel, with no vertical component.

low *1.* A region of the atmosphere where the barometric pressure is below normal, usually surrounded by closed isobars with the point of minimum pressure in the center. Not strictly synonymous with cyclone, *q.v.*, since lows often appear on the weather map without a well-defined cyclonic wind circulation. Moreover, an extra-tropical cyclone, *q.v.*, always has a frontal structure; a low need not have. *2.* Former stream channels in coal beds. They do not extend downward through the entire thickness of coal. They are now filled with sandstone, clay, shale. *See* WASHOUT. *3.* Minimum (gravity or magnetic).

"low," structural An area in which the beds are structurally lower than in neighboring areas; a syncline or structural depression; sometimes also applied to saddles between local "highs" along the crests of anticlines.

low-angle fault A fault dipping less than 45°.

low energy environment Environment characterized by general lack of wave and/or current action; very fine grained sediment is permitted to settle.

lower high water The lower of the two high waters of any tidal day.

lower low water The lower of the two low waters of any tidal day. The single low water occurring daily during periods when the tide is diurnal is considered to be a lower low water.

low-grade ore Ore which is relatively poor in the metal for which it is mined. *Cf.* HIGH-GRADE ORE

lowlands The lowlands include the extended plains or country lying not far above tide level. In general they are less than 1000 feet above the sea, but they are marked off rather by their contrast with the higher lands of the mountain regions than by any special altitude. The surface is usually undulating and often hilly.

low-oblique photograph An oblique aerial photograph with the entire picture below the horizon.

low-quartz Low-temperature quartz; when formed below 573°, SiO_4 tetrahedra are less symmetrically arranged than at higher temperatures; inversion is reversible.

low-rank graywacke Nonfeldspathic graywacke.

low-rank metamorphism Metamorphism accomplished under conditions of low to moderate temperature and pressure. *See* METAMORPHIC GRADE

low tide; low water Minimum height reached by each falling tide; the mean value of all low waters over a considerable period.

low-velocity correction Weathering correction.

low-volatile bituminous coal Nonagglomerating bituminous coal having 78% or more, and less than 86%, of fixed carbon (dry, mineral-matter-free) and 22% or less, and more than 14% of volatile matter, (dry, mineral-matter-free).

low-water datum An approximation to the plane of mean low water that has been adopted as a standard reference plane. *See* DATUM PLANE

L.P.G. An abbreviation for liquefied petroleum gases such as butane, propane, etc., which are kept in a liquid state under pressure and used in domestic and industrial consumption as gases.

L^Q *See* Q

L^R *See* R

Luder's line Slip bands. The dark and light bands inclined at about 45° that appear in rods, especially those made of metal, subjected to tension or compression. These lines (actually surfaces) are zones within which the maximum deformation of the grains takes place.

Ludian Upper upper Eocene.

Ludlovian Upper Silurian (restricted), below Downtonian.

Luisian Lower upper Miocene.

luminescence The nearly instantaneous emission of light.

lumping Practice of ignoring minor differences in the recognition or definition of species and genera.

lunate bar A crescentic-shaped bar commonly found off the entrance to a harbor.

Lusitanian Lower Jurassic, above Oxfordian.

luster The character of the light reflected by minerals; it constitutes one of the means of distinguishing them. There are several kinds of luster: metallic, the luster of metals; adamantine, the luster of diamonds; vitreous, the luster of broken glass; resinous, the luster of yellow resin, as that of sphalerite; pearly, like pearl; silky, like silk.

luster mottlings *1.* A name applied by Raphael Pumpelly to certain augitic rocks that have a shimmering luster because the shining cleavage faces of the augite crystals are mottled by small inclusions. *2.* The shimmering, mottled appearance of certain rocks produced by the reflection of light from the cleavage faces of crystals containing numerous small inclusions of other minerals, i.e., poikilitic crystals. Common to some of the basaltic rocks of the Keweenawan series containing poikilitic augite crystals, but also observed in such rocks as sandstones in which large crystals of cementing calcite incorporate colonies of detrital grains.

lutaceous Argillaceous, *q.v.* Descriptive of a fine-grained texture and particularly, but not entirely, applicable to silts and clays and their derivatives.

Lutetian Middle Eocene.

lutite Sediment or sedimentary rock consisting principally of clay or clay-sized particles. *See* LUTYTE

lutyte Applies to rocks composed of muds, i.e., silts and/or clays

and the various associated materials which when mixed with water form mud. A. W. Grabau proposed a considerable number of terms composed of this word with various appropriate prefixes. Among them are anemoargillutyte, anemolutyte, argillutyte, atmolutyte, atmoargillutyte, autoargillutyte, autolutyte, autosililutyte, biolutyte, hydrargillutyte, hydrocalcilutyte, hydroferrilutyte, hydrosilicilutyte, pyrolutyte, and silicilutyte. The terms are intended to cover every type or variety of clayey or silty sediment. If all other terms applied to the fine-grained clastic elements could be eliminated or forgotten this nomenclature might be excellent, although the words would be long. It is vain to expect, however, that the many other much shorter terms in common use will be given up and these adopted. *See* LUTITE

Lycopodineae Class of pteridophytes; plants densely covered with simple spirally arranged leaves, spore-bearing organs situated on or close to leaves. Sil.-Rec.

lysimeter Structure containing a mass of soil and so designed as to permit the measurement of water draining through the soil.

M

M *Earthquake seismol:* Formerly applied to the phase with the maximum amplitude on the seismogram. Usage in this sense has become obsolete with the recognition of the importance of the constants of seismographs in determining which phase will have the maximum amplitude on a record. Now sometimes used to refer to the phase with the maximum ground amplitude.

maar A crater formed by violent explosion not accompanied by igneous extrusion, commonly occupied by a small circular lake.

macadam effect Cementation of calcareous fragments resulting from wetting, partial solution, and deposition of cement by evaporation.

macro- [<*Gr.* makro-] Prefix meaning large, long; visibly large.

macroaxis The b-axis (long) in orthorhombic and triclinic crystals.

macroclastic Composed of fragments visible without magnification.

macroclimate The general climate over a comparatively large area considered as a whole, as distinguished from the detailed variations within very small areas, which constitute the microclimate, *q.v.* The data of macroclimate are those obtained by observations at ordinary official weather stations.

macrocrystalline *1.* Applied to the texture of holocrystalline igneous rocks in which the constituents are distinguishable with the naked eye. Opposed to microcrystalline. *2.* In recrystallized sediments, the texture of a rock with grains or crystals over .75 mm. in diameter.

macrodome Crystal form whose faces are parallel to the macro or b-axis in orthorhombic and triclinic systems.

macrofacies Suite of genetically related facies.

macropinacoid *See* PINACOID

macropolyschematic A term applied to a body of rock or mineral deposit whose fabric consists of macroscopically different domains, i.e., a coarsely mixed fabric.

macroscopic *See* MEGASCOPIC

macrostructure A structural feature of rocks that can be discerned by the unaided eye, or with the help of a simple magnifier.

maculose A term given to the group of contact-metamorphosed rocks represented by spotted slates, to denote their spotted or knotted character. May be applied to either the rocks or their structures. *See* SPOTTED SLATE

madrepore A branching coral; also, any perforated stone coral.

Maestrichtian Upper Senonian.

mafic *Petrol:* Subsilicic; basic. Pertaining to or composed dominantly of the magnesian rock forming silicates; said of some igneous rocks and their constituent minerals. Contrasted with felsic. In general, synonymous with "dark minerals," as usually used.

maghemite γ -Fe_2O_3. A mineral, Fe_2O_3, dimorphous with hematite. Strongly magnetic.

magma, *n.* Naturally occurring mobile rock material, generated within the earth and capable of intrusion and extrusion, from which igneous rocks are considered to have been derived by solidification. It consists "in noteworthy part" of a liquid silicate-melt phase, which is liquid owing to the temperature attained, and a number of solid phases such as suspended crystals of olivine, pyroxene, plagioclase, etc. In certain instances a gas phase may also be present. Various authors differ in their interpretation of what constitutes "in noteworthy part." Some writers would specifically exclude from the definition those materials fitting the definition of migma. Magmatic, *adj.*

magma chamber A large reservoir in the earth's crust occupied by a body of magma.

magmagranite Granite produced by crystallization of a magma.

magmatic *Petrol:* Of, pertaining to, or derived from magma.

magmatic deposits Certain kinds of mineral deposits form integral parts of igneous rock masses and permit the inference that they have originated, in their present form, by processes of differentiation and cooling in molten magmas.

magmatic differentiation *Petrol:* The process by which different types of igneous rocks are derived from a single parent magma, or by which different parts of a single molten mass assume different compositions and textures as it solidifies. Also applied to ores produced by this process. *Syn:* MAGMATIC SEGREGATION

magmatic segregation *See* MAGMATIC DIFFERENTIATION

magmatic stoping A process of igneous intrusion whereby a magma gradually eats its way upward by breaking off blocks of the country rock. As originally proposed, the hypothesis assumed that these blocks sank downward. In piecemeal stoping the blocks are small, measured in feet or hundreds of feet. In ring-fracture stoping they are large, thousands of feet or miles across.

magmatic water Water that exists in, or which is derived from, molten igneous rock or magma.

magmatism Development and movement of magma within the earth. *Cf.* VOLCANISM

magmatist *1.* One who believes that much granite has crystallized from a mobile magma whatever the origin of that material may have been. *Cf.* TRANSFORMIST. *2.* One who believes that much granite is a primary igneous rock produced by differentiation from basaltic magma.

magma type A categorization of a magma according to any given scheme of classification, e.g., "nonporphyritic central magma-type."

magnafacies A major belt of deposits which is distinguished by similar lithologic and paleontologic characters.

magnesia Magnesium oxide, MgO. Loosely, magnesium carbonate.

magnesian limestone Any limestone containing more than 20% of magnesia is a magnesian limestone. Often used, however, as specifying the limestones of the Permian formation.

magnesian marble Applied to both dolomitic marbles and marbles with magnesian silicates. *See* OPHICALCITE; PREDAZZITE

magnesioferrite A mineral of the spinel group, $(Mg,Fe'')Fe''_2O_4$. Isometric. Strongly magnetic.

magnesite A mineral, $MgCO_3$. Hexagonal rhombohedral, usual massive to compact and earthy.

magnet *1.* Any body which orients itself in definite direction when suitably suspended in any magnetic field such as that of the earth. *2.* Any shaped mass of ferromagnetic material which has been permanently magnetized.

magnetic anomaly Any departure from the normal magnetic field of the earth as a whole. Comparable to a topographic feature on a topographic map. May be a high or a low, subcircular, ridge- or valleylike or linear- or dike-like.

magnetic declination The acute angle between the direction of the magnetic and geographic meridians. In nautical and aeronautical navigation the term magnetic variation is preferred.

magnetic dip Magnetic inclination, *q.v.*

magnetic dip pole Place where the horizontal component of the earth's magnetic field vanishes; not the same as the geomagnetic pole; it changes in position relatively rapidly.

magnetic equator The line on the surface of the earth where the magnetic needle remains horizontal, or does not dip, i.e., where the magnetic lines of force are horizontal. *Syn:* ACLINIC LINE

magnetic equipotential surface Any surface in a magnetic field which at every point is perpendicular to the intensity at that point.

magnetic field *1.* The space through which the force or influence of a magnet is exerted. *2.* The space about a conductor carrying an electric current in which, as it may be shown, magnetic force is also exerted.

magnetic field strength (H) Field intensity. The force exerted on a unit pole at any point is the field strength at that point.

magnetic flux Through any surface element it is the product of the component of the intensity normal to the surface element and its surface area. It is the average intensity over unit area of an equipotential surface.

magnetic force The force, attractive or repulsive, exerted between two magnetic poles; the force which produces or changes magnetization.

magnetic gradiometer An instrument, designed but not applied, for measuring the gradient of the magnetic intensity.

magnetic inclination; magnetic dip The acute angle between the vertical and the direction of the earth's total magnetic field in the magnetic meridian plane.

magnetic induction (B) In a magnetic medium the vector sum of the inducing field H and the corresponding intensity of magnetization I, according to the relationship $B=H+4\pi I$.

magnetic intensity Magnetic field strength, *q.v.*

magnetic line of force In general, a curved line which at each point has the direction of the force which would be exerted on a unit pole at that point. It is a concept of rather limited utility in geophysical prospecting.

magnetic meridian In general,

any isogonic line. Specifically, the direction assumed by the compass needle at any place; a magnetic north-and-south line.

magnetic moment That vector associated with a magnetized mass. The vector product of which and the magnetic field intensity in which the mass is immersed (ignoring the field distortion thereby produced) is a measure of the resulting torque.

magnetic permeability The ratio of the magnetic induction to the inducing field strength.

magnetic polarization The magnetic moment per unit volume.

magnetic pole *1.* Either of several points on the earth's surface where the lines of magnetic force are vertical; and end of the axis of the earth's magnetic polarity, not coinciding with a geographical or geomagnetic pole (*q.v.*) and slowly changing its position. The north magnetic pole is in northern Canada. *2.* One of two points near opposite ends of a magnet toward which the magnetic lines of force are oriented and concentrated; if the magnet is permitted to rotate in all directions by use of a central pivot, one pole will point in the direction of the earth's magnetic pole near the North Pole and the pole at this end is defined as the "north seeking" or positive pole of the magnet; the other pole is the "south seeking" or negative pole.

magnetic pole strength The factor by which the force exerted by a magnetic pole is greater or less than that of a unit pole.

magnetic pyrites Pyrrhotite.

magnetic recording Any process in which the output of a seismic detector-amplifier setup is recorded on a magnetic recording medium. The advantages of such a system are that the resulting records may be played back and converted into conventional records with phase shifting, mixing, etc., between traces and with filtering variations.

magnetic relief The range of values of magnetic intensity over an anomaly or over an area.

magnetic storm A considerable variation of the earth's magnetic field, with time, occurring over extensive areas. The variations are greater, more irregular and more rapid than the diurnal variations. In areas where they are frequent they present a serious obstacle to effective magnetic surveys.

magentic susceptibility A measure of the degree to which a substance is attracted to a magnet; the ratio of the intensity of magnetization to the magnetic field strength in a magnetic circuit.

magnetic unit in prospecting The gamma $(\gamma) = 10^{-5}$ oersteds.

magnetism That peculiar property possessed by certain bodies (as iron and steel) whereby, under certain circumstances, they naturally attract or repel one another according to determinate laws.

magnetite Magnetic iron ore. A mineral, of the spinel group, $Fe''Fe_2'''O_4$. Isometric, black, commonly in octahedrons. An important ore of iron. A frequent minor accessory mineral of igneous rocks.

magnetization The magnetic state of a body defined by a vector having a direction and a magnitude called the magnetic moment per unit volume; this vector may be considered as representing the number and degree of orientation of the elementary magnetic dipoles of the body.

magnetometer An instrument used for measuring magnetic intensity; in ground magnetic prospecting usually an instrument for measuring the vertical intensity; in airborne magnetic prospecting usually an instrument for measuring the total intensity. Also, instruments used in magnetic observatories for measuring various components of the magnetic field.

magnetometry Measurement of the earth's magnetic field.

magnetostriction The effect of stress on magnetization.

magnitude (of an earthquake) A quantity characteristic of the total energy released by an earthquake, as contrasted to "intensity," which describes its effects at a particular place.

malachite A mineral, $Cu_2(CO_3)$-$(OH)_2$. Monoclinic, commonly botryoidal. A common alteration product of copper ores.

Malacostraca Class of crustaceans generally consisting of 20 segments which form a head of 6 fused segments, a thorax of 8 moveable segments, and an abdomen of 6 moveable segments; includes lobsters, crabs, shrimps, etc. Ord.-Rec.

malaspina glacier Any piedmont glacier; so called from a coastal glacier, Malaspina, in Alaska.

Malm Upper Jurassic.

malpais [*Sp.* bad land] The Mauvais terre of the French. In Sonora it is exclusively applied to mesas, lomas, or any more or less elevated plateau formed by igneous rock, here mostly a compact or vesicular trap or basalt.

mammal A warm-blooded vertebrate animal that brings forth its young alive and suckles them.

Mammalia Class of vertebrates; warm-blooded animals clothed in hair which are viviparous and nurse their young. Jur.-Rec.

mammillary *Mineral:* Forming smoothly rounded masses resembling breasts or portions of spheres. Said of the shape of some mineral aggregates, as, malachite or limonite. Similar to but on a larger scale than botryoidal.

manganese hydrate Psilomelane.

manganite A mineral, $MnO(OH)$. Monoclinic.

mangrove swamp A salt or brackish marsh along the coast where there are abundant mangrove trees. This type could be further subdivided according to the type of mangrove.

mantle *1.* Layer of the earth between crust and core; bounded above by Mohorovičić discontinuity at depth of about 35 km. below the continents and about 10 km. below the oceans; bounded below by the Wiechert-Gutenberg discontinuity about 2900 km. below the surface of the earth; believed to consist of ultrabasic material. *2.* Mantle rock; regolith.

mantle rock Regolith.

map A representation on a plane surface, at an established scale, of the physical features (natural, artificial, or both) of a part or the whole of the earth's surface or of any desired surface or subsurface data, by means of signs and symbols, and with the means of orientation indicated.

A map may emphasize, generalize, or omit the representation of certain features to satisfy specific requirements. The type of information which a map is designed primarily to convey is frequently designated in adjective form to distinguish it from maps of other types. A map should carry a record of the projection upon which it is constructed.

map projection An orderly system of lines on a plane representing a corresponding system of imaginary lines on an adopted terrestrial or celestial datum surface. Also, the mathematical concept of such a system.

Marathonian orogeny Post-Pennsylvanian diastrophism.

marble A metamorphic rock composed essentially of calcite and/or dolomite. *See* CALC-SILICATE MARBLE; MAGNESIAN MARBLE

marcasite White iron pyrites. A mineral, FeS₂, the orthorhombic dimorph of pyrite. A common ore mineral.

marginal basin Submarine basin at the foot of a continental slope and bounded by an outer ridge and slightly shallower than the general level of deep ocean bottom, but part of its floor may be an abyssal plain.

marginal deep *1.* As used by Hans Stille (1919) and by J. H. F. Umbgrove this term is equivalent to exogeosyncline. *2.* A narrow linear zone of deep water adjacent to an island arc.

marginal escarpment Steep slope, generally with gradient greater than 1 in 10, occurring on the outside of a marginal platform and descending from a depth of 3000 to 9000 feet to 6000 to 12,000 feet.

marginal fissure Joints along the margin of an intrusive body that dip inward toward the intrusion.

marginal platform Submarine shelf adjacent to a continent and similar topographically to the continental shelf but occurring at a greater depth that may reach to about 7500 feet.

marginal seas Adjacent seas that are widely open to the oceans. *See* ADJACENT SEAS

marginal thrusts or **upthrusts** Thrust faults along the margin

of an intrusive that dip toward the intrusive.

marginal trench Narrow steep-sided depression extending parallel to a continental margin and generally more than 6000 feet deeper than the general level of the adjacent ocean floor from which it is separated by an outer ridge 600 to 3000 feet high.

marginal trough Idiogeosyncline.

marigram A graphic record of the rise and fall of the tide.

marine Of, or belonging to, or caused by the sea.

marine abrasion Erosion of a bedrock surface by the to-and-fro movements of an overlying layer of sand under the influence of waves.

marine-built terrace A terrace seaward of a marine-cut terrace which consists of materials removed in the cutting of the marine-cut terrace.

marine cave A cave formed by wave action; generally at sea level and affected by tides. *Syn:* SEA CAVE

marine climate The climatic type controlled by an oceanic environment, found on the windward shores of continents and on islands, and characterized, in sharp contrast to a continental climate, by small diurnal and annual temperature ranges and high relative humidity.

marine-cut terrace Plain of marine abrasion, marine denudation, marine erosion, submarine denudation. Shore platform; wave-cut plain; wave-cut terrace.

marine denudation *1.* Used to signify the wearing or scouring action of water, or any chemical process affecting the floor of the ocean. *2.* Used to describe the action of the sea in breaking up and destroying the solid land.

marine plane The final stage of

shore development will witness the extinction of all features, except only the abrasion platform and the continental terrace. If the platform were reduced practically to a plane surface before uplift, the uplifted surface may be called a plane of marine denudation, or simply a marine plane.

marker band Identifiable thin bed occurring at a particular stratigraphic position throughout a considerable area.

marker bed; marker horizon *1.* A bed which accounts for a characteristic segment of a seismic refraction time-distance curve and which can be followed over reasonably extensive areas. *2.* A bed which yields characteristic reflections over a more or less extensive area. *See* HORIZON. *3.* A stratigraphic bed selected for use in preparing structure maps, paleogeology maps and others which emphasize the nature or attitude of a plane or surface. Generally selected for lithologic characteristics, but biologic factors and unconformities may control. *Syn:* KEY BED. *See* HORIZON, *1*

marker horizon Marker bed, *1* and *2, q.v.*

marl *1.* A calcareous clay, or intimate mixture of clay and particles of calcite or dolomite, usually fragments of shells. Marl in America is chiefly applied to incoherent sands, but abroad compact, impure limestones are also called marls. *2.* Marl is an old term of considerable range of usage. In Coastal Plain geology of the United States it has been used as a name for little indurated sedimentary deposits of a wide range of composition among which are slightly to richly calcareous clays and silts;

fine-grained calcareous sands; clays, silts, and sands containing glauconite; and unconsolidated shell deposits. In the interior of the United States the name is used for the calcareous deposits of lakes in which the percentage of calcium carbonate may range from 90 to less than 30%. The name does not connote any particular composition and it would seem that it should be abandoned, but it is useless to make a recommendation to that effect as the use is so extensive that the recommendation would be ignored. A writer should always define his meaning when the term is used. Preferred: a calcareous clay.

marlstone; marlite An indurated mixture of clay materials and calcium carbonate (rarely dolomite), normally containing 25% to 75% clay.

marly Resembling marl; abounding with marl.

marmatite A dark iron-rich variety of sphalerite.

marsh *1.* Marshes proper are shallow lakes, the waters of which are either stagnant or actuated by a very feeble current; they are, at least in the temperate zone, filled with rushes, reeds, and sedge and are often bordered by trees which love to plunge their roots into the muddy soil. In the tropical zone a large number of marshes are completely hidden by a multitude of plants or forests of trees, between the crowded trunks of which the black and stagnant water can only here and there be seen. *2.* A tract of low, wet ground, usually miry and covered with rank vegetation. It may, at times, be sufficiently dry to permit tillage or hay-cutting, but requires drainage to make it permanently arable. It may be very small and situated high on a mountain, or of great extent and adjacent to the sea. *Cf.* BOG; SWAMP

Marshall line Andesite line.

marsh buggy A special, self-propelled geophysical vehicle designed to operate over marsh or extremely soft ground, usually having wheels with very wide tread or buoyant wheels which will float the vehicle in water.

marsh gas Methane (CH_4), the chief constituent of natural gas. Results also from the partial decay of plants in swamps. In the miner's language, synonymous with fire damp.

Marsupialia Subclass of mammals generally with a marsupial pouch whose young are born in a very immature condition.

martite Ferric oxide, Fe_2O_3, occurring in iron-black octahedral crystals; a pseudomorph after magnetite.

mashing Excessive granulation of a rock by crushing, accompanied by the displacement of the granules and often by recrystallization involving flow of the rock.

mass action, law of The rate of reaction occurring at constant temperature is proportional to the product of the "active masses of the reacting substances."

mass effect Solid-angle effect, *q.v.*

massif [*Fr.*] *1. Geol.* and *Phys. geog:* A mountainous mass or a group of connected heights, whether isolated or forming a part of a larger mountain system. A massif is more or less clearly marked off by valleys. *2.* Isolated mountains rarely occur; they are either ranged together in a chain, or form some irregular combination, so as to consti-

tute a group (massif) about the central summit. *3.* A mountainous mass which breaks up into peaks towards the summit, and has relatively uniform characteristics. *4.* Body of intrusive igneous or metamorphic rock at least 10 to 20 miles in diameter occurring as a structurally resistant mass in an uplifted area that may have been a mountain core.

massive *1. Petrol:* (a) Of homogeneous structure, without stratification, flow-banding, foliation, schistosity, and the like; said of the structure of some rocks. Often, but incorrectly, used as synonymous with igneous and eruptive. (b) Occurring in thick beds, free from minor joints and lamination; said of some stratified rocks. *2. Mineral:* Without definite crystalline structure; amorphous; not a very good usage. *3.* Applied to shale to indicate it is very hard to split. *4.* A term properly applied to strata more than 100 mm. in thickness.

massive oölith Interior of granular, smooth, or chalk-textured material comprising nearly the entire mass of the spheroid.

mass movement Unit movement of a portion of the land surface as in creep, landslide, or slip.

mass number For any isotope, the sum of the number of neutrons plus protons in the nuclei of its atoms.

mass properties The properties of a sediment as an aggregate, including porosity, permeability, density, color, etc.

mass spectrometer An instrument for separation and measurement of isotopic species by their mass.

mass susceptibility; specific susceptibility The magnetic susceptibility per unit mass, therefore equal to the magnetic susceptibility divided by the density.

mass transport The net transfer of water by wave action in the direction of wave travel. *See* ORBIT

mass-wasting *1.* The slow downslope movement of rock debris. *2.* A general term for a variety of processes by which large masses of earth material are moved by gravity either slowly or quickly from one place to another.

master fracture *1.* Zone of disturbance peripheral to a continent extending to a depth of several hundred miles and including the foci of deep-seated earthquakes. *2.* Great faults or fault systems generally involving much lateral movement that have played a prominent part in the development of earth structure.

master river One of the larger and dominating rivers of the drainage system of the land sculpture and base-leveling of any area of the earth's surface.

master station A radio transmitting station from which the signals of other transmitters (slave stations) are controlled. Used in radio positioning and navigation systems.

Mastigophora Flagellata. Class of protozoans having one or more flagella, which are used for locomotion.

matrix *1.* In a rock in which certain grains are much larger than the others, the grains of smaller size comprise the matrix. The groundmass of porphyritic igneous rocks. *2.* The natural material in which any metal, fossil, pebble, crystal, etc., is embedded.

matterhorn A sharp, hornlike or pyramid-shaped mountain peak, somewhat resembling the Swiss peak of that name. *See* ARÊTE

mature *1.* Having reached the maximum vigor and efficiency of action or the maximum development and accentuation of form. Said of streams, the sculpture of land by erosion, and the resultant topography. *Cf.* YOUNG; OLD. *2.* Said also of sediment that is a long and complete cycle or two or more cycles removed from the original crystalline parent rock, so that all or nearly all weatherable material is absent.

mature conglomerate A conglomerate consisting chiefly of well-sorted, stable constituents.

mature river A river in the third and most perfect stage of development.

mature shore With a given set of conditions, waves tend to develop a certain sort of shore line which, so far as its horizontal form is concerned, is relatively stable. Such a shore line may be said to be "mature."

mature soil A soil with well-developed characteristics produced by the natural processes of soil formation, and in equilibrium with its environment. Generally consists of several differently characterized zones. *See* SOIL PROFILE

mature valley Mature valleys are wider, deeper, and have gentler gradients and more and larger tributaries than young valleys. In early maturity they are roughly U-shaped, instead of V-shaped, as before. In late maturity they have conspicuous flats. These changes in cross section signify that downcutting has come to be very slow, and that the processes which widen valleys and reduce their sides to gentler slopes have become much more important, relatively.

mature wave platform The mature wave platform is characterized by the abundance of rocky debris which is constantly moved by the waves, but which has not yet reached the pebble condition. The occurrence of reefs projecting above the general level of the beach is also equally characteristic of the mature wave platform.

maturity *1.* Maturity may be said to last through the period of greatest diversity of form, or maximum topographic differentiation, but until about three-quarters of the original mass are carried away. During maturity no vestige of plain surface remains. *2.* That stage in the development of streams or in land sculpture at which the process is going on with maximum vigor and efficiency or the maximum development and accentuation has been reached. *Cf.* YOUTH; OLD AGE

maturity index The measure of the progress of a sediment in the direction of chemical stability. A sediment may be said to be mature when it contains only the most stable mineral species and is relatively deficient in the more mobile oxides.

maximum *1. Struct. petrol:* A place on a point diagram or contour diagram, *q.v.*, where there is a concentration of points. There may be several maxima within one diagram. *2.* **gravity; magnetic; radioactivity** An anomaly in which the intensity has greater values at a central area compared to its immediate environment. *Syn:* HIGH

maxwell The practical, electromagnetic unit of magnetic flux in the c.g.s. system. Equal to one gauss-cm.^{2}.

Maysvillian Lower middle Cincinnatian.

M-boundary or **M-discontinuity** Mohorovičić discontinuity.

m.c.f. An abbreviation for one thousand cubic feet.

M crust Crustal layer, probably basaltic and about 8.3 km. thick, immediately above the Mohorovičić discontinuity in which plastic deformation occurs only as the result of tectonic disturbance.

meadow A bit of natural grassland in wooded mountains; a glade or small park; a tract of low or level grassland; a field on which grass is grown for hay.

meager quantities of water Less than 1500 gallons per day. *Cf.* ENORMOUS; VERY LARGE; LARGE; MODERATE; SMALL; VERY SMALL

mean The sum of a set of individual values of any quantity, divided by the number of values in the set. Though essentially the same as the average and the normal, it is distinguished from the latter in meteorological usage; in processing temperature data, for example, the daily mean temperature is the average of the maximum and minimum temperatures for the day, while the normal temperature for the day is the average of the daily means over a long period of years.

meander *1.* One of a series of somewhat regular and looplike bends in the course of a stream, developed when the stream is flowing at grade, through lateral shifting of its course toward the convex sides of the original curves. *2.* A land-survey traverse along the bank of a permanent natural body of water.

meander belt *1.* The part of a flood plain between two lines tangent to the outer bends of all the meanders. *2.* The zone within which channel migration occurs. Within such a zone channel migration is indicated by abandoned channels, accretion topography, oxbow lakes. This is an engineering usage but is not recommended for geology.

meander core The central hill encircled by the meander.

meander cusp The eroded edge of an alluvial terrace made by a meandering stream.

meandering stream A characteristic habit of mature rivers; may be defined as winding freely on a broad flood plain, in rather regular river-developed curves. Under special conditions meanders may occur on plains not essentially river-made, i.e., not flood plains or incised below their original level.

meander line A surveyed line, usually irregular, but not a boundary line. A traverse line.

meander neck Strip of land between adjacent loops of a meandering stream.

meander scar Crescentic cuts in the upland bordering a stream, which were cut by lateral planation on the outer part of the meander loop.

meander scroll *1.* Point bar. *2.* Lake in well-defined portion of an abandoned river channel, commonly an oxbow.

meander spur A projection of high land into the concave part of a meander that has been undercut.

mean diameter, geometric The diameter equivalent of the arithmetic mean of the logarithmic frequency distribution. In the analysis of beach sands it is taken as that grain diameter determined graphically by the intersection of a straight line through selected boundary sizes (generally points on the distribution curve where 16 and 84 per cent of the sample by weight is coarser) and a vertical line through the median diameter of the sample.

mean higher high water The average height of the higher high waters over a 19-year period. For shorter periods of observation, corrections are applied to eliminate known variations and reduce the result to the equivalent of a mean 19-year value.

mean high water The average height of the high waters over a 19-year period. For shorter periods of observations, corrections are applied to eliminate known variations and reduce the result to the equivalent of a mean 19-year value. All high-water heights are included in the average where the type of tide is either semidiurnal or mixed. Only the higher high-water heights are included in the average where the type of tide is diurnal. So determined, mean high water in the latter case is the same as mean higher high water.

mean lower low water Frequently abbreviated lower low water. The average height of the lower low waters over a 19-year period. For shorter periods of observations, corrections are applied to eliminate known variations and reduce the result to the equivalent of a mean 19-year value.

mean low water The average height of the low waters over a 19-year period. For shorter periods of observations, corrections are applied to eliminate known variations and reduce the result to the equivalent of a mean 19-year value. All low-water heights are included in the average where the type of tide is either semidiurnal or mixed. Only the lower low-water heights are included in the average where the type of tide is diurnal. So determined, mean low water in the latter case is the same as mean lower low water.

mean refractive index The mean of the values of the index of refraction for the extreme red and the extreme violet rays.

mean sea level The average height of the sea for all stages of the tide.

Mean sea level is obtained by averaging observed hourly heights of the sea on the open coast or in adjacent waters having free access to the sea, the average being taken over a considerable period of time.

mean stress Algebraic average of three principal stresses.

mechanical analysis An analysis of the particle-size distribution of a sediment.

mechanical origin When the origin of a rock is effected by an external force, as, water flowing in streams, currents, etc., it is used in contradistinction to rocks which may be said to have a chemical origin, or whose particles have been consolidated by a chemical force.

mechanical seismograph A seismic detector in which, except for the mirror and beam of light, all amplification of the ground motion is accomplished by mechanical means. Now little used but employed extensively in earliest seismic prospecting.

mechanical twinning Deformation twinning, *q.v.*

medial moraine *1.* Whenever two mountain glaciers bearing lateral moraines unite, the lateral moraines belonging to the two margins which coalesce give rise to a medial moraine. *2.* An elongate body of drift formed by the joining of adjacent lateral

moraines below the juncture of two valley glaciers. First used by Louis Agassiz.

median diameter The diameter which marks the division of a given sample into two equal parts by weight, one part containing all grains larger than that diameter and the other part containing all grains smaller.

median particle diameter A measure of average particle size obtained graphically by locating the diameter associated with the midpoint of the particle-size distribution.

Medinian Lower Silurian (restricted).

mediterranean *1.* If the sea penetrates into the interior of any continent, it forms there a mediterranean or inland sea, surrounded almost on all sides by land and leaving only a narrow opening into the ocean. *2.* Mesogeosyncline, *q.v.*

Mediterranean climate Climate characterized by summer drought and winter rain.

Mediterranean series, province, or **suite** A third great group of igneous rock magmas, high in potassium, and typified by certain igneous rocks in the Mediterranean area. *See* ATLANTIC and PACIFIC SERIES

medium *1.* The physical substance or environment as defined by its pertinent physical properties, e.g., a magnetic medium; one that is magnetizable. *2.* A substance on which a force acts or through which an effect is transmitted.

medium-volatile bituminous coal Nonagglomerating bituminous coal having 69% or more, and less than 78%, of fixed carbon (dry, mineral-matter-free), 31% or less, and more than 22%, of volatile matter (dry, mineral-matter-free).

medusa A coelenterate without hard parts whose body is umbrellalike with tentacles growing from its margin; a jellyfish or the sexual generation of a hydrozoan.

meerschaum *See* SEPIOLITE

mega- *1.* A combining term meaning large. As a prefix to petrological and other geological terms it signifies parts or properties that are recognizable by the unaided eye. *Ant:* MICRO. *2.* Combining form meaning one million times, e.g., megavolts, one million volts.

megacycle One million cycles. *See* CYCLE

megacyclothem A rhythm of larger order than a single cyclothem, which includes distinct cycles of cyclothems.

megalospheric; megaspheric One of two different kinds of test which occur in many species of Foraminifera because of alternation of sexual and asexual modes of reproduction; the type of test which is small in over-all size but which has a large proloculus.

megaripple Large gentle ripplelike feature composed of sand in very shallow marine situations; wave lengths reach 100 m. and amplitude about 1/2 m.; may be formed by tidal currents.

megascopic Macroscopic. A term applied to observations made with the unaided eye, as opposed to microscopic, made with the aid of the microscope. The term macroscopic is synonymous, but megascopic is preferred.

megashear A transcurrent fault of very large displacement, in excess of 100 kilometers.

megaspore *1.* Relatively large plant spore germinating into a multicellular gametophyte that produces female gametes. *2.* Fossil spore larger than 200μ.

Meinesz zone Relatively long narrow continuous zone of marked negative gravity anomalies.

Meinzer unit The permeability unit most generally applicable to groundwater work and expressed in units of gallon, day, and square foot.

meizoseismal Of, or pertaining to, the maximum destructive force of an earthquake.

meizoseismal curve A curved line connecting the points of the maximum destructive energy of an earthquake shock around its epicentrum.

mela- [<*Gr.* melas, black] Prefix meaning dark colored. *See* MELANO-

melanic Dark colored; refers to igneous rocks with color index between 30 and 90.

melanite A black variety of andradite garnet.

melano- [*Gr.*] Prefix meaning black or dark.

melanocratic Applied to dark-colored rocks, especially igneous rocks, containing between 60 and 100% of dark minerals, i.e., rocks whose color index is between 60 and 100. *See* LEUCOCRATIC; MESOCRATIC

melanterite Copperas. A mineral, $FeSO_4 \cdot 7H_2O$, an alteration product of iron sulfides. Monoclinic.

melilite A mineral group, of general formula $(Na,Ca)_2(Mg,Al)$-$(Al,Si)_2O_7$, the most common end-members including $Ca_2MgSi_2O_7$ (akermanite) and $Ca_2Al_2SiO_7$ (gehlenite). Tetragonal.

mellorite *See* FIRE-CLAY MINERAL

melting point That temperature at which a single pure solid phase changes to a liquid or a liquid plus another solid phase, upon the addition of heat at a specific pressure. Unless otherwise specified, melting points are usually stated in terms of one atmosphere pressure. The term can also be used for the isothermal melting of certain mixtures, such as eutectics. Erroneously and loosely used also to refer to the temperature at which some appreciable but unspecified amount of liquid phase develops in a complex solid mixture that possesses a melting range, e.g., the melting point of granite.

melt water; meltwater Water resulting from the melting of snow or of glacier ice.

member In the usage of the U. S. Geological Survey, a division of a formation, generally of distinct lithologic character or of only local extent. A specially developed part of a varied formation is called a member, if it has considerable geographic extent. Members are commonly, though not necessarily, named.

mendip A hill on a coastal plain which at one time was an offshore island.

Menevian Middle Cambrian.

meniscus The surface of a liquid column. Its curvature is determined by the surface tension, being concave when the walls are wetted by the liquid and convex when not.

Meotian Lower Lower Pliocene.

Meramecian Lower Upper Mississippian.

Mercator map projection A conformal map projection of the so-called cylindrical type. The equator is represented by a straight line true to scale; the geographic meridians are represented by parallel straight lines perpendicular to the line representing the equator; they are spaced according to their distance apart at the equator. The geographic parallels are represented by a second system of straight lines perpendicular to the family of lines representing the meridians, and therefore parallel with the equator. Conformality is achieved by mathematical analysis, the spacing of the parallels being increased with increasing distance from the equator to conform with the expanding scale along the parallels resulting from the meridians being represented by parallel lines.

The Mercator map projection is considered one of the most valuable of all map projections, its most useful feature being that a line of constant bearing (azimuth) on a sphere is represented on the projection by a straight line. It is not a perspective projection on a cylinder, and is not developed geometrically.

mercurial horn ore Horn quicksilver; calomel, *q.v.*

meridian A north-south line from which longitudes (or departures) and azimuths are reckoned; or a plane, normal to the geoid or spheroid, defining such a line.

meridian, magnetic The vertical plane in which a freely suspended symmetrically magnetized needle, influenced by no transient artificial magnetic disturbance, will come to rest. Also, a curve on the earth's surface tangent to such a plane at each place it touches.

meridian, principal (United States public-land surveys) A line extending north and south along the astronomical meridian passing through the initial point, along which township, section, and quarter-section corners are established. The principal meridian is the line from which is initiated the survey of the township boundaries along the parallels.

mero- [<*Gr.* meros] A prefix meaning part, or fraction.

merocrystalline, *adj.* Hypocrystalline; semicrystalline; hemicrystalline. Hypocrystalline is preferred.

merohedral Merosymmetric.

Merostomata Class of arthropods including eurypterids and horseshoe crabs. Camb.-Rec.

merostome A type of arthropod, e.g., the horseshoe crab, the eurypterid, etc.

merosymmetric *Crystallog:* Having only part of the maximum symmetry of the crystal system concerned.

mesa [*Sp.*] A tableland; a flat-topped mountain or other elevation bounded on at least one side by a steep cliff; a plateau terminating on one or more sides in a steep cliff. Local in Southwest.

meseta [*Sp.*] A tableland.

mesh *1.* One of the openings or spaces in a screen. The value of the mesh is usually given as the number of openings per linear inch. This gives no recognition to the diameter of the wire, so that the mesh number does not always have a definite relation to the size of the hole. *2.* The unit component of patterned ground, e.g., circle, polygon, or intermediate form, not step or stripe.

mesh texture *See* RETICULATE

meso- [*Gr.*] Prefix used to denote rocks belonging to the "middle zone" of metamorphism; i.e., produced by high temperature, hydrostatic pressure, and intense stress. *See* APO-; CATA-; EPI-; KATA-; META-

mesocratic Applied to rocks, especially igneous rocks, containing between 30 and 60% of dark minerals, i.e., rocks whose color

index is intermediate between leucocratic and melanocratic.

Mesocryptozoic Middle Precambrian.

mesocrystalline, *adj.* The texture of recrystallized rocks with crystal or grain size ranging from 0.20 to 0.75 mm.

mesoderm Intermediate body layer present in animals more highly organized than the coelenterates.

mesogene Refers to an environment of mingled hypogene and supergene fluids.

mesogeosyncline A deep complex geosyncline occurring between two closely adjacent continents.

mesohaline *See* BRACKISH

mesolittoral zone Shore zone between high and low tides. *Cf.* LITTORAL

mesonorm Theoretical calculation of minerals in metamorphic rocks of the mesozone as indicated by chemical analyses.

mesosiderite A stony-iron meteorite consisting of nickel-iron enclosing patches of stony matter composed of hypersthene and anorthite; olivine is also present, but generally as separately enclosed crystals, usually of fairly large size.

mesosphere *1.* Theoretical thick strong layer within the earth separating the asthenosphere and central iron core. *2.* Outer part of atmosphere between about 400 and 1000 km. elevation.

mesothermal Condition of ore deposition at intermediate temperature and depth.

mesothermal climate A type of climate marked by moderate temperature and rainfall and by ample sunshine. Regions having such a climate lie, in general, between 30° and 40° latitude, though they extend farther poleward on the west coast of the continents. The

Mediterranean climate is a distinct variety of this climatic type, which is named for the mesotherms, or that great variety of plants of the lower middle latitudes requiring considerable heat, but tolerant of short cold winters and also of a dry season.

Mesozoic One of the grand divisions or eras of geologic time, following the Paleozoic and succeeded by the Cenozoic era, comprising the Triassic, Jurassic, and Cretaceous periods. Also the group of strata formed during that era.

mesozone *1.* The "middle zone" of metamorphism. In this zone the distinctive physical conditions are high temperature and hydrostatic pressure and intense stress, and the rocks characteristically produced include mica schists, garnetiferous and staurolite schists, hornblende schists, amphibolite, and various types of crystalline limestones, quartzites, and gneisses. *2.* The intermediate metamorphic zone in the depth zone classification of metamorphic rock, characterized by minerals such as kyanite, staurolite, almandine, zoisite, etc.

meta- [*Gr.*] Prefix used to denote metamorphism of rock qualified. *See* APO-; CATA-; EPI-; KATA-; MESO-. A prefix used before the names of igneous rocks to signify that the mineral and chemical composition of the latter have been modified by alteration.

meta-argillite Rock characterized by weak metamorphic reconstitution, no recrystallization, and without slaty cleavage or foliation.

metabentonite Originally used to designate metamorphosed bentonite; loosely used to refer to potassium bentonite, *q.v.*

metacinnabar A mineral, HgS,

dimorphous with cinnabar. Isometric. Black. A minor ore of mercury.

metacryst Any large crystal developed in a metamorphic rock by recrystallization, such as garnet or staurolite in mica schists. *Syn:* PORPHYROBLAST

metadiorite *1.* Metamorphosed diorite. *2.* Metamorphosed gabbro or diabase. *3.* Metamorphosed sedimentary rock in which both the minerals and texture of a diorite have been produced.

metagenesis Alternation of generation.

metagranite Granite produced by metamorphism without even partial remelting.

metahalloysite *See* HALLOYSITE

metal *1.* Any of a class of substances that typically are fusible and opaque, are good conductors of electricity, and show a peculiar metallic luster, as, gold, bronze, aluminum, etc. Most metals are also malleable and comparatively heavy, and all except mercury are solid at ordinary temperatures. Metals constitute over three-fourths of the recognized elements. They form oxides and hydroxides that are basic, and they may exist in solution as positive ions. *2.* Ore from which a metal is derived. *3.* *Coal min:* In northern England, indurated clay or shale. *See* BIND. *4.* Cast iron, more particularly while melted. *5.* Broken stone for road surfaces or for railway ballast. *6.* Molten glass. *7.* Railway rails. *8.* Copper regulus or matte obtained in the English process. The following varieties are distinguished by appearance and by their percentage of copper (here given in approximate figures): coarse, 20 to 40; red, 48; blue, 60; sparkle, 74; white, 77; pimple, 79. Fine metal includes the latter four varieties. Hard metal is impure copper containing a large amount of tin. *9.* In Scotland, all the rocks penetrated in mining ore. *10.* Road metal; rock used in macadamizing roads.

metallic *1.* Of or belonging to metals, containing metals, more particularly the valuable metals that are the object of mining. *2.* Applied to minerals having the luster of a metal, as, gold, copper, etc.

metallic luster A luster characteristic of metals in a compact state, and shown also by some other substances, as certain minerals. It is due to more or less of selective absorption in the surface layer, combined with a strong reflection.

metallogenic mineral Ore mineral.

metallogenetic or **minerogenetic epoch** The time interval favorable for the deposition of certain useful substances.

metallogenetic province *See* MINEROGENETIC PROVINCE

metallogeny *Geol:* The branch which deals with the origin of ore deposits.

metalloid *1.* An alkali metal, as sodium, or an alkaline-earth metal, as calcium; so called by Sir Humphry Davy because they were not supposed to be well-defined metals. *2.* Certain elements, as arsenic, antimony, that share the properties of metals and nonmetals. *3.* Having the appearance of a metal.

metallurgy The science and art of preparing metals for use from their ores by separating them from mechanical mixture and chemical combination. It includes various processes, as smelting, amalgamation, electrolytic refining, etc. Metallurgy, as generally understood, is concerned with the production of raw metallic materials, the manufacture of which into finished articles belongs to other arts.

metamict, *adj.* A term used to denote minerals whose crystalline structure has been at least in part altered by atomic rearrangement caused by radioactive emanations from uranium or thorium contained in the mineral.

metamorphic differentiation Segregation of certain minerals into lenses and bands accomplished by metamorphism.

metamorphic facies Group of metamorphic rocks characterized by particular mineral associations indicating origin under restricted temperature-pressure conditions.

metamorphic grade The grade or rank of metamorphism depends upon the extent to which the metamorphic rock differs from the original rock from which it was derived. If a shale is converted to slate or phyllite the metamorphism is low grade, if it is converted to mica schist with garnet, staurolite, or kyanite the metamorphism is middle grade, and if it is converted to mica schist with garnet and sillimanite the metamorphism is high grade.

metamorphic rank Metamorphic grade.

metamorphic rock Includes all those rocks which have formed in the solid state in response to pronounced changes of temperature, pressure, and chemical environment, which take place, in general, below the shells of weathering and cementation.

metamorphic water Water that is or has been associated with rocks during their metamorphism.

metamorphism Process by which consolidated rocks are altered in composition, texture, or internal structure by conditions and forces not resulting simply from burial and the weight of subsequently accumulated overburden. Pressure, heat, and the introduction of new chemical substances are the principal causes, and the resulting changes, which generally include the development of new minerals, are a thermodynamic response to a greatly altered environment. Diagenesis has been considered to be incipient metamorphism. *See* CONTACT, THERMAL, DYNAMIC, REGIONAL, HIGH RANK, and LOW RANK METAMORPHISM

metamorphosis *Biol:* Process of more or less complete bodily reorganization of an animal that transforms a larva into a succeeding stage of development and growth; common in many invertebrates.

metasediments Partly metamorphosed sedimentary rocks.

metasomatic *Geol:* Characteristic of, pertaining to, produced by, or occurring during metasomatosis. The term is especially used in connection with the origin of ore deposits. The corresponding noun is metasomatosis, but "replacement" is a good English equivalent.

metasomatism *1.* (Replacement) The process of practically simultaneous capillary solution and deposition by which a new mineral of partly or wholly differing chemical composition may grow in the body of an old mineral or mineral aggregate. *2.* The processes by which one mineral is replaced by another of different chemical composition owing to reactions set up by the introduction of material from external sources. *3.* A practically simultaneous solution and deposition, through small openings,

usually submicroscopic, and mainly by hypogene water solutions, by which a new mineral of partly or wholly differing composition may grow in the body of an old mineral or mineral aggregate.

metasomatite A rock in which one substance has completely replaced another, or certain ones completely replace others, producing an entirely new composition.

metasome An individual mineral developed in another mineral.

metastable, *adj. 1.* Stable with respect to small disturbances, but capable of reaction with evolution of energy if disturbed sufficiently. E.g., a mixture of hydrogen and oxygen is metastable, because it is unchanged by jarring or by mild warming, but explodes violently if touched by a flame. *2.* Any phase is said to be metastable when it exists in the temperature range in which another phase of lower vapor pressure is stable. It is not necessary that a vapor phase be present. Metastability is sometimes confused with instability, refers to a phase existing temporarily under conditions where it is in the process of changing, e.g., a piece of ice in hot water. In the general case, metastability results from the reluctance of the system to initiate the formation of new (stable) phase, i.e., nucleation.

metastasis Lateral shifting of the earth's crust as in the movement of continental masses.

metastasy Metastasis.

metatype *1.* Topotype identified by the original author of a species. *2.* Any specimen so identified.

metavolcanics Partly metamorphosed volcanic rocks.

Metazoa The large group of animals which have bodies consisting of more than one cell, as opposed to Protozoa, which are one-celled animals.

meteor Originally a general term for any atmospheric phenomenon, and still sometimes used in this sense, particularly in such terms as hydrometeor, optical meteor, etc. Now more commonly restricted to astronomical meteors—sometimes called shooting or falling stars—which are relatively small bodies of matter traveling through interplanetary space, and which are heated to incandescence by friction when they enter the atmosphere, and are either wholly or partially consumed; in the latter case they reach the earth's surface as meteorites.

meteor crater Topographic depression formed by the impact of a large meteor.

meteoric Of or belonging to a meteor, or to the atmosphere. Thus meteoric erosion implies that caused by rain, wind, or other weathering forces of the atmosphere.

meteoric water That which occurs in or is derived from the atmosphere.

meteorite Naturally occurring mass of matter that has fallen to the earth's surface from outer space.

meteorology The science dealing with the atmosphere and its phenomena, especially as relating to weather.

meter; metre A unit of length equivalent in the United States to 39.37 inches exactly.

methane A gaseous hydrocarbon, formula CH_4; the simplest member of the paraffin series. *See* MARSH GAS

method of least squares A mathematical method for deter-

mining: (a) the most probable value of a single quantity from a number of measurements of that quantity; (b) the probable error of the mean value of a number of observations; (c) the best curve which may be drawn for a series of observed values of the ordinate over a range of values of the abscissa.

methylene iodide CH_2I_2. In pure form, a straw-colored liquid with a specific gravity of 3.32 at 18° C., a m.p. between 5° and 6° C., a decomposition point of 180° C., and a refractive index of 1.74. Used especially as a component of refractive index liquids and in mineral separation.

mev Abbreviation for million electron volts.

mho A unit of electrical conductance, the reciprocal ohm.

miargyrite A mineral, $AgSbS_2$. Monoclinic.

miarolitic *Petrol:* Applied to small angular cavities in plutonic rocks, especially common in granites, into which small crystals of the rock-forming mineral project. Also said of igneous rocks containing such cavities; characteristic of, pertaining to, or occurring in such cavities.

mica A mineral group, consisting of phyllosilicates with sheet-like structures. Mostly monoclinic, characterized by very perfect basal cleavage. The general formula of the group is (K,Na,Ca) $(Mg, Fe, Li,Al)_{2-3}$ $(Al, Si)_4$-$O_{10}(OH,F)_2$. *See* BIOTITE; LEPIDOLITE; MUSCOVITE; PARAGONITE; PHLOGOPITE; ROSCOELITE

mica book Mica crystal that splits readily into thin elastic layers.

micelle A small body or volume of regularity in the arrangement of smaller constituent entities as contrasted with surrounding non-regularity.

micro- [<*Gr.* mikro-] *1.* Combining form meaning the one-millionth part of, e.g., microgram, the one-millionth part of a gram. *2.* Combining form meaning very small, e.g., microseismic, very small seismic disturbances or microammeter, a meter for measuring currents in the microampere range.

microchemical tests Chemical tests made on minute objects under a microscope. The form, color, and optical properties of the minute crystals are also used.

microclimate The detailed climate of a very small area of the earth's surface, e.g., a single forest, over which small variations exist from place to place, differing from the general climate of the surrounding region. To obtain records for microclimatic studies weather stations are spaced at short intervals, i.e., from 1 to 5 miles apart, occasionally as close as a few feet apart.

microcline A mineral, a member of the feldspar group. Composition $KAlSi_3O_8$. Triclinic; dimorphous with orthoclase. A common mineral of granite rocks.

microcrystalline Applied to a rock in which the individual crystals can only be seen as such under the microscope.

microevolution Evolution occurring within a continuous population; does not result in the development of genetic discontinuities.

microfabric Refers to the microscopic physical constitution of rock.

microfarad The one-millionth part of a farad, *q.v.*

microfold A fold so small that it is observable only in thin section under the petrographic microscope. Generally shown by the parallel arrangement of some elongated crystals.

microfoliation A foliation in rocks distinguished only with the aid of the microscope.

microfossils *1.* Fossil remains of organisms whose average representatives are microscopic in size. *2.* Fossil remains of microscopic organisms (as in *1* above) and also the fossil remains of skeletal elements of organisms commonly occurring in detached form and requiring microscopic study for identification. *3.* Fossil remains as in *1* and *2* and also the depionic and neanic stages of megafossils, as well as dwarfed forms.

microgranular *See* MICROCRYSTALLINE

microlaterolog (Schlumberger) A log obtained with an arrangement of electrodes similar to a miniature laterolog but disposed in concentric fashion in an insulating pad. The current from a central electrode is focused and flows out in a pattern which is reminiscent of the shape of a trumpet, hence the synonym trumpet log. As in the microlog, the electrodes are mounted on a pad which is held against the wall of the hole by springs. The microlaterolog serves a purpose similar to that of a microlog, investigating only a small volume of rock immediately adjacent to the hole.

microlite *1.* A mineral, $(Ca,Na)_2(Ta,Nb)O_6(OH,F)$. Isometric. An ore of tantalum. *Cf.* PYROCHLORE. *2.* A minute crystal.

microlitic A textural term applied to porphyritic igneous rocks whose groundmasses consist of an aggregate of differently oriented or parallelly oriented microlites in a base that is generally glassy. Hyalopilitic, pilotaxitic, and trachytic textures are all included under this term. When the microlites are not in parallel arrangement, the term felty is synonymous.

microlog (Schlumberger) A resistivity log in borehole surveying obtained with a device consisting of closely spaced electrodes, the arrangement of which is basically the same but in miniature, as the normal and lateral devices in the regular electric survey (ES), *q.v.* It is designed to measure the resistivity of a small volume of rock next to the borehole. To this end the electrodes are mounted on an insulating pad which is pressed against the face of the well bore by means of springs. The spacing between electrodes is 1″. The log distinguishes porous and permeable beds from impervious layers by detecting the filter cake deposited on the borehole face by invading drilling fluid.

micron A unit of length equal to the one one-millionth of a meter and usually denoted by the symbol μ.

micrometrics The study of very fine particles.

micromillimeter 1/1,000,000 mm., abbreviation Mμ.

micropaleobotany Refers, in general, to all the varied microscopical studies of fossil plants.

micropaleontology Paleontology dealing with microfossils. *Syn:* MICROGEOLOGY

microperthite A fine-grained intergrowth of potassic and sodic feldspar visible only with the aid of the microscope. *See* PERTHITE

microphotograph Greatly enlarged photograph made through a microscope.

micropoikilitic Microscopically poikilitic, a microscopic shiller structure. *See* POIKILITIC

microporphyritic Microscopically porphyritic. Essentially synonymous with microphyric.

microscope An instrument used for obtaining magnified images of small objects. The simple microscope is a convex lens of short focal length, used to form a virtual image of an object placed just inside its principal focus. The compound microscope consists of two short-focus convex lenses, the objective and the eyepiece mounted at opposite ends of a tube. For most microscopes, the magnifying power is roughly equal to $450/f_of_e$, where f_o and f_e are the focal lengths of objective and eyepiece, respectively, in centimeters.

microscopic *1.* Of, pertaining to, or conducted with the microscope or microscopy; as, a microscopic examination. *2.* Like a microscope; able to see very minute objects. *3.* So small or fine as to be invisible or not clearly distinguished without the use of a microscope. Hence, loosely, very small; minute. Microscopically, *adv.*

microseismometer; microseismograph An apparatus for indicating the direction, duration, and intensity of microseisms.

microseisms More or less persistent feeble earth tremors due to natural causes such as winds or wars.

microspheric Refers to one form of dimorphic Foraminifera which begins with a small initial chamber and grows to a relatively large size.

microsplit A small sample splitter designed to handle minor volumes of material.

microstructure A structural feature of rocks that can be discerned only with the aid of the microscope. *Ant:* MACROSTRUCTURE

microstylolite A type of microscopic grain boundary relationship indicating differential solution between two mineral grains and characterized by fine interpenetrating teeth; boundary often marked by a little opaque material concentrated along it. *Cf.* STYLOLITES

microtectonics That phase of structural geology dealing with small features, especially those that must be investigated under the microscope.

midden *1.* Accumulation of refuse around a dwelling place. 2. Moundlike accumulation of calcareous sediment trapped or bound together by algal growth.

middle limb The overturned limb shared by a pair of adjacent overturned anticline and syncline.

mid-ocean canyon Steep-walled, flat-floored continuous depression up to 5 miles wide and 600 feet deep that traverses an abyssal plain; such canyons commonly lead into or out of abyssal gaps.

mid-oceanic islands Isolated features of the earth's relief which rise from the deep-sea floor. They are chiefly volcanic and composed of basaltic lava. A few are limestone reefs, but these structures appear to have grown up on an eroded basement of volcanic rock.

mid-ocean ridge Great median arch or swell of the sea bottom extending the length of an ocean basin and roughly paralleling the continental margins; one in the Atlantic is several hundred miles wide, very irregular topographically, and rises at some places to form islands.

Midwayan Lower lower Eocene or Paleocene.

migma *1.* A term, originally proposed by M. Reinhard in 1934, which has been variously used, but in general signifies a material having many if not all characteristics in common with magma, but derived from the granitization process. Differentiated from magma only on a genetic basis. 2. Viscous, domed masses (diapirs) rising in orogenic zones, in a way to leave it very uncertain whether there is a magma or not.

migmatite Rock consisting of thin alternating layers or lenses of granite type and schist. *Cf.* COMPOSITE GNEISS; INJECTION GNEISS

migration The movement of oil, gas, or water through porous and permeable rock. Parallel (longitudinal) migration is movement parallel to the bedding plane. Transverse migration is movement across the bedding planes.

migratory dune A dune, such as the barchan, which undergoes a translocation more or less as a unit under continued wind action.

mil A unit of length equal to the one-thousandth part of an inch. Most commonly used in measuring the diameters of wires.

mile, nautical A length of mile used in ocean navigation. The United States nautical mile is defined as equal to one-sixtieth of a degree of a great circle on a sphere whose surface is equal to the surface of the earth. Its value, calculated for the Clarke spheroid of 1866 is 1853.248 meters (6080.20 feet). The international nautical mile is 1852 meters (6076.10 feet).

mile, statute In England and the United States, a measure of length equal to 5280 feet, 1760 yards, 880 fathoms, 80 chains, 1609.3 meters.

milieu [*Fr.*] Environment.

military geology The application of the principles of geology and related earth sciences, such as soil science, botany, and climatology, to the solution of military problems such as terrain analysis, location of construction materials, foundation conditions, water supply, cross-country movement, airfield siting, road construction and maintenance, siting of underground installations, and determining the effect of ground upon mine detectors.

Miller indices Symbols for a crystal face, the coefficients of the equation that defines the plane mathematically.

millerite A mineral, nickel sulfide, NiS. Hexagonal rhombohedral.

milli- [<*Lat.* mille, thousand] Combining form used in connection with many units of the c.g.s. system to denote a thousandth part of that unit, e.g., millisecond, the minimum time interval usually readable on seismic prospecting records.

millibar A subunit of pressure, being one one-thousandth of a bar, *q.v.*; in meteorology it is equal to a force of 1000 dynes per square centimeter. The values of atmospheric pressure are now usually expressed in millibars, and 1013.2 millibars is standard atmospheric pressure.

millidarcy The customary unit of measurement of permeability. One one-thousandth of a darcy, *q.v. See* PERMEABILITY

milligal The one-thousandth part of a gal, *q.v.*

milligram A unit of weight in the metric system, equal to one-thousandth part of a gram, 0.05432 grain, 0.000643 pennyweight, 0.00003215 troy ounce.

millimeter A metric measure of length, equal to 0.0394 of an inch.

milling ore *1.* A dry ore that can be amalgamated or treated by leaching and other processes; usually these ores are low-grade, free or nearly so, from base metals. *2.* Any ore that contains sufficient valuable minerals to be treated by any milling process.

milliroentgen Unit of radiation dosage, a thousandth of a roentgen.

millstone A hard, tough stone used for grinding cereals, cement rocks, and other materials. Usually a coarse-grained sandstone or fine quartz-conglomerate.

Millstone grit An old English name for the conglomeratic sandstone at the base of the Carboniferous coal measures. It was formerly more or less current in this country as a synonym for Pottsville conglomerate.

mima mound; pimple mound *See* PIMPLE PLAIN

mimetic Imitative. Applied to crystals which, by a twinning or malformation resemble simple forms of a higher grade of symmetry.

mimetite A mineral, $Pb_5(AsO_4)_3Cl$, commonly containing some Ca and phosphate. Hexagonal.

minable Capable of being mined.

Mindel Second Pleistocene glaciation.

mine *1.* In general, any excavation for minerals. More strictly, subterranean workings, as distinguished from quarries, placers, and hydraulic mines, and surface or open works. In a military sense, a mine is a subterranean gallery run under an enemy's works to be subsequently exploded. *2.* Any deposit of mineral or ore suitable for extraction, as, an ore deposit. The Federal and State courts have held that the word "mine," in statutes reserving mineral lands, included only those containing "valuable mineral deposits." In England the term mine is applied to any seam of coal, as well as to a deposit of ironstone either in thin bands, or in one bed of considerable thickness. 3. The term mine, as used by quarrymen, is applied to underground workings having a roof of undisturbed rock. It is used in contrast with the open-pit quarry. 4. To dig a mine; to get ore, metal, coal, or precious stones out of the earth; to dig in the earth for minerals; to work in a mine. 5. Discovery of a mine: In statutes relating to mines the word "discovery" is used in the sense of (1) uncovering or disclosing to view ore or mineral, (2) finding out or bringing to knowledge the existence of ore or mineral, or other useful products which were unknown, and (3) exploration, i.e., the more exact blocking out or ascertainment of a deposit that has already been discovered. In this sense it is practically synonymous with development, and has been so used in the U. S. Revenue Act of February 9, 1919, in allowing depletion to mines and oil and gas wells. Article 219 of "Income and War Excess Profits Tax Regulations" No. 45, construes "discovery of a mine" as: (1) the bona fide discovery of a commercially valuable deposit of ore or mineral, of a value materially in excess of the cost of discovery in natural exposure or by drilling or other exploration conducted above or below the ground; (2) the development and proving a mineral or ore deposit which has been apparently worked out . . . to be a minable

deposit of ore or mineral having a value materially in excess of the cost of improving or development.

mineragraphy Microscopic study of minerals in polished sections. Mineralography.

mineral A homogeneous naturally occurring phase; by some authorities restricted to inorganic, crystalline phases.

mineral deposit Any valuable mass of ore. Like ore deposit, it may be used with reference to any mode of occurrence of ore, whether having the characters of a true, segregated, or gash vein, or any other form.

mineral facies; metamorphic facies All rocks that have originated under temperature-pressure conditions so similar that a definite chemical composition has resulted in the same set of minerals regardless of the manner of crystallization or recrystallization.

mineral fillers Finely ground and generally inert cheap mineral substances that are added to such manufactured products as paint, paper, rubber, linoleum, and other materials to give body, weight, opacity, wear toughness, or other useful properties. See FILLERS

mineralization 1. The process of replacing the organic constituents of a body by inorganic fossilization. 2. The addition of inorganic substances to a body. 3. The act or process of mineralizing. See MINERALIZE. 4. The process of converting or being converted into a mineral, as, a metal into an oxide, sulfide, etc.

mineralize 1. To petrify. 2. To impregnate or supply with minerals. 3. To promote the formation of minerals.

mineralized zone A mineral-bearing belt or area extending across or through a district. It is usually distinguished from a vein or lode as being wide, the mineralization extending in some cases hundreds of feet from a fissure or contact plane. Cf. CONTACT DEPOSIT. See ZONE

mineralizer Mineralizing agent. Substances, especially water and other gases, which, when present in solution in magmas, lower the liquidus temperature and the viscosity, aid crystallization, and permit the formation of minerals containing them. Hydrothermal fluids are presumed to be formed by the concentration of such mineralizers.

mineral monument A permanent monument established in a mining district to provide for an accurate description of mining claims and their location.

mineralogical phase rule See GOLDSCHMIDT'S MINERALOGICAL PHASE RULE

mineralography The study under the microscope by reflected light of the structure of opaque minerals and ores.

mineralogy The science of the study of minerals.

mineraloid Used to designate materials that are commonly considered to be minerals, but are amorphous, hence excluded by some definitions. Example: allophane.

mineral oil; naphtha A limpid or yellowish liquid, lighter than water, and consisting of hydrocarbons. Petroleum is heavier than naphtha, and dark green in color when crude. Both exude from the rocks, but naphtha can be distilled from petroleum. See PETROLEUM

mineral pigments Mineral materials used to give color, opacity, or body to a paint, stucco, plaster, or similar materials.

mineral right The ownership of the minerals under a given surface, with the right to enter thereon, mine, and remove them. It may be separated from the surface ownership, but if not so separated by distinct conveyance, the latter includes it.

mineral spring A spring whose water contains large quantities of mineral salts, either those commonly occurring in the locality or of a rare or uncommon character.

mineral water Mineral waters are those which contain some mineral salt generally in sufficient quantities to affect the taste.

mineral wool A substance outwardly resembling wool, presenting a mass of fine interlaced filaments, made by subjecting furnace slag or certain rocks while molten to a strong blast. Being both insectproof and fireproof, it forms a desirable packing for walls, a covering for steam boilers, etc. Syn: MINERAL COTTON; SILICATE COTTON; SLAG WOOL

minerogenetic epoch See METALLOGENETIC EPOCH

miner's inch The miner's inch of water does not represent a fixed and definite quantity, being measured generally by the arbitrary standard of the various ditch companies. Generally, however, it is accepted to mean the quantity of water that will escape from an aperture one inch square through a two-inch plank, with a steady flow of water standing six inches above the top of the escape aperture, the quantity so discharged amounting to 2274 cubic feet in twenty-four hours. Inasmuch as the miner's inch is a local term the flow of the water shall be expressed in cubic feet per second, and where it is desirable for local reasons to use the term "miner's inch" it shall represent a flow of 1 1/2 cubic feet per minute.

Minette ore Jurassic ironstone of the Briey Basin and Lorraine, France.

minimum *1.* The lowest observed value of temperature, pressure, or other weather element during any given period. *2.* **gravity** or **magnetic** Low. An anomaly in which the intensity has values below the level of its more or less immediate environment.

minimum duration The time necessary for steady-state wave conditions to develop for a given wind velocity over a given fetch length.

minimum pendulum A pendulum used in gravity measurements so designed that its period is at a minimum with respect to changes of its effective length. Among factors which may tend to change this length are temperature, creep, or knife-edge wear.

minimum time path *Geophys:* Brachistochronic path; least-time path. A Fermat path between two points along which the time of travel is a true minimum.

mining claim That portion of the public mineral lands which a miner, for mining purposes, takes and holds in accordance with mining laws.

mining district A settlement of miners organized after the plan that, in the first years of mining in the western part of the United States, the miners, in the independence of all other authority, devised for their own self-government. A section of country usually designated by name and

described or understood as being confined within certain natural boundaries, in which gold or silver or other minerals may be found in paying quantities.

mining engineer One versed in, or one who follows, as a calling or profession, the business of mining engineering. Graduates of technical mining schools are given the degree of "engineer of mines" and authority to sign the letters E.M. after their names. The letters M.E. stand for mechanical engineer when given by a school, but are often used by men engaged in mining who lack scholastic degrees as an abbreviation for mining engineer or mining expert.

mining engineering That branch of engineering dealing with the excavation and working of mines. It includes much of civil, mechanical, electrical, and metallurgical engineering.

mining width The minimum width necessary for the extraction of the ore regardless of the actual width of ore-bearing rock.

minor elements Trace elements.

Miocene The fourth of the five epochs into which the Tertiary period is divided. Also the series of strata deposited during that epoch.

miogeosyncline An orthogeosyncline in which volcanic rocks are rare or absent.

miohaline *See* BRACKISH.

mirabilite Glauber's salt. A mineral, $Na_2SO_4.10H_2O$. Monoclinic.

mire A small muddy marsh or bog; wet, spongy earth; soft, deep mud.

mirror image An object that duplicates another except that the relations of its parts are reversed.

mirror plane of symmetry *See* SYMMETRY, PLANE OF MIRROR

miscibility The property enabling two or more liquids to mix and form one phase when brought together. *Ant:* IMMISCIBILITY

miscibility gap *See* IMMISCIBILITY GAP

mispickel Arsenopyrite.

Mississippian Formerly the lower of two epochs into which Carboniferous was subdivided. Recently, the American Commission on Stratigraphic Nomenclature recommended advancement to period rank, and that now accepted by the U. S. Geological Survey. In America, Mississippian is fifth of seven periods in the Paleozoic era. Also, the system of rocks formed during the period.

Missourian Upper Middle Pennsylvanian.

mix crystals A general term for crystals composed of two or more isomorphous or partly isomorphous constituents.

mixed base Term applied to a crude oil in which both the paraffin and the naphthene hydrocarbons are present but neither group dominates.

mixed-layer clay mineral Clay consisting of micaceous grains with two different minerals in layers regularly or randomly interstratified; the layers most commonly are differently hydrated.

mixed-layer crystal Crystal consisting of either regularly or randomly stratified intergrowths of different related minerals. Such interlayering of clay minerals is common. Some dolomite crystals may deviate from the ideal alternation of Ca and Mg in basal planes; some graphitic carbon contains intermixtures of hexagonal and cubic packing.

mobile belt A portion of the crust of the earth, generally long compared to its width and many scores of miles wide, that is more mobile, as evidenced by geosynclines, folds, and faults, than the adjoining stable blocks of the crust.

mobile shelf *1*. Area that alternated between continental and shallow marine conditions and later was strongly folded and faulted. *2*. Part of continental platform that subsided intermittently to produce a basin.

mobilization Any process whereby solid rock is sufficiently liquefied to permit it to flow. *See* RHEOMORPHISM

mode The actual mineral composition of an unaltered igneous rock; contrasted with norm, *q.v.*

moderate quantities of water 150,000 to 1,500,000 gallons per day. *Cf.* ENORMOUS; VERY LARGE; LARGE; SMALL; VERY SMALL; MEAGER

modulation The process or result of the process by which the amplitude, frequency, or phase of one wave or wave train is varied by the superposition of another.

modulus A number or quantity that measures a force or function. *See* BULK MODULUS; YOUNG'S MODULUS

modulus of compression Bulk modulus. A measure of the stress-strain ratio under simple hydrostatic pressure; defined as $K = \dfrac{FV}{A \Delta V}$; where F/A=pressure, V=volume, and ΔV=change in volume.

modulus of elasticity Incompressibility modulus; modulus of volume elasticity. The ratio of any stress to the resulting strain. The principal moduli of interest in seismology are: (1) Young's modulus for tension; (2) rigidity modulus for shear; (3) bulk modulus for hydrostatic compression or dilation.

modulus of rigidity Shear modulus. A measure of the stress-strain ratio for simple shear defined as $n = \dfrac{FL}{A \triangle L}$, where F/A= tangential force per unit area, L=distance between shear planes, and $\triangle L$=the shear strain produced.

modulus of rupture The measure of the force which must be applied longitudinally in order to produce rupture.

modulus of volume elasticity Incompressibility modulus; modulus of elasticity, *q.v.*

mofette A fissure or other opening, occurring in a region of recent volcanic activity, from which water vapor and carbon dioxide are emitted. A type of fumarole, *q.v.*

mogotes Huge castlelike residual masses of limestone between flat-floored valleys; they are riddled with cavernous passages. The typical mogotes are residuals of the old folded limestones of the Sierra de los Organos, in western Cuba.

Mohawkian Upper Champlainian.

Mohnian Middle upper Miocene.

Moho Abbreviation for Mohorovičić discontinuity.

mohole Proposed deep borehole to penetrate into the earth's mantle below the Mohorovičić discontinutity.

Mohorovičić discontinuity Seismic discontinuity situated about 35 km. below the continents and about 10 km. below the oceans which separates the earth's crust and mantle.

Mohr's salt Ferrous ammonium sulfate.

Mohs scale of hardness *See* HARDNESS SCALE

moil *1.* A short length of steel rod tapered to a point, used for cutting hitches, etc. *2.* A long gad used for accurate cutting in a mine; a set. *3.* In glass blowing, metallic oxide adhering to glass when it is detached from the end of the blowpipe.

moisture Essentially water, quantitatively determined by definite prescribed methods which may vary according to the nature of the material. In the case of coal and coke the methods employed shall be those prescribed in the Standard Methods of Laboratory Sampling and Analysis of Coal and Coke, A. S. T. M. Designation: D 271 of the American Society for Testing Materials.

moisture equivalent (of soils) The ratio of (1) the weight of water which the soil, after saturation, will retain against a centrifugal force 1000 times the force of gravity, to (2) the weight of the soil when dry. The ratio is stated as a percentage.

molality Concentration of a solution expressed as moles of solute per 1000 grams of solvent.

molarity Concentration of a solution expressed as moles of solute per liter of solution. Symbol M; thus 0.5M HCl is a solution of HCl containing half a mole of HCl per liter.

mollasse *1.* A provincial Swiss name for a soft green sandstone associated with marl and conglomerates, belonging to the Miocene Tertiary period, extensively developed in the lower country of Switzerland, and composed of Alpine detritus. *2.* It is the detritus worn from elevated ranges during and immediately after the major diastrophism, deposited in the later foredeep, considerably in front of the preceding Flysch geosyncline. It may be deformed and overthrust by the final last advance of the nappes (overthrust sheets). As this is also a typical formation common to all large mountain chains, the term "molasse" may be applied to all orogenic deposits of a similar genesis.

mold The impression left in the surrounding rock by a shell or other organic structure.

mold, external A mold which shows the form and markings of the outer part of the original shell or organism. Also spelled mould.

mold, internal A mold which shows the form and markings of the inner surfaces of a shell or organism.

mold, natural The cavity left after solution of the original shell or organism, bounded by the external impression (external mold) and the surface of the internal filling (core or steinkern).

molding sand A mixture of sand and loam used by founders in making sand molds.

mole *1.* Gram molecular weight. A mass numerically equal (in grams) to the molecular weight (in atomic weight units). *2.* A breakwater provided with a broad superstructure capable of being used as an ordinary wharf.

molecular norm Niggli's classification system, *q.v.*

molecular per cent *See* MOLECULAR PROPORTIONS

molecular proportions or **ratios** The ratios or proportions in which the various "molecules" (usually hypothetical) occur in a substance. Obtained by dividing the weight per cent of each molecular "species" (oxides, etc.) by its

molecular weight. Recalculation to a basis of 100 molecules yields molecular per cent.

molecular replacement The petrifaction of an organic substance at such a gradual molecule by molecule rate that the very finest details of the original structure are preserved. *Syn:* HISTOMETABASIS

molecular volume The volume, in cc., occupied by one gram molecular weight numerically equal to the weight divided by the density.

molecular weight *1.* The weight, in atomic-weight units, of a molecule of the substance. *2.* The gram molecular weight, or an amount of the substance whose weight in grams equals the molecular weight. If the nature of the molecule is in doubt, the gram formula weight is used in place of the gram molecular weight; the assumed formula should be stated.

molecule The smallest part of a substance that can exist separately and still retain its composition and characteristic properties; the smallest combination of atoms that will form a given chemical compound.

mole fraction The mole fraction of a given component in a phase is equal to the number of moles of the component in question, divided by the total number of moles of all components in the phase. Mole fractions are thus useful in defining the composition of a phase.

mollisol *See* ACTIVE LAYER

Mollusca The phylum of invertebrate animals which includes the gastropods, pelecypods, cephalopods, etc.; a phylum of great importance in paleontology.

mollusk One of the Mollusca. Also spelled mollusc.

molybdate A salt or ester of molybdic acid; a compound containing the radical MoO_4^{--}.

molybdenite A mineral, MoS_2. The principal ore of molybdenum. Hexagonal.

moment Geologic time unit corresponding to biostratigraphic zone. *Cf.* INSTANT

monadnock *1.* By long continued erosion a land surface may be reduced to an almost level plain, but there may still be a few hills, which, having as yet escaped final destruction, rise conspicuously above the plain. These are monadnocks. The term connotes nothing in regard to form or structure; it means merely a residual of an old topography standing about a plain of subaerial erosion. *2.* A residual rock, hill, or mountain standing above a peneplain.

monazite A mineral, $(Ce,La)-PO_4$, commonly containing thorium. The principal ore of the rare earths and thorium. Monoclinic.

mono- [<*Gr.* monos] *1.* A combining form meaning one, single, alone. *2. Chem:* Indicating that a compound contains one atom or group of that to the name of which it is united. *3. Phys. chem:* Short for monomolecular.

monobasic acid An acid containing one replaceable hydrogen atom per molecule, e.g., $HCl,-HNO_3$.

monochromatic radiation Radiation of particular wave length in the electromagnetic spectrum; under experimental conditions adjacent characteristic lines of slightly different wave length may not be subject to resolution.

monoclinal *1.* Adjective derived from monocline, *q.v. 2.* Term signifying sameness in direction of dip. *3.* Applied to strata that dip for an indefinite or unknown length in one direction and which do not apparently form sides of ascertained anticlines or synclines. *4.* Having the beds sloping in only one direction.

monoclinal scarp A scarp resulting from a steep downward flexure between an upland block and a tectonic basin. When maturely dissected, a monoclinal scarp may be difficult to distinguish from a fault scarp.

monoclinal shifting (of streams) Flowing along the strike of dipping beds, streams do not usually sink their channels vertically, but shift them down dip at the same time that they are deepened. This process is known as monoclinal shifting of streams.

monocline *1.* Strata that dip for an indefinite or unknown length in one direction, and which do not apparently form sides of ascertained anticlines or synclines. *2.* Beds inclined in a single direction. *3.* A one-limbed flexure in strata which are usually flat-lying except in the flexure itself. *4.* A steplike bend in otherwise horizontal or gently dipping beds.

monoclinic symmetry *Struct. petrol:* May refer to either the movement or the fabric. Monoclinic symmetry of movement is analogous to the sliding of cards over one another in one direction; in this movement there is one plane of symmetry parallel to a, the direction of tectonic transport. In monoclinic symmetry of fabric there is one plane of symmetry parallel to a, the direction of tectonic transport.

monoclinic system That system of crystals whose forms are referred to three unequal axes, two intersecting obliquely and the third perpendicularly to both the others.

Monodelphia Subclass of mammals whose young develop within a placenta and are born in a relatively mature condition.

monogenetic soil Soil produced under a single set of continuing conditions, i.e., parent material, climate, relief, biologic activity, etc.

monogeosyncline A primary geosyncline that is long, comparatively narrow, deeply subsided, composed of shallow water sediments and situated within a continent along the inner border of the borderlands.

monograptid One of the Monograptidae, a family of Silurian graptolites characterized by having a uniserial stipe with a solid axial rod of rhitin.

monomeric Refers to simple rather than compound molecular structure, e.g., HgCl rather than Hg_2Cl_2.

monomineralic rock A rock consisting of essentially one mineral; the amounts of other minerals tolerated under the definition vary with the authors, e.g., anorthosite.

Monongahelan Upper Pennsylvanian.

monophyletic Derived from a single line of descent.

monoschematic Applied to a body of rock or mineral deposit whose fabric is identical throughout. Contrasted with macropolyschematic.

monothalamous *See* UNILOCULAR

monotropic forms In certain instances of polymorphism, the vapor-pressure curves of the two forms do not meet below the melting point. They therefore lack a stable inversion point, and the form with the higher vapor pressure is metastable with re-

spect to the other at all temperatures below the melting point. Such higher-vapor-pressure forms are called monotropic and are not interconvertible.

monotype *1.* The holotype of a species which was described from a single specimen. *2.* Holotype by original designation. *3.* Genotype of a genus with only one species.

monotypic Refers to a genus based on only one known species or a species based on only one known specimen.

monotypical Applied to a genus which included only a single species at the time of publication.

monotypy The condition of having been established on the basis of only a single known type.

monsoon The name is derived from an Arabic word for season, and originally referred to the winds of the Arabian Sea, which blow for about six months from the northeast, and six months from the southwest. It has been extended to include certain other winds which blow with great persistence and regularity at definite seasons of the year. The primary cause of these winds is the seasonal difference of temperature between land and sea areas. The winds are analogous to land and sea breezes, but their period is a year, instead of a day, and they blow over vast areas, instead of over a limited region. Monsoon conditions occur also, but to a much less extent, in northern Australia, parts of western, southern, and eastern Africa, and parts of North America and Chile.

Montanan Upper Upper Cretaceous below Laramian.

Montian Middle or lower Paleocene.

monticellite A mineral, $CaMgSiO_4$,

usually occurring in contact-met-amorphosed limestones. Ortho-rhombic.

montmorillonite *1.* A group of clay minerals whose formulas may be derived by substitution in the general formula $Al_2Si_4O_{10}$-$(OH)_2$ with deficiencies in charge in the tetrahedral and octahedral positions balanced by the pres-ence of cations, most commonly Ca and Na, subject to ion ex-change. They are characterized by swelling in water due to intro-duction of interlayer water in the direction of the c-axis. Repre-sentative members of the group are:

montmorillonite
$$Na_{.33}(Al_{1.67}Mg_{.33})Si_4O_{10}(OH)_2$$
nontronite
$$Na_{.33}(Fe^{+3}{}_{2.00})(Al_{.33}Si_{3.67})O_{10}(OH)_2$$
saponite
$$Ca_{.17}(Mg_{3.00})(Al_{.33}Si_{3.67})O_{10}(OH)_2$$
hectorite
$$Na_{.33}(Mg_{2.67}Li_{.33})Si_4O_{10}(F,OH)_2$$
sauconite
$$Ca_{.12}Na_{.09}(Zn_{2.40}Mg_{0.18}Al_{0.22}Fe^{+3}{}_{0.17})$$
$$Al_{0.58}Si_{3.47})O_{10}(OH)_2$$
stevensite
$$Ca_{.15}Mg_3Si_4O_{10}(OH)_2$$

2. A specific member of the mont-morillonite group. *See 1;* BEIDEL-LITE; VOLCHONSKOITE

montrealite A melanocratic oli-vine essexite. Major titanaugite and titanhornblende, olivine, and plagioclase. May contain biotite and nepheline. Accessory calcite, apatite, sphene, zircon, and opaque oxides.

monument *1.* Any material ob-ject or collection of objects which indicates the position on the ground of a survey station or land corner. *2.* A stone or other permanent object serving to indi-cate a limit, or to mark a bound-ary, as of a mining claim.

monzonite A granular plutonic rock containing approximately equal amounts of orthoclase and plagioclase and thus intermediate between syenite and diorite. Quartz is usually present, but if it exceeds 2% by volume the rock is classified as quartz mon-zonite or adamellite. Either horn-blende or diopside or both are present and biotite is a common constituent. Accessories are apa-tite, zircon, sphene, and opaque oxides.

moonstone A variety of feldspar, commonly transparent or translu-cent orthoclase, albite, or labra-dorite, which exhibits a delicate pearly opalescent play of colors. Used as a gem.

moor *1.* In country affairs, de-notes an unlimited tract of land, usually overrun with heath. *2.* The Scotch moors are the ele-vated, undulating, treeless, flat or generally sloping tracts from which rise the ranges of precipi-tous hills and mountains which characterize the grand but at the same time rather gloomy and monotonous scenery of the Scot-tish Highlands. In the more southern part of Great Britain, moor seems to be used nearly as the equivalent of morass, which latter word is said by W. W. Skeat to be plainly an adjectival form of moor, and is defined by him as swamp, bog, while R. G. Latham defines moor as marsh, fen, bog, tract of low watery ground. *3.* An extensive area of waste ground overlain by peat, and usually more or less wet. A tract of open, unarable land, boggy or of poor soil, more or less elevated. *4.* In Cornwall, an enrichment of ore in a particular part of a lode.

morainal lakes They owe their existence to the blockade of valley or drainage courses by glacial drift. The term drift-barrier lakes would be the more accurate name.

moraine *1*. Drift, deposited chiefly by direct glacial action, and having constructional topography independent of control by the surface on which the drift lies. *2*. An accumulation of drift having initial constructional topography, built within a glaciated region chiefly by the direct action of glacier ice. The term has been used in many different ways and its history is confused. *3*. The floated blocks sometimes carried on lava streams, or the moraines of lava flows as they may suggestively be termed. *4*. The porous, secondary material at the base of the aperture in some species of Endothyra, an important Mississippian foraminifer.

moraine terrace When an alluvial plain or alluvial cone is built against the side or front of a glacier and the glacier is afterward melted away, the alluvial surface becomes a terrace overlooking the valley that contained the ice.

morainic Of, pertaining to, forming, or formed by a moraine.

morass A swamp, marsh, or area of low wet ground, and partially filled-up hollows or depressions, or old lakes, either fresh water or salt water.

Morganian Upper Upper Carboniferous.

morphogenetic region A region in which, under a certain set of climatic conditions, the predominant geomorphic processes will give to the landscape characteristics that will set it off from those of other areas developed under different climatic conditions.

morphogeny The production or evolution of morphological characters.

morphologic Pertaining to morphology, *q.v.*

morphologic species Species based solely on morphologic characters and consisting of individuals included between more or less arbitrarily selected limits.

morphologic unit *1*. Rock stratigraphic unit identified by its topographic features, e.g., a Pleistocene glacial deposit. *2*. A surface either depositional or erosional recognized by its topographic character.

morphology *1*. The observation of the form of lands. *2*. The study of the form and structure of organisms.

morphometry Measurement of shape.

morphotype *1*. The type specimen of a different form of a dimorphic or polymorphic species. *2*. (Not recommended) A figured specimen now adding to knowledge of the morphology of a species.

Morrowan Lowermost Pennsylvanian.

mortar bed (Not recommended) Lime-cemented valley-flat deposits of clays, silts, sands, and gravels, found in Nebraska and Kansas.

mortar structure A mechanical structure produced by dynamic metamorphism upon granites and gneisses in which small crushed grains of quartz and feldspar occupy the interstices between larger individuals, resembling stones set in mortar.

morvan A region of composite structure, consisting of an older undermass, usually made up of deformed crystalline rocks, that had been long ago worn down to small relief and that was then depressed, submerged, and buried beneath a heavy overmass of stratified deposits, the composite mass then being uplifted and tilted, the tilted mass being truncated across its double structure by renewed erosion, and in this worn-down condition rather evenly uplifted into a new cycle of destructive evolution.

mosaic *1. Petrol:* Applied to the texture sometimes seen in dynamo-metamorphosed rocks whose crystal fragments are angular and granular and appear, in polarized light, like the pieces of a mosaic. *2.* A picture formed by matching together parts of a number of overlapping vertical aerial photographs taken from different camera positions.

mosaic breccia A breccia is one whose fragments have been largely but not wholly disjointed and displaced. Some fragments match along adjacent surfaces.

Moscovian Middle Upper Carboniferous.

mosore Albrecht Penck proposed this name for residuals (monadnocks) due to excess of initial mass.

mother liquor The residual solution, often impure or complex, which remains after the substances readily and regularly crystallizing have been removed.

mother lode *1.* The principal lode or vein passing through a district or particular section of country. *2.* The "Great Quartz Vein" in California, traced by its outcrop for 80 miles from Mariposa to Amador.

mottle, *n.* Irregular small body of material in sedimentary matrix of different texture; difference in color is not essential.

mottled Irregularly marked with spots of different colors. Mottling in soils usually indicates poor

aeration and lack of good drainage.

mottled limestone Limestone with narrow branching or anastomosing fucoidlike cylindrical masses of dolomite, often with a central tube or hole. May be organic or inorganic in origin.

moulding or **molding sand** *See* FOUNDRY SAND

moulin *1.* In some places the fields of ice are hollowed out into perpendicular wells, known under the name of moulins (mills), because of the roaring noise of the water which is engulfed in them. *2.* An area of a glacier is unbroken, and driblets of water have room to form rills; rills to unite and form streams; streams to combine to form rushing brooks, which sometimes cut deep channels in the ice. Sooner or later these streams reach a strained portion of the glacier, where a crack is formed across the stream. A way is thus opened for the water to the bottom of the glacier. By long action the stream hollows out a shaft, the crack thus becoming the starting-point of a funnel of unseen depth, into which the water leaps with the sound of thunder. This funnel and its cataract form a glacier mill or moulin. *3.* A circular depression on the surface of a glacier in the ablation zone into which melt water funnels. *Syn:* GLACIER MILL

mound A low hill of earth, natural or artificial; in general, any prominent, more or less isolated hill.

mount A mountain, or a high hill. Used always instead of "mountain" before a proper name.

mountain *1.* A tract of land considerably elevated above the adjacent country. Mountains are usually found connected in long chains or ranges; sometimes they are single, isolated eminences. *2.* Phys. geog: Any portion of the earth's crust rising considerably above the surrounding surface. The term is usually applied to heights of more than 2000 feet, all beneath that amount being regarded as hills, and when of inconsiderable height, as hillocks.

mountain chain *1.* A series of mountains whose bases are continuous (the meaning of the word base must not be pushed too far). Since the word chain is not sufficiently general, it would be better to reserve this word for the subdivisions and to employ the term "system of mountains," or "mass of mountains," to denote a collection or combination of many chains. *2.* There are two distinguishing features which most mountain chains present: (1) Their breadth is small compared with their length. (2) They rise sharply, and are marked off clearly from the country on either side. *3.* Comprises two or more systems in the same general region of elevation, but of different dates of origin. *4.* A series or group of connected mountains having a well-defined trend or direction.

mountain cork A variety of asbestos resembling cork. It is light and floats on water. *Syn:* MOUNTAIN LEATHER

mountain glacier Glacier in which rock projects above the highest levels of the ice and snow.

mountain group A group made up of several or many mountain peaks, or of short mountain ridges. The Catskill Mountains and the Black Hills are examples.

mountain leather *See* MOUNTAIN CORK

mountain pediment *1.* Many of the mountains in the Papago country of southwestern Arizona are bordered by plains cut in rock which superficially resemble alluvial slopes. These plains are eroded by weathering in place and by corrasion of running water. An analysis of the processes of erosion of mountain slopes and of the rock plains at their bases is presented. The term pediment with a series of qualifying adjectives is proposed for the rock plains. *2.* A plain of combined erosion and transportation at the foot of a desert mountain range similar in form to the alluvial plains that front the mountains of an arid region, but without alluvial cover and composed of solid rock.

mountain range *1.* A chain of mountains or hills. *2.* Mountain range is a single mountain individual born at one time (monogenetic), i.e., the result of one (though it may be prolonged) earth-effort; as contra-distinguished on the one hand from mountain ranges born at different times (polygenetic) in the same general region and on the other from ridges and peaks which are subordinate parts—limbs and organs—of such a mountain individual. *3.* A group of peaks, domes, and ridges produced by a single series of movements in the earth's crust, or by a series of movements affecting the same region.

mountain slope The sloping surface which forms the side of a mountain; specifically the slope characteristically developed by the processes of erosion in an arid region.

mountain system Several more

or less parallel ranges grouped together. *See* MOUNTAIN CHAIN; MOUNTAIN RANGE; CORDILLERA

mountain tract Upper portion of a stream where its gradient is steep and it occupies a narrow V-shaped valley.

mouth *1.* The exit or point of discharge of a stream into another stream or a lake or sea. *2.* An opening or aperture resembling or likened to a mouth and affording entrance or exit, such as the mouth of a cave or canyon.

moveout or **moveout time** Stepout; angularity. The difference in arrival times of a reflection on adjacent traces of seismograph record.

moving coil galvanometer A coil suspended in a constant magnetic field which rotates through an angle, the magnitude of which is proportional to the elastic current flowing through the coil.

Mt Abbreviation for magnetite in normative rock calculations.

muck *1.* A dark-colored soil, commonly in wet places, which has a high percentage of decomposed or finely comminuted organic matter. *Cf.* PEAT. *2.* Earth, including dirt, gravel hardpan, and rock, to be, or being, excavated; overburden. *3.* A layer of earth, sand, or sediment lying immediately above the sand or gravel containing, or supposed to contain, gold in placer mining districts. It may itself contain some traces of gold. *4. V:* To excavate or remove muck from.

mucro A short and sharp abrupt spur or spiny tip.

mucronate, *adj.* Terminated abruptly by distinct and obvious mucro.

mud *1.* The familiar as well as scientific term for all wet slimy debris, whether produced by rains on the earthy surface, by sediment from turbid waters, or by ejections from springs and volcanoes. *2.* A mixture of water with clay and/or silt together with materials of other dimensions.

mud avalanche Mudflow.

mud belt The belt of marine deposits composed largely of detrital clay, and lying between the coarser terrigenous sediments to the landward and the deep oceanic organic oozes on the seaward side. At present, the inner boundary of the inner mud belt is the edge of the continental shelf.

mud crack Desiccation crack, *q.v.*

mud crack polygons *See* POLYGONS, MUD CRACK

mud engineer An engineer who studies and supervises the preparation of various fluids and emulsions, collectively termed mud, used in rotary drilling.

mud flat A muddy, low-lying strip of ground by the shore, or an island, usually submerged more or less completely by the rise of the tide.

mudflow A flowage of heterogeneous debris lubricated with a large amount of water usually following a former stream course. *Syn:* MUD ROCK FLOW; MUDSPATE; MUD AVALANCHE; MUD STREAM

mud geyser A geyser that erupts sulfurous mud. A type of mud volcano.

mud lumps Swellings of bluish-gray clay forming small islands of an acre or more, with a height of 5 to 10 feet above sea level, found at the mouths of the Mississippi; apparently caused by pressure of surface deposits upon buried clays. Formation accompanied by minor flows of marsh gas.

mud-pellet conglomerate Sandstone containing abundant, flattened to rounded, small mudstone masses.

mud polygons Polygonal soil patterns in fine textured material. *Syn:* FISSURE POLYGONS; CELLULAR SOIL

mud pot A type of hot spring consisting of a shallow pit or cavity filled with hot, generally boiling, mud carrying very little water and a large amount of fine-grained mineral matter. The mud may have any degree of consistency up to a thick mush or mortar and there is no real dividing line between mud pots and muddy springs. In the Yellowstone Park region, these features vary in size from small holes in the ground up to kettle-like or funnel-shaped hollows, 30 feet in diameter at the top and 12 to 15 feet deep down to the level of the fluid mud.

mud ridge ripple mark Longitudinal ripple mark consisting of narrow angular ridges and relatively wide flat troughs; ridges bifurcate and converge downcurrent.

mud rock flow *See* MUDFLOW

mud rocks A general name applied to sediments composed most commonly of microscopic particles of quartz and clay, sometimes one and sometimes the other predominating. Such mud rocks may be massive or they may have a fine and irregularly bedded or laminated structure (shales).

mudstone *1.* A term originally applied by Sir Roderick Murchison to certain dark-gray, fine-grained, shivery shales of the Silurian system in Wales, which, on being exposed to the atmosphere, are rapidy decomposed and converted into their primitive state of mud; but now extended to all similar shales in whatever formation they may occur. *2.* Mudstone includes clay, silt, siltstone, claystone, shale, and argillite. It should only be used when there is doubt as to precise identification or when a deposit consists of an indefinite mixture of clay, silt, and sand particles, the proportions varying from place to place, so that a more precise term is not possible. It may also be used in a general classification of the three common forms of sedimentary rocks into mudstones, sandstones, and limestones. *3.* An indurated clay rock which is not fissile.

mud volcano Cone-shaped mound with maximum height of about 250 feet built around a spring by mud brought to the surface by slowly escaping natural gas.

mullion structure Rodding structure, *q.v.* *1.* The larger grooves in a fault plane parallel to the direction of displacement. *2.* Series of parallel columns in metamorphic rocks several inches in diameter and several feet long, each column being composed of folded metamorphic rocks.

mullite A mineral, $3Al_2O_3.2SiO_2$. Most often observed as a synthetic mineral in ceramic products. Orthorhombic.

multi- [*Lat.*] Prefix meaning many.

multicycle coast A coast with a series of elevated sea cliffs separated from each other in stairlike fashion by narrow wave-cut benches. The sea cliffs at each elevation represent a separate shore line cycle.

multigelation Repeated freezing and thawing.

multigranular particle Sedimentary particle consisting of several adherent crystals.

multilocular Composed of many chambers, e.g., the Foraminifera.

multipartite map Vertical variability map showing the degrees of concentration of one lithologic type in a stratigraphic unit.

multiple detectors Two, or more, seismic detectors whose combined output energy is fed into a single amplifier-recorder circuit. This technique is used to effect a cancellation of undesirable near-surface waves. *Syn:* MULTIPLE SEISMOMETERS; MULTIPLE GEOPHONES; MULTIPLE RECORDING GROUPS.

multiple dike A dike made up of two or more intrusions of the same kind of igneous rock.

multiple faults System of closely spaced generally parallel faults.

multiple or secondary reflections Reflection "line-ups" which arise from waves which have suffered more than one reflection prior to emergence.

multiple seismometers Multiple geophones; multiple recording groups; multiple detectors, *q.v.*

multiple sill A sill made up of two or more intrusions composed of the same kind of igneous rock.

multiplex A stereoscopic plotting instrument used in preparing topographic maps by stereophotogrammetry.

multivariate analysis Simultaneous statistical analysis with respect to more than two variables.

Murderian Upper Upper Silurian.

Muschelkalk Middle Triassic.

muscovite A mineral, a member of the mica group, the common white, green, red, or light brown mica of granites, gneisses, and schists. Composition $KAl_2(AlSi_3)O_{10}(OH)_2$. Monoclinic. *Clay mineral:* Illite.

mushroom ice Pillars of ice with roundish, expanded tops formed when a portion of an ice-covered area is protected from the direct effect of sunlight by some surface object, while the ice roundabout is not. *See* GLACIER TABLE

muskeg *1.* The muskeg is a characteristic feature of northern topography. From the International boundary to the Arctic Sea the term is applied to alluvial areas with insufficient drainage, over which moss has accumulated to a considerable depth. These swamps are usually covered with tamarack and fir trees. The typical muskeg is traversed by meandering streams, having deep channels but a scarcely perceptible current. Stagnant pools become coated over with a moss of sufficient strength to temporarily sustain the weight of a man. In places the surface is broken by tall hummocks, the *têtes des femmes* of the *voyageur*, which turn under the foot, and sooner or later precipitate the passing pedestrian into the mud or water below. *2.* A Canadian term of Cree Indian origin, meaning a moss-covered muck or peat bog. In the Far North all swamps are called muskegs. *3.* A bog or marsh. Local in north-central United States, Canada, and Alaska.

mussel A pelecypod, generally one that is not attached like an oyster.

mutant The offspring bearing the mutation.

mutation *1.* The insignificant variations or modifications apparent in members more remote from one another in time. *2.* The raw material of evolution; a spontaneously occurring, inheritable change in organism.

mutual boundary pattern The pattern made by two adjacent minerals is smooth and regular or forms regular curves with no decided projections of one mineral into another.

m.y. Million years.

mylonite A fine-grained, laminated rock formed by extreme microbrecciation and milling of rocks during movement on fault surfaces. Metamorphism is dominantly cataclastic with little or no growth of new crystals. *See* AUGEN SCHIST; CATACLASITE; CRUSH BRECCIA; CRUSH CONGLOM-ERATE; FLASER GABBRO; FLINTY CRUSH ROCK

mylonization; mylonitization The process of forming mylonite, *q.v.*

Myriapoda One of the five main divisions of the phylum Arthropoda; here belong the centipedes and millipedes.

myrmekite An intergrowth of plagioclase and vermicular quartz, generally replacing potassium feldspar, formed during the later or deuteric stage of consolidation of an igneous rock.

nacreous Pearly; having the luster of mother-of-pearl.

nacrite An uncommon clay mineral of the kaolin group. It has the same composition, $Al_2Si_2O_5$(OH)$_4$, as kaolinite and dickite, but is structurally distinct.

nadir The point where the direction of the plumb line extended below the horizon meets the celestial sphere. The nadir is directly opposite the zenith.

Namurian Lower Upper Carboniferous.

naphtha *1.* As used by ancient writers, a more fluid and volatile variety of asphalt or bitumen. *2.* In modern use, an artificial, volatile, colorless liquid obtained from petroleum; a distillation product between gasoline and refined oil.

naphthene hydrocarbon A compound of carbon and hydrogen of general formula C_nH_{2n}, containing saturated ring structures. *Syn:* CYCLOPARAFFIN; POLYMETHYLENE HYDROCARBON

nappe Decke [*Ger.*]. *1.* Faulted overturned folds. *2.* A large body of rock that has moved forward more than one mile from its original position, either by overthrusting or by recumbent folding. *3.* In Belgium the term is a synonym of aquifer. *4.* The term originally meant a covering stratum such as basalt flow and may still be found in foreign literature other than French and English. *5. Hydraul:* A sheet or curtain of water overflowing a structure like a weir or a dam. The nappe has an upper and lower surface.

native An element occurring in nature uncombined. Usually applied to the metals, as, native mercury, native copper.

native metal Any metal found naturally in that state, as, copper, gold, iron, mercury, platinum, silver, etc. *See* NATIVE

native paraffin *See* OZOCERITE

natrolite A mineral, one of the zeolites, $Na_2Al(AlSi_3)_{10}.2H_2O$. Orthorhombic.

natron A mineral, $Na_2Co_3.10H_2O$. Monoclinic.

natural arch (marine) *See* SEA ARCH

natural bridge *1.* The term "natural bridge" and "natural arch" have been so often used as synonyms, both in common parlance and in scientific literature, that it is necessary to define the terms. In the restricted sense in which the term natural bridge is used, a natural bridge is a natural stone arch that spans a valley of erosion. A natural arch is a similar structure which, however, does not span an erosion valley. *2.* Any bridge spanning a ravine and left in place by erosive agencies. *3.* A synonym for sea arch, *q.v.*

natural cement A product made by burning a clayey limestone in its natural state.

natural coke In Australia, coal

has been more or less coked by contact with an igneous rock.

natural density Specific gravity of porous sediment or rock containing interstitial water; wet bulk density. *Cf.* BULK DENSITY

natural earth potential An electric potential developed in the earth by electrochemical action between minerals and solutions with which they are in contact.

natural frequency *1.* A constant frequency of a vibrating system in the state of natural oscillation. *2.* In an electrical circuit with inductance L, in henrys, and capacity C, in farads, the frequency n given by the formula

$$n = \frac{1}{2\pi\sqrt{LC}}$$

natural gas *1.* A mixture of gaseous hydrocarbons found in nature; in many places connected with deposits of petroleum, to which the gaseous compounds are closely related. *2. Hydrol:* Gases that are entrapped in interstices in the zone of saturation. A body of natural gas may be partly in solution in water transmitting hydrostatic pressure from below or in any petroleum that may intervene between the water and the gas.

natural-gas liquids Those liquid hydrocarbon mixtures which are gaseous in the reservoir but are recoverable by condensation or absorption. Natural gasoline, condensate, and liquefied petroleum gases fall in this category.

natural levee In floodtime the muddy water flows over the river banks, where its velocity is at once checked as it flows gently down the outer side, causing more material to be deposited there, and a long alluvial ridge, called a natural levee, is built up on either side of the stream.

natural oscillation An oscillation of a vibrating system which may occur in the absence of an external force.

natural selection Process by which less vigorous and less well-adapted individuals tend to be eliminated from a population without leaving descendants to perpetuate an inferior stock.

nautical mile The length of a minute of arc, 1/21,600 of an average great circle of the earth. Generally one minute of latitude is considered equal to one nautical mile. The accepted United States value is 6080.20 feet, approximately 1.15 times as long as the statute mile of 5280 feet *Syn:* GEOGRAPHICAL MILE

nautilicone *See* NAUTILOID

nautiloid *1.* One of the Nautiloidea; a shelled cephalopod having an external chambered shell either straight or variously curved or coiled, with simple septa forming sutures that are simple lines without marked flexures. *Adj: 2* Pertaining to the Nautiloidea *q.v.; 3.* In a planispiral coil with enlarging whorls, as in the genus Nautilus. *Syn:* NAUTILICONE NAUTILICONIC; NAUTILIAN

Nautiloidea Class of cephalopods with straight to coiled shells whose septa meet the external shell along a suture that i not thrown into folds. Camb. Rec.

Ne Abbreviation for nephelin in normative rock calculations.

neanic Describing youthfulness or the stage in which specific characters begin to develop.

neap tide A tide occurring nea the time of quadrature of th moon. The neap tidal range usually 10 to 30% less than th mean tidal range.

nearshore circulation The ocea circulation pattern composed o the nearshore currents and coastal currents. *See* CURRENT

nearshore current system The current system caused primarily by wave action in and near the breaker zone, and which consists of four parts: the shoreward mass transport of water; longshore currents; seaward return flow, including rip currents; and the longshore movement of the expanding heads of rip currents.

neatline The line which surrounds the map itself. Differs from margin in that the margin is outside the neatline.

Nebraskan First Pleistocene glaciation.

neck *1.* A lava-filled conduit of an extinct volcano, exposed by erosion. *Syn:* CHIMNEY; PIPE. *2. Topog:* The narrow strip of land which connects a peninsula with the mainland, or connects two ridges. *See* TOMBOLO. *3.* The narrow band of water flowing seaward through the surf. *Syn:* RIP. *4.* The narrow entrance to a room next to the entry, or a place where the room has been narrowed on account of poor roof. *5.* The tapering portion of an archegonium; a sperm enters an archegonium through a canal extending lengthwise through the neck.

neck channel A narrow channel along which a rip current flows seaward through the surf. *See* RIP CURRENT

neck cutoff The break-through of a river across the narrow neck separating two meanders, where downstream migration of one has been slowed and the next meander upstream has overtaken it. *Cf.* CHUTE CUTOFF

neck, volcanic *See* VOLCANIC NECK

needle *1. Geog.* and *Geol:* A familiar term for pointed, detached masses of rock standing out from the cliff or shores to which they geologically belong, and from which they have been severed by the erosive action of the tides and waves. Applied also to the pointed summits of mountains, the aiguille or needle-top of the French. *2.* Prominent and sharp rocky pinnacle or spire; aiguille. *3.* A slender needlelike snow crystal usually composed of needlelike components lying parallel, with the length of the crystal being at least five times greater than the diameter.

needle ore *1.* Aikinite. A lead-copper-bismuth sulfide. *2.* Iron ore of very high metallic luster, found in small quantities which may be separated in long slender filaments resembling needles.

negative area Area that subsided conspicuously or repeatedly. Thick stratigraphic sections generally identify such areas.

negative center *Elec. prospecting:* The central region of a closed negative earth potential anomaly, theoretically a point.

negative crystal *1.* An optically negative crystal. *See* OPTICAL CHARACTER. *2.* A pseudomorph consisting of a hollow opening shaped like a crystal, presumably formed by the solution of a previously existing crystal.

negative element *1.* Those which have shown a decided tendency to rise are designated positive elements and those which have tended to sink are termed negative elements. *2.* A term applied to a large structural feature in the earth's crust, characterized through a long geologic time by a tendency to sink when diastrophism takes place. *3.* A portion of the earth's crust which has been submerged again and again during geologic history.

negative elongation Anisotropic crystal elongation parallel to vibration direction of the faster of the two plane-polarized rays.

negative movement Subsidence, actual or relative.

negro heads Large black blocks of coral torn loose from the outer face of a reef and tossed onto the reef flat by storm or tsunamic waves. The blocks become blackened by a crust of lichens formed after they come to rest on the reef flat.

nekton 1. That group of marine animals that leads an active swimming life and lives at or near the surface. 2. Swimming animals which can direct their own movements against the action of marine currents.

nektoplanktonic Pelagic.

nematoblastic 1. Pertaining to the texture of a recrystallized rock in which the shape of the grains is threadlike. 2. Applied to a fibrous type of schistosity, seen in rocks composed largely of such minerals as glaucophane and actinolite.

Neocene The later of the two epochs into which the Tertiary period was formerly divided, at one time used by many geologists. Also the series of strata deposited during that epoch. It is no longer used.

Neocomian Lower Cretaceous, approximately equivalent to Valanginian, Hauterivian, and Barremian.

Neocryptozoic Late Precambrian.

neo-Darwinism Darwinism modified in accordance with the principles of genetics.

Neogene The later of the two periods into which the Cenozoic era is divided in the classification adopted by the International Geological Congress and used by many European geologists.

Also the system of strata de posited during that period. comprises the Miocene, Pliocen Pleistocene, and Holocene or R cent epochs. Not generally use in the United States but favore by some for later Tertiary. Se PALEOGENE

neomagma Newly formed pro ucts of metamorphism su jected locally to mass movemen of plastic flow, in contrast hypomagmas of presumabl deep-seated sources.

neomineralization Chemical i terchange within a rock resu ing in alteration of its miner components and production new minerals.

neontology The study of existir life.

neotype 1. Specimen selected replace the holotype if the latt has been lost. 2. Genotype, b subsequent designation.

nepheline; nephelite A minera $(Na,K)AlSiO_4$. Hexagonal. A important rock-forming miner especially in nepheline syenit and alkali-rich basalts.

nepheline syenite A pluton rock composed of a granular a gregate of alkalic feldspar, nep eline, and an alkalic ferroma nesian constituent. The ferr magnesian minerals may be an phiboles such as riebeckit arfvedsonite, barkevikite, etc., pyroxenes such as aegirite, aeg ite-augite, or acmite. Comm accessory minerals are cancrinit sodalite, hauyne, and noselite addition to apatite, zirco sphene, and opaque oxides. Oth more rare accessories are ofte present.

nephelinite An extrusive hypabyssal rock composed p marily of pyroxene (usual titaniferous augite) and neph line.

nephrite *See* JADE

nepionic Young; referring to the stage or period of the young shell before the appearance of distinctive specific characters.

Neptunian theory A general theory of origin of rocks, proposed by A. G. Werner in the eighteenth century.

Neptunist A follower of Abraham Gottlob Werner (1750–1817) who taught that all rocks were formed in or by water. *Cf.* PLUTONIST

nereite A fossil worm track.

neritic *1.* Related to shallow water on the margins of the sea, generally that overlying the continental shelf. 2. Related to the shallow sea bottom, generally that of the continental shelf.

neritic zone *1.* That part of the sea floor extending from the low tide line to a depth of 200 meters. *2.* A part of the pelagic division of the oceans with the water depths less than 200 meters.

nerito-paralic Refers to shallow marine water or conditions such as those of the epicontinental seas.

neritopelagic Pertaining to the shallow waters above the continental shelf area.

Nernst's law States that the solubility of a salt is decreased by the presence in solution of another salt that has a common ion.

nesosilicates Silicate structures in which individual SiO_4 tetrahedra are not linked together, i.e., they do not share oxygens. An example is olivine. *Syn:* ORTHOSILICATE. *See* SILICATES, CLASSIFICATION

ness; naes; naze (nose) *Geog:* In Great Britain, any promontory or sudden projection of the land into the sea, as Dungeness, Fifeness, the Naze, etc.

nested calderas The conditions leading to the formation of a caldera may recur on a smaller scale at the same volcanic center, so that a second depression of this class is developed within the perimeter of the first. The process may be conceived as repeated several times. In such cases the form is conveniently described under the name consecutive calderas, or more generally, nested calderas.

net slip The total slip along a fault; it is the distance measured on the fault surface between two formerly adjacent points situated on opposite walls of the fault.

network Especially in surveying and gravity prospecting, a pattern or configuration of stations, often so arranged as to provide a check on the consistency of the measured values, e.g., a level network, a gravity network based on the integration of torsion-balance gradients.

network structures *See* TECTOSILICATES

neutral salt A salt that gives a neutral solution when dissolved in water.

neutral solution A solution whose $pH = 7.0$.

neutral stress Pore-water pressure.

neutral surface *See* SURFACE OF NO STRAIN

neutrino Elementary particle of very small mass and with no electric charge.

neutron A particle having no electric charge and of mass nearly equal that of a proton.

neutron-gramma log A radioactivity log employing both gamma- and neutron-log curves. The neutron log should respond best to porous fluid-filled rock and the gamma best to shale markers.

neutron logging A radioactivity logging method used in boreholes in which a neutron source provides neutrons which enter rock formations encountered and induce additional gamma radiation which is measured by use of an ionization chamber. The gamma radiation so induced is related to the hydrogen content of the rock.

neutron-neutron (n-n) logging A technique in which the formation is bombarded by neutrons and the scattered neutrons are measured.

Nevadian orogeny Late Jurassic–Early Cretaceous diastrophism.

névé 1. A mass of snow partly converted into ice; forms the upper part of glaciers. See FIRN; SNOW FIELD

Niagaran Middle Silurian (restricted).

niccolite Copper nickel. A mineral, nickel arsenide, NiAs, copper-red. Hexagonal.

nickel bloom See ANNABERGITE

nickeliferous Containing nickel.

nicking A flexure which is so sharply exaggerated that breaking begins, although connection still exists. The structure is analogous to the "greenstick" fracture of wood or bone.

nickpoint The point of interruption of a stream profile at the head of a second-cycle valley according to the Treppen concept, q.v.

Nicol; Nicol prism A device for producing plane-polarized light, consisting of optically clear calcite so cut and recemented that the ordinary ray produced by double refraction in the calcite is totally reflected, but the extraordinary ray is transmitted. Nicol: Any instrument or device for producing plane-polarized

light by absorbing or reflecting one ray produced in a doubly refracting substance such as calcite, polaroid, etc.

nigger head 1. A hard, dark-colored boulder. 2. Large blocks of reef rock, usually located near the inner limit of the marginal zone.

Niggli number A series of magma types or categories into which a Niggli molecular norm is fitted.

Niggli's classification A classification of rocks on the basis of their chemical composition, similar in some respects to the norm system.

Niggli's molecular norm A "norm" calculated from the Niggli numbers in the Niggli classification of rocks.

niter Saltpeter. A mineral, KNO_3. Orthorhombic.

nitrate A salt or ester of nitric acid; a compound containing the radical NO_3.

nitride A compound of nitrogen with one other more positive element or radical.

nitrite A salt or ester of nitrous acid; a compound containing the radical NO_2^-.

nival Characterized by, abounding with, living in or under snow

nivation Frost action and mass wasting beneath a snowbank.

nivation cirque Small cirque formed by nivation.

noble metal Any metal or alloy of comparatively high value, or relatively superior in certain properties, especially resistance to corrosion or infusibility, as, gold, silver, or platinum; opposed to base metal.

nodal point See NODE, 1

nodal section See NODE, 1

nodal zone An area at which the predominant direction of the littoral drift changes.

node *1.* A point, line, or surface in a vibrating medium at which the amplitude of the vibration is reduced to zero by the interference of oppositely directed wave trains, forming stationary waves; e.g., one of the stationary points on a vibrating string. Such a point is a nodal point and such a cross section a nodal section. *2. Paleobot:* A point on a stem from which a leaf and bud arise.

nodular Having the shape or composed of nodules. Said of certain ore.

n o d u l e Small more or less rounded body generally somewhat harder than the enclosing sediment or rock matrix.

noise *1. Grav.* and *Mag. prospecting:* Disturbances in observed data due to more or less random inhomogeneities in surface and near-surface material. *2. Seismic prospecting:* All recorded energy not derived from the explosion of the shot. Sometimes loosely used for all recorded energy except events of interest.

nomenclature *1.* The naming of divisions in any scientific taxonomic scheme. *2.* The names used in systematic classification, as distinguished from other technical terms, as, Linnaean nomenclature.

nomen dubium A name of a taxonomic group which must be rejected when its application is uncertain.

nomina ambigua A name of a taxonomic group which must be rejected if, owing to its use with different meanings, it becomes a permanent source of confusion or error.

nomina confusa A name of a taxonomic group which must be rejected if the characters of that group were derived from two or more entirely discordant elements, especially if those elements were erroneously supposed to form part of the same individual.

nomina conservanda A list of "names retained" although not valid under the rules.

nominal diameter The diameter of a sphere of the same volume as the particle, which is the diameter of a sphere having the same settling velocity as the particle.

nomograph; nomogram A graph or chart reducing a mathematical formula to curves so that its value can be read on the chart coordinates for any value assigned the variables involved.

nonaffine Refers to deformative movements in which, at the scale considered, individual particles do not move uniformly with respect to each other and folding results in distortion of orginally straight lines and even planes.

nonartesian ground water *See* UNCONFINED GROUND WATER

nonconformity *1.* Angular unconformity, *q.v. 2.* An unconformity where the older rocks are of plutonic origin.

nonferrous metals Metals other than iron and its alloys in steel. Usually applied to the base metals, such as copper and lead.

nonhomogeneous or **nonaffine deformation** Deformation that is not homogeneous. *See* HOMOGENEOUS DEFORMATION

nonideal solutions *See* IDEAL SOLUTIONS

nonpiercement salt dome A salt dome in which the salt does not intrude or crosscut the overlying sediments. Contrasts with piercement salt dome, *q.v.*

nonplunging fold A fold with a horizontal axis.

nonpolarizable electrode A metal

electrode immersed in a saturated solution of one of its salts, the solution being carried in a vessel made of a permeable substance.

nonrotational or **irrotational strain** Stress and strain axes remain parallel throughout the deformation. Strictly speaking, the stress and strain axes are parallel regardless of the strain. What is meant is that in nonrotational strain, the applied force is parallel to one of the principal strain axes.

nonselective diagram *Struct. petrol:* A point or contour diagram made by not consciously selecting representatives of one type. For example, a nonselective diagram of quartz would make no distinction between the various grains of quartz. In contrast, a selective diagram might be made of large quartz grains, and another made from small quartz grains.

nonsorted circles Patterned ground, *q.v.*, whose mesh is dominantly circular and has a nonsorted appearance due to the absence of a border of stones such as that characterizing sorted circles.

nonsorted nets Patterned ground with a mesh intermediate between that of a nonsorted circle and a nonsorted polygon and with a nonsorted appearance due to absence of a border of stones such as characterizes a sorted net.

nonsorted polygons Patterned ground whose mesh is dominantly polygonal and has a nonsorted appearance due to the absence of a border of stones such as that characterizing sorted polygons.

nonsorted steps Patterned ground with a steplike form and a non-

sorted appearance due to a downslope border of vegetation embanking an area of relatively bare ground upslope.

nonsorted stripes Patterned ground with a striped pattern and a nonsorted appearance due to parallel lines of vegetation-covered ground and intervening strips of relatively bare ground oriented down the steepest available slope.

nontectonite Rock in which the position and orientation of grains have not been influenced by the movement of neighboring grains

nontronite *See* MONTMORILLONITE

Norian Middle Upper Triassic

norite A variety of gabbro in which orthopyroxene is dominant over clinopyroxene. Hypersthene-gabbro.

norm A theoretical, and in part arbitrary, mineral composition of a rock, calculated, in accordance with certain rules, from the chemical analysis for the purpose of assigning the rock its place in the norm system of rock classification. The norm rarely coincides with the real mineral composition or mode of a rock. *Cf.* MODE

norm, molecular *See* MOLECULAR NORM

normal *1.* In general, a straight line perpendicular to a surface or to another line. Also, a condition of being perpendicular to a surface or line. *2.* The average value over a period of years to any meteorological element such as pressure, temperature, rainfall, or duration of sunshine. The period 1901–30 was adopted by the International Meteorological Organization at Warsaw in 1935 as a standard period for climatological normals.

normal anticlinorium An anticlinorium, in which the axial planes of the subsidiary folds converge downward.

normal atmospheric pressure Standard pressure, usually taken to be equal to that of a column of mercury 760 mm. in height. Approximately 14.7 pounds per square inch.

normal class Holohedral or holosymmetric class.

normal consolidation Sedimentary compaction in equilibrium with overburden pressure.

normal correction *Mag. prospecting:* The correction made to data to remove the normal field.

normal dip The regional or general inclination of stratified rock over a wide area, as contrasted to local dip due to the presence of local structures.

normal distribution Chance occurrence of one of two possibilities that can be represented by a curve rising from zero to a maximum and then declining symmetrically to zero.

normal or geologic erosion The erosion which takes place on the land surface in its natural environment undisturbed by human activity. It includes (1) rock erosion, or erosion of rocks on which there is little or no developed soil, is in stream channels and rocky mountains, and (2) normal soil erosion, or the erosion of the soil under its natural condition or native vegetative cover undisturbed by human activity.

normal fault A fault at which the hanging wall has been depressed, relative to the footwall.

normal field *Mag. prospecting:* The smoothed value of a magnetic field component as derived from a large scale survey, worldwide or of continental scope. The normal field of the earth varies slowly with time, and maps of it are as of a certain date.

normal gravity The value of gravity at sea level according to a theoretical formula which assumes the earth to be a spheroid or of some similar regular shape.

normal horizontal separation *See* OFFSET

normal hydrostatic pressure Hydrostatic pressure in porous strata or wells approximately equal to the weight of a column of water whose length is the depth under consideration.

normality Concentration of a solution expressed as equivalents per liter, an equivalent being defined as the amount of a substance containing one gram-atom of replaceable hydrogen or its equivalent. *Symbol:* N. Thus a 3N ("three normal") solution has three equivalents per liter.

normal limb That limb of an overfold (overturned fold) that is right side up.

normal moveout The increase in reflection time due to an increase in the distance from shot to geophone when there is no dip.

normal projection A division of descriptive geometry in which a three-dimensional object is projected onto two mutually perpendicular planes. *See* ISOMETRIC PROJECTION

normal stress or **traction** Component of stress or traction perpendicular to a plane.

normal synclinorium A synclinorium in which axial planes of the subsidiary folds diverge downward.

normal travel-time curve In fan shooting, a time-distance curve obtained along a profile in some nearby area which does not contain geologic structures of the type being sought.

normal zoning In plagioclase,

the change by which crystals become more sodic in outer parts.

normative *Petrol:* Characteristic of, pertaining to, agreeing with, or occurring in the norm. Used in the quantitative or norm system of classification of igneous rocks, a normative mode being one which is essentially the same as the norm.

normative mineral Standard mineral, *q.v.*

normative quartz Theoretical quartz calculated according to certain rules from the chemical composition of a rock. *See* NORM

norm system A system of classification and nomenclature for igneous rocks based on the norm, *q.v.*, of each rock. C.I.P.W. system.

nose *1.* A half-developed anticline, i.e., one in which one end is open and without closure. *2.* Place on a map where a bed in a fold shows the maximum curvature. *3.* A projecting buttress of rock, usually overhanging; the projecting end of a hill, spur, ridge, or mountain. *4.* In brittle stars (a type of echinoderm), an articulating projection on arm ossicles.

notch *1.* A short defile through a hill, ridge, or mountain. A deep, close pass; a defile; a gap. Local in New England. *2.* A deep narrow cut at the base of a sea cliff above which the cliff overhangs. *Syn:* NIP

notochord A rod of elastic cells which provides a supporting and stiffening structure in an animal's body; it is replaced by a backbone in the true vertebrates.

novaculite A very dense, even-textured, light-colored cryptocrystalline siliceous rock. Originally, the term was applied to rocks found in the lower Paleo-

zoic rocks of the Ouachita Mountains of Arkansas.

nuclear basin A shallow negative area in an island arc region which is generally conformable to the structural trends of the associated positive elements.

nuclear log Radiometric record made in a borehole. *See* GAMMA RAY; SPECTRAL GAMMA RAY

nucleation The beginning of crystal growth at one or more points.

nucleic acid Complex organic substance that is the genetic material in all known organisms. *See* DNA; RNA

nucleon A proton or a neutron.

nucleus *1.* A kernel; a central mass or point about which other matter is gathered, or to which an accretion is made. *2.* A usually spherical or ovoid protoplasmic body found in most cells and considered as a directive center of many protoplasmic activities, including the transmission of hereditary characteristics. *3.* In radiolarians, a rounded mass of protoplasm enclosed in a delicate membrane. *4.* Embryonic gastropod shell commonly consisting of one to four whorls. *5.* The central portion of an atom; the chief constituents are protons and neutrons. *Syn:* PROTOCONCH

nuclide A species of atom characterized by the constitution of its nucleus; thus abundances of isotopes are described as abundances of various nuclides.

nuée or **nuée ardente** [*Fr.*] Applied to a highly heated mass or gas-charged lava, more or less horizontally ejected from a vent or pocket at the summit of a volcano, onto an outer slope where it continues on its course as an avalanche, flowing swiftly however slight the incline, by virtue of its extreme mobility.

nugget A waterworn piece of native gold. The term is restricted to pieces of some size, not mere "colors," or minute particles.

nummulite Lens or coin-shaped shell (test) of rather large foraminifers which were important in the Tertiary, particularly the Eocene. Referring to the type of foraminifer formerly known as the genus Nummulites.

nummulite limestone An Eocene formation made up chiefly of nummulite shells.

Nummulitic Eocene; named for its abundant large disklike foraminifera.

nunatak *1. Glaciol:* An isolated hill or peak which projects through the surface of a glacier. *2. Glacial geol:* A hill or peak which was formerly surrounded but not overridden by glacial ice.

nutation Periodic shifts in the position of the axis of the earth; period is about 19 years.

O

oasis A fertile green spot in a waste or desert, especially in a sandy desert.

ob- [*Lat.*] Prefix usually signifying inversion, as, obconical, inversely conical, cone attached to the small point.

oblate Flattened or depressed at the poles, as, an oblate spheroid.

oblique *1.* Neither perpendicular nor horizontal; slanting; inclined. *2. Photog:* An air photograph in which the camera is pointed downward at an angle to the horizontal. A high oblique is one taken at an angle to the vertical sufficiently high so that the horizon is included. A low oblique, with camera pointed more directly downward, does not include the horizon.

oblique extinction Extinction in anisotropic material not parallel to crystal outlines.

oblique fault A fault whose strike is oblique to the strike of the strata.

oblique joint A joint the strike of which is oblique to the strike of the adjacent strata or cleavage.

oblique-slip fault A fault in which the net-slip lies between the direction of dip and the direction of strike.

obsequent Flowing in a direction opposite to that of the dip of the strata or the tilt of the surface: said of some streams and contrasted with consequent. Called also reversed stream.

obsequent fault-line scarp A scarp along a fault line, but where the topographically low area is in the block that has been relatively uplifted. *See* RESEQUENT FAULT-LINE SCARP

obsequent rift block mountain A mountain which was formerly the floor of a graben but which was left standing as erosion lowered the weak rock areas on either side.

obsequent rift block valley A rift block valley occupying the site of a former horst. The limiting scarps are obsequent fault-line scarps.

observer *1. Seis. prospecting:* The man in charge of the instruments used and of the recording of the seismic data. *2. Grav.* and *Mag. prospecting:* A field man who secures the instrument readings, e.g., on the torsion balance or magnetometer.

obsidian An ancient name for volcanic glass. Most obsidians are black, although red, green, and brown ones are known. They are often banded and normally have conchoidal fracture and a glassy luster. The name has in recent years been somewhat restricted to glasses having a very low water content as contrasted with pitchstones and perlites. Most obsidians are rhyolitic in composition.

obtuse bisectrix *See* BISECTRIX

occidental amethyst Oriental amethyst.

occlude To absorb, as some metals take up certain gases and apparently incorporate them into the metallic structure.

ocean The great body of salt water which occupies two-thirds of the surface of the earth, or one of its major subdivisions. The sea as opposed to the land.

ocean basin That part of the floor of the ocean that is more than about 600 feet below sea level.

ocean current *1.* The name current is usually restricted to the faster movements of the ocean, while those in which the movement amounts to only a few miles a day are termed drifts. *2.* A nontidal current constituting a part of the great oceanic circulation. Examples: Gulf Stream, Kuroshio, Equatorial currents.

oceanic Related to the deep open sea beyond the edge of the continental shelf, in contrast to shallow coastal waters.

oceanic bank Guyot; tablemount, *q.v.* A seamount with a depth less than 100 fathoms.

oceanic islands Islands that rise from deep water far from any continent, though they may occur in a close group, like the Hawaiian Islands, the Azores, and the Galapagos.

oceanic rise Large area, hundreds of miles square, rising from the deep sea floor but not part of a mid-ocean ridge.

oceanite A picritic basalt.

oceanography Embraces all studies pertaining to the sea and integrates the knowledge gained in the marine sciences that deal with such subjects as the ocean boundaries and bottom topography, the physics and chemistry of sea water, the types of currents, and the many phases of marine biology. *Syn:* OCEANOLOGY; THALASSOGRAPHY

ocellar A rock texture characterized by radiating groups of prismatic or platy minerals such as biotite or pyroxene disposed around the borders of larger euhedral crystals such as analcite or leucite. The structures themselves are called ocelli.

ocher; ochre A pulverulent oxide, usually impure, used as a pigment. Brown and yellow ochers consist of limonite, or goethite, and red ocher of hematite. Similar pulverulent oxides of several other metals, also used as pigments, are sometimes called ochers, generally with the name of the metal prefixed, as antimony ocher, cadmium ocher.

Ochoan Upper Permian.

octahedral cleavage In the isometric system, cleavage parallel to the faces of the octahedron.

octahedrite *See* ANATASE

octahedron In the isometric system, a closed form of eight faces each having equal intercepts on all three axes.

octane A liquid hydrocarbon of the paraffin series, formula C_8H_{18}.

octaphyllite Trioctahedral clay minerals.

Oddo-Harkins rule Elements of even atomic number are more abundant than those of odd atomic number on either side.

odograph *1.* A device for recording the length and rapidity of stride and the number of steps taken by a walker. *2.* A device for registering the distance traveled by a vehicle or pedestrian. *3.* An automatic device for plotting the course and distance traveled by a vehicle.

odometer A revolution counter which is attached to the wheel of a vehicle and registers the number of turns made by the wheel in traveling over the ground.

An odometer is used in obtaining an approximate value of the distance traveled, the number of revolutions being multiplied by the circumference of the wheel.

oersted *1.* The practical, c.g.s. electromagnetic unit of magnetic intensity. A unit magnetic pole, placed in a vacuum in which the magnetic intensity is 1 oersted, is acted upon by a force of 1 dyne in the direction of the intensity vector. Formerly called gauss. *2.* Prior to 1932, the practical, c.g.s. electromagnetic unit of magnetic reluctance.

offlap The reverse of transgressive onlap. Offlap occurs where a shore line has retreated seaward and progressively younger strata have been deposited in layers offset seaward.

offset Displacement of formerly contiguous bodies.

offset well A well drilled at a distance, governed by local field practice, from a productive oil or gas well and on an adjoining leasehold for the purpose of protecting, by recovery through the offset, those reserves that otherwise might be produced by the earlier well. An obligation to drill such offset wells is contained in all oil and gas leases.

offshore bar Barrier beach, *q.v.* An accumulation of sand in the form of a ridge, built at some distance from the shore and under water. It results chiefly from wave action. Not to be confused with barrier island, *q.v.*

offshore beach A long, narrow, low sandy beach with a belt of quiet water separating it from the mainland.

offshore current *1.* Any current

in the offshore zone. *2.* Any current flowing away from shore.

offshore wind A wind blowing seaward over the coastal area.

Oghurd dune Arabic term used in the Sahara for a massive, mountainous dune.

ogive Any curved dark band, convex downslope, visible on a glacier surface. Specifically, such a band composed of debris-laden ice. Such bands are also called dirt bands, Forbes bands, Alaskan bands.

ohm The practical unit of electrical resistance. The resistance of a circuit in which one volt of potential difference produces a current of one ampere. The international ohm is the resistance of a column of mercury of uniform cross section, having a mass of 14.4521 grams and 106.3 cm. in length at 0° C.

ohm-centimeter A unit of electrical resistivity, viz., the resistivity of a substance of which a uniform rod of 1 cm.^{2} cross section has a resistance of 1 ohm per cm. length.

ohmmeter An instrument for measuring resistance directly in ohms.

-oid [$<Gr.$ -o-eides] Suffix meaning in the form of.

oil field A district containing a proved subterranean store of petroleum of economic value.

oil pool An accumulation of oil in sedimentary rock that yields petroleum on drilling. The oil occurs in the pores of the rock and is not a pool or pond in the ordinary sense of these words.

oil sand *1.* A general term for any rock containing oil. *2.* Porous sandstone from which petroleum is obtained by drilled wells.

oil shale Shale containing such a proportion of hydrocarbons as to be capable of yielding mineral oil on slow distillation. *See* SHALE; SHALE OIL; KEROGEN

oil smellers Men who profess to be able to indicate where oil-bearing strata are to be found, and locate places for successful well boring, by the sense of smell.

oil spring A spring of petroleum, maltha, or other hydrocarbon with or without hydrocarbon, with or without admixture of water.

oilstone A fine-grained stone used for sharpening edged tools or other similar metal surfaces.

oil-water surface A surface that forms the boundary between a body of ground water and an overlying body of petroleum that saturates the rock.

oil well A dug or bored well, from which petroleum is obtained by pumping or by natural flow.

Ol Abbreviation for olivine in normative rock calculations.

old age That stage in the development of streams and land forms when the processes of erosion are decreasing in vigor and efficiency or the forms are tending toward simplicity and subdued relief. *Cf.* YOUTH; MATURITY

olefin hydrocarbon A compound of carbon and hydrogen with open-chain molecules containing one or more double bonds; specifically a member of the ethylene series, having only one double bond per molecule.

oleogenesis Petroleum formation.

oleostatic Refers to oil pressure in a natural reservoir.

Oligocene The third of the epochs into which the Tertiary period is at present ordinarily divided. Also the series of strata deposited during that epoch.

oligoclase *See* PLAGIOCLASE

oligomictic rocks [<*Gr.* oligo-, few; miktos, mixed] Said of detrital sedimentary rocks in which few kinds of detrital minerals or rocks are present.

oligotrophic Refers to lakes with considerable oxygen in the bottom waters and with limited nutrient matter.

olivine Chrysolite. Peridot. A mineral series, solid solutions of forsterite, Mg_2SiO_4, with fayalite, Fe_2SiO_4, the composition often expressed as mol per cent of the constituents (abbreviated Fo and Fa). Orthorhombic. An important rock-forming mineral, especially in the mafic and ultramafic rocks.

olivinite A foliated rock with olivine as the principal constituent. Also used for hornblende picrite with augite and anorthite.

omega structure *1.* Thrust sheet overlying two oppositely directed low-angle thrust planes that steepen abruptly downward. *2.* Structure consisting of overthrusts or overfolds extending outward in opposite directions.

omission solid solution Defective crystal lattice in which atoms or ions are missing from their normal places.

Onesquethawan Upper Lower Devonian.

onion weathering *See* EXFOLIATION

onlap Extension of successive stratigraphic units beyond the marginal limits of their predecessors onto older rocks as in the deposits of a transgressing sea.

Onondagan Lower Middle Devonian.

onshore A direction landward from the sea.

onshore wind A wind blowing landward over the coastal area.

Ontarian *1.* Middle and Upper Ordovician. *Obs. 2.* Silurian (restricted). *3.* Lower Middle Silurian.

ontogenetic stage Developmental stage in the growth of an individual organism.

ontogeny The life history, or development, of an individual, as opposed to that of the race (phylogeny).

onyx *1.* A cryptocrystalline variety of quartz, made up of different colored layers, chiefly white, yellow, black, or red. *2.* Translucent layers of calcite from cave deposits, often called Mexican onyx or onyx marble.

oölite *1.* A spherical to ellipsoidal body, 0.25 to 2.00 mm. in diameter, which may or may not have a nucleus, and has concentric or radial structure or both. It is usually calcareous, but may be siliceous, hematitic, or of other composition. *2.* Accretionary oölite usually has a nucleus such as a quartz grain, and radial or concentric structure. It is grown in suspension in an agitating medium. *3.* Replacement oölite usually is without a nucleus, or has a nucleus of quartz. It is less regular and spherical, with concentric and radial structure, less well developed than in accretionary oölites. *4.* A rock composed chiefly of oöliths.

oölith The individual spherite of which an oölite (rock) is composed.

ooze A fine-grained pelagic deposit which contains more than 30% of material of organic origin.

ooze, calcareous An ooze with more than 30% of calcium carbonate, which represents the skeletal material of various planktonic animals and plants.

opacite A general term for microscopic, opaque grains in rocks, usually applied to such materials in the groundmass of volcanic rocks. It is generally regarded to consist largely of magnetite dust.

opal A mineral, $SiO_2.nH_2O$. Amorphous. Used as a gem.

opalescence A milky or pearly reflection from the interior of a mineral.

opalized wood Silicified wood, *q.v.*

open bay Bight. A broad indentation between two headlands or points, the bays being sufficiently open so that waves coming directly into the bay are essentially the same in height near the center of the bay as on open portions of the coast.

open cut Strip mine.

open flow The rate of flow of a gas well when flowing into the air, unrestricted by any pressure other than that of the atmosphere, usually in units of cubic feet per 24 hours. *See* INITIAL OPEN FLOW

open fold A fold in which the limbs diverge at a large angle

open form *Crystallog:* A crystal form that, taken alone, extends indefinitely or in one or more directions.

open hole A drill hole which, at the depth referred to, contains no casing or pipe, but in which the wall of the hole is formed by the rock penetrated.

open pack Sea ice composed of floes which for the most part do not touch; easily navigable.

open system Chemical system in which material is either added or removed.

operculum A lid or cover produced by circumscissile dehiscence.

ophicalcite A marble containing

serpentine. *See* MAGNESIAN MARBLE; MARBLE

ophidite Prasinite; ophite, *q.v.*

ophiolite Basic igneous rock associated with geosynclinal sediments, generally altered to rocks rich in serpentine, chlorite, epidote, and albite. *See* GREENSCHIST; GREENSTONE; OPHICALCITE.

ophitic A term applied to a texture characteristic of diabases or dolerite in which euhedral or subhedral crystals of plagioclase are embedded in a mesostasis of pyroxene crystals, usually augite. *See* DIABASIC

Ophiuroidea Subclass of stelleroids with slender arms not containing extensions of the stomach; brittle stars or serpent stars.

optical calcite Calcite crystals so clear that they have value for optical use.

optical character *Crystal opt:* The designation positive or negative, according to whether the algebraic sign of the following expressions is positive or negative: (1) for uniaxial crystals Ne−no ($\epsilon-\omega$); (2) for biaxial crystals, $\dfrac{2}{n_y^2}-\dfrac{1}{n_x^2}-\dfrac{1}{n_z^2}$, or approximately $n_x + n_z - 2n_y$. A useful diagnostic property of crystals.

optical constants *Opt. mineral:* The indices of refractions, axial angle, extinction angle, etc.

optical pyrometer *See* PYROMETER

optic angle *See* AXIAL ANGLE

optic axes Those directions in anisotropic crystals along which there is no double refraction.

optic ellipse Any noncircular section of an index ellipsoid.

optic indicatrix Indicatrix ellipsoid.

optic plane Axial plane.

option A stipulated privilege, given to a party in a time contract, of demanding its fulfillment on any day within a specified period.

Or Abbreviation for orthoclase.

orbicular structure A structure developed in certain phanerocrystalline rocks (e.g., granites, diorites, and corsite) due to the occurrence of concentric shells of different mineral composition around centers that may or may not exhibit a xenolithic nucleus. *Syn:* SPHEROIDAL STRUCTURE; NODULAR STRUCTURE

orbit The path described by a body in its revolution around another body.

orbital current The flow of water accompanying the orbital movement of the water particles in a wave. Not to be confused with wave-generated littoral currents.

orbitoid *1.* One of the foraminiferal family, the Orbitoididae; foraminifera with large, discoidal, saddle-shaped or stellate tests. *2. Adj:* Belonging to the foraminiferal family, the Orbitoididae (the orbitoids).

order *1.* Arrangement, particularly with respect to importance. *2. Tax:* A group of organisms consisting of one or more families and constituting part or all of a class. *3. Geomorph: See* STREAM ORDER; BASIN ORDER

order-disorder inversions An inversion between two polymorphic forms, one of which has a more ordered structure than the other. In general, upon heating the ordered, low-symmetry, low-temperature form a point is reached at which some portion of the lattice becomes disordered (or random), usually with an increase in crystal symmetry, to form the high-temperature form.

order-disorder polymorphism Two phases, generally related to temperature, in which atoms or ions occur at different positions or at random in a crystal lattice.

order of crystallization The apparent chronological sequence in which crystallization of the various minerals of an assemblage takes place, as evidenced mainly by textural features.

order of persistence Stability series.

ordinary ray; O-ray In optically uniaxial crystals, the ray of polarized light that vibrates in the plane of the basal pinacoid. Its refraction is not affected by the orientation.

Ordovician The second of the periods comprised in the Paleozoic era, in the geological classification now generally used. Also, the system of strata deposited during that period. In older literature, it was called Lower Silurian.

ore A mineral, or an aggregate of minerals, more or less mixed with a gangue, which from the standpoint of a miner can be won at a profit or from the standpoint of the metallurgist can be treated at a profit.

ore, developed *See* POSITIVE ORE; PROVED ORE

ore blocked out Ore exposed on three sides within a reasonable distance of each other.

ore body Generally a solid and fairly continuous mass of ore, which may include low-grade and waste as well as pay ore, but is individualized by form or character from adjoining country rock.

ore channel The space between the walls or boundaries of a lode which is occupied by ore and veinstone. Also called lode country.

ore chute An opening in ore or rock through which ore is dropped downward, and frequently used for ore bins and pockets, underground. A trough or lip at the bottom of a bin for conveying ore to a car, conveyor, etc.

ore cluster Group of ore bodies sometimes differing from each other in structure but interconnected or otherwise closely related genetically. Some ore clusters gather downward into a restricted root.

ore-dressing The cleaning of ore by the removal of certain valueless portions as by jigging, cobbing, vanning, and the like.

ore expectant The whole or any part of the ore below the lowest level or beyond the range of vision. *See* POSSIBLE ORE; PROSPECTIVE ORE. The prospective value of a mine beyond or below the last visible ore, based on the fullest possible data from the mine being examined and from the characteristics of the mining district.

ore faces Those ore bodies that are exposed on one side, or show only one face, and of which the values can be determined only in a prospective manner, as deduced from the general condition of the mine or prospect.

Oregonian orogeny Mid-Cretaceous diastrophism.

ore magma A heavy and highly concentrated solution containing metals and nonmetals.

ore shoot A large and usually rich aggregation of mineral in a vein. It is a more or less vertical zone or chimney of rich vein matter extending from wall to wall, and has a definite width laterally. Sometimes called pay streak, although the latter applies more specifically to placers.

organic deposits Rocks and other deposits formed by organisms or their remains.

organic reef A sedimentary rock aggregate, composed of the remains of colonial type organisms, mainly marine.

organ-pipe coral A tubiporoid coral consisting of cylindrical tubes placed side by side and united by horizontal floorlike expansions.

orient To place, as a map or an instrument, so that some portion of it points in a desired direction.

oriental agate Understood to be all the most beautiful and translucent sorts of agate.

oriental amethyst Strictly speaking, a variety of sapphire, but the term is applied to any amethyst of exceptional beauty.

oriental emerald A green variety of corundum.

oriental garnet Precious garnet.

oriental topaz A yellow variety of corundum, Al_2O_3.

orientation 1. The assignment or imposition of a definite direction in space. 2. *Surv:* The rotation of a map (or instrument) until the line of direction between any two of its points is parallel to the corresponding direction in nature. 3. The placing of a crystal in the conventional attitude, so as to show its symmetry and the forms to which its faces belong. 4. *Struct. petrol:* The arrangement in space of the particles (grains or atoms) of which a rock is composed. 5. *Paleontol:* The determination of the position of various organisms or organic hard parts with reference to such features as the dorsal and ventral sides of the animal, the anterior and posterior of the animal, the axis of coiling, the plane of coiling in shells, etc.

orientation, dimensional *Struct. petrol:* A preferred orientation showing a pattern dependent on shapes of fabric elements. This may involve limited lattice orientation, as with mica, but is not essential.

orientation, preferred See PREFERRED ORIENTATION

orientation diagram *Struct. petrol:* A general term for a point diagram and a contour diagram, *q.v.*

oriented specimen 1. *Struct. petrol:* A hand specimen that is so marked that its exact arrangement in space is known. 2. *Paleontol:* A fossil whose position is known as regards such features as anterior and dorsal sides, dorsal and ventral sides, the axis of coiling, the plane of coiling, etc.

origin 1. In a Cartesian coordinate system, the point defined by the intersection of the axes. 2. An arbitrary zero or starting point on a scale or measuring device.

original Characteristic of, or existing in, a rock at the time of its formation. Said of minerals, textures, etc., of rocks; essentially the same as primary *1*, and contrasted with secondary *1*.

original dip; primary dip The dip of beds immediately after deposition. Because of sinking of the basin these dips may steepen. The dip just prior to folding is initial dip, *q.v.*

original lead The common lead in a uranium mineral.

Oriskanian Upper Lower Devonian.

ornamentation The pattern of ridges, grooves, nodes, etc., that may interrupt the smooth surface of a shell.

orocline Structural or mountain arc owing its form to differential horizontal displacement after the main features of the structural zone originated.

orocratic A term applied by Sir Andrew Crosbie Ramsey to periods of maximum diastrophism.

orogen Belt of deformed rocks, in many places accompanied by metamorphic and plutonic rocks. For example, the Appalachian orogen or the Alpine orogen.

orogenic Adjective derived from orogeny, q.v.

orogeny The process of forming mountains, particularly by folding and thrusting.

orogeosyncline Geosyncline that developed into an orogen.

orographic rain Rain derived from rising air currents adjacent to mountains.

orographic rainfall Rainfall resulting when moist air is forced to rise by mountain ranges or other land formations lying athwart the path of the wind.

orography; orology That branch of physical geography which treats of mountains and mountain systems.

O/R potential Oxidation-reduction potential, Eh, expressed in volts.

orthite Allanite.

ortho- [Gr.] 1. A combining form meaning straight, at right angle, proper. 2. Petrog: The prefix indicating that a metamorphic rock was originally igneous.

orthoaxis In the monoclinic system, the axis that is perpendicular to the other two axes.

orthoclase A mineral, a member of the feldspar group. Composition $KAlSi_3O_8$. Monoclinic, dimorphous with microcline. A common mineral of granitic rocks. Abbr: Or

orthodolomite Sedimentary dolomite.

orthodome Monoclinic crystal form whose faces parallel the orthoaxis and cut the other axes.

orthogenesis Evolution continuously in a single direction over a considerable length of time; usages vary but the term usually carries the implication that the direction is determined by some factor internal to the organism, or, at least, is not determined by natural selection.

orthogeosyncline A long, narrow geosyncline, forming belts adjoining their separate cratons, q.v.

orthogneiss A term used to denote a gneiss derived from an igneous rock. See AUGEN GNEISS; GNEISS

orthogonal On a refraction diagram, a line drawn perpendicular to the wave crests.

ortholimestone Sedimentary limestone.

orthomagmatic or **orthotectic stage** Applied to the main stage of crystallization of silicates from a typical magma; the stage during which perhaps 90 per cent of the magma crystallizes. Cf. PEGMATITIC STAGE

orthopinacoid Monoclinic crystal form whose faces are parallel to both ortho- and c-axes.

orthoquartzite A clastic sedimentary rock composed of silica-cemented quartz sand. The cement is commonly deposited in crystallographic continuity with the quartz of the worn grains.

orthorhombic or **rhombic symmetry** 1. Struct. petrol: Refers to either symmetry of movement or symmetry of fabric. Orthorhombic symmetry of movement is exemplified by the motion that occurs when a sphere is subjected to a single compressive force acting along the vertical axis but is constrained on two opposite sides. Orthorhombic symmetry of fabric is the symmetry of an ellipsoid; there are three planes of symmetry. 2. The symmetry of a polyhedron with three orthogonal two-fold axes of rotatory symmetry. Three crystal classes, 222, 2mm, and 2/m 2/m 2/m have this symmetry.

orthorhombic system *Crystallog:* That system of crystals whose forms are referred to three unequal mutually perpendicular axes; also called rhombic system.

orthoschist A schist derived from an igneous rock. *See* PARASCHIST; SCHIST

orthotectic Designates those processes and products, strictly magmatic in the narrowest sense, exemplified in the normal crystallization of normal igneous rocks.

Osagean Lower Middle Mississippian.

osar; asar Esker.

oscillate *1.* To move or swing backward and forward; to vibrate like a pendulum. *2.* To vibrate or vary above and below a mean value.

oscillation cross-ripple marks Ripple marks consisting of two sets of ripple ridges intersecting at an angle. They are formed by two sets of waves acting concurrently or successively or a set of waves acting on previously formed current ripples.

oscillation ripple Ripples characterized by symmetry of crests, neither slope being steeper than the other since the ridges are built up by currents which operate from either side with approximately equal force. The crests are sharp and narrow as compared with the more broadly rounded intervening trough.

oscillatory twinning *See* POLYSYNTHETIC TWINNING

oscillatory wave A wave in which each individual particle oscillates about a point with little or no permanent change in position. The term is commonly applied to progressive oscillatory waves in which only the form advances, the individual particles moving in closed or nearly closed orbits. Distinguished from a wave of translation. *See* ORBIT

oscillograph An instrument which renders visible, or automatically traces, a curve representing the time variations of electric phenomena. The recorded trace is an oscillogram.

osmosis The passage of a solvent through a membrane from a dilute solution into a more concentrated one, the membrane being permeable to molecules of solvent but not to molecules of solute.

osmotic pressure If a pure solvent is separated from a solution by a membrane permeable only to molecules of the solvent, the extra pressure which must be applied to the solution in order to prevent flow of solvent into it by osmosis is known as the osmotic pressure of the solution.

Osann's classification A chemical system of classification of igneous rocks.

Osteichthyes Class of vertebrates, the bony fishes. Dev.-Rec.

Ostracoda Subdivision of crustaceans consisting of small bivalved animals inhabiting both salt and fresh water. Shells were molted several times as individuals grew. Ord.-Rec.

Ostwald's rule An unstable phase does not necessarily transform directly to the truly stable phase, but may first pass through successive intermediate phases, presumably due to lower activation energy barriers via that route.

Oswegan Lower Silurian (restricted).

otolith Ear bone of a fish.

Ouachitaian orogeny Late Mississippian-Early Pennsylvanian diastrophism.

ouady Wady; wadi.

outcrop The exposure of bedrock or strata projecting through the overlying cover of detritus and soil.

outer core Outer part of the earth's core between depths of about 2900 and 5000 km. May be liquid.

outer ridge Broad rise, generally more than 100 miles wide and from 600 to 6000 feet high, extending parallel to a continental margin; may enclose a marginal basin.

outlet The opening by or through which any water discharges its content. The lower end of a lake or pond; the point at which a lake or pond discharges into the stream which drains it.

outlet glacier An ice lobe issuing from an ice sheet and occupying a valley.

outlier Portions of any stratified group which lie detached, or out from the main body, the intervening or connecting portion having been removed by denudation.

outwash Drift deposited by meltwater streams beyond active glacier ice.

outwash plain *Obs.* Outwash apron; overwash apron; marginal plain; outwash gravel plain; washed gravel plain. Sandr, sandur [*Icel.*]. A plain composed of material washed out from the ice.

overbank deposit Flood-plain deposit.

overburden Material of any nature, consolidated or unconsolidated, that overlies a deposit of useful materials, ores, or coal, especially those deposits that are mined from the surface by open cuts.

overdeepened valley The standing lakes, the aggraded flood plains, and the growing fans all show that the bed of the glacial channel has been worn too deep to serve as a valley floor for the existing river; the river must aggrade, with water or with waste, the bed of the channel that the glacier degraded; hence Albrecht Penck has suggested that glaciated valleys of the Alpine kind should be called overdeepened.

overflow Density currents produced where fresh-water streams enter salt water, or warm-water streams enter bodies of cold water, the lighter water flowing over on the surface of the heavier.

overflow streams The spillways from standing water bodies; they include all effluents of lakes. Such effluents may be terminal, carrying the waters of the lake directly to the sea or into a trunk stream which flows into the sea without further laking; or interlacustrine, spilling over from one lake into another.

overfold A fold in which the beds on one limb are overturned, i.e., have been rotated through more than 90° so that they are inverted. *Syn:* OVERTURNED FOLD; OVERTHROWN FOLD; INVERTED FOLD. *Obs.*

overgrowth Secondary material deposited in optical continuity with a crystal grain, common in some sedimentary rocks. *Cf.* SECONDARY ENLARGEMENT

overhand stoping The working of a block of ore from a lower level to a level above.

overhang *1.* The overhanging

part of an erosion cliff, where the lower part has been undercut. 2. A part of the mass of a salt dome that projects out from the top of the dome like the top of a mushroom.

overlap *See* TRANSGRESSION

overlapping pair Two photographs taken at different exposure stations in such manner that a portion of one photograph shows the same terrain shown on a portion of the other photograph.

overlay A record or map on a transparent medium which may be super-imposed on another record.

overloaded stream An aggrading stream.

oversaturated rocks Those rocks which contain an excess of silica, over and above that necessary to form saturated minerals from all bases present. *See* SATURATED; SATURATION; UNDERSATURATED

oversteepening The process of steepening the walls of a valley by the passage of a valley glacier.

overthrust 1. A thrust fault with low dip and large net slip, generally measured in miles. 2. A thrust fault in which the hanging wall was the active element; contrasted with underthrust, but it is usually impossible to tell which wall was actively moved. 3. The process of thrusting the hanging wall (relatively) over the footwall.

overthrust sheet or **block** The block, above a low-angle fault plane, which has been displaced a matter of miles.

overturn The exchange of position in fall and spring of bottom and upper waters in a lake, caused by density differences due to temperature changes.

overturned Having been tilted

past the vertical and hence inverted in the outcrop. Said of folded strata and of the folds themselves.

overturned limb That limb of an overfold (overturned fold) that is overturned, i.e., has rotated through more than 90°.

ovoid, *adj.* Ovate or egg-shaped.

oxbow A crescent-shaped lake formed in an abandoned river bend which has become separated from the main stream by a change in the course of the river.

Oxfordian Lowermost Upper Jurassic.

oxidates Sediments formed by the precipitation of the oxidized form of Fe and Mn; ferric oxide and manganese dioxide sediments.

oxidation 1. Process of combining with oxygen; e.g., the oxidation of Zn gives ZnO. 2. The removal of one or more electrons from an ion or an atom.

oxidation-reduction potential The difference of potential measured in a cell having the oxidized and reduced form of an element on one side and the $H_2 - H^+$ couple on the other. At the hydrogen electrode the H_2 gas must be maintained at 1 atmos. pressure and the H^+ at a concentration of 1 mole/liter, and the temperature must be 25° C. Same as oxidation potential and redox potential; symbol E or Eh. If similar standards are used for both electrodes (all gases at 1 atmos. and all concentrations 1 M) and if the temperature is maintained at 25° C., the potential obtained is the standard oxidation-reduction potential (symbol E°).

oxide A compound of oxygen with one other more positive element or radical.

oxidize To unite with oxygen.

Many minerals and most metals oxidize with greater or less rapidity when exposed to air or water.

oxidized zone That portion of an ore deposit which has been subjected to the action of surface waters carrying oxygen, carbon dioxide, etc. That zone in which sulfides have been altered to oxides and carbonates.

oxidizing flame The outer cone of the blowpipe flame, characterized by the excess of oxygen of the air over the carbon of the gas.

oxychloride cement; sorel cement A plastic cement formed by mixing finely ground caustic magnesite with a solution of magnesium chloride.

oxyphile elements Elements occurring exclusively, or at least for the most part, combined with oxygen in oxides, silicates, phosphates, carbonates, nitrates, borates, sulfates, etc. Oxygen may be replaced by fluorine or chlorine to a minor extent. Approximately equivalent to Goldschmidt's lithophile elements. *Rare*

oxysphere Lithosphere. Proposed because 60% of atoms in the earth's crust are oxygen and they occupy more than 90% of the volume of the familiar rocks.

Ozarkian System between Cambrian and Canadian. *Obs.*

ozocerite One of the solid hydrocarbons. It is light colored, soft, and consists largely of paraffin hydrocarbons of high molecular weight.

P

Pacific series, province, or **suite** One of two great groups of igneous rocks (along with the Atlantic group) based on their tectonic setting. Originally described as occurring on the margins of the Pacific basin, hence the Circum-Pacific province. Characterized by the tholeiitic magma types, yielding saturated or oversaturated residues. *See* ATLANTIC SERIES

Pacific type of coast line Trend of folded belts are parallel to the coast. Contrasts with Atlantic type of coast.

pack ice Any large area of floating ice consisting of pieces of ice driven closely together.

packing The spacing or density pattern of the mineral grains in a rock *Cf.* FABRIC

paha, *n.* (*sing. and pl.*) Ridges of silt and clay in the area of Iowan glacial drift in northeastern Iowa.

pahoehoe, *n.* A Hawaiian term for basaltic lava flows typified by smooth, billowy, or ropy surface. Varieties include corded, elephant-hide, entrail, festooned, filamented, sharkskin, shelly, and slab pahoehoe. *Cf.* AA

paint gold A very thin coating of gold on minerals.

paint pot A type of mud pot containing variegated, highly colored, boiling mud, usually of cream, pink, or reddish tones.

pair production Transformation of a gamma ray (of greater than

1 m.e.v. energy) into a pair of electrons, one positive and the other negative.

palaeo- *See* PALEO

palaeoclimatology *See* PALEOCLIMATOLOGY

palagonite, *n.* A yellow or orange, isotropic mineraloid formed by hydration and other alteration (devitrification, oxidation) of sideromelane (basaltic glass), and constituting a characteristic part of palagonite tuffs. Also found as amygdule fillings in some basaltic lavas and as an alteration of the glassy skins of the pillows in pillow basalts. Two types, gelpalagonite and fibropalagonite, have been recognized.

palagonite tuff An indurated deposit of glassy basaltic ash in which the constituent particles are largely altered to palagonite.

Palatinian orogeny Post-Permian diastrophism.

paleo-; palaeo- [<*Gr. palaio-, palai-*] A combining form meaning old, ancient, used to denote: (1) Remote in the past; (2) Early, primitive, archaic. Before vowels usually pale-, palae-.

paleobiogeographic m a p Map showing the distribution of organisms during some interval of past time.

paleobiology That branch of paleontology which treats of fossils as organisms.

paleobotany *See* PALEONTOLOGY

Paleocene Earliest epoch of the Tertiary period; also strata of that age. Considered by some to be part of the Eocene and by others to be transitional between Cretaceous and Tertiary.

paleoclimatology The science which treats of the climates of the world throughout the geologic ages. Its data are the distribution of glacier deposits, nature of plant and animal fossils, topography and geography of former periods, and character of sedimentary rocks.

paleoecology The science of the relationship between ancient organisms and their environment.

Paleogene The earlier of the two periods comprised in the Cenozoic era, in the classification adopted by the International Geologic Congress and used by many European geologists; it includes the Paleocene, Eocene, and Oligocene epochs. Also, the system of strata deposited during that epoch. *Cf.* NEOGENE. Not used in the United States.

paleogeography The geography of an area at some specified time in the past.

paleogeologic map *1.* Map showing areal geology as it was at some former time. *2.* Areal map of strata below an unconformity.

paleolithologic map Map showing lithologic variations at some buried horizon or within some restricted zone.

paleomagnetism Faint magnetic polarization of rocks that may have been preserved since the accumulation of sediment or the solidification of magma whose magnetic particles were oriented with respect to the earth's magnetic field as it existed at that time and place.

paleontological species A species which embraces all geologically contemporary, closely related, and intergrading morphological forms. Polytypic species of Haas; broad species.

paleontologic facies Facies differentiated on the basis of fossils. *Cf.* BIOFACIES

paleontologic province Large region characterized by similar fossil faunas.

paleontologic species A species based on fossil specimens. It is wholly morphologic and may include specimens that would be considered specifically distinct if living individuals could be observed.

paleontology; palaeontology *1.* The science which treats of fossil remains, both animal and vegetable. *2.* The science that deals with the life of past geological ages. It is based on the study of the fossil remains of organisms. In restricted sense, study of fossil animals. *Cf.* PALEOBOTANY

paleosol A buried soil, especially one developed during an interglacial period and covered by deposits of later advances of the ice.

paleotectonic The crustal deformation at a given time in the geologic past.

paleotectonic map A map intended primarily to represent the deformation of part of the earth's crust during a certain time interval.

paleotopographic map Map showing the relief of an unconformable surface.

paleotopography Topography as it existed during some previous epoch of the earth's development.

Paleozoic One of the eras of geologic time that, between the Late Precambrian and Mesozoic eras, comprises the Cambrian, Ordovician, Silurian, Devonian, Mississippian, Pennsylvanian, and Permian systems. The beginning of the Paleozoic was formerly supposed to mark the appearance of life on the earth, but that is now known to be incorrect. Also, the group of rocks deposited during the Paleozoic era.

paleozoogeographic province Large region characterized by more or less closely related fossil faunas.

paleozoology The science of fossil animals; its two subdivisions are invertebrate and vertebrate paleontology.

palimpsest A structure of metamorphic rocks due to the presence of remnants of the original texture of the rock.

palingenesis *1.* The process of formation of new magma by the melting or fusion of country rocks with heat from another magma, with or without the addition of granitic material. *2.* The differential melting, in the root parts of folded mountains, to form a pore liquid or ichor. Anatexis. *3. Paleontol* and *Biol:* The young stages of an organism recapitulate, without change, the characters of their ancestors. *Ant:* COENOGENESIS

palinspastic map *1.* Map showing restoration of folded and faulted rocks to original relative geographic positions. *2.* A map showing thickness of a sedimentary unit restored to its pre-erosional or pre-truncation dimensions.

palisade A picturesque, extended rock cliff rising precipitately from the margin of a stream or lake and of columnar structure. A line of bold cliffs, especially showing basaltic columns.

Palisadian disturbance Post-Triassic diastrophism.

palladium gold Porpezite, or gold

containing palladium up to 10%.

pallasite *See* SIDEROLITE

palsen Earth mounds, believed to be of periglacial origin and occurring in arctic and alpine regions. They are composed entirely of earth and persist long after amelioration of the climatic conditions that produced them. Earth hummocks, *q.v.*

paludal Pertaining to swamps or marshes, and to material deposited in a swamp environment. *See* PALUSTRINE

palustrine Pertaining to material deposited in a swamp environment. *See* PALUDAL

palygorskite Attapulgite. A group of clay minerals, hydrous magnesium aluminum silicates, characterized by a distinctive rodlike shape.

palynology The study of pollen and other spores and their dispersal, and applications thereof.

pampas The great open treeless plains in the region of South America south of the Amazon, extending from the Atlantic to the Andes; sometimes applied to other similar plains.

pan *1.* A natural basin or depression, especially one containing standing water or mud, and, as in South Africa, in the dry season often dried up, leaving a salt deposit. *2.* In South Africa, a hollow in the ground where the neck of a volcano formerly existed. *3.* Fire clay or underclay of coal seams.

panfan *1.* The ultimate surface attained when the last remnants of a range in a region of rising base-level have disappeared and the flanking alluvial fans coalesce at the divide. *2.* An end stage in the process of geomorphic development in an arid region in the same sense that the peneplain is an end stage of the general process of degradation in a humid climate.

Pangaea Theoretical great continent in the Northern Hemisphere which fragmented to produce the present continents. *Cf.* PANTHALASSA

panmixis The free interchange of genes within an interbreeding population.

panning In Australia and the Pacific, washing earth or crushed rock in a pan, by agitation with water, to obtain the particles of greatest specific gravity which it contains (chiefly practiced for gold, also for quicksilver, diamonds, and other gems).

Pannonian Lower Pliocene.

panplane A nearly flat surface brought about more by the lateral erosion of streams, which pares away the divides and causes a coalescing of all the flood plains of a region to form.

Panthalassa Theoretical sea surrounding Pangaea before its fragmentation.

pantograph An instrument for copying maps, plans, etc., on any predetermined scale.

Pantotheria Infraclass of mammals, includes marsupials and related animals. Jur.-Rec.

paper coal *1.* A variety of brown coal deposited in thin layers like sheets of paper. *2.* Coal in which cuticular matter may be prominent.

paper shale Highly carbonaceous shale that splits in thin, tough, somewhat flexible sheets

papillate; papillose, *adj.* Bearing minute pimplelike protuberances (papillae).

para-; par- [*Gr.*] A prefix meaning beside. *Petrog:* Indicates metamorphic rock so qualified was derived from an original sediment.

parabolic dune A dune having, in ground plan, approximately the form of a parabola, with the concave side toward the wind.

paraconformity Unconformity at which strata are parallel and the contact is a simple bedding plane.

Paracrinoidea Class of stemmed echinoderms with irregularly arranged body plates pierced by pores and uniserial arms. Ord.

paracrystalline deformation Deformation that is contemporaneous with the recrystallization that forms a metamorphic rock. A similar idea is expressed in the terms syntectonic crystallization and paratectonic recrystallization.

paraffin A white, tasteless, odorless, and chemically inert waxy substance composed of natural hydrocarbons and obtained from petroleum. Any saturated hydrocarbon of chain structure whose general formula is C_nH_{2n+2}.

paraffin base Term applied to a crude oil containing paraffin wax in solution; such oil is relatively high in hydrogen and low in carbon.

paraffin dirt The paraffin, or "sour dirt" of the Gulf Coast fields; a yellow, waxy substance resembling beeswax, it has often been regarded as indicating the proximity of an oil gas reservoir.

paraffin hydrocarbon One of a series of saturated hydrocarbons with an open-chain structure; general formula C_nH_{2n+2}. A saturated aliphatic hydrocarbon. *Syn:* METHANE HYDROCARBON

paraffin series A homologous series of open-chain saturated hydrocarbons of the general formula C_nH_{2n+2} of which methane (CH_4) is the first member and the type. *Syn:* METHANE SERIES

paragenesis A general term for the order of formation of associated minerals in time succession, one after another. To study the paragenesis is to trace out in a rock or vein the succession in which the minerals have developed.

paragenetic *1.* Refers to the chronological order of the crystallization of minerals as in a vein. *2.* Refers to the genetic relations of sediments in laterally continuous and equivalent facies.

parageosyncline Intracratonal geosyncline. *1.* A geosyncline that lies within a craton, i.e., within a relatively immobile portion of the crust of the earth. *2.* A geosyncline along the margin of a continent.

parageneiss A term used to denote a gneiss derived from a sedimentary rock. *See* GNEISS; ORTHOGNEISS

paragonite A mineral, a member of the mica group, $NaAl_2(AlSi_3)O_{10}(OH)_2$. Monoclinic.

paraliageosyncline A deep geosyncline that passes into coastal plains along the present continental margin.

paralic Pertaining to environments of the marine borders, such as lagoonal, littoral, shallow neritic, etc.

parallax, instrumental A change in the apparent position of an object with respect to the reference mark(s) of an instrument which is due to imperfect adjustment of the instrument or to a change in the position of the observer.

When a telescope is poorly focused, so that the image of the object does not lie in the plane of the reticle (cross hairs), a movement of the eye transverse to the line of collimation will cause an apparent movement of the image of the object with respect to the cross hairs. This is a usual form of instrumental parallax, and for it the term optical parallax is proposed. Parallax may also result from the position in which an observer stands with respect to the fiducial marks on an instrument, as when reading a vernier or marking a tape end; for this type of parallax the term personal parallax is proposed.

parallel A line extending around the earth parallel to the equator, used to indicate angular distance poleward.

parallel, geographic A line on the earth having the same latitude at every point.

parallel, standard (U.S. public-land surveys) An auxiliary governing line established along the astronomic parallel, initiated at a selected township corner on a principal meridian, usually at intervals of 24 miles from the base line, on which standard township, section, and quarter-section corners are established; also known as a correction line. Standard parallels, or correction lines are established for the purpose of limiting the convergence of range lines from the south.

parallel development Parallel evolution; parallelism; homoeomorphy.

parallel drainage pattern The drainage pattern is called parallel when the streams over a considerable area or in a number of successive cases flow nearly parallel to one another. Parallel drainage implies either a pronounced regional slope, or a slope by parallel topographic features such as glacially remodeled surfaces of the drumloidal or fluted ground moraine type, or control by parallel folded or faulted structures.

parallel evolution The phenomenon whereby related but distinct phyletic stocks develop comparable forms.

parallel extinction Extinction in anisotropic crystals parallel to crystal outlines.

parallel faults A group of faults having essentially the same dip and strike.

parallel or **concentric fold** A fold in which each bed maintains the same thickness (assuming it was initially of uniform thickness) throughout all parts of the fold. Contrasts with similar folding, in which each bed thins on the limbs and thickens toward the anticlinal and synclinal axes.

parallelism The evolution of different lines or families in the same way, with corresponding, successive isomorphs. *Syn:* PARALLEL EVOLUTION; PARALLEL DEVELOPMENT; HOMOEOMORPHY

parallel shot *Seis. prospecting:* A test shot made with all the amplifiers connected in parallel and activated by a single geophone in order to check for lead, lag, polarity, and phasing in the amplifier to oscillograph circuits.

paramagnetic Having a magnetic permeability greater than unity, and susceptibility therefore positive; yet not ferromagnetic.

parameter *Mineral:* That rational multiple of the unit length of any crystallographic axis intercepted by a crystal plane which determines the plane's position with reference to the fundamental form. A quantity constant in a special case, but variable in different cases.

paramorph A pseudomorph with the same composition as the original crystal, as calcite after aragonite.

paraschist A term used to denote a schist derived from a sedimentary rock. *See* ORTHOSCHIST; SCHIST

parasitic cone One or more cinder cones which from their position upon the flanks of the larger volcano are referred to as parasitic cones.

paratectonic recrystallization A recrystallization which accompanies deformation.

para-time-rock units Para-time-rock units express chronology and should approach synchrony, whereas time-rock units express chronology and absolute synchrony.

paratype A specimen other than the holotype, upon which an original specific description is based.

paravane 1. In seismic water shooting, a planing board used to keep a detector in a vertical position. 2. In seismic water shooting, a device attached to the end of a towed line and so arranged that the device either travels a path parallel to but offset from the path of the towing vessel, or maintains a fixed depth below the surface, or both.

Parazoa Multicellular animals whose cells are not organized into tissues or organs, e.g., sponges.

parenchyma A tissue composed of thin-walled, often isodiametric cells, which often store food and usually retain meristematic potentialities.

parental magma That magma from which some other magma was derived.

parent element The radioactive element from which a daughter element is produced by radioactive decay; e.g., radium is the parent element of radon.

parent material (soils) The horizon of weathered rock or partly weathered soil material from which the soil is formed. Horizon C of the soil profile.

parent rock 1. The original rock from which sediments were derived to form later rocks. 2. (Soils) The rock from which parent materials of soils are formed.

park 1. Topog: A grassy, wide, and comparatively level open valley in wooded mountains; also, an open space surrounded by woodland. Local in Rocky Mountains. 2. Shallow broad solution depression. Syn: SINKHOLE; term used locally on the Kaibab Plateau area of Arizona.

parma A low dome or quaquaversal.

paroptesis The changes produced in rocks by dry heat; a baking.

partial or **selective diagram** Struct. petrol: A point or contour diagram prepared by deliberately selecting certain grains of one mineral for measurement, such as measuring the large quartz grains in preference to the small ones, or measuring only quartz grains along shear zones.

particle size histogram A graphic method for presenting the particle-size distribution of sediments as a series of vertical bars whose heights are proportional to the frequency in each class. The term itself is standard statistical usage for such diagrams.

particle-size weight-frequency distribution Particle-size distribution based on weight of material in each size grade rather than on number of grains.

particle velocity For waves, the velocity induced by wave motion

with which a specific water particle moves.

particulate, adj. Of or relating to particles or occurring as minute particles.

parting 1. A small joint in coal or rock, or a layer of rock in a coal seam. 2. The tendency of crystals to separate along certain planes that are not true cleavage planes.

party A group of men performing the geophysical field work necessary for a specific project or prospect, ordinarily using a single method, as, a gravity party.

parvafacies The portion of any magnafacies which lies between designated time-stratigraphic planes or key beds traced across the magnafacies.

Pasadenian orogeny Mid-Pleistocene diastrophism.

Pascal's law The principle that the pressure in a fluid not acted upon by external forces is the same at all points or that a fluid transmits pressures equally in all directions.

pass 1. A gap, defile, or other relatively low break in a mountain range through which a road or trail may pass; an opening in a ridge forming a passageway. See COL. 2. A navigable channel, especially at a river's mouth. 3. A narrow connecting channel between two bodies of water; an inlet. 4. An opening through a barrier reef, atoll, or sand bar.

patch reefs Small, thick, generally unbedded lenses of limestone or dolomite, more or less isolated and surrounded by rocks of unlike facies.

pater noster lake One of a linear series of small lakes occupying depressions in a glacial stairway.

path Seis. prospecting and Seismol: The course of travel between two points of a disturbance in an elastic medium.

patina Thin light-colored outer layer produced by weathering.

patinated chert Chert nodules with weathered or casehardened surface layer.

patterned ground A group term for the more or less symmetrical forms such as circles, polygons, nets, steps, and stripes that are characteristic of, but not necessarily confined to, mantle subject to intensive frost action.

pattern shooting *Seis. prospecting:* The firing of explosive charges arranged in a definite geometric pattern.

pay Profitable ore.

pay gravel *Placer min:* A rich strip or lead of auriferous gravel.

pay ore Those parts of an ore body which are both rich enough and large enough to work with profit. *See* PAY GRAVEL

pay streak That portion of a vein which carries the profitable or pay ore.

PDR Precision depth recorder.

peacock copper Bornite.

peacock ore Name given to bornite, also less commonly to chalcopyrite, in allusion to the variegated colors on tarnished surfaces.

peak diameter Maximum diameter.

peak zone Biostratigraphic zone characterized by maximum development or greatest abundance of some fossil.

peat A dark-brown or black residuum produced by the partial decomposition and disintegration of mosses, sedges, trees, and other plants that grow in marshes and like wet places.

peat bog A bog containing peat.

peat formation A process of decomposition of vegetable and animal substances intermediate between moldering and putrefaction or rot, during which first the former and then the latter process occurs. *Cf.* DISINTEGRATION; MOLDERING; PUTREFACTION

pebble armor A concentration of pebbles coating a desert area. The pebbles are usually the residual product of wind erosion and are closely fitted together so as to cover the surface in the manner of a mosaic. *Syn:* DESERT PAVEMENT. *See* LAG GRAVEL

pebble dike Vein or dikelike bodies composed of rounded-to-angular pebbles in a finer-grained matrix of pebble material or intrusive igneous rock. The pebble rounding results from multiple faceting caused by attrition during intrusion from below. The pebbles are derived from underlying rock units and represent materials pushed ahead of, or dragged along, the edge of magma bodies being forcefully intruded.

pebble gravel Gravel consisting mainly of rounded rock fragments of pebble size.

pebble phosphate Varieties of natural phosphate that are concretionary or alluvial in origin, hence gravel-like.

pebble pup Inexperienced rock hound.

pebbles Smooth rounded stones ranging in diameter from 2 to 64 mm.

pectinate, *adj.* Comblike or pinnatifid with very close narrow divisions or parts; also used to describe spine connections in cacti when small lateral spines radiate like comb teeth from areole.

pectolite A mineral, $Na(Ca,Mn)_2$ $Si_3O_8(OH)$, commonly in radiating groups in cavities in diabase. Triclinic.

ped Individual natural soil aggregate as contrasted with a clod produced by artificial disturbance.

pedalfer Soil of humid regions, enriched in alumina and iron. Accumulates in regions of high temperature and humid climate that are marked by forest cover. *Cf.* PEDOCAL.

pedcal Pedocal.

pedestal boulder Isolated masses or rock above and resting on a smaller base or pedestal. *See* PERCHED BOULDER

pedestal rock A residual mass of weak rock capped with harder rock. *See* PEDESTAL BOULDER

pediment Gently inclined planate erosion surfaces carved in bedrock and generally veneered with fluvial gravels. They occur between mountain fronts and valley or basin bottoms and commonly form extensive bedrock surfaces over which the erosion products from the retreating mountain fronts are transported to the basins.

pediment pass Narrow, flat, rock-floored depression connecting pediment slopes on opposite sides of a mountain ridge.

pedion Crystal form with only one face.

pediplain; pediplane Widely extending rock-cut and alluviated surfaces formed by the coalescence of a number of pediments and occasional desert domes.

pedocal Soil of arid or semiarid regions, enriched in lime. Accumulate in regions of low temperature and rainfall and prairie vegetation. *Cf.* PEDALFER

pedogenesis Soil formation.

pedology The science which treats of soils, their origin, character, and utilization.

pedometer A pocket-size instrument which registers the distance in linear units traversed by the pedestrian carrying it.

peel-off time *Seis. prospecting:* The time correction to be applied to observed data to adjust them to a depressed reference datum.

peel thrust Overthrust fault block pushed ahead of a resistant mass without affecting a hard underlying basement and not involving shortening in a folded region.

pegmatite Those igneous rocks of coarse grain found usually as dikes associated with a large mass of plutonic rock of finer grain size. The absolute grain size is of lesser consequence than the relative size. Unless specified otherwise, the name usually means granite pegmatites, although pegmatites having gross compositions similar to other rock types are known. Some pegmatites contain rare minerals rich in such elements as lithium, boron, fluorine, niobium, tantalum, uranium, and the rare earths.

pegmatitic stage or phase A stage in the normal sequence of crystallization of a magma containing volatiles, at which time the residual fluid is sufficiently enriched in volatile materials to permit the formation of coarse-grained rocks more or less equivalent in composition to the parent rock (pegmatites). The relative amounts of silicate and volatile materials in the fluid, the temperature range, and the relationship of these fluids to the hydrothermal fluids, *q.v.,* are in dispute.

peg model A method of showing relative location of wells and the depth of oil sands or key beds each penetrates. The wells are represented by rods or dowels, set vertically in a base, each graduated for depth. Key strata on the rods are correlated and joined by threads to give a tridimensional relationship of structure.

pelagic *1.* Pertaining to communities of marine organisms which live free from direct dependence on bottom or shore; the two types are the free-swimming forms (nektonic) and the floating forms (planktonic). *2.* Related to water of the sea as distinct from the sea bottom. *3.* Related to sediment of the deep sea as distinct from that derived directly from the land.

pelean, *adj.* Designating or pertaining to a type of volcanic eruption characterized by explosions of extreme violence and the formation of nuées ardentes. The lavas involved in this type of eruption are generally extremely silicic and viscous.

Pelecypoda A division (class) of the phylum Mollusca; commonly called pelecypods, *q.v.*

Pele's hair Rock material consisting of threads of volcanic glass (generally basaltic) drawn out from the lavas by explosion or by bursting of bubbles on lava lakes. The capillary ejecta of Lacroix.

Pele's tears Small drops of volcanic glass (generally basaltic) with pendant threads, or pairs of drops arranged in dumbbell fashion, thrown out during eruptions of fluid lava and measuring a few millimeters in length. Common in Hawaii.

pelite Mudstone.

pelitic Argillaceous, *q.v.*

pelitomorphic Refers to irregular precipitated grains of calcium carbonate.

pellet Small aggregation of sedimentary material. *See* FAECAL PELLETS

pellet structure A feature commonly shown by clays, formed of small rounded aggregates of clay minerals and fine quartz scattered through a matrix of the same material. The pellets may be separated from the matrix by a shell of organic material. In size, the pellets are 0.1 to 0.3 mm. in diameter, and in a few cases several mm. in length.

pellicular A term applied to water adhering as films to the surfaces of openings and occurring as wedge-shaped bodies at junctures of interstices in the zone of aeration above the capillary fringe.

Pelmatozoa Subphylum of echinoderms most of which are permanently attached by a jointed stem after completion of larval development. Camb.-Rec.

Pelmatozoan The stemmed echinoderms, consisting chiefly of the cystoids and crinoids, *q.v.*

pelyte; pelite Mudstone.

pencil ganister Ganister characterized by fine carbonaceous markings and so called from the likeness of these traversing marks to pencil lines. They are often recognizable as roots and rootlets of plants.

pencil structure Very pronounced lineation such as that produced by intersecting bedding and cleavage planes in slate.

pendant A small solutional remnant projecting from the ceiling or an overhanging wall.

pendulum *1.* A body so suspended from a fixed point as to swing freely to and fro under the combined action of gravity and momentum. *2.* A vertical bar so supported from below by a stiff spring as to vibrate to and fro under the combined action of gravity and the restoring force of the spring. Also called an inverted pendulum.

penecontemporaneous A term used in connection with the formation of a sedimentary rock such as a cherty limestone or a concretionary shale. It implies that in the opinion of the user the chert or the concretion was formed at almost the same time as the deposition of the material of the surrounding rock.

peneplain *1.* A land surface worn down by erosion to a nearly flat or broadly undulating plain; the penultimate stage of old age of the land produced by the forces of erosion. *2.* By extension, such a surface uplifted to form a plateau and subjected to renewed degradation and dissection.

peneplanation The subaerial degradation of a region approximately to base level, forming a peneplain.

penetration twin *See* TWIN

penetrometer A weight-driven rod or drill for measuring the vertical resistance of snow to penetration.

peninsula A body of land nearly surrounded by water, and connected with a larger body by a neck or isthmus; also, any piece of land jutting out into the water.

Penjabian Lower Upper Permian.

Pennsylvanian Formerly the upper of two epochs into which Carboniferous was subdivided. Recently, the Am. Comm. on Strat. Nomenclature recommended advancement to period rank, and that is now accepted by the U. S. Geological Survey. In America, Pennsylvanian is sixth of seven periods in the Paleozoic Era. Also, the system of rocks formed during the period

pentagonal dodecahedron *See* PYRITOHEDRON. *Obs.*

pentane A liquid hydrocarbon of the paraffin series, formula C_5H_{12}.

pentremite *1.* A type of blastoid that was particularly common in the Mississippian. *2.* Equivalent to blastoid, *q.v. Syn:* BLASTOID; SEA BUD

pepino Rounded, conical-shaped hills resulting from tropical karst action. *Syn:* HUM; HAYSTACK; MOGOTES; COCKPIT

peptize, *v.* To bring into colloidal solution; to convert into a solution.

per- [*Lat., Gr.*] *1.* A prefix used to signify: (a) Throughout in space or time; (b) Away or over; (c) Completely, thoroughly, perfectly; extremely, very. *2. Chem:* A prefix denoting the presence of the largest possible, or a relatively large, proportion of some element, or the presence of an atom having its highest, or a relatively high, valence.

peralkaline In the Shand classification of igneous rocks, a division embracing those rocks in which the molecular proportion of alumina is less than that of soda and potash combined.

peraluminous In the Shand classification of igneous rocks, a division embracing those rocks in which the molecular proportion of alumina exceeds that of soda, potash, and lime combined.

percentage log A well record made from an examination of cuttings in which the precentage of each type of rock present in each sample of cuttings is estimated and plotted.

perched block *See* PERCHED ROCK

perched boulder A large erratic lying in an unstable position on top of a hill or boss.

perched ground water Ground water separated from an underlying body of ground water by unsaturated rock. Its water table is a perched water table.

perched rock or **block** A large mass of rock which, after glacial transportation, has been lodged in some conspicuous isolated position.

perched water table Water table above an impermeable bed underlain by unsaturated rocks of sufficient permeability to allow movement of ground water.

percolate To pass through fine interstices; to filter; as water percolates through porous stones.

percolation Movement under hydrostatic pressure of water through the interstices of the rock or soil, except movement through large openings such as caves.

percussion mark Crescentic chatter or percussion marks on the finer grained and well-rounded pebbles, especially porphyries.

pereletok [*Russ.*] Intergelisol. A layer of frozen ground between the active layer and permafrost which may persist for one or two summers.

perennially frozen ground *See* PERMAFROST

perennial stream Streams that flow throughout the year and from source to mouth.

perfect gas *See* IDEAL GAS

perforation Puncturing of well casing opposite an oil-bearing zone to permit oil to flow into a cased borehole.

pergelation The act or process of forming permanently frozen ground in the present or in the past.

pergelisol *See* PERMAFROST

pergelisol table Top of pergelisol.

peri- [*Gr.*] Prefix meaning around or beyond.

periclase Magnesia. A mineral, MgO. Isometric.

periclinal Dipping on all sides from a central point or apex. Applied to strata which dip in this manner from some common center of elevation. *Syn:* QUAQUAVERSAL

pericline Quaquaversal; centrocline [Brit.]; dome.

pericline twin *See* TWIN LAW

peridot The gem variety of olivine.

peridotite A general term for essentially nonfeldspathic plutonic rocks consisting of olivine, with or without other mafic minerals. The other mafic minerals may be amphiboles, pyroxenes, or in some examples micas. Minerals of the spinel group are common constituents.

periglacial Refers to areas, conditions, processes, and deposits adjacent to the margin of a glacier.

perimagmatic Close to the magma.

period *1.* A major, world-wide, standard geologic time unit corresponding to a system. *2.* An interval of time characterized in some particular way. *3.* Time required for a recurrent motion or phenomenon to complete a cycle and begin to repeat itself.

periodic or **tidal current** A current, caused by the tide-producing forces of the moon and the sun, which is a part of the same general movement of the sea manifested in the vertical rise and fall of the tides.

perlite A volcanic glass having numerous concentric cracks which give rise to perlitic structure. Most perlites have a higher water content than obsidians. A high proportion of all perlites are rhyolitic in composition.

perlitic structure A structure produced in homogeneous material by contraction during cooling, and consisting of a system of irregular, convolute, and spheroidal cracks; generally confined to natural glass, but occasionally found in quartz and other noncleavable minerals and as a relict structure in devitrified rocks.

permafrost Permanently frozen subsoil.

permafrost table A more or less irregular surface which represents the upper limit of permafrost.

permanent current A current that runs continuously independent of the tides and temporary causes. Permanent currents include the fresh water discharge of a river and the currents that form the general circulatory systems of the oceans.

permanent hardness Hardness of water generally resulting from the presence of dissolved magnesium carbonate; it cannot be removed by boiling.

permanently frozen ground See PERMAFROST

permanent monument A monument of a lasting character for marking a mining claim. It may be a mountain, hill, ridge, hogback, butte, canyon, gulch, river, stream, waterfall, cascade, lake, inlet, bay, arm of the sea, stake, post, monument of stone or boulders, shafts, drifts, tunnels, open cuts, or well-known adjoining patented claim.

permeability *1*. The permeability (or perviousness) of rock is its capacity for transmitting a fluid. Degree of permeability depends upon the size and shape of the pores, the size and shape of their interconnections, and the extent of the latter. It is measured by the rate at which a fluid of standard viscosity can move a given distance through a given interval of time. The unit of permeability is the darcy, *q.v.* See also MILLIDARCY. *2. Geophys:* The ratio of the magnetic induction to the magnetic intensity in the same region. In paramagnetic matter the permeability is nearly independent of the magnetic intensity; in a vacuum it is strictly so. But in ferromagnetic matter the relationship is definite only under fully specified conditions.

permeability, relative The ratio of the permeability of a porous medium under any given conditions to the absolute permeability. This term usually signifies the permeability to one fluid phase when two or more phases are present in the porous medium.

permeability coefficient Coefficient of permeability. The rate of flow of water in gallons a day through a cross section of 1 square foot under a unit hydraulic gradient. The standard coefficient is defined for water at a temperature of 60° F. The field coefficient requires no temperature adjustment and the units are stated in terms of the prevailing water temperature.

permeability trap A condition in which a permeable part of a bed or group of beds is bounded, particularly on the updip side, by relatively impermeable rock.

permeable Pervious. *Hydrol:* Having a texture that permits water to move through it perceptibly under the head differences ordinarily found in subsurface water. A permeable rock has communicating interstices of capillary or supercapillary size.

Permian *1*. Last period of the Paleozoic Era, also system of same age. *2*. Formerly considered by U. S. Geological Survey to be last epoch of the Carboniferous, and its strata. *Obs.*

permineralization The process of fossilization wherein the original hard parts of an animal have additional mineral material deposited in their pore spaces.

Permo-Carboniferous Strata not differentiated between the Permian and Carboniferous systems, particularly in regions where there is no conspicuous stratigraphic break and fossils are transitional.

Permo-Triassic Strata not differentiated between the Permian and Triassic systems, particularly in regions where the boundary occurs within a nonmarine red beds succession.

perovskite A mineral, (Ca,Ce)-(Ti,Nb)O$_3$. Pseudoisometric, usually in yellow, brown, or black cubes.

perpendicular slip The component of the net slip measured perpendicularly to the trace on the fault of the disrupted index plane (bed dike, vein, etc.) in the fault plane.

perpendicular throw The distance between the two parts of a disrupted bed, dike, vein, or of any recognizable surface measured perpendicular to the bedding plane or to the surface in question. It is measured, therefore, in a vertical plane at right angles to the strike of the disrupted surface.

Perret phase (of eruption) Emission of much high energy gas which may greatly enlarge a volcanic conduit.

perthite A variety of feldspar consisting of intergrown orthoclase or microcline with albite.

pervious *See* PERMEABLE

petrifaction The process of petrifying.

petrified rose Aggregates or clusters of tabular crystals of barite, which form chiefly in sandstones,

enclosing the sandy matrix within the crystals.

petrified wood Silicified wood, *q.v.*

petrify To become stone. Organic substances, such as shells, bones, wood, etc., embedded in sediments, become converted into stone by the gradual replacement of their tissues, particle by particle, with corresponding amounts of infiltrated mineral matter. Thus not only the outward forms but even the minutest details of the organic tissues are preserved.

petro-; petr- [*Gr.*] A combining form meaning rock or stone.

petrochemistry *1.* The chemistry of rocks. *2.* The chemistry of petroleum; disapproved by some geochemists.

petrofabric analysis Petrofabrics, *q.v.*

petrofabric diagram A diagram used in petrofabric analysis. It may be a point diagram or contour diagram, *q.v.*

petrofabrics Petrofabric analysis. The study of spatial relations, especially on a microscale, of the units that comprise a rock, including a study of the movements that produced these elements. The units may be rock fragments, mineral grains, or atomic lattices.

petrofacies Facies distinguished by petrographic characters.

petrogenesis A branch of petrology which deals with the origins of rocks, and more particularly with the origins of igneous rocks.

petrogenic grid Pressure-temperature diagram with equilibrium curves showing the stability fields of specific minerals and mineral associations.

petrogeny's residual system The system NaAlSiO$_4$-KAlSiO$_4$-SiO$_2$, which represents a close approximation to the composition of many residual liquids from magmatic differentiation.

petrographer One versed in the science of petrography or the systematic description and classification of rocks.

petrographic period Time represented by a rock kindred.

petrographic province A region or district in which some or all of the igneous rocks are regarded as consanguineous, or as derived from a common parent magma; a comagmatic district or province.

petrography See LITHOLOGY

petroleogenesis Formation of petroleum.

petroleum Material occurring naturally in the earth composed predominantly of mixtures of chemical compounds of carbon and hydrogen with or without other nonmetallic elements such as sulfur, oxygen, nitrogen, etc. Petroleum may contain, or be composed of, such compounds in the gaseous, liquid, and/or solid state, depending on the nature of these compounds and the existent conditions of temperature and pressure.

petroliferous Containing or yielding petroleum.

petroliferous province An area containing known commerical accumulations of petroleum in a tectonic unit, such as a sedimentary basin or a geosyncline.

petrology A general term for the study by all available methods of the natural history of rocks, including their origins, present conditions, alterations and decay. Petrology comprises petrography on the one hand, and petrogenesis on the other, and properly considered, its subject matter includes ore deposits and mineral deposits in general as well as

"rocks" in the more limited sense in which that term is generally understood.

Pfalzian orogeny Palatinian.

pH The negative logarithm of the hydrogen ion activity (less correctly, concentration). For example, pH 7 indicates an H^+ concentration (activity) of 10^{-7} mole/liter.

phacolith A concordant intrusive in the crest of an anticline and trough of a syncline, hence in cross section it has the shape of a doubly convex lens.

phanerite A general term applied to wholly crystalline rocks, the constituents of which may be distinguished with the unaided eye. The adjective form phaneritic is currently used more frequently than the noun.

phaneritic A textural term applied to igneous rocks in which all the crystals of the essential minerals can be distinguished with the unaided eye; i.e., megascopically crystalline. Contrasted with cryptocrystalline; microcrystalline.

Phanerogamia Spermatophyta.

Phanerozoic Comprises Paleozoic, Mesozoic, and Cenozoic; eon of evident life.

phantom crystal A crystal in which an earlier stage of crystallization is outlined in the interior.

phantom horizon In seismic reflection prospecting, a line so constructed that it is parallel to the nearest actual dip segment everywhere along a profile.

phase *1.* A variety differing in some minor respect from the dominant or normal type; a facies; ordinarily used in the detailed description of igneous rock masses. *2. Phys. chem:* A homogeneous, physically distinct portion of matter in a nonhomogeneous (i.e., heterogeneous) system, as the three phases—ice, water, and aqueous vapor. *3.* The point or stage in the period to which the rotation, oscillation, or variation has advanced, considered in its relation to a standard position or assumed instant of starting. This relation is commonly expressed in angular measure. *4. Earthquake seismol:* An event on a seismogram marking the arrival of an impulse or a group of waves at a detecting instrument and indicated by a change of period or amplitude, or both. *5.* Facies, *q.v.,* as it was used prior to 1849. *6.* Geologic time unit smaller than an age. (Uncommon.) *7.* Rock facies identified by both original and secondary characters of the strata. (Uncommon.)

phase angle The phase difference between the impressed electromotive force and the current in an alternating-current circuit, expressed as an angle.

phase area In binary diagrams, any area of the diagram in which both temperature and composition may be varied, within limits, without a phase change occurring. Phase areas are separated from each other by boundary lines. In ternary systems it is that portion of the liquidus surface in which a given solid is the primary phase.

phase boundary Boundary line. The line separating any two phase areas (in binary systems) or any two liquidus surfaces (in ternary systems).

phase diagram A graph in which two or more of the variables temperature, pressure, and concentrations are plotted against one another, designed to show the boundaries of the fields of sta-

bility of the various phases of a heterogeneous system.

phase equilibria Heterogeneous equilibria, *q.v.*

phase inversion A change of 180° in phase angle.

phase rule The statement that for any system in equilibrium, the number of degrees of freedom is two greater than the difference between the number of components and the number of phases; in symbols, $F=C-P+2$.

phassachate A lead-colored agate.

phenacite A beryllium orthosilicate, Be_2SiO_4. Sometimes used as a gem.

phenocryst One of the relatively large and ordinarily conspicuous crystals of the earliest generation in a porphyritic igneous rock.

Phi grade scale *See* GRADE SCALE, PHI

Phi mean particle diameter A logarithmic mean particle diameter obtained by using the negative logs of the class midpoints to the base 2.

Phi Sigma Sigma Phi. The standard deviation of a particle-size distribution computed in terms of Phi grades.

phlogopite A mineral, a member of the mica group, $K(Mg,Fe'')_3(AlSi_3)O_{10}(F,OH)_2$.

phonolite Extrusive equivalent of nepheline syenite. The principal mineral is soda orthoclase or sanidine. Other major minerals are nepheline and aegirine-diopside usually with other feldspathoidal minerals as sodalite or hauyne. Accessory apatite and sphene.

phorogenesis Slipping of the earth's crust over the mantle.

phosphate A salt or ester of phosphoric acid; a compound containing the radical PO_4^{-3}.

phosphate rock A sedimentary rock containing calcium phosphate. The form in which the phosphate occurs is obscure. The chief mineral commonly is apatite.

phosphorescence Luminescence caused by exposure to light or other forms of radiation, and lasting after exposure has ceased. *Cf.* FLUORESCENCE

photogeology The geologic interpretation of aerial photographs.

photogeomorphology Study of earth forms as revealed by aerial photographs.

photogrammetry The science and art of obtaining reliable measurements from photographs.

photomap The reproduction of a single photograph, composite, or mosaic, complete with grid lines and marginal data.

photomicrograph An enlarged or macroscopic photograph of a microscopic object, taken by attaching a camera to a microscope.

photon A quantum of electromagnetic radiation.

photosynthesis Synthesis of chemical compounds effected with the aid of radiant energy, especially light. If unqualified, commonly refers to the synthesis of carbohydrates from water and the carbon dioxide of the air in the chlorophyll-containing tissues of plants exposed to light.

phototaxis Movement of organisms in response to light stimulation.

phreatic, *adj.* [*Gr.* phrear, -atos, well] Originally introduced by G. A. Daubrée to designate water in the upper part of the zone of saturation, excluding the deeper water of this zone below impermeable beds. Now generally regarded as an exact synonym of ground water—pertaining to all water in the zone of saturation.

phreatic explosion A volcanic explosion, ordinarily of extreme violence, caused by the conversion of ground water to steam. Such steam explosions have a low temperature and do not expel essential ejecta.

phyla Plural of phylum, *q.v.*

phyletic Pertaining to a line of organic descent.

phyletic evolution Evolution involving changes in lineages but little or no increase in the number of taxonomic groups.

phyletic species A species based on the close genetic relationship of individuals.

phyllite An argillaceous rock intermediate in metamorphic grade between slate and schist. The mica crystals impart a silky sheen to the surface of cleavage (or schistosity). *See* SCHIST; SLATE

phyllitization Development of phyllitic rocks.

phyllosilicates Silicate structures in which the SiO_4 tetrahedra occur linked together in infinite two-dimensional sheets. An example is mica. *See* SILICATES, CLASSIFICATION

phylogenetic evolution Evolution within a single lineage.

phylogenetic species Fossil species which is a segment of an evolving lineage.

phylogeny The line, or lines, of direct descent in a given group of organisms. Also the study or the history of such relationships.

phylogerontism The condition of racial deterioration and approaching extinction.

phylum One of the primary divisions of the animal and plant kingdom; a group of closely related classes of animals or plants.

-phyric [<*Fr.* -phyre] A combining form denoting porphyritic.

physical geography That branch

of science which has for its object the comparison and generalization of geographical facts. It differs chiefly from geology in that it regards the present rather than the past condition of the earth, but many authors include in their textbooks of physical geography more or less of that which is generally considered as belonging to geology.

physiographic cycle The sequences of changes from the beginning of youth to old age.

physiographic province Region of similar structure and climate that has had a unified geomorphic history.

physiography [<*Gr.* physis, nature; and graphe, description] The study of the genesis and evolution of land forms.

phytolith A rock formed by plant activity or composed chiefly of plant remains. The term was applied by A. W. Grabau to a large group including coal, peat, lignites, and some types of reef limestones, oölites.

phytoplankton All the floating plants such as diatoms, dinoflagellates, coccolithophores, and sargassum weed.

Piacenzian Upper Pliocene; Astian.

picacho A peak or sharply pointed hill or mountain. Because of the steep slopes of mountains in the desert region, picacho appears as the name of numerous mountains in southwestern Arizona.

pick *Seis. prospecting: 1.* The selection of an event on a seismic record. Also used as a verb, as, to pick reflections. *2.* Any selected event on a seismic record.

picrite The term picrite was first used by Gustav Tschermak for a rock of the composition of olivine teschenite. It was later used by Harry Rosenbusch for

an olivine-rich diabase. The adjectival form picritic is now used to connote an olivine-rich rock. *See* PICRITE BASALT

picrite basalt Olivine-rich basalt as is often formed by the settling of olivine in thick flows and sills, etc. These often contain fifty or more per cent of olivine. *See* PICRITE

pictograph *1.* Any conventionalized representation of an object *2.* Diagram showing range of variability, commonly a scatter diagram.

piecemeal stoping A process whereby magma eats into its roof by engulfing relatively small isolated blocks, which presumably sink to depth where they are assimilated. *See* MAGMATIC STOPING

piedmont Lying or formed at the base of mountains, as, a piedmont glacier. A piedmont alluvial plain is formed at the foot of a mountain range by the merging of several alluvial fans

piedmont alluvial plain A plain formed by the coalescence of alluvial fans.

piedmont bulb Expanded foot *q.v.*

piedmont glacier A glacier formed by coalescence of two or more valley glaciers beyond the base of a steep slope.

piedmont steps, benchlands, or treppen Regional terraces sloping outward (down valley) to correspond with the several graded reaches of the streams are postulated to develop as the response to a continually accelerated upheaval of an expanding dome.

piedmont treppen Piedmont steps, *q.v.*

piercement dome A salt dome in which the salt core has broken through the overlying strata until it reaches or approaches the surface.

piercement fold; piercing fold Diapir fold, *q.v.*

piezocrescence The growth of one crystallographic orientation out of another under the influence of stress produced by either mechanical or thermal means.

piezoelectric *1.* Having the ability to develop surface electric charges when subjected to elastic deformation, and conversely. *2.* Oscillates in alternating current circuits with frequencies harmonic with the stimulating frequency.

piezometric surface *Hydrol: 1.* An imaginary surface that everywhere coincides with the static level of the water in the aquifer. *2.* The surface to which the water from a given aquifer will rise under its full head.

pigeonite *See* PYROXENE

piggot corer Device for sampling bottom sediments. A core barrel is driven into unconsolidated material by an explosive charge.

pillar A column of rock remaining after solution of the surrounding rock. *See* HOODOOS

pillow lavas A general term for lavas that exhibit pillow structure, occurring mostly in basic lavas (basalts and andesites) and especially in the sodium-rich basalts known as spilites.

pillow structure The peculiar structure exhibited by some basic lavas (especially spilites) which consist of an agglomeration of rounded masses that resemble pillows, bolsters, or filled sacks. The rounded masses or pillows fit closely upon one another, the hollows of one matching the prominences of another, and the intervening spaces are usually filled with such sedimentary materials as chert, limestone, or hardened shale. In general, the individual pillows have a fine-grained or glassy skin, are vesicular within, and in cross section exhibit a banded concentric structure. The pillow structure is generally believed to be the result of subaqueous deposition.

pilotaxitic A textural term proposed by Harry Rosenbusch and applied to the groundmasses of holocrystalline, glass-free (volcanic) rocks consisting of a feltlike interweaving of lath-shaped microlites (ordinarily plagioclase), commonly in flow lines. *See* FELTY

pimple mound Mima mound. *See* PIMPLE PLAINS

pimple plains Characterized by numerous conspicuous, small, rounded, circular elevations 15 to 30 feet in diameter and 2 to 6 feet in height.

pinacoid *Crystallog:* A crystal form consisting of exactly two parallel faces. In the hexagonal and tetragonal systems, only a basal pinacoid is possible, parallel to the lateral axes and cutting the vertical axis *c* at right angles. In the orthorhombic system, basal, side, or brachy, and front or macro pinacoids are possible; in the monoclinic system, basal, front or ortho, side or clino, and an indefinite number of inclined pinacoids parallel to the ortho-axis *b* are possible; in the triclinic system, pinacoidal class, only pinacoids are possible. In an obsolete nomenclature, only those pinacoids that are parallel to planes containing two crystallographic axes are so designated, others being called hemiprisms, etc., according to their orientation.

pinch A compression of the walls of a vein, or the roof and floor of a coal bed, which more or less completely displaces the ore or coal. Called also pinch out.

pinch out Thin out, *q.v.*

pingo Relatively large mound raised by frost action above the permafrost and generally persisting for more than a single season.

pingok Pingo.

pingo remnant Kettlelike depression resulting from the melting of a mass of ground ice.

pinnacle *1. Topog:* Any high tower or spire-shaped pillar of rock, alone or cresting a summit. A tall, slender, pointed mass; especially a lofty peak. 2. A sharp pyramid or cone-shaped rock under water or showing above it.

pinnate joints *See* FEATHER JOINTS

pinwheel garnet Crystal that has been rotated during metamorphic movement.

pipe A tabular opening or cylindrical rock body filling a tabular opening. It is usually more or less vertical.

pipe, volcanic *See* VOLCANIC PIPE

pipe clay Potter's clay, *q.v.*

pipe ore Iron ore (limonite) in vertical pillars, sometimes of conical, sometimes of hour-glass, form, embedded in clay. Probably formed by the union of stalactites and stalagmites in caverns.

piperno, *n.* A local Italian name applied to the trachytic tuffs of the Phlegrean Fields in the vicinity of Naples. The rock is characterized by a eutaxitic structure and the presence of numerous stringers and lenticles of dark glass (fiamme) in a light-colored, porous, glassy matrix and is generally considered to be a type of welded tuff.

pipestone Catlinite, *q.v.*

pipette analysis Size analysis of fine-grained sediment made by removing samples from a suspension with a pipette.

piracy The diversion of the upper part of a stream by the headward growth of another stream. Also called beheading, stream capture, and stream robbery.

pirate stream *See* PIRACY

Pisces Subphylum of vertebrates, fish. Ord.-Rec.

pisolite A spherical or subspherical accretionary body over 2 mm. in diameter.

pisolith A small spheroidal particle with concentrically laminated internal structure, ranging from 1 to 10 mm. in diameter. The unit particle in the rock "pisolite."

pisolitic Consisting of rounded grains like peas or beans.

pisolitic tuff An indurated pyroclastic deposit made up chiefly of accretionary lapilli or pisolites.

pit *1. Topog:* A cavity or hole in the ground, natural or artificial, such as the La Brea Pits of tar in California. *Speleol:* 2. A deep hole, generally circular in outline, with vertical or nearly vertical walls; 3. Small hole made in cave fills by cave beetles; 4. *Paleobot:* A thin place in a cell wall. A simple pit has no overarching wall, a bordered pit has such a wall.

pitch *Struct. geol:* 1. The angle that a line in a plane makes with a horizontal line in that plane. A committee of the USGS has recently recommended that "pitch" be no longer used and that "rake" be used for this angle instead; 2. Often used as synonymous with plunge. 3. Of an ore shoot in a vein, the angle between the axis of the ore shoot and the strike of the vein. The pitch is measured in the plane of the vein. *Petroleum geol:* 4. A solid hydrocarbon belonging to the group of asphaltites; 5. One of the residues formed in the distillation of wood or coal tar. It is also obtained from petroleum. The term pitch is sometimes employed indiscriminately to mean bitumen or asphalt. 6. *Speleol:* A vertical shaft in a pothole.

pitch, mineral Bitumen; asphalt.

pitchblende Uraninite.

pitches A deposit which follows dipping joint planes. Usage confined largely to Upper Mississippi Valley lead-zinc deposits.

pitch length The length of an ore shoot in its greatest dimension.

pitchstone A volcanic glass characterized by a pitchy rather than glassy luster. They may be almost any color and have compositions equivalent to a wide range of volcanic rocks. They contain a rather high percentage of water compared to other glassy rocks.

pitchy copper ore An early name for a dark-colored oxide of copper which looks like pitch.

Pitot tube A small tube, bent at one extremity to form a right angle. The bent end of the tube is inserted in the flowing stream so that the plane of the opening is perpendicular to the direction of flow. This determines the impact pressure of the flowing stream, indicated by the height to which it will force a fluid column, usually water or mercury. Commonly used in the form of a "U" tube to measure the flow of gas wells.

pitted plain *Topog:* 1. An outwash plain of gravel or sand with kettle holes; 2. Plain with numerous, small, closely spaced sinkholes.

pivotal fault Hinge fault, *q.v.*

Pl Abbreviation for plagioclase.

placenta 1. The organ which bears the ovules in an ovary, often the margin of the carpellary leaves. 2. In cryptogams, the tissue from which the sporangia arise.

placental Member of the Monodelphia.

Placentalia Monodelphia.

placer [*Sp.*] A place where gold is obtained by washing; an alluvial or glacial deposit, as of sand or gravel, containing particles of gold or other valuable mineral. In the United States mining law, mineral deposits, not veins in place, are treated as placers, so far as locating, holding, and patenting are concerned. Various minerals besides metallic ores have been held to fall under this provision, but not coal, oil, or salt.

placer claim 1. A mining claim located upon gravel or ground whose mineral contents are extracted by the use of water, by sluicing, hydraulicking, etc. The unit claim is 1320 feet square and contains 10 acres. *See* PLACER. 2. Ground with defined boundaries which contains mineral in the earth, sand, or gravel; ground that includes valuable deposits not fixed in the rock.

placer deposit A mass of gravel, sand, or similar material resulting from the crumbling and erosion of solid rocks and containing particles or nuggets of gold, platinum, tin, or other valuable minerals, that have been derived from rocks or veins.

placer mining That form of mining in which the surficial detritus is washed for gold or other valuable minerals. When water under pressure is employed to break down the gravel, the term hydraulic mining is generally employed. There are deposits of detrital material containing gold which lie too deep to be profitably extracted by surface mining, and which must be worked by drifting beneath the overlying barren material. To the operations necessary to extract such auriferous material the term drift mining is applied.

Placodermi Class of vertebrates consisting of primitive jawed fish of varied characters, some armored, some skarklike. Dev.-Perm.

plagioclase A mineral group, formula $(Na,Ca)Al(Si,Al)Si_2O_8$; a solid solution series from $NaAlSi_3O_8$ (albite) to $CaAl_2SiO_8$ (anorthite). Triclinic. One of the commonest rock-forming minerals. Commonly the series is designated in terms of the mole fraction of the albite component (Ab) and anorthite component (An), as follows (Ab+An=100): albite (Ab 100–90), oligoclase (Ab 90–70), andesine (Ab 70–50), labradorite (Ab 50–30), bytownite (Ab 30–10), anorthite (Ab 10–0).

plain A region of general uniform slope, comparatively level, of considerable extent, and not broken by marked elevations and depressions; it may be an extensive valley floor or a plateau summit. Any extent of level or nearly level land.

plain, coastal A plain fronting the coast and generally representing a strip of recently emerged sea bottom.

plain of denudation A nearly plane surface, produced by erosion.

plain tract Lower portion of a stream course characterized by low gradient and a wide flood plain.

Plaisancian Piacenzian.

planar cross-stratification Compound stratification. A type of cross-stratification in which the lower bounding surfaces of the sets are planar surfaces of erosion.

planar flow structure Any planar structure that develops during the intrusion of magma. May be expressed by the parallel arrangement of platy minerals (giving a foliation), by slablike inclusions, by schlieren, or by bands of different mineralogy or texture. Synonymous with planar structure and platy flow structure.

planar gliding Uniform slippage along plane surfaces.

planation *1.* The widening of valleys through lateral corrasion by streams after they reach grade and begin to swing, and the concurrent formation of flood plains. Also, by the extension of the above processes, the reduction of divides and the merging of valley plains to form a peneplain; peneplanation. *2.* The grading of an area or district by any erosive process, either subaerial or marine.

plane correction A correction applied to observed data to reduce them to a common reference plane.

plane group A set of symmetry operations in a plane; there are 17 of them.

plane of flattening *See* FLATTENING, PLANE OF

plane of symmetry A plane to which a crystal is symmetrical; i.e., each face, corner, and edge of an ideally developed crystal is the mirror image, with respect to this plane, of another face, comer, or edge.

plane-polarized light Light constrained to vibrate in a plane; a single Nicol prism produces plane-polarized light. *Cf.* CROSSED NICOLS

plane strain State of strain in

which intermediate strain axis is unity or can be ignored.

plane stress State of stress in which tractions (stresses) involving the intermediate principal stress vanish.

plane surveying Surveying in which the curvature of the earth is disregarded, as in ordinary field and topographic surveying.

plane table *1.* A simple surveying instrument by means of which one can plot the lines of a survey directly from the observations. It consists of a drawing board on a tripod, with a ruler, the ruler being pointed at the object observed. *2.* An inclined ore-dressing table.

planetesimal One of numerous small solid planetary bodies which, according to the planetesimal hypothesis, had individual orbits about the sun and of which the planets were formed by aggregation.

planetesimal hypothesis or theory The hypothesis that the earth and other planets were formed by the collision and coalescence of planetesimals and have never been wholly molten.

planimeter An instrument for measuring the area of any plane figure by passing a tracer around the bounding plane.

planimetric analysis Analysis of patterns in a fabric diagram based on distribution of points and areal comparisons.

planimetric map A map which presents the horizontal positions only for the features represented; distinguished from a topographic map by the omission of relief in measurable form.

planimetry The determination of horizontal distances, angles, and areas by measurements on a map.

plankton Holoplankton, *q.v.* Floating organisms. All the float-

ing or drifting life of the pelagic division of the sea.

planktonic Floating.

planosol An intrazonal group of soils with eluviated surface horizons underlain by B horizons more strongly illuviated, cemented, or compacted than associated normal soils, developed upon nearly flat upland surface under grass or forest vegetation in a humid or subhumid climate.

plant An organism generally capable of manufacturing food from inorganic substances by photosynthesis. Plants lack the sensitivity of animals and are incapable of voluntary motion. Some tiny organisms share the characteristics of plants and animals. *See* PROTISTA

Plantae The vegetable kingdom.

plastering-on Process of addition of material to a ground moraine by melting at the base of a glacier.

plaster stone Gypsum.

plastic Capable of being molded into any form, which is retained.

plastic deformation A permanent change in shape of a solid that does not involve failure by rupture. In the narrowest sense the change is accomplished largely by gliding within individual grains; but it also involves rotation of grains. In a larger sense includes deformation that is related to recrystallization.

plastic flow *See* SOLID FLOW; LIQUID FLOW

plastic index Difference between liquid and plastic limits, indicating range of moisture content within which sedimentary material is plastic. If plastic limit is equal to or greater than liquid limit, the index is zero.

plasticity The property of a material that enables it to undergo permanent deformation without appreciable volume change or elastic rebound, and without rupture.

plasticity index The numerical difference between the liquid limit and the plastic limit of a soil.

plastic limit Water content of unconsolidated material at the point where it passes from a plastic solid to a more or less rigid condition as determined by standardized tests.

plastic strain *1*. In the case of a single mineral the term connotes permanent deformation accomplished by gliding within the crystal lattice without loss of cohesion. *2*. In rocks, which are composed of many crystals often belonging to several mineral species, the term is conveniently applicable to any permanent deformation throughout which the rock maintains essential cohesion, and strength, regardless of extent to which local microfracturing and displacement of individual grains may have entered into the process.

plat A diagram drawn to scale showing all essential data pertaining to the boundaries and subdivisions of a tract of land, as determined by survey or protraction.

plateau A relatively elevated area of comparatively flat land which is commonly limited on at least one side by an abrupt descent to lower land.

plateau basalt A term applied to those basaltic lavas that occur as vast composite accumulations of horizontal or subhorizontal flows and which, erupted in rapid succession over great areas, have at times flooded sectors of the earth's surface on a regional scale. They are generally believed to be the product of fissure eruptions and tend to conform to either one of two standard compositions, distinguished as the tholeiitic and olivine basalt magma types respectively. In most parts of the world the two magma types have developed as distinct and separate associations, but there are some important provinces (e.g., the Thulean or Brito-Arctic province of western Scotland, northeastern Ireland, and Iceland) in which lavas having affinities with both magma types are mutually associated. The Columbia Plateau of the northwestern United States and the Deccan Plateau of southeastern India are classic examples of tholeiitic plateau basalt provinces. *Syn:* FLOOD BASALT

plateau glacier An ice sheet that occupies a more or less flat, plateaulike area.

plateau mountain The folds of a mountain chain frequently pass abruptly into the horizontal strata of a basal plateau which, when largely denuded and eroded, may resolve itself into a series of plateau mountains.

platform *1*. *Stratig:* The area of thinner sediments adjoining a geosynclinal wedge of thicker equivalent beds. *2*. In a coral, the flat bottom or floor of calyx. *3*. In brachiopods, as first proposed it meant the elevated and thickened muscle trace in the trimerellid brachiopods.

platinum metals The metals platinum (Pt), palladium (Pd), rhodium (Rh), ruthenium (Ru), osmium (Os), iridium (Ir).

platy flow structure *See* PLANAR FLOW STRUCTURE

playa [*Sp.*] *1*. A shore, strand, beach, or bank of a river. Generally sandy, and sometimes auriferous. *2*. The shallow central basin of a desert plain, in which water gathers after a rain and is evaporated.

playa lake Broad, shallow sheets of water which quickly gather and almost as quickly evaporate, leaving mud flats or playas to mark their sites.

Playfair's law Every river appears to consist of a main trunk, fed from a variety of branches, each running in a valley proportioned to its size, and all of them together forming a system of valleys, communicating with one another, and having such a nice adjustment of their declivities that none of them join the principal valley either on too high or too low a level; a circumstance which would be infinitely improbable if each of these valleys were not the work of the stream which flows in it.

Pleistocene The earlier of the two epochs comprised in the Quaternary period, in the classification generally used. Also called Glacial epoch and formerly called Ice age, Post-Pliocene, and Post-Tertiary. Also the series of sediments deposited during that epoch, including both glacial deposits and ordinary sediments. Some geologists formerly used Pleistocene as synonymous with Quaternary and included in it all Post-Tertiary time and deposits.

pleochroic, *adj.* See PLEOCHROISM

pleochroism; dichroism The property of differentially absorbing light that vibrates in different directions in passing through a crystal.

pleomorphous; pleomorphic Polymorphous, *q.v.*

Pleospongia Group of Lower and Middle Cambrian fossils generally having the form of corals but structures suggesting relationships to sponges.

plesiotype A figured specimen used subsequent to the original description of a species.

plicated *1.* Folded together as in highly inclined and contorted strata. *2. Paleobot:* Folded as in a fan, or approaching this condition.

Pliensbachian Lower Charmouthian.

Plinian, *adj.* Designating or pertaining to a type of volcanic eruption of extreme violence like that described by Pliny the Younger, in 79 A.D., which wrecked the ancient mountain centered approximately on the site of the present-day Vesuvius and buried the cities of Herculaneum and Pompeii under thick deposits of volcanic debris. The characteristics of Plinian eruptions have been only rather vaguely defined, but it is generally believed that they are the result of hydro-explosions, i.e., steam explosions of colossal power.

Pliocene The latest of the epochs comprised in the Tertiary period, in the classification generally used. Also, the series of strata deposited during that epoch.

Plio-Pleistocene Strata transitional across the Pliocene-Pleistocene boundary where distinction cannot be recognized outside of glaciated regions.

plot To place survey data upon a map or plat. In past use, no clearly defined difference existed between plat and plot. It is suggested that a difference be established by limiting plat to the graphical representation of a survey, and plot to the cartographic operations involved in the construction of a map or plat.

pluck To tear away projecting pieces of rock; said of the action of glaciers on contiguous rock.

plucking *1.* Monoliths up to many feet in diameter, bounded by structural surfaces, are lifted from the rock by the flowing ice and removed. This process has been termed plucking, and also quarrying. *2.* The process of erosion, by glaciers and streams, whereby blocks are removed from bedrock along joints and stratification surfaces. Quarrying.

plug, umbilical The filling of secondary shell material which is found in the umbilical region of certain Foraminifera, e.g., the genus Rotalia.

plug, volcanic *See* VOLCANIC PLUG

plug dome *See* VOLCANIC DOME

plumb *1.* Vertical. *2.* A plumb bob; a plummet. *3.* To carry a survey into a mine through a shaft by means of heavily weighted fine wires hung vertically in the shaft. The line of sight passing through the wires at the surface is thus transferred to the mine workings. An important piece of work in mine shafts, and in transferring courses or bearings from one level to another.

plumbago Graphite.

plumb point The point on the ground vertically beneath the perspective center of the camera lens.

plunge *1. Surv:* To set the horizontal cross wire of a theodolite in the direction of a grade. *2.* To turn over the telescope of a transit on its horizontal transverse axis. *3.* Called pitch or rake by many authors. Applied to ore bodies, it is the vertical angle between a horizontal plane and the line of maximum elongation of the body.

plunge pool Potholes, in general, of large size, occurring at the foot of a vertical or nearly vertical waterfall.

plush copper; plush copper ore A Cornish name for chalcotrichite, probably alluding to its appearance. A fibrous red oxide copper mineral.

pluton In the strictest sense, a body of igneous rock that has formed beneath the surface of the earth by consolidation from magma. In a broader sense, it may include bodies composed of pseudoigneous rock that formed beneath the surface of the earth by the metasomatic replacement of an older rock.

plutonic cognate ejecta Coarsely crystalline fragments consanguineous with the lavas of a given volcano, which solidified in depth, generally as dikes and sills, but were brought to the surface by pyroclastic eruption. These are equivalent to the matériaux homoeogènes of Alfred Lacroix.

plutonic emanations The volatile material given off by a deep-seated magma.

plutonic series Series of different rocks that evolved from the same original material through various metamorphic stages until final crystallization ceased.

plutonic water Water in or derived from magma at considerable depth; the minimum depth is not known but it is that of plutonic rocks, probably in the order of several miles.

Plutonism The obsolete belief that all of the rocks of the earth solidified from an original molten mass. *Cf.* NEPTUNISM

Plutonist A follower of James Hutton (1726–1797) who recognized that internal heat of the earth has been important in geologic development and that some rocks are igneous in origin. *Cf.* NEPTUNIST; MAGMATIST

plutonite Coarse-grained intrusive igneous rock.

pluvial *1. Geol:* Due to the action of rain. *2.* Pertaining to deposits by rain water or ephemeral streams. *3. Climatol:* Relating to former periods of abundant rains, such as the pluvial periods of any region. Refers to a rainy period, particularly one outside of the Pleistocene glaciated region corresponding in time to a glacial age; also such a period.

pneumatolitic metamorphism Contact metamorphism in which the composition of rock has been altered by introduced magmatic material.

pneumatolysis The alteration of rocks and the formation of minerals during or as a result of the emanation of gases and vapors from solidifying igneous rocks. *See* PNEUMATOLYTIC

pneumatolytic A term used in various connotations by various authors and perhaps best abandoned. It has been used to describe processes such as (1) surface effects of gases near volcanoes, (2) contact metamorphic effects surrounding deep-seated intrusives without any knowledge of gas vs. liquid state, (3) that stage in igneous differentiation between pegmatitic and hydrothermal, which is supposed to be characterized by gas-crystal equilibria, and (4) (very loosely) any deposit containing "pneumatolytic" minerals or elements, such as tourmaline, topaz, fluorite, lithis, and tin, and hence presumed to have formed from a "gas" phase.

pneumotectic Processes and products of magma consolidation in which fundamental influences of a sort that was magmatic in the strictest sense were recognizably modified and to some extent controlled by gaseous constituents or so-called mineralizers.

pocket *1.* A small body of ore; an enlargement of a lode or vein; an irregular cavity containing ore. *2.* A natural underground reservoir of water. *3.* A receptacle, from which coal, ore, or waste is loaded into wagons or cars. *4.* A ganister quarryman's local term for masses of rock 30 to 50 feet in width that are worked out and loaded, buttresses of untouched rock being left between them to support the upper masses. *5.* A hole or depression in the wearing course of a roadway. *6.* A glen or hollow among mountains. *7.* Solutional concavity in a cave ceiling, wall, or floor whose location is not determined by a joint but is localized by stream action.

pod *1.* A rudely cylindrical ore body that decreases at the ends like a cigar. *See* LENS. *2.* A very shallow depression up to more than 10 km. in diameter of the south Russian steppes containing temporary lakes; may reflect uneven loess deposition, preloess topography, deflation, solution, etc.

podsol; podzol A highly bleached soil that is low in iron and lime. It is formed under moist and cool climatic conditions.

poeciloblastic Poikiloblastic, *q.v.*

poikilitic; poecilitic A textural term denoting a condition in which small granular crystals are irregularly scattered without common orientation in a larger crystal of another mineral.

poikiloblastic; poeciloblastic A texture due to the development, during recrystallization, of a new mineral around numerous relics of the original minerals.

point *1.* A small cape; a tapering projection from the shore of a lake, river, or sea. *See* CAPE; TONGUE. *2.* A position on a reference system determined by a survey. A fix.

point, turning A point on which a foresight is taken from one instrument station in a line of survey and on which a backsight is taken from the next instrument station.

point-bar deposit Sediment deposited on the inside of a growing meander loop.

point diagram *Struct. petrol:* A petrofabric diagram on which each item measured is represented by a point. Each point may represent an optical direction in some mineral, such as the *c* crystallographic axes of quartz grains, or the perpendicular to the cleavage of micas, etc.

point group One of the 32 crystal classes based on possible collections of symmetry elements about axes intersecting in a point.

point maximum Concentration of poles around a point in a fabric diagram; a polar cap generally indicating slipping movement.

point rainfall Rainfall at a specified location, measured in a single precipitation gage.

point system The 65 arrangements of points in space produced by adding screw axes to the Bravais space lattices.

poise The unit of absolute viscosity, equal to one dyne-second per square centimeter. *See* VISCOSITY, ABSOLUTE. The centipoise, 1/100 of a poise, is a more convenient unit and the one customarily used.

poised state *1.* Condition of a river that is neither eroding nor depositing sediment. *2. Engin:* Grade.

Poisson's ratio The ratio of the fractional transverse contraction to the fractional longitudinal extension of a body under tensile stress.

polar bond *See* BOND, POLAR

polar cap Concentration of points in a fabric diagram.

polar diagram Polar projection.

polar front The line of discontinuity, which is developed in suitable conditions between air originating in polar regions and air from low latitudes, on which the majority of the depressions of temperate latitudes develop. It can sometimes be traced as a continuous wavy line thousands of miles in length, but is interrupted when polar air breaks through to feed the trade winds, and is often replaced by a very complex series of fronts, or by continuous gradients of temperature.

polar glaciers *1.* Glaciers formed at high latitudes and developed on plateaus and from which ice tongues extend down valleys trenched into the plateau. *2.* In Ahlmann's classification, a glacier with the accumulation area covered by firn formed by slow recrystallization of solid precipitation and with subsurface temperatures below freezing to considerable depth throughout the year. Two subtypes are highpolar and subpolar glaciers.

polariscope An instrument for studying the properties of and examining substances in polarized light.

polarity *1.* The electrically positive or negative condition of a battery or generator terminal. *2.* The magnetically positive (north) or negative (south) character of a magnetic pole. *3.* Capability of dissociation as ions.

polarization Houppe.

polarize *1.* To endow with poles, as a magnet. *2.* To produce an electrical separation or orientation, especially in the molecules of a dielectric. *3.* To impress some spatial characteristic, as upon the vibrations identified with radiation, e.g., in elliptically polarized light.

polarized light Light that has been changed from the ordinary state, in which the transverse vibrations occur in all planes passing through the line of propagation to a state in which they are in a single plane (plane-polarized) or circular or elliptical. Plane-polarized light produced by the use of Nicols, *q.v.*, in a petrographic microscope is used in the optical study of minerals and rocks. The term polarized light without qualification generally means plane-polarized light.

polar projection Projection of points on the surface of a sphere to a plane tangent at its pole.

polar symmetry Symmetry in which parts are equal and interchangeable in all directions in planes perpendicular to a central axis but not in both directions from these planes.

polar wandering *1.* Short-period movement of earth's poles resulting from wobbling of its axis. *2.* Long-period, more or less systematic displacement of the earth's poles along curved paths which may have occurred during the passage of geologic time.

polders Flat tracts in Holland below the level of the sea or the nearest river, such as a lake or morass which has been drained and brought under cultivation. They are protected from inundation by embankments called dikes. Similar to these are the fens of England.

pole *1. Struct. petrol:* A point on the reference sphere that represents the intersection of the sphere with a line passing through the centér of the sphere. The line may be some optical direction in a mineral or it may be a perpendicular to some plane. *2.* The ends of the axis of coiling in planispirally coiled shells or tests, as in the fusulines. *3.* One of the extremities of the axis of symmetry of radio symmetrical pollen grains.

pole diagram Fabric diagram on polar coordinates showing concentration of points in a restricted area.

pole-fleeing force Force supposedly resulting from the oblate shape of the earth causing land masses to move toward the equator.

polish, *n.* An attribute of surface texture related to the regularity of reflections; a surface presenting a high luster or characterized by highlights as distinct from a surface which is "dull."

polje; polye An isolated depression, generally several miles long or wide, floored with flat alluvium; walls generally steep. *Syn:* INTERIOR VALLEY. *See* UVALA

polyconic map projection A map projection having the central geographic meridian represented by a straight line, along which the spacing for lines representing the geographic parallels is proportional to the distances apart of the parallels; the parallels are represented by arcs of circles which are not concentric, but whose centers lie on the line representing the central meridian, and whose radii are determined by the lengths of the elements of cones which are tangent along the parallels. All meridians except the central one are curved.

polycrystal Assemblage of crystal grains of unspecified number, shape, size, orientation, or bonding that together form a solid body.

polye; polje See POLJE; UVALA

polygenetic Originating in various ways or from various sources; formed at different places or times or from different parts; said specifically, in geology, of mountain ranges. Opposed to monogenetic.

polygenetic soil Soil produced under conditions that have changed importantly with time.

polygeosyncline A wide, long-enduring, primary geosyncline in which shallow water sediments accumulated but in which one or more parallel geanticlines arise to separate the primary geosyncline into two or more sequent geosynclines.

polygon ground Polygonal soil patterns produced on level ground by alternate freeze and thaw of the surface soil above the permanently frozen level. *Syn:* FROST POLYGONS; STRUCTURE GROUND; POLYGONAL MARKINGS

polygons, mud crack Mud cracks (sun cracks, shrinkage cracks) form as sediments lose contained water. The cracks bound polygons, which vary in number of sides and dimensions of angles between the sides. Cracks are rarely straight, and polygons may be bounded by as few as three and as many as eight cracks. Polygons with three to five sides are those most abundant.

polyhalite A mineral, $K_2Ca_2Mg(SO_4)_4.2H_2O$, commonly in pink, red, or gray masses in potassium salt deposits. Triclinic.

polymerization *1.* The joining of identical molecules to form larger ones without altering the total chemical composition. *2.* The joining of similar molecules to form larger and more complex ones. (Loose usage)

polymerize To change (by union of two or more molecules of the same kind) into another compound having the same elements in the same proportions, but a higher molecular weight and different physical properties.

polymictic rocks Rocks characteristic of geosynclinal regions and including arkoses and graywackes.

polymorph One of several different morphologic kinds occurring in a species, a mineral, etc.

polymorphism Pleomorphism. *1.* The existence of a species in several forms independent of the variations of sex. *2.* A substance which can exist in more than one solid form is said to have polymorphic forms, e.g., rhombic and monoclinic sulfur, α and β quartz. *3.* The property possessed by certain chemical compounds of crystallizing in several distinct forms.

polymorphous *1.* Having the same chemical composition but crystallizing in different crystal systems or classes. *See* ALLOTROPIC; DIMORPHOUS; PLEOMORPHOUS; TRIMORPHOUS. *2.* Existing in several forms, independent of variations of sex.

polyp Coelenterate living singly or in colonies; an anthozoan or the asexual generation of a hydrozoan.

polyploidy State of possessing more than two sets of homologous chromosomes; occurs in plants, rare in animals.

polysynthetic twinning Successive twinning of three or more individuals according to the same twinning law and with the composition planes parallel. Often revealed by striated surfaces.

polytypic *1. Tax:* Including several units of the next lower category, as, for example, a species with several subspecies. *2.* Referring to a species which has a group of subspecies which replace each other geographically. Proposed as "polytypic species."

polytypic species A species which consists of a group of subspecies which replace each other geographically.

ponding The natural formation of a pond or lake in a watercourse; chiefly: (a) by a transverse mountain uplift whose rate of elevation exceeds that of the stream's erosion, or (b) by a dam caused by glaciers, volcanic ejecta, landslips, or alluvial cones.

Pontian Upper Lower Pliocene.

pontic Euxinic. Applied to an association of black shale and dark limestone, deposited in stagnant waters.

population *1. Biol:* All individuals of a species living in more or less intimate association with each other. *2. Stat:* All objects or values that constitute a related group.

porcelaneous Having the appearance of porcelain.

porcelaneous smooth chert A type of smooth chert which has a smooth fracture surface, hard, opaque to subtranslucent, typically china-white resembling chinaware or glazed porcelain, grades to chalky.

porcelanite *1.* A light-colored, porcelaneous rock resulting from the contact-metamorphism of marls. *See* HORNFELS. *2.* Fused shales and clay, that occur in roof and floor of burned coal seams. The rock is quite common in the lignite districts of the West, where apparently spontaneous combustion has fired the seams in the past. *3.* Siliceous or cherty shale.

pore *1.* Interstice; void, *q.v.* A space in rock or soil not occupied by solid mineral matter. *2.* In blastoids, an opening at margin of an ambulacrum leading to one of the hydrospires. *3.* In cystoids: horizontal tubes or slits occupying parts of two adjoining plates. *4.* In echinoids: pit for attachment of a ligament which fastens spine to tubercle. *5.* A minute opening or foramen, or orifice.

pore diameter Diameter of the largest sphere that might be contained within a pore.

pore fluid *See* INTERGRANULAR FILM

Porifera Phylum of simply organized metazoans without specialized tissues or organs; sponges. Camb.-Rec.

porosimeter An instrument used to determine the porosity of a rock sample by comparing the bulk volume of the sample with the aggregate volume of the pore spaces between the grains. Porosimeters are of various designs, some using liquids and some using gases, at known pressures, to find the volume of openings.

porosity The ratio of the aggregate volume of interstices in a rock or soil to its total volume. It is usually stated as a percentage.

porosity per cent The ratio of the volume of all pore space to the total bulk volume of a given fragment or sample rock multiplied by 100.

porous Containing voids, pores, interstices, or other openings

which may or may not intercon-
nect.

porpezite Palladium gold, *q.v.*

porphyrin A complex organic
substance found in green plants
and forming the basic feature of
unit of the chlorophyll.

porphyritic; porpyrite A textural
term for those igneous rocks in
which larger crystals (phenocrysts
or insets) are set in a finer
groundmass which may be crystalline or glassy, or both.

porphyroblast *1.* A term given to
the pseudo-phenocrysts of rocks
produced by thermodynamic
metamorphism. The corresponding texture is called porphyro-
blastic. *2.* Large grains or crystals, commonly perfect, developed in schists resulting from deformation of rocks originally
containing phenocrysts. *Syn:*
METACRYSTS

porphyry A term first given to
an altered variety of porphyrite
(porphyrites lapis) on account of
its purple color, and afterwards
extended by common association to all rocks containing conspicuous phenocrysts in a fine-
grained or aphanitic groundmass.
The resulting texture is described
as porphyritic. In its restricted
usage, without qualification, the
term porphyry usually implies a
hypabyssal rock containing phenocrysts of alkali feldspar,
though in the field it is generally
allowed a wider scope, and commercially it is used for all porphyritic rocks.

porphyry copper Disseminated
copper minerals in a large body
of porphyry. In the commercial
sense the term is not restricted
to ore in porphyry but is applied
to deposits characterized by huge
size (particularly with respect to
horizontal dimension), uniform

dissemination, and low average
per-ton copper content.

portal *1.* Gap in a borderland
by which an epicontinental sea
communicated with the permanent ocean. *2.* Surface entrance
to a mine, particularly to a
drift, tunnel, or adit. *Syn:* ENTRY

Portland cement A hydraulic
cement consisting of compounds
of silica, lime, and alumina. It
is obtained by burning to semi-
fusion an intimate mixture of
pulverized materials containing
lime, silica, and alumina in varying proportions within certain
narrow limits, and by pulverizing
finely the clinker that results.

Portlandian Upper Upper Jurassic.

positive An arch of the craton
which persistently tends to stand
higher than the surrounding
shelves.

positive area Area that has been
uplifted conspicuously or repeatedly. Estimation of uplift is relative and some so-called positive
areas actually subsided but less
rapidly or often than adjacent
areas.

positive crystal An optically positive crystal. *See* OPTICAL CHARAC-
TER

positive element Large structural
feature or area that has had a
long history of progressive uplift; also in a relative sense one
that has been stable or has subsided much less than neighboring
negative elements.

positive elongation Elongation of
anisotropic crystals parallel to
vibration direction of the slower
of the two plane-polarized rays.

positive movement Uplift, actual
or relative.

positive ore Ore exposed on four
sides in blocks of a size variously prescribed. *See* PROVED ORE.
Ore which is exposed and prop-

erly sampled on four sides, in blocks of reasonable size, having in view the nature of the deposit as regards uniformity of value per ton and of the third dimension, or thickness.

positive shore line Shore line of emergence.

possible ore Ore which may exist below the lowest workings, or beyond the range of actual vision. *See* EXTENSION ORE

postmagmatic reactions A general term covering reactions occurring after the bulk of the magma has crystallized. The exact range covered by the term varies with different authors, but generally includes the hydrothermal stage.

postorogenic Apotectonic; postkinematic. An event that takes place after an orogeny. Does not necessarily imply any direct relationship with an orogeny.

Postproterozoic Comprises Paleozoic, Mesozoic, and Cenozoic. *Syn:* PHANEROZOIC

posttectonic crystallization Recrystallization in a tectonite that continued after deformation ceased.

potable Drinkable. Said of water and beverages.

potash Potassium carbonate, K_2CO_3. Loosely used for potassium oxide, potassium hydroxide, or even for potassium in deplorable expressions such as potash feldspar.

potash feldspar *See* ORTHOCLASE; MICROCLINE

potash fixation Retention of potassium in clays either by chemical combination in clay minerals or by adsorption.

potassic Of, pertaining to, or containing potassium.

potassium bentonite Metabentonite. A term applied to the potassium-bearing clay of altered volcanic ash, which is a clay of the illite type.

potassium 40 Radioactive potassium; half-life about 1.42×10^8.

potato stone Geode.

pot clay A highly refractory fire clay used in the manufacture of pottery.

potential A term applied to several different scalar quantities, the measure of each of which involves energy as a function of position or of condition. Examples are gravitational potential, electric potential, magnetic potential.

potential, ionic *See* IONIC POTENTIAL

potential barrier *See* ACTIVATION, ENERGY OF

potential electrode *Elec. prospecting:* One of two electrodes between which is measured the difference of potential due to natural currents or those artificially introduced into the ground.

potential energy of waves In a progressive oscillatory wave, the energy resulting from the elevation or depression of the water surface from the undisturbed level. This energy advances with the wave form.

potential function A function which describes the potential energy of a unit quantity of a particle placed at a given point. This usually applies to a conservative field, with the potential at infinity taken as zero.

potentiometer *1.* An instrument for measuring or comparing electromotive forces. It consists essentially of a resistance with a sliding contact, or its equivalent, used in connection with a galvanometer and a standard cell. *2.* A source of adjustable voltage, consisting of a resistor through which current is flowing, provision being made to connect to any desired point along the resistor.

potentiometric surface Surface to which water in an aquifer would rise by hydrostatic pressure.

pothole *1.* A hole generally deeper than wide, worn into the solid rock at falls and strong rapids by sand, gravel, and stones being spun around by the force of the current. *2.* In Death Valley, a circular opening, two to four feet in diameter filled with brine and lined with salty crystals. *3.* A rounded, steep-sided depression resulting from downward surface solution. *4.* An underground system of pitches and slopes. Applied in some cases to single pitches reaching the surface. *5.* A rounded cavity in the roof of a mine caused by a fall of rock, coal, ore, etc. *6.* A hole in the ground from which clay for pottery has been taken. *7.* Depression between dunes that contains water.

potter's or **pipe clay** *1.* Pure plastic clay, free from iron, and consequently white after burning. *2.* A clay adapted for use on a potter's wheel, for manufacture of pottery.

Pottsvillian Lower Pennsylvanian.

powder method A method for recording on film the directions in which a finely powdered crystalline specimen selectively scatters X rays of a single wave length. It is widely used for mineral identification. *See* DEBYEOGRAM

powder snow Dry fallen snow composed of crystals or grains which lie loosely.

Poynting's law A special case of the Clapeyron equation in which the fluid is removed as fast as it forms (as under metamorphic stress) so that its volume may be ignored.

Pozzuolana; Pozzolan; Pozzolana; Pozzuolane A leucitic tuff quarried near Pozzuoli, Italy, and used in the manufacture of hydraulic cement. The term is now applied more generally to a number of natural and manufactured materials (ash, slag, etc.) which impart specific properties to cement. Pozzuolanic cements have superior strength at a late age and are resistant to saline and acidic solutions.

Pr Abbreviation for pyrite in normative rock calculations.

Pratt isostasy A suggested type of hydrostatic support for the earth's solid outer crust in which the crustal density is supposed to be greater under mountains than under oceans.

Precambrian All rocks formed before Cambrian time are now called Precambrian in Canada and by many geologists in the United States. The Am. Comm. on Strat. Nomenclature recommends that the Canadian spelling be used, that the terms Early Precambrian era and Late Precambrian era be substituted for Archean and Proterozoic.

precession camera A single crystal goniometer in which individual layers of the reciprocal lattice are X-rayed without distortion.

precipice *Topog:* The brink or edge of a high and very steep cliff; an abrupt declivity.

precipitation *1. Hydrol:* The discharge of water, in liquid or solid state, out of the atmosphere, generally upon a land or water surface. The quantity of water that has been precipitated (as rain, snow, hail, sleet) measured as a liquid. *2.* The process of separating mineral constituents from a solution by evaporation (halite, anhydrite) or from magma to form igneous rocks.

precipitation facies Facies providing evidence regarding depositional conditions mainly revealed by sedimentary textures and fossils.

precision depth recorder An echo sounder having an accuracy better than 1 in 3000.

preconsolidation pressure Pressure exerted on unconsolidated sediment by overlying material that resulted in compaction; the overburden may have been removed later by erosion.

precrystalline deformation Nonruptural deformation in a tectonite where recrystallization continued after deformation ceases.

predazzite A marble containing calcite and brucite, the molecular proportion of MgO to CaO, being less than than in pencatite; i.e., less than 1:1. *See* MAGNESIAN MARBLE; MARBLE

pre-empted Preoccupied.

preferred orientation *Struct. petrol:* A rock in which the grains are more or less systematically oriented by shape or in which the atomic structure shows a more or less systematic arrangement. A rock in which the mica plates are parallel to one another shows a preferred orientation. Similarly, a hornblende schist in which the long axes of the hornblende crystals are parallel shows a preferred orientation. May be produced by growth, deposition, or deformation.

pregeologic Before the time when the surface of the earth became generally similar to what it is today, certainly 3 and perhaps 4.5 billion years ago.

preglacial Of, pertaining to, or occurring in geologic time before the Glacial epoch.

prehnite A mineral, $Ca_2Al_2Si_3O_{10}$-$(OH)_2$, commonly in green botryoidal masses. Orthorhombic, hemimorphic.

preliminary waves The body waves of an earthquake. They record on the seismograph before the surface waves by virtue of their high speeds in the interior of the earth which they penetrate. A collective term including both P-waves (first preliminary waves) and S-waves (second preliminary waves), *q.v.*

preoccupied Previously used; said of a taxonomic name. The law of priority does not permit the reuse of a preoccupied name.

preorogenic *1.* Dating from a time preceding the formation of mountains. *2.* Refers to beginning of orogenic disturbance; early orogenic.

pressure Force per unit area applied to outside of a body.

pressure, geostatic The pressure exerted by a column of rock. It averages about 1 pound per square inch per foot of column height, but, until it is sufficiently great that the rocks collapse, it is not transmitted to any fluid contained within them.

pressure arches Wavelike formations on a glacier surface; a stage in the formation of Forbes bands, *q.v.*, or ogives.

pressure figure A figure produced by intersecting lines of parting, due to gliding when certain minerals, like mica, are compressed by a blunt point. They are similar in character, but not necessarily in position, to the so-called percussion figures produced by a blow with a sharp point.

pressure-fusion curves See FUSION-PRESSURE CURVES

pressure head Hydrostatic pressure expressed as the height of a column of water that can be supported by the pressure. It is the height that a column of water rises in a tightly cased well that has no discharge. The pressure head is commonly expressed with reference to the land surface at the well or to some other convenient level.

pressure shadow *Struct. petrol:* An area adjoining a porphyroblast characterized by a growth rather than a deformation fabric, as seen in a section normal to the b̲ fabric axis. Its sigmoid form indicates the direction sense of the movement.

pressure solution Solution occurring preferentially at grain contacts where static pressure exceeds hydraulic pressure of interstitial fluid. *See* RIECKE'S PRINCIPLE

pressure tube When an isolated rock or stone rests upon the surface of the solid ice of a glacier, it may be near the center of one of the crevice-surrounded masses, where some emboulement has deposited it, by its greater conducting power and heat-absorbing surface, it becomes warmed by the sun's rays, much more than the ice on which it rests, and sinks down through the ice, forming a tube of its own diameter, often of an enormous depth.

pressure wave P-wave, *q.v.* Compressional wave.

pretectonic pluton Intrusion older than a particular period of folding; may be genetically related to orogeny or much older.

pretectonic recrystallization Recrystallization in a tectonite that ceased before deformation was completed.

prevailing wind The direction from which the wind blows during the greatest proportion of

the time. It is sometimes defined as that direction from which the wind blows with greatest frequency.

Priabonian Upper Eocene.

primacord *Seis. prospecting:* A detonating fuse which consists of an explosive core contained within a waterproof textile covering.

primärrumpf An upwarped, progressively expanding dome, with a rise so slow that degradation keeps pace with uplift.

primary *1.* Characteristic of or existing in a rock at the time of its formation. Said of minerals, textures, etc., of rocks. Essentially the same as original, and contrasted with derived or secondary, *1. 2.* Formed directly by solidification from fusion or deposition from solution. Said of igneous rocks and chemical sediments and contrasted with derivative (little used). *3.* Originally the same as the present Precambrian, then extended to include the present Paleozoic, and later restricted to Paleozoic; finally abandoned and now obsolete.

primary arc Mountain or island arc convex outward from a continent and overlying a deep-seated structure such as a great shear zone or tectogene; consists of an inner volcanic arc and an outer arc that may be represented either by distorted sediments or an oceanic trench.

primary basalt A presumed original magma, from which all other rock types are obtained by various processes.

primary dip *See* ORIGINAL DIP

primary flat joints *See* L-JOINTS

primary flowage Movement within an igneous rock which is partly fluid.

primary geosyncline Major undivided geosyncline.

primary gneiss A term applied to a rock that exhibits foliation, lineation, or other planar or linear structures such as are generally characteristic of metamorphic rocks, but which because of the absence of observable granulation or recrystallization is considered to be igneous. The qualifying adjectives trachitoid or gneissoid for coarse-grained rocks and trachytic for felsitic rocks are regarded as preferable, for the term gneiss should properly be employed only for metamorphic rocks.

primary magma A magma directly erupted from the earth's simatic substratum. Usually considered also as synonymous with parental magma.

primary minerals Those minerals that were deposited in the original ore-forming or rock-forming episode. *Cf.* SECONDARY MINERALS

primary openings Openings or voids existing when the rock was formed. In sedimentary rock, primary openings are usually the result of the arrangement and nature of the original sediment.

primary phase In an isoplethal study, the first crystalline phase to appear on cooling a composition from the liquid state, i.e., at the intersection of the isopleth and liquidus.

primary structure *1.* Structure of a sedimentary rock which is dependent on the conditions of deposition, mainly current velocity and rate of sedimentation. *2.* Those structural features that are contemporaneous with the first stages in the formation of a rock. A banding or foliation that develops in a plutonic rock while it is consolidating from magma is primary.

primary tectonite Tectonite whose fabric was determined by movement of the medium in which the rock developed.

primary wave Longitudinal wave.

primitive circle *Crystallog:* The great circle in the plane of a stereographic projection; the circle inscribed in the plane of a gnomonic projection to define the scale.

principal axes of strain In elastic theory, the principal axes of the reciprocal strain ellipsoid. The extensions of lines drawn in these directions, in the unstrained state, are stationary for small variations of direction. One of them is the greatest extension, the other is the smallest.

principal axes of stress The coordinate axes along which no shearing stresses exist.

principal axis In the tetragonal and hexagonal systems, the vertical crystallographic axis; hence in uniaxial crystals, the optic axis.

In orthorhombic and triclinic crystals: (1) the axis of the principal zone; (2) the axis with the shortest period, often the axis of the principal zone.

In monoclinic crystals: (1) the axis c, usually the axis of the principal zone excluding the symmetry axis; (2) the symmetry axis b.

principal axis (of a lens) The line normal to both surfaces of a lens.

principal meridian A meridian line accurately located and used as a basis from which to construct interior lines of monuments, called guide meridians, for the use of surveyors.

principle of uniformity Uniformitarianism, *q.v.*

principal stresses Intensities of stress (maximum, minimum, and intermediate) along each of three mutually perpendicular axes in terms of which any state of stress can be described.

priority, law of See LAW OF PRIORITY

prism *1. Crystallog:* An open form of three or more similar faces parallel to a single axis; the shape of its cross section is generally used as a modifier, as trigonal prism, rhombic prism, dihexagonal prism; *2. Obs.* Any prism that is parallel to the vertical axis c. *3.* Long relatively narrow, wedge-shaped sedimentary deposit, particularly one of great thickness as in a geosyncline.

prism, geosynclinal See GEOSYNCLINAL PRISM

prism level A kind of dumpy level with a mirror over the level tube, and a pair of prisms so placed that the position of the level bubble can be determined at any time by the levelman without the necessity of moving his head from the eyepiece.

pro- [*Lat.*] Prefix meaning before.

probable error In a normal random distribution, for a large number of observations the range within which half the observations will fall.

probable ore A class of ore whose occurrence is, to all essential purposes, reasonably assured but not absolutely certain.

probability Chance that can be predicted; statistical tests have been devised to predict the probability of many kinds of relationships.

prodelta clays The fine muds or silts which make up the bottom-set portion of cross-bedding. These are deposited in the sea offshore from a river delta.

producer A producing well.

productivity index The number of barrels per day of gross liquid produced from a well per pound per-square-inch pressure differential between well and formation, referred to a specified subsurface datum, usually the mean formation depth.

profile *1.* A vertical section of a soil, showing the nature and sequence of the various layers. *2.* A drawing showing a vertical section of the ground along a surveyed line. *3.* A graph showing as ordinate the variation of some geophysical quantity along a straight line against horizontal distance on this line as abscissa, e.g., a gravity profile. *4. Seis. prospecting:* The data resulting from a single series of observations made at one geographic location with a linear arrangement of seismometers. Also used as an adjective or verb, as, profile shooting, continuous profiling.

profile of a water table The line along which a given vertical plane intersects the water table. A vertical section of the water table.

profile of equilibrium *1.* A shore profile on which the incoming and outgoing of beach gravel and sand is balanced. *2.* A profile of equilibrium, or graded profile, is a river profile in which the slope at every point is just sufficient to enable the stream to carry its load of sediment, neither depositing sediment nor eroding the river bed.

profile section A diagram showing the shape of a surface as it would appear in vertical section. The placement of the profile section is indicated by a line drawn on an accompanying map.

proglacial Applied to deposits made beyond the limits of the glacier. Pertains to features of glacial origin beyond the limits of the glacier itself, as, streams, deposits, loess.

proglacial lake Lake occupying a basin in front of a glacier generally in direct contact with the ice. Varves commonly formed in such lakes.

progradation A seaward advance of the shore line resulting from the nearshore deposition of sediments brought to the sea by rivers.

progression *See* ADVANCE

progressive evolution Evolution from simple toward more complex and more highly specialized structure.

progressive overlap *See* TRANSGRESSION

progressive sand waves Large irregularly shaped ripple marks formed by water currents of high velocity above the third critical point. Movement of progressive sand waves is in the down-current direction.

projection A diagram or representation of three dimensional space relations produced by passing lines from various points to their intersection with a plane.

promontory *Topog:* A high cape with bold termination; a headland. *See* CAPE

propagation of waves The transmission of waves through matter.

propane A gaseous hydrocarbon of the paraffin series, formula C_3H_8.

properties A system's characteristics which can be evaluated quantitatively from experiments.

proportional limit The greatest stress which a material is capable of developing without any deviation from proportionality of stress to strain (Hooke's law). In the case of rocks this term and elastic limit are restricted to short-time tests as in tests of

long duration they slowly and permanently deform, even at stresses below the short-time proportional limit.

propylite An altered, greenstonelike andesitic rock consisting of such minerals as calcite, chlorite, epidote, serpentine, quartz, pyrite, and iron ore and resulting from hydrothermal alteration.

proration *1.* Proportionate distribution. *2.* Legal restriction of oil production to some specified fraction of potential production.

prospect *1.* The name given to any mine workings the value of which has not yet been made manifest. *2.* To examine land for the possible occurrence of coal or valuable minerals by drilling holes, ditching, or other work. *3. Geophys:* An area being examined or to be examined by geophysical methods. *4.* A geologic or geophysical anomaly, especially one recommended for additional exploratory work.

prospect hole Any shaft, pit, drift, or drill hole made for the purpose of prospecting the mineral-bearing ground.

protective colloid A colloid, which, when present in small quantities, is capable of preventing or retarding the coagulation of another colloid.

Proterozoic *1.* Younger of two Precambrian systems or eras. Algonkian. *2.* The entire Precambrian; this is the sense recognized by the U. S. Geological Survey.

Protista Kingdom of one-celled organisms.

proto- [*Gr.*] Combining form, meaning first or before.

Protochordata Phylum or subphylum of animals that possess a notochord during some part of their life histories but do not have a bony skeleton or spinal column. They occupy a position intermediate between the invertebrates and vertebrates; included by some in the Chordata.

protoclastic A term applied to a structure of igneous rocks in which the constituent minerals show granulation and deformation, produced by differential flow of the magma before complete consolidation.

protoconch In a gastropod: *1.* Equivalent to nucleus. *2.* Restricted to simple cap-shaped plate that constitutes the first shell rudiment.

proto-dolomite Crystalline calcium-magnesium carbonate in which the metallic ions occur in the same crystallographic layers instead of in alternate layers as in dolomite.

Protophyta Single-celled plants.

protoquartzite Sandstone intermediate between orthoquartzite and subgraywacke.

protore In older writings, any primary material too low in tenor to constitute ore but from which ore may be formed through enrichment. As commonly employed today, a protore is one that cannot be produced at a profit under existing conditions but that may become profitable with technological advances or price increases.

Prototheria Subclass of mammals; includes spiny anteater and duck-billed platypus. Pleis.-Rec.

prototype; proterotype *1.* An ancestral form. *2.* Most primitive form in a group of related organisms. *3.* Holotype.

Protozoa Phylum of single-celled animals, includes the Flagellata, Ciliata, and Sarcodina, classes that are represented by fossils. Considered by some to be a division of the protistan kingdom.

proustite Light ruby silver ore. A mineral, Ag_3AsS_3. Hexagonal.

prove *1.* In England, to ascertain by boring, driving, etc., the position and character of a coal seam, a fault, etc. *2.* In Scotland, to examine a mine in search of fire damp, known as "proving the pit."

proved ore Ore where there is practically no risk of failure of continuity.

provenance The terrane or parent rock from which any association of sediments is derived.

province A large area or region unified in some way and considered as a whole.

provincial species Species confined to a particular geographic or paleontologic province.

provincial stage Time-stratigraphic unit recognized only locally. *See* STAGE

proximal That part of the grain or spore which is turned inward in the tetrad, opposite the furrow in monocolpate grains. The proximal side of the spores is usually provided with a tetrad scar, in trilete spores also with contact areas.

proximate analysis In the case of coal and coke, the determination, by prescribed methods, of moisture, volatile matter, fixed carbon (by difference), and ash.

psammite *1.* Fine-grained, fissile, clayey sandstones. *See* ARENITE *2.* Any rock composed of sandy particles; sandstone.

psephite A coarse fragmental rock composed of rounded pebbles; conglomerate is an example. *See* RUDITE

pseudo- [*Gr.*] Prefix meaning false, spurious. In most scientific terms it denotes deceptive resemblance to the substance to whose name it is prefixed.

pseudoanticline An arrangement

of rock strata simulating the arch of an anticline. Used with reference to sand bodies that have a convex top.

pseudobreccia An apparent breccia that develops as a result of weathering.

pseudo cross-bedding Structure resembling cross-bedding produced by deposition in advancing ripples.

pseudoeutectic textures The peculiar intergrowths of sulfide minerals which more or less closely simulate the eutectic texture in metals.

pseudofossil Object such as a concretion that may be mistaken for a fossil by an inexperienced person.

pseudogley soil Densely packed silty soil that is alternately water-logged and rapidly dried out. Soils of Europe.

pseudomorph 1. A crystal, or apparent crystal, having the outward form proper to another species of mineral, which it has replaced by substitution or by chemical alteration. 2. *Paleontol:* A natural cast in which the replacing material is a crystallized mineral, as, calcite, pyrite, and more commonly silica in the form of chalcedony.

pseudopod 1. Movable extrusion of protoplasm used for locomotion and food gathering by some protozoans. 2. Movable extension of the water vascular system of echinoderms used for locomotion, respiration, and in some for food gathering.

pseudo ripple mark Ripplelike structures supposed to have been formed by deformation.

pseudostratification Occasionally till deposits which have been overridden by ice (drumlins, etc.) exhibit a structure concentric with their surfaces and somewhat resembling stratification. This is not true bedding. It is caused in part by the plastering of layer on layer by the ice and in part by shearing of the till by the great pressure of the ice.

pseudosymmetry Mimetry. Apparent symmetry, of different grade from that proper to the mineral, generally due to twinning.

pseudovolcano A term applied to large circular hollows or craters generally not associated with any positive indications of recent volcanic activity, e.g., craters of doubtful meteoritic origin which are thought to be the result of phreatic explosion or cauldron subsidence.

psi Abbreviation for pounds per square inch.

psia Abbreviation for pounds per square inch absolute. *See* ABSOLUTE PRESSURE

psig Abbreviation for pounds per square inch gauge. *See* GAUGE PRESSURE

psilomelane A mineral, $BaMn''$-$Mn''^{IV}O_{18}.2H_2O$. Orthorhombic. An ore of manganese. The term psilomelane is sometimes used loosely to designate any hard, massive Mn oxide.

psychrometer An instrument to determine the amount of atmospheric moisture. It consists essentially of two thermometers, one of which has its bulb covered with a closely fitted jacket of clean muslin which is saturated with water when an observation is about to be taken. Both thermometers are well ventilated, either by whirling them, or by blowing or drawing air past them. Because of evaporation, the reading of the moistened thermometer is lower than that given by the dry bulb, and the difference in degrees between them is called the depression of the wet bulb. This, used with the atmospheric pressure, gives a measure of the humidity. By reference to appropriate tables the dew point, relative humidity, and vapor pressure may be obtained.

P-T Abbreviation for pressure-temperature.

Pteridophyta Fernlike division of vascular plants that reproduce by spores; includes Lycopodineae, Equisetineae, and Filicineae.

Pteridospermae Subclass of gymnosperms with fernlike foliage and true seeds borne on leaves, not in cones; seed ferns. Dev-Meso.

Pterocerian Lower Kimmeridgian.

pteropod A pelagic, swimming type of gastropod in which the foot is modified into a pair of winglike lobes or fins; with or without a calcium carbonate shell.

Pteropsida Division of vascular plants, includes ferns, seed ferns, gymnosperms and angiosperms.

ptygmatic folds Folds, especially of granitic and pegmatitic veins; often the folding is considered related to the processes that formed the veins.

pudding ball Armored mud ball, q.v.

puddingstone Conglomerate, q.v.

puffing hole See BLOWHOLE

pulsation theory Theory proposing that eustatic movements of sea level resulted in simultaneous transgression followed by regression of epicontinental seas on all continents.

pulse A single disturbance propagated as a wave, but not having the cyclic characteristic of a wave train.

pulverize To reduce or be reduced to a fine powder or dust

as by beating, grinding, or the like.

pumice An excessively cellular, glassy lava, generally of the composition of rhyolite.

pumice fall 1. A rain of airborne pumice fragments blown out of a vent or fissure during an explosive volcanic eruption. 2. A deposit of pumice resulting from such a fall and lying on the ground surface.

pumice flow 1. An avalanche of fragmented pumice, generally a highly heated mixture of volcanic gases, glass dust, and pumice, down the flanks of a volcano, in the manner of a nuée ardente or ash flow. 2. A deposit of pumice and other volcanic debris resulting from such a flow and lying on the ground surface.

pumice tuff An indurated pyroclastic deposit in which the constituent particles consist predominantly of small ash- or lapilli-sized fragments of pumice.

Pumpelly's rule The generalization that the axes and axial planes of minor folds are parallel to the axes and axial planes of the major folds in the same region.

punctate, adj. With translucent or colored dots or depressions or pits.

Purbeckian Upper Portlandian.

pure shear A strain in which the body is elongated in one direction and shortened at right angles to this of such an amount that the volume remains unchanged.

purple copper ore Bornite.

push wave P-wave, q.v.

puzzolan or **pozzuolan cement** Cement made by mixing powdered slaked lime with either a volcanic ash or a blast-furnace slag.

P-wave A seismic body wave,

advancing by alternating compressions and rarefactions in an elastic medium. It is the type which carries sound. *Syn:* COMPRESSIONAL WAVE; LONGITUDINAL WAVE; IRROTATIONAL WAVE; DILATATIONAL WAVE; PRESSURE WAVE; PUSH WAVE

pygidium Dorsal tail shield of some arthropods, particularly trilobites; consists of several fused segments.

pyramid *1. Crystallog:* In the tetragonal, hexagonal, and orthorhombic systems, an open form of 3, 4, 6, 8 or 12 similar faces that meet at a common point on the vertical axis c. *2.* A dipyramid. *Obs. 3.* A prism, pinacoid, or pedion that intersects all three of the crystallographic axes; also called hemi-dipyramid, tetartopyramid, etc., to indicate the absence of some of the faces. *Obs.*

pyrargyrite Dark ruby silver ore. A mineral, Ag_3SbS_3. Hexagonal.

Pyreneean orogeny Post-Eocene diastrophism.

pyrite Iron pyrites. Fool's gold. A mineral, FeS_2, dimorphous with marcasite. Isometric, commonly in striated cubes or in pyritohedrons. Brass yellow, hardness 6–6 1/2. An important ore of sulfur; sometimes mined for the associated gold or copper.

pyritohedron Pentagonal dodecahedron. In the isometric system, a form enclosed by twelve five-sided faces, each parallel to one axis and cutting the other two at unequal distances.

pyrobole; pyribole A name proposed to cover undifferentiated pyroxene and amphibole, particularly in hand-specimen classifications.

pyrochlore A mineral, essentially $(Ca,Na)_2(Nb,Ta)_2O_6F$ with $Nb >$ Ta. Isometric. An ore of niobium. *Cf.* MICROLITE

pyroclast Fragment of volcanic rock of any size that was explosively or aerially ejected from a volcanic vent.

pyroclastic A general term applied to detrital volcanic materials that have been explosively or aerially ejected from a volcanic vent. Also, a general term for the class of rocks made up of these materials. The term is not the exact equivalent of fragmental volcanic since much of the material of aa and block flows and of volcanic domes is fragmental.

pyroclastic flow Ignimbrite.

pyroclastic rock Any rock consisting of unreworked solid material of whatever size explosively or aerially ejected from a volcanic vent.

pyroclasts A general term for fragmental deposits of volcanic ejectamenta, including volcanic conglomerates, agglomerates, tuffs, and ashes.

pyrogenesis General term including intrusion and extrusion of magma and magmatic derivatives.

pyrogenetic minerals The anhydrous minerals of igneous rocks, usually developed at high temperature in magmas containing only a small proportion of volatile components. Examples are the feldspars, pyroxenes, and olivines.

pyrolusite A mineral, MnO_2. Tetragonal. The principal ore of manganese.

pyrometamorphism Local, intense metamorphism resulting from unusually high temperatures at the contact of a rock with a magma.

pyrometasomatic Formed by metasomatic changes in rocks, principally in limestone, at or near intrusive contacts, under influence of magmatic emanations and high temperature and pressure.

pyrometer An instrument for measuring temperatures, especially those beyond the range of mercurial thermometers, as by means of the change of electric resistance, the production of thermoelectric current, the expansion of gases, the specific heat of solids, or the intensity of the heat or light radiated. The instrument based on the principle of light intensity is called an optical pyrometer and is commonly used to determine the temperature of molten lavas.

pyromorphite A mineral, Pb_5-$(PO_4)_3Cl$, a member of the apatite group. Hexagonal.

pyrope *See* GARNET

pyrophyllite A mineral, $Al_2Si_4O_{10}$-$(OH)_2$, usually is soft, radiated aggregates resembling talc. Orthorhombic.

pyroxene A mineral group, general formula $ABSi_2O_6$, where A is chiefly Mg, Fe″, Ca, and Na, B is chiefly Mg, Fe″, and Al and Si may be replaced in part by Al. Following are the most important pyroxenes: (1) Enstatite-hypersthene-ferrosilite series, $Mg_2Si_2O_6$-$(Fe,Mg)_2Si_2O_6$. Orthorhombic.

(2) Clinoenstatite-clinoferrosilite series, $Mg_2Si_2O_6$-$(Fe,Mg)Si_2O_6$. Monoclinic. (3) Diopside-hedenbergite series, $CaMgSi_2O_6$-$CaFe$-Si_2O_6. Monoclinic. (4) Augite. $(Ca, Mg)(Mg, Fe, Al)(Si, Al)_2O_6$, near *3*, but containing less Ca and appreciable Al. Monoclinic. (5) Pigeonite. Near *2*, but containing appreciable Ca. Monoclinic. Characterized optically by having low 2V. (6) Acmite. Essentially $NaFe'''Si_2O_6$. Monoclinic. (7) Jadeite. Essentially $NaAl$-Si_2O_6. Monoclinic. The group includes some of the commonest rock-forming minerals.

pyroxene-hornfels facies Rocks produced under high temperature contact metamorphic conditions.

pyroxenite A medium or coarse-grained rock consisting essentially of pyroxene.

pyroxenoid Any mineral chemically analogous to pyroxene, but with the SiO_4 tetrahedra connected in single chains different to those found in the pyroxenes.

pyrrhotite Magnetic pyrites. A mineral, $Fe_{n-1}S_n$, with n ranging from about 5 to 16. Hexagonal. Usually in brown to reddish brown masses, magnetic. Commonly associated with pentlandite.

Q

Q Abbreviation for quartz in normative rock calculations.

Q *Earthquake seismol:* A phase designation applied to Love waves. *Syn:* LQ

quagmire Any marsh or bog; soft, wet, miry land, which yields under the foot.

quantum A small unit of matter or energy. Generally used for one of the ultimate units of radiant energy. The size of the unit varies with the frequency of the radiation, and is equal to the frequency multiplied by Planck's constant, $h=6.55 \times 10^{-27}$erg-seconds. *Syn:* PHOTON

quantum evolution Rapid evolution resulting from a sudden shift from one environment to another distinctly different one. Preadaptation is required for such a shift.

quaquaversal Dipping outward in all directions from a central point, as a dome in stratified rocks.

quarfeloids The name given by Albert Johannsen to the light-colored or felsic minerals, as used in his classification of igneous rocks; includes quartz, feldspar, and feldspathoids.

quarry *1.* An open or surface working, usually for the extraction of building stone, as slate, limestone, etc. *2.* In England, an underground excavation formed in the roof or fault for the purpose of obtaining material for pack walls. *Note:* In its widest sense the term mines includes quarries, and has been sometimes so construed by the courts, but when the distinction is drawn, mine denotes underground workings and quarry denotes superficial workings. Open workings for iron ore, clay, coal, etc., are called banks or pits rather than quarries, the latter being defined as in *1* above.

quarry face The freshly split face of ashlar, squared off for the joints only, as it comes from the quarry, and used especially for massive work.

quarter line In western United States, the original survey line by which a section of Government land is divided into four parts.

quarter section In the Government system of land surveying in the United States and Canada, a tract of land half a mile square and containing 160 acres.

quartz A mineral, SiO_2. Hexagonal, trigonal-trapezohedral. Amethyst is a variety of the well-known amethystine color. Aventurine is a quartz spangled with scales of mica, hematite, or other minerals. False topaz or citrine is a yellow quartz. Rock crystal is a watery clear variety. Rose quartz is a pink variety. Rutilated quartz contains needles of rutile. Smoky quartz is a brownish variety, sometimes called cairngorm. Tiger-eye is crocidolite (an asbestoslike mineral) replaced by quartz and iron oxide and having a chatoyant effect.

quartz claim In the United States, a mining claim containing ore in veins or lodes, as contrasted with placer claims, carrying mineral, usually gold, in alluvium.

quartz diorite A phaneritic rock containing major plagioclase, quartz, and hornblende or biotite or both. Accessory apatite, zircon, and opaque oxides. A small amount of orthoclase may be present. The plagioclase is usually andesine or oligoclase. With an increase in orthoclase the rock passes into granodiorite. *Syn:* TONALITE

quartz index A derived quantity (qz) in the Niggli system of rock classification, which may be either positive or negative, and is a valuable indicator of the minerals to be expected.

quartzite *1.* A granulose metamorphic rock consisting essentially of quartz. *2.* Sandstone cemented by silica which has grown in optical continuity around each fragment.

quartz latite The extrusive equivalent of a quartz monzonite The principal minerals are quartz, sanidine, biotite, sodic plagioclase, and often hornblende usually occurring as phenocrysts in a groundmass of potash feldspar and quartz (or tridymite-cristobalite), or glass. Accessory minerals are magnetite, apatite, and zircon. With an increase in silica and alkalies the rock passes into a rhyolite and with a decrease in these constituents it passes into a dacite.

quartz mine A mine in which the deposits of ore are found in veins or fissures in the rocks forming the earth's crust. Usually applied to lode gold mines, but not to placers.

quartz monzonite A phaneritic rock containing major plagioclase, orthoclase, and quartz, with minor biotite, and hornblende and accessory apatite, zircon, and opaque oxides. With an increase in plagioclase and femic minerals the rock passes into granodiorite and with an increase in orthoclase it passes into granite. *Syn:* ADAMELLITE

quartzose, *adj.* A term applied to sands, sandstones, and grits essentially composed of quartz, and in which the component particles are distinct and palpable. Containing quartz as a principal ingredient.

quartz porphyry A rock containing phenocrysts of quartz and alkali feldspar, usually orthoclase, with or without mica, in a microcrystalline or cryptocrystalline groundmass. If the phenocrysts are abundant the rock becomes a granite-porphyry, while if they are absent or inconspicuous, the terms quartz felsite and microgranite are used according to the nature of the groundmass.

quartz vein A deposit of quartz in the form of a vein. Auriferous veins are often called quartz veins, and mining for gold in the rock is called quartz mining.

Quaternary The younger of the two geologic periods or systems in the Cenozoic era. Quaternary is subdivided into Pleistocene and Recent epochs or series. It comprises all geologic time and deposits from the end of the Tertiary until and including the present. It has also been called Post-Tertiary and Pleistocene, but Pleistocene is now generally restricted to the earlier part of the Quaternary.

quaternary system A system of four components, e.g., CaO-MgO-FeO-SiO₂.

quebrada *Topog:* 1. Quebrada [*Sp.* quebrar, to break] seems to be the exact equivalent of barranco. It literally means a break; and the adjective form quebrada corresponds to "broken" as applied topographically, except that it seems to convey the idea of a still rougher country than that simple word would generally be intended to indicate. 2. A canyon of rugged aspect; a fissurelike ravine or canyon; broken or uneven ground; a stream. Local in Southwest.

quick ground Ground in a loose incoherent state; soft watery strata, e.g., running sand.

quicksand Sand which is, or becomes upon the access of water, "quick," i.e., shifting, easily movable or semiliquid.

Q-wave Love wave, *q.v.*

qz value Measure of quantity of silica available for norm calculations determined from igneous rock analyses.

R

R *Earthquake seismol:* A phase designation applied to Rayleigh waves. *Syn:* LR

race *1.* If a shallow or narrow passage, or "strait," intervene in the course of the currents, the tide may there produce a rapid rush of water or a race. *2.* Local group of organisms differing from other groups; less significant than subspecies.

radial drainage pattern The streams radiate from a central area, like the spokes of a wheel. Volcanoes furnish the most perfect examples of this type of drainage pattern, owing to the marked symmetry of form which usually characterizes them and to the conical nature of their internal structures.

radial faults *1.* A group of faults that on a map radiate from a common center. *2.* Faults with dominantly vertical displacement.

radiated Applied to crystal aggregates that radiate from a center without producing stellar forms.

radioactive age determination The determination of the time that has elapsed since crystallization of a rock or mineral by study of the ratio or ratios between stable (or radioactive) daughter products and their parent elements.

radioactive decay The change of one element to another by the emission of charged particles from the nuclei of its atoms.

radioactive element An element capable of changing spontaneously into another element by the emission of charged particles from the nuclei of its atoms. For some elements, e.g., uranium, all known isotopes are radioactive; for others, e.g., potassium, only one of several isotopes is radioactive. Radioactive isotopes of most elements can be prepared artificially, but only a few elements are naturally radioactive.

radioactive series A series of elements, such that the one decays radioactively into the second, and that into the third, etc.

radioactivity The property shown by some elements of changing into other elements by the emission of charged particles from their nuclei.

radioactivity log Radiometric record made in a borehole. *See* GAMMA RAY, SPECTRAL GAMMA RAY, and NEUTRON-GAMMA LOGS

radioautograph Image of an object produced in a photographic emulsion by the radioactivity of the object.

radiocarbon dating The determination of the age of a material by measuring the proportion of the isotope C^{14} (radiocarbon) in the carbon it contains. The method is suitable for the determination of ages up to a maximum of about 30,000 years.

radiocolloid Minute, intensely radioactive concentration found in some rocks.

radiogenic Formed as a consequence of radioactive decay as, radiogenic heat, radiogenic helium, etc.

radiogenic isotope One produced by the decay of radioactive isotopes. A radiogenic isotope may or may not be radioactive itself.

Radiolaria Subclass of the Sarcodina consisting of marine protozoans that possess complex internal siliceous skeletons.

radiolarian ooze Deposits of siliceous ooze which are made up largely of radiolarian skeletons and which are formed at depths between 13,000 and 25,000 feet.

radius ratio The ratio of the radii of two ions. Important in determining the possible geometric arrangements of one kind of ion around the other, hence the possible crystal lattices which the ions can form.

radon Element 86, the heaviest in the noble gas group.

raft The jams formed of timber naturally thrown into the Red River in Louisiana by the caving of the banks.

rafted ice A form of pressure ice resulting from one ice floe overriding another.

rafting Transportation of material by means of attachment to ice, plants, or other floating material.

rain and snow gauge An instrument designed to measure the vertical depth of rain or snow (or its water equivalent). Due to the difficulty of obtaining exact measurements from a simple pan with vertical sides, exposed during the period of precipitation, and also because of the loss of water by evaporation, most gauges are designed to magnify the depth of rainfall so that its real depth may be measured to the nearest hundredth of an inch or millimeter,

and also to prevent evaporation as much as possible.

raindrop imprint A small circular or elliptical crater with raised rim formed by a raindrop falling on soft sediment such as that of a tidal flat.

rain shadow The region of diminished rainfall on the lee side of a mountain or mountain range, where the rainfall is noticeably less than on the windward side. Rain is concentrated on the lee side of some low mountains, e.g., the Black Hills.

rainy day An expression technically defined as a day with 0.01 inch or more of rain, but popularly considered as a day with more or less continuous rain.

raise *1.* To cause to rise, or expand upward. *2.* In England, to wind coal, etc., to the surface. *3.* To take up the floor or bottom rock in a room, gangway, or entry to increase the height for haulage. *4.* A mine shaft driven from below upward; also called upraise, rise, and riser. *See* RISE, *1*

raised reef Organic reef standing above sea level.

rake Rake is synonymous with pitch and is measured in the plane of the vein. The USGS Map Symbol Committee recommends abandoning the term pitch and using rake for the angle measured in the plane of the structure. *Cf.* "New list of map symbols," USGS, undated.

ramp *1.* A fault that is a gravity (normal) fault near the surface of the earth, but curves through the vertical to dip in the opposite direction at depth; where the displacement is that characteristic of thrusts. *2.* An accumulation of snow forming an inclined plane between land or land ice and sea or shelf ice. *3.* A long, gentle slope comprising most of the continental shelf. *4.* In a gastropod, the sloping surface of a whorl next below a suture.

ramp valley *1.* Valley produced by the ramping or upthrusting of two masses, one on either side of the intervening strip. *2.* A valley bounded by thrust faults.

Rancholabrean Upper Pleistocene.

rand The low marshy border of a lake or lagoon.

random orientation *Struct. petrol:* The arrangement of planar or linear features such that no systematic or tendency to systematic arrangement can be found.

range *1. Topog:* A chain of mountains or hills. *2. Sedimentol:* Measure of variability between largest and smallest sizes. *3. Biol:* Geographic distribution. *4. Paleontol:* Stratigraphic persistence. *5. Cartog:* North-south tier of townships identified by its relation to a principal meridian. *6. Min:* Strip of country containing or supposed to contain economically important mineral deposits.

range, geologic Range, stratigraphic, *q.v.*

range, stratigraphic Geologic range. The distribution of any given species, genus, or other taxonomic group of organisms throughout geologic time.

range finder An instrument for finding the distance from a single point of observation to other points at which no instruments are placed.

In general, it employs a very short base line, of fixed length, which is part of the instrument, and is utilized according to the principle of triangulation. The precision of the optical and other parts of the instrument is very great, but because of the small magnitude of the angle of intersection of the lines of sight at the object observed on, the distances obtained are not of a high order of precision. *See* TACHYMETER

range line (U.S. public-land surveys) An exterior boundary of a township extending in a north-south direction.

range zone Biostratigraphic unit defined and identified by the actual occurrence of a single fossil (*cf.* BIOZONE; TEILZONE) or a group of fossils (*cf.* ASSEMBLAGE ZONE).

rank *1.* Those differences in the pure coal material due to geological processes designated as metamorphic, whereby the coal material changes from peat through lignite and bituminous coal to anthracite or even to graphite. *2. Paleobot:* A vertical row; leaves that are 2-ranked are in two vertical rows, and may be alternate or opposite.

Rankine temperature The absolute Fahrenheit temperature scale, obtained by adding 460° to the given Fahrenheit temperature.

rank variety Variety in coals brought about as a result of progressive metamorphism. More or less arbitrarily, although carefully, selected chemical criteria are used to differentiate coals of different rank. Physical criteria are also used but are more difficult of application.

Raoult's law For dilute solutions, the relative lowering of the vapor pressure of a liquid by a dissolved substance is approximately equal to the mol fraction of the latter, independently of the temperature and of the nature of both the solvent and the solute.

Rapakivi texture A texture originally described from Finnish granites. In typical specimens large flesh-colored potassic feldspars occur as rounded crystals a few centimeters in diameter and are mantled with white sodic plagioclase. These feldspars are embedded in a matrix of normal texture, but consist chiefly of quartz and colored minerals. The rounded form of the phenocrysts suggests magmatic corrosion.

rapid *Topog:* 1. A part in a stream where an increase in its gradient accelerates the velocity of the current over that in its adjoining parts; 2. A section of a stream wherein the velocity is notably greater than the sections immediately above or below it. Commonly used in the plural.

rare earths Oxides of a series of metals (rare earth metals) obtained from widely distributed but relatively scarce minerals. The rare earth metals proper are those with atomic numbers from 57 to 71 (lanthanum to lutetium) (same as lanthanide elements); yttrium is often included with the group, and sometimes also beryllium, scandium, zirconium, hafnium, and thorium. The metals and their compounds are characterized by great chemical similarity, so that their separation from one another is difficult. The term rare earths is often used to refer to the metals rather than the oxides.

rating curve A graph showing the relation between elevation of the stream water surface and stream discharge.

ratio-type lithofacies map Map showing areal relations of lithofacies based on limiting values of two ratios, commonly clastic and sand-shale ratios. Statistical lithofacies map.

rattle stone A concretion composed of concentric laminae of different composition, in which the more soluble layers have been removed by solution, leaving a central part detached from an outer portion. *Syn:* KLAPPERSTEIN

Rauracian Sequanian.

ravine *Topog:* A depression worn out by running water, larger than a gully and smaller than a valley.

raw ore Ore that is not roasted or calcined.

raw quartz Quartz that has undergone no treatment, such as burning or reduction, prior to being placed under the stamp heads.

Rayleigh wave R-wave. A surface seismic wave propagated along the plane surface of a homogeneous elastic solid, predicted by Lord Rayleigh and later verified.

razorback A sharp narrow ridge.

reach (of a river) An extended portion of water, as in a straight portion of a stream or river; a level stretch, as between locks in a canal; an arm of the sea extending into the land. A promontory, tongue, or extended portion of land.

reactance 1. In electric-circuit theory, that part of the impedance which is due to capacitance or inductance, or both. It is expressed in ohms. Capacitative

reactance equals $\dfrac{1}{\pi nC}$, where n

is frequency in cycles per second and C is capacitance in farads. Inductive reactance equals $2\pi nL$, where L is the inductance in henrys. 2. Same as acoustic reactance.

reaction boundary Reaction line.

reaction curve Cotectic line; reaction line, *q.v.*

reaction line A special case of the boundary line, in ternary systems, along which one of the two crystalline phases present reacts with the liquid, upon decreasing the temperature, to form the other crystalline phase. *Syn:* COTECTIC LINE; REACTION CURVE

reaction pair Any two minerals, one of which is formed at the expense of the other by reaction with liquid, especially, any adjacent pairs in the discontinuous reaction series.

reaction point A special case of the eutectic point, in which the composition of the liquid phase at the point cannot be stated in terms of positive values of the two solid phases in equilibrium at the point (in binary systems), of the three solid phases in equilibrium at the point (in ternary systems), etc. In binary systems it is equivalent to an incongruent melting point, or peritectic point.

reaction principle The statement that the common minerals of igneous rocks have a reaction relation to one another, in contrast to the subtraction relation of simple eutectic mixtures. The minerals can be arranged in two series, one of the feldspars and one of the ferromagnesian minerals, such that in each series any number is derived from the preceding member by reaction with the magma and is capable of forming the following member by continued reaction with the magma. *See* BOWEN'S REACTION SERIES

reaction rim *See* CORONA

reaction series Any series of minerals in an igneous rock, related in such a way that each member of the series can be regarded as derived from the preceding member by reaction with the magma.

The series may be continuous, like the plagioclase or forsterite-fayalite series, or discontinuous like the olivine-pyroxene-amphibole series. *See* BOWEN'S REACTION SERIES

realgar A mineral, AsS. Monoclinic.

rebound (in shale) Swelling in argillaceous material after removal of compacting overburden as in an excavation; most pronounced in bentonitic shale. *See* ELASTIC REBOUND

recapitulation The theory (now rejected in large part and profoundly modified) that the individual development of an organism passes through stages resembling the adult conditions of its successive ancestors. *Syn:* HAECKEL'S BIOGENETIC LAW; MORPHOGENESIS OF HYATT; HAECKEL'S LAW

Recent *1.* Time and strata younger than the Pleistocene. *2.* Considered by some to be the last subdivision of the Pleistocene representing presumed interglacial time following Wisconsin glaciation.

receptaculid A Lower and Middle Paleozoic spongelike fossil of unknown relationships; not a sponge.

recess That part of an orogenic belt where the axial traces of the folds are concave toward the outer part of the belt. *Syn:* RE-ENTRANT. *Ant:* SALIENT

recession Going back; leaving part of the sea margin exposed as land.

recessional moraine A moraine formed during a temporary decrease in the rate of glacial retreat.

recessive character A character that must be inherited from both parents if it is to be exhibited by offspring. A recessive character can be passed on to offspring without being exhibited by a parent.

recharge Intake. The processes by which water is absorbed and is added to the zone of saturation, either directly into a formation, or indirectly by way of another formation. Also, the quantity of water that is added to the zone of saturation.

reciprocal strain ellipsoid In elastic theory, an ellipsoid of certain shape and orientation which under homogeneous strain is transformed into a sphere, and any set of conjugate diameters of the ellipsoid is transformed into a set of orthogonal diameters of the sphere. The ellipsoid has the property that the length of a line, which has a given direction in the unstrained state, is increased by the strain in a ratio inversely proportional to the central radius vector of the surface drawn in the given direction.

reconnaissance A general examination or survey of a region with reference to its main features, usually as a preliminary to a more detailed survey.

reconnaissance map A map incorporating the information obtained in a reconnaissance survey, and data obtained from other sources.

recovery *1.* The proportion or percentage of coal or ore mined from the original seam or deposit. *2.* A general term to designate the valuable constituents of an ore which are obtained by metallurgical treatment; as, the recovery was 90%. Recovery is better used in connection with milling operations, while extraction is especially applicable to smelting or wet chemical methods and applies to the bullion actually obtained.

recovery factor A factor applied to the oil in place in a reservoir in order to obtain the volume of recoverable oil. The quantity of oil in place is determined from per-cent saturation times the total volume of pore space in the reservoir.

recrystallization *1.* The formation of new mineral grains in a rock while in the solid state. The new grains may have the same chemical and mineralogical composition as in the original rock, as when a fine-grained limestone composed of calcite recrystallizes to a coarse-grained marble composed of calcite. On the other hand, entirely new minerals may be formed; some prefer to call this process neomineralization. *See* PARATECTONIC RECRYSTALLIZATION; POSTTECTONIC RECRYSTALLIZATION; PRETECTONIC RECRYSTALLIZATION. *2.* The process whereby the original microstructure of a shell is blurred or lost, and the shell is converted into a mosaic of interlocking crystals.

rectangular drainage pattern The rectangular pattern is characterized by right-angled bends in both the main stream and its tributaries. It differs from the trellis pattern in that it is more irregular; there is not such perfect parallelism of side streams; these latter are not necessarily as conspicuously elongated; and secondary tributaries need not be present. Structural control is prominent, as the pattern is directly conditioned by the right-angled jointing or faulting of rocks. The term has replaced the earlier one, lattice pattern.

rectification *1.* The act or process of rectifying. *See* RECTIFY. *2. Photogeol:* The process of projecting a tilted or oblique photograph to a horizontal reference plane, the angular relation between the photograph and the plane being determined from known or estimated data.

rectify *1.* To change from alternating to undirectional, as an electric current. Any device for securing this result is a rectifier. *2.* To replace an inverted image by one which is erect, as by the rectifying system in a field glass. *3.* To eliminate from a seismogram by mechanical or electrical means, or both, the time differences caused by differences in weathering correction, elevation correction, and normal moveout.

recumbent fold A fold in which the axial plane is more or less horizontal.

recurved spit A spit having the end more or less strongly curved inward.

red beds Term applied to red sedimentary rocks, which usually are sandstones and shales, though in exceptional cases red limestones have been reported. The coloring of the red beds is ferric anhydride.

red clay A more or less brown to red deep-sea deposit, which usually contains manganese nodules or a film of manganese. It is the finest-divided clay suspension that is derived from the land and transported by ocean currents, accumulating far from land and at the greatest depths. It has a high proportion of volcanic material due to lesser dilution of this material owing to slowness of accumulation of the clay portion. The color is believed to be caused by oxidation.

red mud The most widely distributed deposit on the sea bottom is not globigerina ooze, but a red mud, which appears to be nothing but clay in a very finely

divided state. It covers most of the abyssal region and contains volcanic material, meteoric dust, and shark's teeth in addition to clay. The red color is caused by iron oxide.

red ocher A red, earthy, and often impure, variety of hematite, used as a pigment. *See* OCHER

redox potential *See* OXIDATION-REDUCTION POTENTIAL

red rock *1.* Drillers' term for any reddish sedimentary rock; may be shale, sandstone, or limestone. *2.* Predominantly granophyric rock of red color intimately associated with some large gabbroic masses such as the Duluth gabbro.

reducing flame The inner cone of the blowpipe flame, characterized by the excess of carbon or hydrocarbons of the gas, which at the high temperature present tends to combine with the oxygen of a mineral brought into it.

reduction *1.* The process of removing oxygen from a compound; e.g., hematite is reduced to metallic iron. *2.* More generally a decrease in positive valence or an increase in negative valence; e.g., Co^{+3} is reduced to Co^{++} and Cl_2 is reduced to Cl^-. *3.* In different words, the addition of electrons to an atom or ion.

reduction index Rate of wear of material subject to abrasion.

reduction number The number of cubic centimeters of 0.4 normal chromic acid that is reduced by 100 milligrams of sediment under standard conditions.

reduzate A sediment formed in a strongly reducing environment; e.g., coal, oil, sedimentary sulfides, and sedimentary sulfur.

reef *1.* A range or ridge of rocks lying at or near the surface of water, especially one of coral. *See* ATOLL; BARRIER; FRINGING and SAND REEF. *2.* A rock structure, either moundlike or layered, built by sedentary organisms such as corals, etc., and usually enclosed in rock of a differing lithology. *See* BIOHERM; BIOSTROME; ORGANIC REEF. *3.* A bioherm of sufficient size to develop associated facies. Thus while all reefs are bioherms, all bioherms are not reefs.

reef atoll A ring-shaped coral reef, often carrying low sand island, enclosing a body of water.

reef complex Reef core and all contiguous detrital limestone and genetically related sediments or rocks.

reef flat A stony expanse of dead reef rock with a flat surface. It generally becomes partly or entirely dry at low tide. Patches of sand and debris and a few widely scattered colonies of the more hardy species of coral diversify the featureless horizontal surface of many reef flats. Shallow pools are a normal feature on some; others are crossed by irregular gullies or are riddled with potholes.

reef-knoll Knoll-reef. Conical limestone masses, 200–300 feet high, more or less circular in ground plan and commonly surrounded by black shales. More or less synonymous with bioherm, *q.v.*

reef patch A term for all coral growths that have grown up independently in lagoons of barriers and atolls. They vary in extent from expanses measuring several kilometers across to pillars or even mushroom-shaped growths consisting of a single large colony. The smaller representatives are called knolls or coral heads.

reef talus or **conglomerate** Offreef facies. Massive inclined beds of debris from the growing reef deposited along the seaward margin of the reef.

re-entrant Re-entering, or directed inward, as a re-entrant angle in a coast line, or any indentation in a land form; usually more or less angular in character. *Syn:* RECESS

reference axes *Struct. petrol:* Three mutually perpendicular axes to which structural measurements are referred. a is the direction of tectonic transport, c is perpendicular to the plane along which the differential movement takes place, and b lies in this plane but is perpendicular to a.

reference plane *1. Descr. geom:* In solving structural problems, a plane on which data are plotted. *2.* Datum plane, *q.v.*

reference seismometer *Seis. prospecting:* A detector placed to record successive shots under similar conditions, to permit over-all time comparisons. Used in connection with the shooting of wells for velocity.

reference station A station for which tidal constants have previously been determined and which is used as a standard for the comparison of simultaneous observations at a second station; also a station for which independent daily predictions are given in the tide or current tables from which corresponding predictions are obtained for other stations by means of differences or factors.

reflectance The coefficient of reflection, a measure of the ability of a body to reflect light or sound. It is expressed as the ratio of intensity of the reflected radiation to that of the incident radiation at normal incidence.

reflected wave The wave that is returned seaward when a wave impinges upon a very steep beach, barrier, or other reflecting surface.

reflection *Seis. prospecting: 1.* The returned energy (in wave form) from a shot which has been reflected from a velocity discontinuity back to a detector; *2.* The indication on a record of reflected energy.

reflection shooting *Seis. prospecting:* Procedure which is based on the measurement of the travel times of waves which, originating from an artificially produced disturbance, have been reflected back to detectors from subsurface boundaries separating media of different elastic wave velocities.

reflectometer An instrument for determining the index of refraction by measuring the angle of total reflection.

refraction The deflection of the direction of wave propagation when waves pass obliquely from one region of velocity to another.

refraction coefficient The square root of the ratio of the spacing between adjacent orthogonals in deep water and in shallow water at a selected point. When multiplied by the shoaling factor, this becomes the wave-height coefficient or the ratio of the refracted wave height at any point of the deep-water wave height. Also, the square root of the energy coefficient.

refraction diagram A drawing showing positions of wave crests and/or orthogonals in a given area for a specific deep-water wave period and direction.

refraction seismograph Seismic equipment designed to record refracted waves.

refractometer An instrument for determining the index of refraction of a mineral or of a liquid, etc.

refractory *1.* Resisting the action of heat and chemical reagents; a quality undesirable in ores but desirable in furnace linings, etc. *2.* A piece of pottery wave covered with a vaporable flux and placed in a kiln to form a glaze on other articles.

refractory ore Ore difficult to treat for recovery of the valuable substances.

refringence Refraction of light; measured as an index of refraction.

Refugian Upper Oligocene.

reg Desert surface consisting of small rounded tightly packed pebbles.

regelation Refreezing of ice which has melted under pressure.

regenerated crystal Large crystal that has grown in mass of crushed material like mylonite.

regeneration Replacement of parts lost by an organism through accident.

regime A channel is said to be in regime when it is capable of adjusting its cross-sectional form and/or longitudinal slope by means of alterations that the flow can impose on the solid, and exhibits an average equilibrium between the actions and counteractions there. Recommended for canals; use graded for rivers. *See* REGIMEN

regimen *1.* The material balance of a glacier involving the total accumulation and the gross wastage in one budget year. May be positive or negative. *2.* The series of processes by which glaciers are nourished, grow, and shrink. *3.* The habits or characteristics of individual streams—their particular reactions to the general laws of stream work, whether or not the streams have attained to the conditions of equilibrium. *4.* The stability of a stream and its channel. A river or canal is "in regimen" if its channel has reached a stable form as the result of its flow characteristics.

regional Extending over large areas in contradistinction to local or restricted areas.

regional metamorphism Large-scale metamorphism, usually unrelated to obvious igneous bodies.

regional unconformity Unconformity continuously present throughout an extensive region, recording an important interruption in sedimentary deposition and generally erosion of older strata.

regmagenesis Diastrophism producing large-scale strike-slip displacements.

regmatic Refers to extensive strike-slip displacements.

regolith Mantle rock; saprolith. The layer or mantle of loose, incoherent rock material, of whatever origin, that nearly everywhere forms the surface of the land and rests on the hard or "bed" rocks. It comprises rock waste of all sorts, volcanic ash, glacial drift, alluvium, windblown deposits, vegetal accumulations, and soils.

regression *1.* Gradual contraction of a shallow sea resulting in the emergence of land as when sea level falls or land rises. *2.* The loss by organisms of advanced characters; degeneration.

regressive, *adj.* Applied to bodies of water, and to sediments deposited therein, during lowering or withdrawal of the water.

regressive overlap Offlap, *q.v.*

regur or **regar sail** [*Hind.*] A residual, dark-colored, loamy soil of the volcanic regions of India, rich in organic matter, that is not derived from forest growth; similar to the black earth of Russia. The black cotton soil of India.

rejuvenate *1.* To render young again. *2.* To stimulate, as by uplift, to renew erosive activity; said of streams. *3.* To develop youthful features of topography in an area previously worn down to a base level.

relative humidity The ratio of the actual amount of water vapor in a given volume of air to the amount which would be present where the air saturated at the same temperature, expressed as a percentage.

relative permeability *See* PERMEABILITY, RELATIVE

release fractures Fractures that form perpendicular to the greatest principal stress axis in a specimen that is compressed and has yielded plastically while under hydrostatic pressure. On the assumption that these fractures form when the load is removed, they have been called release fractures.

release joints Joints parallel to the axial planes of the fold; presumably formed at right angles to the greatest principal stress axis after the pressure was released.

relict permafrost Permafrost that was formed in the past and which persists in places where it cannot form today.

relict texture Preservation of any original texture when a mineral is replaced.

relief *1.* The difference in elevation between the high and low points of a land surface. *2.* The character of the surface of a mineral section as observed under the microscope, depending upon its refractive power relative to that of the medium in which it is embedded.

relief, relative *Geomorph:* Ratio of basin relief (h) to basin perimeter (p). *Symbol:* Rhp.

relief map A model of an area in which its inequalities of surface are shown in relief.

relief well A well drilled to intercept or closely approach the shaft of another well and thus relieve the latter of the flow of oil or gas. Relief wells are drilled to extinguish a fire, or to reduce the flow and pressure in the earlier well so that the latter may be brought under control.

Relizian Upper Lower Miocene.

reluctance The ratio of the magnetomotive force acting upon any part of a magnetic circuit to the resulting magnetic flux.

remanence The residual magnetic induction B in a substance undergoing a symmetrical hysteresis cycle, when the magnetic intensity H is reduced to zero; represented by either intercept of the H-B hysteresis curve on the B axis.

remanent magnetization Permanent magnetization induced by an applied magnetic field, like that in a good permanent magnet.

reniform Kidney-shaped.

repeated reflections Seismic reflections which have been multiply re-reflected, either from the surface of the earth or from reflection interfaces. They may be mistaken for deeper reflections, but may often be identified from time and dip relationships. *Syn:* MULTIPLE REFLECTIONS

Repettian Lower Pliocene.

replacement The process of practically simultaneous capillary solution and deposition by which new mineral of partly or wholly differing chemical composition may grow in the body of an old mineral or mineral aggregate.

replacement deposit Deposit formed by replacement. Not infrequently it is a disseminated deposit.

replacement or **substitution vein** A vein in which certain minerals have passed into solution and have been carried away, while other minerals from the solution have been deposited in the place of those removed. The process is called metasomatic replacement.

repose, angle of The slope at which any given deposited material will come to rest under a given set of physical conditions. Eolian sands generally have higher angles of repose than aqueous sands of the same-size grade.

representation work Same as assessment work on a mining claim.

representative fraction Ratio of the distance between two points on a map and the actual distance between them; map scale.

reptile Cold-blooded tetrapod that does not develop through an amphibious gill-breathing larval stage. Snakes are reptiles that have lost their legs.

Reptilia Class of vertebrates, cold-blooded tetrapods that are exclusively air-breathing at all stages of development. Penn.-Rec.

resection The determination of the horizontal position of a survey station by observed directions from the station to points of known position.

resequent fault-line scarp A fault-line scarp in which the structurally downthrown block is also topographically lower than the upthrown block.

esequent stream A stream which flows in a direction identical with that of the consequent drainage, but which develops at a lower level than the initial slope.

eserve 1. *Min:* Refers to known ore bodies that may be worked at some future time. 2. Petroleum or natural gas discovered, developed, and producible, but not yet produced.

servoir A natural underground container of liquids, such as oil or water, and gases. In general, such reservoirs were formed by local deformation of strata, changes of porosity, and by intrusions. These, however, are classifications in the broadest sense.

servoir energy The energy within an oil or gas reservoir which causes the oil, gas, and water to flow into a well.

servoir engineer An engineer engaged in the exploitation of oil and gas reservoirs or in research pertaining thereto.

servoir gas-oil ratio *See* RESERVOIR

servoir pressure *See* BOTTOM-HOLE PRESSURE

sidual 1. (a) Characteristic of, pertaining to, or consisting of esiduum. (b) Remaining essentially in place after all but the east soluble constituents have been removed. Said of the material eventually resulting from the decomposition of rocks. 2. standing, as a remnant of a formerly greater mass of rock or area of land, above a surrounding area which has been generally planated. Said of some rocks, ills, mountains, mesas, plateaus, and groups of such features. *See* MONADNOCK. 3. *Geophys:* The resultant of a measurement upon a quantity, minus

the most probable value of that quantity.

residual bond Van der Waals bond.

residual clay A clay deposit formed by the decay of rock in place.

residual concentration Concentration of a valuable mineral by solution and removal of valueless material.

residual deposits As, residual gravel, sand, clay, etc. *See* RESIDUAL, *1* (b)

residual gravity *Grav. prospecting:* The portion of a gravity effect remaining after removal of some type of "regional"; usually the relatively small or local anomaly components of the total or observed gravity field.

residual liquid A term used for the more volatile constituents of a magma after much crystallization has taken place.

residual magma Ichor, *q.v.*

residual magnetism *Mag. prospecting:* The portion of a magnetic effect remaining after removal of some type of "regional"; usually the relatively small or local anomaly components of the total or observed magnetic field.

residual soil Soil formed in place by the disintegration and decomposition of rocks and the consequent weathering of the mineral materials. Presumably developed from the same kind of rock as that on which it lies.

resilience The work which a body can do in springing back after a deforming force has been removed. If a body is stressed beyond its elastic limit, the resilience equals that proportion of the total work of deformation which the body can give back upon removal of the forces.

resin 1. Secretions of saps of

certain plants or trees. It is an oxidation or polymerization product of the terpenes, and generally contains "resin" acids and esters. 2. The solid bitumens. See BITUMEN

resinous Resembling resin in appearance, as, opal and some yellow varieties of sphalerite.

resistance That which limits the steady electric current in a conductor and is expressed by the ratio of the applied constant electromotive force to the current.

resistate One of the residual sediments, consisting of the chemically undecomposed residues of weathering; examples are sands, sandstones, gravels, etc.

resistivity That factor of the resistance of a conductor which depends upon the material and its physical condition. Its measure is the resistance of a specimen, in the form of a rod of unit length and unit cross section, to a current traversing it longitudinally. Usually expressed in ohm-centimeters. *Syn:* SPECIFIC RESISTANCE

resolution *1.* The separation of a vector into its components. 2. The sharpness with which the images of two closely adjacent spectrum lines, etc., may be distinguished. 3. *Grav.* or *Mag. prospecting:* The indication in some measured quantity, such as the vertical component of gravity, of the presence of two or more close but separate disturbing bodies. 4. *Seis. prospecting:* The ability to indicate separately two closely adjacent interfaces.

resonance A term denoting a variety of phenomena characterized by the abnormally large response of a system having a natural vibration period to a stimulus of the same, or nearly the same, frequency.

resorption A partial refusing c solution of phenocrysts in a po phyritic rock, possibly followe by recrystallization in modifie forms.

rest magma A magma whos composition is that remainin from a long series of differenti tions.

resultant A single force that pr duces the same result as two c more forces.

retained water Interstitial wat held by molecular attractic against gravity, in isolated i terstices or as water vapor o cupying interstices from whic liquid water has been withdraw

reticulate *1.* Netted. Havir veins, fibers, or lines crossir like the threads or fibers of network. 2. *Petrol:* Applied to texture of crystals which a partly altered to a seconda mineral, the remnants of t original mineral lying in a ne work or mesh of the seconda mineral.

retrograde or **retrogressive met morphism** Diaphthoresis. T mineralogical adjustment of r atively high-grade metamorph rocks to temperatures lower th those of their initial metamc phism.

retrograde rotation Rotation opposite direction; all planets e cept Uranus rotate in the sar direction as their revoluti around the sun.

retrograding shore line A sho line which is being extend landward by wave attack.

retrogressive metamorphism I aphthoresis; retrograde metamc phism, *q.v.*

reversal (of dip) A local chan of approximately one hundr and eighty degrees in the dir tion of the regional dip.

reversed arc Mountain or isla

arc in a primary series that faces in the opposite direction, generally offset from others with which it is connected by transcurrent faults.

reversed limb *See* OVERTURNED LIMB

reverse fault A fault along which the hanging wall has been raised relatively to the footwall.

reverse flowage fold Fold in which layers of rock are thickened at crest and thinned at trough.

reverse similar fold Fold in which layers of rock are thickened on flanks and thinned at crest and trough; condition reverse of that in similar folds.

reversible process A thermodynamic process is reversible when an infinitesimal change in the variables characterizing the state of the system can change the direction of the process.

revolution A time of major crustal deformation when folds and faults are formed. Often accompanied by the emplacement of plutonic rocks.

rework To move sediment after preliminary deposition, commonly resulting in transportation and sorting.

Rg *Earthquake seismol:* A phase designation given to a slow, short-period Rayleigh wave which is found to travel only along nonoceanic paths. The subscript g refers to the possible importance of the granitic layer for their propagation.

Rhaetian Rhaetic.

Rhaetic Upper Upper Triassic, transitional into Jurassic.

rheid Body of rock showing flow structure.

rheid folding Folding accompanied by slippage along shear planes at an angle to the bedding or earlier developed foliation.

rheidity Capacity of material to flow within the earth.

rheology Study of the flowage of materials, particularly plastic flow of solids and flow of non-Newtonian liquids.

rheomorphism A process of at least partial fusion, such that the rock may be deformed viscously.

Rhizopoda Sarcodina.

Rhodanian orogeny Mid-Pliocene diastrophism.

rhodochrosite A mineral of the calcite group, $MnCO_3$, commonly containing some Fe and Ca. Hexagonal rhombohedral. A minor ore of manganese.

rhodolite A variety of pyrope-almandite garnet characterized by its roselike color and brilliant luster. Used as a gem.

rhodonite A mineral, $MnSiO_3$. Triclinic.

rhombic dodecahedron *See* DODECAHEDRON

rhombic symmetry *See* ORTHORHOMBIC SYMMETRY

rhombic system *Crystallog:* Same as orthorhombic system. Rhombic is an undesirable term because often confused with rhombohedral.

rhombohedral *1.* Of, pertaining to, forming, or crystallizing in rhombohedrons. *2.* Pertaining to, or belonging in, that group of the hexagonal system which is characterized by a vertical axis of threefold or inverse-threefold symmetry.

rhombohedral packing The manner of arrangement of solid units in a clastic sediment characterized by a unit cell of six planes passed through eight sphere centers situated at the corners of a regular rhombohedron. This is the tightest form of packing, with minimum porosity.

rhombohedral system *1.* The same as the hexagonal system, except that the forms are referred to three axes parallel to the faces of the fundamental rhombohedron instead of to the usual four axes. 2. The rhombohedral division of the hexagonal system, the forms being referred to the same three axes as above. (Neither usage has been generally accepted.)

rhombohedron A crystal form in the hexagonal system bounded by six faces of rhombic outline.

rhomb spar Dolomite.

rhyodacite The aphanitic equivalent of a granodiorite.

rhyolite The aphanitic equivalent of a granite.

rhythmites 1. Rhythmic laminations. 2. Individual units of rhythmic beds.

ria coast This term is derived from northwestern Spain, where the Rio de Vigo, de la Coruña, del Farrol, and several others, form long, fiordlike bays, though branching little, which extend far into the land. Coasts of this type have frequently been regarded as fiord coasts, but there are essential differences; the bays are shorter, more funnel-shaped, broadening and deepening seaward, and are not nearly so deep as fiords.

rib 1. *Coal min:* The solid coal on the side of a gallery or long wall face; a pillar or barrier of coal left for support. 2. The solid ore of a vein; an elongated pillar left to support the hanging wall, in working out a vein. 3. In Scotland, a thin stratum, as of stone, in a seam of coal. Also spelled ribb. 4. A stringer of ore in a lode. 5. *Speleol:* A small solutional remnant of bed rock projecting into a passage. 6. In a leaf or similar organ, the primary vein; also, any prominent vein or nerve.

ribbon diagram Geologic cross section drawn in perspective and joining control points along a sinuous course.

ribbon injection An apophysis of igneous rock injected in a band along the cleavage planes of slate or other foliated rock.

ribbon rock Rock with varvelike layers of alternating brown weathering dolomite, sandy dolomite, and light-weathering limestone.

ribbon structure Structure of vein characterized by thin subparallel films or septa (usually of materials of rock alteration) in quartz or other gangue.

Richmondian Upper Middle Cincinnatian.

Richter magnitude See MAGNITUDE

ridge 1. A relatively narrow elevation which is prominent on account of the steep angle at which it rises. It is thus narrower than an extended rise, the distinction being clear where a rise assumes in some part the character of a ridge. [*Ger.* Rucken; *Fr.* crête.]

ridge, pressure See PRESSURE RIDGE

ridge fold Doubly plunging anticline or elongated dome.

riebeckite See AMPHIBOLE

Riecke's principle or **law** Mineral grains that are under stress have higher solubilities, i.e., they dissolve in preference to unstressed grains of the same mineral. If a given grain is not stressed homogeneously (e.g., there are "point contacts"), the grain will dissolve at these points and recrystallize at points of lower stress.

riffle 1. A groove in the bottom of an inclined trough or sluice for arresting gold contained in sands or gravels. 2. A shallow extending across the bed of a stream; a rapid of comparatively little fall.

rift *1.* A large strike-slip fault parallel to the regional structure; specifically applied to the San Andreas rift in California. *See* RIFT VALLEY. *2.* The intersection of a fault plane with the surface. *3.* A planar property whereby granitic rocks split relatively easily in a direction other than the sheeting (parallel to the surface of the earth). *4.* A narrow cleft or fissure in rock. *5. Topog:* A shallow rocky place in a stream; used in northeastern United States as a synonym for "riffle." *6.* The shallow edge of the surf; the rippling wash up on the beach after a wave has broken. *7. Speleol:* A long, narrow opening above or between underground channels.

rift trough Graben bounded by normal faults.

rift valley Valley produced by subsidence of a strip bounded by two parallel rifts. *See* GRABEN

rig The derrick, mast, or standing equipment used to drill a well, together with the motive power, cable, and tools used in drilling.

right-handed separation Where the horizontal separation along a fault is such that an observer walking along an index plane (bed, dike, vein, etc.) must, upon crossing the fault, turn to the right to find the index plane on the opposite side of the fault. The actual movement along the fault can be a strike-slip movement, a dip-slip movement, or a diagonal-slip movement.

right-lateral fault A strike-slip fault with right-handed (right-lateral) separation.

rigid crust Crustal layer, probably granitic and 30–40 km. thick

beneath the continents, which overlies the M crust.

rigidity Resistance of a body to plastic or viscous flow. *Cf.* STRENGTH

rigidity modulus Let a cube be deformed into a parallelopiped by keeping the base fixed, but by displacing the top of the cube horizontally.

$\mu = \dfrac{F}{D}$ When μ is the rigidity modulus, F=force per unit area, and D is the relative displacement of planes a unit distance apart.

rig time The time during which drilling equipment remains idle on a well. Usually such time is charged on a per diem basis.

rill *1. Topog:* A very small trickling stream of water; a very small brook. *2.* A minute stream that flows away from a beach as a wave subsides. *3.* A small channel made by circulating water in the wall, floor, or ceiling of a cave.

rillenstein Solution-grooved rocks; grooving generally imposed on karren.

rill mark A small groove, furrow, or channel made by a wave-generated rill.

rim *1.* An edge. *2.* A narrow zone of minerals generally arranged radially around a crystal. *See* CORONA; REACTION RIM

rim cement Overgrowth in crystallographic conformity with a grain in a sedimentary deposit.

rimrock *1.* Rock or rocks on the rim forming a natural and usually a precipitous boundary of an elevated land form. *2.* The bedrock rising to form the boundary of a placer or gravel deposit.

rimstone A term suggested by W. M. Davis to designate calcareous deposits formed around the rims of overflowing basins.

rim syncline Downfolds that tend to develop around the periphery of salt domes, presumably due to sagging of the overlying strata into a circular void created by the removal of salt from the source strata.

rim texture A texture in ores where the metasome forms a narrow rim around grains of the host mineral.

ring dike *See* CONE SHEET

ring-fracture stoping Large-scale stoping associated with cauldron subsidence.

ring structures *See* SOROSILICATES

rinnentaler Ice-walled channel.

rio [*Sp.*] A river or stream. Local in Southwest.

rip A body of water made rough by waves meeting an opposing current, particularly a tidal current; often found where tidal currents are converging and sinking. A tide rip.

riparian Pertaining to the banks of a body of water.

riparian water loss Evapotranspiration in the stream-bed zone; the difference between the amount of water feeding into the stream from the water table and the amount of water passing the stream-gaging stations during those periods when stream flow is not affected by storm runoff.

rip current A seaward-moving streak of water which returns the water carried landward by waves.

ripple mark An undulating surface sculpture produced in non-coherent granular materials by the wind, by currents of water, and by the agitation of water in wave action. Singular form may be used to denote general ripple structure; plural, a particular example.

riprap *1.* Broken rock used for

revetment, the protection fc bluffs or structures exposed t wave action, foundations, etc. ; Foundation or wall of broke rock thrown together irregularly

rip tide An improper name fo rip current. A rip current has n relation to the tide, hence th term rip tide in this connectio is in error.

rise *1.* (Oceanic) An elevatio which rises gradually with a angle of only a few minutes c arc, irrespective of whether : is wide or narrow, or of its ver tical development. On account c its flatness, the rise apparentl plays only a subordinate par but rises carry the chief feature of suboceanic relief, so that : an ocean floor was changed int dry land they would act as th main watersheds. [*Ger.* Schwellen *Fr.* seuil.] *2.* A long and broa elevation of the deep-sea floc which rises gently and smoothly *3.* Spring rising from fracture in limestone. *4.* Point at whic an underground stream comes t the surface. *Syn:* RESURGENCI EMERGENCE

riser The vertical element of steplike natural land form; ca be applied to a glacial stairway stream or marine terraces. C TREAD

Riss Third Pleistocene glaciatio

river A stream of water bearin the waste of the land from high er to lower ground, and as rule to the sea. A trunk strear and all the branches that joi it constitute a river system Stream is a general term, wit little relation to size. Rill, rivu let, brook, and creek apply t streams of small or moderat size. River is generally applie to a trunk stream or to th larger branches of a river systen

river basin The land from whic

a river gathers its water and rock waste is called its basin.

iver bed *1.* The bed of a river is the channel which contains its waters. *2.* By the term bed is understood all the space ordinarily covered by water and lying between the lands on each side of the stream. In rivers which rise above the levels of these lands and overflow adjacent flats or bottoms, the channel in which the water is usually confined is called the minor bed while the space occupied during floodtime is known as the major bed.

iver bottom The alluvial land along a river.

iver-cut plain A flat erosion surface produced by a river.

iver flat The alluvial plain adjacent to a river; bottom; interval; intervale (New England).

iver system A river system includes all streams which rise within a given hydrographic basin and whose waters finally pass by one channel into the ocean reservoir.

iver terrace A river terrace consists of a plain and an accompanying escarpment. The terrace plain is approximately horizontal and usually slopes both with the grade of the stream and away from the river bed which it faces. On the side toward the stream the plain is bounded by an escarpment, the two together making the terrace; the opposite side of the plain is usually bounded by more elevated land, either an older and higher terrace or the true valley wall.

iver valley The depression made by the stream, and by its various processes which precede and accompany the development of the stream.

iving seams Open fissures between beds of rock in a quarry.

RNA Ribonucleic acid occurring mainly in the cytoplasm of organisms.

road metal Rock suitable for surfacing macadamized roads and for foundations for asphalt and concrete roadways.

roche moutonnée A glacially abraded bedrock boss. *Syn:* DRESSED ROCK; SHEEPBACK ROCK; SHEEPBACK

rock *1.* (a) Strictly, any naturally formed aggregate or mass of mineral matter, whether or not coherent, constituting an essential and appreciable part of the earth's crust. (b) Ordinarily, any consolidated or coherent and relatively hard, naturally formed mass of mineral matter; stone. *2.* In the Lake Superior region, crude copper ore as it comes from the mines. The concentrate obtained is called mineral, and contains about 65% metallic copper. *3.* In New York and Pennsylvania, a local term for the more massive beds of bluestone that are not jointed and are, therefore, well suited for structural purposes. *4.* A peak, cliff, promontory, or the like, of rock, usually bare, and considered as one mass, as, the Rock of Gibraltar. *5.* To the engineer, the term rock signifies firm and coherent or consolidated substances that cannot normally be excavated by manual methods alone.

rock burst A sudden and often violent failure of masses of rock in quarries, tunnels, and mines.

rock crystal Transparent quartz, especially when colorless.

rock-defended terrace (marine) Soft coastal plain sediments undergoing marine erosion are worn back rapidly until the waves encounter a buried resistant oldland mass at the base of the cliff cut in the coastal plain sediments. The resulting terrace is said to be rock defended and resembles similar terraces along river valleys.

rock drumlin A hill having the form of a drumlin but consisting of bedrock veneered with till.

rockfall The relatively free falling of a newly detached segment of bedrock of any size from a cliff, steep slope, cave, or arch.

rock fault In England, a replacement of a coal seam over a greater or less area, by some other rock, usually sandstone.

rock flour Finely ground rock particles, chiefly silt size, resulting from glacial abrasion.

rockforming Refers to minerals occurring in ordinary rocks as opposed to minerals occurring only in veins, ore deposits, etc.

rock glacier A glacierlike tongue of angular rock waste usually heading in cirques or other steep-walled amphitheaters and in many cases grading into true glaciers. *Syn:* TALUS GLACIER; ROCK STREAM; ROCK RIVER

rock hound Facetious term for a geologist, particularly an oil geologist.

rock mantle Regolith; rock waste.

rock pediment A flat zone of bedrock one mile to several miles in width at the base of many mountains and especially in arid regions, only slightly veneered with alluvium and which slopes away to the adjacent basins.

rock plane Pediment.

rock pressure *1.* A term applied to the pressure found in liquids or gases confined in the rock. Originally supposed to be due to the weight of the overlying rocks. In 1887, I. C. White advanced the theory that pressures of fluids confined in reservoirs are the result of artesian or hydraulic pressures, dependen chiefly upon the vertical interva between the reservoir and th nearest outcrop of the latter This is true in most regions. *2* Strictly, the pressure in the soli structure of a reservoir (over burden pressure). Colloquiall used in gas fields to denot reservoir pressure of the fluids.

rock salt Halite. A crystalline fibrous, or even granular aggre gate of sodium chloride.

rock series *See* IGNEOUS ROCK SERIES

rockslide The downward an usually rapid movement of new ly detached segments of the bed rock sliding on bedding, joint or fault surfaces or any othe plane of separation. Also, th rock mass that has attained it present condition by such movement.

rock-stratigraphic unit Strati graphic unit defined and identi fied by lithologic or structura features without regard to fossil or time boundaries. *Syn:* LITHO STRATIGRAPHIC UNIT; ROCK UNIT

rock stream A rock stream is re garded as a landslide of specia character, a rock mass which wa completely broken up in falling and whose debris acquired momentum so great that it be came a rapidly flowing body and descended in a streamlike form far beyond the normal limit o a landslide mass. *See* ROCK GLA CIER

rock terrace Rock terraces occur on the sides of many valleys cut in horizontal beds of unequal strength. The terraces are formed by the strong beds, which are worn back less rapidly than the weak beds above and below them.

rock train The fringing and medial trains subject to the dynamic forces of the glacier.

rock unit Rock-stratigraphic unit.

rock waste Material making up a talus or scree. Slider rock.

rock wool See MINERAL WOOL

rod *1.* A shape class in the Zingg classification in which the ratio of breadth to length is less than 2/3, and ratio of thickness to breadth is greater than 2/3. *2.* A length of 16 1/2 feet. *3.* A graduated pole used as a target in surveying.

rodding structure Structure characterized by the development of small parallel rods of quartz generally oriented parallel to the fold axes of the containing highly deformed rocks.

roentgen Unit of radiation dosage, $1.61. \times 10^{12}$ ion pairs per gram of standard air. Also röntgen.

rolling ground or **land** Any undulating land surface; a succession of low hills giving a wave effect to the surface. A land surface much varied by many small hills and valleys.

roman ocher A native ocher of a deep orange-yellow color.

roof The rock lying above a coal bed or ore vein.

roof foundering The collapse of the overlying rocks into an underlying reservoir of magma.

roofing slate A finely fissile, compact, homogeneous argillite or clay slate, yielding thin slabs, used for roofing. The prevailing colors are nearly black, though sometimes greenish, purple, or red.

roof pendant Older rocks projecting down from the roof into a batholith. On a map the roof pendant is completely surrounded by the rocks of the batholith.

roof rock The rock forming the ceiling of a cave passage, chamber, etc.

room An expanded portion of a cavern passage.

room and pillar A system of mining in which the distinguishing feature is the winning of 50% or more of the coal or ore in the first working. The coal or ore is mined in rooms separated by narrow ribs or pillars. The coal or ore in the pillars is won by subsequent working, which may be likened to top slicing, in which the roof is caved in successive blocks. The first working in rooms is an advancing and the winning of the rib (pillar) a retreating method. The rooms are driven parallel with one another, and the room faces may be extended parallel, at right angles, or at an angle in the dip. This method is applicable to flat deposits, such as coal, iron ore, lead, and zinc, etc., that occur in bedded deposits. There are many modifications, for which see Albert Hill Fay, "A Glossary of the Mining and Mineral Industry."

root A term used chiefly by Alpine geologists, and in somewhat varying meanings. *1.* The core of a geanticline within a geosyncline, which, after the forward drive of the geosynclinal sediments, became the recumbent fold or nappe. *2.* The back-remaining, steep part of a nappe. *3.* In the United States, the downward projection of sial (granitic crust) into sima (basaltic or peridotitic subcrust).

root zone *1.* Place where the axial plane of a recumbent fold becomes steeper and dips beneath the surface of the earth. *2.* Place where a low angle thrust fault becomes steeper and disappears beneath the surface of the earth.

ropy lava Corded pahoehoe.

roscoelite A mineral, a member of the mica group, $K(V,Al)_2(Al-Si_3O_{10})(OH)_2$. Monoclinic.

rose diagram Circular or semicircular diagram for plotting strikes (or dips) of planar features, such as joints, dikes, etc.

Rosenbusch's law or rule A statement of the sequence and crystallization of minerals from magmas, proposed by Harry Rosenbusch (1882), to which many exceptions have been taken.

rose quartz Quartz with a rosepink color. Used as a gem or as an ornamental stone.

rosette 1. A flowerlike crystal growth of gypsum. *Syn:* OULOPHOLITE; GYPSUM FLOWER. 2. A symmetrical growth form, resembling a rose, assumed by an accretionary body. Barite and pyrite take this form in some rocks. *See* PETRIFIED ROSE

rosin or resin jack A yellow variety of sphalerite.

rosin or resin tin A reddish or yellowish variety of cassiterite.

Rossi-Forel intensity scale A scale for rating earthquake intensities. Devised in 1878 by M. S. de Rossi (Italy) and F. A. Forel (Switzerland). No longer in general use, having been supplanted by H. O. Wood and Frank Neumann's Modified Mercalli Intensity Scale of 1931, and more recently by the Richter Scale. *See* MAGNITUDE

rotary drilling The hydraulic process of drilling which consists of rotating a column of drill pipe, to the bottom of which is attached a drilling bit, and, during the operation, circulating down through the pipe a current of mud-laden fluid, under pressure, by means of special slush pumps. The drilling mud and cuttings from the bit are forced upward and outside the drill pipe to the surface.

rotary fault A fault in which some straight lines on opposite sides of the fault and outside of the dislocated zone, parallel before the displacement, are no longer parallel, i.e., where one side has suffered rotation relative to the other.

rotational cylindroidal folding Subsequent folding that has distorted the axial planes of cylindroidal folds without destroying their cylindroidal character.

rotational fault Rotary fault.

rotational flow Turbulent flow involving all parts of a moving liquid.

rotational movement Refers to movement on faults. Blocks rotate relative to one another about an axis perpendicular to the fault. Some straight lines on opposite sides of the zone and outside the dislocated zone, parallel before the displacement, are no longer parallel afterward.

rotational strain Strain under such conditions that strain axes are rotated relative to stress axes.

rotational wave Shear wave.

rotation axis Axis of symmetry, *q.v.*

Rothliegendes Lower and Middle Permian.

roundness The ratio of the average radius of curvature of the several corners or edges of a solid to the radius of curvature of the maximum inscribed sphere. Not to be confused with sphericity.

royal agate A mottled variety of obsidian.

royalty The landowner's share of the value of minerals produced free of expenses of development and production; commonly expressed as a fractional share of the current market value (oil and gas) or as a fixed amount per ton (mining).

r-tectonite B-tectonite with an axis of rotation rather than an axis of slip.

rubble All accumulations of loose angular fragments not waterworn or rounded like gravel. Loose angular waterworn stones along a beach.

rubellite Dark-pink or red tourmaline.

ruby A red variety of corundum, used as a gem.

ruby silver *See* PROUSTITE, PYRARGYRITE

rudaceous Psephite. The texture of the rubble rocks in which the grain is larger than that of a sand grain. Consolidated rocks of this type are rudytes.

rudimentary *1.* Vestigial; said of structures which are not as highly developed in the descendants as they were in the ancestors. *2.* Very imperfectly developed.

rudite; rudyte Psephite, *q.v.* Fragmental sedimentary rocks composed of fragments coarser than sand grains.

ruggedness number *Geomorphol:* Symbol N^r. Maximum relief times drainage density within a particular drainage basin.

rugose, *adj.* Wrinkled, usually covered with wrinkles, the venation appearing impressed into the surface.

rugose coral Tetracoral.

rule of V's *See* V's, RULE OF

run *1. Topog:* A brook or small creek. A small, swift watercourse. *2.* A ribbonlike, irregular ore body, lying flat or nearly flat, following the stratification, is called a run. Many are formed at the intersections of ore horizons with fissures. *3.* In quarrying, a direction of secondary or minor cleavage grain. *See* RIFT. *4.* Soft ground is said to "run" when it becomes mud and will not hold together or stand.

runite Graphic granite.

runoff *1.* The discharge of water through surface streams. *2.* The quantity of water discharged through surface streams, expressed usually in units of volume such as gallons, cubic feet, or acre-feet. *3.* To cause contents to flow off or out, as, to run off a millpond or a smelting furnace. *4.* The collapse of a coal pillar in a steeply pitching seam, caused either naturally or by a small shot placed in it. This occurs in connection with pillar robbing, and the pillar is said to have run off.

Rupelian Middle Oligocene.

rupture Fracture.

rutile A mineral, TiO_2, trimorphous with anatase and brookite. Tetragonal.

R-wave Rayleigh wave, *q.v.*

Saalian orogeny Mid-Permian diastrophism.

saccharoidal Having a granular texture resembling that of loaf sugar; said of some sandstones and marbles.

saddle *1.* A low point on a ridge or crest line, generally a divide between the heads of streams flowing in opposite directions. *See* COL; PASS. *2. Petroleum geol:* A structural feature created by the sagging of an anticline. *3. Paleontol:* An undulation of the suture which is convex toward the aperture in a cephalopod. *4.* In Australia, a formation of gold-bearing quartz occurring along the crest of an anticlinal fold. *5.* A peculiar formation found in shale or sand rock in the roof of a mine. The under or exposed side looks like natural rock, but its upper side is smooth, having no particular bond with the sand rock with which it is embedded, and is liable to fall out of its place, a fall, however, producing no other derangement of the surrounding parts of the room from which it falls.

saddle fold A type of flexure fold which shows an additional flexure in its crest at right angles to that of the parent fold, and of much larger radius.

saddle reef In Australia, a bedded vein that has the form of an anticline; an inverted saddle has the form of a syncline. *See* SADDLE, *4*

safe yield The rate of which water can be withdrawn from an aquifer without depleting the supply to such an extent that withdrawal at this rate is harmful to the aquifer itself, or to the quality of the water, or is no longer economically feasible.

sagenite A quartz crystal which contains acicular crystals of rutile.

sagenitic Occurring as needles or plates intersecting in a grid- or grill-like manner.

sagittate, *adj.* Like an arrowhead in form; triangular, with the basal lobes pointing downward or concavely toward the stalk.

sagponds *1.* Ponds occupying depressions along active faults. *2.* Depressions due to uneven settling of the ground.

Saint Croixan Croixan.

Sakmarian Lower Lower Permian.

sal Sial.

sal ammoniac Ammonium chloride.

salic A mnemonic term derived from "s" for silica and "a" for alumina and applied to the group of standard normative minerals in which one or both of these elements are present in large amount, including quartz, the feldspars, and the feldspathoids. The corresponding term for the silicic and aluminous minerals actually present in a rock is felsic, *q.v.* Contrasted with femic.

salient *1.* An angle or spur projecting from the side of the main body of any land feature; projecting outwardly; opposite to the re-entrant. *2.* That part of an orogenic belt that is convex toward the foreland, that is, is concave toward the orogenic belt.

salina *1.* In South America, those superficial deposits which often occupy extensive plains on the Pacific or rainless side of the Andes, and which are usually covered with a white saline efflorescence or crystalline incrustation. They occur at all elevations, from a few feet to several thousand feet above sea level, and are evidently the remains of old sea reaches and lagoons that have been dissected by the upheaval of the land. *2.* A salt marsh, or salt pond, enclosed from the sea. *3.* A saline playa. *See* PLAYA LAKE

Salinan Lower Upper Silurian.

saline *N: 1.* In some playas the amount of mineral substances (common salts and others) left by evaporating water is so great as to incrust the entire area, sometimes to a depth of several inches. Such an area is then called a saline. *See* SALINA; *2.* As used by Congress, includes not only salt springs but all salt land of every character. *Adj: 3.* Salty. Possessing a high degree of salinity, more than 3000 parts per million total dissolved solids. *4.* In Louisiana, a body of water lying behind barrier. *Cf.* BRACKISH

salinity *1.* Measure of the quantity of total dissolved solids in water. *2.* A measure of the total concentration of dissolved solids in a saline water. Specifically, for sea water, the total of dissolved solids, expressed in g/kg,

when all carbonate has been converted to oxide, Br and I replaced by Cl, and all organic matter completely oxidized.

Salmian Tremadocian.

Salopian Middle and Upper Silurian (restricted).

salt *1.* Halite; common salt. Sodium chloride, NaCl. *2.* Any class of compounds formed when the acid hydrogen of an acid is partly or wholly replaced by a metal or a metal-like radical; as, ferrous sulfate (FeSO₄) is an iron salt of sulfuric acid, H_2SO_4. *3. V:* To place gold, or any valuable ore in the ground, a mine, or the like to give a false impression of the richness of the property. To "salt" a mine.

salt-and-pepper sand Sand consisting of a mixture of light- and dark-colored grains.

saltation [<*Lat.* saltare, to jump] *1.* The variable or leaping movements arising largely in combinations of friction with inertia as discussed long ago by William Hopkins and more recently by Joseph Le Conte, G. K. Gilbert, and others. *2. Paleontol:* Discontinuous variations, evidenced by the absence of a continuous orthogenetic series. *Cf.* SALTATORY EVOLUTION. *Syn:* Mutation of Hugo de Vries. *3.* The process by which a particle, picked up by the stream current, is flung upward after which, being too heavy to remain in suspension, it drops to the stream floor again at a spot downstream. *4.* Sudden evolution of a new kind or organism derived from older ones without the appearance of intermediate forms; almost impossible genetically.

saltatory evolution The theory that new types and groups of organisms arise by abrupt and radical change from parent to offspring, without transitional intervening generations and populations.

salt dome A structure resulting from the upward movement of a salt mass, and with which oil and gas fields are frequently associated. In the Gulf Coast area of the United States, the salt is in the form of a roughly circular plug of relatively narrow diameter, but often several thousand feet in depth. *See* PIERCEMENT DOME; INTERIOR SALT DOME

salt glacier Mass of mobile salt at the earth's surface that flows slowly outward from a center, generally an exposed salt plug; known only in such an extremely arid region as that adjacent to the Persian Gulf.

salt lakes Lakes which contain a predominating amount of sodium chloride in solution and usually magnesium chloride as well as magnesium and calcium sulfate.

salt lick A place where salt is found on the surface of the earth to which animals resort to lick it up.

salt marsh A marsh periodically flooded by salt water.

salt pan 1. A shallow lake of brackish water. Also written panne. 2. A large pan for making salt by evaporation. 3. A salt works.

saltpeter Niter. Potassium nitrate; Chile saltpeter is sodium nitrate; wall saltpeter is calcium nitrate.

salt plug *See* SALT DOME

salt prairie Soda prairie. A tract of level land covered with a whitish efflorescence of natron or soda and presenting an aspect of utter desolation; common in New Mexico, Arizona, and Texas.

salt-water encroachment or **intrusion** The phenomenon occurring when a body of salt water, because of its greater density, invades a body of fresh water. It can occur either in surface or ground-water bodies. The balance between the two, in static situations, is expressed by the Ghyben-Herzberg formula.

samarskite A mineral, $(Y,Er,U,Fe)(Nb,Ta)_2O_6$. Orthorhombic.

sample 1. A representative unit of a formation fluid, ore, or other material for analysis or display. 2. A representative unit taken for laboratory analysis only. The sample may be taken as an example of the object, or it may be taken to illustrate some specific feature or variation. 3. V: To collect samples; to try, or test.

sampling 1. Cutting a representative part of an ore (or coal) deposit, which should truly represent its average value. Most usually a trenchlike cut 4 inches wide and 2 inches deep is cut into the clean face of ore (or coal) and across its course. 2. Selecting a certain fractional part of ore or coal from cars, stock piles, etc., for analysis.

sand 1. Detrital material of size range 2–1/16 mm. diameter. Very coarse 1–2 mm.; coarse 1/2–1 mm.; medium 1/4–1/2 mm.; fine 1/4–1/8 mm.; very fine 1/8–1/16 mm. 2. Other common definitions, not recommended: size 1/8–2 mm. J. A. Udden; 0.05–1.0 U. S. Bur. Soils; 0.032–1, C. G. Hopkins, 1899; 0.0–5.0, Lucien Cayeux, 1929; 0.2–2 mm., Albert Atterburg, 1903; 0.074–4.76 mm. 3. Sandstone. Not recommended. 4. A siliceous detrital deposit composed mainly of quartz particles. Not recommended. 5. A drilling term for an oil-bearing horizon.

sand bars A bar or ridge of sand built up to or near to the surface of the water by currents in a river or by wave action in coastal waters.

sand crystal Large euhedral or subhedral, poikiloblastic crystal containing up to 60% sand, developed by the growth of calcite or barite crystals in a sand deposit. May also form during or as a result of cementation.

sand dune A mound, ridge, or hill of loose sand, heaped up by the wind. *See* DUNE

sand flood A vast body of sand moving or borne along a desert, as in Arabia.

sand glacier The typical forms of sand accumulations known as sand glaciers, which have been described in various parts of the world, are due to sand being blown up the sides of hills or mountains, thence finding a passage through any passes or saddles and spreading out on the opposite side to form wide fan-shaped plains. This is E. E. Free's definition. V. Cornish restricts the term to a horizontal plateau of sand terminated by a talus, as steep as the sand can rest.

sand line *1.* These are fine as a hair, and are like the marks of the finest sandpaper; they extend a few inches only, and are very easily overlooked. *2.* In well boring, a wire line used to lower and raise the bailer or sand pump, which frees the borehole from drill cuttings.

sand pipe A tubular cavity from a few inches to many feet in depth occurring in calcareous rocks, and often filled with gravel, sand, etc.

sandr [*Icel.*] Outwash plain, *q.v.*, in front of an existing glacier. Used commonly in Scandinavian countries and Germany.

sandrock Sandstone.

sand-shale ratio Ratio of thickness of all sandstone to thickness of all shale in a stratigraphic section.

sand sheet The region of mass accumulation of sand.

sand snow Dry new snow that has fallen at very low temperature (usually below $-25°$ C.) whose crystals are small and loosely compacted, being somewhat similar to dry sand.

sand spit A narrow sand embankment, created by an excess of deposition at its seaward terminus, with its distal end (the end away from the point of origin) terminating in open water.

sandstone A cemented or otherwise compacted detrital sediment composed predominantly of quartz grains, the grades of the latter being those of sand. Mineralogical varieties such as feldspathic and glauconitic sandstones are recognized, and also argillaceous, siliceous, calcareous, ferruginous, and other varieties according to the nature of the binding or cementing material.

sandstone dikes *1.* Tabular-shaped bodies composed of sandstone ranging in thickness from a fraction of an inch to several inches and in length up to several miles, which cut across structure and bedding of the enclosing rocks. May be formed by fissure filling or by injection of sand into a fissure from below. *See* CLASTIC DIKE. *2.* Vein of sandstone or mudstone penetrating coal seams from either the floor or roof, both as irregular bulbous masses and vertically or steeply dipping sheets. They frequently extend from roof to floor.

sandstone grit *1. Geol:* A coarse angular-grained sandstone. *2.* In commerce, a sandstone well adapted for abrasive purposes and not necessarily having a coarse grain.

sandstorm Sandstorms occur when a strong wind carries relatively coarse sand through the air near the ground. A sandstorm rarely extends to a greater height than 50–100 feet above the ground, though fine dust particles may be carried to greater heights, and the sand particles are not carried to appreciable distances from their source. There is a marked distinction between sandstorms and dust storms, q.v.

sand stream Every torrential rain moves large quantities of sand which, on account of overloading, is deposited along the beds of the small creeks, forming so-called sand streams, or is spread out at the mouths of gullies forming small subaerial deltas.

sandur [Icel.] Outwash plain, q.v.

sand waves 1. Cross-bedding may be considered in connection with ripple marks, because it probably represents in many instances one phase of a phenomenon called sand waves, which are nothing more than current-made ripple marks when the current is overloaded with sediment. The crests are often 15 to 35 feet apart and rise from 2 to 3 feet above the troughs. 2. A large ripplelike structure formed by water currents of high velocity. Sand waves may be symmetrical, a-symmetrical or irregular in shape. In currents of high velocity the sand waves move down current, and at slightly lower velocity they move upstream.

sand wedge A body of sand or sandstone shaped like a wedge. Used in reference to a sandy layer that varies greatly in thickness in short distances. See LENS

sandy gravel Gravel containing 50 to 75% of sand.

Sangamon Post-Illinoian interglacial.

sanidine A variety of orthoclase.

sanidinite facies Metamorphic rocks that crystallized under maximum temperature and minimum pressure conditions.

Sannoisian Lattorfian.

Santonian Lower Middle Senonian.

saponite A clay mineral. A member of the montmorillonite group. See MONTMORILLONITE

sapphire Blue gem-quality corundum, or, with the proper adjective, any other color except red, e.g., yellow sapphire.

saprolite Saprolite is residual clay, silt, or other substance. The color is commonly some shade of red or brown, and substances other than clay or silt are commonly present. Cf. LATERITE; GEEST

sapropel 1. An aquatic ooze or sludge that is rich in organic (carbonaceous or bituminous) matter. 2. A fluid organic slime originating in swamps as a product of putrefaction. In its chemical composition it contains more hydrocarbon than peat. When dry, it is a lusterless, dull, dark, and extremely tough mass which is hard to break up.

sapropelite series Series of organic and coaly materials in order of increasing rank: sapropel, saprocol, saprodil, saprodite, sapanthracone, sapanthracite.

Saratogan Upper Cambrian.

Sarcodina Class of Protozoa of changeable body form which extrude mobile parts or pseudopodia; includes Foraminifera and Radiolaria.

Sardinan orogeny Post-Cambrian diastrophism.

sardonyx The yellow or red-brown gem variety of chalcedony.

Sarmatian Upper Miocene.

sastrugi [*Russ.*] Plural form of sastruga. *1.* The minor inequalities of the snow surface as determined by the wind blowing over the inland ice have been mentioned more or less persistently by all Arctic travelers, since upon the character of this surface depends the celerity of movement in sledge journeys. All minor hummocks and ridges of this nature are included under the general term sastrugi. *2.* Irregularities or wave formations caused by persistent winds on a snow surface. They vary in size according to the force and duration of the wind and the state of the snow surface in which they are formed.

satelite The gem-trade name for a fibrous serpentine having a chatoyant effect.

sathrolith; saprolith Regolith, *q.v.*

satin spar Fibrous gypsum.

saturated *1. Hydrol:* A rock or soil is saturated with respect to water if all its interstices are filled with water. *2. Petrol:* Applied to minerals capable of crystallizing from rock magmas in the presence of an excess of silica. Such minerals are said to be saturated with regard to silica and include the feldspars, pyroxenes, amphiboles, micas, tourmaline, fayalite, spessartite, almandine, and accessory minerals such as sphene, zircon, topaz, apatite, magnetite, and ilmenite. The term is also applied to igneous rocks composed wholly of saturated minerals.

saturation *1.* The extent or degree to which the voids in rock contain oil, gas, or water. Usually expressed in per cent related to total void or pore space. *2. Petrol:* A principle developed by S. J. Shand for the classification of igneous rocks, based on the presence or absence of saturated or unsaturated minerals.

saturation line The line, on a variation diagram of an igneous rock series, representing saturation with respect to silica; rocks to the right of it are oversaturated, those to the left are undersaturated.

saturation pressure The pressure on a liquid which is in equilibrium with gaseous or solid material, or both, or the pressure on a vapor which is in equilibrium with a liquid.

Saucesian Middle Lower Miocene.

sauconite A clay mineral. A zinc-bearing member of the montmorillonite group. *See* MONTMORILLONITE

sausage structure Boudinage.

saussurite A tough, compact, white, greenish, or grayish mineral aggregate, produced in part by the alteration of feldspar, and consisting chiefly of zoisite or epidote.

savanna; savannah A tract of level land having a wet soil except during periods of dry weather, and supporting grass and other low vegetation, with but a scattered growth of pine or other trees and bushes. Sometimes applied to tracts of open prairie land.

Savian orogeny Post-Oligocene diastrophism.

Saxonian Middle Permian.

scabland; scabrock Used in the Pacific Northwest to describe areas where denudation has removed or prevented the accumulation of a mantle of soil and the underlying rock is exposed or covered largely with its own coarse, angular debris.

scalar *Struct. petrol:* Applied to the physical features of a fabric which are nondirectional; e.g., grain shape, porosity, crystal habit, etc., are scalar quantities.

scale Crude paraffin obtained in petroleum refining by filtering from the heavier oils. Loose, thin fragments of rock, threatening to break or fall from either roof or wall.

scale model A model of some natural feature constructed in such a way that all dimensions are in the proper ratio. Thus, if the model is many times smaller than the natural feature it represents, the strength of the materials must be much less than in nature.

scallop shell A type of pelecypod shell characteristically rather flat, radially ribbed, and with an undulating edge.

scalped anticline Anticline whose upper part was eroded before the deposition of overlying uncomformable strata.

Scaphopoda Class of mollusks whose noncoiled elongated body is covered by a gently curved, tapering, cylindrical shell open at both ends. Sil.-Rec.

scapolite A group of minerals of general formula $(Na,Ca)_4Al_3(Al,Si)_3Si_6O_{24}(Cl,CO_3,SO_4)$. Tetragonal.

scar [*Sax.*] *1.* Any bluff precipice of rock. *2.* An isolated or protruding rock; a steep rocky eminence; a bare place on the side of a mountain or other steep slope. *3. See* SHORE PLATFORM

scarp An escarpment, cliff, or steep slope of some extent along the margin of a plateau, mesa, terrace, or bench. *See* FAULT SCARP; FAULT-LINE SCARP

scatter diagram *1.* Coordinate diagram showing by points the relations of specimens observa-

tions with respect to two or three variables. *2. Struct. petrol:* An orientation diagram which has not been contoured; lineations, axes, or poles of planes are represented by points.

scheelite A mineral, $CaWO_4$, commonly containing molybdenum. An ore of tungsten.

S-chert Stratigraphically controlled chert occurring as beds or nodules distributed parallel to bedding.

schiller A bronzelike luster or iridescence due to internal reflection in minerals that have undergone schillerization.

schillerization The development of poikilitic texture by the formation of inclusions and cavities along particular crystal planes, largely by solution somewhat as are etch figures.

schist A medium or coarse-grained metamorphic rock with subparallel orientation of the micaceous minerals which dominate its composition. *See* AUGEN SCHIST; ORTHOSCHIST; PARASCHIST; PHYLLITE

schistose *See* SCHIST

schistosity That variety of foliation that occurs in the coarser-grained metamorphic rocks. Generally the result of the parallel arrangement of platy and ellipsoidal mineral grains.

schlieren Tabular bodies generally a few inches to tens of feet long that occur in plutonic rocks; they have the same general mineralogy as the plutonic rocks, but because of some differences in the ratios of the minerals they are darker or lighter; the boundaries with the plutonic rock tend to be transitional. Some schlieren are modified inclusions, others may be segregations of minerals.

Schmidt net Lambert projection. An equal-area azimuthal projection of the lower hemisphere of a sphere onto a plane.

schorl Black tourmaline.

schotts The erosion desert includes the most remarkable forms of weathering and erosion; it possesses a highly diversified surface, and includes the bounding walls of the plateaus with their zeugen and wadies. Beside valleys of the wady type, which are more or less similar to ordinary river valleys, there are also to be found great hollows, true rock basins, which are often called schotts. These are sometimes completely dry and sometimes contain small salt lakes.

schuppen structure Imbricate structure, *q.v.*

scintillation A very small light flash excited in certain natural or synthetic crystals by radioactive rays or particles; the basic phenomenon of the "scintillation counter" in which the photoelectric effect of the scintillation flashes is amplified and measured to give a measure of intensity of radioactivity.

scintillation counter A gamma-ray detector for measuring radioactivity employing certain crystals which emit light flashes when they absorb gamma rays. The light flashes are detected, amplified, and recorded by a photomultiplier tube.

scintillometer Instrument for measuring radioactivity, based on emission of light by certain crystals under impact of gamma rays.

scissors fault Normal fault with vertical displacement increasing rather regularly away from its point of origin. *Cf.* HINGE FAULT

scolecite A mineral, $CaAl_2Si_3O_{10}.3H_2O$, a zeolite. Monoclinic.

scolecodont Tiny toothed or jaw-like fossils composed of silica probably derived from annelid worms.

scoria Volcanic slag. Pyroclastic ejecta, usually of basic composition, characterized by marked vesicularity, dark color, heaviness, and a texture that is partly glassy and partly crystalline. Fragments of scoria between 4 mm. and 32 mm. are essentially equivalent to volcanic cinders. *Adj:* Scoriaceous.

scoriaceous Cellular *q.v.*

scorodite A mineral, $FeAsO_4.2H_2O$. Orthorhombic.

scour Erosion, especially by moving water. *See* EROSION

scour and fill The process of cutting and refilling channels in sediments.

scour depression Where the channel of a stream is curved, the swiftest thread of the current is near the outside of the bend. The maximum erosive force of the current is exerted over a crescentic area in the bend. These areas are likely to be scoured below the grade of the stream, producing the hollows here called scour depressions.

scout 1. *Petroleum geol:* A person who gathers information from drilling wells of others, or operations, for the benefit of his own company. 2. Frequently used for an engineer who makes preliminary examinations of promising mining claims and prospects.

scree A heap of rock waste at the base of a cliff or a sheet of coarse debris mantling a mountain slope. By most writers "scree" is considered to be a synonym of "talus," but it is a more inclusive term. Whereas talus is an accumulation of material at the base of a cliff, scree also includes loose material lying on slopes without cliffs.

screen analysis The determination of weights of crushed material which passes through or is held on a series of screens of varying mesh.

screened sand Sand freed of finer material by the winnowing action of waves and currents.

screw axis Axis around which spiral movement of the components of a space lattice may occur involving both rotation and translation along the axis.

scroll A long closely fitting ridge within the large meander loop that has been built, during bankfull stages, at the inner edge of the low-water channel.

scroll meander Long, curving, parallel ridges (scrolls) that during stages of high water have been aggraded against the inner bank of the meandering channel, while the opposite bank experienced erosion.

Scyphozoa Class of coelenterates represented by medusae without hard parts; true jellyfish. Camb.-Rec.

Scythian; Skythian Lower Triassic.

S-dolostone Stratigraphically controlled dolostone occurring in extensive beds generally intertongued with limestone.

se Foliation of groundmass around metamorphic crystals which indicates external structure.

sea *1.* An ocean or a large body of (usually) salt water less than an ocean. *2.* Waves caused by wind at the place and time of observation. *3.* State of the ocean or lake surface in regard to waves.

sea arch At places where two sides of a headland are attacked by waves, a weaker or narrower section may be cut through completely by sea-cave enlargement.

The opening so made is called a sea arch. *Syn:* NATURAL ARCH; NATURAL BRIDGE; MARINE ARCH

sea breeze The breeze that blows from the sea to the land on many coasts from about 10 or 11 A.M. to sunset on sunny days in summer. *See* LAND BREEZE

sea cave A cleft in a sea cliff excavated in easily weathered rocks by waves and currents.

sea cliff A cliff formed by wave action.

seacoast The coast adjacent to the sea or ocean.

sea cucumber Holothuroid, *q.v.*

sea ice Within polar regions the surface of the sea freezes during the long winter season, the product being known as sea ice or field ice.

sea level *See* MEAN SEA LEVEL

seam *1.* A stratum or bed of coal or other mineral. *2.* A plane in a coal bed at which the different layers of coal are easily separated.

seamount A submarine mountain rising more than 500 fathoms above the ocean floor. Generally a volcanic cone.

sea or seamount range An elongated series of seamounts, sea peaks, or table mounts, the bases of which may be confluent, rising from a prominent elevation of the sea floor (ridge).

sea slide Submarine slide similar to a landslide.

seasonal stream In England, bourn or bourne. *See* INTERMITTENT STREAM

sea stack Small steep-sided rocky projection above sea level near a coast.

sea valley A submarine depression of broad valley form without the steep side slopes which characterize a submarine canyon.

sea wall *1.* A long embankment of smooth boulders, without gravel, built by powerful storm waves at the high-water mark. 2. A structure built by man along a portion of a coast primarily to prevent erosion and other damage by wave action. It retains earth against its shoreward face.

secondary 1. A general term applied to rocks and minerals formed as a consequence of the alteration of pre-existing minerals. Secondary minerals may thus be formed *in situ* as pseudomorphs or paramorphs, or they may be deposited from solution in the interstices of a rock through which the solution is percolating. 2. Formed of material derived from the erosion or disintegration of other rocks; derivative: said of clastic sedimentary rocks. 3. The output coil of a transformer.

secondary arc Mountain arc raised behind the junction point of two primary arcs and convex in the opposite direction.

secondary consolidation Compaction of sediment occurring at essentially constant pressure resulting from internal processes such as recrystallization.

secondary enlargement The deposition around a nucleus, in optical continuity with it, of material of the same composition as the nucleus. Under proper conditions good crystal faces may be developed in this way.

secondary enrichment An enrichment of a vein or an ore body by material of later origin, often derived from the oxidation of decomposed overlying ore masses. Nature's process of making high-grade out of low-grade ores.

secondary recovery The recovery obtained by any method whereby oil or gas is produced by aug-menting the natural reservoir energy, as by fluid injection. It usually implies substantial depletion of the reservoir before the injection of fluids, followed by a secondary development period.

secondary reflections Multiple reflections, *q.v.*

secondary structure Structure in a sedimentary rock which developed penecontemporaneously with sedimentation or shortly thereafter. Refers to an accretionary structure, of chemical origin.

secondary waves Distortional, equivolumnar, shear, transverse, or shake waves. S-waves, *q.v.*

second boiling point The development of a gas phase from a liquid upon cooling. During the cooling crystallization of large quantities of compounds low in or lacking volatile materials (such as feldspar) results in a sufficient increase in the concentration of volatile materials (such as water) in the residual liquid that finally the vapor pressure of this liquid becomes greater than the confining pressure and a gas phase develops (i.e., the liquid boils).

second law of thermodynamics For all reversible processes the change in entropy is equal to the heat which the system exchanges with the outside world divided by the absolute temperature. In irreversible processes the change in entropy is greater than the quotient of heat and temperature. The second law introduces entropy as a function of the state of the system.

second-order geosyncline 1. Local structural depression that received little sediment. 2. Foredeep.

secretion 1. The process by

which animals and plants transform mineral material from solution into skeletal forms. 2. Material which has been deposited from solution by infiltration into the cavity of a rock. Cf. CONCRETION. 3. The term is the antonym of concretion in which growth is outward from a nucleus.

sectile Capable of being cut with a knife without breaking off in pieces.

section 1. Geol: Either a natural or an artificial rock cut, or the representation of such on paper. 2. A vertical exposure of strata. 3. A drawing or diagram of the strata sunk through in a shaft or inclined plane, or proved by boring. 4. In Scotland, a division of the mine workings. 5. One of the portions, of 1 mile square, into which the public lands of the United States are divided; contains 640 acres. One thirty-sixth of a township. 6. A very thin slice of anything, especially for microscopic examination 7. The local series of beds constituting a group or formation, as, the Cambrian section of Wales. 8. An important division of a genus.

secular movements Movements of the earth's crust which take place slowly and imperceptibly.

secular variation A relatively large, slow change in part of the earth's magnetic field caused by the internal state of the planet and having a form roughly to be expected from a simple but not quite uniformly polarized sphere.

secule Shortest perceptible time interval in earth history. See INSTANT

sedentary 1. Paleontol: Attached, as, an oyster, barnacle, or similar shelled invertebrate. 2. In sedimentation, formed in place without transportation by the underlying rock or by the accumulation of organic material; said of some soils, etc.

sedifluction The subaquatic or subaerial movement of material in unconsolidated sediments which takes place in the primary stages of diagenesis.

sediment 1. Solid material settled from suspension in a liquid. 2. Solid material, both mineral and organic, that is in suspension, is being transported, or has been moved from its site of origin by air, water, or ice, and has come to rest on the earth's surface either above or below sea level.

sedimentary Descriptive term for rock formed of sediment, especially: (1) Clastic rocks, as, conglomerate, sandstone, and shales, formed of fragments of other rock transported from their sources and deposited in water. (2) Rocks formed by precipitation from solution, as, rock salt and gypsum, or from secretions of organisms, as, most limestone.

sedimentary basin Geologically depressed area with thick sediments in the interior and thinner sediments at the edges.

sedimentary cycle The major sedimentary rhythm which is the complement of the geographic cycle of W. M. Davis. This cycle determines the ordered sequence of orthoquartzite, graywacke, and arkose.

sedimentary facies Any areally restricted part of a designated stratigraphic unit which exhibits characters significantly different from those of other parts of the unit.

sedimentary mantle Sedimentary rocks overlying the crystalline basement.

sedimentary rocks Rocks formed by the accumulation of sediment in water (aqueous deposits) or from air (eolian deposits). The sediment may consist of rock fragments or particles of various sizes (conglomerate, sandstone, shale); of the remains or products of animals or plants (certain limestones and coal); of the product of chemical action or of evaporation (salt, gypsum, etc.); or of mixtures of these materials. Some sedimentary deposits (tuffs) are composed of fragments blown from volcanoes and deposited on land or in water. A characteristic feature of sedimentary deposits is a layered structure known as bedding or stratification. Each layer is a bed or stratum. Sedimentary beds as deposited lie flat or nearly flat.

sedimentation That portion of the metamorphic cycle from the separation of the particles from the parent rock, no matter what its origin or constitution, to and including their consolidation into another rock. Sedimentation, thus, includes a consideration of the sources from which the sediments are derived; the methods of transportation from the places of origin to those of deposition; the methods, agents, and environments of deposition; the chemical and other changes taking place in the sediments from the times of their production to their ultimate consolidation; the climatic and other environmental conditions prevailing at the place of origin, over the regions through which transportation takes place, and in the places of deposition; the structures developed in connection with deposition and consolidation; and the horizontal and vertical variations of sediments.

sedimentation or Oden curve An experimental curve showing cumulatively the quantity of sediment deposited or removed from suspension in successive units of time from an originally uniform suspension.

sedimentation unit That thickness of sediment which was deposited under essentially constant physical conditions.

sediment concentration Ratio of the weight of the sediment in a water-sediment mixture to the total weight of the mixture. It is ordinarily expressed in per cent for high values of concentration and in parts per million (ppm) for the low values.

sedimentology The study of sedimentary rocks and the processes by which they were formed.

sediment station A river section where samples of suspended load are taken each day, or periodically.

seep A spot where water or petroleum oozes from the earth, often forming the source of a small trickling stream.

segregate 1. To separate the undivided joint ownership of a mining claim into smaller individual "segregated" claims. 2. Geol: To separate from the general mass, and collect or become concentrated at a particular place or in a certain region, as in the process of crystallization and solidification.

segregation, magmatic See MAGMATIC DIFFERENTIATION

segregation banding A compositional banding in gneisses that is not primary in origin, but rather is the result of segregation of material from an originally homogeneous rock.

segregation in magmas Magmatic segregation. Syn: MAGMATIC DIFFERENTIATION

seiche A periodic oscillation of a body of water whose period is determined by the resonant characteristics of the containing basin as controlled by its physical dimensions. These periods generally range from a few minutes to an hour or more. Originally the term was applied only to lakes, but now also to harbors, bays, oceans, etc.

seif dune *1.* The individual seif dune has a form very like that of a sand drift behind a rock. Its length or axis lies in the direction of the prevailing wind, and its long crest is a knife-edge ridge, one side of which is rounded and the other falls abruptly as a collapsing front which faces a direction at right angles to the line of the dune and to the prevailing wind. The side on which the front occurs depends on the side to which the wind has temporarily veered out of its prevailing direction. The whole aspect of a seif dune may therefore change within a few days. *2.* Longitudinal dunes, oriented in the direction of wind movement, and of great height and length.

seismic Pertaining to, characteristic of, or produced by earthquakes or earth vibration, as, seismic disturbances.

seismic area The area affected by any particular earthquake.

seismic center The point of origin of an earthquake.

seismic discontinuity Physical discontinuity within the earth separating materials in which seismic waves travel at significantly different velocities.

seismic-electric effect A phenomenon in which a periodic change in current is caused to flow between two electrodes inserted in the ground when a seismic

waves passes through the region between the electrodes.

seismic event *See* EVENT, SEISMIC

seismic intensity Sound intensity, *q.v.*

seismic method A method of geophysical prospecting using the generation, reflection, refraction detection, and analysis of elastic waves in the earth.

seismic wave Tsunami. A generally long period wave caused by an underwater seismic disturbance or volcanic eruption. Commonly misnamed "tidal wave."

seismism The processes or phenomena involved in earth movements.

seismogram The record made by a seismograph.

seismograph Instrument which records seismic waves. *Syn:* DETECTOR

seismologist One who applies the principles of seismology to his work, e.g., oil exploration, earthquake detection, and analysis.

seismology *1.* The science of earthquakes: all that relates to their forces, duration, lines of direction, periodicity, and other characteristics. *2.* A geophysical science which is concerned with the study of earthquakes and measurement of the elastic properties of the earth.

seismometer Detecting device which receives seismic impulses. *Syn:* GEOPHONE; DETECTOR; PICKUP; JUG

seismotectonic lines The communes which are notable by reason of their susceptibility to seismic disturbances betray an arrangement within definite lines which in many cases are revealed as lineaments upon the surface. Such lines are designated seismotectonic lines.

selective diagram *See* PARTIAL DIAGRAM

selective elemental diagram Fabric diagram based upon rock elements selected with regard to gross orientation size, kind of mineral, etc.

selective fusion The fusion of only a portion of a mixture or rock; the liquid portion will contain, in the general case, a greater amount of the more readily fused materials than the solid portion contains.

selective or preferential replacement Replacement of one mineral in preference to, or more rapidly than, another.

selective wetting A particular manifestation of adsorption in which one fluid in contact with a solid is displaced by another fluid having a greater affinity for that solid.

selenate A salt or ester of selenic acid; a compound containing the radical SeO_4^{--}.

selenide A compound of selenium with one other more positive element or radical.

selenite Clear transparent gypsum.

selenomorphology The geomorphology of the moon.

selerenchyma A strengthening tissue composed of thick-walled, elongated cells (fibers) or shorter cells (stone cells).

self-diffusion The movement, by diffusion, of atoms within a phase of which they are an essential constituent. For the most part it implies a continuous exchanging of atoms between equivalent atomic sites.

self-inductance The property of an inductive component in an electric circuit which produces a counter e.m.f. when current in the circuit changes. The e.m.f. $= -L \, di/dt$, where L is the coeffi-

cient of self-inductance, measured in henrys. A 1-volt counter e.m.f. is induced in a circuit of 1-henry self-inductance when the rate of current change is 1 ampere per second.

self-potential method Electrical potential caused by dissimilar conductors in an electrolyte, similar to the action of an electric battery. *See* SPONTANEOUS POTENTIAL METHOD

self-potential prospecting A method of electrical prospecting based on the measurement of natural earth potentials caused by the self-potential effects from ore bodies, commonly metallic sulfides.

selvage *1.* A zone of altered material along a fault, joint, vein, or fissure showing effects of circulating solutions or vapors. It is usually a layer of soft clayey material separating ore from country rock in a vein. *2.* The chilled glassy border of a dike or lava flow. *3.* A marginal zone, as in a dike or vein, having some distinctive feature of fabric or composition.

semianthracite Nonagglomerating anthracitic coal having 86% or more, and less than 92%, of fixed carbon (dry, mineral-matter-free) and 14% or less and more than 8% of volatile matter (dry, mineral-matter-free).

semiarid Pertaining to a subdivision of climate in which the associated ecological conditions are distinguished by short grass (whereas a subhumid climate is characterized by tall grass), and best exemplified by the climate of the steppes.

semibituminous Half or somewhat bituminous; applies to a variety of coal intermediate between bituminous coal and anthracite, averaging 15 to 20% of volatile matter.

semidiurnal tides A tide with two high and two low waters in a tidal day, with comparatively little diurnal inequality.

semitropical Pertaining to the climate prevailing at the tropical margins of the temperate zones. *Syn:* SUBTROPICAL

Senecan Lower Upper Devonian.

senescence *1.* Old age. *Paleontol:* Applied especially to the life cycle of a species or other group. *2. Geomorphol:* Refers to the stage in a land surface in which erosion has reached a minimum and base level has been reached.

senility Condition of organisms that in old age revert to development resembling younger stages.

Senonian Upper Upper Cretaceous.

separation Indicates the distance between any two parts of an index plane (bed, vein, etc.) disrupted by a fault. Horizontal separation is separation measured in any indicated horizontal direction; vertical separation is measured along a vertical line; stratigraphic separation is measured perpendicular to the bedding planes.

sepiolite Meerschaum. A clay mineral. A compact, spongy, or fibrous hydrous magnesium silicate with a crystallization related to but distinct from that of the palygorskites.

septarian A structure developed in certain concretions known as septarian nodules, consisting of an irregular polygonal system of internal cracks, which are almost always occupied by calcite or other minerals.

septarium A roughly spheroidal concretion, generally of limestone or clay-ironstone, cut into poly-hedral blocks by radiating and intersecting cracks which have been filled (and the blocks cemented together) by veins of some material, generally calcite. *Pl.* septaria. *Syn:* SEPTARIAN BOULDER; SEPTARIAN NODULE; TURTLE STONE

septum *1.* The internal partition or division between the chambers of a cephalopod; also in the pterobranches. *2.* Radially arranged vertical plates of stony substance which project inward and upward from the wall and base of individual coral skeletons. *3.* In echinoid spines, the platelike structures which radiate from the axial zone toward the anterior of the spine and are seen in cross sections of the spine.

Sequanian Upper Lusitanian.

seracs When two or more sets of crevasses intersect, the surface of the glacier is torn into a broken mass of jagged ice pinnacles known as seracs.

serial samples Samples collected according to some predetermined plan, such as along the intersections of grid lines, or at stated distances or times. The method is used to insure random sampling.

sericite A fine-grained variety of mica occurring in small scales, especially in schists. Usually muscovite, but may consist of paragonite or hydrous micas.

series A time-stratigraphic unit ranked next below a system. Loosely used in petrology for related igneous rocks.

series circuit An electrical circuit so connected that there is a single continuous path and all the current flows through each component.

series of igneous rocks *See* IGNEOUS ROCK SERIES

serpentine $Mg_3Si_2O_5(OH)_4$. The name includes at least two distinct minerals, antigorite and chrysotile, very difficult to distinguish. Most asbestos is chrysotile. A common rock-forming mineral.

serpentinite A rock consisting almost wholly of serpentine minerals derived from the alteration of previously existing olivine and pyroxene.

serrate, *adj.* [<*Lat.* serra, saw] *1.* Pertaining to the rocky summit of a mountain having a sawtooth profile; a small sierra-shaped ridge. Local in Southwest. *2. Paleobot:* Said of a margin when saw-toothed with the teeth pointing forward.

sessile Applied to animals and organisms that are closely attached to other objects and not supported on a pedicle, footstalk, or stem.

sessile animal Animal incapable of moving voluntarily from place to place, generally more or less permanently attached to the substratum or another organism; many are aquatic filter feeders.

sessile benthos Sea-bottom-dwelling forms which are anchored in position by attachment to the bottom.

set A group of essentially parallel planar features, especially joints, dikes, faults, veins, etc.

setaceous, *adj.* Bearing bristles.

settling The sag in outcrops of laminated sedimentary rocks caused by rock creep. *Syn:* OUTCROP CURVATURE; TERMINAL CREEP

sexual dimorphism Differences in form exhibited by males and females of the same species.

shaft *1.* An excavation of limited area compared with its depth, made for finding or mining ore or coal, raising water, ore, rock, or coal, hoisting and lowering men and lowering men and material, or ventilating underground workings. Often specifically applied to approximately vertical shafts as distinguished from an incline or inclined shaft. *2. Speleol:* A vertical passage.

shale *1.* A laminated sediment in which the constituent particles are predominantly of the clay grade. *2.* Shale includes the indurated, laminated, or fissile claystones and siltstones. The cleavage is that of bedding and such other secondary cleavage or fissility that is approximately parallel to bedding. The secondary cleavage has been produced by the pressure of overlying sediments and plastic flow.

shale break Thin layer or parting of shale between harder strata, primarily a drillers' term.

shale oil A crude oil obtained from bituminous shales, especially in Scotland, by submitting them to destructive distillation in special retorts.

shallow-focus earthquake Earthquake whose focus occurs at a depth of less than 65 km.

shaly bedded Term applied to a sedimentary deposit whose stratification is in the form of laminae 2 to 10 mm. in thickness.

Shand's classification A classification of igneous rocks based on crystallinity, degree of saturation with silica, degree of saturation with alumina, and color index.

shard A curved, spiculelike fragment of volcanic glass.

sharpstone Term proposed by R. R. Shrock for a sedimentary rock made up of angular particles more than 2 mm. in greatest dimension.

shatter cone Structure produced by shear planes outlining a cone a few inches in diameter which occurs in the rocks of some cryptovolcanic areas.

shear *1. V:* To subject a body to shear, similar to the displacement of the cards in a pack relative to one another. *2. N:* The effect produced by action of a shearing stress.

shear cleavage Slip cleavage; strain-slip cleavage.

shear or **slip fold** A fold formed as a result of the minute displacement of beds along closely spaced fractures or cleavage planes.

shear fracture *1.* A fracture that results from stresses which tend to shear one part of a specimen past the adjacent part. Contrasts with tension fractures. *2.* Fracture at a more or less acute angle to applied force, generally with some pulverized material along its surface; splitting fracture.

shearing off Extensive lateral shearing movement within, between, or below layers of the earth's crust or at top of basement.

shearing or **tangential stress** A stress causing or tending to cause two adjacent parts of a solid to slide past one another parallel to the plane of contact.

shear joints Joints that formed as shear fractures.

shear modulus Rigidity or shear modulus is a measure of the stress-strain ratio for a simple shear. A shearing force is tangential to the surface displaced, and a shearing stress is such a force per unit area. The shearing strain is the resulting displacement without change of volume and is measured by the displacement ΔL in the line of force per unit length L perpendicular to the line of force. Therefore, the shear modulus, μ,

is $\mu = \dfrac{F/A}{\Delta L/L} = \dfrac{FL}{A\Delta L}$ and also has the dimension of force per unit area.

shear strength The internal resistance offered to shear stress. It is measured by the maximum shear stress, based on original area of cross section, that can be sustained without failure.

shear wave S-wave. Distortional, equivolumnar, secondary, or transverse wave.

shear zone *Geol:* A zone in which shearing has occurred on a large scale so that the rock is crushed and brecciated.

sheepback Roches moutonnée, *q.v.*

sheet *1.* A tabular mass of igneous rock, either a flow, sill, or dike. *2.* A widespread tabular body of sedimentary rock. *See* SHEET SAND; BLANKET SAND. *3. Speleol:* Thin coating of calcium carbonate formed on walls, shelves, benches, and ledges by trickling water. *4.* In Australia, a solid body of pure ore filling a crevice. *5.* In Upper Mississippi lead region, galena in thin and continuous masses. The ore itself is called sheet mineral.

sheeted vein A group of closely spaced, distinct, parallel fractures filled with mineral matter and separated by layers of barren rock.

sheeted zone A zone of closely spaced fractures whether mineralized or not.

sheet or **sheetflood erosion** Erosion accomplished by sheets of running water, as distinct from streams.

sheetflood Movement of near uniform sheets of flood water down the surface of a slope.

sheet flow Laminar flow.

sheet ground In the Joplin, Missouri, district, a term applied to horizontal, low-grade, disseminated zinc-lead deposits, covering an extensive area.

sheeting 1. In a restricted sense, the gently dipping joints that are essentially parallel to the ground surface; they are more closely spaced near the surface and become progressively farther apart with depth. Especially well developed in granitic rocks. 2. In a general sense, a set of closely spaced joints.

sheet minerals Those minerals, belonging to the phyllosilicates, q.v., having sheets of linked SiO_4 tetrahedra. Includes the mica, the chlorite, and most of the clay group of minerals.

sheet sand A sandstone of great areal extent, presumably deposited by a transgressing sea advancing over a wide front and for a considerable distance. See BLANKET SAND

sheet structure 1. Sheetlike tracts of crushed rock parallel and adjacent to a fault. 2. See PHYLLOSILICATES; SHEETING

shelf 1. In the ocean, the zone extending from the line of permanent immersion to the depth (usually about 65 fathoms) where there is a marked or rather steep descent toward the great depths. See CONTINENTAL SHELF. 2. In Cornwall, the solid rock or bedrock, especially under alluvial tin deposits. 3. A rock, ledge of rocks, reef, or sandbank in the sea. 4. A projecting layer or ledge of rock on land. 5. In gastropod shells, the subhorizontal part of whorl surface next to a suture, bordered on side toward periphery of whorl by a sharp angulation or by a carina.

shelf ice Ice shelf, q.v. The extension of glacial ice from land into coastal waters. Shelf ice, which may be several hundred feet thick, is in contact with the bottom nearshore, but not at its seaward terminus. From the seaward margin of the shelf ice tremendous slabs break and float away as bergs which may be 50 miles long.

shelf sea The water that rests upon a sea shelf (continental shelf).

shell 1. The generally hard rigid covering of an animal, commonly calcareous, in other cases chiefly or partly chitinous, horny, or even siliceous. 2. *Petroleum geol:* A torpedo used in oil wells. 3. A cylinder or tube of light metal which is filled with nitroglycerin or other explosive, lowered into a drill hole, and detonated when a well is shot. 4. A thin and usually hard layer of rock found in drilling a well.

shelves The most stable areas of the craton that are periodically flooded by marine waters.

shield 1. A continental block of the earth's crust that has been relatively stable over a long period of time and has undergone only gentle warping in contrast to the strong folding of bordering geosynclinal belts. Mostly composed of Precambrian rocks. 2. A disk-shaped formation standing edgewise at a high angle in a cave. 3. In animals, a protective structure likened to a shield, as, a large scale, carapace, or lorica.

shield basalts Multiple vent basalts. Basaltic accumulations of smaller size than the plateau or flood basalts, arising from the confluence of lava flows from a large number of small and closely spaced volcanoes. The flows coalesce into masses hundreds to thousands of square miles in size.

shield volcano A broad, gently sloping volcanic cone of flat domical shape, usually several tens or hundreds of square miles in extent, built chiefly of overlapping and interfingering basaltic lava flows. Typical examples are the volcanoes Mauna Loa and Kilauea on the island of Hawaii, and the great basaltic volcanoes of Iceland. The slopes of shield volcanoes generally range from about 4 to 10 degrees. The Schildvulkan of German writers.

shift *1.* A fault of dislocation. *2.* The maximum relative displacement of points on opposite sides of the fault and far enough from it to be outside the dislocated zone. Net shift. *See* STRIKE SHIFT; DIP SHIFT; NORMAL SHIFT; VERTICAL SHIFT. *3.* Refers to displacements on opposite sides of fault measured outside the zone of dislocation. Whereas the net shift along a fault might be 1000 feet, because of drag the net slip along the fault might be much less.

shingle Loosely and commonly, any beach gravel which is coarser than ordinary gravel, especially if consisting of flat or flattish pebbles and cobbles.

shingle beach A beach whose surface is covered with shingle rock. *See* SHINGLE

shingle-block structure A series of thrust sheets lying against one another like the shingles of a roof. *Syn:* IMBRICATE STRUCTURE

shingle rampart A ridge of shingle, 1 or 2 meters high, built up by waves on the seaward edge of a reef flat.

shingle structure Arrangement of veins en echelon in the manner of shingles on a roof.

shingling Imbricate structure. The overlapping upstream of platy or tabular pebbles in stream deposits

and seaward overlapping in beach deposits.

shipping ore Any ore of greater value when broken than the cost of freight and treatment.

shoal *1.* A part of the area covered by water, of the sea or lake or river, when the depth is little; a bank always covered, though not deeply. *2. V:* To become shallow gradually. *3.* A detached elevation of the sea bottom comprised of any material except rock or coral, and which may endanger surface navigation.

shoaling coefficient The ratio of the height of a wave in water of any depth to its height in deep water with the effect of refraction eliminated. Sometimes shoaling factor or depth factor. *See* ENERGY COEFFICIENT; REFRACTION COEFFICIENT

shoal reefs *1.* Bank reefs. *2.* Reef growths developed in irregular patches amidst submerged shoals of calcareous debris.

shoestring sands A narrow and relatively long body of sandstone. Examples have been described from the Pennsylvanian system of east-central Kansas. They originated as channel fillings, bars, beaches, etc.

shonkinite A melanocratic syenite often containing a small amount of nepheline. The principal minerals are augite and orthoclase. Other minerals that may often be present in varying small amounts are nepheline, olivine, plagioclase, sodalite, and analcite. Apatite and opaque oxides are common accessories.

shoot *Seis. explor:* The firing of the explosive by an electrical impulse; also the process of carrying out a seismic survey, to "shoot" an area or prospect.

shooting a well Exploding a charge of nitroglycerin in a drill hole, at or near an oil-bearing stratum, for the purpose of increasing the flow of oil.

shoot of ore A body of ore with relatively small horizontal dimensions and steep inclination in a lode; in contradistinction to a course of ore, which is flatter. *See* CHUTE

shoran A high-frequency radio wave location system using microwave pulses used for offshore and airborne prospecting operations. Two stations are located at fixed points, the third is on the mobile station whose location is desired. The fixed stations broadcast pulses, the mobile station rebroadcasts them, and the round-trip time is measured by means of cathode-ray screens to an accuracy of ∓ 25 feet.

shore The common margin of dry land and a body of water.

shore boulder chain An embankment, wall, or chain of boulders and gravel which surrounds the shores of some lakes. The walls are believed to originate by stones and boulders being frozen into the bottom of nearshore ice. Ice expansion and wind shove causes the boulders to be arranged in a row paralleling the coast. *Syn:* LAKE RAMPART; ICE RAMPART; SHORE WALL

shore face The narrow zone seaward from the low-tide shore line permanently covered by water, over which the beach sands and gravels actively oscillate with changing wave conditions.

shore line The line of intersection of the sea with the land. The region immediately to the landward of the shore line is called the coast.

shore-line cycle Coasts are sequential forms developed by marine erosion, and in part by accumulation, form varied initial forms. A succession of stages, or shore-line cycle, through which the coastal features normally pass, can be developed for each kind of initial coast. *See* CYCLE OF SHORE DEVELOPMENT

shore line of depression *See* SHORE LINE OF SUBMERGENCE

shore line of elevation *See* SHORE LINE OF EMERGENCE

shore line of emergence or **elevation** Results when the water surface comes to rest against a partially emerged sea or lake floor.

shore line of submergence or **depression** Produced when the water surface comes to rest against a partially submerged land area.

shore platform Plane of marine abrasion; wave-cut terrace.

shore wall Lake rampart; shore boulder chain.

short limb That side of an asymmetrical fold in which the direction is sooner reversed; generally the steeper side.

short range order Lack of orderliness in arrangement in a solid or liquid over distances a little beyond immediately neighboring atoms or molecules; typical of glass and liquids.

shot The explosion in seismic operations.

shot break *Seis. explor:* The electrically recorded instant of explosion.

shot copper Small rounded particles of native copper, somewhat resembling small shot in size and shape.

shot datum Seismic calculations are usually reduced to a convenient reference surface or plane. These calculations simulate a condition where the charge is shot on the reference surface and the arrival of seismic waves is also recorded on this same reference surface. At this reference surface, the time-depth charts have their origin.

shot depth The distance from the surface to the charge. In the case of small charges, the shot depth is measured to the center of the charge or to the bottom of the hole. In the case of large charges, the distances to the top and to the bottom of the column of explosives are frequently given, and may be reduced to effective shot depth to give the equivalent of a concentrated charge.

shot drill An earth-boring drill using steel shot as an abrasive.

shot elevation Elevation of the dynamite charge in the shot hole.

shot hole *Seis. prospecting:* The borehole in which an explosive is placed for blasting.

shot-hole fatigue Phenomenon causing observed travel times to another point to increase with successive shots in the same hole.

shot instant *Seis. explor:* The instant of detonation of the dynamite charge.

shot point That point at which a charge of dynamite is exploded for the generation of seismic energy. In field practice, the shot point includes the hole and its immediately surrounding area.

shotty gold Small granular pieces of gold resembling shot.

shoulder The transverse profile of a glaciated valley is not always U-shaped, but it is often made up of two distinct elements, giving a U-in-U appearance, a steep-sided inner U with a flatter, widely opened U, or catenary curve, the steep inner slopes meeting the general outer slopes at a distinct angle. The bench above the angle, which has the appearance of a remnant of a valley existing before the inner trough was cut, is termed a shoulder.

show (of oil or gas) A noncommercial quantity of oil or gas, encountered in drilling.

shrinkage crack Mud crack; sun crack.

shrub-coppice dune A mound of wind-blown sand built up by bush or clump vegetation.

shunt One of the paths in a parallel circuit; a low-value resistor hooked up in parallel with a galvanometer when it is to be used as an ammeter; a nonresistance connector or "jumper" between two electrical poles.

si Orderly arrangement of inclusions in crystals that have grown during metamorphism and indicate internal structure.

sial A layer of rocks underlying all continents, which ranges from granitic at the top to gabbroic at the base. The thickness is variously placed at 30–35 km. The name derives from the principal ingredients, silica and alumina. Specific gravity is considered to be about 2.7.

sialma A mnemonic term derived from "si" for silica, "al" for alumina, and "ma" for magnesia and applied as a compositional term to a layer within the earth which occupies a position intermediate between sial and sima, *q.v.*

sibling species One of two or more species that are closely related, very similar morphologically but reproductively isolated.

siderite Chalybite. *1.* A mineral, $FeCO_3$, commonly containing also Mg and Mn. *2.* An iron meteorite.

siderolite A type of meteorite consisting of approximately equal parts of metal and silicate phases. *Syn:* PALLASITES; STONY IRONS; SYSSIDERITES

sideromelane Basaltic glass. Characteristic of palagonite tuffs.

siderophile elements Elements with a relatively weak affinity for oxygen and sulfur, characterized by ready solubility in molten iron, hence concentrated in iron meteorites and probably in the earth's iron core.

siderosphere Central iron core of the earth.

side shot A reading or measurement from a survey station to locate a point which is not intended to be used as a base for the extension of the survey. A side shot is usually made for the purpose of determining the position of some object which is to be shown on the map.

side-wall core A core or rock sample extracted from the wall of a drill hole, either by shooting a retractable hollow projectile, or by mechanically removing a sample.

side-wall sampling The process of securing samples of formations from the sides of the borehole anywhere in the hole that has not been cased.

Siegenian Middle Lower Devonian.

sienna Mineral paint.

sierra [*Sp.*, <*Lat.* serra, saw] A chain of mountains whose successive peaks present the resemblance of a saw.

sieve texture *1.* A texture of metamorphic rocks and of some igneous rocks produced by inclusions of a mineral or glass in larger spongy crystals of another species. *Syn:* DIABLASTIC. *2.* A mineral formed by replacement which contains inclusion of the old.

sif Seif.

sight *1.* A bearing or angle taken with a compass or transit when making a survey. *2.* Any established point of a survey.

Sigma Phi Phi Sigma, *q.v.*

sigmoidal fold Fold with steeply inclined axis whose outcrop pattern shows S-shaped strike curves.

signal correction A correction to eliminate the time differences between reflection times, resulting from changes in the outgoing signal from shot to shot.

signal effect Variations in arrival times of reflections as a result of changes in the outgoing signal, the reflection being recorded with identical filter settings.

silica Silicon dioxide, SiO_2.

silica sand Sand very high in SiO_2, hence a source of silicon; also has industrial uses.

silicate A salt or ester of any of the silicic acids, real or hypothetical: a compound whose crystal lattice contains SiO_4 tetrahedra, either isolated or joined through one or more of the oxygen atoms to form groups, chains, sheets or three-dimensional structures.

silicates, classification This classification is based on types of linkages of SiO_4 tetrahedra, in which Si may be partly replaced by Al. Nesosilicates [*Gr.* neso, island] have independent SiO_4 groups. Example Mg_2SiO_4. Sorosilicates [*Gr.* soro, group] have two tetrahedra linked to form $Si_2O_7^{-6}$ groups. Example $Ca_2Mg-Si_2O_7$. Cyclosilicates [*Gr.* cyclo, ring] have three tetrahedra linked to form rings such as $Si_3O_9^{-6}$ or $Si_6O_{18}^{-12}$ groups. Example: beryl, $Be_3Al_2Si_6O_{18}$. Inosilicates [*Gr.* ino, thread] have three tetrahedra linked to form continuous chains of $Si_2O_6^{-4}$ or $Si_4O_{11}(OH)^{-7}$ groups. Examples: enstatite, $MgSiO_3$, tremolite $Ca_2Mg_5Si_8O_{22}(OH)_2$. Phyllosilicates [*Gr.* phyllo, sheet] have four tetrahedra linked to form continuous sheets of $Si_4O_{10}^{-4}$ groups. Examples: kaolinite,

$Al_2Si_2O_5(OH)_2$, muscovite, $KAl_2(AlSi_3)O_{10}(OH)_2$. Tectosilicates [*Gr.* tecto, framework] have continuous three-dimensional frameworks of compositions $(Si,Al)O_2$. Examples: quartz, SiO_2, orthoclase, $K(AlSi_3)O_8$, nepheline, $Na(AlSiO)_4$.

siliceous; silicious Of or pertaining to silica; containing silica, or partaking of its nature. Containing abundant quartz.

siliceous ooze A fine-grained pelagic deposit with more than 30% material of organic origin, a large percentage of which is siliceous skeletal material produced by planktonic plants and animals.

siliceous residue Insoluble residue, *q.v.*

siliceous shale Hard fine-grained rock of shaly structure generally believed to be shale altered by silicification.

siliceous sinter Siliceous sinter, geyserite, and fiorite are names given to the nearly white, often soft, and friable, hydrated varieties formed on the evaporation of the siliceous waters of hot springs and geysers, or through the eliminating action of algous vegetation. *See* SINTER

silicification *1.* The introduction of or replacement by, silica. Generally the silica formed is fine-grained quartz, chalcedony, or opal, and may both fill up pores and replace existing minerals. The term covers all varieties of such processes, whether late magmatic, hydrothermal or diagenetic.

silicified wood A material formed by replacement of wood by silica in such manner that the original form and structure of the wood is preserved. The silica is generally in the form of opal or chalcedony.

silky Having the luster of silk, like fibrous calcite, fibrous gypsum.

sill *1.* An intrusive body of igneous rock of approximately uniform thickness and relatively thin compared with its lateral extent, which has been emplaced parallel to the bedding or schistosity of the intruded rocks. *2.* A submarine ridge or rise separating partially closed basins from one another or from the adjacent ocean.

silled basin Submarine basin of deposition separated from the main water body by a relatively narrow submerged ridge; deeper water in the basin is likely to be more or less stagnant. *Syn:* BARRED BASIN

sillimanite Fibrolite. A mineral, Al_2SiO_5, trimorphous with kyanite and andalusite. Orthorhombic.

silt *1.* A clastic sediment, most of the particles of which are between 1/16 and 1/256 mm. in diameter. *2.* Soil consisting of 80% or more silt (.05–.002 mm.) and less than 12% clay.

siltstone A very fine-grained consolidated clastic rock composed predominantly of particles of silt grade.

silttil Chemically decomposed and eluviated till; horizon 2 of a well-drained soil profile.

Silurian *1.* Geologic period between Ordovician and Devonian, and system of same age. *2.* Originally included Ordovician and still considered to be so constituted by some Europeans who recognize Gotlandian instead of restricted Silurian. In America and Great Britain before 1900, "Upper Silurian" is modern Silurian and "Lower Silurian" is Ordovician.

silver The native element, commonly containing Au and Hg. Isometric.

silver glance Argentite.

sima The basic outer shell of the earth; under the continents it underlies the sial, but under the Pacific Ocean it directly underlies the oceanic water. Originally, the sima was considered basaltic in composition with a specific gravity of about 3.0. In recent years it has been suggested that the sima is peridotitic in composition with a specific gravity of about 3.3.

similar folding That type of folding in which each successively lower bed shows the same geometrical form as the bed above. Thus, if the shape of one bed is that of a sine curve, all the beds show the same shape. Similar folding implies thinning on the limbs of the folds and thickening at the axes. Contrasts with parallel folding and supratenuous folding.

simple coral Horn coral.

simple harmonic motion Oscillatory motion of a particle or mass, with constant amplitude, and which is sinusoidal with time. Such motion results when the restoring force is proportional to the displacement (as in a simple pendulum of small amplitude).

simple shear A homogeneous strain that consists of a movement in one direction of all straight lines initially parallel to that direction. Analogous to sliding of cards in a pack of cards; a square marked on the sides of the cards is deformed into a rhomboid.

simplexity Measure of structural complexity in crystals; high simplexity means disorder and structural simplicity.

simplexity principle The general-

ization that high simplexity (structural simplicity) is favored over low during nucleation and crystal growth.

sine curve The graph which displays the magnitude of the sine as a function of its argument; frequently applied to quantities having the shape of a sine curve, such as an alternating electric current.

sine galvanometer Combinations of unifilar magnetometers and deflection coils so arranged as to give a horizontal comparison field in the magnetic prime vertical or at right angles to the needle. In the second case, the instrument is used as the sine galvanometer proper; in the first case as a tangent galvanometer.

Sinemurian Lower Lower Jurassic, above Hettangian.

single-ended spread *Seis. prospecting:* A reflection profile which is shot from one end of the spread, or line of detectors.

single jack A light single-hand hammer used in drilling, especially in metal mines. The hammer is used in one hand while the drill is held by the other.

Sinian System of late Precambrian age in China, referred to the Paleozoic because strata are unmetamorphosed and may be conformable beneath the Cambrian.

sinistral fault Left lateral fault. A strike-slip fault in which the net slip is such that to an observer moving toward the fault the opposite block appears to have moved relatively to the left.

sinistral fold Asymmetric fold in which the long limb is apparently offset to the left as one looks along the long limb (i.e. offset in the same manner as in a left-hand fault).

sinkhole A funnel-shaped depression in the land surface generally in a limestone region communicating with a subterranean passage developed by solution. Water commonly drains downward and is lost but the passage may become blocked so that a pond is formed. Sinkholes also may result from solution of gypsum and rock salt. A few may be produced by collapse of a cavern roof.

sinter A chemical sediment deposited by a mineral spring, either hot or cold. Siliceous sinter, consisting of silica, is also called geyserite and fiorite; calcareous sinter, consisting of calcium carbonate, is also called tufa, travertine and onyx marble.

sinus 1. In gastropod shells, a re-entrant in the outer edge of the aperture with nonparallel sides. 2. In a brachiopod shell, the major rounded depression along the longitudinal midline, generally found on the pedicle valve. *Syn:* SULCUS (usually called sulcus, since 1932). 3. The space or recess between two lobes or divisions of a leaf or other expanded organ.

sinusoidal displacement Displacement involving rising on one side and sinking on the other side of a relatively stable hinge line.

siphon; syphon Small upright or inverted U-shaped channel with water in hydrostatic equilibrium.

size 1. In brickmaking, plasticity, as of tempered clay. 2. To separate minerals according to various screen meshes.

s-joints *See* LONGITUDINAL JOINTS

skarn The term is generally reserved for rocks composed nearly entirely of lime-bearing silicates and derived from nearly pure limestones and dolomites into which large amounts of Si, Al, Fe, and Mg have been introduced. *See* CALC-SILICATE HORNFELS; LIMURITE; TACTITE

skeleton crystals Hollow or imperfectly developed crystals.

skewness The state or quality of a frequency distribution of being bunched together on one side of the average and of tailing out on the other side. It results from lack of coincidence of the mode, median, and arithmetic mean of the distribution. It is measured by the quotient of the difference between the arithmetic mean and the mode divided by the standard deviation. In positive skewness, the mode is greater than the mean.

skewness, coefficient of A measure of the dissymmetry in the size distribution of the particles of a sediment.

Skiddavian Arenigian.

skin effect The increase of the alternating-current resistance of an electrical conductor over its ohmic or direct-current resistance, due to the tendency of the alternating current to travel over the surface on skin of the conductor. In alternating-current methods of electrical prospecting this effect tends to limit the penetration of the current into the earth.

Skythian *See* SCYTHIAN

slab or **slabstone** Cleaved or finely parallel jointed rocks, which split into tabular plates from 1 to 4 inches thick.

slab pahoehoe A type of pahoehoe, the surface of which consists of a mass of tilted, jumbled, or imbricated plates of lava, apparently resulting from draining of the liquid from beneath a thin crust, followed by fracturing of the crust and tilting and heaping of the fragments. The plates or slabs are generally 1 to 4 feet in length and width and 2 to 6 or 8 inches thick. Their upper surfaces exhibit the minor features characteristic of any pahoehoe flow, but their lower surfaces are exceedingly rough and spinose.

slack tide The state of a tidal current when its velocity is near zero, especially the moment when a reversing current changes direction and its velocity is zero. Sometimes considered the intermediate period between ebb and flood currents during which the velocity of the currents is less than 0.1 knot. *See* STAND OF TIDE

slack water Essentially currentless water such as that occurring in flooded areas beyond a stream channel or in an estuary at high or low tide.

slag, volcanic *See* SCORIA

slaking Loosely, the crumbling and disintegration of earth materials when exposed to air or moisture. More specifically, the breaking up of dried clay when saturated with water, due either to compression of entrapped air by inwardly migrating capillary water or to the progressive swelling and sloughing off of the outer layers.

slate *1.* A fine-grained metamorphic rock possessing a well-developed fissility (slaty cleavage). *See* CLAY SLATE; PHYLLITE; SPOTTED SLATE. *2.* A coal miner's term for any shale accompanying coal; also sometimes applied to bony coal.

slate coal *1.* In England, a hard dull variety of coal. *2.* Coal that has pieces of slate of greater or less size attached to it, which can be separated by breaking the coal into smaller pieces and subjecting the coal to a washing process.

slaty cleavage That variety of

foliation typical of slates but found in many other kinds of rocks. Generally the result of parallel arrangement of platy or ellipsoidal minerals. *See* FOLIATION

slice *1.* A large block caught along a thrust. *2.* Arbitrary informal division, either of uniform thickness or constituting some uniform fraction, of an otherwise indivisible stratigraphic unit that is distinguished for individual facies mapping or analysis.

slickenside Polished and striated (scratched) surface that results from friction along a fault plane.

slide *1.* The descent of a mass of earth or rock down a hill or mountain side. *2.* The track of bare rock left by a landslide. *3.* Material moved in a landslide.

slim hole Drill hole of the smallest practicable size, often bored as a stratigraphic test.

slip *1.* A fault. *2.* A smooth joint or crack where the strata have moved upon each other. *3.* The relative displacement of formerly adjacent points on opposite sides of the fault, measured in the fault surface. *See* DIP SLIP; STRIKE SLIP. *4.* The downhill movement of a mass of soil under wet or saturated conditions. The movement is only a short distance and the soil mass stays relatively intact. A form of landslide.

slip bands Luder's line, *q.v.*

slip bedding The contortion of stratification planes into complex folds caused by gliding.

slip or **shear cleavage** That variety of foliation along which there has been visible displacement, usually shown by bedding that is cut by the cleavage. Such displacements are commonly shown along many adjacent cleavage planes.

slip fold Shear fold, *q.v.*

slip folding Development of folds in layers by nonaffine slip not involving any actual bending.

slip glaze *1.* A pottery glaze composed of a fine clay or similar mineral powder; applied mixed with water. *2.* A glaze produced with slip clay, *q.v.*

slip-off slope A streamward sloping erosion surface developed along the inner bends of rivers. The surface is the resultant of the interaction of lateral and downward erosion by the river.

slip plane Closely spaced surfaces along which differential movement takes place in rock. Analogous to surfaces between playing cards. *Syn:* GLIDE PLANE; GLIDING PLANE

slip sheet A gravity-collapse structure. A bed that has slid down the flanks of an anticline, fractured at its base, and slid out over the adjacent strata.

slip surface Flow surface.

slip tectonite Rock whose particles have been oriented by movement along s-planes.

slope *1.* The inclined surface of a hill, mountain, plateau, plain, or any part of the surface of the earth; the angle at which such surfaces deviate from the horizontal. *2. Min:* An inclined passage driven from the dip of a coal vein. *Cf.* SLANT

slope wash Soil and rock material that is being or has been moved down a slope predominantly by the action of gravity assisted by running water that is not concentrated into channels. The term may also designate the process by which such material is moved.

slough A place of deep mud or mire. *Syn:* BOG; QUAGMIRE; SWALE

sluicing Washing auriferous earth through long races or boxes, provided with riffles and other gold-saving appliances, and so-called sluices.

slump *1. N:* Material that has slid down from high rock slopes. *V:* To slip down en masse. *2.* The downward slipping of a mass of rock or unconsolidated material of any size, moving as a unit or as several subsidiary units, usually with backward rotation on a more or less horizontal axis parallel to the cliff or slope from which it descends.

slump bedding Deformation in an unconsolidated or plastic sediment due to subaqueous slump or gliding. The disturbance may be restricted to layers only an inch or two thick, and are confined to a single bed or zone between undisturbed beds. *Syn:* CURLY BEDDING; GLIDE BEDDING; HASSOCK STRUCTURE

slush pit A pit used in rotary drilling where water can be stored for circulation through the hole while drilling. Mud can be mixed in the slush pit if necessary in drilling the hole.

small quantities of water 15,000 to 150,000 gallons per day. *Cf.* ENORMOUS; VERY LARGE; LARGE; MODERATE; VERY SMALL; MEAGER

smaltite A mineral $(Co,Ni)As_{2-3}$. Isometric. An ore of cobalt.

smectite *1.* A green clay. *2.* A greenish variety of halloysite. In certain states of humidity it appears transparent and almost gelatinous.

smithsonite Dry bone ore. A mineral of the calcite group, $ZnCO_3$. Hexagonal rhombohedral. An ore of zinc.

smoky quartz Cairngorm. A smoky, brown-colored crystalline variety of quartz.

smut In South Staffordshire, bad, soft coal, containing much earthy matter.

Snell's law Law of refraction, q.v.

snow avalanche The rapid downslope movement of large quantities of snow, usually in a mountain region since steepness of slope is an important factor. There are three broad categories of snow avalanches: (1) dry-snow avalanches, (2) wet-snow avalanches, and (3) wind-slab avalanches.

snowball garnet Pinwheel garnet.

snow concrete Snow which has been compressed at low temperatures and which sets with time into a tough hard substance of considerably greater strength than uncompressed snow.

snow field Where snow endures from year to year over any considerable area.

snow sampler Any device used to collect a section of fallen snow or firn.

soapstone A massive impure variety of talc.

soda Sodium carbonate, Na_2CO_3; especially the decahydrate, $Na_2CO_3.10H_2O$. Loosely used for sodium oxide, sodium hydroxide, sodium bicarbonate, and even for sodium in deplorable expressions such as soda feldspar.

soda feldspar Misnomer for sodium feldspar. Albite. See PLAGIOCLASE

soda lake Undrained depressions containing large amounts of salts of sodium and magnesium, chiefly sulfates.

sodalite A mineral, $Na_4Al_3(SiO_4)_3$-Cl. Isometric.

soda niter Chile saltpeter. A mineral, $NaNO_3$. Hexagonal rhombohedral.

soft coal Bituminous coal as opposed to anthracite.

soft ground That part of a mineral deposit that can be mined without drilling and shooting

hard rock; commonly occurs in the upper weathered portion of a vein.

soft radiation Radiation of low energy.

soft rock Rock that can be removed by air-operated hammers, but cannot be handled economically by pick. Loosely used to distinguish sedimentary from igneous and metamorphic rock.

soft water Water with practically no dissolved calcium or magnesium salts. Cf. HARD WATER

soil 1. Pedol: That earth material which has been so modified and acted upon by physical, chemical and biological agents that it will support rooted plants. 2. Engin. geol: The term soil is equivalent to regolith, q.v.

soil analysis Geochem. prospecting: Method which consists of taking soil samples and analyzing them for the various hydrocarbons and other gases and waxes, minerals or other rare components which they may contain.

soil colloids Soil colloids are defined as those which show heat of wetting irrespective of sizes of particles, which may be as large as .008 mm. or even a little larger. All clays and some silts exhibit heat of wetting.

soil creep Slow movement of rock fragments down even, gentle slopes.

soil horizon The letters A, B, and C are used to designate soil horizons. The A-horizon is the upper part. It consists of mineral layers of maximum organic accumulation; or layers from which clay materials, iron, and aluminum have been lost; or both. The B-horizon lies under the A. It consists of weathered material with an accumulation of clay, iron, or aluminum; or with more or less blocky or prismatic structure; or both. The C-horizon under the B is the layer of unconsolidated, weathered parent material. Not all these horizons are present in all soils.

soil mechanics The science of the mechanical properties of a mass of loose or unbonded particles, particularly of their composition, shear resistance, and effects of water. Applied in highway and foundation engineering and other problems depending on support by stability of and varieties in loose surface materials.

soil profile Succession of zones or horizons beginning at the surface that have been altered by normal soil-forming processes of which leaching and oxidation have been particularly important.

soil stratigraphic unit Rock stratigraphic unit consisting of the upper weathered part of an older sedimentary deposit recognized mainly in material of Pleistocene age.

soil stripes See STRIPED GROUND

soil-testing methods Dynamic methods used in engineering to test the site of buildings, dams, bridges and similar structures for possibilities of compaction or of earthquake or other vibration damage.

soil trafficability Capacity of the soil to support moving vehicles. *Cf.* CROSS-COUNTRY MOVEMENT

soil zone Soil horizon.

sol A colloidal dispersion of a solid in a liquid.

solar constant The rate at which solar radiant energy is received outside the atmosphere on a surface normal to the incident radiation at the earth's mean distance from the sun. The value of the mean solar constant is 1.94 gram calories per minute per square centimeter.

solar radiation Radiation received directly from the sun. As emitted from the sun, its spectral distribution is characterized by a maximum intensity in the blue-green part of the spectrum at 0.5μ; and hence it is often called short-wave radiation to distinguish it from the predominantly longer wave terrestrial radiation. As received at the surface of the earth, the spectral distribution is characterized by numerous intense telluric absorption lines and bands, the most important of which are produced by O_2, O_3, CO_2, and H_2O.

sole 1. The lowest thrust plane in an area of overthrusting. Commonly rocks above are imbricated. 2. Lower surface of a sedimentary stratum.

sole fault Low-angle thrust fault.

sole injection Discordant pluton, generally mafic, formed by intrusion of magma along a relatively flat thrust plane.

solfatara A semiextinct volcano, emitting only gaseous sulfurous exhalations, and aqueous vapors so called from the Solfatara, near Naples.

solid Matter with a definite shape and volume and some fundamental strength. Crystalline solids are composed of grains of one or more minerals in which the atoms have an orderly arrangement. For example rock salt is composed of interlocking crystals of halite in which the sodium and chlorite atoms form a cubic pattern. Vitreous solids or glasses are supercooled liquids. Amorphous solids do not possess a definite arrangement of atoms.

solid angle Fraction of the area of a unit sphere around a point of reference; usually expressed in units of π ($100\% = 4\pi$, the area of a sphere of unit radius).

solid angle effect "Mass" effect. Direct dependence of the counting rate from a radioactive object on the solid angle the object subtends with reference to the detector (other things being equal).

solid flow Flowage within a solid body accomplished by rearrangement between or within its particles.

solid solution A single crystalline phase which may be varied in composition within finite limits without the appearance of an additional phase.

solid stage That stage in the cooling of a magma when it has become completely solid, but while the magma is still present below. The structural features that develop are controlled by the movement of the still-liquid magma elsewhere in the body.

solid-state reaction Chemical reaction involving solids without any melting or dissolving of material.

solidus The locus of points in a temperature-composition diagram in a system at temperatures above which solid and liquid are in equilibrium and below which the system is completely solid. In binary systems without solid solutions, it is a straight line, and with solid solutions, it is a curved line or a combination of curved and straight lines. Likewise,, in ternary systems, the solidus is a flat plane or a curved surface, respectively.

solifluction The process of slow flowage from higher to lower ground of masses of waste saturated with water. Also applied to similar subaqueous flowage. Other terms: flowing slopes; mud glaciers; mud streams.

solifluction lobe Tonguelike mass of solifluction debris commonly with steep front and relatively gentle upper surface.

solifluction sheet Broad solifluction mantle.

solifluction slope Smooth slope produced by solifluction.

solifluction stream Narrow, laterally confined, streamlike solifluction mantle.

solifluction stripes Nonsorted stripes, q.v.

solitary coral Cup coral; fossil cow's horn; horn coral, q.v. An individual corallite that exists unattached to other corallites.

solstice The point in the ecliptic at which the sun is farthest from the equator, north (summer) or south (winter).

solubility The equilibrium concentration of solute when undissolved solute is in contact with the solution. The most common units of solubility are grams per 100 grams of solvent and moles per liter of solution.

solubility product The equilibrium constant for the process of solution of a substance (generally in water). A high value indicates a more soluble material.

solum The upper part of the soil profile, q.v., above the parent material, in which the processes of soil formation are taking place. In mature soils this includes the A and B horizons.

solute A dissolved substance. Ambiguity arises in the case of a liquid dissolved in a liquid, or a gas dissolved in a gas, but the term is seldom used for such solutions. For solids or gases dissolved in water the meaning is unambiguous.

solution 1. The change of matter from the solid or gaseous into the liquid state by its combination with a liquid. When unaccompanied by chemical change, it is called physical solution;

otherwise, chemical solution. *2.* The result of such change; a liquid combination of a liquid and a nonliquid substance.

solution potholes Includes all the holes that are formed primarily by solution action. Such holes are more numerous in soluble rocks, notably limestones.

solution transfer Solution of detrital grains at points of contact followed by deposition of dissolved material on other parts of the grain surfaces.

solution valley Broadly U-shaped valley in carbonate rocks formed by solution.

Solvan Lower Middle Cambrian.

solvate Chemical compound consisting of a dissolved substance and its solvent, e.g., hydrated calcium sulfate.

solvent The dissolving medium; the substance in which solution takes place.

solvus The curved line (binary systems) or surface (ternary systems) separating a field of homogeneous solid solution from a field of two or more solid phases which may form from the homogeneous one by unmixing.

soma General term for the material of an organism other than the germ plasm.

sonic log An acoustic log continuously recording travel time of sound from surface to an instrument lowered down a borehole.

Sonne camera A camera used in aerial photography and aeromagnetic surveying in which a film is moved continuously past a narrow slit to obtain a continuous picture of a strip on the ground surface. The film speed can be varied to match the speed of flight so that a stopped picture is obtained.

sonobuoy An anchored floating buoy which transmits a radio impulse when actuated by a sound wave in the water. Used in radioacoustic ranging as a method of location in marine operations, especially seismic prospecting. Locations are determined by measuring times from shot moment to the return of the resulting radio impulse from two or more sonobuoys at known positions.

sonograph Seismograph developed by Frank Rieber for the application of reflection methods to areas of complex geology and steeply dipping beds. The ordinary oscillograph traces are replaced by "sound tracks" of variable transparency on a moving picture film. The "analyzer" adds up impulses which are in phase, while the random effects tend to cancel one another.

sonoprobe Type of echo sounder that generates sound waves and records their reflections from inequalities beneath a sedimentary surface.

sooty chalcocite A black, pulverent variety of chalcocite of supergene origin.

Soret's principle That principle by which, if differences of temperature are induced in a solution of common salt or other substance in water, the dissolved material will become relatively concentrated in those portions in which the temperature is lowest.

sorosilicates Silicate structures in which the SiO_4 units are linked into finite groups, as into pairs of two, rings of three or more, etc. An example is beryl. *See* SILICATES, CLASSIFICATION

sorted circles Patterned ground whose mesh is dominantly circular and has a sorted appearance commonly due to a border of stones surrounding finer material.

sorted nets Patterned ground with a mesh intermediate between that of a sorted circle and a sorted polygon and with a sorted appearance commonly due to a border of stones surrounding finer material.

sorted polygons Patterned ground whose mesh is dominantly polygonal and has a sorted appearance commonly due to a border of stones surrounding finer material.

sorting 1. In a genetic sense the term may be applied to the dynamic process by which material having some particular characteristic, such as similar size, shape, specific gravity, or hydraulic value, is selected from a larger heterogeneous mass. 2. In a descriptive sense the term may be used to indicate the degree of similarity, in respect to some particular characteristic, of the component parts in a mass of material. 3. *Stat:* A measure of the spread of a distribution on either side of an average.

sorting coefficient A mathematical measure of the degree of sorting of a sediment. *See* SORTING INDEX

sorting index A measure of the uniformity of particle size in a sediment, usually based on the statistical spread of the particle-size frequency curve.

sound 1. A relatively long arm of the sea or ocean forming a channel between an island and a mainland or connecting two larger bodies, as, a sea and the ocean, or two parts of the same body; usually wider and more extensive than a strait. 2. *V:* To measure or ascertain the depth of water, as with sounding lines. 3. *Geophys:* Elastic waves in which the direction of particle motion is longitudinal, i.e., is

parallel with the direction of propagation in the air, but also applies to wave motion in liquids and solids. It is the type of wave motion applied in the reflection seismograph method of geophysical prospecting.

sounding 1. A measured depth of water. On hydrographic charts the soundings are adjusted to a specific plane of reference (sounding datum). *V: 2. Min:* Knocking on a roof to see whether it is sound or safe to work under; 3. Rapping on a pillar to signal a person on the other side of it or to enable him to estimate its width.

sounding datum The plane to which soundings are referred. *See* CHART DATUM

sounding line A line, wire, or cord used in sounding. It is weighted at one end with a plummet (sounding lead). *Syn:* LEAD LINE

sound intensity Average rate of flow of sound energy through a unit section normal to the direction of propagation. Average power transmission per unit area. *Syn:* ACOUSTIC INTENSITY; SEISMIC INTENSITY

sound ranging *Geophys:* Method of locating a source of unknown position by acoustic triangulation, i.e., by recording sound impulses on receivers at known positions; has been used in military application to locate gun positions.

sound receivers Mechanical and electrical devices which detect, receive, and amplify sound signals. Examples: horn, undograph, stethoscope, hydrophone, thermophone, microphone, geophone.

sound transmitters Mechanical and electrical devices which generate sound signals. Examples: Behm echo sounder, echometer, bells, horns, whistles, sirens, electromagnetic diaphragms, piezoelectric crystals, magnetostrictive solenoid.

source 1. *Seis. prospecting:* Either the point of origin or shot from which elastic waves are propagated, or the formation, horizon, interface or boundary at which the seismic wave is refracted and/or reflected and returned to the surface. 2. *Earthquake seismol:* The point of origin of an earthquake. 3. In neutron logging, the source of neutrons at one end of the logging tool.

source bed concept Hypothesis that many sulfide ore bodies were derived from sulfides deposited syngenetically in a particular stratigraphic zone of a sedimentary basin.

source beds Rocks in which oil or gas has been generated.

source rock The geological formation in which oil, gas, and/or other minerals originate.

sour oil or **gas** Crude oil containing an abnormally large amount of sulfur and sulfur compounds; or natural gas which contains objectionable amounts of hydrogen sulfide and other sulfur compounds.

space group A set of symmetry operations of the indefinite repetition of motif in space; there are 230 of them.

space lattice *See* SPACE GROUP

space-time unit Stratigraphic unit whose lateral limits are determined by lithology and whose vertical extent is measured in terms of time.

spall 1. Relatively thin, commonly curved and sharp-edged piece of rock produced by exfoliation. 2. *V:* To break off in layers parallel to a surface.

span 1. Length of a time interval. 2. Informal designation for a local geologic time unit.

Spanish ocher A variety of red ocher.

Spanish topaz *See* FALSE TOPAZ

spar 1. As used, loosely, almost any transparent or translucent, readily cleavable, crystalline mineral having a vitreous luster, as, calcspar (calcite), fluorspar (fluorite) heavy spar (barite). Most commonly used for feldspar. 2. *Min:* Small clay veins found in coal seams.

Sparnacian Upper Upper Paleocene.

spathic Having good cleavage.

spathization The widely distributed crystallization of calcite or dolomite, forming either "open" or "closed" fabrics.

spatter cone A low, steep-sided hill or mound of spatter built by lava fountains along a fissure or around a central vent. The great bulk of the structure consists of spatter, the glassy skins of which adhere to form agglutinate. True cinders and bombs also may be present and there generally is some scoria and Pele's hair. Cones of this type are generally elongate and seldom more than 50 feet high. They are characteristic of basaltic eruptions.

spatulate Spoon-shaped.

special creation Theory antedating an understanding of evolution that each species of organisms inhabiting the earth was created fully formed and perfect by some divine process.

speciation 1. Splitting of lineages and production of increased number of species. 2. Origin of genetic isolation separating two or more parts of a population

species No entirely satisfactory definition can be formulated because theoretical and practical species are not necessarily the same. Ideally, the species concept embraces (a) interbreeding, (b) morphologic similarity, (c) physiologic compatibility, (d) ecologic association, (e) geographic distribution, and (f) continuity in time. Practically, a species is the type specimen (holotype) and other individuals considered to be so closely related and similar that they should be referred to by a single species name.

species group A group of species which replace each other geographically and may be regarded as all descended from a common stock, but which are undeniably all of specific rank. *Syn:* GENS; ARTENKREIS

specific capacity (of a well) The discharge expressed as rate of yield per unit of drawdown, generally gallons per minute per foot of drawdown.

specific gravity Ratio of the mass of a body to the mass of an equal volume of water at a specified temperature.

specific heat Quantity of heat necessary to raise the temperature of 1 gram of a given substance 1 degree centigrade.

specific humidity The mass of water vapor in a unit mass of moist air, usually expressed as so many grams per gram or per kilogram of moist air. Specific humidity must be distinguished from mixing ratio, which is the mass of water vapor per unit mass of absolutely dry air.

specific name *1.* The second or trivial name of a species. *2.* Less properly, the name of a species consisting of two words.

specific productivity index The productivity index of a well per foot of producing sand. The sand thickness should correctly be taken to the bedding planes, but actually it has commonly been taken along the axis of the well, regardless of dip or well slant.

specific resistance *Elec. prospecting:* The resistivity ρ of a homogeneous ground in which ρ is defined by the relation $R = \rho L/A$, where R is the resistance of a sample of material of length L and cross-section A. If L and A are unity, then ρ becomes the resistance across two opposite faces of a cube of unit dimensions. The unit used is usually the centimeter, and ρ is then the resistance in ohms across a 1-cm. cube expressed as ohms per centimeter cube and with the dimensions ohms times centimeters.

specific retention *Hydrol:* As applied to a rock or soil it is the ratio of (1) the volume of water which, after being saturated, it will retain against the pull of gravity to (2) its own volume. It is stated as a percentage.

specific rotation Rotatory power (rotation of plane of polarization of polarized light) given in degrees per decimeter for liquids and solutions, and in degrees per millimeter for solids. Varies with the wave length of light used, with temperature, and, in the case of solutions, with the concentration.

specific volume Reciprocal of density or volume per unit mass expressed in cubic centimeters per gram, or cubic feet per pound.

specific yield As applied to a rock or soil it is the ratio of (1) the volume of water which, after being saturated, it will yield by gravity to (2) its own volume. This ratio is stated as a percentage.

specimen Properly speaking, a

sample of anything; but among miners it is often restricted to selected or handsome minerals, as, fine pieces of ore, crystals, or pieces of quartz containing visible gold.

spectral gamma-ray log Record of the radiation spectrum and relative intensities of gamma rays emitted by strata penetrated in drilling. Because of their different energies the relative amounts of radioactivity contributed by different elements can be determined.

spectrographic analysis Analysis by obtaining the spectrum of a substance and matching lines in the spectrum with known wave lengths of lines in the spectra of the elements. The analysis can be made quantitative by comparing intensities of the spectral lines.

spectrometer Instrument used in determining the index of refraction. Spectroscope fitted for measurements of the spectra observed with it.

spectrophotometer Optical instrument for comparing the intensities of the corresponding colors of two spectra.

spectroscope Optical instrument for forming and examining spectra.

spectrum An image formed by dispersing a beam of radiant energy so that its rays are arranged in the order of their wave lengths.

specular hematite Specularite, q.v.

specularite Hematite, Fe_2O_3, occurring in tabular or disklike crystals of gray color and splendent metallic luster. Syn: GRAY HEMATITE; SPECULAR HEMATITE; SPECULAR IRON

speed Time rate of motion measured by the distance moved per

unit time. Seis. prospecting: The rate of propagation of elastic waves.

speleology The scientific study of exploration of caverns and related features.

spergenite A calcarenite containing less than 10% of quartz and composed primarily of oölite and fossil detritus.

spessartite 1. One of the end members in the garnet, q.v., mineral group. 2. A dioritic or gabbroic lamprophyre. The principal minerals are hornblende or augite or both with plagioclase (usually andesine) feldspar. Olivine or biotite may be present but, in small amount. Apatite and opaque oxides are normal accessories. A small amount of quartz and orthoclase may occur interstitially.

sphalerite A mineral, $(Zn,Fe)S$ dimorphous with wurtzite. Isometric. The principal ore of zinc. Syn: BLENDE; BLACKJACK; JACK ROSIN JACK; ZINC BLENDE

sphene Titanite. A mineral $CaTiSiO_5$. Monoclinic.

sphenoid 1. Crystallog: An open form in the monoclinic system consisting of two intersecting similar faces related to one another only by a twofold symmetry axis perpendicular to their line of intersection and bisecting the dihedral angle between them Cf. DOME. 2. A disphenoid.

spherical coordinates A system of three-dimensional coordinates defined by a radius and two angles (like latitude and longitude) Seis. prospecting: The radial distance and angular measure which give the orientation of pulses originating at a point source, such as a shot hole.

spherical wave front Spherical surface which a given phase of a seismic impulse (in an isotrop ic medium) occupies at any particular time.

spherical weathering Spheroidal weathering, *q.v.*

sphericity The degree in which the shape of a fragment approaches the form of a sphere. *Cf.* ANGULARITY; ROUNDNESS; SHAPE

spheroid In general, any figure differing but little from a sphere. *Geodesy:* A mathematical figure closely approaching the geoid in form and size, and used as a surface of reference for geodetic surveys.

spheroidal structure Orbicular structure, *q.v.*

spheroidal symmetry Axial symmetry, *q.v.*

spheroidal weathering Boulders produced chiefly by chemical weathering of rock along fractures. Such boulders are called boulders of decomposition. *See* CONCENTRIC WEATHERING

spherulite A small, radiating, and usually concentrically arranged aggregation of one or more minerals generally of spherical or spheroidal shape, formed by the radial growth of acicular crystals in a rigid glass about a common center or inclusion. Such structures are especially common in the glassy groundmass of silicic lava flows and in obsidians.

spicule Tiny siliceous or calcareous object, commonly needle-shaped or branched, contained in the tissues of certain invertebrate animals such as sponges.

spike, isotopic Known amount of an isotopic mixture of known and abnormal composition.

spilite A basaltic rock with albitic feldspar. The albitic feldspar is usually accompanied by autometamorphic minerals or minerals characteristic of low-grade greenstones such as chlorite, calcite, epidote, chalcedonic silica or quartz, actinolite, and others.

spilosite Used for a rock arrested at an early stage in adinole formation and also as a synonym for spotted slate.

spinel *1.* A mineral, $(Mg,Fe)Al_2O_4$. Isometric. Used as a gem. *2.* A mineral group of general formula AB_2O_4, where A=Mg, Fe",Zn,Mn",Ni,   B=Al,Fe''',- Mn''',Cr. Isometric.

spinning fiber Asbestos suitable for the spinning of asbestos fabrics.

S-P interval *Earthquake seismol:* The time interval between the first arrivals of longitudinal and transverse waves, which is a measure of the distance from the earthquake source.

spiral garnet Pinwheel garnet.

spit A small point of land or narrow shoal projecting into a body of water from the shore.

s-plane An unwarped s-surface.

splays Divergent small faults at the extremities of large normal faults, especially rifts.

splendent Applied to the luster of a mineral that reflects with brilliancy and gives well-defined images, as, hematite, cassiterite.

spliced Applied to veins when they pinch out and are overlapped at that point by another parallel one.

split spread *Seis. prospecting:* A line of detectors symmetrically disposed on two sides of the shot point.

spodumene A mineral, $LiAlSi_2O_6$. Monoclinic. An ore of lithium. The clear green and pink varieties are used as gems.

spoil *1.* Debris or waste material from a coal mine. *2.* In England, a stratum of coal and dirt mixed.

spoil banks Submerged embankments of dumped material dredged from a channel which lie alongside the channel.

sponge An organism belonging to the simplest and least advanced phyla of multiple-celled animals or Porifera; generally possesses a spicular skeleton.

spontaneous polarization Self-potential method; spontaneous potential method, *q.v.*

spontaneous potential method An electrical method in which a potential field caused by spontaneous electrochemical phenomena is measured. *Syn:* SELF-POTENTIAL METHOD; SPONTANEOUS POLARIZATION

sporadic permafrost zone Regional zone predominantly free of permafrost, with only scattered areas underlain by permafrost.

spore An asexual reproductive structure, commonly unicellular and usually produced in sporangia.

spore coal Coal in which the attritus may contain a large amount of spore matter together with a certain amount of transparent attritus. *See* CANNEL COAL

spot correlation Correlation of reflections on isolated seismograms by "spotting" similarities in character and interval. *Syn:* CORRELATION METHOD

spot soundings Individual soundings in contrast to continuous soundings such as are obtained by recording fathometers.

spotted slate An argillaceous rock in which low-grade metamorphism has caused the growth of incipient porphyroblasts. *See* FLECKSCHIEFER; HORNFELS; KNOTTED SLATE; MACULOSE; SLATE; SPOTTED SCHIST

spot test Delicate chemical test for ores or other substances in which a drop of solution is applied to filter paper impregnated with a sensitive reagent and a colored spot is formed.

spread, seismic Arrangement of the geophones in relation to the shot point. Several patterns are used in field practice such as correlation, continuous, interlocking, reversed, removed, leap frog, in-line, end-to-end, parallel, cross, "L," perpendicular, star arc, fan, circular, split, and straddle spreads.

spread correction Reduction of the seismic reflection time to vertical incidence by applying the ratio of the depth of the reflection horizon to the distance between the shot point and the observed geophone.

spring A place where, without the agency of man, water flows from a rock or soil upon the land or into a body of surface water.

Springeran Lower Lower Pennsylvanian.

spring tide A tide that occurs at or near the time of new and full moon and which rises highest and falls lowest from the mean level.

spud in To commence the actual drilling of a well.

spurs The subordinate ridges which extend themselves from the crest of a mountain like ribs from the vertebral column.

squeeze job Usually a secondary cementing job where the cement is pumped into the formation through the bottom of the casing or through perforations in casing to obtain a shutoff of undesirable fluids.

s-surface; s-plane *Struct. petrol:* Any planar surface. May be a plane of stratification, schistosity, shear, or a statistical surface based on petrofabric analysis.

stability *Thermodyn:* A phase is

said to have stability if a slight perturbation in the variables defining the system, temperature, pressure, or composition does not result in the appearance of a new phase.

stability field (critical level) The temperature and pressure within which a mineral is stable.

stability series Order of persistence. The order of resistance of minerals to alteration or destruction by weathering of the parent rock, abrasion during transportation, and postdepositional solution.

stabilized dune A dune protected from further wind action by a cover of vegetation or by cementation of the sand; known also as a "fixed" or "anchored" dune.

stable gravimeter A gravimeter having a simple weight on a spring such that the sensitivity is proportional to the square of the period. Examples: Hartley, Boliden (Lindblad-Malmqvist), Gulf (Hoyt), Haalck, Askania (Graf).

stack Under favorable conditions waves are able to cut back on the two sides of a tiny promontory, and then, aided by weathering, to cut behind the end of this, leaving it as an island, or stack, entirely removed from the mainland. *Syn:* CHIMNEY; SKERRIES

stade Time represented by glacial deposits formerly termed a substage; differs from a stratigraphic substage because it is not a rock unit and has somewhat variable time value from place to place.

stadia *Surv:* 1. A temporary station. 2. A stadia rod. 3. An instrument for measuring distances, consisting of a telescope with special horizontal parallel lines or wires, used in connection with a vertical graduated rod; also,

the rod alone, or the method of using it.

stadial 1. *N:* Stade. 2. *Adj:* Pertaining to a stade.

stadial moraine Recessional moraine.

stadia rod A graduated rod used with an instrument of the stadia class to measure the distance from the observation point to the place where the rod is positioned.

stadia tables Mathematical tables from which may be found, without computation, the horizontal and vertical components of a reading made with a transit and stadia rod.

stage 1. *Hydraul:* Elevation of a water surface above any chosen datum plane, often above an established low-water plane; gage height. 2. *Stratig:* The time-stratigraphic unit next in rank below a series. The fundamental working unit in local time-stratigraphic correlation. Its boundaries commonly coincide with those of some objective stratigraphic unit, such as a formation, faunizone, or mineral zone. In America, used as a time term for major subdivisions of the Pleistocene epoch.

stagnation 1. Condition of water not stirred by currents or waves; commonly implies oxygen deficiency and accumulation of noxious substances. 2. Condition of a glacier that has ceased to move.

stalactite A cylindrical or conical deposit of minerals, generally calcite or aragonite, hanging from the roof of a cavern.

stalagmite Columns or ridges of carbonate of lime rising from a limestone cave floor, and formed by water charged with carbonate of lime dripping from the stalactites above. Stalactites and stalagmites often meet, and then form a column from floor to roof.

standard atmosphere The International Standard Atmosphere which is used as the basis of graduation of altimeters assumes at mean sea level a temperature of 15° C., a pressure of 760 mm. of Hg. (1013.2 millibars) and a lapse rate of 6.5° C./km. from sea level up to 11 km.

standard cell A method of studying the chemical relationships between rocks by calculating the number of various cations in the rocks per 160 oxygen ions; the results of such calculations.

standard deviation map Vertical variability map showing the degree of dispersion of one lithologic type about its center of gravity in a stratigraphic unit.

standard mineral A hypothetical mineral composition, as used in the calculation of the norm, *q.v. Syn:* NORMATIVE MINERAL

standard state The condition within the crust of the earth such that the pressures are uniform in all directions. That is, the stresses are essentially hydrostatic.

standing wave A type of wave in which there are nodes, or points of no vertical motion and maximum horizontal motion, between which the water oscillates vertically. The points of maximum vertical motion and least horizontal motion are called antinodes or loops. It is caused by the meeting of two similar wave groups traveling in opposing directions. Sometimes called stationary wave.

stand of tide An interval at high or low water when there is no sensible change in the height of the tide. The water level is stationary at high and low water for only an instant, but the change in level near these times is so slow that it is not usually perceptible. *See* SLACK TIDE

standstill The condition or time of static sea level.

stanniferous Yielding or containing tin, as, stanniferous ores.

stannite A mineral, Cu_2FeSnS_4. Tetragonal.

star, *adj.* Asteriated, as, a star ruby. *See* ASTERISM

starved basin *See* BASIN, STARVED

state line fault Discontinuity in the patterns of geologic maps occurring at state lines or other geographic boundaries resulting from the recognition and mapping of differently constituted stratigraphic units in adjacent areas.

state of matter Matter is generally considered to exist in three states: gaseous, liquid, and solid. The relations between liquid and solid states are not entirely clear and it has been suggested that a better division is: gaseous, vitreous (amorphous), and crystalline.

static Noises which interfere with radio waves. The term is also applied to interferences with acoustic and seismic waves.

static metamorphism Diagenism. *Geol:* Metamorphism produced by the internal heat of the earth and the weight of the superincumbent rocks and not accompanied by appreciable deformation. A term used in contradistinction to dynamic metamorphism which involves stresses principally due to thrust.

static pressure Pressure that is "standing" or stabilized due to the fact that it has attained the maximum possible from its source and is not being diminished by loss.

statics That branch of mechanics which treats of the equilibrium of forces, or relates to bodies as held at rest by the forces acting on them.

static zone The zone which extends below the level of the lowest point of discharge, and in which the water is stagnant or moves with infinitesimal velocity.

station Ground position at which the geophysical instrument is set up for observation in the field.

stationary field Natural field of force as a gravimetric or a magnetic field. *Elect. prospecting:* A field which does not change with time and is produced by direct current after equilibrium has been reached.

stationary wave A wave of essentially stable form which does not move with respect to a selected reference point; a fixed swelling. Sometimes called standing wave.

station elevation In the U. S. Weather Bureau, the elevation above sea level adopted for a station as the basis to which all pressure observations at the station correspond.

station pressure In the U. S. Weather Bureau, that pressure corresponding to an adopted station elevation, *q.v.*, which may differ slightly from the actual elevation of the barometer.

statistical lithofacies Stratigraphic facies, distinguished from others by the proportions of its components, that grades laterally into its neighbors and is bounded by vertical abitrary cutoff planes. *Cf.* INTERTONGUED LITHOFACIES

staurolite A mineral, Fe″Al₄Si₂-O₁₀(OH)₂, occurring in metamorphic rocks. Orthorhombic.

steady-state stream A graded stream.

steady-turbidity current Persistent turbidity current, e.g., one produced by a heavily sediment-laden river flowing into a body of deep standing water.

steatite Massive, in many cases impure, talc-rich rock.

steatite talc High grade variety of talc suitable for use in electronic insulators.

Stebinger drum A type of gradienter, *q.v.*, used particularly on alidades such as Gale, *q.v.*, explorer or miniature types.

s-tectonite Rock whose predominant structures are s-planes which may have been produced by either slipping or flattening.

steel jack (colloquial) Sphalerite.

steephead A nearly vertical bluff or streamhead, at the base of which springs emerge, supplying small streams, assumes in time a semicircular form, which is the steephead.

stellate Starlike; stellate hairs have radiating branches or, when falsely stellate, are separate hairs aggregated into starlike clusters; hairs once or twice forked are often treated as stellate.

Stelleroidea Class of echinoderms of starlike form; includes asteroids, auluroids, and ophiuroids. Ord.-Rec.

stenohaline Refers to relatively low tolerance for variation in salinity.

Stephanian Upper Upper Carboniferous.

stepout Angularity; moveout or moveout time, *q.v.*

stepout correction The correction, determined from the geometry of the detector spread, which eliminates the effect on the reflection time of the horizontal distance between seismometers and shot point. *See* STEPOUT TIME

stepout time *Seis. prospecting:* The time differential in arrivals of a given peak or trough of a reflected or refracted event for successive detector positions on the earth's surface. This difference gives information on the dip of the reflecting or refracting horizon in the earth.

steppe A Tartar term, adopted by geographers for those extensive flats or plains which occupy so large a portion of northern Asia and Siberia. They are generally covered with long rough grass, are but partially wooded, and consist of alluvial deposits.

steptoe An islandlike area in a lava flow. *Cf.* NUNATAK

stereogram A stereographic projection.

stereographic projection *Mineral:* A projection made on a plane through the center of a sphere by projectors from the South Pole.

stereoscope An optical instrument for assisting the observer in obtaining stereoscopic vision from two properly prepared photographs.

stereoscopic image or **model** That mental impression of a three-dimensional model which results from stereoscopic fusion of a stereoscopic pair.

stereoscopic pair Two photographs of the same area taken from different camera stations in such a manner that a portion of the area appears on both photographs. *Syn:* STEREOGRAM

stereoscopic vision That particular application of binocular vision which enables the observer to view an object, or two different perspectives of an object—as two photographs of the same image taken from different camera stations—and to obtain therefrom the mental impression of a three-dimensional model.

stereostructural contour Structural contour determined by ster-

eoscopic study of aerial photographs.

sterile coal In England, black shale or clay on top of a coal seam.

Sternberg's law Wearing away of transported pebbles is proportional to their weight in water and distance traveled.

stibnite Antimony glance; gray antimony. A mineral, Sb_2S_3. Orthorhombic. The principal ore of antimony.

stiff clay Clay of low plasticity.

stilbite A mineral of the zeolite group, close to $Ca_2NaAl_5Si_{13}O_{36}\cdot14H_2O$. Monoclinic.

stillstand To remain stationary with respect to sea level or to the center of the earth.

still-water level The elevation of the surface of the water if all wave action were to cease.

stock A body of plutonic rock that covers less than 40 square miles, has steep contacts (generally dipping outward), and although generally discordant, may be concordant.

stock pile The ore accumulated at the surface when shipping is suspended, as on the iron ranges of Michigan and Minnesota during the winter months.

stockwork [*Ger.* Stockwerke] An ore deposit of such a form that it is worked on floors or stories. It may be a solid mass of ore, or a rock mass so interpenetrated by small veins of ore that the whole must be mined together. Stockworks are distinguished from tabular or sheet-deposit, i.e., veins or beds, which have a small thickness in comparison with their extension in the main plane of the deposit, i.e., in strike and dip. *See* STOCK

Stokes' law A formula to express the rate of settling of spherical particles in a fluid. It is expressed as $V=Cr^2$ where V is the velocity in centimeters per second, r is the radius of the particle in centimeters, and C is a constant relating relative densities of fluid and particle, the acceleration due to gravity, and the viscosity of the fluid.

stomach stone Gastrolith, *q.v.*

stone *1.* Concreted earthy or mineral matter. A small piece of rock. Rock or rocklike material for building. Large natural masses of stone are generally called rocks; small or quarried masses are called stones; and the finer kinds, gravel or sand. *2.* A precious stone; a gem. *3.* In England, ironstone. See CLAY IRON-STONE

stone-bordered strips See STRIPED GROUND

stone bubbles Lithophysae, *q.v.*

stone circle See STONE RING

stone fields See FELSENMEER

stone guano Breccia of agatelike fragments formed by leaching of guano and enrichment of deposit in insoluble phosphates.

stone line A line of angular or subangular rock fragments which parallels a sloping topographic surface at a depth of several feet.

stone net See STONE RING

stone polygon See STONE RING

stone ring A ring or polygon of stones surrounding a central area of fine debris in a bouldery soil region. *Syn:* STONE POLYGON; STONE NET; STONE CIRCLE; STONE WREATH; ROCK WREATH; FROST-HEAVED MOUND

stone stripes See STRIPED GROUND

stone wreath See STONE RING

stony iron See SIDEROLITE

stony meteorite Meteorite consisting mainly of rock-forming silicate minerals such as pyroxene, olivine, and feldspar. *Cf.* ACHONDRITE; CHONDRITE

stope *1.* An excavation from which the ore has been extracted, either above or below a level, in a series of steps. A variation of step. *2.* An underground excavation from which ore has been extracted, either above (overhand) or below (underhand) a level. Access to stopes is usually by way of adjacent raises.

stoping Overhand or magmatic stoping. *1.* A method of intrusion of light acidic magma into heavier basic rocks at Ascutney Mountain, Vermont. Blocks of the older rock are wedged loose overhead, settle in the magma, and are assimilated at depth. Thus the magma works its way upward. *See* STOPE. *2. Min:* The loosening and removal of ore in a mine either by working upward (overhead or overhand) or downward (underhand).

stoping, magmatic See MAGMATIC STOPING

stoping ground Part of an ore body opened by drifts and raises and ready for breaking down.

storage coefficient Coefficient of storage. The volume of water released from storage in each vertical column of the aquifer having a base of 1 foot square when the water table or other piezometric surface declines 1 foot. This is approximately equal to the specific yield for nonartesian aquifers.

storm *1.* In general, a disturbance of the ordinary average conditions of the atmosphere which unless specifically qualified may include any or all meteorological disturbances, such as wind, rain, snow, hail, thunder, etc. This general term may be further restricted by some descriptive adjective, as, e.g., sandstorm, dust storm, hot wind (such as the Khamsin or foehn or chinook), cold windstorm (such as the norther and the pampero), etc. 2. Wind force of 11 in the Beaufort wind scale.

storm beach During exceptionally heavy storms coarse material is sometimes built by the waves into surprisingly strong ridges which stand some distance from the shore under normal conditions and are known as storm beaches.

storm tide The rise of water accompanying a storm caused by wind stresses on the water surface. *See* WIND SETUP

storm wave A rise of the sea over low coasts not ordinarily subject to overflow; it is caused primarily by wind and has no relation to the tide brought about by gravitational forces except that the two may combine. More than three-fourths of all the loss of human lives in tropical cyclones has been caused by these inundations and not by the winds directly.

stoss, *adj.* Facing the direction whence a glacier moves, as a rock or hill in its track; as, the stoss side of a crag; contrasted with lee. Applied to the struck side of a rounded ledge.

stoss-and-lee topography The persistently asymmetric arrangement of bosses and small hills in a strongly glaciated district, each hill having a comparatively gentle abraded slope on the stoss side and a somewhat steeper and rougher quarried slope on the lee side. Topography having gentle upstream (stoss) and steep downstream (lee) slopes as the result of glacial erosion.

strain Deformation resulting from applied force; within elastic limits strain is proportional to stress.

strain, rotational *See* ROTATIONAL STRAIN

strain cleavage Strain-slip cleavage, *q.v.*

strain ellipse In two-dimensional analysis of rock deformation, the imaginary ellipse whose half axes are the greatest and least principal strains.

strain ellipsoid *1.* In elastic theory, a sphere under homogeneous strain is transformed into an ellipsoid with this property: the ratio of the length of a line, which has a given direction in the strained state, to the length of the corresponding line in the unstrained state, is proportional to the central radius vector of the surface drawn in the given direction. *2.* The ellipsoid whose half-axes are the principal strains.

strain gauges Mechanical, electrical, or optical devices which measure displacement or strain produced by force or stress. The stress-strain ratios measure the elastic moduli; when applied to rocks and formations they determine the elastic properties involved in the propagation of seismic waves.

strain-slip cleavage In slates and schists, a structure similar to fracture cleavage, *q.v.*, but with marked flexing of the earlier cleavage or foliation along the shear planes.

strait A relatively narrow waterway between two larger bodies of water. *See* SOUND; CHANNEL

strand The strand and beach are synonymous terms, applied to the portion of the shore between high and low water.

strand flat A low coastal platform that abuts inland against higher terrain. It may be partly submerged or slightly emerged and its local altitude depends partly upon recent vertical movements of the coast. Strand flats varying from a few hundred yards to many miles extend along hundreds of miles of arctic shore.

strata Plural of stratum.

strategic materials Those materials vital to the security of a nation which must be procured entirely or to a substantial degree from sources outside the continental limits of that nation because the available production will not be sufficient in quantity or quality to meet requirements in time of national emergency. *Cf.* CRITICAL MATERIALS

strath *1.* Generally used for a broad river valley. If it has been elevated and dissected, the erosion remnant is called a strath terrace. *2.* Valley deeply filled with alluvial deposits, particularly glacial outwash, not now occupied by stream.

stratification A structure produced by deposition of sediments in beds or layers (strata), laminae, lenses, wedges, and other essentially tabular units.

stratification index Number of beds in a stratigraphic unit times 100 divided by the unit's thickness.

stratified Formed or lying beds, layers, or strata.

stratified cone *See* COMPOSITE CONE

stratified drift Drift exhibiting both sorting and stratification, implying deposition from a fluid medium such as water or air.

stratified or **sedimentary rocks** Derivative or stratified rocks may be fragmental or crystalline; those which have been mechanically formed are all fragmental; those which have been chemically precipitated are generally crystalline, and those composed of organic remains are sometimes partially crystalline.

stratified water Standing water consisting of density layers differing in temperature or salinity.

stratiform *1.* Composed of layers. *2.* Resembling stratus clouds.

stratigrapher One who studies, or who has expert knowledge of, stratigraphy.

stratigraphic classification Classification of stratified rocks and geologic time into rock, time-rock, time, and biostratigraphic units.

stratigraphic control The apparent localization of mineral deposition by stratigraphic features.

stratigraphic facies Stratigraphic unit or part of stratigraphic unit distinguished from others by its aspect.

stratigraphic geology The study of stratified rocks.

stratigraphic leak Situation or process whereby microfossils, generally conodonts, are supposed to have descended through crevices or solution channels and lodged in a lower stratum where they may be associated with fossils of greater age.

stratigraphic paleontology Study of fossils applied particularly to discrimination and correlation of fossiliferous strata.

stratigraphic separation *See* STRATIGRAPHIC THROW

stratigraphic test Hole drilled to determine the local stratigraphic section or the position of a key bed; term generally applied to holes considerably deeper than core holes.

stratigraphic throw or **separation** The stratigraphic thickness that separates two beds brought into contact at a fault.

stratigraphic time *See* TIME, STRATIGRAPHIC

stratigraphic trap A type of trap

which results from variation in lithology of the reservoir rock and a termination of the reservoir (usually on the updip extension) or other interruption of continuity.

stratigraphic unit Unit consisting of stratified mainly sedimentary rocks grouped for description, mapping, correlation, etc. *See* BIOSTRATIGRAPHIC; CHRONOSTRATIGRAPHIC

stratigraphy That branch of geology which treats of the formation, composition, sequence, and correlation of the stratified rocks as parts of the earth's crust.

stratosphere That part of the earth's atmosphere between the troposphere, *q.v.*, and the ionosphere, *q.v.*

strato-volcano A volcanic cone, generally of large dimension, built of alternating layers of lava and pyroclastic materials. Essentially synonymous with composite cone; stratified cone.

stratum *1.* A section of a formation that consists throughout of approximately the same kind of rock material; a stratum may consist of an indefinite number of beds, and a bed may consist of numberless layers; the distinction of layer and bed is not always obvious. *2.* A single sedimentary bed or layer, regardless of thickness.

streak The color of the powder of a mineral as obtained by scratching the surface of the mineral with a knife or file or, if not too hard, by rubbing it on an unpolished porcelain surface.

streak plate A piece of unglazed porcelain for testing the streak of minerals.

stream Any body of flowing water or other fluid, great or small.

stream capacity The maximum

amount of material that the stream is able to transport.

stream capture Piracy, *q.v.*

streamflood An eroding agent made by transformation from a sheetflood that is depositional. The cause of the transformation may be differential uplift or a climatic change.

stream frequency *Geomorph:* Ratio of the number of stream segments of all orders to the area of a drainage basin; a measure of topographic texture. *Symbol:* F

stream gradient ratio Ratio of the gradient of a stream channel of one order to that of the next higher order in the same drainage basin; $R_s = \theta_u / \theta_{u+1}$. *Symbol:* R_s

streaming flow Glacier flow, *q.v.*, in which the ice flows without cracking or breaking into blocks.

streaming potential Electric potential developed in a liquid when it is forced through a capillary.

stream length *Geomorph:* (Symbol L_u). Length of a stream segment of a particular order. Total stream length (symbol ΣL_u): the length of all stream segments of a particular order in a specified drainage basin. Mean stream length (symbol L_u): the mean of all stream lengths of a particular order within a specified drainage basin.

stream length ratio *Geomorph:* Ratio of the mean length of stream segments of one order to the mean length of segments of the next lower order within a specified drainage basin. *Symbol:* R_L

streamline flow Laminar flow.

stream order *Geomorph:* First order streams are the smallest unbranched tributaries; second order streams are initiated by the confluence of two first order streams; third order streams are initiated by the confluence of two second order streams; etc. The symbol u refers to an order number.

streams, number of *Geomorph:* Total number of stream segments of the same order within a specified drainage basin. *Symbol:* Nu

stream segment *Geomorph:* The portion of a stream extending between the junctions of tributaries of different orders.

stream terrace (Shoshone type) Stream-cut rock terrace with thick cover of slope wash.

stream tin Tin ore (cassiterite) occurring in stream beds; distinguished from lode tin.

strength The limiting stress that a solid can withstand without failing by rupture or continuous plastic flow. Rupture strength or breaking strength refers to the stress at the time of rupture. If a body deforms plastically continuously after a certain stress has been reached without any increase in stress, this is also called strength. *See* ULTIMATE STRENGTH; FUNDAMENTAL STRENGTH

strength of magnetic field A vector quantity with a magnitude and direction defined as that of the force acting on a unit positive pole. The force between magnetic poles may be considered as the reaction of one pole on the magnetic field of the other. Thus a unit field strength exerts a force of 1 dyne on a unit pole, and such a field has a strength of 1 oersted. The magnetic field strength is represented by the density of the lines of force or the number of lines per square centimeter in a section perpendicular to their direction. These lines are maxwells, and the strength of the field in oersteds is the number of maxwells per square centimeter.

strength of magnetic pole The force between magnetic poles is proportional to the pole strength. Equal poles have unit strength when they exert unit force (1 dyne) when they are unit distance (1 cm.) apart.

stress *1.* Force per unit area, found by dividing the total force by the area to which the force is applied. *2.* The intensity at a point in a body of the internal forces or components of force which act on a given plane through the point. As used in product specifications, stress is calculated on the basis of the original dimensions of the cross section of the specimen.

stress difference The algebraic difference between the maximum and minimum principal stresses.

stress ellipsoid The ellipsoid whose half-axes are the principal stresses.

stress minerals A term suggested for minerals, such as chlorite, chloritoid, talc, albite, epidote, amphiboles, kyanite, etc., whose formation in metamorphosed rocks is favored by shearing stress. *Ant:* ANTISTRESS MINERALS

stress pressure *1.* Pressure resulting from nonhydrostatic stress. *2.* Mean of three principal components of nonhydrostatic stress.

stretched pebbles Pebbles in conglomerates that, more or less spherical originally, are now shaped like triaxial ellipsoids, oblate spheroids, or prolate spheroids because of rock deformation.

stretch thrust Thrust that forms when the inverted limb of an overturned or recumbent fold becomes so stretched that it ruptures.

stria *1.* A minute groove or channel. A threadlike line or narrow band. *See* GLACIAL STRIAE. *2.* A type of ornamentation or surface detail found on the shells of invertebrates: a very fine grooved line or thread. *3.* **striae,** *pl.* Parallel grooves or lines.

striation The markings with lines or striae, generally applied to the parallel scratches with which the bed of a glacier is scored by means of sharp angular fragments of rock embedded in the ice stream, which are forcibly dragged along with the ice. These embedded masses are also striated and polished, often only on one side, but more generally on more than one, owing to their having been turned over and over in their journey.

striding level A spirit level, the frame of which carries at its two extremities inverted Ys below, so that it may be placed upon two concentric cylinders and straddle any small intervening obstacles.

strike The course or bearing of the outcrop of an inclined bed or structure on a level surface; the direction or bearing of a horizontal line in the plane of an inclined stratum, joint, fault, cleavage plane, or other structural plane. It is perpendicular to the direction of the dip. *Cf.* TREND

strike fault A fault whose strike is parallel to the strike of the strata.

strike joint A joint that strikes parallel to the strike of the adjacent strata or schistosity if bedding is not present.

strike separation In faulting, the distance on a map between the two parts of an index plane (bed, vein, dike, etc.) where they are in contact with the fault and measured parallel to the strike of the fault.

strike shift The horizontal component of the shift measured parallel to the strike of the fault.

strike-shift fault A fault in which the component of the shift is parallel to the fault strike.

strike slip The component of the slip parallel with the fault strike, or the projection of the net slip on a horizontal line in the fault surface.

strike-slip or **transcurrent fault** A fault in which the net slip is practically in the direction of the fault strike.

string A driller's term for the drilling bit, jars, drill stem, rope socket, and other tools connected to the lower end of a drilling cable in standard or percussion drilling. Also used occasionally for the rig and complete drilling equipment.

stringer *1.* A narrow vein or irregular filament of mineral traversing a rock mass of different material. *2.* A thin layer of coal at the top of a bed, separating in places from the main coal by material similar to that comprising the roof.

stringer lead A small ore body, generally a vein leading to a more valuable one.

stringer lode A shattered zone containing a network of small nonpersistent veins. *Syn:* STRINGER ZONE

string galvanometer An instrument for measuring small electrical current, consisting of a very fine conducting fiber stretched loosely between the poles of a strong magnet. Current in the fiber causes it to move laterally, perpendicular to the magnetic lines of force; the motion is measured by projecting a magnified shadow of the fiber onto a photographic film or paper. A multiple-string galvanometer with a "harp" of several strings was formerly used in seismic recorders. Now largely obsolete.

strip *1.* To remove from a quarry, or other open working, the overlying earth and disintegrated or barren surface rock. *2.* To mine coal, alongside a fault, or barrier.

striped ground Alternate stripes of fine and coarse debris on a slope. Other terms: stone stripes; stone-bordered strips; striate land; soil strips; soil stripes.

stripped plain A plain composed of flat-lying or gently tilted sedimentary rocks from which sediments have been removed down to some resistant bed which seems to have controlled the depth of erosion. *Cf.* DIP SLOPE

stripped structural terrace Relatively level surface resulting from the removal of weak rock that overlay a resistant layer.

stripper well An oil well producing such small quantities of oil that it receives special attention. Apparently so called from the milk cow which must be "stripped" by special manual effort, in order to yield the small quantity of milk.

strip thrust *See* DÉCOLLEMENT

stromatolite Laminated but otherwise structureless calcareous objects; commonly called fossil calcareous algae. *Syn:* CRYPTOZOON; COLLENIA; GYMNOSOLEN

stromatoporoidea Laminated, organic bodies made of calcium carbonate; probably an extinct order of hydrozoans.

strombolian Designating or pertaining to a type of volcanic eruption characterized by the appearance of fluid basaltic lava in a central crater, and in which the liquid lava is thrown up by explosions or fire fountains, some accumulating around the vent as spatter, scoria, and bombs. There is no eruption cloud.

strong *1.* Large; important; said of veins, dikes, etc. *2.* In Scotland: hard, not easily broken, e.g., strong coal, strong blaes.

strontianite A mineral, $SrCO_3$. Orthorhombic.

structural Pertaining to, part of, or consequent upon the geologic structure, as, a structural valley.

structural basin *1.* An elliptical or roughly circular structure in which the rock strata are inclined toward a central point.

structural control The apparent localization of mineral deposition by structural features.

structural crystallography Study of the internal arrangement and spacing of atoms and molecules composing solids.

structural fabric *See* FABRIC

structural feature Features produced in the rock by movements after deposition, and commonly after consolidation, of the rock.

structural geology Study of the structural (as opposed to the compositional) features of rocks, of the geographic distribution of the features and their causes.

structural high *See* HIGH, STRUCTURAL

structural low *See* LOW, STRUCTURAL

structural petrology Study of structure within rocks, particularly minute structure revealed by petrofabric investigation.

structural plain A gently sloping stratum plain.

structural terrace Where dipping strata locally assume a horizontal attitude.

structural trap One in which entrapment results from folding, faulting, or a combination of both.

structure *1.* The sum total of the structural features of an area. Not to be used as a synonym for structural feature, as, "this structure" meaning "this anticline." *2. Petrol:* One of the larger features of a rock mass, like bedding, flow banding, jointing, cleavage, and brecciation; also the sum total of such features. Contrasted with texture, *q.v.*

structure contour A contour line drawn through points of equal elevation on a stratum, key bed, or horizon, in order to depict the attitude of the rocks.

structure sections Diagrams to show the observed geologic structure on vertical faces or, more commonly to show the inferred geologic structure as it would appear on the sides of a vertical trench cut into the earth.

Strunian Uppermost Devonian, transitional into Carboniferous.

stuffed minerals A mineral having large interstices in its structure may accommodate various foreign ions in these holes; such a mineral is then said to be "stuffed." The "stuffing" may have considerable consequences on the stability of the mineral.

stylolite A term applied to parts of certain limestones which have a columnlike development; the "columns" being generally at right angles or highly inclined to the bedding planes, having grooved, sutured or striated sides, and irregular cross sections.

Styrian orogeny Early Miocene diastrophism.

subaerial Formed, existing, or taking place on the land surface. Contrasted with subaqueous.

subage Geologic time unit smaller than an age, corresponding to the time-rock unit substage.

subalkalic *1.* Refers to igneous rocks lacking alkali minerals other than feldspars. *2.* Formerly used to describe Pacific series of igneous rocks.

suballuvial bench The outer extension of the pediment which is covered by alluvium with a thickness equivalent to the depth of stream scour during flood but which may be hundreds or thousands of feet thick in its distal portion.

subangular A roundness grade in which definite effects of wear are shown, the fragments retaining their original form and the faces virtually untouched, but the edges and corners rounded off to some extent. Secondary corners are numerous (10 to 20). Class limits 0.15 to 0.25.

subaqueous gliding Subaqueous solifluction.

subarctic *1.* The region immediately south of the Arctic Circle and those which have similar climate. *2. Oceanog:* That region in which arctic and nonarctic waters are found together at the surface. *3. Geog:* The regions in which mean temperature is not higher than 50° F. for more than 4 months of the year and the mean temperature of the coldest month not more than 32° F.

subarid Subhumid, *q.v.;* moderately arid.

subarkose Sandstone containing 10 to 25% feldspar. *Cf.* FELDSPATHIC SANDSTONE; ARKOSIC SANDSTONE

subbituminous A coal Both weathering and nonagglomerating subbituminous coal having 11,000 or more, and less than 13,000 B.t.u. (moist, mineral-matter-free).

subbituminous B coal Both weathering and nonagglomerating subbituminous coal having 9500 or more, and less than 11,000 B.t.u. (moist, mineral-matter-free).

subbituminous C coal Both weathering and nonagglomerating subbituminous coal having 8300 or more, and less than 9500 B.t.u. (moist, mineral-matter-free).

subcapillary interstice An opening smaller than a capillary interstice, and theoretically so small that, at least in some parts, the attraction of the molecules of its walls extends through the entire space which it occupies.

Subcarboniferous Mississippian.

subcrop 1. Occurrence of strata on the undersurface of an inclusive stratigraphic unit that succeeds an important unconformity where overstepping is conspicuous. 2. Area within which a formation occurs directly beneath an unconformity.

subcrop map 1. Paleogeologic map. 2. Geologic map showing distribution of formations immediately overlying an unconformity.

subfacies 1. Subdivision of a broadly defined facies. 2. Subdivision of a metamorphic facies based on compositional differences rather than pressure-temperature differences.

subgelisol Unfrozen ground below pergelisol.

subgenus; subgenera A group of species which is judged to have special characters in common and which is distinct from other such groups, or subgenera.

subgraywacke Similar to graywacke but has less feldspar and more and better rounded quartz grains.

subhedral Intermediate between anhedral and euhedral.

Sub-Hercynian orogeny Mid-Late Cretaceous diastrophism.

subhumid Pertaining to a type of climate too dry for natural forest growth, as, the prairie region of the United States or the pampas of South America, and yet not so dry as to require irrigation; its original native vegetation is tall grass.

subjacent 1. Lying under or below. 2. *Petrol:* Applied to intrusive igneous bodies which enlarge downward and have no demonstrable base.

sublevation Erosion of unconsolidated sediment.

sublimation The transition of a substance directly from the solid state to the vapor state, or vice versa, without passing through the intermediate liquid stage.

sublittoral Refers to the benthonic zone extending from low tide level to the edge of the continental shelf or some comparable depth of water. It may be separated into inner and outer zones at some depth ranging from about 50 to about 300 feet. *Cf.* NERITIC; LITTORAL; BATHYAL

submarine bulge Fanlike sedimentary deposit, presumed to have been formed by turbidity currents, on the outer continental slope at the mouth of a submarine canyon. Term is applicable where data are inadequate to distinguish between deltas and alluvial fans.

submarine canyon Steep valley-like submarine depression crossing the continental margin region, except for isolated portions of outer ridges, less than 1 to more than 10 miles wide, less than 60 to more than 6000 feet deep. Commonest on the continental slope and shelf but some continue across the continental rise, also may cross marginal escarpments and landward slopes of trenches.

submarine delta Submarine sedimentary deposit formed at the mouth of a submarine canyon whose surface features resemble those of a subaerial delta.

submerged coast *See* SHORE LINE OF SUBMERGENCE

submergence A term which implies that part of the land area has become inundated by the sea but does not imply whether the sea rose over the land or the land sank beneath the sea. *Syn:* EMERGENCE

submetallic Applied to minerals having an imperfect metallic luster, as, columbite, wolframite.

subrounded A roundness grade in which considerable wear is shown. Edges and corners are rounded to smooth curves, and the area of the original faces is considerably reduced, but the original shape of the grain is still distinct. Secondary corners are much rounded and reduced in number. Class limits 0.25 to 0.40.

subsequent Tributary to and subsequent in development to a primary consequent stream, but itself consequent upon structure brought out in the degradation of the region; subconsequent: said of some streams and their valleys, as, a subsequent valley.

subsequent pluton A pluton that is later than the orogeny. *Syn:* POSTOROGENIC PLUTON

subsequent streams Streams that have grown headward by retrogressive erosion along belts of weak structure, and also for streams which, having been thus developed in one cycle, persist in the same courses in a following cycle. *See* LONGITUDINAL VALLEY

subsequent valleys Valleys cut by those streams which have grown by headward erosion along belts of weak structure, without relation to the initial trough lines.

subsidence *1.* A sinking of a large part of the earth's crust. *2.* Movement in which there is no free side and surface material is displaced vertically downward with little or no horizontal component.

subsilicic A term to connote rocks having a silica content of less than 52%.

subsoil A layer of the regolith, grading into the soil above and into unmodified rock waste below, which is less oxidized and hydrated than the soil proper and contains almost no organic matter, but is somewhat charged with and indurated by iron oxides and clay that has been leached down from the overlying soil.

subsolidus Chemical system below its melting point; reactions may occur in the solid state.

subspecies Recognizable subdivision of a species that occupies a more or less definite geographic or ecologic range and grades into neighboring subspecies.

substage Time-stratigraphic unit next lower in rank than stage. Zone has been much used for such a subdivision.

substitution, ionic *See* IONIC SUBSTITUTION

substratum An underlayer or stratum; a stratum, as of earth or rock, lying immediately under another. The hypothetical vitreous basaltic substratum lying beneath the lithosphere or outer granitic shell of the earth.

subsurface Underground; zone below the surface whose geologic features, principally stratigraphic and structural, are interpreted on the basis of drill records and various kinds of geophysical evidence.

subsurface geology The study of structure, thickness, facies, correlation, etc., of rock formations beneath land or sea-floor surfaces by means of drilling for oil or water, core drilling, and geophysical prospecting.

subsurface water All the water that exists below the surface of the solid earth.

subsystem Time-stratigraphic unit proposed for Mississippian or Pennsylvanian rocks to harmonize American stratigraphic classification with European in which these divisions correspond to parts of the Carboniferous System.

subterranean Being or lying under the surface of the earth.

subterranean stream A body of flowing water that passes through a very large interstice, such as a cave, cavern, or a group of large communicating interstices.

subterranean water *See* GROUND WATER

Sudetian orogeny Late Early Carboniferous diastrophism.

sugarloaf A conical hill or mountain comparatively bare of timber.

suite *1.* Collection of rock specimens from a single area, generally representing related igneous rocks. *2.* Collection of rock specimens of a single kind, e.g., granites from all over the world. *3.* Succession of closely associated sedimentary strata, especially a repeated sequence.

suites of igneous rocks *See* CONSANGUINITY

sulcus *Palentol:* Sinus, *q.v.*

sulfate A salt or ester of sulfuric acid; a compound containing the radical SO_4^{--}.

sulfide A compound of sulfur with one other more positive element or radical.

sulfide enrichment The enrichment of a deposit by replacement of one sulfide by another of higher valuable metal content, as pyrite by chalcocite.

sulfide zone That part of a lode or vein not yet oxidized by the air or surface water and containing sulfide minerals.

sulfite A salt or ester of sulfurous acid; a compound containing the radical SO_3^{--}.

sulfophile elements Elements which occur preferentially in minerals free of oxygen (or fluorine or chlorine), i.e., mostly as sulfides, selenides, tellurides, arsenides, antimonides, intermetallic compounds, native elements, etc. This group includes some of the chalcophile and some of the siderophile elements as classified by V. M. Goldschmidt.

sulfur Sulphur. The native element, S. Orthorhombic.

sulfur bacteria Bacteria that obtain their metabolic energy by the oxidation of sulfur in hydrogen sulfide or various other compounds and the production of elemental sulfur or sulfate ions.

sulfur balls Round or irregularly angular masses of pyrites occurring as common impurities in many coals. These balls usually consist of mixtures of pyrites and any of the following materials: clay, siderite, calcite, and colomite.

sulfuret In Pacific coast miners' phrase, the undecomposed metallic ores, usually sulfides. Chiefly applied to auriferous pyrites. Concentrate and sulfide are preferable. An old synonym for sulfide. *Obs.*

summation method Method of correcting seismic reflection arrival times for time spent by the wave in the low-velocity zone. On a continuous, reversed, and interlocked reflection profile between two holes shot at reasonable depths below the low-velocity zone, the low-velocity time under each geophone is equal to one-half the sum of the first arrival times (first kicks) received at that geophone from both shot holes minus the average high-velocity time, which is obtained by subtracting the uphole time from the first arrival time at the geophone at the shot hole on the opposite end of the profile.

summit concordance The equal or almost equal elevation of ridge tops or mountain summits that is thought to indicate the existence of ancient erosion surfaces of which only scattered patches are preserved.

sump A hole or pit which serves for the collection of quarry or mine waters.

sun opal Fire opal.

sunspot cycle Cycle of increasing and decreasing intensity of magnetic storms on the sun's surface of about 11 years' duration.

sunstone A variety of oligoclase feldspar containing numerous small inclusions which cause a delicate play of colors. Used as a gem.

super- [*Lat.*] Prefix meaning over, above, beyond.

superanthracite Coal intermediate between anthracite and graphite.

supercapillary interstice An opening larger than a capillary interstice. It is so large that water will not be held in it far above the level at which it is held by hydrostatic pressure. Water moving in it may form crosscurrents and eddies.

supercompressibility A term used in connection with the deviation from Boyle's law when natural gas is subjected to higher pressures. Natural gas becomes increasingly compressible with increasing pressure, and a deviation factor must be applied to such volumes.

supercooling Undercooling. The process of lowering the temperature of a phase or assemblage below the point or range at which a phase change should occur at equilibrium, i.e., making the system metastable by lowering the temperature. Generally refers to a liquid taken below its liquidus temperature.

supercritical At a temperature higher than the critical temperature.

superficial Surficial, *q.v.*

supergene Applied to ores or ore minerals that have been formed by generally descending water. Ores or minerals formed by downward enrichment. *Cf.* HYPOGENE

superheating 1. A process of adding more heat than is necessary to complete a given phase change (e.g., superheated steam). 2. In magmas, the accumulation of more heat than is necessary to cause essentially complete melting; in such cases the increase in temperature of the liquid above the liquidus temperature for any major mineral components is called the superheat.

superimposed drainage A natural drainage system that has been established on underlying rocks independently of their structure.

superindividual *Struct. petrol:* A fabric element composed of an aggregate of grains, commonly mineral grains produced by granulation of a single large crystal so that the smaller grains approximate the original orientation of the larger one.

superlattice A lattice some or all of whose translations are multiples of the translations of a particular lattice.

superposed stream A stream with a present course which was established on young rocks burying an old surface. With uplift, this course was maintained as the stream cut down through the young rocks to and into the old surface.

superposition The order in which rocks are placed above one another.

supersaturated solution A solution which contains more of the solute than is normally present when equilibrium is established between the saturated solution and undissolved solute, in other words, more than could be dissolved by prolonged stirring.

superstructure C. E. Wegmann's term for the upper nonmigmatitic phase of an evolving granitic magma.

supersystem Time-rock unit corresponding to era.

supragelisol Material above pergelisol.

supralittoral zone Shore zone immediately above high tide level, commonly the zone kept more or less moist by waves and spray.

supratenuous fold *1.* A fold in which the beds thicken toward the syncline because the basin subsided during sedimentation. *2.* A fold which shows a thinning of the formations upward above the crest of the fold.

surf The wave activity in the area between the shore line and the outermost limit of breakers.

surface *1.* The exterior part or outside of a body. *2.* The top of the ground; the soil, clay, etc., on the top of strata.

surface anomalies Irregularities at the earth's surface, in the weathering zone, or in near-surface beds which interfere with geophysical measurements.

surface corrections Corrections of geophysical measurements for surface anomalies and ground elevations.

surface density Density of the surface material within the range of the elevation differences of the gravitational survey.

surface deposits Ore bodies that are exposed and can be mined from the surface.

surface energy That additional amount of energy characterizing a substance as a consequence of its surface area.

surface geology The geology of the superficial deposits and of the surface of the fundamental rocks. *Cf.* AREAL GEOLOGY

surface interference Interference of geophysical measurements caused by surface anomalies or disturbances.

surface of no strain When a beam is bent the outer convex side is under tension, whereas the inner concave side is under compression. Somewhere near the middle is a surface that is neither lengthened nor shortened, hence is a surface of no strain.

surface tension That force that tends to reduce the total surface energy of a given phase; in general it results in a decrease in surface area.

surface thrust Erosion thrust, *q.v.*

surface velocity Initial velocity of the seismic wave in the earth's surface layer.

surface waves Waves which propagate along the earth's surface. Among these are the Love, Rayleigh, hydrodynamic, and coupled waves.

surficial; superficial Characteristic of, pertaining to, formed on, situated at, or occurring on the earth's surface; especially, consisting of unconsolidated residual, alluvial, or glacial deposits lying on the bedrock.

surf zone The area between the outermost breaker and the limit of wave uprush.

surge The name applied to wave motion with a period intermediate between that of the ordinary wind wave and that of the tide, say from 1/2 to 60 minutes. It is of low height; usually less than 0.3 foot.

surge channel Transverse channel cutting the outer edge of an organic reef in which the water level rises and falls as the result of wave and tidal action.

surge zone The region between the breaker zone and the 50–60 feet depth contour, where the effect of sea waves and swell produces oscillatory surges causing sediment transport and abrasive erosion.

survey To determine and delineate the form, extent, position, etc., of a tract of land, coast, harbor, or the like, by taking linear and angular measurements, and by applying the principles of geometry and trigonometry.

survey, cadastral A survey relating to land boundaries and subdivisions, made to create units suitable for transfer or to define the limitations of title. Derived from "cadastre," and meaning register of the real property of a political subdivision with details of area, ownership, and value, the term is now used to designate the surveys of the public lands of the United States.

survey, geologic A survey or investigation of the character and structure of the earth, of the physical changes which the earth's crust has undergone or is undergoing, and of the causes producing those changes.

survey, geological A general term used to designate an organization making geologic surveys and investigations.

surveying That branch of applied mathematics which teaches the art of determining the area of any portion of the earth's surface, the lengths and direction of bounding lines, the contour of the surface, etc., and accurately delineating the whole on paper.

surveyor One who makes a survey.

susceptibility, magnetic See MAGNETIC SUSCEPTIBILITY

suspended load In the process by which running water transports detritus, two factors are distinguished. The smaller particles are lifted far from the bottom, are sustained for long periods, and are distributed through the whole body of the current; they constitute the suspended load.

suspended turbidity current Turbidity current that overrides denser underlying water and is not in contact with the sea bottom.

suspended water Vadose water. Subsurface water occupying the zone of aeration.

suspended sediment Sediment which remains in suspension in water for a considerable period of time without contact with the bottom.

suspension current Turbidity current, *q.v.*

suspension load That part of sediment moved in suspension by a stream rather than that transported by traction on the bottom.

suture A line or mark of splitting open; a groove marking of a natural division or union. The lengthwise groove of a plum or similar fruit.

suture joint Same as stylolite, *q.v.*

swale *1.* A slight, marshy depression in generally level land. *2.* A depression in glacial ground moraine.

swallow hole Swallet; swallet hole. *Syn:* SINK; SINKHOLE, *q.v.*

swamp A low, spongy land, generally saturated with moisture and unfit either for agricultural or pastoral purposes. The term is commonly used as synonymous with bog and morass, but a swamp may be here and there studded with trees, while bogs and marshes are destitute of trees, though frequently covered with grasses and aquatic vegetation.

swamp theory The theory which holds that coal beds formed in the place where the plants grew. *See* AUTOCHTHONOUS COAL; IN SITU ORIGIN

swash The rush of water up onto the beach following the breaking of a wave. Uprush; run up.

swash mark A thin wavy line of fine sand, mica flakes, bits of seaweed and other debris produced by the swash. Wave mark.

S-wave A transverse body wave which travels through the interior of an elastic medium. Originally applied in earthquake seismology, where it was the second (S) type of wave to arrive at a recording station. *Syn:* DISTORTIONAL WAVE; EQUIVOLUMNAR WAVE; SECONDARY WAVE; SHEAR WAVE; TRANSVERSE WAVE

"sweet" gas or oil Natural gas containing little or none of the sulfur compounds which, when present, cause it to be "sour." *See* SOUR GAS

swell *1.* A low dome or quaqua-versal anticline of considerable areal extent. *2.* A large domed area within the nuclear part of the continent. *3.* An essentially equidimensional uplift without connotation of size or origin.

swell-and-swale topography Topography of ground moraine having low relief and gentle slopes.

syenite A plutonic igneous rock consisting principally of alkalic feldspar usually with one or more mafic minerals such as hornblende or biotite. The feldspar may be orthoclase, microcline, or perthite. A small amount of plagioclase may be present. A small amount of quartz is usually present but in some examples nepheline may take its place. Accessory minerals are sphene, apatite, and opaque oxide.

syenodiorite Monzonite.

syenogabbro An intrusive rock which contains orthoclase in addition to the normal gabbroic minerals. An orthoclase gabbro. The plutonic equivalent of trachybasalt.

sylvanite A mineral, $(Au,Ag)Te_2$. Monoclinic.

sylvinite Name given to mixtures of halite and sylvite mined as potassium ore.

sylvite A mineral, KCl. Isometric. The principal ore of potassium.

symbiosis The growth together of different species in a manner beneficial to the participants.

symbol *1: Crystallog:* (1) Any letter or sign used to designate a group of similar faces. (2) Miller indices. *2.* Geological maps are generally accompanied by special symbols to show the outcrops of formations and the attitude of bedding, foliation, faults, joints, etc.

symmetrical banding Bands of similar material on both sides of an opening, layer on layer.

symmetrical bedding Term proposed by Karl Andrée to indicate a balanced order in which lithologic types or facies follow one another. A symmetrical arrangement would be illustrated by 1-2-3-2-1-2-3-2-1, etc.

symmetrical fold A fold the axial plane of which is essentially vertical, i.e., the two limbs dip at similar angles.

symmetry 1. Correspondence in size, shape, and relative position of parts that are on opposite sides of a dividing line or median plane or that are distributed about a center or axis. 2. *Crystallog:* The property of having two or more directions that are alike in all physical and crystallographic properties because of either identity, or mirror-image relation, of the crystal structure with respect to these directions.

symmetry, axis of; rotation-axis An axis in a crystal such that a rotation of the crystal by 360°/n (n=1, 2, 3, 4, or 6) about this axis results in a perfect reproduction of the original pattern of the crystal structure, and therefore of all its directional properties such as tendency to form crystal faces, ability to reflect X rays, optical, thermal, and elastic properties, etc.

symmetry, plane of; mirror; mirror plane of symmetry A plane through a crystal such that the pattern of atomic structure is precisely reproduced on each side of the plane as if it were the mirror image of that on the other side of the plane. In consequence, there is an equal tendency for pairs of crystal faces to form so that one of the pair is the mirror image of the other as

reflected in this plane; likewise, vectorial properties, such as conductivity, optical constants, and elastic properties, are symmetrical with respect to such a mirror plane.

syn- [*Gr.*] A prefix meaning with, along with, together, at the same time.

synaeresis Separation of fluid from a gel.

synantetic A term proposed by J. J. Sederholm and applied to those primary minerals in igneous rocks which are formed by the reaction of two other minerals, as in kelyphite rims, reaction rims, etc.

synchronal Occurring at the same time.

synclinal *Geol:* Characteristic of, pertaining to, occurring or situated in or forming a syncline. *Ant:* ANTICLINAL

synclinal axis *Geol:* The central line of a syncline, toward which the beds dip from both sides.

synclinal mountain *See* ANTICLINAL MOUNTAIN

syncline A fold in rocks in which the strata dip inward from both sides toward the axis. *Ant:* ANTICLINE

synclinorium A broad regional syncline on which are superimposed minor folds.

syneresis A spontaneous throwing off of water by a gel during aging. In a hardened or set gel the shrinkage resulting from loss of water causes cracking. *See* SEPTARIAN

syngenesis The process by which mineral deposits were formed simultaneously and in a similar manner to the rock enclosing them. *See* EPIGENESIS

syngenetic A term now generally applied to mineral or ore deposits formed contemporaneously with the enclosing rocks, as contrasted with epigenetic deposits, which are of later origin than the enclosing rocks.

synkinematic granitization Granitization taking place essentially simultaneously with orogeny.

synonym *Tax:* Different names for one and the same thing.

synonymy (-ies) The list of all prior references to a genus or species including all names which have been used to refer to that particular form.

synoptic *Meteor:* Atmospheric conditions existing at a given time over an extended region, e.g., a synoptic weather map, which is drawn from observations taken simultaneously at a network of stations over a large area, thus giving a general view of weather conditions.

synoptic diagram Composite fabric diagram produced by combining several diagrams in such a way that the ab-planes coincide.

synorogenic; synkinematic; syntectonic; synchronous Adjectives to describe some process, usually the emplacement of plutons or the recrystallization of metamorphic rocks, that is contemporaneous with orogeny.

synplutonic dike Dike more or less contemporaneous with the plutonic rock in which it occurs.

synsedimentary Accompanying deposition.

syntaxial Applied to overgrowths retaining crystallographic continuity.

syntaxis Convergence of mountain ranges at a common center; *Ant:* VIRGATION

syntaxy Similar crystallographic orientation in a mineral grain and its overgrowth.

syntectic A term suggested by Franz Loewinson-Lessing (1899) and applied to magmas produced by syntexis, and also used substantively to connote the magmas themselves.

syntectite Rock produced by melting of older rocks.

syntectonic Principal tectonic; synkinematic; synorogenic, *q.v.*

synthetic faults Subsidiary faults parallel to the master fault.

synthetic group Rock stratigraphic unit consisting of two or more formations which are associated because of similarities or close relationships between their fossils or lithologic characters.

syntype *1.* Any specimen of the author's original material when no holotype was designated. *2.* Any of a series of specimens described as "cotypes" of equal rank. *3.* One of two or more specimens to which a single name was equally attached in original publication. Term to be used in review and revision only. *4.* Paratype. (Usage not recommended.)

system *1.* Designates rocks formed during a fundamental chronologic unit, a period, e.g., Devonian system. *2. Crystallog:* The division of first rank, in the classification of crystals according to form. The six systems ordinarily recognized are the isometric, tetragonal, hexagonal, orthorhombic (or rhombic), monoclinic, and triclinic; some divide the hexagonal system into hexagonal and trigonal.

systematics Study of similarities and differences in organisms and their relations; includes taxonomy and classification.

T

tabetisol Unfrozen ground above, within, or below pergelisol.

tableland *1.* Land elevated much above the level of the sea and generally offering no considerable irregularities of surface. *2.* A flat or undulating elevated area; a plateau or mesa.

tablemount A seamount (roughly circular or elliptical in plan) generally deeper than 100 fathoms, the top of which has a comparatively smooth platform. *Syn:* SEAMOUNT; GUYOT

tachygenesis The extreme crowding and eventually the loss of those primitive phyletic stages which are represented early in the life of the individual. *Syn:* ACCELERATION

tachylyte A volcanic glass of basaltic composition. *See* SIDEROMELANE

tachymeter A surveying instrument designed for use in rapid determination of distance, direction, and difference of elevation from a single observation, using a short base, which may be an integral part of the instrument. Range finders, *q.v.*, with self-contained bases belong to this class.

Taconian Lower Cambrian.

Taconian orogeny Post-Ordovician diastrophism.

taconite A ferruginous chert representing a complete replacement of greenalite rock by silica, iron ores, and ferruginous amphiboles. *See* ITABIRITE; JASPILITE

tactite A rock of complex mineralogical composition formed by contact metamorphism and metasomatism of carbonate rock. *See* CALC-FLINTA; CALC-SILICATE HORNFELS; LIMURITE; PNEUMATOLYTIC HORNFELS; SKARN

Taghanican Upper Middle Devonian.

taiga [*Russ.*] The cold, swampy, forested region of the north which begins where the tundra leaves off.

tailings Those portions of washed ore that are regarded as too poor to be treated further. Used especially of the debris from stamp mills or other ore-dressing machinery, as distinguished from material (concentrates) that is to be smelted.

talc A mineral, $Mg_3Si_4O_{10}(OH)_2$, commonly in foliated masses. Very soft (H=1), has a greasy or soapy feel, and is easily cut. Impure massive material is called steatite or soapstone. A common mineral of metamorphosed mafic rocks.

talcum Talc; soapstone.

talik [*Russ.*] *1.* A layer of unfrozen ground between the seasonal frozen ground (active layer) and the permafrost. *2.* An unfrozen layer within the permafrost. *Syn:* TABETISOL

talus A collection of fallen disintegrated material which has formed a slope at the foot of a steeper declivity. *Syn:* SCREE

talus-creep The slow downslope

movement of a talus or scree, or of any of the material of a talus or scree.

talus slope See TALUS

Tamiskamian Precambrian system of late Archeozoic age, younger than Kewatinian.

tangent A straight line that touches, but does not transect, a curved surface.

tangential fault Fault with dominantly horizontal movement; contrasts with radial fault.

tangential section A section of a cylindrical organ, such as a stem, cut lengthwise and at right angles to the radius of the organ.

tangential stress See SHEARING STRESS

tangential wave Shear wave.

tangent screw A slow-motion screw tangent to an arc or circle. Usually it has a graduated head and is used to control the inclination of the telescope of a surveying instrument. *Cf.* GRADIENT SCREW

tank 1. Tanks are natural depressions in an impervious stratum, in which rain or snow water collects and is preserved the greater portion of a year. 2. A natural or artificial pool or water hole in a wash. Local in arid West.

tantalite A mineral, the part with Ta>Nb of the orthorhombic columbite-tantalite series, $(Fe,Mn)(Ta,Nb)_2O_6$. The principal ore of tantalum.

taphrogenesis Broad vertical movements with high-angle faulting.

taphrogeny Type of orogeny that forms rift valleys by tension.

taphrogeosyncline A sediment-filled, deeply depressed fault block bounded by one or more high-angle faults.

tapiolite A mineral, the tetragonal dimorph of tantalite, $(Fe,-$ $Mn)(Ta,Nb)_2O_6$. An ore of tantalum.

tarn [<*Scand.*] A small mountain lake or pool, especially one that occupies an ice-gouged basin on the floor of a cirque.

tarnish *Mineral:* The thin film, of color different from that of a fracture, that forms on the exposed surface of a mineral, especially a metallic mineral, such as columbite.

tautonomy Relations that exist if the same word is used for both the generic and specific name in the name of a species.

tautonym A name in which the specific name merely repeats the generic, as, Linaria Linaria Karst.

tautozonal facies Facies belonging to the same crystal zone.

taxion Taxon.

taxon A named group of organisms, i.e., a species, genus, family, etc.

taxonomic categories The principal grades of taxonomic units in descending order are kingdom, class, order, family, genus, and species. Intermediate grades are identified by these same names modified by the prefixes super-, sub-, and infra-. A few other grades such as cohort, tribe, and section also may be recognized.

taxonomy 1. The systematic classification of plants and animals. *Syn:* SYSTEMATICS. 2. The science of the classification and arrangement, according to relationships, of living organisms.

T-chert Tectonically controlled chert occurring in irregular masses related to fractures and ore bodies.

tchornozem; tschernosem See CHERNOZEM

T.D. Abbreviation for total depth. The greatest depth reached by a drill hole.

T.D. curve *See* TIME-DISTANCE CURVE

T²-D² curve In reflection prospecting, a plot of squares of reflection times versus squares of shot-detector distances. If the reflecting horizon is horizontal, the slope of the T²-D² plot is a straight line and is inversely proportional to the square of the average velocity to the reflecting bed.

TΔT process. A method of obtaining or measuring the vertical velocity of sound through subsurface sediments by use of the reflection seismograph technique.

t direction *Struct. petrol:* Direction of movement in gliding plane.

T-dolostone Tectonically controlled dolostone occurring in irregular masses related to fracture systems.

tear fault Strike-slip fault that trends transverse to the strike of the deformed rocks. *Syn:* TRANSCURRENT; TRANSVERSE FAULT

tectofacies *1.* A group of strata of different tectonic aspect from laterally equivalent strata. *2.* Laterally varying tectonic aspects of a stratigraphic unit.

tectogene A deeply down-buckled belt of sediments within a eugeosyncline.

tectogenesis The processes by which rocks are deformed; more specifically, the formation of folds, faults, joints, and cleavage. Orogenesis, a term often used for these processes, should be restricted to processes resulting in morphological features.

tectonic Of, pertaining to, or designating the rock structure and external forms resulting from the deformation of the earth's crust. As applied to earthquakes, it is used to describe shocks not due to volcanic action or to collapse of caverns or landslides.

tectonic axes *See* AXES, TECTONIC

tectonic basin A surface basin that owes its origin directly to deformation of the earth's crust, whether the result of warping or of fracture, or both. Tectonic basins are usually somewhat flat-bottomed or gently undulating.

tectonic breccia An aggregation of angular coarse rocks formed as the result of tectonic movement. Included in this category are fault breccias, especially those associated with great overthrust sheets, and fold breccias or Riebungsbreccia.

tectonic conglomerate A coarse clastic rock produced by deformation of brittle, closely jointed rocks. Rotation of the joint block and granulation and crushing sometimes produce a rock that closely simulates a normal conglomerate. *Syn:* CRUSH CONGLOMERATE

tectonic enclave Body of rock completely isolated by plastic structural disturbance from similar material with which it was once continuous.

tectonic fabric Particle or crystal arrangement determined by movement within a rock.

tectonic facies Rocks owing their present characters to tectonic movements, e.g., mylonites, some phyllites, etc.

tectonic framework The structural elements of a region including the rising, stable, and subsiding areas.

tectonic land Land raised by tectonic movements as contrasted with land formed by volcanism or sedimentary deposition.

tectonic map One on which are shown areas or lines of major structural features produced by uplift, downwarp, or faulting, together with the major lineation within such features. The term is generally applied to maps covering large areas, while maps showing the same features in smaller areas are called structural maps.

tectonic rotation Movement in a tectonite that involves internal rotation in the direction of transport.

tectonics Study of the broader structural features of the earth and their causes.

tectonic transport Movement within a rock by flowage or slippage.

tectonism 1. Crustal instability. 2. The structural behavior of an element of the earth's crust during, or between, major cycles of sedimentation.

tectonite Rock whose minute structure has been produced by internal movement of its parts without these parts losing spacial continuity or the rock its individuality.

tectonosphere 1. Zone within the earth where crustal movements originate. 2. Crust of the earth in which tectonic adjustments occur. 3. Earth shell consisting of sial, salsima, and sima layers.

tectosilicates Silicate structures in which the SiO4 tetrahedra share all oxygens with adjacent tetrahedra, to build up a three-dimensional network structure. Examples are quartz and feldspar. See SILICATES, CLASSIFICATION

tectotope A stratum or succession of strata with characteristics indicating accumulation in a common tectonic environment.

teilchron Geologic time unit corresponding to a teilzone.

teilzone The local stratigraphic range of a given species or genus of plant or animal.

tektite Black to greenish glassy objects of various rounded shapes of doubtful extraterrestrial origin; chemical composition is different from obsidian and resembles that of argillaceous sediments.

telemagmatic Applied to deposits far from the intrusive center.

telescoped ore deposits Ore deposits representing most of the metals of most of the plutonic ore-sequence zones within short horizontal or vertical distances.

telescoping Differential acceleration or retardation.

telethermal The ore deposits produced at or near the surface from ascending hydrothermal solutions and representing the terminal phase of its activity.

tellurate A salt or ester of telluric acid; a compound containing the radical TeO4^{--}.

telluric Pertaining to the earth, particularly the depths of the earth.

telluric currents Natural electric currents that flow on or near the earth's surface in large sheets. Methods have been developed for using these currents to make resistivity surveys. Syn: EARTH CURRENTS

telluric diurnal variation See DIURNAL VARIATION, TELLURIC

telluride A compound of tellurium with one other more positive element or radical.

tellurite A salt or ester of tellurous acid; a compound containing the radical TeO3^{--}.

temblor [Sp.] In the United States, an earthquake.

temperature coefficient A numerical value indicating the relation between the change in temperature and a simultaneous change in some other property, as, solubility, volume, electrical resistance, etc.

temperature correction Observations made with geophysical instruments, such as the magnetometer, pendulum, torsion balance, etc., are not independent of temperature as temperature changes result in expansion or contraction of parts of the delicate measuring instruments. The temperature correction is applied to the observed values to reduce them to a standard temperature.

temperature gradient Rate of change of temperature with distance in a specified direction. *Cf.* LAPSE RATE

temperature well logging A method of determining the temperature along the bore of a drill hole. A temperature well log is a graph showing the temperature as a function of depth in the drill hole. *Syn:* THERMAL LOGGING

temperature zone An area or latitudinal belt on the earth delimited by given temperature conditions.

template; templet A gauge, pattern, or mold; commonly a thin plate or board or a light frame used as a guide to the form of work to be executed. In gravity and magnetic interpretation a chart with holes in a certain array to select values from a map to be used in calculation of derivatives or other functions of the field.

temporary base level The lowest level to which the stream can bring its valley under the conditions which exist when the flat is developed. It is therefore a temporary base level and serves as the limit below which tributary streams may not cut.

temporary hardness Hardness of water resulting from the presence of dissolved calcium bicarbonate; it can be removed by boiling.

tennantite A mineral, the part with As>Sb of the tetrahedrite-tennantite series, $Cu_3(As,Sb)S_3$. Isometric. An important ore of copper and silver. *Syn:* GRAY COPPER ORE; FAHLORE

Tennesseean *1.* Upper Mississippian, includes Meramecian and Chesterian. *2.* System between Waverlyan and Pennsylvanian. *Obs.*

tenor The percentage or average metallic content of an ore, matte, or impure metal.

tensile strength The ability of a material to resist a stress tending to stretch it or to pull it apart. *Cf.* YOUNG'S MODULUS; HOOKE'S LAW

tensile stress A normal stress that tends to pull apart the material on the opposite sides of a real or imaginary plane.

tension A system of forces tending to draw asunder the parts of a body, especially of a line, cord, or sheet, combined with an equal and opposite system of resisting forces of cohesion holding the parts of the body together; stress caused by pulling. Opposed to compression, and distinguished from torsion.

tension fault A fault produced by tension; sometimes used incorrectly as synonymous with gravity fault or normal fault.

tension fracture A fracture that is the result of stresses that tend to pull material apart.

tension joint A joint that is a tension fracture, *q.v.*

tepee butte *1.* A conical erosion hill, so named from its resemblance to the Indian wigwam or tepee. *2.* A hill formed by a columnar bioherm found in the Cretaceous Pierre shale of Colorado, containing enormous numbers of the small pelecypod, Lucina.

tepetate *See* CALICHE

tephra A collective term for all clastic volcanic materials which during an eruption are ejected from a crater or from some other type of vent and transported through the air; includes volcanic dust, ash, cinders, lapilli, scoria, pumice, bombs, and blocks. *Syn:* VOLCANIC EJECTA

tephrochronology A chronology based on the dating of volcanic ash layers.

tephroite A mineral, Mn_2SiO_4, a member of the olivine group. Orthorhombic.

terminal moraine A moraine formed across the course of a glacier at its farthest advance, at or near a relatively stationary edge, or at places marking the termination of important glacial advances.

terminus The outer or distal margin of the ablation area of a glacier.

ternary, *adj.* Term applied to a triangle diagram which is a graphic depiction of a three-component mixture.

ternary system A system of three components, e.g., $CaO-Al_2O_3-SiO_2$.

terrace Benches and terraces are relatively flat, horizontal, or gently inclined surfaces, sometimes long and narrow, which are bounded by a steeper ascending slope on one side and by a steeper descending slope on the opposite side. Both forms, when typically developed, are steplike in character.

terraced pools Shallow circular pools with rims arranged terracelike fashion built by calcareous secreting algae on coral reef surfaces.

terracettes Ledges of earth on steep hillsides, varying from a few inches to four or five feet in height and averaging two to four feet in width, formed as a result of the development of slippage planes in, and subsequent slumping of, the soil or mantle. *Syn:* TERRACETTE SLOPES

terra cotta The "baked earth" of the Italians. Kiln-burnt clay assuming a peculiar reddish-brown color fashioned into vases, statuettes, and other moldings.

terra-cotta clay A loose term that might include any clay used in the manufacture of terra cotta.

terrain *1.* A complex group of strata accumulated within a definite geologic epoch. *2.* Area of ground considered as to its extent and natural features in relation to its use for a particular operation. *3.* The tract or region of ground immediately under observation.

terrain analysis The process of interpreting a geographical area to determine the effect of the natural and man-made features on military operations. This includes the influence of weather and climate on these features.

terrain or **topographic correction** A correction applied to observed values obtained in geophysical surveys in order to remove the effect of variations to the observations due to the topography in the vicinity of the sites of observation.

terrain factors Consist of land forms, drainage features, ground, vegetation, and cultural features on man-made changes in the earth's surface.

terrane *1.* A formation or group of formations. *2.* The area or surface over which a particular rock or group of rocks is prevalent. *3.* An area or region considered in relation to its fitness or suitability for some specific purpose.

terra rossa Residual red clay mantling limestone bedrock.

terrestrial Consisting of or pertaining to the land.

terrestrial magnetism 1. The magnetic field of the earth as a whole. 2. The science which treats the laws of magnetism and the application of these laws in surveying, navigation, etc.

terrigenous Produced from or of the earth. *Geol:* Deposited in or on the earth's crust.

terrometer The name of one of the devices designed for the detection of buried metallic objects at shallow depths. It consists of a frame on which are mounted an electromagnetic oscillator and a receiver having fixed positions with respect to each other. *Cf.* TREASURE FINDER

Tertiary The earlier of the two geologic periods comprised in the Cenozoic era, in the classification generally used. Also, the system of strata deposited during that period.

test 1. Hard covering or supporting structure of some invertebrate animals; may be enclosed within an outer layer of living tissue; a shell. 2. An oil well, particularly a wildcat.

test pit A shallow shaft or excavation made to determine the existence, extent, or grade of a mineral deposit or to determine the fitness of an area for engineering works such as buildings or bridges.

tetartohedral Having or requiring one-fourth the number of planes or faces required by the symmetry of the holohedral class of the same system.

Tethys Elongated east-west seaway that separated Europe and Africa and extended across southern Asia in Pre-Tertiary time.

teton A rocky mountain crest of rugged aspect. Local in Northwest.

Tetrabranchiata Subclass of Cephalopoda with external shells; includes nautiloids and ammonoids.

tetracoral Coral with fourfold symmetry. Ord.-Perm.

tetragonal system That system of crystals in which the forms are referred to three mutually perpendicular axes, two of which are of equal length and the third longer or shorter.

tetrahedral radius The radius of an atom which has four covalent bonds with other atoms.

tetrahedrite A mineral, the part with Sb$>$As of the tetrahedrite-tennantite series, $Cu_3(Sb,As)S_3$. Silver, zinc, iron, and mercury, may replace part of the copper. Isometric. An important ore of copper and silver. *Syn:* GRAY COPPER ORE; FAHLORE

tetrahedron A crystal form in the isometric system, having four faces each with equal intercepts on all three axes.

tetrahedron hypothesis The hypothesis that the earth, because of shrinking, tends to assume the form of a tetrahedron.

tetrahexahedron Isometric crystal form of cubic habit with 24 faces each parallel to one crystallographic axis and cutting the others at unequal distances.

Tetrapoda Subphylum of vertebrates; animals equipped with four limbs, mostly terrestrial. Dev.-Rec.

texture 1. Geometrical aspects of the component particles of a rock, including size, shape, and arrangement. 2. The relative spacing of drainage lines in country which has undergone fluvial and pluvial dissection.

texture ratio *Geomorph:* Ratio of the greatest number of channels crossed by a contour line to the length of the upper basin perimeter intercept; a measure of topographic scale or texture, closely related to drainage density. *Symbol:* T

thalassic Of or pertaining to the sea.

thalassography Oceanography, *q.v. See* LIMNOLOGY

thalassology Study of the sea.

thalassophile elements Elements whose amount in sea water is greater than, or a large fraction of, the total amount supplied to the sea by weathering and erosion. Carbon (C), bromine (Br), iodine (I), boron (B), sulfur (S), and sodium (Na).

Thallophyta Division of nonvascular plants, those without differentiated roots, stems, or leaves; includes algae and fungi.

thalweg [*Ger.*] *1. Hydraul:* The line joining the deepest points of a stream channel. *2.* By many geomorphologists the term is used as a synonym for valley profile.

thanatocoenose; thanatocoenosis A group of organisms brought together after death.

Thanetian Lower Upper Paleocene.

thaw depression Hollow formed by the melting of ice in perennially frozen ground.

thawing index Number of degree-days between lowest and highest points on a curve of cumulative degree-days versus time for one thawing season; a measure of combined duration and magnitude of above-freezing temperature during a thawing season.

thawing season Time during which average daily temperature is generally above freezing.

thaw lake *1.* Lake or pond in permafrost area whose basin is formed by thawing of ground

ice. *See* THERMOKARST. *2.* A pool of water on the surface of sea ice or large glaciers formed by accumulation of melt water.

theca External skeleton of a coelenterate.

thenardite A mineral, Na_2SO_4. Orthorhombic.

theodolite An instrument for measuring horizontal and vertical angles. It consists of a telescope mounted so as to swivel vertically and secured to a revolvable table carrying a vernier for reading horizontal angles. Usually a graduated circle for vertical angles and a compass are included. Similar to but more precise than a transit.

Theria Subclass of vertebrates, includes placentals and marsupials.

therm A quantity of heat equivalent to 100,000 British thermal units.

thermal Hot; warm. Applied to springs which discharge water heated by natural agencies.

thermal analysis Determination of the temperatures at which phase changes occur during the heating of clay and other substances by measuring the heat evolved or absorbed. Differential thermal analysis.

thermal aureole *1.* The zone of heating surrounding an intrusion. *2.* The zone of contact effects, in part due to the heating, surrounding an intrusion.

thermal or **heat conductivity** A quantity for classifying materials according to their ability to conduct heat. The amount of heat passing through unit cross section in unit time under the influence of unit heat gradient. In the c.g.s. system the thermal conductivity is expressed in calories per centimeter per second per degree centigrade.

thermal-detection methods Geophysical thermal-detection methods involve the location of objects by their heat radiation. Airplanes can be located by the heat issuing from their exhaust pipes; icebergs have been located at appreciable distances by such detection methods. *See* THERMAL PROSPECTING

thermal diffusivity *See* DIFFUSIVITY, THERMAL

thermal logging *See* TEMPERATURE WELL LOGGING

thermal metamorphism Metamorphism in which heat is the principal agent causing reconstitution.

thermal prospecting A system of geophysical prospecting based on measuring underground temperatures or temperature gradients and relating their irregularities to geological deformation.

thermal stratification The waters of deep lakes and seas are generally not of uniform temperature; they may be divided into three strata or layers on the basis of their temperatures. The upper layer, known as the epilimnion, has a nearly uniform temperature since it is stirred by wind and convection currents. The bottom stratum is called the hypolimnion. Its waters are relatively stagnant, generally low in oxygen, and they have a fairly uniform but lower temperature than do the upper layers. The middle layer is called the thermocline. It is the layer having rapid decrease of temperature with depth. It is fairly sharply defined from the epilimnion but grades into the hypolimnion.

thermal unit A unit chosen for the comparison or calculation of quantities of heat, as, the calorie, or the British thermal unit.

thermionic emission The emission of electrons from a hot cathode, as in a vacuum tube. *Syn:* RICHARDSON EFFECT

thermistor A heat-sensitive device used in bolometric measurements of power in high-frequency electric circuits.

thermochemistry Chemistry as related to temperature.

thermocline The zone in a lake between the epilimnion and the hypolimnion in which the change in temperature with depth exceeds $1°$ C. per meter.

thermocouple A union of two conductors, as, bars or wires of dissimilar metals joined at their extremities for producing a thermoelectric current. *Syn:* THERMOJUNCTION; THERMOELECTRIC COUPLE

thermodiffusion A process whereby certain dissolved "molecules" (or their constituent ions) diffuse toward the chilled margins of a magma chamber; the driving force is the concentration gradient established in the liquid owing to the precipitation of the material at the margins. The effective rate of movement of materials is greatly enhanced by a combination of thermodiffusion with convection.

thermodynamic process If on comparing the state of a thermodynamic system at two different times there is a difference in any macroscopic property of the system, then a process has taken place.

thermodynamics The mathematical treatment of the relation of heat to mechanical and other forms of energy.

thermoelectric couple Thermocouple, *q.v.*

thermoelectric pyrometer An instrument for measuring temperatures based on the principle of thermoelectricity and consisting essentially of a thermocouple and an indicating scale device.

thermograph A self-registering thermometer.

thermojunction Thermocouple, *q.v.*

thermokarst Settling or caving of the ground due to melting of ground ice.

thermokarst pit Steep-walled depression formed by thermokarst processes.

thermokarst topography Irregular land surface containing depressions formed by thermokarst processes; it resembles the karst topography resulting from solution of limestone.

thermoluminescence The property possessed by many minerals of emitting visible light when heated. It results from release of energy stored as electron displacements in the crystal lattice.

thermometry The measurement of temperature.

thermopile An apparatus consisting of a number of thermoelectric couples, as of antimony and bismuth or copper sulfide and German silver, combined so as to multiply the effect. It is used to generate electric currents for certain purposes, and in a sensitive form it is used for determining slight differences in temperature.

thermostat An automatic device for regulating temperature, utilizing either the differential expansion of solids, liquids, or gases subjected to heat. Some thermostats utilize the principle of the thermopile. *Syn:* THERMOREGULATOR

thick bands A field term that, in accordance with an arbitrary scale established for use in describing banded coal, denotes vitrain bands with a range of thickness from 5.0 to 50.0 mm. (about 1/2 to 2.0 inches). *Cf.* THIN, MEDIUM, and VERY THICK BANDS

thick-bedded Relative term applied to strata occurring in uniformly constituted beds variously defined as exceeding 2 1/2 inches to 4 feet in thickness.

thick coal or **seam** In England, a coal seam of greater thickness than, say, 8 or 10 feet (sometimes as much as 130 feet), or those which are worked in two or more stages or lifts.

thin bands A field term that, in accordance with an arbitrary scale established for use in describing banded coal, denotes vitrain bands with a range of thickness from 0.5 to 2.0 mm. (about 1/50 to 1/12 inch) thick. *Cf.* MEDIUM, THICK, and VERY THICK BANDS

thin-bedded *1.* Applied to shale to indicate it is easy to split. *2.* Occurring in relatively thin layers or laminae.

thinolite A tufa deposit of calcium carbonate occurring on an enormous scale in northwestern Nevada; also occurs about Mono Lake, California. It forms layers of interlaced crystals of a pale yellow or light-brown color and often skeleton structure except when covered by a subsequent deposit of calcium carbonate.

thin out A stratum is said to thin out when it becomes thinner and thinner as it is traced in any direction, till it finally disappears and its place is taken by some other stratum. *Syn:* PINCH OUT; WEDGE OUT; LENSING

thin section A fragment of rock or mineral ground to paper thinness, (usually 0.03 mm.) polished, and mounted between glasses as a microscopical slide.

thixotropy The property exhibited by some gels of becoming fluid when shaken. The change is reversible.

tholeiite *See* BASALT

tholeiitic magma A type of basaltic magma containing little or no olivine and yielding oversaturated late differentiates. Characteristically the primary magma from which the Pacific series, *q.v.*, of rocks is derived. Also called the nonporphyritic central magma type. Opposite to the olivine-basalt magma type or Atlantic series, *q.v.*

thorax Central part of the arthropod body consisting of several segments that generally are movable.

thorianite A mineral, ThO_2, commonly containing some uranium. Isometric.

thorite A mineral, essentially $ThSiO_4$, commonly altered and metamict. Tetragonal.

thread of the current The thread of the current, the mathematical line rapidity, which varies every day and in every stream, according to the quantity of water and the section of its bed, exceeds by about one-fifth the average speed of the river.

three-dimension dip *Seis. prospecting:* The true dip of a reflection or refraction horizon found by exploration and calculation. *Syn:* TRUE DIP

three-faceted stone Dreikanter, *q.v.*

three-layer structure Structure in minerals composed of repeated layered units each consisting of an aluminum octahedral layer between two silicon tetrahedral layers as in muscovite. Both Al and Si can be replaced by other elements.

three-point method *1.* Geometric determination of dip and strike in any regular plane whose elevation is known at three ac-

curately located points. *2.* Determination of geographic positio inside or outside of the triangl formed by the intersection o bearing lines from three triangu lation stations.

threshold Low necks of san which frequently divide lakes in to two basins and in the dese separate the bajirs one from th other.

threshold pressure Yield poin The stress at which plastic defor mation begins.

threshold velocity (wind erosio) The minimum velocity at whic wind will begin moving particle of sand or other soil material.

throw *1.* The amount of vertic displacement occasioned by fault. *2.* More generally, use for the vertical component of th net slip.

throwing clay Clay plastic enoug to be shaped on a potter's whee

thrown Faulted or broken up b a fault.

thrust Fault occurring in pla of the overturned limb of fold.

thrust fault A reverse fault th is characterized by a low ang of inclination with reference a horizontal plane. *See* FAULT

thrust plane The plane of thrust or reversed fault.

thrust scarps Sinuous scarp marking the front of a low-ang thrust sheet or block. Original defined as a fault scarp at th outcrops of steeply inclined r verse faults.

thrust sheet The block above thrust fault.

Thulean province A region Tertiary volcanic activity inclu ing Northwest Britain, Icelan and the Faeroes.

thunder egg Geodelike bo commonly containing opal, agat

or chalcedony weathered out of welded tuff or lava.

Thuringian Upper Permian.

Ti Abbreviation for titanite or sphene in normative rock calculations.

tidal bore *See* BORE

tidal channel *See* TIDAL INLET

tidal compartment The tidal compartment of a river may be defined as that portion of the stream which intervenes between the area of unimpeded tidal action and that in which there is a complete cessation or absence of tidal action.

tidal constant Either of two parameters, which combined completely specify a simple tide, the first being the amplitude of a tide (the elevation above mean sea level) and the second its epoch or the time between the moon's meridian passage and the ensuing high tide.

tidal correction A correction applied to gravitational observations to remove the effect of earth tides on gravimetric observations. The value of gravity at any point varies in a cyclical manner during the course of a day due to the changing positions of the sun and the moon relative to the area being investigated. The tidal correction commonly is included in the drift correction and may be determined by a series of observations at a fixed base station.

tidal or periodic current A current, caused by the tide-producing forces of the moon and the sun, which is a part of the same general movement of the sea manifested in the vertical rise and fall of the tides. *See* FLOOD CURRENT; EBB CURRENT

tidal datum A plane defined by reference to a certain phase of tide.

tidal day The time of the rotation of the earth with respect to the moon, or the interval between two successive upper transits of the moon over the meridian of a place, about 24.84 solar hours (24 hours and 50 minutes) in length or 1.035 times as great as the mean solar day.

tidal flat A marshy or muddy land area which is covered and uncovered by the rise and fall of the tide.

tidal friction The frictional effect of the tides, especially in shallow waters, lengthening the tidal epoch and tending to retard the rotational speed of the earth and so increase very slowly the length of the day.

tidal inlet *1.* A natural inlet maintained by tidal flow. *2.* Loosely, any inlet in which the tide ebbs and flows. Also tidal outlet.

tidal marsh *See* TIDAL FLAT

tidal pool A pool of water remaining on a beach or reef after recession of the tide.

tidal prism The total amount of water that flows into the harbor or out again with movement of the tide, excluding any freshwater flow.

tidal range The difference between the level of water at high tide and low tide.

tidal theory A theory of origin of the solar system involving tidal forces set upon the sun by the near approach of another star; the J. H. Jeans and Harold Jeffreys theory.

tidal wave *1.* In astronomical usage, restricted to the periodic variations of sea level produced by the gravitational attractions of the sun and the moon. *2.* Commonly and incorrectly used for a large sea wave caused by a submarine earthquake or volcanic eruption, properly called a tsunami, *q.v. 3.* Sometimes used for a large sea wave caused by a hurricane wind or a severe gale, properly called a storm wave.

tide The periodic rise and fall of oceans and bodies of water connecting them, caused chiefly by the attraction of the sun and moon.

tide, flood *See* FLOOD TIDE

tide rip *See* RIP

tied island An island connected to the mainland or to another island by a tombolo.

tie line A line at constant temperature connecting the compositions of any two phases that are in equilibrium at the temperature of the tie line. In two-liquid fields, the tie lines are sometimes called conjugation lines.

tierra blanca *See* CALICHE

tie-time The reflection times obtained by shooting in opposite directions over an interval resulting in a common reflection point. When this time is corrected for uphole time, or corrected to datum, the resulting comparison of corrected reflection times is the tie-time.

tiff A sparry mineral; calcite in southwest Missouri; barite in southeast Missouri.

tiger's-eye A chatoyant stone, usually yellow-brown, much used for ornament. It is silicified crocidolite.

tight fold A fold in which the limbs diverge at a small angle or are parallel.

till Nonsorted, nonstratified sediment carried or deposited by a glacier.

tillite A sedimentary rock composed of cemented till.

tilt *1. Photogram:* The distortion in a photograph caused by tilt-ing of the photographic plane due to variable winds and air currents. *2.* The rotation of the photograph about the axis parallel to the line of flight.

tilt blocks Blocks that have received a marked tilt in regions of block faulting.

tiltmeter *1. Earthquake seismol:* A device for observing surface disturbances on a bowl of mercury, employed in an attempt to predict earthquakes. *2.* An instrument used to measure displacement of the ground surface from the horizontal. *Volcanol:* Used to indicate the degree and intensity of tumescence or doming-up of a volcano by magmatic pressure.

tilt slide Gravity slide of rocks or sediments down the slope of an uptilted surface.

timber line The height on mountains at which the growth of trees stops. It varies with the latitude and climate.

time Duration; a period in which something occurs, or endures. *Geol:* Any division of geologic chronology.

time at shot point *Seis. explor:* The time required for the seismic impulse to travel from the charge in the shot hole to the surface of the earth. *Syn:* UP-HOLE TIME

time break An indication on a seismic record showing the instant of detonation of a shot or charge. *Syn:* SHOT MOMENT; SHOT INSTANT. *Cf.* TIME SIGNAL

time constant The time taken for a current in a circuit having a steady e.m.f. to reach a definite fraction of its final value after the circuit is closed. This fraction is $1-1/e=0.623$ where e is the base of natural logarithms The time constant is the ratio of the inductance of the circuit in henrys to its resistance in ohms. The time required for a charge on a condenser to decrease to $1/e$ of its original value in the process of discharging. It is the product of the resistance in ohms of the discharging circuit and the capacity of the condenser in farads.

time-depth chart A graphical expression of the functional relation between the velocity function and the times observed in the seismic method of geophysical exploration. It permits the time increments to be converted to the corresponding depths. *Syn:* TIME-DEPTH CURVE

time-depth curve *See* TIME-DEPTH CHART

time-distance curve In refraction seismic computations, a graph, usually with arrival times of seismic events plotted as ordinates and distances along the surface of the earth plotted as abscissas. In earthquake studies, the times of arrival of seismic waves at recording stations may be known but the time of initiation of the waves may be unknown. As data are accumulated from different recording stations, a time-distance graph may be constructed. If it is possible to extrapolate this graph to the origin on the time and distance coordinates, it becomes a travel-time curve.

time-distance graph In refraction seismic computations, a plot of the arrival times of refracted events against the shot point to detector distance. The reciprocal slopes of the segments plotted are the refraction velocities for the refracting bed. *Syn:* ODO-GRAPH

time gradient In the reflection seismic methods applied to dipping reflectors, the travel-time curves may not be straight lines, i.e., the apparent velocity observed varies with the spread from shot point to detectors. The time gradient is the reciprocal of the apparent velocity. *Seis. prospecting:* The rate of change of travel time with depth.

time integral In regard to any variable f which is a function of the time, the definite integral of the product of the variable by the element of time between specified limits, viz: f dt. *Cf.* IMPULSE

time lag In refraction seismic interpretation, where arrival times are plotted against shot-detector distances, if some of the paths from shot point to detector include a low-speed bed, the corresponding arrival times will be abnormally long, and the departure from normal travel time is called a time lag. *Seis. prospecting:* Time delays in arrivals due to phase shifts in filtering, to shot-hole fatigue, etc.

time leads In a method of interpretation of refraction seismic records where the arrival times are plotted against shot-detector distances, if some of the paths from shot point to detector include a high-speed segment, the corresponding travel times will not fall on a smooth curve. The departure in this case from the curve is called a time lead, and it is proportional to the horizontal extent of the high-speed segment. Used in salt-dome exploration.

time line Line indicating equal time in a geologic cross section or correlation diagram.

time plane Stratigraphic horizon identifying an instant in geologic time.

time-rock unit Time-stratigraphic unit.

time signal A signal sent by telegraph or radio indicating an exact instant of time; in geophysics such a signal is used to indicate the time of explosion in a shot hole. *Cf.* TIME BREAK. A signal sent from the Naval Observatory to regulate time-pieces.

time-stratigraphic Term applied to rock units with boundaries based on geologic time, i.e., with synchronous boundaries.

time-stratigraphic facies Facies differentiated from each other on the basis of the proportions of geologic time during which sedimentary deposition and non-deposition occurred.

time-stratigraphic unit Stratigraphic unit of rocks representing some definite interval of geologic time. Time-stratigraphic units in descending order of importance are: (a) system, (b) series, (c) stage, and (d) substage corresponding to (a) period, (b) epoch, (c) age, and (d) subage. *See* PARA-TIME-ROCK UNIT

time tie In seismograph continuous profiling, a coincident travel path for seismic energy initiated at opposite ends of the path. The use of such coincident travel paths on adjacent reflection layouts facilitates correlation from one layout to the next as the shotpoint or recording position is changed.

time transgressive formation Formation whose sediment accumulated in an environment that shifted geographically with time; consequently its age varies from place to place. Such a formation may record a zone concentric with either an advancing or retreating coast line.

time transitional formation Formation including within itself an important geologic time plane and thus being composed of strata belonging to two adjacent time-rock units such as systems.

time unit Geologic time unit.

time value Geologic time represented by a stratigraphic unit, unconformity, range of a fossil, etc.

timing lines Marks or lines placed on seismic records at precisely determined intervals of time (usually at intervals of 0.01 or 0.005 seconds) for the purpose of measuring the time of events recorded. The timing mechanism commonly includes an accurate tuning fork for the determination of small time intervals.

tinguaite A dike rock composed of alkalic feldspars, nepheline, and alkalic pyroxene and amphibole. The rock is commonly porphyritic and the mafic constituents have a characteristic crisscross orientation in the groundmass. A textural variety of phonolite.

tinstone cassiterite.

Tioughniogan Middle Middle Devonian.

tip *1.* The pile of snow formed by an avalanche which has come to rest. *2. Photogram:* The rotation of a photograph about the axis perpendicular to the line of flight. *Cf.* TILT, 2

tipple Structure above a mine shaft, particularly a coal mine, in which loaded cars are emptied by being tipped over.

titaniferous Carrying titanium, as titaniferous iron ore. *See* ILMEN-ITE

titanite *Syn:* SPHENE

Tithonian Portlandian.

tjäle [*Sw.*] *See* FROZEN GROUND

Toarcian Upper Lower Jurassic, below Aalenian.

toluene A liquid hydrocarbon

of the aromatic series, formula C_7H_8.

tombolo [*It.*] A bar connecting an island with the mainland or with another island.

tonalite Quartz diorite.

Tonawandan Middle Middle Silurian.

Tongrian Lattorfian.

tongue *1.* A long narrow strip of land, projecting into a body of water. *2.* Part of a formation that is known to wedge out laterally, between sediments of a different lithologic constitution, and in the other direction, thickens and becomes part of a larger body of like sediments.

tongue, lava *See* LAVA TONGUE

Tonolowayan Middle Upper Silurian.

top The contact between the uppermost bedding-plane surface of a stratum and separating two geologic formations used in correlation, especially for the purpose of compiling structure maps, e.g., calling "tops" in well logs.

topaz A mineral, $Al_2SiO_4(F,OH)_2$. Orthorhombic. Used as a gem.

topaz quartz The yellow variety of quartz, citrine, used as a gem.

topocline A cline whose members vary regularly and progressively from place to place.

topographic adjustment A tributary (stream) is in topographic adjustment when its gradient is harmonious with that of its main.

topographic adolescence A stage in the stream erosional cycle when lakes have mostly disappeared and river drainage is well established, stream channels being comparatively narrow and well marked and falls occurring characteristically.

topographic correction *See* TERRAIN CORRECTION

topographic high Frequently used in the oil fields to indicate the higher elevations, regardless of age; opposed to topographic low which indicates a lower elevation. *Cf.* GEOLOGIC HIGH

topographic infancy A stage in the stream erosional cycle characterized by a smooth nearly level surface of deposit, lakes abounding in slight depressions, shallow streams, and drainage systems not well established.

topographic low *See* TOPOGRAPHIC HIGH

topographic map Map showing the topographic features of a land surface generally by means of contour lines.

topographic maturity A stage in the stream erosional cycle of maximum diversity of form when valleys have greatly increased and the river channels are widely opened.

topographic old age A stage in the stream erosional cycle in which there is a featureless surface, differing from the earliest stage (topographic infancy) in having a system of drainage streams, separated by faintly swelling hills.

topographic scale *See* TOPOGRAPHIC TEXTURE

topographic texture The disposition, grouping, or manner of assembly of the topographic units in a stream-dissected district.

topographic unconformity Adjacent topographic differences. Preferable term: topographic discontinuity.

topographic youth *See* YOUNG VALLEY

topography [*Gr.* topos, place; graphein, to write] The physical features of a district or region, such as are represented on maps, taken collectively; especially, the relief and contour of the land.

topology Topographical study of a particular place; specifically, the history of a region as indicated by its topography.

toposphere The area in which all organisms live.

topotype A specimen from the original locality from which a species was described.

top-set beds The material laid down in horizontal layers on top of a delta. *See* FORE-SET BEDS; BOTTOM-SET BEDS

tor Roche moutonnée.

torbernite A mineral, $Cu(UO_2)_2$-$(PO_4)_2.8H_2O$. Tetragonal, in green tabular crystals.

toreva-block slide A landslide consisting essentially of a single large mass of unjostled material which, during descent, has undergone a backward rotation toward the parent cliff about a horizontal axis which roughly parallels it.

torose load casts Elongate ridges on undersurfaces of sandstone layers, which pinch and swell along their trends and may terminate in bulbs, teardrops, or spiral forms.

torque Product of a force and the perpendicular distance between its line of application and the axis of rotation. *See* COUPLE

torrent A stream of water flowing with great velocity or turbulence, as during a freshet or down a steep incline; cascade; freshet; hence, any similar stream, as of lava.

torrential cross-bedding Fine, horizontally laminated strata alternating with uniformly cross-bedded strata composed of coarser materials. Believed to originate under desert conditions of concentrated rainfall, abundant wind action, and playa lake deposition.

torrent tract Mountain tract.

Torrid Zone The climatic zone lying between the tropics, and

hence also called the tropic or tropical zone; it is the largest of the climatic zones, embracing nearly one-half the earth's area.

torsion A body is under torsion when subjected to force couples acting in parallel planes about the same axis of rotation but in opposite senses.

torsion balance An instrument for measuring force fields in which the field being measured is opposed by a known force. The torsion balance measures small forces, such as gravitational or electrical, by determining the amount of torsion or twisting they cause in a slender wire or filament.

torsion coefficient A measure of the resistance offered by a material to a torsional stress. For a cylindrical wire of radius r, length l, and having a modulus of rigidity μ, the torsional coefficient t in c.g.s. units is $t = \pi \mu r^4 l$. The torsional coefficient therefore has the dimensions of work, and it may be interpreted as the amount of work necessary to twist the wire through one radian.

torsion fault Wrench fault, *q.v.*

torsion gliding Twist gliding.

torsion head *1.* That part of a torsion balance from which the filament or wire is suspended. *2.* A rotary cap, often graduated in degrees, atop the vertical tube supporting a torsion suspension.

torsion period The natural period of oscillation of the suspended system in a torsion balance.

torsion wire The filament or wire supporting the beam in a torsion balance or gravity meter.

Tortonian Upper Middle Miocene.

total displacement Slip, *q.v.*

total field The vector sum or combination of all the components of the field under consideration, such as the magnetic or gravitational fields.

total intensity See TOTAL FIELD

total porosity Porosity, q.v.

total reflection Internal reflection in which the angle of incidence exceeds a value known as the critical angle, whose sine is the relative refractive index from the more to the less refractive medium, so called because all the energy is reflected and none is transmitted in the steady state.

total time correction Seis. prospecting: The sum of all corrections applied to a reflection travel time to express the time in reference to a selected datum plane. The main corrections are those for the low-velocity layer and the so-called elevation correction to datum.

tough Having the quality of flexibility without brittleness; yielding to force without breaking.

toughness Amount of work required to deform a body to its rupture point.

tourmaline Schorl. A mineral, a complex borosilicate of Na, Li, Mg, Fe, and Al, occurring commonly in granitic pegmatites. Hexagonal rhombohedral. Used as a gem.

Tournaisian Lower Lower Carboniferous.

tower A peak rising with precipitous slopes from an elevated tableland; a towerlike formation. Local in Northwest.

township The unit of survey of the public lands of the United States and of Canada. Normally a quadrangle approximately 6 miles on a side with boundaries conforming to meridians and parallels. It is further subdivided into 36 sections, each approximately one mile square.

T-phase Earthquake seismol: A phase designation applied to a short-period (1 sec. or less) wave which travels through the ocean with the speed of sound in water, and is occasionally identified on the records of earthquakes in which a large part of the path from epicenter to station is across the deep ocean.

T plane Plane of movement in crystal gliding.

trace 1. The record made by a recording device on paper or film, as, one of the traces of a seismograph record. 2. A line on one plane representing the intersection of another plane with the first one, e.g., a fault trace. 3. A very small quantity of a constituent, especially when not quantitatively determined, owing to its minuteness.

trace elements Elements present in minor amount in the earth's crust. All elements except the eight abundant rock-forming elements, Oxygen (O), silicon (Si), aluminum (Al), iron (Fe), calcium (Ca), sodium (Na), potassium (K), and magnesium (Mg). Syn: MINOR ELEMENTS; ACCESSORY ELEMENTS

trace slip Component of net slip parallel to the trace of an index plane (vein, bedding, etc.) on plane of the fault.

trace-slip fault A fault on which the net slip is parallel to the trace of a bed (or some other index plane) on the fault.

trachyandesite An extrusive rock containing sodic plagioclase and a considerable amount of alkalic feldspar, with one or more mafic constituents (biotite, amphibole, or pyroxene). Its composition is intermediate between andesite and trachyte.

trachybasalt An extrusive rock intermediate between trachyte and basalt and consisting primarily of calcic plagioclase, sanidine, augite, and olivine. Analcite or leucite may be minor constituents.

trachyte An extrusive rock composed essentially of alkalic feldspar and minor biotite hornblende, or pyroxene. Small amounts of sodic plagioclase may be present. The extrusive equivalent of syenite.

trachytic A textural term applied to the groundmasses of volcanic rocks in which neighboring microlites of feldspar are arranged in parallel or subparallel fashion, bending around phenocrysts, and corresponding to the flow lines of the lava from which they were formed. The texture is common in trachytes.

trachytoid A textural term applied to phaneritic igneous rocks in which the feldspars have a parallel or subparallel disposition, as in many varieties of nepheline syenite. Corresponds to the trachytic texture of some lava flows.

traction The entire complex process of carrying material along the bottom of a stream.

traction, antidune-phase A form of stream transportation which develops with higher current velocity and/or larger loads, in which erosion takes place on the downcurrent side of a ridge or ripple and deposition is found on the upcurrent side. The antidunes are thus of reverse shape to the dunes, the antidune form migrating upcurrent, although the individual sand grain moves downcurrent.

traction, dune-phase A form of stream transportation in which sand, gravel, and other material may travel as a mass in the form of small, dunelike bodies that have gentle upcurrent slopes and much steeper downcurrent slopes.

These bodies migrate downcurrent by sand moving from the upcurrent side, which is being eroded, to the downcurrent side, where there is deposition. These unaltered forms of dunes signify over-all equilibrium, with neither erosion nor deposition, and yield only transportation load.

traction, smooth-phase A form of stream transportation during which, with intermediate velocity of current or an intermediate load, the dune phase of traction disappears. The sand then moves as a sheet with gradually increasing density from the surface downward so that there is no sharp plane of demarcation between the sands in motion and those that are stationary.

tractional load Bottom load; bed load, *q.v.*

tractive current Current in standing water that transports sediment along the bottom, as in a river, contrasted with turbidity current or current not in contact with the bottom.

trafficability A rather loose term that usually means the capacity of the soil to support moving vehicles, but is also used to refer to the suitability of the terrain as a whole for cross-country movement of military forces. The more precise terms soil trafficability, *q.v.*, and cross-country movement, *q.v.*, are preferred.

trail Track; trace or sign of the passing of one or many animals, generally used for markings in sedimentary rocks made by moving invertebrates.

trail of the fault Crushed material of a bed or vein that indicates the direction of the fault movement; valuable as a guide to the miner in search of the main vein.

train *1*. Rows of large stones,

some perched, some dropped and broken, which probably fell from the drifting ice. If so, the lines point out the course of the moving rafts and the run of the stream which moved them, but this test is uncertain. *2.* A series of successive repetitive events, as, a train of waves. *3. Seismol:* A series of reflections on a seismograph record.

traîneau écraseur An important and large nappe which, when driven over a lower, recumbent fold or nappe crushes, shears, or rolls into a thin sheet the underlying folds.

trans- [*Lat.*] A prefix meaning across; beyond.

transcurrent fault Strike-slip fault, *q.v.*

transection glacier A glacier that entirely fills a valley system overflowing the divides between the valleys.

transfer Process occurring in the frame of space-time consisting of erosion, sediment transportation, and deposition.

transfer percentage For any element, the ratio of the amount present in sea water to the amount supplied to sea water during geologic time by weathering and erosion, multiplied by 100.

transformation In phase studies, used interchangeably with inversion, *q.v.*

trans-formational breccia Breccia in more or less vertical bodies cutting across strata, produced by collapse, as above a dissolved salt bed.

transformist One who believes that all granites had a metasomatic or palingenetic origin. *Cf.* MAGMATIST

transgression Gradual expansion of a shallow sea resulting in the progressive submergence of land, as when sea level rises or land

subsides. *Syn:* OVERLAP; PROGRESSIVE OVERLAP

transgressive reef One of a series of reefs or bioherms developed close to (and more or less parallel to) the shore line by an advancing sea.

transient methods Electrical methods of geophysical exploration that depend on either the introduction into the ground of a sharp current pulse, such as may be produced by suddenly closing or opening an electrical circuit connected to grounded electrodes, or upon impressing an electric current of a certain wave form on the ground. Measurements are made either of the form of the current or more commonly of the form of the resulting potential.

transit *1.* A surveying instrument with the telescope mounted so that it can be transited; called also a transit theodolite. *2.* The passage of one heavenly body over the disk of another, or the apparent passage of a heavenly body over the meridian of a place.

transition Intermediate.

transition metals Elements in the middle of the long periods of the periodic table. Usage varies, but most commonly the transition elements are taken to include those from scandium (Sc) to zinc (Zn) in the first long period, from yttrium (Y) to cadmium (Cd) in the second, and from lanthanum (La) to mercury (Hg)—excluding the 14 rare earth metals from cerium (Ce) to lutecium (Lu)—in the third.

transit theodolite *See* TRANSIT, *1*

translation Homogeneous sideward motion.

translational movement Refers to movement along faults. All straight lines on opposite sides of the fault and outside the dislocated zone that were parallel before faulting are parallel after faulting.

translation gliding That type of single-crystal slip, produced either by compression or tension, by which displacement on preferred lattice planes takes place, in a given direction or directions, without reorientation or rupture of the deformed parts.

translation plane Gliding plane.

translatory fault Rotary fault, q.v.

translucent Admitting the passage of light, but not capable of being seen through. Transmitting light diffusely.

transmutation The transformation of one element into another.

transparent May be seen through. Transmitting light without diffusing or scattering its rays.

transpiration The process by which water vapor escapes from a living plant and enters the atmosphere.

transport, restricted A tectonic transport in which the principal stress is applied so as to favor equal and simultaneous development of two intersecting shear surfaces. The net elongation of the fabric elements is normal to the stress and limited in magnitude.

transport, tectonic A general term for differential movement in tectonites.

transport, unrestricted A tectonic transport in which the principal stress is applied so as to favor unequal development of two intersecting shear surfaces. One prominent s-surface results and movement on it is relatively unrestricted.

transportation Geol: The shifting of material from one place to another on the earth's surface by moving water, ice, or air.

transverse crevasse A crack in a glacier at right angles (approximately) to the direction of ice flow.

transverse dune A strongly asymmetrical dune ridge extending transverse to the direction of dominant sand-moving winds; the leeward slope stands at or near the angle of repose of sand if the dune is active, while the windward slope is comparatively gentle.

transverse fault A fault whose strike is transverse to the general structure.

transverse fold Cross fold.

transverse joint A joint that is transverse to the strike of the strata or schistosity.

transverse valley A valley having a direction at right angles to the strike of the rocks.

transverse wave *1. Seismol:* A wave motion in which the motion of the particles, or the entity that vibrates, is perpendicular to the direction of progression of the wave train. *2. Geophys:* A body seismic wave advancing by shearing displacements. *Syn:* DISTORTIONAL WAVE; EQUIVOLUMNAR WAVE; SECONDARY WAVE; S-WAVE; SHEAR WAVE

trap *1.* Trap in the Dutch language signifies stairs, a staircase [*Sw.* trappa; *Ger.* Trappe]. In basaltic lava fields a remarkable steplike or terracelike appearance is observable. This configuration is due to the abrupt terminations of the successive flows. *2.* A body of reservoir rock completely surrounded by impervious rock; a closed reservoir.

trapdoor structure A blocklike type of foreland structure, the essential feature of which is a sharply asymmetrical flexure usually broken on its steep flank by a high-angle fault. The flexure or fault or both generally outline two adjacent sides of the block, and displacement is commonly greatest at the corner.

trapezohedron *1.* In the isometric system, the same as tetragonal trisoctahedron. *See* TRISOCTAHE-DRON (b). *2.* In the tetragonal and hexagonal systems, any of several forms having principal and lateral axes of symmetry, but no planes of symmetry, and enclosed by six, eight, or twelve quadrilateral faces each having unequal intercepts on all the axes.

trap rock A term applied to dark-colored dike and flow rocks, chiefly basalt and diabase. Also spelled trapp.

traverse *1.* A line surveyed across a plot of ground. *2. V:* To make a traverse survey. *3.* Line across a thin section or other sample in which elements are counted or measured.

travertine Calcium carbonate, $CaCO_3$, of light color and usually concretionary and compact, deposited from solution in ground and surface waters. Extremely porous or cellular varieties are known as calcareous tufa, calcareous sinter, or spring deposit. Compact, banded varieties, capable of taking a polish, are called onyx marble. Travertine forms the stalactites and stalagmites of limestone caves, and the filling of some veins and hot spring conduits.

tread The flat part of a step-like natural land form; can be applied to a glacial stairway, stream or marine terraces. *Cf.* RISER

treasure finder Terrometer, *q.v.*

trellised or **grapevine drainage** A stream pattern in which master and tributary streams are arranged nearly at right angles with respect to one another.

Tremadocian Lower Lower Ordovician; considered uppermost Cambrian in Great Britain.

tremolite *See* AMPHIBOLE

tremor An earthquake having small intensity. A quick vibratory movement. Any quivering or trembling.

Trempealeauian Upper Croixan.

trench (marine) *1.* A long but narrow depression of the deep-sea floor having relatively steep sides. *2.* A long narrow intermontane depression occupied by two or more streams (whether expanded into lakes or not) alternately draining the depression in opposite directions. *Ger.* Graben; *Fr.* ravine.

trend The direction or bearing of the outcrop of a bed, dike, sill, or the like, or of the intersection of the plane of a bed, dike, joint, fault, or other structural feature with the surface of the ground.

Trentonian Upper Mohawkian.

treppen concept The idea that on a surface reduced to old age by streams and then uplifted, the rejuvenated streams develop second-cycle valleys first near their mouths and that these young valleys are extended headward to form "stair steps."

tri- [*Gr., Lat., Fr.*] Prefix meaning threefold or three.

triangular diagram A method of plotting compositions in terms of the relative amounts of three materials or components, involving a triangle wherein each apex represents a pure component. The perpendicular distances of a point from each of the three sides (in an equilateral triangle) will then represent the relative amounts of each of the three materials represented by the apexes opposite those sides

triangular facets Truncated spur ends with broad base and apex pointing upward. Usually associated with gravity faults, but may also characterize fault-line scarps. Triangular facets may also be formed by other processes such as wave erosion of a mountain front and truncation of spurs by a valley glacier.

triangulate To divide into triangles; to survey by triangulation; having triangular markings.

triangulation The laying out and accurate measurement of a network of triangles, especially on the surface of the earth, as in surveying.

Triassic The earliest of the three geologic periods comprised in the Mesozoic era. Also the system of strata deposited during that period.

triboluminescence The property displayed by some specimens of zinc sulfide of emitting sparks when scratched. Not only the mineral zinc blende but the artificial sulfide exhibit this phenomenon.

tributary Any stream which contributes water to another stream.

trichter pluton Funnel pluton.

triclinic symmetry *Struct. petrol:* Refers to either symmetry of fabric or symmetry of movement in which there are no planes or axes of symmetry.

triclinic system That system of crystals in which the forms are referred to three unequal, mutually oblique axes. The characteristic of all triclinic crystals is the total lack of symmetry other than a possible center.

tridymite A mineral, SiO_2, trimorphous with quartz and cristo-

balite. Hexagonal at high temperature, orthorhombic at low.

trigonal Having, in the ideal or symmetrically developed form, triangular faces, as, the trigonal trisoctahedron.

trigonal system *See* RHOMBOHEDRAL SYSTEM

trigonometrical survey A survey accomplished by the trigonometrical calculation of lines after careful measurement of a base line and of the angles made with this line by the lines toward points of observation; generally preliminary to a topographical survey. *See* TRIANGULATION

trilling A compound crystal consisting of three twinned individuals.

Trilobita Class of arthropods with a dorsal skeleton consisting of cephalon, thorax, and pygidium, and divided longitudinally into a central axis and two pleural regions. Camb.-Perm.

trimline A line marking the former extent of the margins of a glacier.

trimorphism The presence of three forms in every species (of foraminifer), two of them representing the megalospheric forms and the last the microspheric form.

Trinitian Middle Lower Cretaceous.

trioctahedral Refers to the structure of layered clay minerals in which all possible octahedral positions of aluminum are occupied by Mg, Fe, Cr, or Zn.

tripartite method A method of determining the apparent surface velocity and direction of propagation of microseisms or earthquake waves by determining the times at which a given wave passes three separated points.

triphylite A mineral, the part with Fe>Mn of the lithiophilitetriphylite series, Li(Fe,Mn)PO$_4$. Orthorhombic.

triploblastic Refers to structure of animals consisting of ectodermal, mesodermal, and endodermal layers.

tripod A three-legged stand for supporting a theodolite, magnetometer, compass, camera, or any other instrument.

tripoli; tripolite An incoherent, highly siliceous sedimentary rock composed of the shells of diatoms or of radiolaria, or of finely disintegrated chert. Used as a polishing powder and for filters.

trisoctahedron In the isometric system, either of two forms of normal symmetry, enclosed by 24 faces: (a) the trigonal or ordinary trisoctahedron, having triangular faces, each with equal intercepts on two axes and a greater intercept on the third axis; (b) the tetragonal trisoctahedron (also called trapezohedron and icositetrahedron), having trapezial faces, each with equal intercepts on two axes and a less intercept on the third axis.

tritium A hydrogen isotope containing two neutrons in addition to the proton in its nucleus. *See* DEUTERIUM

trivariant, *adj.* Referring to a system having three degrees of freedom, i.e., having a variance of three.

trivial name Second or specific name in the name of a species.

TRM Thermo-remanent magnetization.

troilite A mineral, FeS, a variety of pyrrhotite occurring in nodular masses and thin veins in meteorites. Hexagonal.

trona An impure form of hydrous sodium carbonate. Na$_2$CO$_3$.NaHCO$_3$.2H$_2$O.

tropical cyclone A cyclonic storm of great intensity that originates in the tropics over the oceans and first moves westward, then recurves to the northeast (toward the southeast in the southern hemisphere). The very low pressures result in very high winds which in the northern hemisphere blow counterclockwise and spirally toward the center. These storms vary from 25 to 600 miles in diameter. At the outer edge of the storm the wind is moderate, but increases toward the center where a velocity as high as 150 miles per hour has been recorded.

tropics The area or belt of the surface of the earth bounded by the Tropics of Cancer and Capricorn; also called the Torrid Zone, *q.v.*

tropopause The upper limit of the troposphere—in middle latitudes, generally 10 to 12 km. above the earth's surface.

troposphere That portion of the atmosphere next to the earth's surface in which temperature generally rapidly decreases with altitude, clouds form, and convection is active. In middle latitudes the troposphere generally includes the first 10 to 12 km. above the earth's surface.

trough *1.* An elongate and wide depression, with gently sloping borders. *Ger.* Mulde; *Fr.* vallée. *2.* A long narrow channel or depression between ridges on land or between crests of waves at sea. *3.* In brachiopods, the furrow on posterior part of pedicle valve which provides space for the pedicle beneath the apex.

trough of wave The lowest part of a wave form between successive crests. Also that part of a wave below still-water level.

true dip Three-dimension dip, *q.v.*

true folding Same as flexure folding, q.v.

truncate v. To cut the top or end from; to terminate abruptly as if cut or broken off.

truncated spur The widening of a stream valley by a glacier results in the truncation of the spurs which extend into it from the two sides.

trunk glacier The main ice stream in a system of tributary valley glaciers.

tschernosem; tchornozem See CHERNOZEM

tsunami A great sea wave produced by a submarine earthquake or volcanic eruption. Commonly misnamed tidal wave, q.v.

tube foot Pseudopod of echinoderms.

tufa A chemical sedimentary rock composed of calcium carbonate or of silica, deposited from solution in the water of a spring or of a lake or from percolating ground water; sinter.

tuff A rock formed of compacted volcanic fragments, generally smaller than 4 mm. in diameter.

tuff ball Accretionary lapilla, q.v.

tuffite Indurated rocks composed of a mixture of pyroclastic and sedimentary detritus, especially ash and fine sediment.

tuff lava A term applied to consolidated, lavalike tuffa consisting primarily of lenses of black and gray obsidian lying in a tuffaceous matrix that displays a streaky, varicolored banding or eutaxitic structure. Essentially synonymous with welded tuff.

tuff palagonite A bedded aggregate of dust and fragments of basaltic lava, among which are conspicuous angular pieces and minute granules of pale yellow, green, red, or brown altered basic glass called palagonite.

tumescence Volcanol: The swelling or uparching of a volcano during periods of rising magma preceding an eruption.

tumulose Full of small hills and mounds.

tundra One of the level or undulating treeless plains characteristic of arctic regions, having a black muck soil and a permanently frozen subsoil.

tundra climate The climate peculiar to the tundra regions. The limits of the tundra type of climate are the mean isotherms of 32° F. on the north and 50° F. on the south, drawn for the warmest month of the year.

tungstate A salt or ester of tungstic acid; a compound containing the radical $WO_4{}^{--}$.

tunnel 1. Strictly speaking, a passage in a mine open at both ends. Often used loosely as a synonym for adit, drift, gallery. 2. A spiral opening in the plane of coiling bounded by chomata, in the Fusulinidae (a family of Foraminifera).

tunnel valley Sizable streams flowing beneath the ice and not loaded with coarse sediment which cut shallow trenches in the till and other loose material at the surface.

turbidite Turbidity current deposit.

turbidity current Density current, q.v.

turbidity size analysis Size analysis based upon the amount of turbidity in a suspension, the turbidity decreasing as the grains settle. The turbidity is usually measured by means of a photoelectric cell.

turbulence spectrum Distribution of eddies of different magnitude in a water body.

turbulent flow That type of flow in which the stream lines are thoroughly confused through heterogeneous mixing of flow. The head loss varies approximately with the second power of the velocity. *See* LAMINAR FLOW; REYNOLDS NUMBER

turf Peat. There are several varieties, as, white, brown, black, stone, gas, or candle turf.

turkey-fat ore In Missouri, a name for a variety of smithsonite, colored yellow; so called from its appearance.

turning point A point, the height of which is determined before the leveling instrument is moved, used to determine the height of the leveling instrument after it is moved to another site; the location of the rod in spirit leveling.

Turonian Middle Upper Cretaceous.

turquoise A mineral, $CuAl_6(PO_4)_4(OH)_8.4H_2O$. Triclinic. Used as a gem.

turrelite A Texas asphaltic shale.

turtleback Large smoothly curved topographic surface underlain by folded metamorphic rocks in the Death Valley region; resembles a structural nose with amplitude up to several thousand feet.

turtleback fault Low-angle fault which has brought Cenozoic sedimentary and volcanic rocks into contact with metamorphics at a turtleback surface; interpreted as a folded overthrust or as a plane along which normal faulting or extensive landsliding has occurred.

turtle stones Large nodular concretions found in certain clays and marls. In form they have a rough resemblance to turtles, and this appearance is increased by their being divided into angular compartments by cracks filled with spar, reminding one of the plates on the shell of a turtle. *See* SEPTARIUM

twin; twinned crystal; twin crystal A nonparallel, rational, symmetrical intergrowth of two or more grains of the same crystalline species. Contact twin. *See* TWIN LAW; TWINNING

twin-gliding That type of single-crystal slip, produced either by compression or tension, by which displacement on preferred lattice planes takes place, with a fixed direction sense, producing reorientation of part of the crystal so that it is in a twin-position with respect to the stationary part. Rupture is not involved.

twin law The statement of the relation between the parts of a twin, including (1) the orientation of the twinning axis or of the twinning plane, one of which is necessarily rational, (2) the nature of the twinning relationship or operation, such as reflection across the twinning plane or rotation about the twinning axis, (3) the nature of the surface of contact between the parts of the twin, including the orientation if it is a plane surface.

twinning The formation of twins.

twinning, cyclic *See* CYCLE TWINNING

twinning, polysynthetic *See* POLYSYNTHETIC TWINNING

twinning axis Any direction in a twin that has the same relation to the lattices of both parts of the twin. It is always normal to a twinning plane, and at least one of these is always rational with respect to the lattices.

twinning displacement Movement along a crystallographic plane that results in twinning.

twinning plane Any plane that bears the same relation to the lattices of both parts of a twin. It is always normal to a twinning axis. Either the twinning plane or the twinning axis or both are always rational with respect to the lattices.

twin symmetry The two-dimensional discontinuity at a twin boundary is bridged by a slice of structure shared by both crystals. The possible twin symmetry operations derive logically from this single structural condition. The possible symmetries of the boundary structure are the two-sided plane groups, and these number 80.

twist gliding Unequal slippage along planes that results in torsion around the axis of displacement.

two-cycle valley A valley that has been subjected to two cycles of erosion. This is evidenced by narrow inner valley bordered by high level terraces.

two-layer structure Structure of minerals composed of repeated layered units each consisting of an aluminum octahedral layer and a silicon tetrahedral layer as in kaolinite. Both Al and Si can be replaced by other elements.

two-phase flow Flow of two associated liquids such as oil and water.

Tyler standard scale A grade scale for the determination of size grades of sediment particles which is based on $\sqrt{2}$, and in which the midpoint values of each class turn out to be simple whole numbers or fractions.

type The term type, used alone and unqualified, generally refers to the holotype. *See* HOLOTYPE; TYPE SPECIMEN; TYPE SPECIES

type concept To associate each specific name and description with a definite preserved specimen or specimens, each generic name and description with a named species, and each higher category with a definite member of a lower category included in it.

type fossil Occasionally used as equivalent to index fossil, *q.v.* *Syn:* INDEX FOSSIL

type genus or **genera** The generic name or names from which a family or sub-family name is formed.

type locality 1. The place at which a formation is typically displayed and from which it is named. 2. The place at which a fossil is displayed in typical form.

type material All of the fossil specimens whose study provided the basis for the description of a new species.

type section Stratigraphic section recognized as the standard, generally the one from which a stratigraphic unit received its name.

type species Genotype.

type specimen A specimen, generally the holotype, that provides the basis for description and recognition of a species of organisms; used loosely for other less important specimens. *See* PRIMARY TYPE; SECONDARY TYPE

typhoon A name of Chinese origin meaning "great wind" applied to the tropical cyclones, *q.v.*, which occur in the western Pacific Ocean.

typology Taxonomy governed by the concept that species are defined by the morphology of individual type specimens.

typonym A later generic name which has the same genotype as an earlier, valid name.

tyuyamunite A mineral, $Ca(UO_2)_2(VO_4)_2 \cdot 7\text{-}10H_2O$. Orthorhombic. usually massive, powdery, in yellow incrustations. An ore of uranium and vanadium.

U

Udden scale A logarithmic scale for size classification of sediments starting from 1 mm. and progressing by the ratio 1/2 in one direction and 2 in the other. This was the scale adopted by C. K. Wentworth, and by the Committee on Sedimentation.

uintahite *See* GILSONITE

ulexite Cotton ball. A mineral, $NaCaB_5O_9.8H_2O$. Triclinic, fibrous.

ulmain A subvariety of euvitrain. It is composed of completely jellified plant material which may lie at one end of a partly jellified stem and be observable microscopically. It differs from collain in that it is not believed to have been precipitated from solution. *Cf.* COLLAIN

Ulsterian Lower Devonian.

ultimate base level Ultimate base level is a base level at sea level or below, to which lands may be reduced by the processes acting upon them.

ultimate form *See* CYCLE OF EROSION

ultimate recovery The quantity of oil or gas that a well, a pool, a field, or a property will produce. It is the total obtained or to be obtained from the beginning to final abandonment.

ultimate strength The greatest stress that a substance can stand under normal short-time experiments, i.e., the highest point on a stress-strain diagram.

ultra- [*Lat.*] A prefix meaning beyond.

ultrabasic, *adj.* Some igneous rocks and most varieties of meteorites containing less than 45% silica; containing virtually no quartz or feldspar and composed essentially of ferromagnesian silicates, metallic oxides and sulfides, and native metals, or of all three.

ultrahaline Hypersaline.

ultramafic Ultrabasic.

ultrametamorphism Melting of rock and creation of magma *in situ.*

ultrasima Layer within the earth underlying and heavier than the sima and presumably consisting of more basic material.

ultraviolet Applied to radiation outside of the visible spectrum of light at its violet end; said of rays more refrangible than the extreme violet rays.

umbilical plug *See* PLUG, UMBILICAL

umbo A projection arising from the surface. *See* DISTAL GROOVES

unaka Monadnock. The term monadnock is applied to a single isolated residual, such as Mount Monadnock in New Hampshire, which stands alone. More massive residuals of greater size and height would seem to require a different name, and the term unaka has been proposed for such large residuals as the Unaka Mountains.

unary or **unicomponent system** A system of one component.

unavailable moisture Moisture, held in soil by adsorption or other forces, that cannot be utilized by plants.

unbalanced force A force or system of forces that results in a change of motion, i.e., causes acceleration, deceleration, or a change in direction of a moving body.

unconformability This term is seldom used. *See* UNCONFORMITY

unconformable Having the relation of unconformity to the underlying rocks; not succeeding the underlying strata in immediate order of age and in parallel position.

unconformity A surface of erosion or nondeposition, usually the former, that separates younger strata from older rocks. *See* ANGULAR UNCONFORMITY; DISCONFORMITY; LOCAL UNCONFORMITY; NONCONFORMITY

unconsolidated material From the standpoint of workability, this constitutes the "Earth," *q.v.*, of the A.S.C.E. classification system.

unda That part of the floor of the ocean which lies in the zone of wave action, and in which the bottom is repeatedly stirred and reworked by storm waves.

undaform The subaqueous land form produced by the erosive and constructive action of the waves during the development of the subaqueous profile of equilibrium.

undaform zone That part of the ocean floor which lies in the zone of wave action and in which, therefore, the bottom is repeatedly stirred and reworked by storm waves.

undathem A term proposed by J. L. Rich for a rock unit formed in an unda, *q.v.*, environment.

undation 1. Large wavelike fold in the earth's crust. 2. Theoretical rhythmic oscillation of the earth's surface in broad waves.

undation theory A theory of mountain building proposed by R. W. van Bemmelen that assumes that long broad anticlines of basement rock rose like huge waves in the crust. The sedimentary cover and sometimes the basement itself slid off to form the folds and faults observed in orogenic belts.

underclay A stratum of clay beneath a coal bed often containing roots of coal plants, especially stigmaria. *See* FIRE CLAY

undercooling Reduction in temperature of a liquid to the point where viscosity increases to such a degree that the liquid behaves like a solid. Glass is an example of an undercooled liquid. *Syn:* SUPERCOOLING

undercut slope *See* SLIP-OFF SLOPE

underfit stream A stream that appears too small to have eroded the valley in which it flows.

underflow 1. The movement of ground water in an underflow conduit. 2. Movement of water through a pervious subsurface stratum; the flow of percolating water; the flow of water under ice, or under a structure.

underground storage (natural gas) The use of natural underground reservoirs for storage of natural gas which has been transferred from its original location in a gas and/or oil field for the primary purposes of conservation, fuller utilization of pipeline facilities, and more effective delivery to markets, rather than for pressure maintenance.

underlie *Geol:* To occupy a lower position than, or to pass beneath; said of stratified rocks over which other rocks are spread out.

undersaturated *Petrol:* Applied to igneous rocks consisting wholly or in part of unsaturated minerals. The class of rocks is subdivided into nonfeldspathoidal and feldspathoidal divisions.

underthrust A thrust fault in which the footwall was the active element. In most instances, it is impossible to tell which element was active.

underthrust fold A fold in which the axial planes dip away from the force producing them.

undertow A supposed undersurface flow return of surface wave water taking place after the wave has broken on the beach. These returning waters are now thought to be concentrated into definite surface currents and called rip currents, *q.v.*

undisturbed Rocks that lie in the positions in which they were originally formed. *Cf.* DISTURBED

undulatory extinction Irregular darkening of crystals in thin section when rotated between crossed Nicols; results from distortion of the crystal lattice.

unfolding Deformation process that reduces or obliterates previous folds.

uni- [*Lat.*] Prefix meaning one.

uniaxial Having but one direction in which light passing through the crystal is not doubly refracted. Typical of tetragonal and hexagonal minerals. *Cf.* BIAXIAL

unicellular One-celled; refers to an organism the entire body of which consists of a single cell.

unicomponent system *See* UNARY SYSTEM

uniformitarianism The concept that the present is a key to the past. *Syn:* PRINCIPLE OF UNIFORMITY

uniformity coefficient An expression of variety in sizes of grains that constitute a granular material.

unigeneric Said of a family composed of a single genus; monogeneric.

unilocular Containing a single chamber or cell.

uniserial Consisting of a single series, as, the plates of primitive crinoid arms.

unit cell The smallest volume or parallelopiped within the three-dimensional repetitive pattern of a crystal that contains a complete sample of the atomic or molecular groups that compose this pattern; crystal structure can be described in terms of the translatory repetition of this unit in space in accordance with one of the space lattices.

unit form Crystal form whose parameters correspond to unit lengths of crystallographic axes.

unitization Combination of adjacent oil leases for efficient operation in which the value of oil, regardless of where the producing wells are located, is allocated among the properties according to some reasonable formula.

univalve *1.* Animal protected by a shell consisting of one piece, particularly a gastropod. *2.* Shell of such an animal.

univariant equilibrium Said of a system in which the variance (degrees of freedom) is one.

universal stage Microscope stage that can be rotated through both horizontal and vertical planes. The ordinary universal stage has four axes of rotation in addition to that of the common petrographic microscope.

unmixing *1.* Natural separation of unlike things from any mixture. *2.* Separation of chemical compounds from mixcrystals when temperature falls and these become unstable; exsolution. *3.* Segregation and concentration, as in the diagenesis of some sediments.

unpaired terraces Remnant of a former continuous alluvial terrace, which (because of differential erosion) is no longer duplicated on opposite sides of a valley.

unrestricted movement Movement accompanying rock flowage in which elongation of particles is in the direction of movement.

unsaturated *1.* Applied to minerals that are incapable of crystallizing from rock magmas in the presence of an excess of silica. Such minerals are said to be unsaturated with regard to silica and include the feldspathoids, analcime, magnesian olivine, melanite, pyrope, perovskite corundum, calcite, and perhaps spinel. *2.* State of a chemical compound, particularly an organic one, that is capable of holding additional atoms, especially hydrogen, without change in its basic molecular structure.

unstable equilibrium Not in true or in metastable equilibrium; in the process of change, as, a piece of ice in hot water.

unstratified Not formed or deposited in beds or strata.

updip block Block on the updip side of a strike fault.

uphole shooting *Seis. explor:* The setting off of successive shots in a hole at varying depths in order to determine velocities and velocity variation of the materials forming the hole walls.

uphole time Term used to denote the observed travel time of a seismic wave from the point of generation at a given depth in a shot hole to a detector at the surface, and the observed time

equivalent of the corresponding shot depth. *Syn:* T-OF-SHOT POINT

uplift Elevation of any extensive part of the earth's surface relative to some other parts. *Ant:* SUBSIDENCE

upper *Geol:* Designates a later period or formation; so called because the strata are normally above those of the earlier formations.

upright fold Fold with vertical axial plane.

uprush Swash. The rush of water up onto the beach following the breaking of a wave.

upthrow The block or mass of rock on that side of a fault which has been displaced relatively upward. The term should be used with the definite understanding that it refers merely to a relative and not an absolute displacement.

upthrust *1.* An upheaval of rock; said preferably of a violent upheaval. *2.* A high-angle gravity or thrust fault in which the relatively upthrown side was the active (moving) element. This is usually impossible to determine.

upwarp An area that has been uplifted; generally used for broad anticlines.

upwelling *Oceanog:* Light surface water transported away from a coast (by action of winds parallel to it) and replaced near the coast by heavier subsurface water.

Uralian Upper Upper Carboniferous.

uralite A fibrous or acicular variety of hornblende occurring in altered rocks and pseudomorphous after pyroxene. *See* AMPHIBOLE

uralitization The conversion of pyroxene into hornblende; usually as a finely fibrous aggregate. It is usually considered to be a late magmatic process.

uraninite Pitchblende. A mineral, essentially UO_2, but usually containing Th and rare earths as substituents, and UO_3, Ra, and Pb formed by radioactive decay. Isometric. Pitchblende is the massive variety found in sulfide-bearing veins. The chief ore of U.

urano-organic ore Uranium ore precipitated by organic matter.

uranophane; uranotil A mineral, $Ca(UO_2)_2Si_2O_7.6H_2O$. Orthorhombic.

urstromtal [<*Ger.*] Trenchlike valley cut by a temporary stream flowing along the margin of a former ice sheet.

urtite A plutonic rock composed largely of nepheline with minor aegirine, and apatite. Urtite is transitional into ijolite with increasing aegirine and decreasing nepheline.

U-tube *See* PITOT TUBE

uvala *1.* A large, broad sinking in the karst with uneven floor, formed by the breaking down of the wall between a series of dolinas. These uvalas possess the chief characteristics of polyes, for their major axes agree with the strike, but they differ from them in their irregular floor, and they lack the special hydrographical condition of polyes. *2.* Large sinkhole formed by the coalescence of several doline sinks.

uvarovite *See* GARNET

V

vadose water Suspended water. A term proposed by Franz Pošepný to designate subsurface water above the zone of saturation in the zone of aeration.

vadose-water discharge Discharge of soil water not derived from the zone of saturation.

vagrant animal An animal that customarily moves about by its own volition, either continuously or intermittently.

vagrant benthos Bottom-dwelling organisms which are capable of movement on, in, or above the substratum. Term is vagrant benthos as distinct from sessile benthos, *q.v.*

Valanginian Lowermost Lower Cretaceous.

Valentian Llandoverian.

valid name An available name whose "title" to a species is clear, i.e., which is neither a synonym nor a homonym of an earlier name.

valley [*Lat.* vallis] Any hollow or low-lying land bounded by hill or mountain ranges, and usually traversed by a stream or river which receives the drainage of the surrounding heights.

valley braid A term proposed for an individual runway of a valley which is in anastomosis, its valley parts passing about features in bas-relief or about upland tracts. The floors of the valley braids may be near the level of the one which carries

the present stream or they may be much higher.

valley fill A valley underlain by unconsolidated rock waste derived from the erosion of the bordering mountains.

valley flat The low flat land between valley walls bordering a stream channel.

valley glacier A glacier occupying a valley. Mountain glacier; Alpine glacier.

valley plug A local constriction in a stream channel formed by any of several types of channel obstructions and which may cause rapid deposition.

valley profile Thalweg, *q.v.*

valley sink An elongated sink or series of interconnecting sinks forming a valleylike depression.

valley system A valley and its tributaries.

valley tract Middle part of a stream course characterized by moderate gradient and a fairly wide valley.

valley train A long narrow body of outwash confined within a valley.

Valmeyeran Middle Mississippian.

valve *1.* Any device or arrangement that is used to open or close a passage to permit or stop the flow of a substance; a device for rectifying an alternating current. *2.* A single part of the two-piece shell of the clams, ostracods, and brachiopods.

vanadate A salt or ester of vanadic acid; a compound containing the radical VO₄⁻³ or VO₈⁻.

vanadinite A mineral, Pb₅(VO₄)₃-Cl, commonly containing As and P replacing V. Hexagonal. An ore of vanadium.

Van Allen radiation zone Powerful doughnut shaped zone of radiation 1000 or 3000 miles above the earth's surface and parallel with the equator.

van der Waals forces The weak attraction exerted by all molecules on one another, resulting from the mutual interaction of the electrons and nuclei of the molecules; it has its origin in the electrostatic attraction of the nuclei of one molecule for the electrons of another, which is largely but not completely compensated by the repulsion of electrons by electrons and nuclei by nuclei. These forces are involved in some kinds of adsorption and in the condensation and freezing of the inert gases and nonpolar convalent molecules. The linkage resulting from van der Waals attraction is sometimes called a van der Waals bond.

van't Hoff's law The law that when a system is in equilibrium, of the two opposed interactions the endothermic is promoted by raising the temperature, the exothermic by lowering it.

vapor Any substance in the gaseous state; a gasified liquid or solid. *See* GAS; LIQUID; FLUID

vapor pressure The pressure at which a liquid and its vapor are in equilibrium at a given temperature. *Syn:* VAPOR TENSION

vapor tension Vapor pressure, *q.v.*

vara An old Spanish unit of length, used in the southwestern United States and in Mexico. One vara is equivalent to 33 1/3 inches in Texas, 33 inches in California, and 32.9931 inches in Mexico.

variance of a system The number of intensive or internal variables, such as temperature, pressure, and concentration, which can be altered independently and arbitrarily (within limits) to bring the system into new states of equilibrium without causing a phase change. Also called degrees of freedom.

variation 1. The angle by which the compass needle deviates from the true north. 2. One of the laws of organic nature; organisms vary in time, from place to place, and also in one locality and time; they vary also in their morphology.

variation diagram A name given a method of plotting the chemical compositions of rocks in an igneous rock series, designed to reveal genetic relationships and the nature of the processes that have affected the series. Usually the weight per cent silica is plotted as the abscissa and the weight per cent of individual other oxides as the ordinates. Also called a Harker diagram after A. Harker.

variety *Morphol:* A distinctive group of individuals within a population (a species), differentiated from other parts of the population by possession of some character or combination of characters lacking in the others; an artificial group, not a sort of subspecies

variometer *Geophys:* A device for measuring or recording variations in terrestrial magnetism; a variable inductance provided with a scale.

Variscan orogeny Series of late Paleozoic diastrophic movements beginning perhaps in Late Devonian and continuing to the end of Permian.

Variscides Mountain system raised in the latter part of the Paleozoic era, particularly in central Europe; more or less equivalent to Hercynian.

varve *1.* Any sedimentary bed or lamination that is deposited within one year's time. *2.* A pair of contrasting laminae representing seasonal sedimentation, as, summer (light) and winter (dark) within a single year.

vascular plant Plant with well-developed circulatory system and structural differentiation into roots, stem, and leaves; includes majority of terrestrial plants.

vector A physical quantity which has magnitude and direction.

vectorial *Struct. petrol:* Applied to the physical features of a fabric which are directional in character, e.g., lattice and dimensional orientation are vectorial features.

vector quantity *See* VECTOR

vein An occurrence of ore, usually disseminated through a gangue, or veinstone, and having a more or less regular development in length, width, and depth. A vein and a lode are, in common usage, essentially the same thing, the former being rather the scientific, the latter the miners' name for it. *See* LODE; FISSURE; FISSURE VEIN

vein claim Lode claim, *q.v.*

vein dike The product of solidification of the so-called "ore magma."

veined gneiss Metamorphic rock formed by intrusion of magma into nonfissile country rock in numerous veins and dikelets extending in all directions.

veldt In South Africa, a tract of land not forested, or thinly forested; a grass country.

velocity A vector quantity which indicates a time rate of motion.

velocity discontinuity An abrupt change of the rate of propagation of seismic waves within the earth, as at an interface.

velocity of propagation The velocity with which energy moves through a medium as wave motion. The velocity of a wave at a point is the velocity with which the beginning of the wave passes the point.

velocity of waves The speed with which an individual wave advances.

velocity potential A mathematical entity defined in such a manner that the negative of its first derivative at any given point yields the velocity at that point.

velocity profile A seismic reflection spread designed to record data which may be used to compute average velocities in the earth to reflecting horizons by observation of time variations compared with geometrical ray paths traveled.

vent agglomerate Agglomerate that is localized within a volcanic vent. *See* AGGLOMERATE

vent breccia Volcanic breccia that is localized within a volcanic vent. A conduit filling or neck of volcanic breccia.

ventifact *See* EINKANTER; DRIEKANTER

ventral, *adj.* Front; relating to the inner face or part of an organ; opposite the back or dorsal part.

Venturian Middle Pliocene.

Venus hair Fine rutile crystals occurring as inclusions in quartz. *See* SAGENITE

verde antique A dark-green rock composed essentially of serpentine (hydrous magnesium silicate). Usually crisscrossed with white veinlets of magnesium and calcium carbonates. Used as an ornamental stone. In commerce often classed as a marble.

Vermes Inclusive name for a great variety of wormlike animals belonging to several different phyla. *Obs.*

vermiculites A group of platy minerals, hydrous silicates of Al, Mg, Fe chiefly, closely related to the chlorites and montmorillonites. Characterized by exfoliating markedly when heated; the expanded material is used for heat insulation. Material similar to vermiculites; occurs as a clay mineral. *See* HYDROBIOTITE

Vermontian orogeny Post-Cambrian diastrophism.

vernier An auxiliary scale used in conjunction with the main scale of a measuring device to obtain one more significant figure of a particular measurement.

Vertebrata Phylum of animals possessing a spinal column and other more or less bony parts of an internal skeleton. Chordata, as sometimes restricted.

vertical balance An instrument for measuring variations in the vertical component of the terrestrial magnetic field, usually by balancing the torque on a magnet system by means of a counter-gravitational torque acting on counterweights; vertical field balance.

vertical component That part, or component, of a vector that is perpendicular to a horizontal, or level, plane.

vertical exaggeration In a stereoscopic image, the increase in relief seen by the eye.

vertical intensity The magnitude of the vertical component of any vector; the strength of intensity of the vertical component of the earth's magnetic or gravitational field at any point.

vertical photograph An aerial photograph made with the camera axis vertical or as nearly vertical as practicable.

vertical range The local sequence of strata through which a certain species or genus is found. *Syn:* TEILZONE

vertical separation In faulting, the separation between the two parts of the displaced index plane (bed, vein, dike, etc.) measured in a vertical direction.

vertical shift The vertical component of the shift. *See* SHIFT

vertical slip In faulting, the vertical component of the net slip; this is the same as the vertical component of the dip slip.

vertical variability map Map showing areal relations of vertical variability in a stratigraphic unit; may show (a) degree of differentiation of the unit in subunits of different lithologic types, or (b) vertical distribution or concentration in the unit of one lithologic type.

very large quantities of water 15,000,000 gallons per day. *Cf.* ENORMOUS; LARGE; MODERATE; SMALL; VERY SMALL; MEAGER

very small quantities of water 1500 to 15,000 gallons per day. *Cf.* ENORMOUS; VERY LARGE; LARGE; MODERATE; SMALL; MEAGER

very thick bands A field term that, in accordance with an arbitrary scale for use in describing banded coal, denotes vitrain bands exceeding 50.0 mm. (over 2 inches) thick. *Cf.* THIN, MEDIUM, and THICK BANDS

vesicle *1.* A small, circular, enclosed space. *2.* A small cavity in an aphanitic or glassy igneous rock, formed by the expansion of a bubble of gas or steam during the solidification of the rock.

vesicular *1.* Characteristic of, or

characterized by, pertaining to, or containing vesicles. 2. Containing many small cavities.

vestigial Pertaining to organic structures whose embryonic start is ordinary but whose later development is retarded and often so much reduced that these structures are functionless.

vestigial structure Nonfunctional structure of an organism of little or no use to the individual that was inherited from ancestors to whom it was useful; vestigial organs commonly become smaller and eventually may be lost entirely by distant descendants.

vesuvianite Idocrase.

vibration The act of vibrating; oscillation. Vibrations may be free or forced; longitudinal, transverse, torsional, or dilatational; also classified according to kind, as, acoustical, electrical, flexural, etc.

vibration gravimeter A device which affords a measurement of gravity by observation of the period of transverse vibration of a thin wire tensioned by the weight of a known mass, useful for observations at sea.

vicinal forms *Crystallog:* Forms taking the place of the simple fundamental forms to which they approximate very closely in angular position.

Vindobonian Middle Miocene.

virgation Divergence of mountain ranges from a common center. *Ant:* SYNTAXIS

Virgilian Upper Pennsylvanian.

virgin clay Fresh clay, as distinguished from that which has been fired.

Virglorian Anisian.

Virgulian Upper Kimmeridgian

vis-à-vis Mirror image.

viscosity Internal friction due to molecular cohesion in fluids. The internal properties of a fluid which offer resistance to flow. *See* POISE

viscosity, absolute The force which will move 1 sq. cm. of plane surface with a speed of 1 cm. per second relative to another parallel plane surface from which it is separated by a layer of the liquid 1 cm. thick. This viscosity is expressed in dynes per square centimeter, its unit being the poise, which is equal to 1 dyne-second per square centimeter. *See* CENTIPOISE; POISE

viscosity coefficient *Hydrol:* A quantitative expression of the friction between the molecules of water when in motion. It is the amount of force necessary to maintain a unit difference in velocity between two layers of water at a unit distance apart. It decreases rapidly with increase in temperature.

viscosity of a fluid The ratio of shearing stress to the time rate of shear. The unit of viscosity is the poise. A fluid exhibits a viscosity of one poise when a tangential force of one dyne causes a plane surface of one square centimeter area, spaced one centimeter from a stationary plane surface, to move with a constant velocity of one centimeter per second, the space between the planes being filled with the viscous liquid.

viscous *1.* Adhesive or sticky, and having a ropy or glutinous consistency. *2.* Imperfectly fluid; designating a substance that, like tar or wax, will change its form under the influence of a deforming force, but not instantly, as more perfect fluids appear to do.

viscous flow Flowage that occurs upon application of any unbalanced force however small providing that the stress difference continues to operate for a sufficient length of time. *See* PLASTIC FLOW

Visean Upper Lower Carboniferous.

vitrain [*Fr.* vitre, glass] Thin horizontal bands in coal, visible to the naked eye, up to 20 mm. thick, but may also be in thicker lenticels. It has brilliant gloss, strong rectangular fracture perpendicular to bedding, conchoidal fracture in other directions, and clean specular reflection. It is very friable, breaking into small cubes with curved sides; quite clean to the touch, not intrinsically stratified parallel to the bedding plane, but may show striations due to plant structure irrespective of bedding planes. Microscopically, vitrain can be differentiated into two varieties based upon the absence or presence of visible plant structure.

vitreous *1.* Having the luster of broken glass, quartz, calcite. *2.* Having no crystalline structure; amorphous.

vitric tuff An indurated deposit of volcanic ash dominantly composed of glassy fragments blown out during a volcanic eruption. The term should properly be restricted to tuffs containing more than 75 per cent by volume of glass particles. *See* TUFF

vitrifaction *See* VITRIFICATION

vitrification *1.* Act, art, or process of vitrifying; state of being vitrified; also, a vitrified body. *2.* Any process tending to make a body more vitreous. *Syn:* VITRIFACTION

vitrify To convert into, or cause to resemble, glass or a glassy substance, by heat and fusion.

vitro- [<*Lat.* vitrum, glass] A combining form meaning glassy.

vitroclastic Pertaining to a structure typical of fragmental glassy rocks, in which the particles usually have crescentic, rudely triangular outline, or somewhat concave borders.

vitrophyre Porphyritic volcanic glass.

vitrophyric Of, pertaining to, formed of, or characterized by vitrophyre.

vivianite Blue iron earth. A mineral, $Fe_3(PO_4)_2.8H_2O$. Monoclinic.

viviparity Status of organisms that produce living young rather than eggs.

vly; vlei; vley *1.* A small swamp, usually open and containing a pond. *2.* A valley where water collects. Local in Middle Atlantic States.

vogesite A lamprophyre consisting primarily of hornblende or augite or both and either orthoclase or sanidine. Plagioclase is common in many varieties, and biotite and olivine are occasionally present.

void Interstice. A general term for pore space or other openings in rock. In addition to pore space, the term includes vesicles, solution cavities, or any openings either primary or secondary. *See* PORE, *1*

voidal concretion Hollow limonitic concretion resulting from the weathering of clay ironstone.

void ratio Ratio of intergranular voids to volume of solid material in a sediment or sedimentary rock.

volatile Readily vaporizable; as, volatile oils.

volatile components Those materials, such as water, carbon dioxide, etc., in a magma whose pressures are sufficiently high so that they will become concentrated in any gaseous phase that forms.

volatile matter Those products, exclusive of moisture, given off by a material as gas and vapor, determined by definite prescribed methods which may vary according to the nature of the material.

volatiles The volatile constituents (or "rest magma") remaining after the less volatile ores have crystallized as igneous rocks.

volcanic Of, pertaining to, like, or characteristic of a volcano; characterized by or composed of volcanoes, as, a volcanic region, volcanic belt; produced, influenced, or changed by a volcano or by volcanic agencies; made of materials derived from volcanoes, as, a volcanic cone.

volcanic action [<*Lat.* Vulcanus, god of fire] Igneous action at the surface of the earth, in contradistinction to plutonic action which takes place beneath the surface.

volcanic agglomerate Coarse volcanic material produced by explosions. Occurs in necks or pipes of old volcanoes. Not stratified. Coarse pyroclastic rocks containing chiefly rounded fragments.

volcanic ash *See* ASH, VOLCANIC

volcanic belt A linear or arcuate arrangement of volcanoes, generally of great extent and confined to orogens along the margins of the continents or within the ocean basins; e.g., the volcanoes of the Aleutian Island chain comprise a volcanic belt.

volcanic block A subangular, angular, round, or irregularly shaped mass of lava, varying in size up to several feet or yards in diameter. *Cf.* VOLCANIC BOMB; BLOCK

volcanic bombs Detached masses of lava shot out by volcanoes, which, as they fall, assume rounded forms like bombshells.

volcanic breccia A more or less indurated pyroclastic rock consisting chiefly of accessory and accidental angular ejecta 32 mm. or more in diameter lying in a fine tuff matrix. If the matrix is abundant, the term tuff breccia seems appropriate.

volcanic chain Volcanic belt.

volcanic cinders *See* CINDERS, VOLCANIC

volcanic clinker *See* CLINKER, VOLCANIC

volcanic cloud *See* ERUPTION CLOUD

volcanic cluster A group of volcanoes, volcanic cones, or volcanic vents without any apparent systematic arrangement.

volcanic conduit *See* CONDUIT, 2

volcanic cone A cone-shaped eminence formed by volcanic discharges.

volcanic conglomerate A rock composed mainly or entirely of rounded or subangular fragments, chiefly or wholly of volcanic rocks, in a paste of the same material.

volcanic crater *See* CRATER, VOLCANIC

volcanic or **cumulo dome** A steep-sided protrusion of viscous lava forming a more or less dome-shaped or bulbous mass over and around a volcanic vent.

volcanic dust *See* DUST, VOLCANIC

volcanic earthquake Seismic disturbances which are due to direct action of volcanic force or one whose origin lies under or near a volcano, whether active, dormant, or extinct.

volcanic ejecta Tephra, *q.v.*

volcanic emanations *See* EMANATIONS, VOLCANIC

volcanic eruption *See* ERUPTION, VOLCANIC

volcanic fissure trough Volcanic rent.

volcanic focus The supposed seat or center of activity in a volcanic region or beneath a volcano.

volcanic gases The primary magmatic gases emitted from lavas, either quietly or with explosive violence, at the earth's surface, chief among which are water vapor, hydrogen, oxygen, nitrogen, hydrogen sulfide, sulfur dioxide, sulfur trioxide, carbon dioxide, carbon monoxide, gaseous hydrochloric acid, chlorine, methane, gaseous hydrogen fluoride, argon, and helium.

volcanic glass Natural glass produced by the cooling of molten lava, or some liquid fraction of molten lava, too rapidly to permit crystallization, and forming such material as obsidian, pitchstone, sideromelane, and the glassy mesostasis in the groundmass of many effusive rocks.

volcanicity; vulcanicity The quality or state of being volcanic; volcanism.

volcanic mud Mud formed by the mixture of water with volcanic dust, ash, or other fragmental products of volcanic eruptions, often initially hot and flowing down the flanks of a volcanic cone as a hot lahar or mudflow.

volcanic mudflow Lahar.

volcanic neck The solidified material filling a vent or pipe of a dead volcano. If or when a volcanic neck has resisted degradation better than the mass of the mountain, it will stand alone as a column, tower, or crag of igneous rock.

volcanic pipe Sometimes the steams of lava are very fluid, and they cool at the bottom and upper surfaces much more rapidly than in the interior. The rocks thus formed remain, while the interior molten lava flows on and caves are formed in this manner which are known as volcanic pipes.

volcanic pisolites Accretionary lapilla, *q.v.*

volcanic plug The term is restricted by some to necks consisting of a monolithic mass of solidified igneous rock. *See* VOLCANIC NECK

volcanic rent or **fissure trough** A great volcanic depression, usually concentric in plan, caused by the tearing apart of volcanic cones by movements that are mainly horizontal. The sliding may be induced by the injection of dike swarms or by the overloading of cones on a weak substratum, either sedimentary or volcanic. Examples are the crescentic troughs on many Javanese volcanoes, such as the Tengger.

volcanic rift zone A narrow zone of fissures extending down the flanks of a volcano, ordinarily reaching from the summit crater to the foot of the mountain and beyond. Such features are common on the great shield volcanoes of the island of Hawaii, where they range from a few hundred feet to more than 2 miles in width. Commonly they are marked by lines of open fissures, strings of cinder and spatter cones and spatter ramparts, pit craters, and lava cones.

volcanic rocks *1*. The class of igneous rocks that have been poured out or ejected at or near the earth's surface. *Syn:* EXTRUSIVE ROCKS; EFFUSIVE ROCKS. *2*. One of the three great subdivisions of rocks under a classification proposed by H. H. Read. It includes the effusive rocks and associated intrusive rocks. Dominantly basic, magmatic, igneous. Nonorogenic.

volcanics General collective term for extrusive igneous and pyroclastic material and rocks.

volcanic sand Sand-sized volcanic debris of either pyroclastic or detrital origin.

volcanic shield cluster A large volcanic mass, usually many hundreds of square miles in extent, formed by the overlapping and interfingering of a group of shield volcanoes. An example is the island of Hawaii.

volcanic slag *See* SLAG, VOLCANIC

volcanic spine A slender, pointed, monolithic protrusion of lava squeezed up in viscous condition on the surface of a thick lava flow or on the surface of a viscous volcanic dome through an opening in the solidified upper crust or carapace. They range in height from a few inches to many hundreds of feet. The classic example of a large spine is that of Mt. Pelée, in Martinique, which reached a height of over 1100 feet during its period of growth.

volcanic tuff *See* TUFF

volcanic vent An opening or channel in the earth's crust through which magmatic materials are transported and out of which volcanic materials (lava, pyroclastic detritus) are erupted at the surface.

volcanic water Water in or derived from magma at the earth's surface or at a relatively shallow depth.

volcanism; vulcanism Volcanic power or activity; volcanicity. The term ordinarily includes all natural processes resulting in the formation of volcanoes, volcanic rocks, lava flows, etc.

volcanist; vulcanist One versed

in the study of volcanic phenomena. A volcanologist.

volcano *1.* A vent in the earth's crust from which molten lava, pyroclastic materials, volcanic gases, etc., issue. *2.* A mountain which has been built up by the materials ejected from the interior of the earth through a vent.

volcanologist; vulcanologist One versed in the study of volcanic phenomena. A volcanist.

volcanology; vulcanology The branch of science treating of volcanic phenomena. Volcanological.

volchonskoite A clay mineral. A chromium-bearing montmorillonite.

volt The unit of electromotive force and potential in the practical and M.K.S. systems of electric units. Named after Alessandro Volta, Italian physicist. Practically equivalent to 10^8 c.g.s. electromagnetic units. The International volt is that e.m.f. which, steadily applied to a conductor whose resistance is one International ohm, maintains a current of one International ampere.

volt-ampere A unit of electrical measurement equal to the product of a volt and an ampere. For direct current it is a measure of power and is the same as the watt; for alternating current it is a measure of apparent power.

volt-second The unit of magnetic flux in the M.K.S. and practical systems. So called because one volt is induced in a single turn of conductor when it links or unlinks uniformly in one second with a magnetic flux of one weber; 1 volt-second=1 weber.

volume elasticity Bulk modulus, *q.v.*

volume law, Lindgren's *See* LINDGREN'S VOLUME LAW

volume susceptibility (magnetic) The ratio of the magnetization of the material to the strength of the magnetizing field. Thus defined, the magnetic susceptibility is a dimensionless ratio.

volumetric measurements The determination of the quantity of oil or gas contained in a reservoir. Porosity, thickness, saturation (for oil), area, temperature, and reservoir pressure (for gas) are elements in the calculation.

von Wolff's classification A chemicomineralogical classification of igneous rocks.

Vraconian Lowermost Upper or uppermost Lower Cretaceous.

V's, rule of In regions where there is relief, the outcrop of a horizontal bed extends up the valleys to form a V or U that points upstream. This is also true if the bed dips upstream or downstream, except where the bed dips downstream at a steeper angle than the slope of the stream, in which case the V points downstream.

V-shaped A gorge with evenly sloping sides is often called V-shaped and the V is narrow or broad according to the amount of wasting which has taken place.

vug A cavity, often with a mineral lining of different composition from that of the surrounding rock. *See* GEODE

vuggy porosity Porosity due to vugs in calcareous rock.

vugular Vuggy.

vulcanian *1.* Designating or pertaining to a type of volcanic eruption in which the phenomena are explosive, with the emission of much fine ash and ash-laden gases which ascend to form a voluminous, cauliflowerlike eruption cloud. *2.* Of or pertaining to plutonism; plutonic.

W

wad Bog manganese. An impure mixture of manganese and other oxides. It contains 10 to 20 per cent water, and is generally soft, soiling the hand.

wady; wadi; ouady A ravine or watercourse, dry except in the rainy season. Some wadies are permanently dry.

wall *1.* The side of a level or drift. *2.* The country rock bounding a vein laterally. *3.* The side of a lode.

Wallachian orogeny Post-Pliocene diastrophism.

walled lake A lake with an accumulation of boulders resembling walls about its shores. It owes its peculiar features to the shove of shore ice.

wallow A place to which an animal comes to wallow; also, the depression made by its wallowing, as, a buffalo wallow. A depression suggesting a place where animals have wallowed.

wall rock The rock forming the walls of a vein or lode; the country rock.

wandering The compound movement of sweeping meanders in a swinging meander belt.

waning slope In Wood's classification of hillside slopes, the concave lower slope beneath the scarp which may include the pediment.

warm front The boundary line between advancing warm air and a mass of colder air over which it rises. The surface of separation or frontal surface rises from the warm front over the cold air at a smaller angle than at a cold front, *q.v.*, about 1 in 100 to 1 in 150 being usual figures.

warping The gentle bending of the earth's crust without forming pronounced folds or dislocations.

wash *1.* A Western miner's term for any loose, surface deposits of sand, gravel, boulders, etc. *2.* Auriferous gravel. *3.* Coarse alluvium; an alluvial cone.

washed drift *See* STRATIFIED DRIFT

washed gravel plain In England, an outwash plain, *q.v.*

Washitan Lowermost Upper or uppermost Lower Cretaceous.

washload Washload is that part of the total sediment load composed of all particles finer than limiting size, which is normally washed into and through the reach under consideration.

washout A channel cut into or through a coal seam at some time during or after the formation of the seam, and generally filled with sandstone—or more rarely with shale—similar to that of the roof.

washovers Small deltas built on the landward side of a bar separating a lagoon from the open sea. Such washovers result from storm waves breaking over low parts of the bar and depositing sediment on the lagoon side.

wastage The process or processes by which glaciers lose substance.

Wastage is usually considered as including melting, wind erosion, evaporation, and calving, *q.v.*, but is sometimes used as a synonym for ablation, *q.v.*

waste plain The debris cones along the foot of a mountain range usually so completely coalesce that they form a true plain, called often a waste plain or waste slope. *See* PIEDMONT ALLUVIAL PLAIN

water, film Water held tenaciously by the soil particles, not free to move in the interstices.

water, interstitial Water that exists in the interstices or voids in a rock, or other porous medium.

water, juvenile Water from the interior of the earth which is new or has never been a part of the general system of groundwater circulation, e.g., magmatic water.

water, meteoric Water that previously existed as atmospheric moisture, or surface water, and that entered from the surface into the voids of the rock.

water-bearing bed *See* AQUIFER

water-bearing formation A relative term used to designate a formation that contains considerable gravity ground water.

water-bearing stratum *See* AQUIFER

water bed A bed of coarse gravel or pebbles occurring in the lower part of the upper till in the Upper Mississippi Valley.

water cement Hydraulic cement.

water content Water contained in porous sediment or sedimentary rock, generally expressed as a ratio of water weight to dry sediment weight.

watercourse *1.* A stream of water; a river or brook. *2.* A natural channel for water; also a canal for the conveyance of wa-

ter, especially in draining lands.

water cycle Hydrologic cycle, *q.v.*

water drive Any process whereby energy for the production of oil is derived principally from the pressure of water in the formation.

water-drive reservoir One from which the oil or gas is wholly or partly expelled by pressure due to encroaching water. The water may have been in the reservoir initially, in which case the drive is natural, or it may have been introduced artificially.

water encroachment The displacement of reservoir fluids by the movement of water into a petroleum reservoir as a result of a pressure differential.

waterfall A point in the course of a stream or river where the water descends perpendicularly or nearly so.

waterflood A secondary-recovery method in which water is injected into a petroleum reservoir in order to displace and move residual oil toward a recovery wall.

waterflooding The secondary-recovery operation in which water is injected into a petroleum reservoir for the purpose of effecting a water drive.

water gap A pass in a mountain ridge through which a stream flows.

water hole A natural hole or hollow containing water, such as one in the dry bed of an intermittent stream; a spring in a desert; also, a pool, pond, or small lake.

water humus Organic matter deposited in water.

waterlime Impure limestone which can be burned without addition of other material to produce cement that sets when mixed with water. *Cf.* HYDRAULIC CEMENT

water of dehydration Water that was once in chemical combination with certain minerals and has been by later chemical changes set free as water.

water of imbibition *1.* The proportionate amount of water that a rock can contain above the line of water level or saturation. Quarry water. *2.* Water of saturation.

water of retention That part of the interstitial water in a sedimentary rock which remains in the pores under a definite capillary pressure differential and conditions of unhindered flow. Determined by "restored state" type of experiments. Usually called connate water.

water parting The high land which forms the divisional line between two contiguous river basins is called the water parting. Term suggested as a substitute for watershed.

watershed The area contained within a drainage divide above a specified point on a stream. In water-supply engineering it is termed a watershed, and in river-control engineering it is termed a drainage area, drainage basin, or catchment area.

water source A body of surface water, a spring, or a well from which raw water can be obtained for a water supply, *q.v.*

water supply A volume of water that has been treated or is safe, and is ready for distribution. *Cf.* WATER SOURCE

water table *1.* The upper surface of a zone of saturation except where that surface is formed by an impermeable body. *2.* Locus of points in soil water at which the pressure is equal to atmospheric pressure.

water vascular system Hydrostatic system peculiar to echino-

derms that serves as a circulatory system and controls movement of the tube feet.

water witch One who locates underground water with a divining instrument.

Waucobian Lower Cambrian.

wave *1.* An oscillatory movement in a body of water manifested by an alternate rise and fall of the surface. *2. Geophys:* A disturbance of the equilibrium of a body or of a medium in which the disturbance is propagated from point to point through the medium with a continuous recurring motion.

wave amplitude *1. Hydrodyn:* One-half the wave height. *2. Eng:* Loosely, the wave height from crest to trough.

wave base *1.* The plane to which waves may degrade the bottom in shallow water. *2.* The depth at which wave action ceases to stir the sediments.

wave-built terrace An embankment extending seaward or lakeward from the shore line produced by wave deposition.

wave crest The highest part of a wave. Also that part of the wave above still-water level.

wave-crest length The length of a wave along its crest. Sometimes called crest width.

wave-current ripple mark Ripple mark supposed to have been produced by wave modification of previously existing transverse ripples.

wave-cut bench A bench extending seaward from the base of a sea cliff produced by wave erosion. This bench may be bare rock or it may be covered with a temporary deposit of sand, gravel, and pebbles.

wave-cut notch *See* NOTCH

wave-cut scarp *See* SEA CLIFF

wave-cut terrace Marine-cut terrace; plain of marine abrasion; shore platform; wave-cut plain, wave platform.

wave decay The change which waves undergo after they leave a generating area (fetch) and pass through a calm, or region of lighter or opposing, winds. In the process of decay, the significant wave height decreases and the significant wave length increases.

wave delta Large storm waves dash over the crest of the bar, and their waters flowing down the landward side build wave deltas into the edge of the lagoon.

wave direction The direction from which a wave approaches.

wave forecasting The theoretical determination of future wave characteristics, usually from observed or predicted meteorological phenomena.

wave front *Seismol:* The surface of equal time lapse from the point of detonation to the position of the resulting outgoing signal at any given time after the charge has been detonated. In a more restricted sense, the surface along which phase is constant at a given instant.

wave generation The creation of waves by natural or mechanical means.

wave height The vertical distance between a crest and the preceding trough. *See* SIGNIFICANT WAVE HEIGHT

wave length The horizontal distance between similar points on two successive waves measured perpendicularly to the crest.

wave line When a wave dies out on a beach, it sometimes leaves a tracing of its sweep on the sand, as a wave line; and the returning waters flowing by any half-buried shell on stone may

make rills in the sand, or rill marks.

wavellite A mineral, $Al_3(PO_4)_2(OH,F)_3.5H_2O$. Orthorhombic, radiating.

wave mark *See* SWASH MARK

wave normal Line rising perpendicularly from a point in a plane that is tangent to the wave surface at that point.

wave of translation In strong winds and in shallow water there is a distinct forward movement of some of the water of a wave. Waves in which there is a pronounced forward movement are sometimes called waves of translation.

wave period *1.* The time for a wave crest to traverse a distance equal to one wave length. *2.* The time for two successive wave crests to pass a fixed point. *See* SIGNIFICANT WAVE PERIOD

wave platform Marine-cut terrace; plain of marine abrasion; shore platform; wave-cut plain; wave-cut terrace.

wave propagation The transmission of waves through water.

wave refraction The process by which the direction of a train of waves moving in shallow water at an angle to the contours is changed. The part of the wave train advancing in shallower water moves more slowly than that part still advancing in deeper water, causing the wave crests to bend toward alinement with the underwater contours.

wave ripple marks Ripple marks with symmetrical slopes, sharp crests, and rounded troughs produced by oscillatory waves. Oscillation ripple mark; symmetrical oscillation ripple mark; oscillatory ripple mark; symmetrical ripple mark; aqueous oscillation ripple mark.

Waverlyan *1.* Lower Mississippian, includes Kinderhookian and Osagean. *2.* System between Devonian and Tennesseean. *Obs.*

wave steepness The ratio of a wave's height to its length.

wave surface The surface that includes all loci of light in the same phase that originated at a given point.

wave train A series of waves from the same direction.

wave trough The lowest part of a wave form between successive crests. Also that part of a wave below still-water level.

wave velocity The speed with which an individual wave advances.

wavy extinction Irregular extinction of a mineral under the polarizing microscope, due to bending or distortion of the crystal, or due to a subparallel aggregate of crystals.

W-chert Chert nodules formed by weathering.

W-dolostone Dolostone produced by weathering; occurs as bodies related to modern or ancient land surfaces.

Wealdian Variable unit of Upper Jurassic and Lower Cretaceous age.

weather *1.* The state of the atmosphere, defined by measurement of the six meteorological elements, viz., air temperature, barometric pressure, wind velocity, humidity, clouds, and precipitation. *2. Geol:* To undergo or endure the action of the atmosphere; to suffer meteorological influences.

weathered layer In seismic work, a zone extending from the surface to a limited depth, usually characterized by a low velocity of transmission which abruptly changes to a higher velocity in the underlying rock. The name is erroneous, and the zone is more properly called the low-velocity layer.

weathering The group of processes, such as the chemical action of air and rain water and of plants and bacteria and the mechanical action of changes of temperature, whereby rocks on exposure to the weather change in character, decay, and finally crumble into soil.

weathering correction In seismic work, a time correction applied to reflection and refraction data to correct for the travel time of the observed signals in the low-velocity layer, or weathered layer.

weathering index A measure of the weathering or slacking characteristics of coal. In determining the index, the U. S. Bureau of Mines applies the following test: A 500 to 1000-gram sample of coal in lumps approximately 1 to 1 1/2 inches in diameter is air-dried at 30–35° C., with humidity at 30 to 35 per cent for 24 hours. It is then immersed in water for one hour, the water is drained off, and the coal is again air-dried for 24 hours. The amount of disintegration is determined by sieving on an 8-inch wire mesh sieve with 0.236-inch square openings, and weighing the undersize and oversize. The percentage of the undersize, after passing a blank sieving test, is the weathering or slacking index of the coal.

weathering potential index A measure of the degree of susceptibility to weathering of a rock or a mineral, computed from a chemical analysis.

weathering profile Succession of layers in unconsolidated surface material produced by prolonged weathering; where well developed it consists of surface soil, chemically decomposed layer, leached and oxidized layer, oxidized but unleached layer, and unaltered material. *Cf.* SOIL PROFILE

weathering velocity The velocity with which a seismic compressional wave passes through the low-velocity layer, or weathered layer. It ranges from 175 to 4500 feet per second in different parts of the earth.

websterite A variety of pyroxenite composed of hypersthene and subordinate diopside.

wedge out Thin out.

wedge-work of ice If abundant moisture is present in the pores and cracks of the rock a change of temperature from 45° to 35° F. might be far less effective in breaking the rock than a change from 35° to 25° in the same time, for in the latter case the sudden and very considerable expansion (about one-tenth) which water undergoes on freezing is brought into play. This may be called the wedge-work of ice.

wedge zone That part of a dipping reservoir stratum on the margin of an oil pool which is partly occupied by edge water.

Wegener theory *See* CONTINENTAL DRIFT

weight per cent Weight units of a given substance per 100 weight units of a mixture containing it.

Weissenberg camera A single crystal goniometer involving a coupled motion of the crystal and film in conjunction with a screen by means of which layers of the reciprocal lattice are X-rayed individually.

welded tuff, welded pumice A tuff which has been indurated by the combined action of the heat retained by the particles and the enveloping hot gases.

welding Welding is consolida-

tion by pressure due either to the weight of superincumbent material or to earth movement.

well core Sample of rock penetrated in a well or other borehole obtained by use of a hollow bit that cuts a circular channel around a central column or core.

well cuttings Rock chips cut by a bit in the process of well drilling and removed from the hole by pumping or bailing. Well cuttings collected at closely spaced intervals provide a record of the strata penetrated.

well graded (soil) A coarse-grained unconsolidated material with a continuous distribution of grain sizes from the coarsest to the finest components in such proportions that the successively smaller grains just fill the spaces between the larger grains.

well log Record of a well, generally a lithologic record of the strata penetrated. *See* CALIPER, ELECTRIC, and GRAMMA-RAY LOG

well rounded A roundness grade in which no original faces, edges, or corners are left and the entire surface consists of broad curves. Flat areas are absent, and there are no secondary corners. The original shape is suggested by the present form of the grain. Class limits 0.60 to 1.00.

well sample Cutting produced in well drilling that are collected and saved as a record of the kinds of rock penetrated in the hole.

well shooting *Seismol:* A method or methods of logging wells so that average velocities, continuous velocities, or interval velocities are obtained by lowering geophones into the hole. Shots are usually fired from surface shot holes, but may be fired in the well itself, or perforating-gun detonations may be used. In continuous logging, a sound source is lowered in the hole together with recording geophones.

well spacing The geographic distribution of well locations on the surface above a reservoir; the number of acres per well, as, "20-acre spacing."

well ties The comparison of seismic datum points with geologic datum points at well locations, being the measure of the reliability of the seismic map.

welt A relatively narrow but sharp uplift. Part of the "welts and furrows" or geanticline-geosynclinal couple.

Wenlockian Middle Silurian (restricted).

Wenner configuration A direct current resistivity method using a linear arrangement of 4 equally spaced electrodes. Current is supplied by the outside electrodes, while potential differences are observed between the inside ones. The array may be moved along a traverse using constant electrode spacing to obtain a horizontal profile, or it may be moved progressively out from its center to obtain a depth profile.

Wentworth scale A logarithmic grade scale for size classification of sediment particles, starting at 1 mm. and using the ratio 1/2 in 1 direction (and 2 in the other), providing diameter limits to the size classes of 1, 1/2, 1/4, etc., and 1, 2, 4, etc. This was adopted by C. K. Wentworth from J. A. Udden's scale, *q.v.*, with slight modifications of grade terms and limits.

Werfenian Scythian.

Wernerian Of or pertaining to A. G. Werner (1750–1817), a German mineralogist and geologist who classified minerals according to their external characters and advocated the theory that the strata of the earth's crust were formed by depositions from water; neptunian.

westerly winds Characteristic winds of atmospheric zones north and south of the trade wind zones where the direction of air flow is reversed.

Westphalian Middle Upper Carboniferous.

wet-bulb temperature The lowest temperature to which air can be cooled by evaporating water into it at constant pressure, when the heat required for evaporation is supplied by the cooling of the air. This temperature is given by a well-ventilated wet-bulb thermometer.

wet bulk density Bulk density.

wet gas Natural gas that contains more or less oil vapors. It occurs with or immediately above the oil. Also sometimes called casing-head gas.

wet snow *1.* Fallen snow containing considerable free water. *2.* Falling snow which is partially melted.

wetted perimeter *Hydraul.* and *Geomorph:* The part of a channel surface that is below the water level of a stream.

wetting The property of a fluid and a solid whereby the fluid adsorbs on the surface of the solid in a relatively unbroken film. A fluid has positive wetting ability when it tends spontaneously to increase the mutual area of contact under the existing conditions.

wetting agent A substance, usually fluid, introduced into another liquid in order to reduce surface tension of the latter.

whaleback dune A general, self-explanatory descriptive term for elongate dunes with a rounded crest.

Wheelerian Lower Pleistocene or Upper Pliocene.

wheelerite A yellowish resin filling fissures and interstratified with coal in the Cretaceous lignite beds of New Mexico.

whetstone Natural rock shaped into a sharpening stone.

white agate Chalcedony.

whitecap On the crest of a wave, the white froth caused by wind.

white coal *1.* Water power; first so called by the French (houille blanche). *2.* Tasmanite.

white radiation Radiation in the electromagnetic spectrum varying in wave length and intensity over a wide range extending down to the shortwave length limit.

whiting A white levigated and washed chalk used as a pigment and for polishing. According to its quality, it is known as Spanish white or whiting and Paris white.

wiggle stick Divining rod, *q.v.*

Wilcoxian Lower or Upper Lower Eocene.

wildcat Applied to a mining or oil company organized, or to a mine or well dug, to develop unproven ground far from previous production. Any risky venture in mining or the petroleum industry.

wildflysch A type of flysch, which displays small-scale folding and much twisting and confusion in the beds. The constituents are siliceous shales, clays, and sandstones, with included exotic blocks.

willemite A mineral, Zn_2SiO_4, commonly containing manganese. Hexagonal rhombohedral. A minor ore of zinc.

Williston's law Evolution tends to reduce the number of similar parts in organisms and render them more different from each other.

win *1.* To extract ore or coal. To mine, to develop, to prepare for mining. *2.* To recover metal from an ore.

wind In general, air in natural motion relative to the surface of the earth, in any direction whatever and with any velocity.

wind corrasion Wind abrasion.

wind denivellation Rise of water level resulting from wind drift, as along a windward shore.

wind gap The low depressions or notches in the ridges where streams formerly flowed are now called wind gaps and are utilized for highways in crossing the ridges.

windkanter *See* FACETED PEBBLE

window Circular or ellipsoidal erosional break in an overthrust sheet whereby the rocks beneath the overthrust are exposed. Fenster, *q.v.*

wind polish The high gloss or luster developed on a rock in desert areas as a result of abrasion by sand blown against it.

wind ripple Ripples created by wind.

wind rose A diagram which indicates, at a given station, the average percentage of winds coming from each of the principal compass points, together with the percentage occurrence of calm air. It usually consists of a central circle, in which the figure indicating calm is written and from which emanate eight lines, whose lengths are proportional to the percentage occurrence of the winds they represent.

wind scale A numerical scale for

expressing the different degrees of wind speed, in a fashion suitable for easy communication and rapid plotting on a weather map. The form in almost universal use is the Beaufort wind scale, *q.v.*

wind setup The vertical rise in the still-water level on the leeward side of a body of water caused by wind stresses on the surface of the water.

wind shadow That portion of a scarp or slope which is protected from the direct action of the wind blowing over it.

wind tide Wind setup, *q.v.*

windward The direction from which the wind is blowing.

wineglass valley Hourglass valley.

winnowing Separation of fine particles from coarser ones by action of the wind.

winze A vertical or inclined opening, or excavation, connecting two levels in a mine, differing from a raise only in construction.

wire gold or **silver** (or other metals) Native metal in the form of wires or threads.

Wisconsin Fourth Pleistocene glaciation.

witch *1. V:* To search for underground water, ore, etc., with a divining instrument. *2. N:* One who searches in this way.

witherite A mineral, $BaCO_3$. Orthorhombic.

witness corner A post set near a corner of a mining claim with the distance and direction of the true corner indicated thereon. Used when the true corner is inaccessible.

Wo Abbreviation for wollastonite.

wold Cuesta, *q.v.*

Wolfcampian Lower Lower Permian.

wolframite A mineral series, $(Fe,Mn)WO_4$, ranging from $FeWO_4$ (ferberite) to $MnWO_4$ (huebnerite). Monoclinic. The principal ore of tungsten.

wollastonite A mineral, $CaSiO_3$, commonly found in contact-metamorphosed limestones. Triclinic.

wood coal *1.* Lignite. *See* BOARD COAL. *2.* Charcoal.

wood opal Xylopal. A variety of opal consisting of wood in which the organic matter has been replaced by silica; silicified wood.

wood tin A nodular variety of cassiterite, of a brownish color and fibrous structure, and somewhat resembling dry wood in appearance.

Worden gravimeter A compact, small, temperature-compensated gravity meter in which a system is held in unstable equilibrium about an axis, so that an increase in the gravitational pull on a mass at the end of a weight arm causes a rotation opposed by a sensitive spring.

worm's-eye map *1.* A map showing overlap of sediments. *2.* A map showing progressive transgressions of a sea over a given surface. *3.* A map representing the beds immediately overlying and in contact with the formations forming the geological surface at the time in question. *4.* The pattern of formations visible to an observer who would look upward at the bottom of the rocks overlying the surface in question.

wrench fault A nearly vertical strike-slip fault.

wulfenite A mineral, $PbMoO_4$. Tetragonal.

Würm Fourth Pleistocene glaciation.

wurtzite A mineral, ZnS, dimorphous with sphalerite. Hexagonal.

wye (Y) level A leveling instrument having the telescope with attached spirit level supported in wyes (Ys), in which it may be rotated about its longitudinal axis (collimation axis), and from which it may be lifted and reversed, end for end.

X

X *Geophys:* The letter used in equations to designate a positive direction from the origin to the north. *Seis. prospecting:* The distance from the shot point to the center of the spread, or to any particular geophone.

xeno- [*Gr.*] A combining form meaning guest, stranger, strange, foreign.

xenoblastic A term applied to a texture of metamorphic rocks in which the constituent mineral grains lack proper crystal facies. Corresponds to the allotriomorphic- or xenomorphic-granular texture of igneous rocks.

xenocryst A term applied to allothigenous crystals in igneous rocks that are foreign to the body of rock in which they occur.

xenolith A term applied to allothogenous rock fragments that are foreign to the body of igneous rock in which they occur. An inclusion.

xenothermal Deposit formed at high temperature, but at shallow to moderate depth.

xenotime A mineral YPO_4, usually containing rare earths, thorium and uranium. Tetragonal.

xerophyte An organism that characteristically lives under dry conditions.

xerothermic period A historical warm-dry period.

X rays An electromagnetic disturbance, the wave lengths of which are beyond the ultraviolet region of the electromagnetic spectrum.

xylopal Wood opal, *q.v.*

Y

Y The letter used in geophysical equations to designate a positive direction to the east from the origin.

yamas Perpendicular or oblique shafts which at a greater or less depth lead into caves.

yardang; yarding; jardang Irregular ridges, commonly alternating with round-bottomed troughs, formed by eolian erosion.

yarding Yardang, *q.v.*

Yarmouth Post-Kansan interglacial.

yield The proportion of coal or ore obtained in mining; the product of a metallurgical process; extraction; recovery.

yield point *See* ELASTIC LIMIT

Y-level A level mounted in a pair of Ys: a common form of spirit level, used in surveying, etc.

yoked basin Zeugogeosyncline.

young; youthful Being in the stage of increasing vigor and efficiency of action: said of some streams; also, being in the stage of accentuation of and a tendency toward complexity of form: said of some topography resulting from land sculpture. Contrasted with mature and old.

young plain A plain that has a level surface poorly defined, and perhaps swampy divides, and shallow lakes.

young river *Geol:* A river which has begun to form a drainage system in newly raised or newly deformed land.

Young's modulus Stretch modulus. Let a rod be pulled or compressed then $E = \dfrac{F l_0}{\Delta 1}$

Where E is Young's modulus, F=force per unit area, l_0 is original length of rod, and $\Delta 1$ is increase in length. Expressed in dynes/cm^2 or lbs/ft^2.

young valley A valley in its early stages, when it is relatively straight, has steep slopes, a high gradient, and a V-shaped cross section, while its tributaries are short.

youth That stage in the development of streams when they are increasing in vigor and efficiency; or in land sculpture when topographic forms are being accentuated and are tending toward complexity; contrasted with maturity and old age.

youthful stage of erosion cycle *See* YOUTH

youthful topography One in which the rivers flow in gorges and canyons, rather than in ordinary valleys, the drainage system is but partially developed, and the divides between the streams are broad, flat-topped areas, while the streams are obstructed by many falls and rapids.

Ypresian Lower Eocene.

Z

Z *Geophys:* The letter used in equations to designate the depth below the origin or datum of a point under consideration.

zastrugi Plural form of zastruga. *See* SASTRUGI

zebra dolomite Hydrothermally altered dolomite in the Leadville district of Colorado consisting of bands, generally parallel to bedding, that are light gray and coarsely crystalline, alternating with darker fine-grained bands.

Zechstein Upper Permian.

Zemorrian Lower Lower Miocene.

zenithal map projection *See* AZIMUTHAL MAP PROJECTION

zeolites A generic term for a group of hydrous alumino-silicates of Na, Ca, Ba, Sr, and K, characterized by their easy and reversible loss of water of hydration and their intumescence when heated strongly. Many are also characterized by a significant capacity for ion-exchange.

zeolitic deposits Deposits, particularly native copper, which occur in basalts accompanied by minerals of the zeolite group.

zero curtain Ground layer between active layer and permafrost where zero (C.) temperature persists for a considerable time (up to 115 days per year) during freezing and thawing of overlying ground.

zeta potential *1.* Interfacial potential. *2.* Potential resulting from adsorption of ions by unsatisfied charges occurring at a surface.

zeugen Earth pillars. They consist of soft rock with a layer of hard rock at the summit, and beneath the hard cap the soft rock is carved into slopes which resemble the typical denudation curve.

zeugogeosyncline A parageosyncline that receives its sediment from eroded complementing highlands within the craton.

zigzag folds *See* CHEVRON FOLDS

zinc blende Sphalerite.

zinc bloom *See* HYDROZINCITE; ZINC OXIDE

zincite A mineral, ZnO, usually containing some Mn. Hexagonal. A minor ore of zinc.

zinc oxide; zinc white A white pulverulent oxide ZnO, made by burning zinc in air. It is used as a pigment, chiefly as a substitute for white lead. Called also flowers of zinc, nihil album, philosopher's wool, and zinc bloom.

zircon A mineral, $ZrSiO_4$. Tetragonal. Used as a refractory and as the gem, hyacinth. The chief ore of zirconium.

zoarium Skeleton of a bryozoan colony.

zoic *Geol:* Containing fossils, or yielding evidence of contemporaneous plant or animal life; said of rocks.

zoisite A mineral, $Ca_2Al_3(SiO_4)_3$-(OH). Orthorhombic. Found in metamorphic rocks.

zonal axis Straight line parallel to all faces of a crystal zone.

zonal guide fossil Species of known limited vertical range in the local succession.

zonal theory A theory of ore deposition which holds that the ores originate in a zone of differentiation in the lower part of the zone of crystallization, where the siliceous-aqueous-metalliferous residues are formed, which in passing upward through faults and fractures deposit the ores in successive zones, each marked by its distinctive mineral associations.

zonation *Stratig:* The condition of being arranged or distributed in bands or zones, generally more or less parallel to the bedding.

zone *1. Stratig:* A group of beds, of an inferior status, characterized by one or several special fossils, which serve as indices. *2.* An area or region more or less set off or characterized as distinct from surrounding parts, as in a metalliferous region, the mineral zone. *3. Crystallog:* A series of faces whose intersection lines with each other are all parallel. *4.* The fundamental para-time-rock unit. *q.v.*

zone of aeration *Hydrol:* The zone in which the interstices of the functional permeable rocks are not filled, except temporarily, with water. The water is under pressure less than atmospheric.

zone of capillarity An area that overlies the zone of saturation and contains capillary voids, some, or all, of which are filled with water that is held above the zone of saturation by molecular attraction acting against gravity.

zone of discharge The zone embracing that part of the belt of saturation which has a means of horizontal escape. *See* GATHERING ZONE; STATIC ZONE

zone of eluviation A horizon, *q.v.*

zone of equilibrium *See* PROFILE OF EQUILIBRIUM

zone of flow The inner mobile mass of a glacier.

zone of fracture As proposed by C. R. Van Hise, the upper portion of the earth's crust and in which rocks are deformed mainly by fracture.

zoning of crystals Refers to those solid solution crystals which do not have a uniform composition throughout, but possess irregularities in composition from one point to another, occurring in the form of more or less concentric zones. Also called zonal structure.

zooecium Skeleton of an individual bryozoan animal.

zoogene *Geol:* Of, pertaining to, consisting of, resulting from, or indicative of animal life or structure.

zoolite; zoolith A fossil animal.

zoophyte Bryozoa or coralline, *q.v.;* polyzoa.

zooplankton These include myriads of animals that live permanently in a floating state and countless numbers of helpless larvae and eggs of the animal benthos and nekton.

zygote A fertilized egg; a cell arising from the fusion of gametes.